INTERNATIONAL AND GLOBAL MARKETING

Concepts and Cases

The Irwin Series in Marketing

INTERNATIONAL AND GLOBAL MARKETING
Concepts and Cases

Taylor W. Meloan
School of Business Administration
University of Southern California

John L. Graham
Graduate School of Management
University of California, Irvine

81148

IRWIN

Chicago • Bogota • Boston • Buenos Aires • Caracas
London • Madrid • Mexico City • Sydney • Toronto

Sponsoring editor: Nina McGuffin
Marketing manager: Jim Lewis
Project editor: Ethel Shiell
Production supervisor: Pat Frederickson
Designer: Mercedes Santos
Art studio: Arcata Graphics
Art coordinator: Heather D. Burbridge
Compositor: J.M. Post Graphics, a division of Cardinal Communications Group, Inc.
Typeface: 10/12 Times Roman
Printer: R. R. Donnelley & Sons Company

Library of Congress Cataloging-in-Publication Data

International and global marketing: concepts and cases/edited by
    Taylor W. Meloan, John L. Graham.
        p.   cm.—(The Irwin series in marketing)
    Includes bibliographical references.
    ISBN 0-256-15723-5
    1. Export marketing.   2. Export marketing—Case studies.
I. Meloan, Taylor W.   II. Graham, John L.   III. Series.
HF1416.I54   1995
658.8'48—dc20   94–17867

Printed in the United States of America
3 4 5 6 7 8 9 0 DO 1 0 9 8 7 6 5

This book is dedicated to the late Richard D. Irwin,
a man of integrity, vision,
and a great love of life.

About This Book

This is an impressive and comprehensive compilation of classic and cutting-edge articles on major aspects of international and global marketing. It includes commissioned papers on subjects that have not been seen in other collections. A number of high-quality cases and a global decision simulation are also important supplements to the readings.

I commend this book to academicians and practitioners as a very valuable companion text in undergraduate and graduate courses in international and global marketing.

Roy A. Herberger, Jr.
President and Professor of International
  Marketing
American Graduate School of
  International Management (Thunderbird)
Glendale, Arizona

About The Editors

Taylor W. Meloan is professor of marketing and the Robert E. Brooker emeritus professor of marketing at the University of Southern California. He has served as marketing department chair and dean in USC's School of Business Administration. He has participated as a faculty member at five overseas universities and institutes, most recently at the Madrid Business School in 1993. During the same year he was a visiting faculty member at the University of Hawaii. He holds degrees from Indiana University, Washington University, and St. Louis University.

He is a member of the Foreign Trade Association of Los Angeles and the International Marketing Association of Orange County. He has served as national publications chair and director and as president of the Southern California chapter of the American Marketing Association. During 1986–90, he served as a member of the National Advertising Review Board. In 1993 he was elected to the board of the World Affairs Council of Orange County. He is a member of the board of the Institute for Shipboard Education, the governing body of the semester at sea program. Author of many research papers and cases, he is co-author or co-editor of seven books. Currently he serves on the editorial boards of four professional publications.

John L. Graham is professor of marketing in the Graduate School of Management at the University of California, Irvine. He has taught at the University of Southern California (1979–89) and was visiting Professor at the Madrid Business School (1991–1992).

He holds a PhD in marketing (with an emphasis in cultural anthropology) from the University of California, Berkeley. He previously worked as a market analyst for a division of Caterpillar Tractor Co. With a number of colleagues, Graham has published more than forty articles and three books dealing primarily with international marketing topics.

His articles on international marketing negotiations have appeared in the *Journal of Marketing, Marketing Science,* the *Journal of Consumer Research,* the *Journal of Strategic Management,* the *Journal of International Business Studies,* and the *Harvard Business Review.* Recently he and his co-authors published a paper in *Management Science* that received a citation of excellence from the Lauder Institute of International Management at the Wharton School.

Preface

In planning internationally oriented courses, seminars, and workshops, educators and practitioners today typically look beyond the contents of traditional textbooks. They seek insights and concepts in professional journals, research studies, working papers, and government publications from around the world. Your editors have endeavored to perform this search for you, bringing together an integrated matrix of timely articles and papers on international and global marketing. After reviewing more than 250 global citations, our final selections include recently published papers, timeless classics, commissioned papers written especially for this book, cases, and an international negotiations simulation. Each has been written by an authority in his/her field.

We believe that increased coverage should be given in courses and seminars to exporting/importing entrepreneurship. Rather than focusing largely on the marketing opportunities and barriers facing multinationals, greater emphasis should be given to preparing entrepreneurs and the owners/managers of smaller businesses to expand abroad. Along with our careful selection of readings, we believe that this orientation differentiates this book from other anthologies. Course participants are provided with opportunities to prepare export or import marketing plans, or to conduct autopsies of international marketing "failures."

We hope sincerely that our selections will add a relevant extra dimension that will enhance lively discussion and debate in courses, seminars and workshops. The editors acknowledge with appreciation the contributions of the authorities cited herein and their willingness to permit us to reproduce their work. We acknowledge also the encouragement of Rob Zwettler, Publisher, and the valuable assistance of Nina McGuffin, Marketing Editor, Ethel Shiell, and Heather McCammond-Watts, all with Richard D. Irwin, Inc.

Taylor W. Meloan
John L. Graham

Contents

PART ONE

INTRODUCTION

The worldwide growth of marketing is one of the most singular and far-reaching developments in business over the last quarter of a century. The governments of most nations of the world are committed to the enhancement of international trade. They recognize that trade is the principal vehicle necessary to raise the standards of living of their peoples, thereby contributing to societal harmony. The reduction of trade barriers provides for greater marketing opportunities. It is also a major bulwark in the maintenance of world peace. The introductory section of this book contains five contributions. The first of these, *International and Global Marketing: An Overview,* summarizes export market entry vehicles, risk assessment, and tailoring the marketing mix to meet the needs and expectations of selected international target markets.

The next two contributions explore the dichotomy of international marketing versus global marketing. A leading authority argues that global-minded firms should treat the entire world as a single market and regard regional and national differences as superficial and unimportant. The global firm should do the same things in the same way everywhere. The alternative view, cogently argued, is that marketing globalization is essentially a myth. These authorities hold that one or more elements of the marketing mix must be tailored for successful export of most products or services.

The concluding papers in this section outline managerial and strategic factors that contribute to successful international marketing or impede effectiveness in global competition. The author of *Great Strategy or Great Strategy Implementation* believes that, in general, American firms try to envision a unique business strategy that will allow them to outmaneuver their competition. By contrast, successful Asian firms often implement undifferentiated business strategies, but do it better than competitors, thereby gaining a competitive advantage. The last paper in this section outlines managerial barriers to successful exporting, including vision limitations and corporate inertia. It summarizes the balance of trade of the United States from 1890 to 1989. The vehicles for financing trade deficits, which the United States has had since 1972, is an important component of *Managerial Barriers to U.S. Exports.*

International and Global Marketing: An Overview

Taylor W. Meloan. *Taylor W. Meloan is Professor of Marketing, University of Southern California.*

Competition in a Shrinking World

Increasingly we all live in a shrinking world that has become dramatically more competitive. Five key factors explain this unparalleled competitive environment.

Communications and Logistical Revolution

Remember when the printed words in newspapers and books, supplemented by radio, were the principal vehicles of communications? Today, with worldwide telephonic messages, fax transmissions, and satellite reception, instant economic, political, business, and personal communications have become the norm. Major events around the world are common knowledge within minutes. Jet transport has also contributed to a shrinking world. People, products, and components are transported within hours over vast distances, facilitating the production and distribution process.

Financial and Nonmonetary Settlement Systems

The dramatic growth of international business and investment has been facilitated by efficiently functioning modes of payment and the settlement of financial accounts. In recent years, this has been supplemented by increased countertrading wherein all or part of the payment is made in goods rather than in currency. The simplest form of countertrading is barter—the exchange of goods of one kind for products of another, whether finished, semi-finished, or raw material. Other varieties of countertrading are more complex; part of the payment may be in goods with the balance in currency. Infinite variations have accelerated competition and provided for new marketing opportunities.[1]

Worldwide Dedication to Trade

Most nations of the world are committed to the enhancement of international trade. This dedication has manifest itself in the General Agreement on Trade and Tariffs (GATT).

The basic objectives of the GATT are to promote nondiscrimination in trade barriers to freer trade and to create vehicles for resolution of international trade disputes.

Dedication to international trade by the major nations of the world has led to the encouragement of exports by their governments and, in many instances, direct or indirect subsidies of exporters' operations. This can lead to exported products being sold in foreign markets at lower prices than identical merchandise offered in the home market. Such "dumping" and export subsidization inevitably lead to efforts by governments to protect themselves and their indigenous industries from injury. They result in a more competitive and complex environment for marketers.

Role of the Multinationals

Multinational corporations have contributed to international competition and the shrinking world phenomenon. While there is no commonly accepted definition of a multinational, it is generally perceived as a large firm enjoying a dominant position in one or more industries with subsidiaries in many countries. Typically it manufactures and has R&D facilities in major markets where it competes. Multinationals tend to lose their national identity because of their omnipresence and widespread operations. Because of their economic power, they are often feared and resented by lesser competitors and by the governments of emerging nations in which they operate. Most of the major American oil companies, automotive manufacturers, and international banks, for example, are multinationals.

The Importance of Peace

The universal desire for peace has been an important contributor to the shrinking world phenomenon. The peoples of all nations yearn for meaningful international arms agreements and arsenal inspections to enhance the likelihood of continued peaceful coexistence. While the world has experienced periodic localized aggression and a recent rise in terrorism, nonetheless relative peace and lack of worldwide war have provided a fertile competitive environment in which marketing has played a major role.

Barriers to Exporting

According to the U.S. Department of Commerce, approximately 20,000 American firms could export successfully but currently are not. Five factors explain why. The American market is the largest in the world. Many firms can grow and prosper without exporting. Only when sales and profits plateau domestically do many companies consider marketing abroad. Second, most companies don't know how to go about exporting. They don't know whether they need to tailor products or services for international markets. They don't know how to price, promote, or select distributors abroad, or how to research such questions. They don't know which world to consider for exporting. Consequently, they procrastinate.[2] Third, Americans tend to be ethnocentric—they lack comprehension of the cultures, business practices, and languages of other peoples. Because English is the major business language of the world, there is little incentive to learn the languages of others. Fourth, foreign aggression and sporadic terrorism reduce American receptivity to export consideration. Assessing foreign political and economic risk is difficult for most Americans to contemplate, let alone do. Finally, protected markets abroad have made many countries difficult to penetrate. Tariff barriers, nontariff barriers (NTBs) including import quotas, burdensome licensing requirements, antitrade product specifications, and bureaucratic red tape all combine to discourage American exporters in many countries.

Export Market Entry Vehicles

Export entry vehicles range from reactive to proactive modes, from simple to complex in nature. The following alternatives begin with simple, weak commitments to international marketing and proceed to dedicated major efforts on a global basis.

Indirect Exporting

Often this hand-in-the-water approach involves the sale of a manufactured product or line to a domestic intermediary who takes title to the goods, stores, and resells to markets abroad where it has contracts. This mode avoids the need for the producer to research, promote, price, and find distributors in other countries. The export firm takes over these functions. Persuading another manufacturer who is already exporting, with perhaps a complementary line, to act as one's agent abroad is another indirect vehicle. Using an export management company is a third possibility. These small, service-oriented marketing organizations, typically with only a few employees, are usually agents for domestic manufacturers that need exporting expertise. They provide market information and access to prospects in parts of the world where they have developed contacts.

Direct Exporting: Reactive Mode

Many intermediate and smaller firms began exporting in response to unsolicited inquiries and orders from abroad. Based on cursory analyses of such orders, neophyte exporters seek customers abroad with businesses characteristics similar to those of the inquiries. Gradually a cadre of customers abroad is developed, largely via this mode, with modest proactive solicitation of business.

Direct Exporting: Proactive Mode

This mode requires a commitment to actively explore the feasibility of exporting to selected target markets whose sales and market potentials have been researched. Distributors and/or agents in the target market(s) must be appointed, products or lines may be modified to meet the needs or expectations of foreign buyers, appropriate price levels and margins must be determined, and an appropriate personal selling, advertising and sales promotional mix must be devised to achieve penetration objectives. The international marketer must also become familiar with export procedures and documentation, as well as the vehicles for international payments and settlement of accounts.

Proactive international marketers should develop rosters of prospective distributors and agents from a network of business contacts, including their banks, advertising agencies, competitors, export management companies, trade associations, chambers of commerce, and agencies of the federal government. They may then prune the list by writing to each prospective agent or distributor to ascertain interest in being appointed in the target market area. Letters should be accompanied by catalogs and brochures documenting the scope of the line, elements of superiority, and pricing information. Those who express interest can be researched. Banks with which they have dealt and other firms they have represented are logical sources of input. Choices from the final list should be made only after personal interface with each candidate in the target countries. While this step may require considerable time and travel expense, there is no substitute for face-to-face exploration of mutual expectations with prospective agents and distributors. At that time the terms, conditions, duration of an appointment, and provisions for possible termination should be reviewed.

Sales Branches and Subsidiaries

As the international phase of business operations expands, sales branches may be established in selected target markets where the potential warrants the cost. Agents and distributors are compensated largely via commissions and markups, but establishing a sales branch requires the commitment of upfront monies to finance office, storage, and/or repair facilities, overhead expenses, and sales force maintenance and supervision. Significantly greater sales volume is required to warrant the upgrade from an agency/distributorship mode to sales branch.

In contrast with sales branches, subsidiaries are separate legal entities that are created to assume responsibilities designated by the home company.[3] Subsidiaries are controlled but not always entirely owned by the parent. A foreign government may require that subsidiary ownership be shared to limit the financial commitment of the parent and to facilitate management participation by foreign nationals.

Sometimes subsidiaries operate in several nations or regions of the world. In other instances, they are smaller in scope, essentially upgraded sales branches. Their relationship to the parent may range from relatively autonomous to highly dependent, depending on the philosophy of the home company.

Licensing

The principal attraction of this international marketing entry vehicle is that it limits investment and commitment, while simultaneously offering the possibility of substantial profitability through licensing fees or royalty payments. The principal costs are those associated with negotiating the licensing agreements and monitoring their implementation. Licensing offers quick access to international business, market share, and cash flow. Typically the licensee is already established in the target market and can finance use of the license. Licensing can also circumvent tariff barriers that limit the quantity or raise the price of imports.[4]

Licensees may receive technical know-how, patent usage, access to production processes, the right to use a trademark, or copyrighted materials from the licensor. Licenses may be granted on an exclusive basis, meaning that other firms will not be given a license in the same geographic area. Or they may be nonexclusive, implying that other licenses are possible in a given region. Delineating the license's field of use can restrict the markets in which technological knowhow may used.[5]

A likely disadvantage of licensing is that licensees may ultimately become competitors. When a licensee acquires technological know-how, management expertise, and market position, it becomes tempting to terminate the license and continue in the field as a competitor. Or the licensee may endeavor to revise the license on more advantageous terms.

While the licensor typically conducts periodic audits and spot checks in an effort to ensure licensee compliance with the parameters of the licensing agreement, these are often not as reassuring as one would like. The licensor's lack of control over the operations of licensees can be a nagging problem. Short of terminating the license (where that can be done for cause), the licensor must rely on persuasion and example to upgrade marginal licensee performance. Finally, licensing can limit the profits of the licensor vis-à-vis its own manufacturing and marketing abroad. Balancing this potential disadvantage are the limitation on risk and the modest financial commitment licensing generally requires.[6]

Franchising

Franchise marketing refers to a contractual arrangement whereby a franchisor who has developed a format and operational procedures for a particular type of business extends to franchisees the right to conduct such a business, provided that they follow the established *modus operandi* of the franchisor. Franchisees are expected to adhere to the format, management guidelines, and accounting controls of the franchisor. In turn, the franchisees expect to acquire the expertise of the franchisor and receive guidance, training, and continuing support. Franchisees also acquire the name, logo, image, and reputation of the franchisor as part of the franchise package.

Because the franchisor can rely in part on funds provided by franchisees, expansion is facilitated. These monies are in the form of initial franchisee fees, annual renewals, and orders for materials and supplies needed by the franchisees. In international franchising, area franchises are often granted for a specified geographic region or sometimes an entire nation. Such master franchisees have the right to subfranchise to those who operate individual units in the subfranchise chain.

The franchisor has a tailormade chain of units with reasonably predictable demand, domestic or international, for its product or service. Such a franchisor is not subject to the whims of independent dealers who are completely free to buy where they wish. This interdependence facilitates planning and control of overall operations.

As in corporate chains, franchisors are able to spread their risks among a variety of outlets and parts of the world. Inevitably, certain locations will prove to be superior to others. Obviously, the goal of any chain operator, corporate or franchise, is to have all units, wherever located, stand on their own feet. But the overall health of the organization is not impaired unduly even if a few locations or parts of the world are less satisfactory than anticipated.[7]

Another possible advantage of this mode of international distribution is the expectation that franchisees will be more highly motivated than salaried employees. It is assumed that people who regard themselves as their own boss will do a better than average job. This is especially important in small retail operations that require long, hard physical work. But franchisees who regard themselves as self-employed may not be disposed to accept guidance and direction from a franchisor or to standardize their operations for reasonable uniformity throughout the system. Conversely, franchisors may spend too much time seeking new franchisees around the world, neglecting the development of those they already have. This can result in system tensions.[8]

The attraction of international franchising stems from franchisors' desire to maximize the utilization of their accumulated experience and knowhow, expectation of enjoying the dedication and cultural empathy of indigenous franchisees, desire to minimize nationalistic restrictions on foreign ownership and control, and hope of avoiding exposure to lawsuits in another country and expropriation of overseas assets and facilities.

In spite of the potential advantages of international franchising, this mode of distribution tends to limit one's profit possibilities due to the need to share profits with franchisees. Coordinating and controlling a far-flung franchise system is also a likely source of difficulty. Many franchisors find themselves stretched thin as they attempt to motivate and maintain communications with franchisees even in the United States. This problem is compounded with foreign franchisees whose expectations, needs and mindsets are likely to be different from those of Americans.

Joint Ventures

When a firm joins with one or more partners to establish a new business abroad, a joint venture is created. These partners may be firms indigenous to the nation in which the joint venture is to be located, or they may be state agencies or governmental enterprises. Such direct investment typically requires the commitment of equity and/or other assets, including physical plant, raw materials, management talent, or intellectual property. The joint venture may or may not involve establishment of a new manufacturing facility. The proportion and value of the investment generally determine the percentage shares held by the joint venture partners. American companies typically wish to have a majority share in order to ensure control, but many nations do not permit foreign firms to have a majority ownership position in a joint venture. This is especially true of developing countries.[9]

Foreign government opposition to direct investment may make a joint venture the only feasible mode of foreign market penetration. But joint ventures are also popular because they limit the American firm's commitment of capital and other resource. They can also combine the management know-how of a foreign partner and his or her understanding of the business environment with that of the host nation. The joint venture partner's personal contact with competitors, channel of distribution members, raw material and component suppliers, government officials, and trade association sources may be invaluable. This is the prime reason why certain companies have gone the joint venture route in Japan even though sole ownership of a new undertaking is open to them. Joint ventures also appeal to firms with little experience in international operations.[10]

A major key to joint venture success is choice of the local partner. Each firm in the partnership should contribute strengths and expertise that synergistically result in a whole greater than the sum of the parts. The parameters of the joint venture must be codified contractually, but communication and trust are of equal importance. When joint ventures fail, it is usually due to problems in these areas.

Joint venture partners acquire the technological, management, and marketing know-how of each other. If the partnership is dissolved for whatever reason, the foreign partners can become competitors of the American firm that perhaps provided much of the initial expertise. There is some risk that successful joint ventures can become targets for expropriation in certain countries where multinationals are suspect.

Contract Manufacturing

If an internationally oriented firm finds export entry to a given target market blocked by onerous restrictions, contract manufacturing may be feasible. This often requires the transfer of technological and operational assistance to a foreign manufacturer with whom one contracts for local production of a product or line built to the specifications of the contractor. Contract manufacturing requires only a modest level of commitment, allows for easy entry, and sidesteps ownership of foreign manufacturing facilities. It permits an internationally oriented firm to retain control over marketing and product service. It may be tempting to pursue this route when the market potential is too thin to warrant on-site manufacturing of one's own. The key problems associated with contract manufacturing are (1) finding a local manufacturer who has excess capacity and the ability to adhere to specifications, (2) maintaining ongoing quality control, and (3) avoiding having such a producer become a future competitor.

Turnkey Projects

Multinational firms with planning and construction expertise sometimes contract to build an entire plant or project. The fully equipped plant is turned over to the foreign owners when it is fully operational. This is often done on a fee or cost-plus basis with escalation clauses for unanticipated construction delays. Large manufacturing plants or hydroelectric facilities are illustrative of such turnkey projects.

Management Contracts

Marketers with management expertise offer their services on a contractual basis to manage or operate a facility for the owners. This is sometimes done as part of a turnkey project to make sure a facility will be operational upon construction completion. Often this is a short-term arrangement until permanent employees can be trained to assume the responsibilities of operation.[11] Hotel corporations operate their own facilities but often manage hotels bearing their name that are owned by others.

The Multinational Firm and the Global Corporation

Major multinational marketers competing on a global basis combine various market entry strategies. In certain markets, they engage in direct investment via joint ventures or sole ownership and management of foreign operations. In other markets, they utilize licensing or direct exporting. The choice of strategies depends largely on their perceived global mission, financial strength, comparative cost analyses, product characteristics, channel of distribution availability, nature and strength of competition, and with environmental and political risk.

In contrast with the multinational firm, the global corporation treats the entire world as a single entity. It markets "the same things in the same way everywhere." Products and brands are standardized worldwide.[12]

Risk Assessment

When a multinational entity considers alternative market entry strategies, it must do so within the context of risk assessment and acceptable assumption of risk. Two major categories of risk assessment are germane. The first is analysis of the governmental and political environment and stability in the host nation. The economic climate and prognosis in the target market are of equal importance. Included are assessment of possible future nationalization or expropriation of the multinational's assets and facilities, along with the likelihood of unanticipated or discriminatory taxes, strikes, riots, and/or revolutions which could imperil or doom the enterprise.[13]

The second category of risk assessment involves interaction between the host government and other nations, world organizations, or nongovernmental groups or movements. The possibility of retaliatory tariffs or quotas being imposed by the host nation, boycotts, embargoes, deteriorating political relationships, and/or terrorism are all elements of this category.[14]

International Marketing Research and Intelligence

The essence of sound marketing is discerning what customers and prospects need, want, and will buy, then creating a satisfying mix of goods and services from which buyers can select. To ascertain what the public wants, will buy, and at what price, research is needed. International marketing research utilizes the same methodologies and tools as research in the United States. The problem under study must be defined, the sources of information to address the problem ascertained, the germane data from either secondary or primary sources gathered, and the data analyzed and translated into a report of findings.

Secondary source data is available from federal agencies in the United States, from international organizations like the United Nations, the Organization for Economic Cooperation and Development, and the European Economic Community, and from host nations where international marketers contemplate competing. Private secondary sources of data include trade associations, international chambers of commerce, international banks, and research organizations that gather data and sell them to clients. International marketers typically subscribe to many ongoing journals, studies, and research reports as part of their continuing international marketing intelligence function. By contrast, garnering secondary data for a specific project is generally regarded as an aspect of marketing research. Gathering and interpreting secondary data from international sources is generally considered more difficult and suspect than doing so in the United States from domestic sources alone. International data are generally more difficult to obtain, may be unreliable or dated, can be subject to translation errors from another language into English, or may be misinterpreted because of cultural bias.

Primary data are obtained via survey research, observation, or controlled experiments. Survey research involves personal interviewing, or data gathering by means of telephone or mail surveys. All are more difficult in an international milieu than in the United States. Consumers may be unwilling to respond to research questions. Companies in many parts of the world are much more secretive than in the United States and disinclined to reveal details of their business operations. Observational research, unless done by skilled researchers with in-depth knowledge of the culture being observed, is subject to possible bias, making controlled experiments difficult to implement. (Such experiments involve holding all variables constant except for the one being researched—for example, the sales effect of a given advertising campaign or price change.[15])

The International Marketing Mix

The four decision variables for which international marketers have responsibility are (1) product scope and mix, (2) promotional strategies, media, and appeals, (3) pricing and discount strategies, and (4) channel of distribution choices. Channel of distribution alternatives are summarized under Export Market Entry Vehicles (p. 5). Each of these variables is interrelated.

Product Scope and Mix

In product planning, a basic decision is whether to export or produce abroad virtually the same product or line as that in the home market. Certain firms resolved this question long ago; Coca-Cola and Pepsi-Cola are the same around the world. This is also true for many industrial marketers. For other firms, it is a more complex issue. While standardized products have the appeal of simplicity and cost savings, long-run profitability may be better served by tailored products, whether destined for the ultimate consumer or for industrial markets, that meet local needs and cultural expectations. In certain instances, products must be modified because of the need for design changes, metric calibration, alternative voltage systems, or customer demands.[16]

Product and packaging color may also be affected by cultural taboos. In Japan and many other Asian countries, for example, white is associated with death. By contrast, black signifies death to Americans. A red circle on a logo or package is reminiscent of the Japanese flag and it should be avoided in countries with anti-Japanese feelings. Local views about color appropriateness must be researched with sensitivity by the international marketer.

It behooves international marketers to be alert to the possibility of counterfeit and look-alike versions of their products. Counterfeits are goods bearing an unauthorized trademark or products that are identical or highly similar to the goods for which the trademark are registered. Look-alikes are similar to genuine products but do not involve infringements of patents, trademarks, or copyrights. In addition to highly advertised consumer goods, product categories that are frequently counterfeited today include computers, drugs, medical devices, military hardware, and automotive parts.[17] International marketers sometimes retain private investigators to unearth infringing merchandise at the source. This is an important initial step in stanching the flow of such goods into legitimate trade channels. Anticounterfeiting actions involve high-technology labels and packaging so advanced that duplication is nearly impossible.[18]

Promotional Issues

Advertising Themes.   Many well-known international marketers have launched advertising campaigns that have proved ineffective because of cultural insensitivity. The Marlboro man on horseback with his omnipresent cigarette has been effectively used in America and Europe, but this rugged masculine theme was not well received in urbanized Hong Kong. The ad was remade showing a younger model with a truck. Ford introduced a vehicle abroad under the name "Fiera" only to learn that it means "ugly old woman" in Spanish.[19]

Media Availability.   Advertising media are either too scarce or too plentiful, depending upon the country. Government restrictions on commercials limit access to television and sometimes radio in certain nations. In some countries, more advertising is offered than can be accepted in the limited range of available newspapers and magazines. In certain other countries, so many newspapers are available with such modest circulations that coverage of the market in a cost-effective manner is difficult or impossible.[20]

Circulation data are closely related to the issue of media availability. Reliable circulation and market coverage information in most parts of the world is difficult to obtain or suspect. Often the figures are exaggerated, but one can never be sure to what extent. As a result, measuring cost per thousand readers, listeners, or viewers and comparing one medium to another become very tenuous.[21]

Personal Selling.   Because of foreign limitations on media availability, personal selling often becomes an important aspect of the promotional mix. Lower wage costs in developing nations can make the use of sales representatives even more attractive.

International salespeople perform one or more of three essential sales functions: (1) to promote the product or line to the trade, i.e., distributors or dealers, (2) to influence end users of the firm's offerings with the expectation that they will order more from distributors or dealers, and (3) to assist in identifying and solving the technical problems of buyers, especially those in industrial or engineering-based firms. Securing trial orders is also part of this process.

Sales Promotion.   Aspects of an overall promotional program that are not personal selling or mass communications are typically referred to as sales promotion. Store demonstrations, displays, shows, contests, coupons, product sampling, and premiums are all aspects of sales promotion.

In an international context, trade fairs and shows are an especially important part of sales promotion. Hundreds of such shows are held in countries around the world for a wide variety of products and services. The most common trade fair is one where broad categories of products are shown, with representatives from many firms and nations. The second is restricted to a narrower range of products for a more limited clientele. A third possibility is a trade show devoted to the products of a single firm.[22]

Pricing Decisions

While pricing is a key decision variable in any business enterprise, domestic or international, it is especially complex in international marketing. Strategically, a firm must decide whether to stress nonprice competition in its international operations or to focus on sound value for a competitive price. Nonprice competition emphasizes product quality and features, plus service and repair, all projected via advertising and sales promotion. The alternative approach highlights price and value for the money.[23]

Although a firm may espouse uniform prices in its domestic market, this is typically not feasible when competing in diverse countries around the world. Production costs, shipping expenses, the character and depth of competition, exchange rate fluctuations, duties and taxes all affect the multinational firm differently from one market to another, thereby mandating a tailored pricing strategy. But this can lead to a charge of dumping if the price abroad is lower than that in the home market without demonstrable justification for the differences.

Summary

Success in international marketing requires commitment, careful research of target markets, tailoring the product or line where appropriate to meet local needs, optimizing modes of market entry, skilled use of promotional and pricing strategies, long-term nurturing, and cultural sensitivity that transcends ethnocentric misperceptions.[24] But one should not be deterred. Mistakes will inevitably be made, but mistakes enhance learning and offer the opportunity to enlarge sales and profits internationally.

References

1. Pompiliu Verzariu, *Countertrade, Barter, Offsets: New Strategies for Profit in International Trade* *(Riverside, CA: Global Risk Assessments, 1985).*

2. John L. Graham and Taylor W. Meloan, "Preparing the Exporting Entrepreneur," *Journal of Marketing Education,* Spring 1986, pp. 11–20.

3. Edward W. Cundiff and Marye T. Hilgar, *Marketing in the International Environment* (Englewood Cliffs, NJ: Prentice Hall, 1984), pp. 233–34.

4. Vincent D. Travaglini, "Foreign Licensing and Joint Venture Arrangements," in *Foreign Business Practices* (Washington, DC: U.S. Department of Commerce, 1981), p. 75.

5. See Noel Capon, "Amicon Corporation," in *Problems in Marketing* ed. E. Raymond Cory, Christopher Lovelock, and Scott Ward (New York: McGraw-Hill Book Co., 1981), pp. 302–15, for a review of field of use considerations in granting a blood plasma license.

6. Jean Pierre Jeannet and Hubert D. Hennessey, *International Marketing Management* (Boston: Houghton Mifflin Co., 1992), pp. 295–99.

7. See Michael R. Czinkota and Ilkka A. Ronkainen, *International Marketing* (Chicago: The Dryden Press, 1990), p. 395 for a summary of international locations of U.S. franchising establishments.

8. V. H. Kirpalani, *International Marketing* (New York: Random House, 1985), pp. 311–12.

9. See Sak Onkvisit and John J. Shaw, *International Marketing* (New York: Macmillan Publishing Co., 1993), pp. 430–31, for a summary of key C.I.S. joint ventures.

10. Martin C. Schnitzer, Marilyn L. Liebrenz, and Konrad W. Kubin, *International Business* (Cincinnati: Southwestern Publishing Co., 1985), pp. 67–68.

11. Franklin R. Root, *Foreign Market Entry Strategies* (New York: AMACOM, 1982), pp. 127–28.

12. See Theodore Levitt, "The Globalization of Markets," *Harvard Business Review*, May/June, 1983, p. 13. See also Philip R. Cateora, *International Marketing* (Homewood, IL: Richard D. Irwin, Inc., 1993), pp. 646–47, for a review of the key differences between a global and a multinational company.

13. See Jerry Rogers (ed.), *Global Risk Assessments: Issues, Concepts and Applications* (Riverside, CA: Global Risk Assessments, Inc., 1983), for a detailed summarization of risk categories.

14. See Yonah Alexander (ed.), *International Terrorism: National, Regional and Global Perspectives* (New York: Praeger Publishers, 1978), for a review of terrorism in the major regions of the world.

15. A. Coskun Samli, Richard Still, and John S. Hill, *International Marketing* (New York: Macmillan Publishing Co., 1993), pp. 375–93.

16. Warren J. Keegar, *Global Marketing Management* (Englewood Cliffs, NJ: Prentice Hall, 1989), pp. 378–82.

17. Eileen Hill, "Protecting U.S. Intellectual Property Rights," *Business America* (April 14, 1986), pp. 2–6.

18. *Product Counterfeiting* (Arlington, VA: Council of Better Business Bureaus, 1985), pp. 34–35.

19. David A. Ricks, *Big Business Blunders: Mistakes in Multinational Marketing* (Homewood, IL: Dow Jones-Irwin, 1983), pp. 39, 52.

20. Dennis Chase, "The Impact of Globalization," *Advertising Age* (May 26, 1986), p. 32.

21. See Brian Toyne and Peter G. P. Walters, *Global Marketing Management* (Boston: Allyn and Bacon, 1993), pp. 550–54, for a review of regulation of advertising in Western Europe.

22. L. R. Thomas, "Trade Fairs: Gateways to European Markets," *Business America* (April 20, 1981), pp. 7–9.

23. See Lee D. Dahringer and Hans Muhlbacher, *International Marketing* (Reading, MA: Addison-Wesley Publishing Group, 1991), pp. 518–25, for a review of factors that influence international pricing. See Subhash C. Jain, *Export Strategy* (New York: Quorum Books, 1989), pp. 144–50, for a summary of the bases for export price determination, and Subhash C. Jain, *International Marketing Management* (Belmont, CA: Wadsworth Publishing Co., 1993), pp. 551–53, for a review of the factors influencing transfer pricing among units of a firm and the methods used to set transfer prices.

24. See Vern Terpstra and Ravi Sarathy, *International Marketing* (Fort Worth, TX: The Dryden Press, 1994), pp. 111–19, for a review of the religions of the world and their impact on culture.

The Globalization of Markets

Theodore Levitt. *Mr. Levitt is Edward W. Carter Professor of Business Administration and head of the marketing area at the Harvard Business School. This is Mr. Levitt's twenty-third article for HBR; his classic "Marketing Myopia," first published in 1960, was reprinted in September–October 1975, and his last article was "Marketing Intangible Products and Product Intangibles" (May–June 1981).*

A powerful force drives the world toward a converging commonality, and that force is technology. It has proletarianized communication, transport, and travel. It has made isolated places and impoverished peoples eager for modernity's allurements. Almost everyone everywhere wants all the things they have heard about, seen, or experienced via the new technologies.

The result is a new commercial reality—the emergence of global markets for standardized consumer products on a previously unimagined scale of magnitude. Corporations geared to this new reality benefit from enormous economies of scale in production, distribution, marketing, and management. By translating these benefits into reduced world prices, they can decimate competitors that still live in the disabling grip of old assumptions about how the world works.

Gone are accustomed differences in national or regional preference. Gone are the days when a company could sell last year's models—or lesser versions of advanced products—in the less-developed world. And gone are the days when prices, margins, and profits abroad were generally higher than at home.

The globalization of markets is at hand. With that, the multinational commercial world nears its end, and so does the multinational corporation.

The multinational and the global corporation are not the same thing. The multinational corporation operates in a number of countries, and adjusts its products and practices in each—at high relative costs. The global corporation operates with resolute constancy—at low relative cost—as if the entire world (or major regions of it) were a single entity; it sells the same things in the same way everywhere.

Which strategy is better is not a matter of opinion but of necessity. Worldwide communications carry everywhere the constant drumbeat of modern possibilities to lighten and enhance work, raise living standards, divert, and entertain. The same countries that ask the world to recognize and respect the individuality of their cultures insist on the wholesale transfer to them of modern goods, services, and technologies.

Modernity is not just a wish but also a widespread practice among those who cling, with unyielding passion or religious fervor, to ancient attitudes and heritages.

Who can forget the televised scenes during the 1979 Iranian uprisings of young men in fashionable French-cut trousers and silky body shirts thirsting with raised modern weapons for blood in the name of the Islamic fundamentalism?

In Brazil, thousands swarm daily from pre-industrial Bahian darkness into exploding coastal cities, there quickly to install television sets in crowded corrugated huts and, next to battered Volkswagens, make sacrificial offerings of fruit and fresh-killed chickens to Macumban spirits by candlelight.

During Biafra's fratricidal war against the Ibos, daily televised reports showed soldiers carrying bloodstained swords and listening to transistor radios while drinking Coca-Cola.

In the isolated Siberian city of Krasnoyarsk, with no paved streets and censored news, occasional Western travelers are stealthily propositioned for cigarettes, digital watches, and even the clothes off their backs.

The organized smuggling of electronic equipment, used automobiles, western clothing, cosmetics, and pirated movies into primitive places exceeds even the thriving underground trade in modern weapons and their military mercenaries.

A thousand suggestive ways attest to the ubiquity of the desire for the most advanced things that the world makes and sells—goods of the best quality and reliability at the lowest price. The world's needs and desires have been irrevocably homogenized. This makes the multinational corporation obsolete and the global corporation absolute.

Living in the Republic of Technology

Daniel J. Boorstin, author of the monumental trilogy *The Americans,* characterized our age as driven by "the Republic of Technology [whose] supreme law . . . is convergence, the tendency for everything to become more like everything else."

In business, this trend has pushed markets toward global commonality. Corporations sell standardized products in the same way everywhere—autos, steel, chemicals, petroleum, cement, agricultural commodities and equipment, industrial and commercial construction, banking and insurance services, computers, semiconductors, transport, electronic instruments, pharmaceuticals, and telecommunications, to mention some of the obvious.

Nor is the sweeping gale of globalization confined to these raw material or high-tech products where the universal language of customers and users facilitates standardization. The transforming winds whipped up by the proletarianization of communication and travel enter every crevice of life.

Commercially, nothing confirms this as much as the success of McDonald's from the Champs Elysees to the Ginza, of Coca-Cola in Bahrain and Pepsi-Cola in Moscow, and of rock music, Greek salad, Hollywood movies, Revlon cosmetics, Sony televisions, and Levi jeans everywhere. "High-touch" products are as ubiquitous as high-tech.

Starting from opposing sides, the high-tech and the high-touch ends of the commercial spectrum gradually consume the undistributed middle in their cosmopolitan orbit.

No one is exempt and nothing can stop the process. Everywhere everything gets more and more like everything else as the world's preference structure is relentlessly homogenized.

Consider the cases of Coca-Cola and Pepsi-Cola, which are globally standardized products sold everywhere and welcomed by everyone. Both successfully cross multitudes of national, regional, and ethnic taste buds trained to a variety of deeply ingrained local preferences of taste, flavor, consistency, effervescence, and aftertaste. Everywhere both sell well. Cigarettes, too, especially American-made, make year-to-year global inroads on territories previously held in the firm grip of other, mostly local, blends.

These are not exceptional examples. (Indeed their global reach would be even greater were it not for artificial trade barriers.) They exemplify a general drift toward the homogenization of the world and how companies distribute, finance, and price products.[1] Nothing is exempt. The products and methods of the industrialized world play a single tune for all the world, and all the world eagerly dances to it.

Ancient differences in national tastes or modes of doing business disappear. The commonality of preference leads inescapably to the standardization of products, manufacturing, and the institutions of trade and commerce. Small nation-based markets transmogrify and expand. Success in world competition turns on efficiency in production, distribution, marketing, and management, and inevitably becomes focused on price.

The most effective world competitors incorporate superior quality and reliability into their cost structures. They sell in all national markets the same kind of products sold at home or in their largest export market. They compete on the basis of appropriate value—the best combinations of price, quality, reliability, and delivery for products that are globally identical with respect to design, function, and even fashion.

That, and little else, explains the surging success of Japanese companies dealing worldwide in a vast variety of products—both tangible products like steel, cars, motorcycles, hi-fi equipment, farm machinery, robots, microprocessors, carbon fibers, and now even textiles, and intangibles like banking, shipping, general contracting, and soon computer software. Nor are high-quality and low-cost operations incompatible, as a host of consulting organizations and data engineers argue with vigorous vacuity. The reported data are incomplete, wrongly analyzed, and contradictory. The truth is that low-cost operations are the hallmark of corporate cultures that require and produce quality in all that they do. High quality and low costs are not opposing postures. They are compatible, twin identities of superior practice.[2]

To say that Japan's companies are not global because they export cars with left-side drives to the United States and the European continent, while those in Japan have right-side drives, or because they sell office machines through distributors in the United States but directly at home, or speak Portuguese in Brazil is to mistake a difference for a distinction. The same is true of Safeway and Southland retail chains operating effectively in the Middle East, and to not only native but also imported populations from Korea, the Philippines, Pakistan, India, Thailand, Britain, and the United States. National rules of the road differ, and so do distribution channels and languages. Japan's distinction is its unrelenting push for economy and value enhancement. That translates into a drive for standardization at high quality levels.

Vindication of the Model T

If a company forces costs and prices down and pushes quality and reliability up—while maintaining reasonable concern for suitability—customers will prefer its world-standardized products. The theory holds at this stage in the evolution of globalization, no matter what conventional market research and even common sense may suggest about different national and regional tastes, preferences, needs, and institutions. The Japanese have repeatedly vindicated this theory, as did Henry Ford with the Model T. Most important, so have their imitators, including companies from South Korea (television sets and heavy construction), Malaysia (personal calculators and microcomputers), Brazil (auto parts and tools), Colombia (apparel), Singapore (optical equipment) and, yes, even from the United States (copiers, computers, bicycles, castings), Western Europe (automatic washing machines), Rumania (housewares), Hungary (apparel), Yugoslavia (furniture), and Israel (pagination equipment).

Of course, large companies operating in a single nation or even a single city don't standardize everything they make, sell, or do. They have product lines instead of a single product version, and multiple distribution channels. There are neighborhood, local, regional, ethnic, and institutional differences, even within metropolitan areas. But although companies customize products for particular market segments, they know that success in a world with homogenized demand requires a search for sales opportunities in similar segments across the globe in order to achieve the economics of scale necessary to compete.

Such a search works because a market segment in one country is seldom unique; it has close cousins everywhere precisely because technology has homogenized the globe. Even small local segments have their global equivalents everywhere and become subject to global competition, especially on price.

The global competitor will seek constantly to standardize his offering everywhere. He will digress from this standardization only after exhausting all possibilities to retain it, and he will push for reinstatement of standardization whenever digression and divergence have occurred. He will never assume that the customer is a king who knows his own wishes.

Trouble increasingly stalks companies that lack clarified global focus and remain inattentive to the economics of simplicity and standardization. The most endangered companies in the rapidly evolving world tend to be those that dominate rather small domestic markets with high value-added products for which there are smaller markets elsewhere. With transportation costs proportionately low, distant competitors will enter the now-sheltered markets of those companies with goods produced more cheaply under scale-efficient conditions. Global competition spells the end of domestic territoriality, no matter how diminutive the territory may be.

When the global producer offers his lower cost internationally, his patronage expands exponentially. He not only reaches into distant markets, but also attracts customers who previously held to local preferences and now capitulate to the attractions of lesser prices. The strategy of standardization not only responds to worldwide homogenized markets but also expands those markets with aggressive low pricing. The new technological juggernaut taps an ancient motivation—to make one's money go as far as possible. This is universal—not simply a motivation but actually a need.

The Hedgehog Knows

The difference between the hedgehog and the fox, wrote Sir Isaiah Berlin in distinguishing between Dostoevski and Tolstoy, is that the fox knows a lot about a great many things, but the hedgehog knows everything about one great thing. The multinational corporation knows a lot about a great many countries and congenially adapts to supposed differences. It willingly accepts vestigial national differences, not questioning the possibility of their transformation, not recognizing how the world is ready and eager for the benefit of modernity, especially when the price is right. The multinational corporation's accommodating mode to visible national differences is medieval.

By contrast, the global corporation knows everything about one great thing. It knows about the absolute need to be competitive on a worldwide basis as well as nationally and seeks constantly to drive down prices by standardizing what it sells and how it operates. It treats the world as composed of a few standardized markets rather than many customized markets. It actively seeks and vigorously works toward global convergence. Its mission is modernity and its mode, price competition, even when it sells top-of-the-line, high-end products. It knows about the one great thing all nations and people have in common: scarcity.

Nobody takes scarcity lying down; everyone wants more. This in part explains division of labor and specialization of production. They enable people and nations to optimize their conditions through trade. The medium is usually money.

Experience teaches that money has three special qualities: scarcity, difficulty of acquisition, and transience. People understandably treat it with respect. Everyone in the increasingly homogenized world market wants products and features that everybody else wants. If the price is low enough, they will take highly standardized world products, even if these aren't exactly what mother said was suitable, what immemorial custom decreed was right, or what market-research fabulists asserted was preferred.

The implacable truth of all modern production—whether of tangible or intangible goods—is that large-scale production of standardized items is generally cheaper within a wide range of volume than small-scale production. Some argue that CAD/CAM will allow companies to manufacture customized products on a small scale—but cheaply. But the argument misses the point. If a company treats the world as one or two distinctive product markets, it can serve the world more economically than if it treats it as three, four, or five product markets.

Why Remaining Differences?

Different cultural preferences, national tastes and standards, and business institutions are vestiges of the past. Some inheritances die gradually; other prosper and expand into mainstream global preferences. So-called ethnic markets are a good example. Chinese food, pita bread, country and western music, pizza, and jazz are everywhere. They are market segments that exist in worldwide proportions. They don't deny or contradict global homogenization but confirm it.

Many of today's differences among nations as to products and their features actually reflect the respectful accommodation of multinational corporation to what they believe are fixed local preferences. They *believe* preferences are fixed, not because they are but because of rigid habits of thinking about what actually is. Most executives in multinational corporations are thoughtlessly accommodating. They falsely presume that marketing means giving the customer what he says he wants rather than trying to understand exactly what he'd like. So they persist with high-cost, customized multinational products and practices instead of pressing hard and pressing properly for global standardization.

I do not advocate the systematic disregard of local or national differences. But a company's sensitivity to such differences does not require that it ignore the possibilities of doing things differently or better.

There are, for example, enormous differences among Middle Eastern countries. Some are socialist, some monarchies, some republics. Some take their legal heritage from the Napoleonic Code, some from the Ottoman Empire, and some from the British common law; except for Israel, all are influenced by Islam. Doing business means personalizing the business relationship in an obsessively intimate fashion. During the month of Ramadan, business discussions can start only after 10 o'clock at night, when people are tired and full of food after a day of fasting. A company must almost certainly have a local partner; a local lawyer is required (as, say, in New York), and irrevocable letters of credit are essential. Yet, as Coca-Cola's Senior Vice President Sam Ayoub noted, "Arabs are much more capable of making distinctions between cultural and religious purposes on the one hand and economic realities on the other than is generally assumed. Islam is compatible with science and modern times."

Barriers to globalization are not confined to the Middle East. The free transfer of technology and data across the boundaries of the European Common Market countries are hampered by legal and financial impediments. And there is resistance to radio and television interference ("pollution") among neighboring European countries.

But the past is a good guide to the future. With persistence and appropriate means, barriers against superior technologies and economics have always fallen. There is no recorded exception where reasonable effort has been made to overcome them. It is very much a matter of time and effort.

A Failure in Global Imagination

Many companies have tried to standardize world practice by exporting domestic products and processes without accommodation or change—and have failed miserably. Their deficiencies have been seized on as evidence of bovine stupidity in the face of abject impossibility. Advocates of global standardization see them as examples of failures in execution.

In fact, poor execution is often an important cause. More important, however, is failure of nerve—failure of imagination.

Consider the case for the introduction of fully automatic home laundry equipment in Western Europe at a time when few homes had even semiautomatic machines. Hoover,

Ltd., whose parent company was headquartered in North Canton, Ohio, had a prominent presence in Britain as a producer of vacuum cleaners and washing machines. Due to insufficient demand in the home market and low exports to the European continent, the large washing machine plant in England operated far below capacity. The company needed to sell more of its semiautomatic or automatic machines.

Because it had a "proper" marketing orientation, Hoover conducted consumer preference studies in Britain and each major continental country. The results showed feature preferences clearly enough among several countries (see the exhibit).

The incremental unit variable costs (in pounds sterling) of customizing to meet just a few of the national preferences were:

	£	s.	d.
Stainless steel vs. enamel drum	1	0	0
Porthole window		10	0
Spin speed of 800 rpm vs. 700 rpm		15	0
Water heater	2	15	0
6 vs. 5 kilos capacity	1	10	0
	£6	10s	0d

$18.20 at the exchange rate of that time.

Considerable plant investment was needed to meet other preferences.

The lowest retail prices (in pounds sterling) of leading locally produced brands in the various countries were approximately:

U.K.	£110
France	114
West Germany	113
Sweden	134
Italy	57

Product customization in each country would have put Hoover in a poor competitive position on the basis of price, mostly due to the higher manufacturing costs incurred by short production runs for separate features. Because Common Market tariff reduction programs were then incomplete, Hoover also paid tariff duties in each continental country.

How to Make a Creative Analysis

In the Hoover case, an imaginative analysis of automatic washing machines sales in each country would have revealed that:

1. Italian automatics, small in capacity and size, low-powered, without built-in heaters, with porcelain enamel tubs, were priced aggressively low and were gaining large market shares in all countries, including West Germany.

2. The best-selling automatics in West Germany were heavily advertised (three times more than the next most promoted brand), were ideally suited to national tastes, and were also by far the highest priced machines available in that country.

3. Italy, with the lowest penetration of washing machines of any kind (manual, semiautomatic, or automatic) was rapidly going directly to automatics, skipping the pattern of first buying hand wringer, manually assisted machines and then semiautomatics.

4. Detergent manufacturers were just beginning to promote the technique of cold-water and tepid-water laundering then used in the United States.

The growing success of small, low-powered, low-speed, low-capacity, low-priced Italian machines, even against the preferred but highly priced and highly promoted brand in West Germany, was significant. It contained a powerful message that was lost on managers confidently wedded to a distorted version of the marketing concept according to which you give the customer what he says he wants. In fact the customers *said* they wanted certain features, but their behavior demonstrated they'd take other features provided the price and the promotion were right.

In this case it was obvious that, under prevailing conditions, people preferred a low-priced automatic over any kind of manual or semiautomatic machine and certainly over high priced automatics, even though the low-priced automatics failed to fulfill all their expressed preferences. The supposedly meticulous and demanding German consumers violated all expectations by buying the simple, low-priced Italian machines.

It was equally clear that people were profoundly influenced by promotions of automatic washers; in West Germany, the most heavily promoted ideal machine also had the largest market share despite its high price. Two things clearly influenced customers to buy: low price regardless of feature preferences and heavy promotion regardless of price. Both factors helped homemakers get what they most wanted—the superior benefits bestowed by fully automatic machines.

Hoover should have aggressively sold a simple, standardized high-quality machine at a low price (afforded by the 17% variable cost reduction that the elimination of £6–10–0 worth of extra features made possible). The suggested retail prices could have been somewhat less than £100. The extra funds "saved" by avoiding unnecessary plant modifications would have supported an extended service network and aggressive media promotions.

Hoover's media message should have been: *this* is the machine that you, the homemaker, *deserve* to have to reduce the repetitive heavy daily household burdens, so that *you* may have more constructive time to spend with your children and your husband. The promotion should also have targeted the husband to give him, preferably in the presence of his wife, a sense of obligation to provide an automatic washer for her even before he bought an automobile for himself. An aggressively low price, combined with heavy promotion of this kind, would have overcome previously expressed preferences for particular features.

The Hoover case illustrates how the perverse practice of the marketing concept and the absence of any kind of marketing imagination let multinational attitudes survive when customers actually want the benefits of global standardization. The whole project got off on the wrong foot. It asked people what features they wanted in a washing machine rather than what they wanted out of life. Selling a line of products individually tailored to each nation is thoughtless. Managers who took pride in practicing the marketing concept to the fullest did not, in fact, practice it at all. Hoover asked the wrong questions, then applied neither thought nor imagination to the answers. Such companies are like the ethnocentricists in the Middle Ages who saw with everyday clarity the sun revolving around the earth and offered it as Truth. With no additional data but a more searching mind, Copernicus, like the hedgehog, interpreted a more compelling and accurate reality. Data do not yield information except with the intervention of the mind. Information does not yield meaning except with the intervention of imagination.

Features	Great Britain	Italy	West Germany	France	Sweden
Shell dimensions*	34″ and narrow	Low and narrow	34″ and wide	34″ and narrow	34″ and wide
Drum material	Enamel	Enamel	Stainless steel	Enamel	Stainless steel
Loading	Top	Front	Front	Front	Front
Front porthole	Yes/no	Yes	Yes	Yes	Yes
Capacity	5 kilos	4 kilos	6 kilos	5 kilos	6 kilos
Spin speed	700 rpm	400 rpm	850 rpm	600 rpm	800 rpm
Water-heating system	No[†]	Yes	Yes[††]	Yes	No[†]
Washing action	Agitator	Tumble	Tumble	Agitator	Tumble
Styling features	Inconspicuous appearance	Brightly colored	Indestructible appearance	Elegant appearance	Strong appearance

*34″ height was (in process of being adopted as) a standard work-surface height in Europe.

[†]Most British and Swedish homes had centrally heated hot water.

[††]West Germans preferred to launder at temperatures higher than generally provided centrally.

Accepting the Inevitable

The global corporation accepts for better or for worse that technology drives consumers relentlessly toward the same common goals—alleviation of life's burdens and the expansion of discretionary time and spending power. Its role is profoundly different from what it has been for the ordinary corporation during its brief, turbulent, and remarkably protean history. It orchestrates the twin vectors of technology and globalization for the world's benefit. Neither fate, nor nature, nor God but rather the necessity of commerce created this role.

In the United States two industries became global long before they were consciously aware of it. After over a generation of persistent and acrimonious labor shutdowns, the United Steel Workers of America have not called an industry-wide strike since 1959; the United Auto Workers have not shut down General Motors since 1970. Both unions realize that they have become global—shutting down all or most of U.S. manufacturing would not shut out U.S. customers. Overseas suppliers are there to supply the market.

Cracking the Code of Western Markets

Since the theory of the marketing concept emerged a quarter of a century ago, the more managerially advanced corporations have been eager to offer what customers clearly wanted rather than what was merely convenient. They have created marketing departments supported by professional market researchers of awesome and often costly proportions. And they have proliferated extraordinary numbers of operations and product lines—highly tailored products and delivery systems for many different markets, market segments, and nations.

Significantly, Japanese companies operate almost entirely without marketing departments or market research of the kind so prevalent in the West. Yet, in the colorful words of General Electric's chairman John F. Welch, Jr., the Japanese, coming from a small cluster of resource-poor islands, with an entirely alien culture and an almost impenetrably complex language, have cracked the code of Western markets. They have done it not by looking with mechanistic thoroughness at the way markets are different but rather by searching for meaning with a deeper wisdom. They have discovered the one great thing all markets have in common—an overwhelming desire for dependable, world-standard modernity in all things, at aggressively low prices. In response, they deliver irresistible value everywhere, attracting people with products that market-research technocrats described with superficial certainty as being unsuitable and uncompetitive.

The wider a company's global reach, the greater the number of regional and national preferences it will encounter for certain product features, distribution systems, or promotional media. There will always need to be some accommodation to differences. But the widely prevailing and often unthinking belief in the immutability of these differences is generally mistaken. Evidence of business failure because of lack of accommodation is often evidence of other shortcomings.

Take the case of Revlon in Japan. The company unnecessarily alienated retailers and confused customers by selling world-standardized cosmetics only in elite outlets; then it tried to recover with low-priced world-standardized products in broader distribution, followed by a change in the company president and cutbacks in distribution as costs rose faster than sales. The problem was not that Revlon didn't understand the Japanese market; it didn't do the job right, wavered in its programs, and was impatient to boot.

By contrast, the Outboard Marine Corporation, with imagination, push, and persistence, collapsed long-established three-tiered distribution channels in Europe into a more focused and controllable two-step system—and did so despite the vociferous warnings of local trade groups. It also reduced the number and types of retail outlets. The result was greater improvement in credit and product-installation service to customers, major cost reductions, and sales advances.

In its highly successful introduction of Contac 600 (the timed-release decongestant) into Japan, SmithKline Corporation used 35 wholesalers instead of the 1,000-plus that established practice required. Daily contacts with the wholesalers and key retailers, also in violation of established practice, supplemented the plan, and it worked.

Denied access to established distribution institutions in the United States, Komatsu, the Japanese manufacturer of lightweight farm machinery, entered the market through over-the-road construction equipment dealers in rural areas of the Sunbelt, where farms are smaller, the soil sandier and easier to work. Here inexperienced distributors were able to attract customers on the basis of Komatsu's product and price appropriateness.

In cases of successful challenge to prevailing institutions and practices, a combination of product reliability and quality, strong and sustained support systems aggressively low prices, and sales compensation packages, as well as audacity and implacability, circumvented, shattered, and transformed very different distribution systems. Instead of resentment, there was admiration.

Still, some differences between nations are unyielding, even in a world of microprocessors. In the United States almost all manufacturers of microprocessors check them for reliability through a so-called parallel system of testing. Japan prefers the totally different sequential testing system. So Teradyne Corporation, the world's largest producer of microprocessor test equipment, makes one line for the United States and one for Japan. That's easy.

What's not so easy for Teradyne is to know how best to organize and manage, in this instance, its marketing effort. Companies can organize by product, region, function, or by using some combination of these. A company can have separate marketing organizations for Japan and for the United States, or it can have separate product groups, one working largely in Japan and the other in the United States. A single manufacturing facility or marketing operation might service both markets, or a company might use separate marketing operations for each.

Questions arise if the company organizes by product. In the case of Teradyne, should the group handling the parallel system, whose major market is the United States, sell in Japan and compete with the group focused on the Japanese market? If the company organizes regionally, how do regional groups divide their efforts between promoting the parallel vs. the sequential system? If the company organizes in terms of function, how does it get commitment in marketing, for example, for one line instead of the other?

There is no one reliably right answer—no one formula by which to get it. There isn't even a satisfactory contingent answer.[3] What works well for one company or one place may fail for another in precisely the same place, depending on the capabilities, histories, reputations, resources, and even the cultures of both.

The Earth Is Flat

The differences that persist throughout the world despite its globalization affirm an ancient dictum of economics—that things are driven by what happens at the margin, not at the core. Thus, in ordinary competitive analysis, what's important is not the average price but the marginal price; what happens not in the usual case but at the interface of newly erupting conditions. What counts in commercial affairs is what happens at the cutting edge. What is most striking today is the underlying similarities of what is happening now to national preferences at the margin. These similarities at the cutting edge cumulatively form an overwhelming predominant commonality everywhere.

To refer to the persistence of economic nationalism (protective and subsidized trade practices, special tax aids, or restrictions for home market producers) as a barrier to the globalization of markets is to make a valid point. Economic nationalism does have a powerful persistence. But, as with the present almost totally smooth internationalization of investment capital, the past alone does not shape or predict the future.

Reality is not a fixed paradigm, dominated by immemorial customs and derived attitudes, heedless of powerful and abundant new forces. The world is becoming increasingly informed about the liberating and enhancing possibilities of modernity. The persistence of the inherited varieties of national preferences rests uneasily on increasing evidence of, and restlessness regarding, their inefficiency, costliness, and confinement. The historic past, and the national differences respecting commerce and industry it spawned and fostered everywhere, are now subject to relatively easy transformation.

Cosmopolitanism is no longer the monopoly of the intellectual and leisure classes; it is becoming the established property and defining characteristic of all sectors everywhere in the world. Gradually and irresistibly it breaks down the walls of economic insularity, nationalism, and chauvinism. What we see today as escalating commercial nationalism is simply the last violent death rattle of an obsolete institution.

Companies that adapt to and capitalize on economic convergence can still make distinctions and adjustments in different markets. Persistent differences in the world are consistent with fundamental underlying commonalities; they often complement rather than oppose each other—in business as they do in physics. There is, in physics, simultaneously matter and anti-matter working in symbiotic harmony.

The earth is round, but for most purposes it's sensible to treat it as flat. Space is curved, but not much for everyday life here on earth.

Divergence from established practice happens all the time. But the multinational mind, warped into circumspection and timidity by years of stumbles and transnational troubles, now rarely challenges existing overseas practices. More often it considers any departure from inherited domestic routines as mindless, disrespectful, or impossible. It is the mind of a bygone day.

The successful global corporation does not abjure customization or differentiation for the requirements of markets that differ in product preferences, spending patterns, shopping preferences, and institutional or legal arrangements. But the global corporation accepts and adjusts to these differences only reluctantly, only after relentlessly testing their immutability, after trying in various ways to circumvent and reshape them as we saw in the cases of Outboard Marine in Europe, SmithKline in Japan, and Komatsu in the United States.

There is only one significant respect in which a company's activities around the world are important, and this is in what it produces and how it sells. Everything else derives from, and is subsidiary to, these activities.

The purpose of business is to get and keep a customer. Or, to use Peter Drucker's more refined construction, to *create* and keep a customer. A company must be wedded to the ideal of innovation—offering better or more preferred products in such combinations of ways, means, places, and at such prices that prospects *prefer* doing business with the company rather than with others.

Preferences are constantly shaped and reshaped. Within our global commonality enormous variety constantly asserts itself and thrives, as can be seen within the world's single largest domestic market, the United States. But in the process of world homogenization, modern markets expand to reach cost-reducing global proportions. With better and cheaper communication and transport, even small local market segments hitherto protected from distant competitors now feel the pressure of their presence. Nobody is safe from global reach and the irresistible economics of scale.

Two vectors shape the world—technology and globalization. The first helps determine human preferences; the second, economic realities. Regardless of how much preferences evolve and diverge, they also gradually converge and form markets where economics of scale lead to reduction of costs and prices.

The modern global corporation contrasts powerfully with the aging multinational corporation. Instead of adapting to superficial and even entrenched differences within and between nations, it will seek sensibly to force suitably standardized products and practices on the entire globe. They are exactly what the world will take, if they come also with low prices, high quality, and blessed reliability. The global company will operate, in this regard, precisely as Henry Kissinger wrote in *Years of Upheaval* about the continuing Japanese economic success—"voracious in its collection of information, impervious to pressure, and implacable in execution."

Given what is everywhere the purpose of commerce, the global company will shape the vectors of technology and globalization into its great strategic fecundity. It will systematically push these vectors toward their own convergence, offering everyone simultaneously high-quality, more or less standardized products at optimally low prices, thereby achieving for itself vastly expanded markets and profits. Companies that do not adapt to the new global realities will become victims of those that do.

References

1. In a landmark article, Robert D. Buzzell pointed out the rapidity with which barriers to standardization were falling. In all cases they succumbed to more and cheaper advanced ways of doing things. See "Can You Standardize Multinational Marketing?" *HBR* November–December 1968, p. 102.

2. There is powerful new evidence for this, even though the opposite has been urged by analysts of PIMS data for nearly a decade. See "Product Quality: Cost Production and Business Performance—A Test of Some Key Hypotheses" by Lynn W. Phillips, Dae Chang, and Robert D. Buzzell, Harvard Business School Working Paper No. 83–13.

3. For a discussion of multinational reorganization, see Christopher A. Bartlett, "MNCs: Get Off the Reorganization Merry-Go-Round," *HBR* March–April 1983, p. 138.

The Myth of Globalization

Susan P. Douglas and Yoram Wind. *Susan P. Douglas is a Professor of Marketing and International Business at New York University's Graduate School of Business Administration. Her research interests include international consumer behavior, international market research and strategic planning for international markets. Yoram Wind is The Lauder Professor and Professor of Marketing at the Wharton School of the University of Pennsylvania. He is the author of ten books and about 200 papers and articles, encompassing the areas of marketing strategy, marketing research, new product and market development, consumer and industrial buying behavior, and international marketing. He is also an active consultant to many Fortune 500 companies and multinationals in Europe, Latin America, and Japan.*

In recent years, globalization has become a key theme in every discussion of international marketing strategy. Proponents of the philosophy of "global" products and brands, such as professor Theodore Levitt of Harvard, and the highly successful advertising agency, Saatchi and Saatchi, argue that in a world of growing internationalization, the key to success is the development of global products and brands, in other words, a focus on the marketing of standardized products and brands worldwide (Levitt 1983). Others, however, point to the numerous barriers to standardization, and suggest that greater returns are to be obtained from adapting products and marketing strategies to the specific characteristics of individual markets (Fisher 1984, Kotler 1985, Vedder 1986).

The growing integration of international markets as well as the growth of competition on a worldwide scale implies that adoption of a global perspective has become increasingly imperative in planning marketing strategy. However, to conclude that this mandates the adoption of a strategy of universal standardization appears naive and oversimplistic. In particular, it ignores the inherent complexity of operations in international markets, and the formulation of an effective strategy to penetrate these markets. While global products and brands may be appropriate for certain markets and in targeting certain segments, adopting such an approach as a universal strategy in relation to all markets may not be desirable, and may lead to major strategic blunders. Furthermore, it implies a product orientation, and a product-drive strategy, rather than a strategy grounded in a systematic analysis of customer behavior and response patterns and market characteristics.

The purpose of this paper is thus to examine critically the notion that success in international markets necessitates adoption of a strategy of global products and brands. Given the restrictive characteristics of this philosophy, a somewhat broader perspective in developing global strategy is proposed which views standardization as merely one option in the range of possible strategies which may be effective in global markets.

The paper is divided into four parts. First, the traditional perspective on international marketing strategy focusing on the dichotomy between "standardization" and "adaptation" is reviewed. The second part examines the key assumptions underlying a philosophy of global standardization, as well as situations under which this is likely to prove effective. In the third part, the constraints to the implementation of a global standardization strategy are reviewed, including not only external market constraints, but also internal constraints arising from the structure of the firm's current operations. Finally, based on this review, a more general approach is suggested, enabling consideration of a range of alternative strategies incorporating varying degrees of standardization or adaptation.

The Traditional Perspective on International Marketing Strategy

Traditionally, discussion of international business strategy has been polarized around the debate concerning the pursuit of a uniform strategy worldwide versus adaptation to specific local market conditions. On the one hand, it has been argued that adoption of a uniform strategy worldwide enables a company to take advantage of the potential synergies arising from multi-country operations, and constitutes the multinational company's key competitive advantage in international markets. Others however, have argued that adaptation of strategy to idiosyncratic national market characteristics is crucial to success in these markets.

Fayerweather (1969) in his seminal work in international business strategy described the central issue as one of conflict between forces toward unification and those resulting in fragmentation. He pointed out that within a multinational firm, internal forces created pressures toward the integration of strategy across national boundaries. On the other hand, differences in the sociocultural, political and economic characteristics of countries as well as the need for effective relations with the host society constitute fragmenting influences which favor adaptation to the local environment.

This theme has been elaborated further in subsequent discussions of international business strategy. Doz (1980), for example, characterizes the conflict as one between the requirements for economic survival and success (the economic imperative), and the adjustments to strategy made necessary by the demands of host governments (the political imperative). Economic success or profitability in international markets is viewed as contingent on the rationalization of activities across national boundaries.

The political imperative, on the other hand, implies a strategy of "national responsiveness" forgoing potential benefits of global integration and allowing local subsidiaries substantial autonomy to develop their own production policies and strategy. A third alternative, "administrative coordination" is, however, postulated. In this case, each strategic decision is made on its own merits, allowing flexibility either to respond to pressures for national responsiveness or alternatively to move towards worldwide rationalization.

Recent discussion of global competitive strategy (Porter 1980, 1985) echoes the same theme of the dichotomy between the forces which have triggered the globalization of markets and those which constitute barriers to global competition. Factors such as economies of scale in production, purchasing, faster accumulation of learning from operating worldwide, decrease in transportation and distribution costs, reduced costs of product adaptation and the emergence of global market segments have encouraged competition on a global scale. However, barriers such as governmental and institutional constraints, tariff barriers and duties, preferential treatment of local firms, transportation costs, differences in customer demand, etc., call for nationalistic or "protected niche" strategies.

Similar arguments have characterized the debate concerning uniformity vs. adaptation of marketing and advertising strategies. In this context, greater attention has generally been focused on barriers to standardization (Buzzell 1968, Elinder 1964). Differences in customer behavior and response patterns, in local competition, in the nature of the marketing infrastructure, as well as government and trade regulation have all been cited as calling for, and in some cases rendering imperative, the adaptation of products, advertising copy, and other aspects of marketing policy (Miracle 1968, Dunn 1966, Donnelly and Ryans 1969, Ryans 1969). Yet, some advocates of a uniform or standardized strategy worldwide, especially in relation to advertising copy, have emerged—who point to a growing internationalization of life-styles, and increasing homogeneity in consumer interests and tastes (Britt 1974, Fatt 1967, Boote 1967, Killough 1978). They have, for example, noted benefits such as development of a consistent uniform image with customers worldwide, improved planning and control, exploitation of good ideas on a broader geographic scale, as well as potential cost savings.

Compromise solutions such as "pattern standardization" have also been proposed (Peebles, Ryans and Vernon 1978). In this case, a global promotional theme or positioning is developed, but execution is adapted to the local market. Similarly, it has been pointed out that even where a standardized product is marketed in a number of countries, its positioning may be adapted in each market (Keegan 1969). Conversely, the positioning may be uniform across countries, but the product itself adapted or modified.

Although this debate first emerged in the 1960s, it has recently taken on a new vigor with the widely publicized pronouncements of proponents of "global standardization" such as Professor Levitt and Saatchi and Saatchi. Levitt, for example, in his provocative article (1983) stated:

> A powerful force (technology) now drives the world toward a single converging commonality. The result is a new commercial reality—the explosive emergence of global markets for globally standardized products, gigantic world-scale markets of previously unimagined magnitudes.
>
> Corporations geared to this new reality generate enormous economies of scale in production, distribution, marketing, and management. When they translate these into equivalently reduced world prices, they devastate competitors that still live functionally in the disabling grip of old assumptions about how the world now works.

The sweeping and somewhat polemic character of this argument has sparked a number of counterarguments as well as discussion of conditions under which such a strategy may be most appropriate. It has, for example, been pointed out that the potential for standardization may be greater for certain types of products such as industrial goods or luxury personal items targeted to upscale consumers, or products with similar penetration rates (Huszagh, Fox, and Day 1985). Opportunities for standardization are also likely to occur more frequently among industrialized nations, and especially the Triad countries, where customer interests as well as market conditions are likely to be more similar than among developing countries (Hill and Still 1983, Huszagh, Fox, and Day 1985, Ohmae 1985).

The role of corporate philosophy and organizational structure in influencing the practicality of implementing a strategy of global standardization has also been recognized (Quelch and Hoff 1986). Here, it has been noted that few companies pursue the extreme position of complete standardization with regard to all elements of the marketing mix, and business functions such as R and D, manufacturing, and procurement in all countries throughout the world. Rather, some degree of adaptation is likely to occur relative to certain aspects of the firm's operations or in certain geographic areas. In addition, the feasibility of implementing a standardized strategy will depend on the autonomy accorded to local management. If local management has been accustomed to substantial autonomy, considerable opposition may be encountered in attempting to introduce globally standardized strategies.

An examination of such counterarguments suggests that there are a number of dangers in espousing a philosophy of global standardization for all products and services, and in relation to all markets worldwide. Furthermore, there are numerous difficulties and constraints to implementing such a strategy in many markets, stemming from external market conditions (such as government and trade regulation, competition, the marketing infrastructure, etc.), as well as from the current structure and organization of the firm's operations.

The rationale underlying the philosophy of global products and brands is next examined in more detail, together with its inherent limitations.

The Global Standardization Philosophy:
The Underlying Assumptions

An examination of the arguments in favor of a strategy of global products and brands reveals three key underlying assumptions:

1. customer needs and interests are becoming increasingly homogeneous worldwide.
2. people around the world are willing to sacrifice preferences in product features, functions, design and the like for lower prices at high quality.
3. substantial economies of scale in production and marketing can be achieved through supplying global markets.

(Levitt 1983)

There are, however, a number of pitfalls associated with each of these assumptions. These are discussed here in more details.

Homogenization of the World Wants

A key premise of the philosophy of global products is that customers' needs and interest are becoming increasingly homogeneous worldwide. But while global segments with similar interests and response pattern may be identified in some product markets, it is by no means clear that this is a universal trend. Furthermore, there is substantial evidence to suggest an increasing diversity of behavior within countries, and the emergence of idiosyncratic country-specific segments.

Lack of Evidence of Homogenization.   In a number of product markets ranging from watches, perfume, handbags, to soft drinks and fast foods, companies have successfully identified global customer segments, and developed global products and brands targeted to these segments. These include such stars a Rolex, Omega and Le Baume & Mercier watches, Dior, Patou or Yves St. Laurent perfume. But while these brands are highly visible and widely publicized, they are often, with a few notable exceptions, such as Classic Coke or McDonald's, targeted to a relatively restricted upscale international customer segment (Ohmae 1985).

Numerous other companies, however, adapt lines to idiosyncratic country preferences, and develop local brands or product variants targeted to local market segments. The Findus frozen food division of Nestlé, for example, markets fish cakes and fish fingers in the UK, but beef bourguinon and coq au vin in France, and vitello con funghi and braviola in Italy. Their line of pizzas marketed in the UK includes cheese with ham and pineapple topping on a French bread crust. Similarly, Coca-Cola in Japan markets Georgia, cold coffee in a can, and Aquarius, a tonic drink, as well as Classic Coke and Hi-C.

Growth of Intra-Country Segmentation Price Sensitivity.   Furthermore, there is a growing body of evidence which suggests substantial heterogeneity within countries. In the US, for example, the VALS study has identified nine value segments (Mitchell 1983), while other studies have identified major differences in behavior between regions and subcultural segments (Kahle 1986, Garreau 1981, Wallendorf and Reilly 1983, Saegert, Moore & Hilger 1985). Lifestyle approaches such as the Yankelovich Monitor (Beatty 1985) or the customized AIO approach (Wells 1975) have also identified different lifestyle segments both generally and relative to specific product markets.

Many other countries are also characterized by substantial regional differences as well as different lifestyle and value segments. The Yankelovich Monitor and AIO approaches have, for example, been applied in a number of countries throughout the world (Broadbent and Segnit 1973, the RISC Observer No. 1 & 2, 1986). In some cases, this has resulted in the identification of some common segments across countries, but country-specific segments have also emerged (Douglas and Urban 1977, Boote 1982/3). Lifestyle segmentation studies conducted by local research organizations in other countries also reveal a variety of lifestyle profiles (Hakuhodo 1985).

Similarly, in industrial markets, while some global segments, often consisting of firms with international operations, can be identified, there also is considerable diversity within and between countries. Often local businesses constitute an important market segment and, especially in developing countries, may differ significantly in technological sophistication, business, philosophy and strategy, emphasis on product quality, and service and price, from large multinationals (Hill and Still, 1984, Chakrabarti, Feinman and Fuentivilla, 1982).

The evidence thus suggests that the similarities in customer behavior are restricted to a relatively limited number of target segments, or product markets, while for the most part, there are substantial differences between countries. Proponents of standardization counter that the international marketer should focus on similarities among countries rather than differences. This may, however, imply ignoring a major part of a local market, and the potential profits which may be obtained from tapping other market segments.

Universal Preference for Low Price at Acceptable Quality

Another critical component of the argument for global standardization is that people around the world are willing to sacrifice preferences in product features, functions, design and the like for lower prices assuming equivalent quality. Aggressive low pricing for quality products which meet the common needs of customers in markets around the world is believed to further expand the global markets facing the firm. Although an appealing argument, this has three major problems.

Lack of Evidence of Increases.   Evidence to suggest that customers are universally willing to trade off specific product features for a lower price is largely lacking. While in many product markets there is invariably a price sensitive segment, there is no indication that this is on the increase. On the contrary, in many product and service markets, ranging from watches, personal computers, household appliances, to banking and insurance, an interest in multiple product features, product quality and service appears to be growing.

For example, findings from the PIMS project overwhelmingly suggest that product quality is the driving force behind successful marketing strategies not only in the US, but also in other developed countries (Douglas and Craig 1983, Gale, Luchs and Rosenfeld 1986). In industrial markets insofar as global market segments consist of multinational corporations, they may be more concerned with the ability to supply and service their operations worldwide than with the price. Similarly, in consumer markets where global market segments consist of upscale affluent customer, they are likely to look for distinctive prestige, high quality products such as Cartier watches and handbags and Godiva chocolates. Consequently, it is arguable that world customers are less price sensitive than other customers.

Low Price Positioning is a Highly Vulnerable Strategy.   Also, from a strategic point of view, emphasis on price-positioning may be undesirable especially in international markets, since it offers no long-term competitive advantage. A price positioning strategy is always vulnerable to new technological developments which may lower costs, as well as to attack from competitors with lower overhead and lower operating or labor costs. Government subsidies to local competitors may also undermine the effectiveness of a price-positioning strategy. In addition, price-sensitive customers typically are not brand or source loyal.

Standardized Low Price Can Be Overpriced in Some Countries and Underpriced in Others.   Finally, a strategy based on a combination of a standardized product at a low price, when implemented in countries which vary in their competitive structure, as well as the level of economic development, is likely to result in products which are over-designed and overpriced for some markets and underdesigned and underpriced for others. There is, for example, substantial evidence to suggest that where markets in developing countries are price sensitive, a strategy of product adaptation and simplification may be the most effective (Hill and Still 1984). Cost advantages may also be negated by transportation and distribution costs as well as tariff barriers and/or price regulation (Porter 1980, 1985).

Economies of Scale of Production and Marketing

The third assumption underlying the philosophy of global standardization is that a key force driving strategy is product technology, and that substantial economies of scale can be achieved by supplying global markets. This does, however, neglect three critical and interrelated points: (a) technological developments in flexible factory automation enable economies of scale to be achieved at lower levels of output and do not require production of a single standardized product, (b) cost of production is only one and often not the critical component in determining the total cost of the product, and (c) strategy should not be solely product-driven but should take into account the other components of a marketing strategy, such as positioning, packaging, brand name, advertising, P.R.. consumer and trade promotion and distribution.

Developments in Flexible Factory Automation.   Recent developments in flexible factory automation methods have lowered the minimum efficient scale of operation and have thus enabled companies to supply smaller local markets efficiently, without requiring operations on a global scale. However, diseconomies may result from such operations due to increased transportation and distribution costs, as well as higher administrative overhead and additional communication and coordination costs.

Furthermore, decentralization of production and establishment of local manufacturing operations enable diversification of risk arising from political events, fluctuations in foreign exchange rates, or economic instability. Recent swings in foreign exchange rates, coupled with the growth of offshore sourcing, have underscored the vulnerability of centralizing production in a single location. Government regulations relating to local component and/or offset requirements create additional pressures for local manufacturing. Flexible automation not only implies that decentralization of manufacturing and production may be cost-efficient but also makes minor modifications in products of models in the latter stages of production feasible, so that a variety of model versions can be produced without major retooling. Adaptations to product design can thus be made to meet differences in preferences from one country to another without loss of economies of scale.

Production Costs Are Often a Minor Component of Total Cost.   In many consumer and service industries, such as cosmetics, detergents, pharmaceuticals, or financial institutions, production costs are a small fraction of total cost. The key to success in these markets is an understanding of the tastes and purchase behavior of target customers and distribution channels, and tailoring products and strategies to these rather than production efficiency. In the detergent industry, for example, mastery of mass-merchandising techniques and an effective brand management system is typically considered the key element in the success of the giants in this field, such as Procter and Gamble (P&G) or Colgate-Palmolive.

For many products the establishment of an effective distribution network is often of prime importance in penetrating international markets. This is particularly the case for consumer products in countries where the absence or limited reach of mass-communication channels such as TV or magazines preclude the use of "pull" strategies. Distribution may also be crucial for products such as agricultural machinery, which require extensive after-sales service and maintenance. Furthermore, for some companies such as Avon with their Avon sales ladies network, or direct marketing insurance companies, distribution may constitute the crux of their marketing strategy and be a major component of their costs.

In these cases, the potential for scale economies arising from a standardization of operations may be negligible or non-existent. In some instances, greater efficiency in operational systems and procedure may result from experience in multiple country market environments, but as also noted previously, there may also be significant scale diseconomies.

The Standardization Philosophy Is Primarily Product Driven.   The focus on product and brand related aspects of strategy in discussions of global standardization is misleading since it ignores the other key marketing strategy variables. Strategy in international markets should also take into consideration other aspects of the marketing mix, and the extent to which these are standardized across country markets rather than adapted to local idiosyncratic characteristics. Thus, not only should the effectiveness of using standardized positioning strategy promotional and advertising campaigns be considered, but a standardized distribution system and uniforming pricing should be considered as well. There are, however, often formidable barriers to such a strategy, which will be discussed subsequently.

Requisite Conditions for Global Standardization

The numerous pitfalls in the rationale underlying the global standardization philosophy suggest that such a strategy is far from universally appropriate for all products, brands or companies. Only under certain conditions is it likely to prove a "winning" strategy in international markets. These include: (a) the existence of a global market segment, (b) potential synergies from standardization and (c) the availability of a communication and distribution infrastructure to deliver the firm's offering to target customers worldwide.

Existence of Global Market Segments

As noted previously, global segments may be identified in a number of industrial and consumer markets. In consumer markets these segments are typically luxury or premium type products. Global segments are, however, not limited to such product markets, but also exist in other types of markets, such as motorcycle, record, stereo equipment, and computer, where a segment with similar needs and wants can be identified in many countries.

In industrial markets, companies with multinational operations are particularly likely to have similar needs and requirements worldwide. Where the operations are integrated or coordinated across national boundaries, as in the case of banks or other financial institutions, compatibility of operation systems and equipment may be essential. Consequently, they may seek vendors who can supply and service their operations worldwide, in some cases developing global contrasts for such purchases. Similarly, manufacturing companies with worldwide operations may source globally in order to ensure uniformity in quality, service and price of components and other raw materials throughout their operations.

Marketing of global products and brands to such target segments and global customers enables development of a uniform global image throughout the world. In some markets such as perfume, fashions, etc., association with a specific country of origin or a foreign image in general may carry a prestige connotation. In other cases, for example, Sony electronic equipment, McDonald's hamburgers, Hertz or Avis car rental, IBM computers, or Xerox office equipment, it may help to develop a worldwide reputation for quality and service. Just as multinational corporations may seek uniformity in supply worldwide, some consumers who travel extensively may be interested in finding the same brand of cigarettes and soft drinks, or hotels in foreign countries. This may be particularly relevant in product markets used extensively by international travelers.

While the existence of a potential global segment is a key motivating factor for developing a global product and brand strategy, it is important to note that the desirability of such a strategy depends on the size and economic viability of the segment in question, the strength of the segment's preference for the global brand, as well as the ability to reach the segment effectively and profitability.

Synergies Associated with Global Standardization

Global standardization may also have a number of synergistic effects. In addition to those associated with a global image noted above, opportunities may exist for the transfer of good ideas for products of promotional strategies from one country to another. For example, a new product or an effective promotional strategy developed in one country (not necessarily the country in which the product or brand originated) may be effectively exploited in other countries. For example, US detergent companies have acquired or developed new, more effective detergent formulas and fabric softeners to cope with harder water conditions in European markets. These have subsequently been introduced into the US home market. Similarly, promotional campaigns such as the Marlboro cowboy may also prove effective in several countries.

Global marketing also generates experience of operating in multiple and diverse environments. Experience gained in one foreign environment may thus be transferred to another country, or may facilitate more rapid adaptation to new environmental conditions, even if these have not been previously experienced. Consequently, the range of experience acquired may result in the introduction of operating efficiencies.

The standardization of strategy and operations across a number of countries may also enable the acquisition or exploitation of specific types of expertise which would not be feasible otherwise. Expertise in assessing country risk or foreign exchange risk, or in identifying and interpreting information relating to multiple country markets, may, for example, be developed.

Such synergies are not, however, unique to a strategy of global standardization, but may also occur wherever operations and strategy are coordinated or integrated across country markets (Takeuchi and Porter 1985). In fact, only certain scale economies associated with product and advertising copy standardization and the development of a global image as discussed earlier are unique to global standardization.

Availability of an International Communication and Distribution Infrastructure

The effectiveness of global standardization also depends to a large extent on the availability of an international infrastructure of communications and distribution. As many corporations have expanded overseas, service organizations have followed their customers abroad to supply their needs worldwide.

Advertising agencies such as Saatchi and Saatchi, McCann Erickson and Young and Rubicam now have an international network of operations throughout the world, while many research agencies can also supply services in major markets worldwide. With the growing integration of financial markets, banks, investment firms, insurance and other financial institutions are also becoming increasingly international in orientation and are expanding the scope of their operations in world markets. The physical distribution network of shippers, freight forwarding, export and import agents-customs clearing, invoicing and insurance agents is also becoming increasingly integrated to meet demand for international shipment of goods and services.

Improvements in telecommunications and in logistical systems have considerably increased capacity to manage operations on a global scale and hence facilitate adoption of global standardization strategies. The spread of telex and fax systems, as well as satellite linkages and international computer linkages, all contribute to the shrinking of distances and facilitate globalization of operations. Similarly, improvements in transportation systems and physical logistics such as containerization and computerized inventory and handling systems have enabled significant cost savings as well as reducing time required to move goods across major distances.

Operational Constraints to Effective Implementation of a Standardization Strategy

While adoption of a standardized strategy may be desirable under certain conditions, there are a number of constraints which severely restrict the firm's ability to develop and implement a standardized strategy. These include both external or environmental constraints, the nature of the marketing infrastructure, resource market conditions or the type of competition, as well as internal constraints which stem from the firm's current strategy or organization of international operations.

External Constraints to Effective Standardization

The numerous external constraints which impede global standardization are well recognized, and have been clearly identified in the classic discussion by Buzzell (1968). Here, three major categories are highlighted, namely: (a) governmental and trade restrictions, (b) differences in the marketing infrastructure, such as the availability and effectiveness of promotional media, (c) the character of resource markets, and differences in the availability and costs of resources, and (d) differences in competition from one country to another.

Governmental and Trade Restrictions.   Government and trade restrictions, such as tariff and other trade barriers, product, pricing or promotional regulation, frequently hamper standardization of the product line, pricing or promotion strategy. Tariffs, or quotas on the import of key materials, components or other resources may, for example, affect production costs and thus hamper uniform pricing or alternatively result in the substitution of other components and modifications in product design. Local content requirements or compensatory export requirements, which specify that products contain a certain proportion of components manufactured locally or that a certain volume of production is exported to offset imports of components or other services, may have a similar impact.

Regulation of business practices may also affect the feasibility of standardization. In Japan, for example, in many product markets such as electronics and food, product design and composition must conform to standards established by the relevant trade body, necessitating adaptation by foreign companies. Similarly, severe advertising regulation in countries such as Germany and Switzerland has restricted the use of many campaigns successful in other countries.

The existence of cartels such as the European steel cartel, or the Swiss chocolate cartel, may also impede or exclude standardized strategies in countries covered by these agreements. In particular, they may affect adoption of a uniform pricing strategy as the cartel sets prices for the industry. Cartel members may also control established distribution channels, thus preventing use of a standardized distribution strategy. Extensive grey markets in countries such as India, Hong Kong, and South America may also affect administered pricing systems, and require adjustment of pricing strategies. For example, Wilkinson's attempt to market its line of razor blades in India suffered greatly from price undercutting in the grey market.

The Nature of the Marketing Infrastructure.   Differences in the marketing infrastructure from one country to another may hamper use of a standardized strategy. These may, for example, include differences in the availability and reach of various promotional media, in the availability of certain distribution channels or retail institutions, or in the existence and efficiency of the communication and transportation network. Such factors may, therefore, require considerable adaptation of strategy of local market conditions.

The type of media available as well as their reach and effectiveness differ from country to country. For example, TV advertising, while a major medium in the US, Japan and Australia, is not permitted in Scandinavian countries. Where TV advertising is permitted it may reach only a limited number of households due to limited ownership of TVs, as for example in South Africa, Nigeria or Indonesia. Similarly, in countries with high levels of illiteracy the effectiveness of print media is severely limited. Conversely, in some countries certain media are particularly effective or unique to the country. These include the circular street advertising to be found in Paris, or the neon advertising common in Japan.

The nature of the distribution system and structure also differs significantly from one country to another. While in the US supermarkets account for the major proportion of food sales, in other countries there are virtually no supermarkets and Mom and Pop type stores predominate. This severely limits the effectiveness of a "pull" type strategy and ability to use "in store" promotions or display to stimulate customer interest. Even in industrialized nations such as Japan, Italy, Belgium, Portugal and Spain, more than 75% of retail sales are done through small retailers. Again, discount outlets common in many industrialized nations may not exist in other countries, which may restrict a company's ability to use an aggressive price penetration strategy.

The physical and communications infrastructure also varies from country to country. Inadequate mail service (as for example, in Brazil or Italy) will limit the effectiveness of direct mail promotion. A poor or ill-maintained road network may necessitate use of alternative modes of transportation such as rail or air. Inaccessibility of outlying rural areas due to the nature of the physical terrain in countries such as Canada, Australia and Peru may also require the design of logistical systems specifically adapted to their unique conditions.

Interdependencies with Resource Markets.   Yet another constraint to the development of standardized strategies is the nature of resource markets, and their operation in different countries throughout the world as well as the interdependency of these markets with marketing decisions. Availability and cost of raw materials, as well as labor and other resources in different locations, will not only affect decisions regarding sourcing of and hence the location of manufacturing activities but can also affect marketing strategy decisions such as product design. For example, in the paper industry, availability of cheap local materials such as jute and sugar cane may result in their substitution for wood fiber. Similarly, the relative cost of paper vs. plastic materials may affect product packaging decisions. In Europe, use of plastic rather than paper is more common than in the US due to differences in the relative cost of the two materials.

Cost differentials relative to raw materials, labor, management and other inputs may also influence the trade-off relative to alternative marketing mix strategies. For example, high packaging cost relative to physical distribution may result in use of cheaper packaging with a shorter shelf-life and more frequent shipments. Similarly low labor costs relative to media may encourage a shift from mass media advertising to labor intensive promotion such as personal selling and product demonstration.

Availability of capital, technology and manufacturing capabilities in different locations will also affect decisions about licensing, contract manufacturing, joint ventures, and other "make-buy" types of decisions for different markets, as well as decisions about countertrade, reciprocity and other long-term relations.

The Nature of the Competitive Structure.   Differences in the nature of the competitive situation from one country to another may also suggest the desirability of adaptation strategy. Even in markets characterized by global competition, such as agricultural equipment and motorcycles, the existence of low-cost competition in certain countries may suggest the desirability of marketing stripped-down models or lowering prices to meet such competition. Even where competitors are predominantly other multinationals, pre-emption of established distribution networks may encourage adoption of innovative distribution methods or direct distribution to short-circuit an entrenched position. Thus, the existence of global competition does not necessarily imply a need for global standardization.

All such aspects thus impose major constraints on the feasibility and effectiveness of a standardized strategy, and suggest the desirability or need to adapt to specific market conditions.

Internal Constraints to Effective Standardization

In addition to such external constraints on the feasibility of a global standardization strategy, there are also a number of internal constraints which may need to be considered. These include compatibility with the existing network of operations overseas, as well as opposition or lack of enthusiasm among local management toward a standardized strategy.

Existing International Operations.   Proponents of global standardization typically take the position of a novice company with no operations in international markets, and hence fail to take into consideration the fit of the proposed strategy with current international activities. In practice, however, many companies have a number of existing operations in various countries. In some cases, these are joint ventures or licensing operations or involve some collaboration in purchasing, manufacturing or distribution with other companies. Even where foreign manufacturing and distribution operations are wholly owned, the establishment of a distribution network will typically entail relationships with other organizations, as for example, exclusive distributor agreement.

Such commitments may be difficult if not impossible to change in the short run, and may constitute a major impediment to adoption of a standardized strategy. If, for example, a joint venture with a local company has been established to manufacture and market a product line in a specific country or region, resistance from the local partner (or government authorities) may be encountered if the parent company wishes to shift production or import components from another location. Similarly, a licensing contract will impede a firm from supplying the products covered by the agreement from an alternative location for the duration of the contract, even if it becomes more cost efficient to do so.

Conversely, the establishment of an effective dealer or distribution network in a country or region may constitute an important resource to a company. The addition of new products to the product line currently sold or distributed by this network may therefore provide a more efficient utilization of company resources than expanding to new countries or geographic regions with the existing product line, as this would require substantial investment in the establishment of a new distribution networks.

In addition, overseas subsidiaries may currently be marketing not only core products and brands from the company's domestic business, but may also have added or acquired local or regional products and brands in response to local market demand. P&G, for example, acquired Domestos, an established local brand of household cleanser in the

UK, and added it to its product line in a number of other European markets. In some cases, therefore, introduction of a global product or brand may be likely to cannibalize sales of local or regional brands.

Advocates of standardization thus need to take into consideration the evolutionary character of international involvement, which may render a universal strategy of global products and brands sub-optimal. Somewhat ironically, the longer the history of a multinational corporation's involvement in foreign or international markets, and the more diversified and far-flung its operations, the more likely it is that standardization will not lead to optimal results.

Local Management Motivation and Attitudes.   Another internal constraint concerns the motivation and attitudes of local management with regard to standardization. Standardized strategies tend to facilitate or result in centralization in the planning and organization of international activities. In particular, product development and positioning as well as key promotional themes are likely to be developed at corporate headquarters. Especially if input from local management is limited, this may result in a feeling that strategy is "imposed" by corporate headquarters and/or not adequately adapted nor appropriate in view of specific local market characteristics and conditions. Local management is likely to take the view, "it won't work here—things are different," which will reduce their motivation to implement a standardized strategy effectively.

Standardization tends to conflict with the principle of local management responsibility. Emphasis on local management autonomy stems from the advantages traditionally associated with decentralization and a concern with encouraging local entrepreneurship. The establishment of a standardized strategy by corporate headquarters may therefore reduce the overall effectiveness of the firm. It also restricts local management's ability to adapt to local market competitive conditions, for example, in promotion or distribution decisions, which can result in sub-optimal reactions to competition.

A Framework for Classifying Global Strategy Options

This review of the rationale underlying "global standardization" thus suggests that it's appropriate only in relation to certain product markets or market segments under certain market environment conditions, and dependent on company objectives and structure. The adoption of a global perspective should not therefore be viewed as synonymous with a strategy of global products and brands. Rather for most companies, such a perspective implies consideration of a broad range of strategic options of which standardization is merely one.

In essence, a global perspective implies planning strategy relative to markets worldwide rather than on a country by country bias. This may result in the identification of opportunities for global products and brands and/or integrating and coordinating strategy across national boundaries to exploit potential synergies of operating on an international scale. Such opportunities should, however, be weighed against the benefits of adaptation to idiosyncratic customer characteristics.

CHART 1   **The Standardization–Differentiation Continuum**

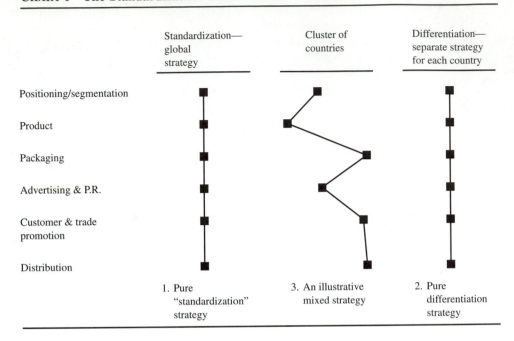

The development of an effective global strategy thus requires a careful examination of all alternative international strategic options in terms of standardization vs. adaptation open to the firm. These are, however, vast in number given the range of possible geographic areas, countries, market segments, product variants, and marketing strategies to be considered. It is, therefore, helpful to classify these options based on the degree of standardization. A continuum can thus be identified, ranging from "pure standardization" to "pure differentiation," where most options fall into the intermediate category of mixed or "hybrid" strategies. This is shown in Chart 1.

In the extreme case of pure standardization, all dimensions of marketing strategy are standardized or uniform throughout the world. In practice, as noted previously, not only is such a strategy fraught with problems, but it is rarely likely to be feasible in relation to all elements of the mix. The other extreme is that of totally differentiated strategy, in which each component of the mix is adapted to the specific idiosyncratic customer and environmental characteristics in each country. Management in each country thus develops its own strategy independently, with no coordination across countries nor attempt to identify any commonality from one country to another.

In between these two extremes is a set of mixed or hybrid options including some standardized and some differentiated components. Here, a variety of different patterns may be identified. These include those in which some components of the mix are standardized, while others are adapted to local market factors; those where strategies are standardized across regions or cluster of countries; strategies standardized by market segment; as well as combinations of the above.

CHART 2   Key Dimensions of Global Marketing Strategy

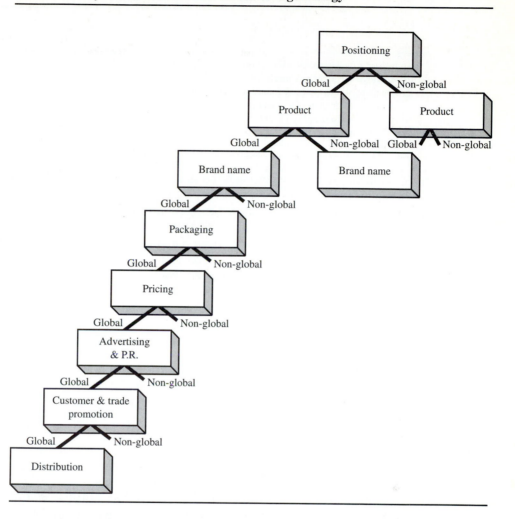

For example, as shown in Chart 2, some components of the marketing mix, product or advertising copy are standardized across countries, but others, such as distribution policy or pricing, are adapted to specific country or environmental characteristics. For example, companies marketing global products or brands may pursue different distribution or pricing policies in each country. Apple Computers, for example, while selling a standardized product line worldwide, has different positioning, promotional, and distribution strategies in each country.

Another option is to standardize strategy across regions or clusters of countries. Ford, for example, develops different models for its European operations as compared with the US market. The Fiesta, Granada, and Taurus models were all initially developed for the European market, as were the positioning strategy and promotional themes.

TABLE 1   **A Standardized Global Strategy Checklist**

	YES *Continue* *to Explore*	*NO* *Standardization* *Not Appropriate*
1. It there a global market segment for your product?	Yes	No
2. Are there synergies associated with a global strategy?	Yes	No
3. Are there no **external** constraints or government regulation on ability to implement a global strategy?	Yes	No
4. Are there no **internal** constraints to implementing a global strategy?	Yes	No
If yes to all 4, consider global	Yes	No

Alternatively, strategies might be standardized by customer segments. Revlon, for example, targets its Charlie line to working women worldwide, using the same positioning strategy and advertising copy. Almay cosmetics targets its line to the global segment of women with sensitive or delicate skin throughout the world.

Combinations of these alternatives can also be adopted. For example, a company might market a standardized or uniform product worldwide but adapt its promotional strategy for different countries or regions. For example, P&G sells its Pampers brand of diapers worldwide, but the promotional strategy is adapted to different geographic regions. Similarly, Kellogg's Corn Flakes is sold worldwide, but in some regions such as Latin America, and the Far East, promotional themes are standardized, while in other areas, such as Europe, promotional themes, packaging and distribution strategies are specific to each country. Again, Virginia Slims is targeted to "liberated" women throughout the world, but in Japan, the advertising copy is changed from "You've Come a Long Way Baby" to "Oh, So Slim and Sexy" (translation from Japanese).

In addition to such options which all assume a worldwide strategy, companies may also target specific and unique product markets and segments in a given geographic region or country. In the detergent market, for example, a company may market its line of powdered detergents worldwide, its liquid detergents and softeners in industrialized countries, and for the developing countries, develop a line of synthetic detergents and bar soaps. Similarly in India, a major segment of the tooth cleansing market consists of black and white tooth-cleansing powders. Multinationals such as P&G and Colgate have each developed a brand of white tooth-cleansing powder to tap this market.

A firm's international operations are thus likely to be characterized by a mix of strategies, including not only global products and brands, but also some regional products and brands and some national products and brands. Similarly, some target segments may be global, others regional and others national. Hybrid strategies of this nature thus enable a company to take advantage of the benefits of standardization and potential synergies from operating on an international scale, while at the same time not losing those afforded by adaptation to specific country characteristics and customer preferences. Guidelines and an approach for developing such a strategy based on a dynamic portfolio perspective have been proposed (Wind and Douglas 1987). These take into consideration the company's existing network of operations, the current mix of products and brands, and their competitive positioning in each country, in designing an effective global marketing strategy.

Conclusion

The main thesis of this paper is that the design of an effective global marketing strategy does not necessarily entail the marketing of standardized products and global brands worldwide. While such a strategy may work for some companies and certain product lines, for other companies and other product markets adaptation to local or regional differences may yield better results. The key to success is rather a careful analysis of the forces driving towards globalization as well as the obstacles to this approach, and assessment, based on the company's strengths and weaknesses, of where the most attractive opportunities and the company's differential advantage in exploiting these appear to lie.

References

Boote, Alfred S. (1982/83), "Psychographic Segmentation in Europe," *Journal of Advertising* (December/January).

Britt, Stewart Henderson (1974), "Standardizing Marketing for the International Market," *Columbia Journal of World Business* (Winter). 39–45.

Buzzell, R. (1968), "Can You Standardize Multinational Marketing?" *Harvard Business Review* (November–December), 102–113.

Donnelly, James H., Jr., and John K. Ryans (1969), "Standardized Global Advertising, A Call as Yet Unanswered," *Journal of Marketing,* April, 57–60.

Chakrabarti, Alok K., Stephen Feinman, and William Fuentivilla (1982), "The Cross-National Comparison of Patterns of Industrial Innovations," *Columbia Journal of World Business* (Fall), 33–38.

Douglas, Susan P., and Christine Urban (1977), "Life Analysis to Profile Women in International Markets," *Journal of Marketing,* 41 (July), 46–54.

Douglas, Susan P. and C. Samuel Craig (1983), "Examining the Performance of U.S. Multinationals in Foreign Markets," *Journal of International Business Studies* (Winter), 51–62.

Doz, Yves (1980), "Strategic Management in Multinational Companies," *Sloan Management Review,* 21 (Winter), 27–46.

Dunn, S. Watson (1966), "The Case-Study Approach in Cross-Cultural Research," *Journal of Marketing Research,* February, 26–31.

Elinder, Erik (1965), "How International Can European Advertising Be?" *Journal of Marketing,* April, 7–11.

Fatt, Arthur C. (1967), "The Danger of 'Local' International Advertising," *Journal for Marketing* (January).

Fayerweather, John (1969), *International Business Management: A Conceptual Framework,* New York: McGraw-Hill.

Fisher, Anne B. (1984), "The Ad Viz Gloms onto Capital," *Fortune,* November 12.

Gale, Bradley, Robert Luchs, and Joel Rosenfeld (1987), "Who Will Succeed in Europe's Changing Marketplace?" *International Management Development Review* (to appear).

Garreau, J. (1981), *The Nine Nations of North America,* Boston, Mass.: Houghton Mifflin Co.

Hakuhodo Institute of Life and Living (1983), *Hitonami: Keeping Up With the Satos,* Tokyo: Hill.

Hill, J.S., and R.R. Still (1984), "Adapting Products to LDC Tastes," *Harvard Business Review,* 62 (March/April), 92–101.

Huszagh, Sandra, Richard J. Fox, and Ellen Day, "Global Marketing: An Empirical Investigation," *Columbia Journal of World Business,* Twentieth Anniversary Issue, 1985, 31–43.

Kahle, Lynn R. (1986), "The Nine Nations of North America and the Value Basis of Geographic Segmentation," *Journal of Marketing,* 56 (April), 37–47.

Killough, James (1978), "Improved Payoff from Transnational Advertising," *Harvard Business Review,* (July–August), 103.

Kotler, Philip (1985), "Global Standardization—Courting Danger," panel discussion, 23 American Marketing Association Conference, Washington, D.C.

Levitt, T. (1983), "The Globalization of Markets," *Harvard Business Review* (May–June), 92–102.

Miracle, Gordon (1968), "Internationalizing Advertising Principles and Strategies," *MSU Business Topics,* Autumn, 29–36.

Mitchell, A. (1983), *The Nine American Lifestyles,* New York: Macmillan Publishing.

Ohmae, Kenichi (1985), "Becoming a Triad Power: The New Global Corporation," *The McKinsey Quarterly,* Spring, 2–25.

Ohmae, Kenichi (1985), *Triad Power,* New York: The Free Press.

Peebles, Dean M., John K. Ryans, and Ivan R. Vernon, (1978), "Coordinating International Advertising," *Journal of Marketing,* 46 (Winter), 27–35.

Porter, Michael (1980), *Competitive Strategy: Techniques for Analyzing Industries and Competitors,* New York: The Free Press.

Porter, Michael (1985), *Competitive Advantage,* New York: The Free Press.

Quelch, Joan A., and Edward J. Hoff (1986), "Customizing Global Marketing," *Harvard Business Review* (May/June).

The RISC Observer, No. 1 and 2 (1986), Paris: RISC (mimeographed).

Ryans, John K. (1969), "Is It Too Soon to Put a Tiger in Every Tank?" *Columbia Journal of World Business* (March), 69–75.

Saegert, Joel, Robert J. Hoover and Marye Thorp Hilger (1985), "Characteristics of Mexican American Consumers," *Journal of Consumer Research,* 12 (June), 104–109.

Segnit, Susanna, and Simon Broadbent, "Lifestyle Research." *European Research,* 1 (January 1973), 1 (March 1973).

Takeuchi, H., and M. E. Porter (1985), "The Strategic Role of International Marketing: Managing the Nature and Extent of Worldwide Coordination," Michael E. Porter (ed.), Competition in Global Industries, Cambridge, Mass.: Harvard Graduate School of Business Administration.

Great Strategy or Great Strategy Implementation—Two Ways of Competing in Global Markets

William G. Egelhoff. *William G. Egelhoff is associate professor of management systems at the Fordham University Graduate School of Business*

On 19 April 1775, British troops (Redcoats) marched toward Concord, Massachusetts, to destroy military stores that had been collected by the American revolutionaries (Minutemen). At Lexington Green, a large, flat, open area, the Redcoats met the Minutemen in the first battle of the day. Both sides employed a similar battle strategy, firing at each other in the open from closed ranks. It was the dominant battle strategy of the day. The Redcoats quickly prevailed, and the Minutemen dispersed after a few volleys and a number of casualties.

Later in the day, as the Redcoats returned to Boston, a second battle developed. At various points along the road, Minutemen fired upon the Redcoat formations from inside houses and behind stone fences. When the Redcoats charged these positions, the Minutemen withdrew into the countryside and reappeared farther down the road. The Minutemen's skirmish tactics took a heavy toll on the massed and extremely vulnerable Redcoats, who could do little but set fire to the buildings the Minutemen had already abandoned.

The two battles between the same opponents on the same day produced two very different results. It seems reasonable to suggest that between the two battles the Minutemen made a fundamental shift in their battle strategy, and this new strategy, rather than luck or chance, produced the significant difference in results.

Like the Minutemen, competitors frequently don't compete the way one expects them to. This is one of the key difficulties for managers trying to understand, prepare for, and manage global competition. Western firms, and U.S. firms in particular, generally try to compete through some kind of strategic advantage. That is, they often try to develop a unique business strategy that will allow them to outmaneuver competitors. Yet many global Asian firms appear to compete successfully without much attempt to develop

FIGURE 1

*Minutemen
versus
Redcoats—
first battle*

FIGURE 2

*Minutemen
versus
Redcoats—
second battle*

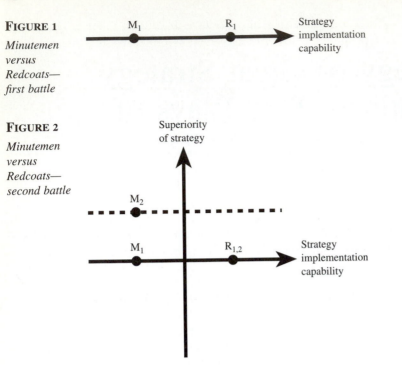

distinctive business strategies. Instead, they try to implement not-so-unique business strategies better than competitors and thereby to gain competitive advantage.

In this paper, I will distinguish between these two modes of competing, discuss some of their implications, and illustrate my analysis with research conducted in U.S. and Japanese semiconductor companies.[1] I will then consider what happens when these two modes confront each other in a global market and discuss some of the implications for U.S. competitiveness in global markets.

In order to clarify the difference between competing through strategy and competing through strategy implementation, let's return to the Redcoats and the Minutemen and analyze the differences between the two battles more conceptually. Figure 1 shows that in the first battle the two sides followed a similar battle strategy and therefore, differed only in how well they implemented it. The Redcoats clearly had the edge with their superior capability and greater experience in executing the conventional battle strategy.

Figure 2 shows what happened in the second battle. The Redcoats continued to follow conventional battle strategy, which called for retaining relatively closed ranks and centralized direction. Their implementation capability was presumably similar to what it had been earlier in the day at Lexington Green, thus their strategy and implementation capabilities in the second battle (R_2) were similar to what they had been in the first battle (R_1). The important difference in the second battle was that the Minutemen shifted up the vertical axis and adopted a different—and superior—battle strategy (M_2). They changed to a skirmish strategy, which was ideally suited to the winding road and broken countryside where the second battle took place. Although not shown in Figure 2, it is probable that their implementation capability also improved (shifted to the right). It was the different and superior battle strategy, however, that allowed the Minutemen to overcome the Redcoats in the second battle.

The Minutemen had two basic options for trying to defeat the Redcoats. First, they could have done what most armies of the eighteenth century would have done: stuck with the conventional strategy but tried to execute it better. This might have required increasing the number of troops or making available more weapons and ammunition (essentially committing more resources). Or it might have called for more training and practice so that the troops could reload quicker, shoot more accurately, and hold their ranks under fire. Officers might also have been trained to better direct and coordinate battle tactics (essentially getting the most out of available resources).

The Minutemen chose a second approach: to select a different and superior battle strategy. A strategy is superior to the extent that it better fits the competitive environment and the organization's capabilities to implement it. In this case, the skirmish strategy was ideally suited to the terrain (winding road, broken countryside) and to allowing the Minutemen to exploit an important enemy weakness (the absence of cavalry). It also capitalized on the Minutemen's superior knowledge of the locale and downplayed their lack of training and experience with conventional battle tactics.

Competition in the Global Semiconductor Industry

Now let's examine a more recent competitive situation—the battle for supremacy in the global semiconductor industry—and discuss it in terms of the strategies and strategy implementation capabilities of the two major competitor groups—U.S. and Japanese semiconductor firms. This examination is based on a field study of eight U.S. and eight Japanese semiconductor firms. Data was collected through a series of in-depth structured and semistructured interviews with each firm's general manager, research and development (R&D) manager, manufacturing manager, and marketing manager. Interviews focused on the business and functional strategies of each company's semiconductor business and the organizational arrangements and managerial practices used to implement them. The appendix describes the methodology and the sample companies more fully.

The case of the semiconductor industry is a familiar one, but a brief review may be helpful.[2] U.S. companies dominated in the 1950s and 1960s, as they developed most of the new product and process technology. During the 1960s and 1970s, there was an active transfer of product and process technology from the United States to Japan. In the late 1970s and early 1980s, Japanese firms cooperating under government-sponsored research successfully developed the technology needed to produce very large scale integrated (VLSI) chips. Subsequent large scale investments in plant and equipment and concerted efforts within firms to improve process technology led to a Japanese advantage in terms of quality and productivity over most U.S. firms by the mid-1980s. However, this advantage was confined to standardized, high-volume products, primarily memory chips. U.S. firms continued to develop most product innovations and to dominate the newer, more innovative product markets. By the late 1980s, Japan had taken sufficient market share away from U.S. firms to become the industry leader. Serious trade friction had developed between the two countries, and Americans feared that the United States might be unable to compete successfully against Japanese semiconductor firms.[3] It was during this period that the study was conducted.

Distinct Competitive Styles

Of the various aspects of strategy measured in the study, five characteristics emerged that, taken together, suggest that U.S. and Japanese firms have two different styles for competing in the semiconductor industry. Table 1 summarizes these characteristics for the two groups. Although no generalization holds across all the sample firms in each group, the patterns were remarkably distinctive, and secondary data available on other U.S. and Japanese semiconductor firms tends to be consistent.

Unique Product-Market Advantage

U.S. semiconductor firms generally seek to differentiate their products from those of competitors through innovative product design. As a product line matures and becomes more difficult to differentiate from similar competing products, a U.S. firm attempts to bring out the next generation of the product with improved performance characteristics. The classic example of this has been Intel's sequential development and launching of the 286, 386, and 486 lines of microprocessors. Another common U.S. mechanism for product differentiation is to develop families of chips that work together to satisfy systems applications. Then, by regularly developing peripheral chips that extend the family and its applications capability, a company can continually maintain some uniqueness for the product family. It is therefore not surprising that the semicustom design techniques that permit the economical design and manufacture of application specific integrated circuits (ASICs) were primarily developed by U.S. firms. These techniques figure prominently in the strategies of nearly all firms.

The degree to which U.S. firms realize product differentiation varies. Firms with more innovative product research, such as Intel, realize it to a greater degree than firms such as National Semiconductor or Texas Instruments, which have more incremental product development capabilities. Yet nearly all firms try for some kind of uniqueness, even if it's only a relatively minor performance characteristic that might make the product more attractive for certain applications. Thus, the dominant strategy by far among U.S. firms has been product differentiation, and very few firms have made low cost their primary competitive strategy.[4]

Japanese firms, on the other hand, place considerably less emphasis on developing differentiated products. The major producers all attempt to offer broad product lines that concentrate on covering the higher-volume market segments. Smaller producers have more of a niche strategy, usually emphasizing products that impart some special advantage to the company's systems products and, therefore, that tend to be more unique in the marketplace. Even these companies, however, produce large quantities of basic products, such as memory chips and standard logic, in direct competition with the broad product line firms. The rationale is that these basic product volumes are required for

TABLE 1   Comparison of U.S. and Japanese Competitive Styles

	Competitive Style of U.S. Company	*Competitive Style of Japanese Company*
Unique Product/ Market Advantage	Generally seeks to develop some unique advantage for each product line.	Does not generally require a unique product-market advantage for a product line.
Withdrawal Decisions	Calls for withdrawal from product-market segments where clear advantage is not possible (usually this occurs after competitive pressures make the segment unprofitable).	Seldom calls for withdrawal from a product-market segment, even if it loses money. Instead, tends to emphasize continued presence in a segment and profitability, even if this takes a long time.
Role of Process Technology	Shows high variance in the importance attached to process technology. Some strategies require state-of-the-art technology while others can be two to three years behind the technology leaders.	Emphasizes trying to keep process technology either ahead of competitors or even with competitors (both at the development and capital investment levels).
Sources of Process Technology	Frequently depends to an appreciable extent on external sources for new process technology (e.g., equipment manufacturers, collaborative research with others, outright purchase or trade). Existing levels of external dependency vary widely across firms (from being almost self-sufficient to depending entirely on external sources for new technology).	Tends to favor the internal development of new process technology. With a few notable exceptions, Japanese companies have no plans to engage in substantial collaborative research with other firms on process technology.
Importance of Vertical Integration	Generally places value on vertical integration only when the company's microelectronics products contribute to the uniqueness of its electronics systems products.	Places high value on vertical integration of microelectronics products and company's electronics systems products as part of a general drive toward more self-sufficiency.

manufacturing economies of scale and, in the case of DRAMs (dynamic random access memories), for staying near the forefront of process technology. Thus, Japanese strategies can be generally characterized as either: (1) a broad product line strategy heavily oriented toward basic products with low differentiation from competitors' products (e.g.,

NEC, Toshiba, and Hitachi) or (2) a niche strategy coupled with a limited line of basic products with low differentiation (e.g., Sony, Sharp, and Sanyo). As a result, the dominant competitive strategy for Japanese firms has been based on high quality and low price, with much less emphasis on product differentiation.

Withdrawal Decisions

U.S. firms tend to withdraw relatively quickly from products and market segments where they cannot gain or maintain sufficient differentiation. An example was the widespread withdrawal of U.S. firms from the DRAM segment of the memory market during the latter half of the 1980s. Despite the fact that many technical managers believe that a viable presence in this product area is critical to staying at the forefront of process technology, all of the U.S. merchant semiconductor firms except Texas Instruments and Micron Technology strategically repositioned themselves out of this highly competitive segment, in which the only available strategy was low price.

In contrast, Japanese companies seldom withdraw from a significant product line or market segment even if it is losing money. If a company views the product or segment as important, it will focus on actions that will restore profitability, even if this requires a very long time. The study found that Japanese firms tend to consider a product or segment important if (1) it supports the wider company strategy of vertical integration, (2) it is large or will grow rapidly, and (3) a reasonable number of internal or external customers have come to depend on the company for it. As a result, there are substantially higher barriers to making withdrawal decisions in Japanese companies than in U.S. firms. Strategically repositioning oneself by deliberate withdrawal from unprofitable products or markets is an option much more available to U.S. managements than it is to Japanese managements.

Role of Process Technology

The U.S. firms vary considerably with regard to the importance they attach to process technology (the technology that transforms product designs into products). Because semiconductor manufacturing processes are complex, capital intensive, and still evolving at a rapid pace, there is considerable room for difference in firm capabilities. The strategies of some U.S. firms, such as Texas Instruments and IBM, call for staying at the forefront of process technology as an important part of competitive advantage. These tend to be the larger firms. For firms that rely most heavily on product-market differentiation, the role of process technology is less important, and process technology can be as much as two or three years behind the leading edge.

By contrast, both the large broad product line and smaller limited product line Japanese firms pursue strategies that call for staying at or near the forefront of process technology, both in terms of technology development and capital investment. The cost of these investments would be beyond most niche strategy or limited-line U.S. companies. The cost is borne more easily in Japan because the limited-line producers tend to be divisions of very large electronics systems companies that can absorb the research expense and provide the capital. In addition, all of the limited-line companies have entered and maintained a significant presence in a number of high-volume basic product markets. These products provide both the high volumes of production necessary to drive down the technology learning curve and the economies of scale necessary for optimum production facility size.

Sources of Process Technology

U.S. and Japanese firms frequently have different strategies regarding the source and process for acquiring new process technology. Many U.S. firms depend to a considerable extent on external sources, concentrating their internal R&D efforts on circuit design in order to support strategies that emphasize unique or differentiated products. Equipment manufacturers are an important source of new process technology for large and small firms. Many smaller firms depend almost entirely on such suppliers for process technology innovations. Larger firms often collaborate closely with an equipment manufacturer during the development stage of new equipment. Several major industry groups (Microelectronics and Computer Technology Corporation, Semiconductor Research Association and Sematech) also facilitate collaboration on process technology research. Typically, this work is several years from the commercialization stage.

Another external source available to U.S. firms is purchasing or trading process technology with other semiconductor firms. This is often done in conjunction with a transfer of product technology. Firms will license other firms to produce certain products (e.g., Intel has licensed numerous firms to produce its famous sixteen-bit microprocessor). When product designs are transferred to the licensee, some process technology may also have to be transferred in order for the licensee to properly manufacture the product. Sometimes licensees will convert the designs to run on newer technologies (for example, from an NMOS to a CMOS technology) and, as part of the agreement, assist the licensor in also converting the product to the newer technology. Such technology transfer, however, tends to operate behind the forefront of new process technology.

The relative importance of external sources for new process technology varies widely across U.S. firms. Some large firms, such as IBM and Texas Instruments, have extensive internal R&D operations and even equipment-building operations committed to keeping the company at the forefront of new process technology. Other relatively large firms, such as Intel, pursue strategies that emphasize product technology innovations and that rely on external sources for most new process technology. The many small U.S. firms also pursue this latter strategy. Thus, although there is considerable variance, most U.S. firms are quite dependent on external sources for process technology improvements.

In the past, Japanese firms depended heavily on external sources for new process technology (primarily U.S. semiconductor firms and equipment manufacturers), but today they rely most heavily on internal development. Among the eight Japanese sample companies, only two of the smaller firms indicated an interest in collaborating with other semiconductor firms in developing new process technology. Since the study, significant increases in the cost of developing next-generation CMOS technology appear to have forced even the largest Japanese firms into collaboration. Agreements now exist between Hitachi and Texas Instruments, Toshiba and Motorola, and Toshiba and Siemens. Generally, Japanese firms consider leading-edge process technology the key strength of their strategies, and, consequently, they have little incentive to collaborate with other firms pursuing similar strategies (that is, other Japanese firms).

The importance of government-sponsored research projects, which earlier played an important role in improving the process technology of Japanese firms, has declined considerably. The rapid buildup in company-sponsored research has greatly reduced its relative importance. Although nearly all companies indicated an interest in continuing to participate in long-range, government-sponsored projects as a source of technology stimulation, several raised questions about the value of such programs in the future. Not only has company-sponsored research eclipsed government-sponsored research in terms of magnitude, but in some cases, the time horizons of company-sponsored research have started to exceed those of the government-sponsored projects. Thus Japanese semiconductor companies seem to be much more self-sufficient than U.S. firms when it comes to new process technology.

Importance of Vertical Integration

Semiconductor products are the basic components for all electronics systems products, from radios to computers. Virtually all significant Japanese semiconductor producers are subunits of larger electronics systems products companies. Original entry into semiconductor products was generally motivated by the desire to gain more control over the components that made up the company's final products. This vertical integration strategy is still very strong in Japanese firms, even though internal sales typically account for only 20 percent to 25 percent of total semiconductor sales. Japanese firms still tend to manufacture many of the key semiconductor components that go into their final products, even when such components are readily available in the marketplace at prices competitive with the cost of internal manufacture.[5]

Many U.S. semiconductor firms are independent companies, dependent on the merchant market for all of their sales. Such firms are obviously not motivated to make products because they further a strategy of vertical integration and reduced external dependency. Instead, they are driven by strategies of low cost or product differentiation. Even where U.S. semiconductor producers belong to larger companies (such as Texas Instruments and NCR) that use semiconductors in their end products, the vertical integration strategy is somewhat different than in Japanese companies. In U.S. firms, these vertical integration strategies are largely confined to supplying user divisions with semiconductor products that contribute to the uniqueness of their electronics systems products. Excluding the few semiconductor firms that are solely captive suppliers (such as IBM), it is unlikely that the semiconductor division will manufacture and supply standardized, basic products to the systems products divisions unless it is already making these products for the external market. Thus, in U.S. firms, vertical integration strategies focus largely on creating systems uniqueness, with less emphasis on increasing self-sufficiency and reducing external dependency.

To summarize, U.S. firms have strategies that tend to emphasize product differentiation and that seek to capture some unique product-market advantage. They place relatively less importance on process technology and, consequently, avoid competing on low cost. This kind of business strategy has contributed to an unusually high degree of strategic diversity in the U.S. industry, with most firms pursuing niche strategies and even the broad product line firms varying considerably in their product strengths and important market segments. Firms tend to withdraw relatively quickly from products and markets with too much competition or when they miss a technological change. As a result, price competition tends to be relatively moderate across much of a company's product range.

Japanese strategies, in contrast, emphasize forefront process technology, with only a secondary and much lower emphasis on product differentiation and unique product-market advantages. Low cost is the most important basis for competing. This kind of business strategy has led to a relatively low degree of strategic diversity among Japanese firms. Even the companies with niche strategies tend to compete with the broad product line producers on price for much of their sales volume. Because there is little tendency to withdraw from products or markets, competition over price in the standardized, basic product areas is intense.

These differences translate into differences in competitive behavior. U.S. firms generally attempt to manage competition through strategic repositioning or by creating a more unique strategy. Japanese firms tend to compete against each other using very similar strategies. They do not withdraw or try to avoid or reduce direct competition through strategic repositioning, as U.S. firms do. This low strategic diversity (or high strategic similarity) means that firms cannot readily compete with each other by having a superior strategy (of more attractive products or markets). As a result, Japanese semiconductor firms compete not so much at the level of strategy as at the level of strategy implementation.[6] They are the Redcoats and U.S. firms are the Minutemen from our earlier example.

Other comparative frameworks might also be used to explain these differences. For example, these differences might be viewed as a battle between innovation and operations management or between product technology and process technology. It is undoubtedly true that many superior business strategies in the semiconductor industry are currently based on innovation or some unique product technology. But they could also be based on other differential advantages. For example, brand image, distribution channels, and access to low-cost raw materials or other inputs are differential advantages that firms in other industries frequently use to build superior business strategies. As the rate of technological change in semiconductors declines, one would expect such factors to increasingly replace technological innovation and unique product technology as important differential advantages in firms' business strategies. In any case, striving for technological innovation and unique product technology is simply one way of attempting to compete with a differentiated and superior business strategy. Similarly, incrementally improving process technology and operations management is one way of seeking to compete with superior strategy implementation. The concept of a distinction between superior strategy and superior strategy implementation is broader than the alternative comparative frameworks and thus more useful from a strategic management perspective.

This analysis provides a somewhat different perspective than has previously been used to understand competition between U.S. and Japanese semiconductor firms.[7] Most research studies and articles have attributed the loss of U.S. competitive position in semiconductor to the following factors: (1) Japanese trade barriers, (2) dumping (selling below cost) by Japanese firms in export markets, (3) unfair targeting of the U.S.

TABLE 2   **Advantages and Disadvantages of the Two Competitive Styles**

	Competing through Superior Strategy	*Competing through Strategy Implementation*
Strategic Variety	Greater variety of strategies providing a wider range of products and more segmentation of markets.	Fewer strategies involving more direct competition between substitute products, with a greater emphasis on quality and cost.
Industry Concentration	Room for many successful competitors (low industry concentration).	Room for relatively few successful competitors (high industry concentration).
Survival Patterns	Innovative competitors survive and dominate an industry (higher turnover among leaders).	Efficient competitors survive and dominate an industry (lower turnover among leaders).
Stage of Product Life Cycle	Works best in early stages of a product life cycle when technological and/or environmental change is rapid and there exists a wide variety of feasible strategies.	Works best in later stages of a product life cycle when technological and/or environmental change is slow, dominant designs have evolved, and a limited number of feasible strategies exists.
Technological and Environmental Change Risk	Risks losing competitive advantage when the rate of technological and/or environmental change levels off and imitators enter a company's strategic domain.	Risks losing competitive advantage when technological and/or environmental change preempts the dominant strategy.
Profit Margins	Less direct competition and wider profit margins.	More direct competition and lower profit margins.

semiconductor market by Japanese firms supported by the Japanese Ministry for International Trade and Industry (MITI), (4) inadequate spending on research and capital investment in the United States, and (5) the lack of U.S. industrial or technology policy.[8] Although such industry-level economic and political factors are important contributors to the competitiveness problem, my study suggests that there may be another dimension to this problem—the way firms themselves attempt to compete.

Advantages and Disadvantages of the Competitive Styles

Each competitive style has advantages and disadvantages, both for an industry's firms and for its customers, suppliers, and regulators (see Table 2 for a summary). The first three conditions largely describe how industry structure might be expected to vary depending on which competitive style is most prevalent. The last three conditions outline the relative advantages and disadvantages firms face when they select either of the two competitive styles.

Strategic Variety

When firms in an industry attempt to compete by possessing strategies that are superior to those of their potential competitors, the result is a variety of different strategies. These differing strategies produce a wide variety of products and services and numerous strategic groups. When firms in an industry compete through superior strategy implementation, a high level of strategic similarity occurs. These firms provide products and services that are already successful in a market, but they make them better (cheaper or of better quality). Thus industries dominated by firms competing through superior strategy will provide customers with a wider range of products than industries dominated by firms concentrating on strategy implementation. The latter, however, will provide more direct competition with lower prices and higher quality.

Industry Concentration

The dominant competitive style is likely to influence the degree of industry concentration. Competing through superior strategy creates a richer competitive environment full of differentiated niches, thus making room for many successful competitors. Firms don't need to be large or efficient to survive, just sufficiently different. When competition occurs largely around strategy implementation, however, there is no place to hide from direct competition. Even relatively small differences in implementation capability can lead to long-run cost and quality advantages that will tend to drive less capable competitors from an industry once competition sets in (and once supply exceeds demand).

Survival Patterns

Survival patterns should also look quite different between the two cases. Competing through superior strategy favors innovative firms that can pick and even create growing niches. Entrepreneurial firms are likely to dominate such industries. But just as innovation and strategic maneuvering create new niches, they also destroy old ones. This contributes to a more dynamic industry in which firms can rise and fall rapidly and industry leadership is subject to considerable change. Competing through strategy implementation favors the efficient as opposed to the innovative competitor. Because efficiency within firms is likely to be more predictable and stable than innovation, the relative positions of firms in such an industry will change more slowly. As a result, industry leadership should be more stable.

These three conditions describe how competitive style can influence an industry's structure. The advantages and disadvantages of industry structures are of particular interest to customers, suppliers, regulators, and potential competitors. The next three conditions focus more on the advantages and disadvantages of competitive style for competing firms.

Stage of Product Life Cycle

Competing through superior strategy works best in the early stages of a product life cycle, when technological and environmental change tend to be rapid and a wide variety of feasible strategies exists. In later stages of a product life cycle, technological and environmental change are slowing and a limited number of dominant product designs have evolved. Firms have less opportunity to come up with a new design that the market will support and, hence, less opportunity to develop a strategy that differs from those already in place. These circumstances imply that more firms will be competing with similar strategies and that difference in strategy implementation rather than difference in strategy will tend to determine the winners.

Technological and Environmental Change Risk

The kind of business risk a firm faces also varies with the type of competitive style it employs. Firms attempting to compete through superior strategy are most vulnerable to losing their strategic uniqueness. Their risk is greatest when the rates of technological and environmental change level off, making it more difficult to create new bases for uniqueness. They are especially vulnerable when efficient imitators enter their strategic domains and change the basis of competition to one of strategy implementation.[9] This is what happened in the DRAM (memory) market of the U.S. semiconductor industry.

The creation of innovative technology in the semiconductor industry often creates only a temporary differential advantage. One reason is that new technologies associated with standard products and standard manufacturing processes are often quite "leaky." Ouchi and Bolton distinguish between private intellectual property (technology) and leaky intellectual property.[10] Private intellectual property is property that a private party can practically or legally appropriate and retain or transfer at will. Examples in the semiconductor industry are patentable product designs that cannot be readily bypassed or engineered around. Leaky intellectual property can be effectively appropriated by a private party but only for a short time. Soon others will either duplicate or bypass the new technology and eliminate the creator's ability to earn a return on it. Leaky technologies are primarily associated with standard products, such as designs for the next generation of DRAMs, and standard manufacturing processes, such as moving process technology from a one-micron technology to a submicron technology.

It is apparent that leaky technology must be frequently replenished or recreated in order to remain a differential advantage. In highly competitive industries, this is often difficult, and it becomes increasingly difficult and costly when the technology curve levels off. Even when technology is not leaky, the licensing of proprietary technology in the semiconductor industry is widespread for a number of reasons: it is a way of establishing a product as an industry standard, it satisfies customer demands for second sourcing, and it avoids inadvertent patent infringements and legal suits. As a result, new technology development in the semiconductor industry often provides only a temporary differential advantage.

Conversely, firms used to competing with superior strategy implication face the greatest risk when the rate of technological and environmental change increases. Such conditions create opportunities for technological breakthroughs and other changes that can become the bases for new strategies. These new technologies are often sufficiently different to be more proprietary and less leaky than the mature technology they replace. This hinders the strategy implementer from adopting the new strategy and might eliminate the advantage the implementer presently realizes from its superior ability to implement the old strategy (much as the Minutemen's new strategy eliminated the superior implementation capability of the Redcoats in the second battle).

For example, many believed that improvements in ASIC technologies might allow U.S. firms to outflank Japanese dominance in standard products. This would make Japan's superior strategy implementation capability less relevant. This belief has waned, however, as growth in ASICs has been slower than anticipated (they still account for only 20 percent to 25 percent of the market).

Profit Margins

Finally, firms able to compete with a superior strategy should encounter less direct competition and higher profit margins than firms competing with similar strategies and attempting to excel through strategy implementation.

Thus competitive style has a number of important implications for both firms and industries. This comparison reveals that the two modes of competing tend to work best under different conditions and tend to provide different kinds of advantages.

Managerial Requirements for the Competitive Styles

In this section, I will consider the different managerial requirements that the two competitive styles demand (see Table 3 for a summary).

Leadership Style

Leadership in a firm that competes through superior strategy should be different from leadership in a firm that largely competes through strategy implementation.

TABLE 3   Managerial Requirements Associated with the Two Competitive Styles

	Competing through Superior Strategy	Competing through Strategy Implementation
Leadership Style	Leader is the great strategist.	Leader is the great organizer and motivator.
Management Focus	Management focus is external.	Management focus is internal.
Basis for Excellence	Competitive advantage is based on the actions of a few.	Competitive advantage is based on the actions of many.
Careers	Company experience is less important than industry experience.	Need long careers and intensive training within the company.

In the former, the leader needs to be the great strategist—brilliant, capable of seeing what others do not see, and possessing considerable insight into environmental threats and opportunities. The strategist's job is to plot the best course through this environment. By comparison, the leader in a firm that competes through strategy implementation needs to be an "organization man"—a great organizer and motivator of people in their day-to-day activities. Here the job is to implement rather than plot strategy, and the leader does this by focusing human, physical, and financial resources on the right activities and managing them with unusual efficiency.

Management Focus

In firms competing through superior strategy, management's focus needs to be more external than internal. Insight into environmental threats and opportunities and a deep understanding of the industry tend to be more important than great insight into a firm's internal characteristics and ways of operating. Although both are needed, it is in the former area that the firm primarily attempts to gain advantage over its competitors. In contrast, firms that attempt to compete through strategy implementation, managements' focus needs to be more internal. A deep understanding of how to fine-tune an organization through better organizational design, management of organizational processes, and motivation of employees lies at the core of this way of competing.

Basis of Excellence

The primary burden of achieving competitive advantage rests on different groups of people under the two styles. Competing through superior strategy places most of the burden on top management and a few other critical people. In semiconductor firms with unique strategies, for example, the people responsible for making the strategy unique tend to be the product designers. In such firms, this small strategic core of people can command very high compensation and status. In firms where competing through strategy implementation is stronger, the strategic core of people is usually much broader. In large Japanese semiconductor firms, for example, competitive advantage depends on the actions of thousands of people scattered across the product design, process development, and manufacturing subunits. No small elite strategic core can by itself establish and maintain competitive advantage in such an organization. Compensation and status tend to be much more equalized in such firms.

Careers

Finally, the two competitive modes tend to require and support different career patterns. Competing through superior strategy implies that company experience is usually less important than industry experience because the latter is required to uniquely position a firm in its competitive environment. One would expect such firms to hire more people from the outside and to have managers with multicompany careers. Competing through strategy implementation, in contrast, favors long careers within a company so that managers can acquire the knowledge and credibility to fine-tune coordination between subunits, motivate critical behavior, and develop a reinforcing company culture.

Data from the sixteen semiconductor companies in my sample tend to support the relationships hypothesized. The firms attempting to compete most strongly through superior strategy were the three U.S. companies with niche strategies based largely on developing and making unique products. In these firms, the general manager tended to see (and frequently referred to) the strategy as his own, and others in the firms also tended to refer to the strategy as "Bob's" or "Jim's" strategy. All of these general managers had rich multicompany careers, as did most of the key functional managers as well, and spent considerable time maintaining and using their extensive intercompany networks to help establish a new product as an industry standard, develop second-sourcing and licensing arrangements, and hire critical talent. The general manager and a few people, usually product designers, tended to be viewed as the strategic core that made the strategy viable. In one firm, with a new general manager, the strategy subsequently underwent significant change.

The firms in the sample competing most strongly through strategy implementation were the five broad product line Japanese firms. Their strategies were relatively similar in terms of breadth of product line and markets and where they sought to achieve competitive advantage. In these firms, managers presented strategies as stable and long term and did not identify them with a creator. Top managers seemed to spend most of their time coordinating, organizing, training, and motivating people rather than plotting strategy. For example, the president of one Japanese company was reported to spend three days a week at the company training and development center, interacting with and motivating the employees in the various training programs. As is typical in large Japanese firms, all senior managers had single-company careers and all general managers had spent time in divisions outside of semiconductors. They had largely been selected to be general managers because they were good "organization men," not because they knew a lot about semiconductors. Their impact on company success was not direct but rather felt through their influence on the actions of many employees.

These two sets of companies were the extremes. Other companies lay between them, competing with a combination of superior strategy and strategy implementation (although generally leaning more toward one or the other). These in-between firms generally had in-between managerial characteristics. Thus the sample provides some preliminary support for my attempt to link differences in managerial requirements to differences in competitive style. If we look back at Table 3, it seems that the two sets of managerial requirements are relatively incompatible, which raises a question about how successful companies or business units can be when they attempt to embrace both competitive styles more or less equally. As already stated, the sample companies tended to lean toward one style or the other.

Confrontation between the Competitive Styles

With the internationalization of semiconductor markets (especially the U.S. market), the two competitive styles have come into direct competition. As one would predict, firms pursuing the typical U.S. strategy have withdrawn rapidly from products and market segments soon after they have been assaulted by Japanese producers attempting to compete largely through superior strategy implementation. This is illustrated by the substantial decline in U.S. market share and increase in Japanese market share for DRAMs, static random access memories (SRAMs), and gate arrays, all products the United States once dominated. The U.S. firms have generally attempted to reposition themselves into more innovative product areas such as electrically erasable programmable read-only memories (EEPROMs) and ASICs. This is the typical U.S. attempt to compete with product-market differentiation or strategic repositioning. The Japanese firms have rapidly gained large shares of the abandoned markets, only to find themselves facing charges of unfair competition and potential protectionist action by the U.S. government. The sentiment among many U.S. semiconductor executives is that the Japanese firms have not played the game the way it should be played.

The interviews revealed that Japanese executives also believed that the game was not being played properly—by the Americans. Several were puzzled that strong U.S. firms abandoned product areas so quickly, that they had allowed their process technology to slip so far behind, and that there was a clamor for government protection. This is not the way the game would have been played among Japanese companies, which have little expectation that competitors will retreat or leave the field when competition becomes intense. Direct confrontation between these two competitive styles seems to have led to a high degree of misunderstanding and a sense that the opposing side has not been playing the game fairly.

Recent Trends

The semiconductor industry is extremely dynamic, and firms often change competitive position rapidly. It is useful to consider how the industry has changed since the study was completed. During 1988 and 1989, U.S. firms continued to lose market share as Japanese firms gained share, primarily owing to the rapid growth of standardized memory products. The relative market shares of the United States and Japan essentially stabilized in 1990 and 1991, which may suggest that U.S competitiveness has improved. Also during this period, there are reports that large U.S. firms such as Motorola, IBM, and Texas Instruments have instituted massive total quality management (TQM) programs in semiconductor manufacturing and have made major gains in improving quality and reducing unit costs. Such programs have also grown rapidly in other industries, stimulated by the Malcolm Baldrige Award and widespread interest in renewing U.S. manufacturing competitiveness. These programs are primarily aimed at improving strategy implementation capabilities rather than developing a new differentiated strategy that will provide some meaningful advantage. Yet few would argue that U.S. firms can out-implement their Japanese competitors in DRAMs or other standard products or that U.S. firms are pinning their hopes on undifferentiated product strategies and superior strategy implementation capabilities.

A closer examination indicates that market shares have stabilized, not because U.S. firms have been able to halt market share erosion in highly competitive, standardized products, but because the U.S. has had continued success in innovative, differentiated products. The growth in ASICs and microprocessors, which are innovative and differentiated product categories that tend to be dominated by U.S. firms, has served to offset losses in other market segments. In fact, the bulk of this success has been concentrated in one product category and one firm. The rapid growth in Intel's microprocessor sales during recent years has been largely responsible for the stabilized U.S. position. Thus, although U.S. firms have begun major efforts to improve strategy implementation capability (through TQM programs, the creation of Sematech, and major agreements with Japanese firms to cooperate on developing product and process technology for future generations of DRAMs), these efforts appear to date to have had little effect on recent results or existing competitive trends. Instead, the traditional ability of U.S. semiconductor firms to compete with differentiated business strategies based on superior product innovation continues to explain the relative success and failure of individual U.S. firms and the U.S. industry as a whole.

At the same time, there is some evidence that the major Japanese firms may be attempting to compete with more differentiated business strategies. Japanese firms are increasingly investing in new product technology, working hard to improve their ASIC design and manufacturing capability (most recently with ASIC plants in the United States), and cooperating in joint technology development with innovative U.S. and European firms. In several cases, Japanese firms are assisting Western partners to improve process technology in exchange for access to design tools and standard cell libraries that will improve their capability to compete for the growing ASIC market. Yet, to date, Japanese firms have been able to dominate only the more standardized and competitive gate array segment of the ASIC market, while U.S. firms have continued to dominate the more differentiated standard cell and programmable logic device (PLD) segments. In other words, Japanese firms still rely heavily on relatively undifferentiated, highly competitive products, where superior strategy implementation is the primary basis for competition.

Although U.S. firms are improving their ability to compete in terms of strategy implementation and Japanese firms are making some efforts to develop more differentiated product strategies, it is questionable how far such convergence will proceed. To date, there is insufficient evidence to suggest that the fundamental pattern of competition described by the study is changing.

Implications for Global Competitiveness

In this section I will attempt to generalize from the specific findings and limited hypotheses developed above to some of the broader implications for global competition. The globalization of an increasing number of U.S. markets has brought many U.S. firms into direct competition with foreign firms. Many of these foreign firms, especially those based in the Pacific Rim countries, primarily compete through superior strategy implementation. At the same time, the maturing of many product categories has made it more difficult to compete with unique product-market strategies. In many cases, it has been impossible to consistently stay a step ahead of a determined competitor that posses superior strategy implementation capabilities. As technology curves flatten out, time is on the side of the better implementer.

Attempting to gain strategic competitive advantage through frequent repositioning of one's product lines and market segments seems to work best when one's competitors also believe in this principle and are playing the same game. When one's competitors are not playing this game, frequent strategic repositioning may not lead to long-run success. Compared to Japanese firms, U.S. firms have fairly flexible business strategies and are quite adept at realigning product lines and market segments to reflect changes in competitive advantage. This kind of continuous strategic maneuvering has worked well for those companies that can maneuver the best. Competitors generally understand the meaning of being outmaneuvered and back off quickly, either going into other areas or licensing the winner's technology. A good example of this has been Intel, which has consistently focused its resources on developing the next product before others, quickly coalesced a group of customers and suppliers around the new product to make it an industry standard, and retreated from old products and markets as they have matured and become too price competitive.

But Japanese firms do not play this same game of frequently repositioning product lines and market segments. It is more difficult for a Japanese firm to alter strategy and very hard to withdraw from products or markets when one has been outmaneuvered or lost competitive advantage. A good example of this has been NEC's persistence over the years in developing and establishing its own line of microprocessors, despite the dominance of the Intel and Motorola designs. Thy typical Japanese response is to refocus its efforts on catching up. Toshiba committed itself in 1982 to catching up in DRAMs and in 1988 became the largest and most successful producer of the one-megabit DRAM. Japanese firms do not generally attempt to leapfrog new developments in either product or process technology, the way many U.S. firms do. Thus, when a Japanese firm falls behind, it can generally catch up by simply working harder at implementing the existing strategy. Conversely, when a U.S. firm fails at implementing an overly ambitious strategy (such as leapfrogging a product improvement), it tends to fall so far behind that it frequently must exit this segment of the market.

Overall, the frequent strategic repositioning of U.S. firms seems to have a definite impact on the strategies of other U.S. firms but relatively little impact on the strategies of Japanese competitors. The Japanese firms are busy implementing product line and market segment strategies that are longer term, less flexible, and not subject to being judged on short-run profitability. When faced with a poor competitive situation, the Japanese firm is much more likely to alter the nature or intensity of strategy implementation than the strategy itself.

This kind of competitive behavior raises questions about the efficacy of strategic repositioning as a means of gaining competitive advantage. Most strategies based on frequent repositioning rely on competitors recognizing and backing away from firms in strategically more favorable positions. For awhile, at least, this leaves the fruits of the abandoned product line or market segment to the winner. If, however, the competitor fails to yield and insists on competing (even at a loss), the expectant winner will not realize the full benefits of its strategic advantage. In fact, if the competitor displays superior strategy implementation capabilities and has staying power, it is probable that the early winner will even lose much of the product line or market segment as the initial advantage wanes. This is because competitors with superior strategy implementation

TABLE 4   Implications for U.S. Competitiveness

- More firms need to shift from relying on superior strategy to developing superior strategy implementation capabilities.
- Education, reward systems, and cultural values need to facilitate this shift.
- Otherwise, the United States will have to establish barriers and avoid direct confrontation. Trade would have to be more confined to regional and intracultural competitive patterns, and it would have to be more carefully regulated across these regional and cultural differences.

capabilities can usually catch up once they target a product or market segment in which a dominant product design or industry standard already exists. For example, U.S. firms were early leaders in SRAMs and once dominated this market. Now they only dominate the very fast SRAM segment, where technology development has been most rapid and unique designs abound. Japanese firms hold the bulk of the SRAM market and dominate those segments in which product technology has matured. If firms are not deterred by short-run losses and do not confront an unassailable mobility barrier, such as a patent or trade barrier, strategies based on implementation can probably negate the advantages of strategies built on frequent strategic repositioning.

It is probable that competing through superior strategy works only over a limited period of time in an industry's life. Unless a firm can drive out all competitors while it possesses the superior strategy and raise entry barriers sufficient to keep them out, it must at some point change its competitive style to one stressing superior strategy implementation.

It is important to recognize that both modes of competing—creating a unique and superior business strategy and excelling at strategy implementation—constitute strategic behavior. It is not that one is strategic while the other is tactical or operational, although strategy implementation frequently involves getting tactical and operational behavior to strongly support key strategy elements. Both competitive modes can fundamentally influence or alter the firm's strategic position in its competitive environment. The overall strategic management of a firm needs to be viewed as some combination of these two modes of competing, although it appears that most firms tend to emphasize one more than the other. While this tendency is undoubtedly influenced by industry and technological maturity, it also appears to be influenced by national culture. If this is true, it is a disturbing complexity for those who deal with global industries, and especially for those who seek to achieve "fairness" or a "level playing field" in global competition.

I conclude with three implications, as shown in Table 4. In the increasingly global competitive system, more U.S. firms will need to shift their way of competing from relying on superior strategy to developing superior strategy implementation capabilities. Superior strategy worked well for the Minutemen and for most industries during the early periods of product life cycles. Their experiences have helped to create a myth that this is the most successful and profitable way to compete. Unfortunately, flattening technology curves and global competition have made this myth out of date for many industries.

Education, reward systems, and cultural values need to change to facilitate this shift toward strategy implementation. U.S. business education has strongly touted the virtues of strategic maneuvering, breakthroughs and rapid success, outflanking rather than confronting competitors, and high early profits. The constant, incremental improvement of a company's operations and performance is generally viewed as a boring way to compete; it is not the route to the cover of *Business Week*. Somehow, reward systems need to change.

If the United States cannot become more competitive in terms of strategy implementation capability, it will probably have to establish trade barriers to protect itself from foreign competitors that excel at this competitive mode. Trade will have to be more confined to regional and intracultural competitive systems, and it will have to be more carefully regulated across these rational and cultural differences. To some extent, this is the pattern that may be developing in Europe.

Porter argues that a competitive home environment is a prerequisite for global success.[11] This article points out that national environments can be competitive in different ways. It suggests that the U.S. environment is not necessarily insufficiently competitive but that it is more used to a different kind of competition than the Japanese environment. Porter's notion of competitive and noncompetitive home environments may be too simple to fully capture the reality of global competition when fundamentally different modes of competition are involved.

The framework and hypotheses in this article present a somewhat different perspective of global competition than previous articles. This perspective was suggested by an examination of the business strategies and competitive styles of firms in an industry that has recently become global. Most attempts to explain global competitiveness and international trade problems have employed industry and societal-level factors such as industry spending on R&D, differences in interest rates, and government policies. This new perspective needs to be seen as augmenting, not replacing, the existing perspectives. It suggests, however, that international competitiveness problems exist at multiple levels of analysis and are unlikely to be successfully addressed by simple, single-level solutions.

Appendix

This article is based on a major study of strategy and strategy implementation in twenty-three semiconductor firms, Eight were in the United States, eight were Japanese, and seven were European (the latter are not used here). I used information from public sources to choose companies that represented the strategic diversity of the industry in each geographical area.

I conducted structured interviews during 1986 and 1987 at each company's headquarters and often at additional company sites. The interviews generally involved the general manager, R&D manager, manufacturing manager, and marketing manager, as well as others. In all but a few instances in which individual managers objected, I taped the interviews. The tapes facilitated the later quantification and coding of certain data and the transcription and analysis of qualitative data.

Although many of the variables and concepts I measured were suggested by prior work, the thrust of the study was exploratory. The central idea presented in this article evolved out of a comparative analysis of the firms' various strategies.

References

1. The research is described in more detail in: R.N. Langlois, T.A. Pugel, C.S. Haklisch, R.R. Nelson, and W.G. Egelhoff, *Microelectronics: An Industry in Transition* (Boston: Unwin Hyman, 1988).

2. A good, nontechnical description of the semiconductor industry and its evolution to 1987 can be found in: "The Global Semiconductor Industry, 1987" (Boston: Harvard Business School, Case No. 9–388–052, 1987).

3. See B.R. Scott, "National Strategy for Stronger U.S. Competitiveness," *Harvard Business Review,* March–April 1984, pp. 77–91. Also, M.L. Dertouzos, R.K. Lester, and R.M. Solow, *Made in America: Regaining the Productive Edge* (Cambridge, Massachusetts: MIT Press, 1989).

4. This view about the importance of differentiation in high-technology industries such as semiconductors is supported by Krishna and Rao. They argue that U.S. high-tech industries need to be "higher tech" relative to overseas competitors if they are to be competitive. See: E.M. Krishna and C.P. Rao, "Is U.S. High Technology High Enough?" *Columbia Journal of World Business,* Winter 1986, pp. 81–86.

5. This finding is consistent with Prahalad and Hamel's view that Japanese firms pay great attention to developing and maintaining core competencies within a firm and avoid outside dependency in these areas. See: C.K. Prahalad and G. Hamel, "The Core Competence of the Corporation," *Harvard Business Review,* May–June 1990, pp. 79–91. A related view is expressed in: C.H. Ferguson, "Computers and the Coming of the U.S. Keiretsu," *Harvard Business Review,* July–August 1990, pp. 55–70. Ferguson sees digitalization as creating interdependencies across many industries bordering on semiconductors and believes it can also be managed with keiretsu-like relationships among clusters of firms.

6. Ohmae alludes to the Japanese preference for competing through strategy implementation and for giving less attention to the strategy being implemented: *Japanese managers are victims of their own success and of the habits that success creates. Not long ago, I was talking with the CEO of a large Japanese machinery company who had been an oarsman in college. According to his view of the world, if you want to win, all eight guys in the boat bend over a little farther, pull a little harder, work a little better as a team. That's how you beat the other boats. That was his idea of strategy: hunch over and pull harder. No change in course, no pause to look at the distant horizon, no time to take new bearings. If your goal is to beat the competition, you win by narrowing your field of vision and doing more better.* K. Ohmae, "Companyism and Do More Better," *Harvard Business Review,* January–February 1989, pp. 125–132.

7. In a recent article, Hamel and Prahalad state, "The new global competitors approach strategy from a perspective that is fundamentally different from that which underpins Western management thought." They, however, see Japanese firms as possessing "strategic intent," which means an obsession with winning at all levels of the organization. An active management process supports this obsession. This view does not appear to be the same as my distinction between competing through superior strategy and competing through superior strategy implementation, although we both arrive at some of the same conclusions. See: G. Hamel and C.K. Prahalad, "Strategic Intent," *Harvard Business Review,* May–June 1989, pp. 63–76.

8. For insightful discussions of such industry-level factors, see: C.H. Ferguson, "American Microelectronics in Decline: Evidence, Analysis, and Alternatives" (Cambridge, Massachusetts: Massachusetts Institute of Technology, VLSI Memo No. 85–284, 1985); M.T. Flaherty and H. Itami, "Finance," in *Competitive Edge: The Semiconductor Industry in the U.S. and Japan,* eds. D.I. Okimoto, T. Sugano, and F.B. Weinstein (Stanford, California: Stanford University Press, 1984); C.V. Prestowitz, Jr., "U.S.-Japan Trade Friction: Creating a New Relationship," *California Management Review,* winter 1987, pp. 9–19; and Semiconductor Industry Association, *The Effects of Government Targeting on World Semiconductor Competition: A Case History of Japanese Industrial Strategy and Its Costs for America* (Cupertino, California: Semiconductor Industry Association, 1983).

9. See E. Mansfield, "Industrial Innovation in Japan and the United States," *Science,* September 1988. He found that Japanese firms enjoy significant cost and time advantages over U.S. firms when commercializing externally developed innovations.

10. See W.G. Ouchi and M.K. Bolton, "The Logic of Joint Research and Development," *California Management Review,* Spring 1988, pp. 9–33.

11. M.E. Porter, "The Competitive Advantage of Nations," *Harvard Business Review,* March–April 1990, pp. 73–93.

Managerial Barriers to U.S. Exports

Christopher M. Korth.   *Christopher M. Korth is a professor of international business at the College of Business Administration, University of South Carolina, Columbia.*

During the 1980s, the U.S. economy enjoyed one of its longest growth periods on record. Not surprisingly, imports grew along with the economy. However, for most of the decade, exports stagnated. The United States is now suffering from a serious deficit in its balance of trade: we are importing much more merchandise than we are exporting. The deficit is due primarily to the shortfall of exports.

Many observers in the United States have blamed the balance-of-trade deficit on governments—import barriers in foreign countries, and government actions in this country that have produced an unrealistically high exchange rate. However, companies from many other countries have been able to export successfully despite existing trade barriers. Also, some U.S. companies are quite successful exporters (see Table 1). And although the federal government was indeed responsible for an unrealistically high value of the dollar in the first half of the 1980s, that overvaluation was eliminated during the second half of the decade.

Thus, neither American nor foreign governments are responsible for most of the recent failure of American companies to be more successful exporters. *The fact is, on average, American companies are lousy exporters.* It is time for American managers to stop pointing the finger of blame at others and examine themselves instead. The legal barriers of foreign governments or a high U.S. exchange rate are not preventing American companies from redressing the trade imbalance. Rather, the principal factor that has allowed the trade deficits to reach such scandalous levels and prevented the U.S. from sharply reducing that deficit is the extensive failure of American companies to aggressively pursue export opportunities. The barriers to successful exporting from this country are internal: they are *managerial barriers within the companies themselves.*

The U.S. Trade Deficit

Trade deficits have not always been the norm for the United States. Indeed, for most of the past century, this country experienced trade surpluses (see Table 2). The U.S. balance of trade (BOT) was in surplus every year from 1894 through 1970.

Reprinted from *Business Horizons*, March–April 1991, pp. 18–26. Copyright © 1991 by the Foundation for the School of Business at Indiana University. Used with permission.

TABLE 1   The Top 10 American Exporters
($ billion; 1989)

Boeing	11.0
General Motors	10.2
Ford Motor	8.6
General Electric	7.3
IBM	5.5
DuPont	4.8
Chrysler	4.6
United Technologies	3.3
Caterpillar	3.3
McDonnell Douglas	2.9

SOURCE: *Fortune,* July 16, 1990, p. 77.

TABLE 2   The U.S. Balance of Trade: 1890–1970
($ billion)

	(a) *Exports*	*(b)* *Imports*	*(c)* *Balance of Trade*
1890	0.9	0.8	0.1
1900	1.4	0.9	0.5
1910	1.8	1.6	0.2
1920	8.2	5.3	2.9
1930	3.9	3.1	0.8
1940	4.0	2.6	1.4
1950	10.3	8.9	1.4
1955	15.6	11.4	4.2
1960	19.4	15.0	4.4
1965	26.7	21.4	5.3
1970	42.7	40.0	2.7

SOURCE: *Statistical Abstract of the United States: 1926* (for data from 1890–1925, p. 443); *1958* (for 1930–1955, p. 880); and *1989* (for 1960–1970, p. 786).

A balance-of-trade surplus means that a country will earn more money abroad from merchandise exports than it spends on merchandise imports. By this means, the country generates funds that allow it to finance other international activities: for example, a deficit on its balance of services (foreign travel); the payment of foreign aid; the accumulation of foreign reserves by the government of the country; or, investments by its companies in foreign countries. (During the period of trade surpluses, the United States accumulated hundreds of billions of dollars of foreign investments. The country became the world's largest international creditor and largest international direct investor.)

The era of chronic balance-of-trade surpluses of the United States ended abruptly in 1971 with a trade deficit of $2.3 billion. As can be seen in Table 3, the nation has since run chronic deficits in its merchandise-trade account. Also, after the mid-1970s, the levels of the deficits far exceeded any of the earlier surpluses.

TABLE 3   The U.S. Balance of Trade: 1970–1989
($ billion)

	(a) Exports	(b) Imports	(c) Balance of Trade
1970	42.7	40.0	2.7
1972	49.2	55.6	−6.4
1974	98.1	102.6	−4.5
1976	115.2	123.5	−8.3
1978	143.7	174.8	−31.1
1980	220.6	244.8	−24.2
1982	212.3	244.1	−31.8
1984	217.9	325.7	−107.9
1986	217.3	370.0	−152.7
1988	322.4	441.0	−118.5
1989	349.7	473.0	−123.3

SOURCE: *Statistical Abstract of the United States: 1989*, p. 786. For 1990, *Survey of Current Business.*

In 1980, U.S. merchandise exports totalled $220.6 billion while imports were $244.8 billion (a $24.2 billion deficit). Six years later, exports had actually declined from their 1980 level, while imports had soared by $125 billion to $370.0 billion—producing a deficit of $152.7 billion. (U.S. exports had actually declined even more when the distortions caused by inflation are removed.)

The U.S. trade picture has improved since 1986. However, every year since 1983 the merchandise trade deficit has exceeded $100 billion—the highest levels of any country in history. Most economists see little reason to expect significant improvement.

Trade deficits are not necessarily bad—indeed, many industrialized countries and most developing countries have merchandise trade deficits. Many of the imports are important commodities, supplies, and machines that help modernize an economy's productive capacity, raise the standard of living, and depress inflation.

However, what is of great concern is both the absolute and relative levels of the deficits of the United States—and the duration of those deficits. While small or even moderate deficits in the trade balance may not pose serious problems, the massive deficits of the 1980s have very serious risks for both this country and the rest of the world. And, the longer we delay in resolving this untenable situation, the more disruptive and painful the remedy will be.

Financing a Trade Deficit

A trade deficit of any magnitude must be financed by sources of revenues from abroad. Figure 1 shows that there are many sources for revenues, such as a surplus in services, a sale of foreign assets, or the inflow of foreign capital. Some of the beneficiary countries from such flows are identified.

The U.S. is not, of course, a prime candidate for the receipt of foreign aid. Also, our traditional surplus on international services has recently shifted into deficit, and the federal government's international reserves are not large enough to finance much of the trade deficits. Nor has there been a net sale of foreign assets by the

---

FIGURE 1   The Financing of Trade Deficits

Surpluses on the international balance of services
  • Financial services (United Kingdom, Switzerland, Singapore)
  • International tourism (Jamaica, Portugal)

Surpluses in unilateral transfers
  • Remittances from citizens who are working abroad (Algeria, Mexico)
  • Foreign aid (Egypt, Israel, the Philippines)

Sale of foreign assets
  • Equity and debt investment of the private sector
  • Government's international reserves and foreign equity investments
    (Libya's sale of its large share of the FIAT automobile company)

Inflow of foreign capital
  • Bank loans (into Brazil, India)
  • Direct investments (into Turkey, Spain)

---

private sector. The only way that deficits of the magnitude of those of the United States can be financed is via an inflow of debt or equity capital from abroad. Indeed, both the government and the private sector now must borrow heavily abroad, or foreigners must buy equity in companies or real estate in the United States, to finance the international expenditures of our economy.

Implications of These Deficits

When the United States, the world's largest economy, runs a deficit year after year that is chronically at very high levels with little hope of rapid reduction, there is a serious problem. Among the consequences are excessively high interest rates and a reduction in the funds available to other borrowers. The impact is felt by borrowers as diverse as home buyers and manufacturing corporations in the U.S., and third-world debtors—all of whom are paying higher interest rates because of the enormous U.S. borrowing demand.

Other adverse consequences include a weak dollar that encourages exports but is inflationary for the United States, and major disruptions in many industries and communities. For example, construction in the United States has been adversely affected by high interest rates, and both automobiles and textiles are industries where domestic employment has fallen significantly in the face of foreign competition.

Until 1986, the United States had invested more abroad than had been invested in the U.S. by foreigners. The country enjoyed a net surplus on international investments. However, the massive balance-of-trade deficits of the past decade have given foreign investors the opportunity to make very large direct investments in America.

The Solution: Import Protectionism or Export Expansion?

As was seen in Table 3, the American international trade problem is the result of a growth in exports that has been much slower than the rise in imports. How can this trade imbalance be remedied? Either a rise in exports or a drop in imports could accomplish the desired result.

Import Protectionism

Many government officials, corporate managers, and labor-union leaders have recommended trade barriers to stem the flow of imports. However, protectionism is not the answer. Protectionism (whether in the form of tariffs, quotas, or any other barrier designed to reduce imports) is inflationary, limits the range of products available to American companies and consumers, and encourages economic inefficiency. Also, protectionism here is likely to lead to protectionism abroad, which will hurt American exports, exporters, and the employees in those firms—companies that have proven themselves efficient enough and aggressive enough to succeed in foreign markets. Why should domestic consumers and successful exporting companies suffer to protect the inefficient producers?

Export Expansion

Far better than protectionism would be greater efforts to increase U.S. exports by encouraging those companies that can compete successfully abroad. This failure of the U.S. export effort commands a heavy price. In addition to the above-mentioned problems of the trade deficit, the failure of American companies to export more aggressively costs Americans jobs. The U.S. Department of Commerce estimates that every $1 billion increase in exports creates 25,000 more jobs in the United States. Declines in imports are not nearly as helpful in creating new jobs. Therefore, the efforts of the federal government and American companies should be to improve export efforts—not to limit imports.

Managerial Barriers to Successful Exporting

It is argued here that, even for companies that have the potential for successful exporting and even when the government does not interfere with their internationalization efforts, most U.S. companies do not adequately pursue their foreign market opportunities. The balance of this article will explore which barriers to exporting are management imposed and what can be done by managers to improve this situation.

Numerous explanations, rationalizations, and excuses are commonly given by managers for their failure to explore international opportunities. However, basically the reasons fall into one of five major categories of managerial barriers:

- Limited ambition;
- Unrecognized opportunities;
- Culpable lack of necessary resources;
- Unrealistic fears; and
- Managerial inertia.

These obstacles are within the firm. The company really has no one to blame but itself—the fault lies in the lack of vision and entrepreneurship by the managers of the firm.

These managerial barriers are clearly not unique to international business. The same shortcomings help to explain companies that fail to fully tap their domestic markets—whether local, regional, state/provincial, or national. Thus, the reader may choose to consider what follows with domestic as well as international markets in mind. However, the focus of the discussion here of each of the five managerial barriers will be on the failure to pursue international markets.

Limited Ambition

The first of the five managerial barriers to exporting is the limited ambitions of management for the growth of the company. This limited ambition can reflect either satisfaction with domestic market opportunities in the United States or a preoccupation with problems in existing domestic markets.

Sufficient Opportunities in the United States.   Many managers are content with their current domestic sales and profitability and with the potential for continued growth in domestic markets. They simply are not looking for further opportunities. They may have the potential to expand internationally but not the desire. Such managers are either complacent about the existing state of their businesses or take a very parochial view of markets.

The management of many companies is complacent about the existing status of their firms in very limited regional or even local markets. They are quite satisfied with the rate of return, total profitability, rate of growth, extent of market penetration, and economies of scale of their current operations. Therefore, those managers might not feel a need to try harder.

Such an attitude is quite common, and can be understandable. Such limited-growth companies play a valuable role in any local economy. Given their limited goals, these companies are often very successful within the confines of their own aspirations. However, many of these companies could become far more successful if they were to set, and attempt to attain, more ambitious goals—with either a larger domestic or an international horizon.

A different group of companies is more aggressive. These companies are interested in growing. They may not only explore domestic expansion opportunities of existing merchandise or service lines but even consider product diversification as a means of growth. They have not limited their goals to servicing their current markets, but they do limit the horizons of the ambitions to their broader regional or national domestic markets.

These are some of the companies that should most carefully consider export opportunities. If they were to examine the potential of international markets, they might find highly profitable opportunities for their existing products. Companies often find that foreign opportunities exceed domestic ones. Also, the product life cycles of existing product and productive equipment might be extendable via international markets.

Many of these companies will be forced to confront international markets when foreign competitors invade the domestic markets—often with different styles and marketing techniques. If the domestic company had first penetrated foreign markets, it might have acquired ideas to benefit its products, production, and markets at home. To wait for the need to react at a time of competitors' choosing is not likely to be as desirable as acting on the firm's own time schedule. Economic parochialism can be very dangerous.

Managerial Preoccupation with Domestic Problems in the U.S.   Not all companies that fail to even explore the opportunities in foreign markets do so because of inappropriate products or a failure to look beyond U.S. borders. The ambition of many companies is limited by serious problems in their existing domestic operations that fully absorb their efforts and resources.

For example, a company may be involved in a difficult and expensive struggle with aggressive competitors. Or, it may be having serious labor difficulties. Such a company might be making a serious mistake if it added other managerial burdens to those that already exist. These companies are not currently ripe for export development. However, some of these companies would now be far stronger if they had diversified earlier into international markets.

Serious preoccupations with existing problems are justification for a company to maintain its focus on its current business. Also, a company that is aggressively expanding domestically may justify its focus on expansion efforts on those markets. However, it is a great tragedy that tens of thousands of other companies, which have neither the problems of the former nor the dynamic domestic opportunities of the latter, lack the initiative to explore their growth potential. Simple complacency and parochial horizons are among the greatest reasons for the unsatisfactory levels of U.S. exports.

As we shall see, there are many resources to assist companies in exploring international opportunities. However, many of the potentially greatest beneficiaries of such assistance not only are unaware of these resources, but are not even very interested in getting assistance. The United States remains a parochial country. We complain about inroads of foreign sellers and investors; we gripe about a huge trade deficit; however, we do not make the appropriate effort to improve our own performance—it is much easier to blame the foreigners for being successful.

American colleges and universities are among the best in the world. In many ways, American business schools are the best in the world. However, in general, they do a miserable job of preparing managers to compete in the global markets of the 1990s—markets that will involve strong domestic competition from foreign companies.

American business schools must take the lead in changing this situation. As long as this country continues to graduate tens of thousands of MBAs who are ignorant of the basics of international business, American companies will continue to fail to reach their potential. It is said that generals are preparing always to refight the last war rather than for the changing conditions that will dictate the nature of the next war. Similarly, American business schools are training managers for the parochial markets of the past instead of the world markets of the future.

Unrecognized Opportunities

If a company has thrown off the burden of limited ambition, and is prepared to consider foreign markets, the first step is the acquisition of accurate knowledge about the foreign possibilities. Problems can arise from both inadequate knowledge and an appropriate interpretation of that knowledge.

Lack of Knowledge.   The most obvious reason companies do not seek to develop new markets under these circumstances is simply their failure to recognize that new markets exist. This lack of knowledge can be due to either the lack of chance to explore new markets or the lack of effort to find out what opportunities exist.

Ignorance due to lack of chance for the potential exporter to learn of foreign market potential is *not* the fault of the parties involved. For example, the native weaver in Ecuador or the woodcarver in Ghana may have little opportunity to learn about and to develop export markets: such individuals may simply have no access to the information.

The form of ignorance about which we are most concerned is not the result of a lack of chance to get the information, but rather from a lack of effort. The rewards for making the effort can be very substantial. If Kentucky Fried Chicken had not first made the effort to find out the potential, it would never have had the incentive to open in Beijing, China—its largest facility in the entire world. Unfortunately, however, the majority of potential American exporters are guilty of failing to make a satisfactory effort. Eighty-five percent of all American exports are accounted for by only 250 companies (Stout 1989).

Managerial Misperceptions about Foreign Markets.   Another form of culpable ignorance stems from misinterpretation of available information. For example, even if the opportunities are recognized, many managers are deterred by their perception—or more accurately, their misperception—of the possible opportunities and the difficulties or risks involved.

Misperceptions can result from ideas about the foreign market, including notions about inadequate size, excessive costs, and excessive difficulties. Misperceptions can also arise from inaccurate ideas about such environmental considerations as laws, currencies, financing, taxes, trade and exchange controls, and documentation.

Managers who underestimate the potential opportunities or who exaggerate the difficulties of developing and servicing foreign markets are not as likely to make the effort and take the risk of trying to develop those markets. A realistic perception is very important if a company is going to make the effort.

In the United States today there are numerous sources, both government and private, from which a company can collect the desired information and determine what the opportunities are. The federal government, and many state governments as well, are actively involved in not only enhancing international awareness but also in actively promoting exports. Such governments try to inform companies of the available opportunities. As an example, the U.S. Department of Commerce offers a wide range of services: training seminars, market surveys, foreign trade fairs, help in preparing promotional material, and even help in identifying specific foreign distributors. Similarly, state governments and universities also offer very useful training programs. Private organizations, such as commercial banks, transportation companies, foreign freight forwarders, insurance companies, accounting firms, law firms, and advertising agencies, are also commonly in a position to identify foreign market opportunities and assist the exporter in reaching those markets.

Culpable Lack of Necessary Resources

Some managers do recognize foreign opportunities but will plead that they lack the necessary resources to take advantage of the opportunities. In many instances, that may be a fair assessment. For example, strong demands upon a firm's management, productive capacity, and financial resources are indeed real considerations. However, such limitations are often relative, not absolute—they can often be overcome, just as they would need to be overcome for domestic expansion. This claim of inadequate resources is therefore a culpable shortage, often merely an alibi—an additional managerial barrier to international business. If the profitable opportunities are there, then it is generally possible for the company to obtain the necessary resources. Some of those resources include: exporting skills, managerial time, necessary financing, and productive capacity.

Inadequate Skills.   International trade requires a unique range of knowledge and skills. Most American companies not already active in international trade are very deficient in these areas. (As was noted above, most business schools in this country prepare their graduates very poorly for any type of international business.) If the profitable opportunity is there, then the cost of personnel is simply one that must be considered. Current managers may be able to obtain the necessary training. Or, new managers or technicians with the necessary skills (training, ability to speak foreign languages, past experience of living abroad, technological knowledge, and so forth) can be hired.

International business is indeed a very unique part of the business world. However, there is a very strong supportive structure to aid businesses until they themselves are able to perform such services. As was indicated above, both government agencies and private-sector companies can provide very important assistance—at little or no cost to the exporting company. Such assistance can take the form of educational efforts (seminars or consulting) or the provision of specialist services (freight forwarders for exporters or customs house brokers for importers). The Small Business Administration offers educational programs. The Service Corps of Retired Executives (SCORE) offers one-on-one counseling and assistance.

Managerial Time.   A managerial problem related to the absence of necessary skills is the availability of managerial time. Managers often assert that they lack the time necessary to learn how to market abroad. However, as with so many other business decisions, the profits and other benefits need to be weighed against the added costs and risks: if the opportunities are sufficiently attractive, then the additional managers, technicians, or other workers can be hired.

Lack of Financing.   The availability of capital is a serious consideration for any significant expansion. However, capital is inadequate for many firms primarily because they fail to search for funding opportunities. If managers are unfamiliar with exporting, they should not assume that funding is unavailable. There are many unique sources of financing for exports that are not available for domestic sales. For example, export contracts or export letters of credit can be used as security to obtain export financing. Also, agencies of the federal government such as the Export-Import Bank and the Commodity Credit Corporation provide financing and other assistance to exporters of goods and services from the United States.

Inadequate Productive Capacity.   Many companies explore foreign-market opportunities because they possess excess capacity and are seeking additional markets for their products. Unfortunately, the export efforts of many companies ebb and flow according to the strength of their domestic markets—they seek to export when domestic markets are weak and withdraw from foreign markets when domestic markets are strong. **The export markets are used as a buffer for domestic markets. Other companies that might find opportunities abroad do not have such excess capacity. For those companies, new factories may be necessary. For some, foreign factories may be desirable. However, productive capacity in the United States is probably best for most companies. This is especially true with the decline in the value of the U.S. dollar relative to the Japanese yen and major European currencies since 1985, which stimulates exports and makes investment abroad more expensive.**

It is easy for managers who are not enthusiastic about a particular venture to convince themselves that they lack the necessary resources—whether they be skills, time, financing, or productive capacity. However, it is a basic truism of capitalism that, if a project is worthwhile, the resources can usually be found; if the project justifies the effort, the resources are generally available.

Indeed, many companies that do not feel they have the resources for international expansion seem to find sufficient resources for whatever domestic expansion they desire. The difference between developing domestic and international markets is only one of degree, not substance: if the resources can be found for domestic growth, they can also be found for international growth.

Unrealistic Fears

Even if the opportunities for exporting are recognized and the necessary resources and goals exist, companies often fail to take advantage of them. The basic reason for such hesitation is fear.

It does need to be recognized that there are inherent diseconomies, as well as economies, in foreign operations—communication and transportation difficulties, legal complications, and so forth. Internationalization will likely provide greater challenge and add new strain upon the management of a company, in addition to offering new benefits. These added costs and risks can easily frighten timid managers.

However, any business growth entails risks, adjustments, and new problems as well as opportunities. Prudent caution is desirable, indeed necessary, for wise business decisions. Yet many companies refrain from internationalization not because of prudence but because of excessive or unrealistic fears: fears of operational difficulties, environmental differences, risks, and the possible strain upon the company.

Fear is a difficult variable to analyze. Few managers are willing to admit that fear is a major factor in their inaction. Managers after all are employed to lead the company through difficulties and risks. They are not expected to avoid opportunities simply because of fear of the difficulties.

Fear of Operational Difficulties.   Managers often feel that the difficulties of operating an export program will be too great. This perception may not be based upon fact but rather upon rumors, comments of others, or other things that cause the manager to fear that the difficulties do not warrant the effort involved.

The concern may stem from likely difficulties in communicating with a customer (inadequate telephone service or difference in time zones). Or the issue may be a reluctance to travel abroad to visit customers. Another fear may relate to complexities of the procedures for exporting, including export and customs documentation, guarantees of financing, insurance, shipping, trade controls, and red tape.

Exporting generally is more complicated than domestic sales, but there are companies (foreign freight forwarders) that specialize in handling such tasks at reasonable prices. And, as was seen in a previous section there are financing and insurance programs that protect the exporter from most of the risks.

Fear of Environmental Differences.   For many managers, important sources of fear about international business are the many differences between the home and foreign environments (economic, political-legal, and socio-cultural): currency, infrastructure, language, customs, religious or ethical differences, labor unions, laws, policies, documentation requirements, taxation, the political system, and the role of government in the economy, to name some. The importance of *not* underestimating the potential difficulties of these differences needs to be stressed. However, these differences generally represent costs rather than insuperable barriers. Perhaps careful analysis will lead to the conclusion that the difficulties are not sufficiently offset by the opportunities. However, that question should be asked and carefully answered. The potential opportunity should not be carelessly dismissed. A manager should not allow fear of environmental differences to prevent the company from exploring foreign opportunities.

Fear of Risks.   The risks of exporting include not only foreign risks comparable to standard domestic risks, but also unique risks to which the company has little or no exposure in its home markets. For example, credit risks tend to be greater for customers who are much farther away and with whom the company has no past experience. However, letters of credit are used in most international trade transactions between unrelated companies; letters of credit offer the exporter a guarantee of payment. Similarly, if there is fear that the quality of the imports may not be satisfactory, there are companies that specialize in quality inspections and issuing quality guarantees. And fear of exchange-rate fluctuation can be eased with forward or futures contracts. Thus, other companies can be retained to shift the risk of non-payment or of poor quality.

Since foreign governments are involved—governments with which the company may have little or no past experience—a company may rightly fear blockage of funds, expropriation, seizure of shipments, or any of a myriad of other interferences to which some governments are prone. However, again, these risks can be shifted to banks (with letters of credit or performance letters), insurance companies (insurance of the goods or insurance of the credit through an agency such as the Foreign Credit insurance Association), or government agencies (the Export-Import Bank).

Fear of the Strain upon the Company.   Any major new venture will likely cause additional strain upon a company. The bigger the venture, and the more that it departs from the traditional operations of the company, then the greater that strain is likely to be. The strain may be upon the capital of the company or upon other resources, such as personnel. These fears are important and need to be carefully evaluated. However, as with the other managerial barriers, the problem being addressed here is that the strain will be misperceived and exaggerated. The proper response to such possibilities is that the project needs to be carefully considered and the issue of whether the resources of the company can bear the strain needs to be carefully weighed.

Any new venture should cause fear in the mind of a prudent manager. However, it is important to distinguish between realistic and unrealistic fears. The former stem from risks and uncertainties that cannot be avoided, the latter are those that either are excessive or involve concerns for which there are ready remedies.

Thus, many of the fears that immobilize most managers confronted with the prospect of foreign markets can be overcome with the aid of the government, a commercial bank, insurance company, freight forwarder, or other organization. The issue of strain upon a company is realistic in many cases. However, the manager is then confronting the question of resources—which, as was seen in the previous section, can usually be overcome if the project is right.

Managerial Inertia

The last of the five managerial barriers is nothing more than the failure of management to act even when other managerial barriers are not a problem. The managers suffering from this malady are immobilized by limited ambition, unrecognized opportunities, lack of resources, or even unrealistic fears. Rather, they are simply failing to act—even when they have realistic perceptions of the opportunities, problems, risks, and costs. This barrier is perhaps the most lamentable one of all.

Unfortunately, this obstacle to international trade is one that reading and study alone cannot overcome. All that can be done here is to introduce the reader to the realistic nature of the added complexities and opportunities involved with international trade together with the techniques and institutions that readily exist to assist the novice exporter to overcome these problems. However, the initiative to actually pursue the internationalization must usually come from within the company.

Such inertia besets us all when we are faced with difficult or unpleasant situations—whether it involves calling a dentist for an appointment or starting a diet. Therefore, we should each be able to understand the inertia of the manager who is faced with plunging into what is truly a foreign area. It is not easy to know how to get such managers to act. Sometimes the actions of competitors will do it. Or a prospective partner may initiate the venture. The government offers many training seminars to help get the company started. However, in the final analysis, many of these managers never act. Young, more open-minded managers may help. However, as noted above, American universities are not providing the necessary training in their business schools.

Evidence

In a pioneering study of the rationale for not being more active internationally, Frederick Schroath (1987) surveyed the failure of American insurance companies to venture abroad. Although his original survey was not organized around my concept of the five managerial barriers, it was obvious to him that the responses he received fell over-whelmingly into these five categories.

Sixty-seven U.S. insurance companies responded to his survey, giving a total of 211 reasons for their international reluctance. Only one of the 211 answers blamed governmental barriers. Indeed, 99 percent of the responses could easily be classified as one of the first four managerial barriers (see Table 4).

The United States is experiencing a chronic string of massive balance-of-trade deficits. These deficits have many negative impacts upon the economy: a net loss of jobs, a weakening of the dollar (which contributes to inflation) and a need by the United States to borrow heavily abroad to finance those deficits.

Americans import heavily. While *imports* are one side of the balance of trade, they enrich the economy with lower prices, better variety, greater quality, improved productive efficiency, and a higher standard of living. Efforts to reduce imports are short-sighted and expensive.

TABLE 4   Reasons for Reluctance to Enter International Markets

Limited Ambition	
Sufficient opportunities in the U.S.	26%
Management preoccupation with domestic problems in the U.S.	3%
Time needed to establish foreign operations would be too great	*
Unrecognized Opportunities	
Lack of knowledge of foreign opportunities	16%
Feeling that foreign markets were too small or too expensive	8%
Culpable Lack of Necessary Resources	
Lack of qualified personnel	12%
Lack of knowledge of regulations	10%
Lack of capital	3%
Lack of reinsurance	*
Unrealistic Fears	
Concerns about culture or language	10%
Concerns about foreign exchange	10%
Concerns about logistical problems	*
Concerns about stability of foreign economies	*
Concerns about competition from other U.S. firms operating abroad	*

* less than 0.5%.

The other side of the balance-of-trade equation is *exports*. It is my contention that American companies are, on the average, lousy exporters. There are excellent opportunities in foreign markets for the export of the goods and services of thousands of American companies. Unfortunately, the vast majority of companies in this country that have export potential give little thought to foreign markets.

There are various reasons for this parochialism: America's traditional insularity, our massive domestic market, and narrow educational training are among the most obvious. Such provincialism is always economically inefficient. However, in an era of massive balance-of-trade deficits, it is dangerous.

These parochial views are reflected in barriers to exporting which are within the company itself. This article has highlighted the five major varieties of these managerial barriers:

1. Limited ambition;
2. Unrecognized opportunities;
3. Culpable lack of necessary resources;
4. Unrealistic fear;
5. Managerial inertia.

Most American producers have failed to search adequately for foreign opportunities. They have failed to acquire the resources necessary to tap those markets. They have let ignorance, fear, and simple inertia prevent them from expanding their marketing horizons. They have allowed themselves to become complacent with their existing, domestic markets. American companies have not adequately tried.

It is very important for the American economy to reduce these managerial barriers. It should be an important goal for both corporate managers and for government agencies. Whenever a company attempts to penetrate new markets, there are costs and risks involved. Indeed, there were clearly costs and risks for the company in starting its original business in the domestic market. Just as with domestic ventures, foreign ventures (whether exporting, importing, licensing, consulting, or investing) require the entrepreneur to weigh the prospective benefits against the associated costs: only if the expected returns are sufficient should the venture be undertaken.

Overcoming these managerial obstacles is no guarantee that the company will export. A careful evaluation of the foreign prospects may convince the company that its best alternatives continue to be in the United States. However, the company would have at least considered the opportunities and problems—instead of simply ignoring the possibilities.

Even if the company overcomes these hurdles and decides that foreign opportunities and benefits exceed the costs and offer better prospects than alternative domestic possibilities, there is no assurance that the company will be an overwhelming international success. The mere pursuit of any market is no guarantee of success—either domestically or internationally. However, unless the alternative road is explored, the company will never know what could have been. Nevertheless, success is still going to depend upon skill and hard work in attempting to succeed in foreign markets.

Although no one company or industry or region will alone reverse the poor export performance of American companies in the 1980s, if enough companies systematically examine what foreign opportunities may exist for them, the impact can be dramatic. Such improvement will affect the number of jobs created, profits earned, the standard of living, and the international balance of payments of the United States.

References

Frederick W. Schroath, "Analysis of Foreign Market Entry Techniques for Multinational Insurers," Ph.D. dissertation, University of South Carolina, 1987.

Frederick W. Schroath and Christopher M. Korth. "Managerial Barriers to the Internationalization of American Property and Liability Insurance Companies: Theory and Perspectives," *Journal of Risk and Insurance.* December 1989, pp. 630–648.

Hilary Stout. "Export Davids Sling Some Shots at Trade-Gap Goliath," *Wall Street Journal,* March 8, 1989, p. B2.

PART TWO

THE ENVIRONMENT OF INTERNATIONAL AND GLOBAL MARKETING

The Cultural and Political Environment

Readers will discover in this section a rich selection of contributions examining major world cultures that marketers must understand and appreciate if they are to maximize the likelihood of success in the international marketplace. "Culture is everything that people have, think and do as members of a society."[1]. Culture is the summation of customs, skills, arts, values, attitudes, sociopolitical beliefs, religious roots, language, education, and productive systems of people that order their lives and are passed on to succeeding generations. Understanding cultural differences from one market to another is one of the most daunting issues facing international marketers today.

The selections begin with a venerable paper on nonverbal communications—the silent language that often baffles international marketers in their efforts to influence overseas buyers. It is followed by a companion classic on avoiding business blunders abroad, especially those relating to product positioning, promotional programs, brand names, and packaging.

A series of papers follow on the alleged causal link between the promotion and consumption of Nestlé infant formula. Is there indeed a causal link? Research findings supporting this belief are critiqued and rebutted by those who support and disagree with the findings. The misuse of infant formula to supplement or replace breast feeding points up the cultural implications of using the same product labeling and promotional programs around the world, in economically advanced nations as well as developing ones.

A paper on ethical issues explores the moral and legal implications of gift exchanges, lubrication payments, and bribes that must be resolved by American international marketers. It will challenge the reader.

Because of the importance of the Japanese economy to world trade, a commissioned paper is included that details Japanese versus American cultural values and business systems, with analysis of their impact on international negotiations between representatives of both nationalities. It is followed by an insightful piece on similarities and differences between buyer and seller relationships in Japan and Germany. The author provides a British perspective on the inner workings of marketing relationships among America's two most important international competitors and in two of our largest foreign markets.

The next paper prognosticates the possible outcome of the battle for economic supremacy among Europe, Japan, and the United States in the twenty-first century. It is accompanied by a piece that assesses political risk in advanced and developing nations around the world.

---

[1]Gary P. Ferraro, *The Cultural Dimension of International Business* (Englewood Cliffs, NJ: Prentice Hall, 1990), p. 18.

The Silent Language in Overseas Business

Edward T. Hall

With few exceptions, Americans are relative newcomers on the international business scene. Today, as in Mark Twain's time, we are all too often "innocents abroad," in an era when naïveté and blundering in foreign business dealings may have serious political repercussions.

When the American executive travels abroad to do business, he is frequently shocked to discover to what extent the many variables of foreign behavior and custom complicate his efforts. Although the American has recognized, certainly, that even the man next door has many minor traits which make him somewhat peculiar, for some reason he has failed to appreciate how different foreign businessmen and their practices will seem to him.

He should understand that the various peoples around the world have worked out and integrated into their subconscious literally thousands of behavior patterns that they take for granted in each other.* Then, when the stranger enters, and behaves differently from the local norm, he often quite unintentionally insults, annoys, or amuses the native with whom he is attempting to do business. For example:

In the United States, a corporation executive knows what is meant when a client lets a month go by before replying to a business proposal. On the other hand, he senses an eagerness to do business if he is immediately ushered into the client's office. In both instances, he is reacting to subtle cues in the timing of interaction, cues which he depends on to chart his course of action.

Abroad, however, all this changes. The American executive learns that the Latin Americans are casual about time and that if he waits an hour in the outer office before seeing the Deputy Minister of Finance, it does not necessarily mean he is not getting anywhere. There people are so important that nobody can bear to tear himself away; because of the resultant interruptions and conversational detours, everybody is constantly getting behind. What the American does not know is the point at which the waiting becomes significant.

Reprinted and excerpted by permission of *Harvard Business Review,* "The Silent Language in Overseas Business," by Edward T. Hall, May–June 1960, pp. 87–96. Copyright 1960 by the President and Fellows of Harvard College; all rights reserved.

*For details see my book, *The Silent Language* (New York: Doubleday & Co., 1959).

In another instance, after traveling 7,000 miles an American walks into the office of a highly recommended Arab businessman on whom he will have to depend completely. What he sees does not breed confidence. The office is reached by walking through a suspicious-looking coffeehouse in an old, dilapidated building situated in a crowded non-European section of town. The elevator, rising from dark, smelly corridors, is rickety and equally foul. When he gets to the office itself, he is shocked to find it small, crowded, and confused. Papers are stacked all over the desk and table tops—even scattered on the floor in irregular piles.

The Arab merchant he has come to see had met him at the airport the night before and sent his driver to the hotel this morning to pick him up. But now, after the American's rush, the Arab is tied up with something else. Even when they finally start talking business, there are constant interruptions. If the American is at all sensitive to his environment, everything around him signals, "What am I getting into?"

Before leaving home he was told that things would be different, but how different? The hotel is modern enough. The shops in the new part of town have many more American and European trade goods than he had anticipated. His first impression was that doing business in the Middle East would not present any new problems. Now he is beginning to have doubts. One minute everything looks familiar and he is on firm ground; the next, familiar landmarks are gone. His greatest problem is that so much assails his senses all at once that he does not know where to start looking for something that will tell him where he stands. He needs a frame of reference—a way of sorting out what is significant and relevant.

That is why it is so important for American businessmen to have a real understanding of the various social, cultural, and economic differences they will face when they attempt to do business in foreign countries. To help give some frame of reference, this article will map out a few areas of human activity that have largely been unstudied.

The topics I will discuss are certainly not presented as the last word on the subject, but they have proved to be highly reliable points at which to begin to gain an understanding of foreign cultures. While additional research will undoubtedly turn up other items just as relevant, at present I think the businessman can do well to begin by appreciating cultural differences in matters concerning the language of time, of space, of material possessions, of friendship patterns, and of agreements.

Language of Time

Everywhere in the world people use time to communicate with each other. There are different languages of time just as there are different spoken languages. The unspoken languages are informal; yet the rules governing their interpretation are surprisingly *ironbound*. In the United States, a delay in answering a communication can result from a large volume of business causing the request to be postponed until the backlog is cleared away, from poor organization, or possibly from technical complexity requiring deep analysis. But if the person awaiting the answer or decision rules out these reasons, then the delay means to him that the matter has low priority on the part of the other person—lack of interest. On the other hand, a similar delay in a foreign country may mean something altogether different. Thus:

In Ethiopia, the time required for a decision is directly proportional to its importance. This is so much the case that low-level bureaucrats there have a way of trying to elevate the prestige of their work by taking a long time to make up their minds. (Americans in that part of the world are innocently prone to downgrade their work in the local people's eyes by trying to speed things up.)

In the Arab East, time does not generally include schedules as Americans know and use them. The time required to get something accomplished depends on the relationship. More important people get fast service from less important people, and conversely. Close relatives take absolute priority; nonrelatives are kept waiting.

In the United States, giving a person a deadline is a way of indicating the degree of urgency or relative importance of the work. But in the Middle East, the American runs into a cultural trap the minute he opens his mouth. "Mr. Aziz will have to make up his mind in a hurry because my board meets next week and I have to have an answer by then," is taken as indicating the American is overly demanding and is exerting undue pressure. "I am going to Damascus tomorrow morning and will have to have my car tonight," is a sure way to get the mechanic to stop work, because to give another person a deadline in this part of the world is to be rude, pushy, and demanding.

An Arab's evasiveness as to when something is going to happen does not mean he does not want to do business; it only means he is avoiding unpleasantness and is side-stepping possible commitments which he takes more seriously than we do. For example:

The Arabs themselves at times find it impossible to communicate even to each other that some processes cannot be hurried, and are controlled by built-in-schedules. This is obvious enough to the Westerner but not to the Arab. A highly placed official in Baghdad precipitated a bitter family dispute because his nephew, a biochemist, could not speed up the complete analysis of the uncle's blood. He accused the nephew of putting other less important people before him and of not caring. Nothing could sway the uncle, who could not grasp the fact that there is such a thing as an *inherent* schedule.

With us, the more important an event is, the further ahead we schedule it, which is why we find it insulting to be asked to a party at the last minute. In planning future events with Arabs, it pays to hold the lead time to a week or less because other factors may intervene or take precedence.

Again, time spent waiting in an American's outer office is a sure indicator of what one person thinks of another or how important he feels the other's business to be. This is so much the case that most Americans cannot help getting angry after waiting 30 minutes; one may even feel such a delay is an insult, and will walk out. In Latin America, on the other hand, one learns that it does not mean anything to wait in an outer office. An American businessman with years of experience in Mexico once told me, "You know, I have spent two hours cooling my heels in an executive's outer office. It took me a long time to learn to keep my blood pressure down. Even now, I find it hard to convince myself they are still interested when they keep me waiting."

The Japanese handle time in ways which are most inexplicable to the Western European and particularly the American. A delay of years with them does not mean that they have lost interest. It only means that they are building up to something. They have learned that Americans are vulnerable to long waits. One of them expressed it, "You

Americans have one terrible weakness. If we make you wait long enough, you will agree to anything."

Indians of South Asia have an elastic view of time as compared to our own. Delays do not, therefore, have the same meaning to them. Nor does indefiniteness in pinpointing appointments mean that they are evasive. Two Americans meeting will say, "We should get together sometime," thereby setting a low priority on the meeting. The Indian who says, "Come over and see me, see me anytime," means just that.

Americans make a place at the table which may or may not mean a place made in the heart. But when the Indian makes a place in his time, it is yours to fill in every sense of the word if you realize that by so doing you have crossed a boundary and are now friends with him. The point of all this is that time communicates just as surely as do words and that the vocabulary of time is different around the world. The principle to be remembered is that time has different meanings in each country.

Language of Space

Like time, the language of space is different wherever one goes. The American business-man, familiar with the pattern of American corporate life, has no difficulty in appraising the relative importance of someone else, simply by noting the size of his office in relation to other offices around him:

Our pattern calls for the president or the chairman of the board to have the biggest office. The executive vice president will have the next largest, and so on down the line until you end up in the "bull pen." More important offices are usually located at the corners of and on the upper floors. Executive suites will be on the top floor. The relative rank of vice presidents will be reflected in where they are placed along "executive row." The French, on the other hand, are much more likely to lay out space as a network of connecting points of influence, activity, or interest. The French supervisor will ordinarily be found in the middle of his subordinates where he can control them.

Americans who are crowded will often feel that their status in the organization is suffering. As one would expect in the Arab world, the location of an office and its size constitute a poor index of the importance of the man who occupies it. What we experience as crowded, the Arab will often regard as spacious. The same is true in Spanish cultures. A Latin American official illustrated the Spanish view of this point while showing me around a plant. Opening the door to an 18-by-20-foot office in which seventeen clerks and their desks were placed, he said, "See, we have nice spacious offices. Lots of space for everyone."

The American will look at a Japanese room and remark how bare it is. Similarly, the Japanese look at our rooms and comment, "How bare!" Furniture in the American home tends to be placed along the walls (around the edge). Japanese have their charcoal pit where the family gathers in the *middle* of the room. The top floor of Japanese department stores is not reserved for the chief executive—it is the bargain roof!

In the Middle East and Latin America, the businessman is likely to feel left out in time and overcrowded in space. People get too close to him, lay their hands on him, and generally crowd his physical being. In Scandinavia and Germany, he feels more at home, but at the same time the people are a little cold and distant. It is space itself that conveys this feeling.

In the United States, because of our tendency to zone activities, nearness carries rights of familiarity so that the neighbor can borrow material possessions and invade time. This is not true in England. Propinquity entitles you to nothing. American Air Force personnel stationed there complain because they have to make an appointment for their children to play with the neighbor's child next door.

Conversation distance between two people is learned early in life by copying elders. Its controlling patterns operate almost totally unconsciously. In the United States, in contrast to many foreign countries, men avoid excessive touching. Regular business is conducted at distances such as 5 feet to 8 feet; highly personal business, 18 inches to 3 feet—not 2 or 3 inches.

In the United States, it is perfectly possible for an experienced executive to schedule the steps of negotiation in time and space so that most people feel comfortable about what is happening. Business transactions progress in stages from across the desk to beside the desk, to the coffee table, then on to the conference table, the luncheon table, or the golf course, or even into the home—all according to a complex set of hidden rules which we obey instinctively.

Even in the United States, however, an executive may slip when he moves into new and unfamiliar realms, when dealing with a new group, doing business with a new company, or moving to a new place in the industrial hierarchy. In a new country the danger is magnified. For example, in India it is considered improper to discuss business in the home on social occasions. One never invites a business acquaintance to the home for the purpose of furthering business aims. That would be a violation of sacred hospitality rules.

Language of Things

Americans are often contrasted with the rest of the world in terms of material possessions. We are accused of being materialistic, gadget crazy. And, as a matter of fact, we have developed material things for some very interesting reasons. Lacking a fixed class system and having an extremely mobile population, Americans have become highly sensitive to how others make use of material possessions. We use everything from clothes to houses as a highly evolved and complex means of ascertaining each other's status. Ours is a rapidly shifting system in which both styles and people move up or down. For example:

The Cadillac ad men feel that not only is it natural but quite insightful of them to show a picture of a Cadillac and a well-turned out gentleman in his early fifties opening the door. The caption underneath reads, "You already know a great deal about this man."

Following this same pattern, the head of a big union spends in excess of $100,000 furnishing his office so that the president of United States Steel cannot look down on him. Good materials, large space, and the proper surroundings signify that the people who occupy the premises are solid citizens, that they are dependable and successful.

The French, English, and the Germans have entirely different ways of using their material possessions. What stands for the height of dependability and respectability with the English would be old-fashioned and backward to us. The Japanese take pride in often inexpensive but tasteful arrangements that are used to produce the proper emotional setting.

Middle East businessmen look for something else—family, connections, friendship. They do not use the furnishings of their office as part of their status system; nor do they expect to impress a client by these means or to fool a banker into lending more money than he should. They like good things, too, but feel that they, as persons, should be known and not judged solely by what the public sees.

One of the most common criticisms of American relations abroad, both commercial and governmental, is that we usually think in terms of material things. "Money talks," says the American, who goes on talking the language of money abroad, in the belief that money talks the *same* language all over the world. A common practice in the United States is to try to buy loyalty with high salaries. In foreign countries, this maneuver almost never works, for money and material possessions stand for something different there than they do in America.

Language of Friendship

The American finds his friends next door and among those with whom he works. It has been noted that we take people up quickly and drop them just as quickly. Occasionally a friendship formed during schooldays will persist, but this is rare. For us there are few well-defined rules governing the obligations of friendship. It is difficult to say at which point our friendship gives way to business opportunism or pressure from above. In this we differ from many other people in the world. As a general rule, in foreign countries friendships are not formed as quickly as in the United States but go much deeper, last longer, and involve real obligations. For example:

It is important to stress that in the Middle East and Latin America your "friends" will not let you down. The fact that they personally are feeling the pinch is never an excuse for failing their friends. They are supposed to look out for your interests.

Friends and family around the world represent a sort of social insurance that would be difficult to find in the United States. We do not use our friends to help us out in disaster as much as we do as a means of getting ahead—or, at least, of getting the job done. The United States systems work by means of a series of closely tabulated favors and obligations carefully doled out where they will do the most good. And the least that we expect in exchange for a favor is gratitude.

The opposite is the case in India, where the friend's role is to "sense" a person's need and do something about it. The idea of reciprocity as we know it is unheard of. An American in India will have difficulty if he attempts to follow American friendship patterns. He gains nothing by extending himself in behalf of others, least of all gratitude, because the Indian assumes that what he does for others he does for the good of his own psyche. He will find it impossible to make friends quickly and is unlikely to allow sufficient time for friendships to ripen. He will also note that as he gets to know people better they may become more critical of him, a fact that he finds hard to take. What he does not know is that one sign of friendship is speaking one's mind.

Language of Agreements

While it is important for American businessmen abroad to understand the symbolic meanings of friendship rules, time, space, and material possessions, it is just as important for executives to know the rules for negotiating agreements in various countries. Even if they cannot be expected to know the details of each nation's commercial legal practices, just the awareness of and the expectation of the existence of differences will eliminate much complication.

Actually, no society can exist on a high commercial level without a highly developed working base on which agreements can rest. This base may be one or a combination of three types:

1. Rules that are spelled out technically as law or regulation.
2. Moral practices mutually agreed on and taught to the young as a set of principles.
3. Informal customs to which everyone conforms without being able to state the exact rules.

Some societies favor one, some another. Ours, particularly in the business world, lays heavy emphasis on the first variety. Few Americans will conduct any business nowadays without some written agreement or contract.

Varying from culture to culture will be the circumstances under which such rules apply. Americans consider that negotiations have more or less ceased when the contract is signed. With the Greeks, on the other hand, the contract is seen as a sort of way station on the route to negotiation that will cease only when the work is completed. The contract is nothing more than a charter for serious negotiations. In the Arab world, once a man's word is given in a particular kind of way, it is just as binding, if not more so, than most of our written contracts. The written contract, therefore, violates the Moslem's sensitivities and reflects on his honor. Unfortunately, the situation is now so hopelessly confused that neither system can be counted on to prevail consistently.

Informal patterns and unstated agreements often lead to untold difficulty in the cross-cultural situation. Take the case of the before-and-after patterns where there is a wide discrepancy between the American's expectations and those of the Arab:

In the United States, when you engage a specialist such as a lawyer or a doctor, require any standard service, or even take a taxi, you make several assumptions: (a) the charge will be fair; (b) it will be in proportion to the services rendered; and (c) it will bear a close relationship to the "going rate."

You wait until after the services are performed before asking what the tab will be. If the charge is too high in light of the above assumptions, you feel you have been cheated. You can complain, or can say nothing, pay up, and take your business elsewhere the next time.

As one would expect in the Middle East, basic differences emerge which lead to difficulty if not understood. For instance, when taking a cab in Beirut it is well to know the going rate as a point around which to bargain and for settling the charge, which must be fixed before engaging the cab.

If you have not fixed the rate *in advance,* there is a complete change and an entirely different set of rules will apply. According to these rules, the going rate plays no part whatsoever. The whole relationship is altered. The sky is the limit, and the customer has no kick coming. I have seen taxi drivers shouting at the top of their lungs, waving their arms, following a red-faced American with his head pulled down between his shoulders, demanding for a two-pound ride 10 Lebanese pounds which the American eventually had to pay.

It is difficult for the American to accommodate his frame of reference to the fact that what constitutes one thing to him, namely, a taxi ride, is to the Arab two very different operations involving two different sets of relationships and two sets of rules. The crucial factor is whether the bargaining is done at the beginning or end of the ride! As a matter of fact, you cannot bargain at the end. What the driver asks for he is entitled to!

One of the greatest difficulties Americans have abroad stems from the fact that we often think we have a commitment when we do not. The second complication on the same topic is the other side of the coin, that is when others think we have agreed to things that we have not. Our own failure to recognize binding obligations, plus our custom of setting organizational goals ahead of everything else, has put us in hot water far too often.

People sometimes do not keep agreements with us because we do not keep agreements with them. As a general rule, the American treats the agreement as something he may eventually have to break. Here are two examples:

Once while I was visiting an American post in Latin America, the Ambassador sent the Spanish version of a trade treaty down to his language officer with instructions to write in some "weasel words." To his dismay, he was told, "There are no weasel words in Spanish."

A personnel officer of a large corporation in Iran made an agreement with local employees that American employees would not receive preferential treatment. When the first American employee arrived, it was learned quickly that in the United States he had been covered by a variety of health plans that were not available to Iranians. And this led to immediate protests from the Iranians which were never satisfied. The personnel officer never really grasped the fact that he had violated an ironbound contract.

Certainly, this is the most important generalization to be drawn by American businessmen from this discussion of agreements: there are many times when we are vulnerable *even when judged by our own standards.* Many instances of actual sharp practices by American companies are well known abroad and are giving American business a bad name. The cure of such questionable behavior is simple. The companies concerned usually have it within their power to discharge offenders and to foster within their organization an atmosphere in which only honesty and fairness can thrive.

But the cure for ignorance of the social and legal rules which underlie business agreements is not so easy. This is because:

The subject is complex.

Little research has been conducted to determine the culturally different concepts of what is an agreement.

The people of each country think that their own code is the only one, and that everything else is dishonest.

Each code is different from our own; and the farther away one is traveling from Western Europe, the greater the difference is.

But the little that has already been learned about this subject indicates that as a problem it is not insoluble and will yield to research. Since it is probably one of the more relevant and immediately applicable areas of interest to modern business, it would certainly be advisable for companies with large foreign operations to sponsor some serious research in this vital field.

How to Avoid Business Blunders Abroad

David A. Ricks

A major fast-food company planned to open an outlet in Munich, West Germany. To ensure a successful location, the company carefully counted the number of people passing by several prospective sites. A highly trafficked location was then selected, but sales proved unexpectedly poor. Why? Investigation revealed that the activity level in the area was due to a nearby bordello—the individuals walking by had more than hamburgers on their minds!

This is just one example of the unexpected problems that occur in international business ventures. Overseas marketing can be extremely tricky. Even though a company may employ sophisticated management techniques, it still runs a real risk of blundering if any detail is overlooked. However, many of the problems that have been encountered by companies operating in foreign territory can be avoided.

For example, merely asking the right question can prevent a giant blunder. In one reported case, a firm neglected to inspect some wooded land for sale in Sicily prior to its purchase. Only after the company had bought the land, built a plant, and hired a labor force did it realize that the trees available were only knee high and were not usable for making paper. The result? They imported logs!

Another company encountered a somewhat similar experience when it built a pineapple cannery near the delta of a Mexican river. The pineapple plantation was established upriver, and barges were purchased to float the crop down to the cannery. It was not discovered until the fruit was ripe that the river current was too strong to allow the barges to be tugged back upriver from the cannery to the fields. As a result, the plant was useless in that location and was sold for a mere 5% of its cost. These errors are regrettable, but we can learn from them. There is no need to repeat the mistakes others have made.

Reprinted by permission of *Business*, "How to Avoid Business Blunders Abroad," by David Ricks, April 1984. Reprinted by permission of the author.

Picking the Package

Numerous problems result from the failure to correctly adapt packaging for local environments. Occasionally, only the color of the package needs to be altered to enhance a product's sales. White, for instance, symbolizes death in Japan and much of Asia; green represents danger or disease in Malaysia. Consequently, the use of these colors in certain countries can produce negative reactions to products.

A lesser known variable worthy of consideration is the use of numbers. Packages that prominently display a specific number increase the risk of consumer avoidance. For example, the number *four* is an evil number in Japan, where it represents death. Even the number of products pictured on a label can prove troublesome.

Sometimes it is not the number displayed on the package or the color that creates a problem, but rather the picture on the label. A baby food manufacturer discovered this important lesson the hard way. It tried to sell jars of baby food in an African country using labels that depicted a happy baby. Unfortunately, most of the prospective customers were illiterate and could only determine the contents of a container by looking at the label. The picture of a baby indicated to them that the jar literally contained bottled babies.

A simple test market experiment, a brief survey, a few interviews with potential buyers, or a discussion with knowledgeable local residents would have uncovered many of the problems just described at an early stage.

Changing the Product

In many instances the product itself requires alteration. Food, beverages, and tobacco products often need to be modified in order to accommodate the tastes of local consumers. Cigarette manufacturers learned long ago that American brands sell well overseas if the tobacco is carefully blended to suit local preferences. Market tests can help determine the appropriate blends.

Not only can the taste of a product hinder sales, but occasionally its consistency or texture creates difficulties. After correctly determining the flavors considered desirable by the British, Jell-O tried to sell its products in powdered form (just as in the United States). But the British avoided the products because they normally purchase this type of food in jelled form. After discovering this, Jell-O successfully marketed its products in a ready-to-consume form.

Campbell Soup Company encountered a similar experience. The Campbell's cans originally marketed in Great Britain were the same size as those available in the United States. Instructions carefully stated that water should be added—the normal procedure for most American soups. The British, however, were accustomed to purchasing diluted soup. Since buyers never bothered to read the fine print on the label, Campbell's condensed soups appeared more expensive because consumers received less volume for their money. Sales were low until Campbell's discovered the problem and began marketing a diluted soup in larger cans. Because consumer expectations play a vital role in sales and acceptance, companies must always examine potential competitive products and how they are marketed.

Sometimes significant product modification is required to market products abroad. A dishwasher built to U.S. norms may need an electric motor that requires 220 voltage rather than 110 voltage, may need to tolerate different water pressures than those available in the United States, or may need to accommodate local dishes and utensils of different shapes. Products that are not modified to meet local needs may fail.

The Language Barrier

A close examination of foreign markets and language differences is necessary and should be required before a product's domestically successful name is introduced abroad. Unfortunately, this step is sometimes neglected in a company's enthusiasm to plunge into overseas marketing operations.

Sometimes, the company or product name may require alteration because it conveys the wrong message in a second language. Large and small firms alike have discovered this. For example, when the Coca-Cola Company was planning its marketing strategy for China in the 1920s, it wanted to introduce its product with the English pronunciation of "Coca-Cola." A translator used a group of Chinese characters that, when pronounced, sounded like the product name. These characters were placed on the cola bottles and marketed. Was it any wonder sales levels were low? The characters actually translated to mean "a wax-flattened mare" or "bite the wax tadpole." Since the product was new, sound was unimportant to the consumers; meaning was vital. Today Coca-Cola is again marketing its cola in China. The new characters used on the bottle translate to "happiness in the mouth." From its first marketing attempts, Coca-Cola learned a valuable lesson in international marketing.

General Motors was faced with a similar problem. It was troubled by a lack of enthusiasm among Puerto Rican auto dealers for its recently introduced Chevrolet "Nova" about ten years ago. The name "Nova" means star when literally translated. However, when spoken it sounded like "no va" which, in Spanish, means "it doesn't go." This obviously did little to increase consumer confidence in the vehicle. To remedy the situation, General Motors changed the automobile name to "Caribe" and sales increased.

Comparable situations have also been experienced by other car manufacturers. In fact, problems with the names used in international automobile promotions seem to crop up frequently. For example, the American car name "Randan" was interpreted by the Japanese to mean "idiot." The American Motors Corporation's car "Matador" might conjure up images of virility and strength in America, but in Puerto Rico it means "killer"—not a favorable connotation in a place with a high traffic fatality rate.

A U.S. company was taken by surprise when it introduced its product in Latin America and learned that the name meant "jackass oil" in Spanish. Another well-intentioned firm sold shampoo in Brazil under the name "Evitol." Little did it realize that it was claiming to be selling a "dandruff contraceptive." One manufacturing company sold its machines in the Soviet Union under the name "Bardak"—a word that signifies a brothel in Russian. The name of an American product that failed to capture the Swedish market translated to "enema," which the product was not!

Of course, foreign firms can make mistakes, too. A Finnish brewery introduced two new beverages in the United States—"Koff" beer and "Siff" beer. Is it any wonder that sales were sluggish? Another name Americans found unappealing was on packages of a delicious chocolate and fruit product sold in German and other European delicatessens. The chocolate concoction had the undesirable English name "Zit"!

Many times the required name change is a rather simple one. Wrigley, for example, merely altered the spelling of its "Spearmint" chewing gum to "Speermint" to aid in the German pronunciation of the flavor. "Maxwell House" proved slightly more difficult: the name was changed to "Maxwell Kaffee" in Germany, to "Legal" in France, and to "Monky" in Spain.

Product names are not the only ones that can generate company blunders. If a firm's name is misinterpreted or incorrectly translated, it, too, can have the same humorous, obscene, offensive, or unexpected connotations.

For example, a private Egyptian airline, Misair, proved to be rather unpopular with the French nationals. Could the fact that the name, when pronounced, meant "misery" in French have contributed to the airline's plight? Another airline trying to gain acceptance in Australia only complicated matters when it chose the firm name "EMU." The emu is an Australian bird incapable of flying. When Esso realized that its name phonetically meant "stalled car," it understood why it had had difficulties in the Japanese market.

As final illustration, consider the trade magazine that promoted giftware and launched a worldwide circulation effort. The magazine used the word "gift" in its title and part of its name. When it was later revealed that "gift" is the German word for "poison," a red-faced publishing executive supposedly retorted that the Germans should simply find a new word for poison!

Of course, some company names have traveled quite well. Kodak may be the most famous example. A research team deliberately developed this name after carefully searching for a word that was pronounceable everywhere but had no specific meaning anywhere. Exxon is another name that was reportedly accepted only after a lengthy and expensive computer-assisted search.

Multinational corporations have experienced many unexpected troubles concerning company or product names, and even attempts to alter names have led to blunders. It should be evident that careful planning and study of the potential market is necessary because name adaptation can be every bit as important as product or package modification.

Respecting Nationalism

Many avoidable problems occur because managers are insensitive to the nationalistic feeling of the people of the host country. Except at the retail level, it is usually best for companies to maintain a low profile. Seldom does a firm need to turn an overseas manufacturing plant into a "Little America." Companies that have tried to do this have met stiff resistance from both employees and local customers. One U.S. firm, for example, acquired a Spanish manufacturing plant and promptly announced that it would be bringing in superior U.S. technology. The company changed the prestigious Spanish name and even raised the U.S. flag. Naturally employee morale and sales were hurt.

Foreign manufacturers in the United States learned long ago to keep a low profile. About 2% of the American labor force is now working for foreign-owned firms, but many of the workers are unaware of this. This is considered desirable for the foreign owners because it reduced the likelihood of problems.

Management should avoid any unnecessary comparisons that might reflect the home country management's belief that the host country is inferior. It is often possible—sometimes even desirable—to compare products, but it is not wise to publicly compare governments, management practices, labor, or technology.

One way to maintain a low profile is to hire most, if not all, top-level managers of the overseas subsidiary from the available host country management pool. Not only will these individuals project a local image, but they usually understand local problems well and can often help the company avoid blunders.

If an expatriate is to be hired, extra care must be taken. To be effective, an expatriate manager must possess special abilities and traits if he or she is to avoid blundering. Among the most important characteristics are the following:

- An ability to get along well with people
- An awareness of cultural differences
- Open-mindedness
- Tolerance of foreign cultures
- Adaptability to new cultures, ideas, and challenges
- An ability to adjust quickly to new conditions
- An interest in facts, not blind assumptions
- Previous business experience
- Previous experience with foreign cultures
- An ability to learn foreign languages

Problems with Promotions

Many companies have run into serious troubles trying to coordinate their sales and promotional efforts. For example, one firm authorized a large promotional drive to introduce a new product in Latin America. The promotion ran smoothly, but someone forgot to coordinate product delivery—the home office was totally unaware of the sales push and had no plans to ship the product. Consumers were confused and money was wasted when the promoted product was not available.

All plans should be in writing, and someone should be responsible for central coordination. Hence, risks are lessened and opportunities to save money may arise. Coca-Cola, for instance, requires that all overseas marketing plans be submitted to the central office well in advance. This gives the company a chance to examine the concepts. Previous experiences with similar plans can be reviewed and necessary changes can be suggested. Sometimes central company managers find that similar plans for overseas ventures have failed in the past. Minor improvements tried overseas with success should also be reported. There is no need to reinvent the wheel. Coordination not only reduces the chance of errors, it also provides opportunities to learn improved methods.

With so many details to consider, it is rather easy to understand how so many firms have blundered. Nevertheless, their errors illustrate the importance of paying attention to detail. The McDonnell Douglas Corporation, for example, experienced unexpected difficulties when it produced an aircraft brochure for distribution to potential customers in India. The promotional material depicted turbaned men, but the photos were not well received. The company had used old *National Geographic* pictures and had overlooked the fact that the turbans were being worn by Pakistani men—not by Indians!

If a theme works exceedingly well in one country, it becomes very tempting for a firm to use it elsewhere. The risks involved in doing this are high, however, because good themes are often culturally oriented. Consider the popular and successful Marlboro advertisements. The Marlboro man projects a strong masculine image in America and in Europe. But the promotion was unsuccessful in Hong Kong, where the totally urban people did not identify at all with horseback riding in the countryside. So Phillip Morris quickly changed its ad to reflect a Hong Kong-style Marlboro man. The Hong Kong version is still a virile cowboy, but he is younger, better dressed, and owns a truck and land.

Local weather conditions can also foul up a multinational corporation's promotional campaign. One firm, for example, tried to use a typical U.S. radio advertisement to promote its swimsuits in Latin America. The ad boasted that one could wear the swimsuit all day in the sun and it would not fade. To local Latins, however, this point meant little because the weather is always too hot to stay in the sun for very long.

In many cases, the language of the promotional effort is correct but its physical presentation is not effective. As a classic illustration, consider the company that rented space on a wall beside the main road leading from the airport into Buenos Aires. The following message was placed on the wall: "With (brand name) you'd be there already." Just one slight problem—the message was written on a cemetery wall!

Symbols or logos have also caused troubles. A U.S. firm marketing in Brazil was a bit embarrassed when it used a large deer as a sign for masculinity. The word "deer" is a Brazilian street name for homosexual. Another company blundered in India when it used an owl in its promotional efforts. To an Indian, the owl is a symbol for bad luck!

One laundry detergent company certainly wishes that it had contacted a few residents before it initiated a promotional campaign in the Middle East. All of the company's advertisements pictured soiled clothes on the left, its box of soap in the middle, and the clean clothes on the right. But because in that area of the world people generally read from right to left, many potential customers interpreted the message to mean that the soap actually soiled the clothes.

Another U.S. company had problems in Britain. In a U.S. promotion, the firm had effectively used the phrase, "You can use no finer napkin at your dinner table" and decided to use the same commercials in England. After all, the British do speak English. To the British, however, the word "napkin" or "nappy" actually means "diaper." The American firm was unknowingly advertising that "You could use no finer diaper at your dinner table." The ad could hardly be expected to boost sales.

One fairly common American practice is to utilize the same promotional strategy for all domestic subsidiaries, with promotional budgets based on a fixed percentage of sales.

This strategy may work well with domestic ventures, but usually proves foolish when it is attempted for overseas subsidiaries. Those U.S. companies that try to force such standardization are sometimes asking their foreign managers to do the impossible.

For one thing, some types of media are not legally available. In many countries, no television advertisements are permitted, and this alone makes a U.S.-style promotional budget infeasible. A second problem is one of scale. The use of a standard percentage of sales may be appropriate for large, domestic subsidiaries, but for small foreign subsidiaries 10% of sales may not support a single promotional campaign. Each market offers different opportunities and challenges at different cost structures. A better strategy is to standardize the methods used to analyze opportunities and then develop local promotional budgets. The subsidiaries can be urged to follow the established methods.

This does not mean, however, that each country is totally unique and must *always* be treated independently. One company, for example, sold a popular detergent in Austria and Germany under two different brand names. The people in both countries speak German, and they heard and read ads that originated in both countries. Consequently, they thought there were two products that were in competition. The company could have consolidated its promotional effort to cover both countries.

Observing Local Customs

A lack of awareness of cultural differences or insensitivity to local customs can create problems. There are norms for each country; sometimes they are very strict. Several manufacturing plants have encountered serious troubles in England because of the famed British tea break. American managers have tried—usually to no avail—to persuade their British employees to drop their tea-break habit. It is now considered wiser to accept such local traditions.

This also applies to local holidays. The host country may seem to have many holidays, but generally there is little that can be done to change the situation. A company usually must either pay overtime, close on the holiday, or face high levels of employee absenteeism, turnover, and unrest.

And consider the public display of affection between members of the opposite sexes. In many countries, such as Thailand, this is unacceptable and offensive. A firm trying to introduce its mouthwash there, however, was not aware of this taboo and promoted its products with an ad that displayed a young couple holding hands. But when the advertisement was changed to feature two women, the commercials were no longer offensive to the Thais.

The Asian Indians found a BiNoca Talc ad disturbing even though the woman in the advertisement was wearing a body stocking. The promotion, which appeared in many of the major local newspapers featured an attractive but apparently nude young woman lavishly powdering herself with BiNoca's talcum. Strategic portions of her body were carefully covered with the slogan "Don't go wild—just enough is all you need of BiNoca talc." The public, however, found the ads indecent.

The display of certain parts of the body generally thought innocuous can be offensive to certain groups. For example, Mountain Bell experienced a problem in the

Middle and Far East when one of its promotional photos depicted an executive talking on the telephone with his feet propped up on his desk. The photos were considered by local residents to be in poor taste. To them the display of the sole of the foot or shoe is one of the worst possible insults. Exposure of the foot is also considered an insult in Southeast Asia.

Since social norms vary so greatly from country to country, it is extremely difficult for any outsider to be knowledgeable of them all. Therefore, local input is vital in avoiding blunders. Many promotional errors could have been averted had this warning been heeded.

One of the best-known promotional blunders occurred in Quebec. There, a manufacturer of canned fish ran advertisements in the local newspapers which depicted a woman in shorts playing golf with a man. The caption explained that a woman could go golfing with her husband in the afternoon and still get home in time to serve a great dinner of canned fish that same evening. The entire promotional effort was off target. In Quebec women did not wear shorts on local golf courses and were usually not permitted to golf with men. Furthermore, regardless of how much preparation time is available, women in Quebec would not consider serving canned fish for dinner, especially as the major course. The company neglected to consider local customers and, obviously, the product failed.

Pepsodent reportedly tried to sell its toothpaste in regions of Southeast Asia with a promotion that stressed that the toothpaste helped enhance white teeth. However, in this area some local people deliberately chew betel nut in order to achieve the social prestige of darkly stained teeth, so the ad was understandably less than effective. The slogan "Wonder where the yellow went," was also viewed by many as a racial slur.

A marketer of eyeglasses promoted his spectacles in Thailand with commercials featuring animals wearing glasses. It was an unfortunate decision, however, because in Thailand animals are considered a low form of life and it is beneath humans to wear anything worn by an animal.

The failure to consider specialized aspects of local religions has led to a number of problems. Companies have many times tried to incorporate a picture of a Buddha in their Asian promotions. Religious ties are strong in this area and the use of local religious symbols in advertising is resented—especially when words are deliberately or even accidentally printed across the picture of Buddha.

A refrigerator manufacturer made a similar blunder in the Middle East. The typical refrigerator advertisement often features a refrigerator full of delicious food, and because these photos are difficult to take, they are often used in as many places as possible. This company used its stock photo, depicting a prominently placed chunk of ham, in one place too many, though—because Muslims do not eat ham. Local residents considered the ad to be insensitive and unappealing.

Be Sure It Translates

Many international advertising errors are due to faulty translations. The translation should embody the general theme and concept rather than be an exact or precise duplication of the original slogan. This point hit home when Pepsi reportedly learned that its ad "Come alive with Pepsi" was literally translated into German to mean "Come alive out of the grave with Pepsi." And in Asia it was translated as "Bring your ancestors back from the dead."

Other companies have translated "stepping stone" to "stumbling block," have changed the words "car wash" into "car enema," and have said that a battery is "over rated" when the phrase should have been "highly rated."

Hunt Wesson Foods can attest to the risks of translation. The company planned to market its "beans in tomato sauce" product in Quebec, Canada, under the name "Grose Jos." Just before the product was to be released, a local employee advised the company to reassess this name because it could be translated colloquially as "big breasts."

Translators must be attuned to the local language and possible double meanings. An ink pen manufacturer, for example, ran an ad campaign in Latin America. The ad was mistakenly translated to imply that the ink pen would help avoid unwanted pregnancies—the ad copy stated that the ink pen would help avoid embarrassment, but "embarrassment" there implies pregnancy.

General Motors encountered problems in Belgium when "Body by Fisher" was translated into Flemish as "Corpse by Fisher." Obviously, literal translations can prove deadly!

Another U.S. company may have actually been the victim of translation sabotage. The firm tried to sell its products in the Soviet Union with the help of a Russian translator. The company innocently displayed a translated poster in Moscow which, it soon discovered, said that the company's oil well equipment was good for improving a person's sex life.

What Can Be Done

There are several ways to avert potential translation disasters.

A brilliant translator may have an extraordinary gift for the language or may have studied in the country, but certain idiomatic expressions and slang may be unfamiliar. It is often wise to also hire a second translator who is familiar with the local slang and unusual idioms to *backtranslate*.

Backtranslation is one of the best techniques available to reduce translation errors. This method requires that one individual translate the message into the desired foreign language and that a second person translate the foreign version back to the original language. This allows a company to determine if the intended message is the one actually being presented. An Australian soft drink company discovered the value of backtranslation during the planning stages of its Hong Kong market entry. The company wanted to introduce its successful slogan, "Baby, it's cold outside," but first had it translated back into English. This proved to be a wise decision. The message backtranslated to "Small mosquito, on the outside it is very cold." Even though "small mosquito" was a local colloquial expression for a small child, the phrase simply did not convey the same thing as the friendly English slang word "baby." The intended message was lost.

Backtranslation reveals many translation errors, but it can prove frustrating if done by mediocre translators. Naturally, the better the translator, the fewer the problems and delays. The difficulty, therefore, lies in being able to determine the ability of a potential translator. Firms should thoroughly investigate the translator's qualifications. The following points should be covered in an interview:

- Does the translator maintain or have access to a library or reference books dealing with the appropriate subject and industry?
- Does the translator understand the required technical terms? Does he or she know of the foreign words for these specialized terms? If not, how does he or she intend to learn them?
- Does the translator have a staff or access to experts in various fields (such as law)?
- Will someone check the work? If so, what are the credentials of the assistant? (It is often advisable to request references and copies of material translated for other clients.)
- How recently has the translator visited the foreign country? Sometimes it is necessary to determine just how current the translator's knowledge is, because languages do change. It is not enough to have someone familiar with the foreign language and culture. Even a native tends to lose track of slang and idioms after being away from home for a few years. Experience that is ten years old may be too old.

Once a translator has been chosen, there are several things that a company can do to simplify his or her job. For instance, when the company has spent several months developing good promotional materials, a translator should not be asked to translate the material overnight. Simple literal translation is not generally appropriate, so a translator needs time to be creative.

This is not to say that the translator should not be given a deadline—the person should be given a reasonable time frame and the expected promotion schedule. And be sure to tell the translator what season the ad will appear in.

Also, the translator should understand the type of media to be used and the general characteristics of the audience. This allows him or her to determine the proper level of formality and the correct tone. A translator must be given the freedom to modify original wording to avoid disastrous literal translations.

If possible, firms should avoid overly technical terms and industry jargon. It is also advisable to limit the use of large numbers. Any number over 10,000 may be easily mistranslated. The number "billion," for example, numerically contains nine zeros in the United States, but contains twelve zeros in Europe.

Also, humor can be impossible to translate, so it is best to avoid jokes in advertising. What is deemed funny by some is often not funny to others.

And because the translated version of a message may require more words than the original, don't limit the translator to a particular amount of time or space. Doing so may seriously jeopardize the effectiveness of the message.

Finally, the translator should be informed of the message's objectives and theme. If the translator is allowed to examine previous company translations as well as translated slogans of competing companies, he or she not only can assure that any key phrase associated with the company is included but also can avoid accidentally using a competitor's phrases.

Sometimes companies have found that the best solution to the translation problem is simply not to translate the material. In countries experiencing high levels of illiteracy, visual methods of communication can be used. Libby, for instance, has successfully promoted its products through inexpensive commercials featuring a clown enjoying Libby products. In these ads, no words are spoken.

Using English in Non-English-speaking Countries

If the local residents can understand some English or if they really don't need to comprehend the spoken message, then it may be safe for a firm to stick with the English copy. To reduce the problems that may occur when English is used in such situations:

- Keep the entire message short and simple, including the words and sentences
- Avoid jargon or slang
- Avoid idioms
- Avoid humor, if possible
- Use appropriate currencies and measurements
- Cite examples, if feasible
- Repeat important points

If a company decides to go ahead with an English message through a verbal advertisement directed to an audience whose native language is not English, the speaker should speak slowly and carefully, pronounce all words, and pause between sentences.

Research Can Help

Proper market research can reduce or eliminate most international business blunders. Market researchers can uncover adaptation needs, potential name problems, promotional requirements, and proper market strategies. Even many translation blunders can be avoided if good research techniques are used.

A number of mistakes have occurred because firms tried to use the same product, name, promotional material, or strategy overseas that they used at home. But even though standardization promotes certain efficiencies and cost reductions, in many instances it is not a worthwhile strategy to pursue abroad. Limitations do exist, and it is important for firms to recognize and understand these barriers.

The use of market research enables a firm to determine its limits of standardization. It serves two major functions: the research can help a company identify what it can hope to accomplish and realize what it should not do. Neither dimension should be overlooked.

Few question the value of marketing research as part of international business planning. Unfortunately, market research is an extremely difficult and complex undertaking. Specific data requirements depend on the firm, its products, and the type of decisions being made. Different sets of data are needed for a company to determine whether or not to go abroad, which countries to enter, how to enter the foreign markets, and what the best marketing strategies are. Research methods must be tailored to the particular situation. There is no short, simple list of variables all firms should always research.

Market tests can be tricky to initiate and conduct. It is difficult indeed to "cover all the angles," and one of the hardest tasks is to identify the proper testing location. Firms normally identify sample areas as representative of a country or region. Some companies use an area of France for their West European test market, and others use Belgium. Each firm, however, must determine the region most appropriate for its product. This is no easy task. In fact, a combination of locations may be necessary. Wherever these places are, though, they must be found because market testing is essential.

We can learn from our mistakes. Blunders have been made, but they need not be repeated by others. Awareness of differences, consultation with local people, and concern for host-country feelings will reduce problems and will save money. Many companies—especially those that blundered—have already learned this and are doing much better. But there is still room for improvement.

A Macroeconomic Study of the Effects of Promotion on the Consumption of Infant Formula in Developing Countries

Mary C. Gilly and John L. Graham. *Mary C. Gilly and John L. Graham are professors of Marketing at the Graduate School of Management, University of California, Irvine, California.*

Few issues have stirred more controversy among marketers, governmental organizations, and consumer activists than the Nestlé's infant formula boycott of the late 1970s (see Cateora 1983; Sethi et al. 1985). The crux of the debate was the causal effect of promotion by manufacturers on the breast-feeding behavior of women in less developed countries. Nestlé and other infant formula manufacturers strongly argued that their advertising and personal selling efforts did not influence women to stop breast-feeding their children. That is, the only effect of their promotional expenditures was to distribute market share among competitors, *not* to increase the size of the market (Nestlé 1980). Several critics vehemently disagreed (for example, Schudson 1984; James 1983). The purpose of this study is to test these competing hypotheses. Examination of infant formula imports by 79 developing countries during the 1970s provides an answer to this debate.

The remainder of the article is divided into four sections. First, the literature pertinent to the study is briefly described, including a statement of hypotheses. Next, the methods used are discussed. Third, results are presented. The article concludes with an interpretation of the findings and implications for managers and policymakers.

The *Journal of Macromarketing* is published by the Business Research Division of the University of Colorado at Boulder. Reprinted with permission.

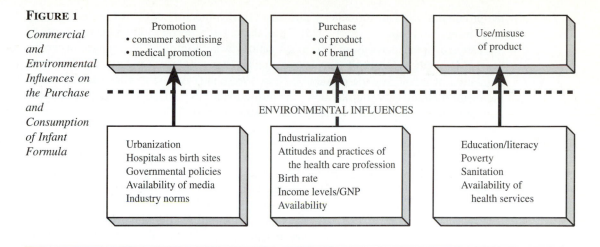

FIGURE 1

Commercial and Environmental Influences on the Purchase and Consumption of Infant Formula

Background Literature

According to Sethi et al. (1986, p. 26), "all market actions have some nonmarket or indirect consequences for societies." In the case of marketing infant formula in developing countries, one consequence was an increased potential for infant malnutrition and mortality. No one has claimed that infant formula is an inherently bad or unsafe product (Pagan 1986). In fact, physicians consider infant formula superior to other breast-milk substitutes, such as powdered milk (Post 1978). But while a "mother can safely and adequately breast-feed a child in conditions of poverty and inadequate sanitation . . . , safety and adequacy cannot be guaranteed or achieved with any degree of consistency when bottle-feeding is attempted under the same conditions" (Post 1985, p. 116).

It is useful to discuss the issues surrounding this problem within the framework of marketing's effect on purchase and consumption and the environmental influences on this process. Figure 1 offers such a framework. Promotion is shown as influencing purchase of infant formula, which leads to use (or misuse) of the product. Environmental factors are shown as affecting all three components of the purchase and consumption process: promotion, purchase, and use. This framework serves as the basis for the following discussion of the infant formula problem.

Promotion of Infant Formula

The promotion of infant formula products was "rampant and unchecked before 1970" (Post 1985, p. 116). Two types of companies produced and marketed formula, depending on the promotion strategy favored. Pharmaceutical firms (typically American) used medical promotion, while the food companies (typically European) preferred consumer advertising (Post 1978). Several environmental factors influenced the amount and type of promotional efforts. One example is the growing urbanization of the developing countries, which increased the food companies' ability to use consumer advertising efficiently (Post 1978). Hospitals became more popular birth sites, and newborns typically are fed at the hospital for the first few days. The medical community became a logical focus for the promotion of infant formula by pharmaceutical companies through free samples and other incentives (Sethi and Post 1979). Thus, the industry norms guiding the two types of marketers of infant formula in developed nations were reinforced by changes occurring there. Most governments of developing nations were cautious and reserved in their regulation of infant formula promotion (Post 1985), not wishing to alienate business or the medical community. Furthermore, the institutional mechanisms necessary for inspection and regulation generally were lacking (Sethi and Post 1979).

Purchase of Infant Formula

Consumer advertising and medical promotion contributed to the purchase of infant formula. Critics claimed that most of the advertising was misleading or used "hard sell" techniques to persuade mothers not to breast-feed (Sethi and Post 1979).

A general criticism of advertising is that it manipulates the minds of consumers so that they buy things they do not need or should not have (Schudson 1984). This has been the reasoning behind the ban on cigarette advertising on television (McGuinness and Cowling 1975) and the proposed ban on beer and wine advertising (Hume 1985). The argument that promotion shapes consumers' desires has also been the basis for the censure of marketers of infant formula in developing countries (see James 1983; Muller 1975). It was claimed that they were overpromoting their products to poor, uneducated people living in economic and hygienic conditions which made appropriate usage of powdered formula almost impossible (Sethi et al. 1985). According to critics, marketers were contributing to, if not responsible for, women opting for bottle-feeding rather than breast-feeding, resulting in infant sickness and death.

In their defense marketers maintained that advertising cannot manipulate consumers because it is ineffective or only modestly influential in changing consumption habits. Promotion seeks to change not people's product choices but their *brand* choices (Schudson 1984). In a public relations pamphlet, Nestlé (1980) made just such a claim regarding the influence of promotion on breast-feeding and the use of infant formula:

> QUESTION: Doesn't the promotion of infant formula in developing countries lead to lower levels of breast-feeding?
>
> ANSWER: The best evidence we have to date shows quite the opposite—the promotion of infant formula is *not* related to less breast-feeding in developing countries.
>
> The WHO Collaborative Breast-feeding Study (1979), which interviewed more than 23,000 mothers in nine nations, showed *no* association between breast-feeding decline and formula promotion. Of fundamental importance is the fact that the WHO Collaborative Study, in reporting reasons why mothers from nine countries did not breast-feed or stopped breast-feeding, listed the main factors as insufficient milk, maternal illness, infant illness, and new pregnancy. *Not once was any commercial factor even mentioned.*

Thus, the defenders of this view would point to other environmental factors that contribute to demand for infant formula and the decline in breast-feeding. For example, the industrialization of the developing countries, which has caused a westernization of social mores and has increased the need for mobility in employment, has been suggested as a contributing factor. It was a simple matter for mothers to breast-feed in an agricultural setting, but most places of industrial employment do not provide facilities for nursing (Sethi and Post 1979). The attitudes and practices of the health care profession also have been cited as factors (Benton et al. 1978). Doctors, nurses, and clinicians, as well as the policies of hospitals and clinics, often endorsed the use of infant formula. In many hospitals, newborns were routinely bottle-fed regardless of whether the mother planned to breast-feed (Sethi and Post 1979). Rising birth rates and income levels also increased potential demand.

A third view of the effects of advertising on purchase is offered by Schudson (1984). He claims that under certain conditions advertising can have a significant effect on sales and, furthermore, may influence cultural life even when it does not do much in the way of selling goods individually. While Schudson feels that advertising is generally ineffective, he believes some groups are particularly vulnerable to advertising. Among these are citizens of developing countries, due to poverty and illiteracy, lack of governmental consumer protection, and lack of personal experience with products. He said this about infant formula: "The powers of marketing here—through the medical professionals as much or probably more than through direct advertising—influence consumer choice" (1984, p. 125). Likewise, Farley, Louis, and Reddy (1980) report consumption of weaning foods in Sri Lanka to be positively influenced by direct mail advertising and free samples.

James (1983) supports this latter view, stating that multinationals use promotional techniques in competing for the mother's initial choice. Once committed to bottle-feeding, mothers then seek reinforcement of the correctness of their decision. James hypothesized that if the infant becomes ill, cognitive dissonance theory predicts that anxiety will be aroused. Because switching to breast-feeding may be impossible at that point, the mother must reduce anxiety by denying the association between infant formula and the baby's illness, thus perpetuating the influence of promotion on consumer choice of infant formula.

In summary, on the one hand, some authors suggest that promotion/advertising is ineffective in increasing product demand and only distributes demand among brands— for our purposes, a null hypothesis. On the other hand, particularly in the case of marketing infant formula in developing countries, other researchers suggest that promotion is effective in increasing product demand. The hypotheses considered in this study are:

H_0: Consumption of infant formula is unrelated to changes in promotional efforts of manufacturers in developing countries. Or, sales of infant formula in developing countries during 1972–1974 were no different from those during 1976–1978.

H_1: Consumption of infant formula is positively related to changes in promotional efforts of manufacturers. Or, sales of infant formula in developing countries were higher during 1972–1974 than during 1976–1978.

The rationale for choosing the specified test periods is delineated in the Methods section.

Product Use/Misuse

Although not specifically addressed in this study, a brief discussion of the factors causing misuse of infant formula is pertinent. Consumer research typically focuses on product and brand choice, but it is important that marketers consider how consumers *use* products as well as how they purchase them (Nicosia and Mayer 1976). The infant formula controversy highlights this importance dramatically. The following quotation from Post (1985, pp. 127–128) concisely summarizes the effect of environmental factors on consumers' use of infant formula:

> The reason that children die in developing nations is not because infant formula is a bad product. Rather, there is an environment of poverty, illiteracy, inadequate sanitation, unhealthy water and limited health services that create dangerous conditions for the use of formula. Marketing did not create these conditions, but marketing was a more *actionable* aspect of the problem than poverty, water or education. Moreover, the manufacturers were placing their products in the stream of commerce without attempting to find out who actually used them, under what circumstances, and with what consequences.

Post went on to say that industry executives admitted at later hearings that their firms had done no research following up the purchase of their products. Thus, poor understanding of product use led to infant death and controversy.

Methods

The Independent Variable

Measurement of the independent variable in this study, promotional efforts by infant formula manufacturers, is most difficult. Information regarding actual expenditures and/or marketing practices has been closely guarded by the firms because of their involvement in lawsuits associated with the controversy. In 1975, however, the leading companies in the industry agreed to a fundamental curtailment of promotional efforts in developing countries. The events leading up to this crucial change are described below.

As can be seen in Exhibit 1, the controversy regarding promotion of infant formula in developing countries was sparked in 1970 at a conference in Paris sponsored by a United Nations agency, the Protein Advisory Group (PAG). A key recommendation of PAG stated: "It is clearly important to avoid any action which would accelerate the trend away from breastfeeding" (PAG 1972). Jelliffe (1971), a consultant to PAG at the Paris conference and then director of the Caribbean Food and Nutrition Institute, claimed that the marketing practices of the infant formula manufacturers were the "major factor" contributing to the decline in breast-feeding and the associated increase in consumption of breast-milk substitutes. From these beginnings the controversy grew to be one of the most debated issues of the 1970s, including lawsuits in several countries, international consumer group protests and boycotts, and even U.S. Senate hearings. The history of the controversy is interesting in and of itself and is well documented by others (see Sethi et al. 1985). The focus of this article is not the controversy, however, but the promotional behaviors of the infant formula manufacturers.

Prior to 1970 almost all the manufacturers used a wide variety of promotional techniques in developing countries. Six were considered most objectionable by the several critics (McComas et al. 1983; Nestlé 1983): advertising to the general public; samples given to new mothers; personal selling through mothercraft workers (that is, women presenting themselves as nutritional experts, often dressed in nursing uniforms);

EXHIBIT 1   Important Events in the Infant Formula Controversy

Date(s)	Event	References
1867	Henri Nestlé introduces first commercially produced infant formula	Post (1978)
1945–1959	Infant formula sales soar in industrialized countries because of post-World War II baby boom	Post (1978)
1960s	Birth rates in industrialized countries decline, manufacturers begin "rampant and unchecked" promotion of bottle-feeding in developing countries	Post (1985)
1970	At UN conference in Paris, Jelliffe blames formula manufacturers for infant deaths in less developed countries	Sethi et al. (1986)
Early 1970s	Nestlé begins to review marketing practices on a region-by-region basis	Nestlé (1983)
1972	Abbott/Ross introduces code to control promotions practices	Beaver and Silvester (1982)
1974	Bristol-Myers in the United States is subject to shareholder lawsuit demanding information regarding formula promotion in developing countries	McComas et al. (1983)
1974	First public identification of issue with publication of *The New Internationalist* and *The Baby Killer*	Sethi and Post (1979)
1974–1978	Nestlé phases out all direct promotional practices	Armstrong (1985)
1975	Nestlé trial in Switzerland and shareholder resolutions filed in the United States	Sethi and Post (1979)
1975	Formation of International Council of Infant Food Industries (ICIFI) and promulgation of code of marketing ethics	Sethi and Post (1979)
1976	Borden stops all promotion and sales of infant formula in Hong Kong and Taiwan	Post (1978)
1977	Boycott against Nestlé begins	Pagan (1986)
1978	U.S. Senate hearings regarding United States firms' role in controversy	
1981	First developing country government (Kenya) takes legislative action to curtail promotion of infant formula	James (1983)
1981	World Health Organization passes code on marketing breast-milk substitutes	Pagan (1986)
1982	Nestlé creates Nestlé Infant Formula Audit Commission (NIFAC)	Pagan (1986)
1984	International Nestlé Boycott Committee announces termination of seven-year boycott	Post (1985)

point of sale advertising; the use of commissions/bonuses for sales; and copious samples to physicians.

In response to the criticism of Jelliffe, PAG, and other consumer activists, formula manufacturers began to examine their marketing in developing countries. Nestlé (1983, p. 1), the industry leader (largest market share worldwide), reports beginning "to review its marketing practices on a region-by-region basis" in the early 1970s. In 1974 in the United States Bristol-Myers was the subject of a shareholder lawsuit demanding information regarding the firm's marketing practices in developing countries (McComas et al. 1983). Post (1978) reports that Borden stopped all advertising for its infant formula in Hong Kong and Taiwan in 1976. Beaver and Silvester (1982, pp. 2–3) state: "The companies had responded quietly but continuously. Nestlé stopped direct contact between employees and mother and introduced stringent controls over sampling. Abbott/Ross introduced a code in 1972 and by the mid-1970's there was a general tightening up."

At a meeting sponsored by PAG in Singapore in 1974, executives from several formula manufacturing companies first discussed the possibility of forming an industry council to consider marketing practices in developing countries. In 1975 the International Council of Infant Formula Industries was formally organized in Zurich, Switzerland, bringing together eight of the largest U.S., European, and Japanese firms, Nestlé among them. One of their first actions was to develop a code of conduct embodying the principles of the 1970 PAG recommendations. Beaver and Silvester (1982) agree with Armstrong (1985, p. 8): "From 1974 to 1978, Nestlé phased out all direct promotional practices."

Considering the published information summarized in Exhibit 1, 1975 is chosen as the critical year when the industry, based on previous examination of marketing practices, began to curtail its marketing efforts. That is, promotion by the infant formula manufacturers in developing countries was greater immediately before than immediately following 1975. Thus, a dichotomous independent variable is defined—more promotional effort before 1975 versus less promotional effort after 1975.

Imports as an Indicator of Consumption

Direct measurement of infant formula consumption in low income countries is not possible using publicly available data. Post (1978, p. 223) explains: "There is no precise information about the world market for infant formula products. Moreover, virtually no individual countries require disclosure of information from manufacturers or sellers by line of business." Post does venture an estimate. Based on extrapolations from bits of information from three U.S. companies, he speculates sales in less developed countries in 1978 to be approximately $600 million. Using company data, Cox (1978, p. 243) provides a much lower estimate for the same period. "The prepared infant formula market in the one hundred countries generally considered to be third world is about U.S. $350,000,000."

Infant formula imports *are* tracked by most countries, and those data are made available through the United Nations. Imports (SITC 048.82) to the 79 low income countries included in our data base amounted to $148.4 million in 1978. Thus, using Cox's lower estimate of the total market, imports appear to account for about 54% of infant formula consumption, that is, $148.4 million/($350 million × (79/100)).

Obviously, imports do not take into account local production, but they are directly related to strategies common to several firms. Post (1978) reviewed the operations of formula producers and concludes that in addition to production in the United States and other industrialized countries, a common approach is to produce in a third country or region combined with export distribution. Indeed, Stafford (1978) reports that his firm, Wyeth International, manufactures formula in the United States and 14 foreign countries and markets the product in 90 countries. Since formula production is a high technology process (Post 1978), requiring the strictest sanitation (Stiegler 1985), it tends to be concentrated in the industrialized countries. Moreover, when multinationals invest in production facilities, they favor larger markets; for example, American Home Products announced in 1978 that it would be opening a new plant for infant formula production in

EXHIBIT 2   Countries Included in the Study

Bolivia[a]	Congo	Tanzania
Brazil	Gabon	Upper Volta
Chile[a]	Algeria	Zaire
Colombia	Angola	Zambia
Ecuador[a]	Egypt[a]	Cyprus[a]
Mexico[a]	Ethiopia	Iran[a]
Peru[a]	Djibouti	Iraq
Uruguay[a]	Gambia	Jordan
Venezuela	Ghana	Lebanon
Belize	Guinea	Oman
French Guyana[a]	Ivory Coast	Syria[a]
Surinam	Kenya[a]	Yemen
Costa Rica[a]	Liberia	D. Yemen
El Salvador[a]	Madagascar	Bangladesh
Guatemala	Mali	Burma
Honduras[a]	Mauritius[a]	Hong Kong[a]
Nicaragua	Morocco	India
Panama[a]	Mozambique	Indonesia
Barbados[a]	Niger	S. Korea
Guyana	Nigeria	Malaysia[a]
Jamaica[a]	Rwanda	Pakistan
Trinidad Tobago	Senegal	Philippines[a]
Dominican Republic	Sierra Leone	Singapore
Haiti	Somalia	Sri Lanka
Cameron	S. Africa[a]	Thailand[a]
Central Africa	Tunisia[a]	

[a]Birth rate statistics available (United Nations 1983).

Indonesia (Post 1978). Thus, it is reasonable to assume that imports better reflect consumption in smaller, low income countries.

Dependent Variable

The dependent variable considered in this study is infant formula imports (IFI) (SITC 048.82) as a percentage of total food imports (TF) (SITC 0). These data were obtained from the *United Nations Trade Statistics Annual* (1969–1980) for the 79 low income countries listed in Exhibit 2. The data are summarized in Table 1.

This percentage of food imports measures controls for several potential monetary and economic biases. First, because both import figures (formula and food) are reported in dollars, inflation is controlled by the division. Second, and perhaps more important, economic performance variables in the countries and in the world economy might be expected to influence imports of food and formula in a similar manner. Without this control, then, fluctuations in demand/consumption of infant formula might be attributed to economic conditions, such as overall increases in world trade, changes in GNP, import restrictions, or foreign exchange availability in the individual countries. These issues are further discussed in sections to follow.

TABLE 1   Imports of Infant Formula and Food

Year	Infant Formula Imports (IFI) (SITC 048.82)[a]	Food Imports (TF) (SITC 0)[b]
1969	21.6	2.38
1970	48.3	2.99
1971	—	—
1972	76.4	3.80
1973	101.0	6.41
1974	99.4	9.72
1975	107.4	10.80
1976	117.5	9.19
1977	125.5	10.64
1978	148.4	12.62
1979	157.5	15.49

NOTE: See Exhibit 2 for a listing of the countries.

[a]Imports ($ millions) of "diet, infant cereal preps" (SITC 048.82) to 79 countries (*World Trade Annual* 1969–1979).

[b]Imports ($ billions) of "Food all categories" (SITC 0) to 79 countries (*World Trade Annual* 1969–1979).

Hypothesis Tests

One-tailed T-tests were used to test the hypotheses. Imports of formula during 1972–1974 and 1976–1978 were calculated for each country, and the pairs of consumption values were compared across the two periods. Three-year periods were selected for two reasons. First, Salvatore (1983), Buzzell and Wiersema (1981), and Weede (1983) all argue for measures of variables averaged over a number of years. Feder (1982, pp. 63–64) adds: "Annual data include substantial random effects which tend to be eliminated by the procedure of averaging. The existence of lagged responses is another element which becomes less severe when averages rather than annual data are used." Second, data for 1971 are not available, thus limiting the test to the three years before 1975 and a comparable period after 1975.

Please note that we considered aggregating the data across the 79 countries and doing a regression analysis over the ten periods for which we have data (1969 to 1979, less 1971). Then a dummy variable for promotion (0 = pre-1975, 1 = post-1975) might compete with any other possible independent variables to explain the variance in infant formula imports. However, such an approach is precluded by two problems. First, ten data points give almost no statistical power, particularly with a five-plus-variable regression equation. Second, as mentioned above, the arguments for pooling the data *across time periods* are substantial. Moreover, the pairwise analysis is appropriate for the data, given the *imports 1972–1974* and *imports 1976–1978* for each country are not independent. If they were independent, then analysis of variance or discriminant analysis would have been possible and more appropriate. The method we have chosen takes advantage of all the information in the data, across all 79 countries.

TABLE 2   Results of T-Tests, Infant Formula Imports (SITC 048.82) as a Percentage of Food Imports (SITC 0)

	All 79 Countries	*Sample 31 Countries[a]*
Mean		
(1972 + 1973 + 1974)/3	2.10%	2.16%
Mean		
(1976 + 1977 + 1978)/3	1.75%	1.68%
T value	2.14	2.40
d.f.	78	30
One-tail probability	.018	.011

[a]1979 population less than five million.

Results

The competing hypotheses are:

H_0: Consumption of infant formula is unrelated to changes in promotional efforts of manufacturers in developing countries. Or, sales of infant formula in developing countries during 1972–1974 were no different from those during 1976–1978.

H_1: Consumption of infant formula is positively related to changes in promotional efforts of manufacturers. Or, sales of infant formula in developing countries were higher during 1972–1974 than during 1976–1978.

As indicated in Table 2, Hypothesis 1 is supported by the analysis. That is, imports of infant formula (IFI/TF), controlling for several factors, were lower in 1976–1978 than in 1972–1974. Consumption of infant formula was found to be positively related to changes in industry promotional efforts, and the relationship was statistically significant ($p < 0.05$).

Discussion

Conclusions

The information in Table 2 strongly suggests that infant formula imports (IFI/TF), controlling for several economic factors in the 79 countries, were reduced by the curtailment of promotion. The empirical evidence in this study supports the views of Jelliffe (1971), Schudson (1984), and James (1983) that promotion affected overall consumption of infant formula and, by implication, breast-feeding behavior.

Indeed the model proposed in Figure 1 is supported by our data and analysis. That is, the infant formula manufacturers aggressively promoted their products, and consumption was thereby increased in environments conducive to misuse. Because the manufacturers took actions to reform and curtail promotion in low income countries, inappropriate purchase and use of infant formula was also curtailed. The tragedy here is that all the companies did not respond to their critics in an even more prudent and timely manner.

In addition to statistical significance, the results also provided a measure of practical significance. That is, the reduction of infant formula imports between the two three-year periods was 20%—calculated (2.10–1.75)/1.75 (see Table 2). In other words, had the manufacturers maintained their much criticized promotional practices through 1978, imports to the 79 countries in 1978 might have been $178 million instead of $148 million, other things being equal.

Alternative Explanations

Several alternative explanations for the results reported above warrant examination.

1. It might be argued that the activities of the various protest groups influenced consumers or governments to reduce use of infant formula after 1975. Indeed, this was the time when the Nestlé controversy began to gain widespread attention in the popular press. However, the protests and publicity were largely confined to the industrialized countries and did not reach Third World consumers. Indeed, James (1983, p. 165) reports: "Not until April 1981 (with the introduction of a code of ethics in Kenya) was legislative action taken in a developing country against the manufacturers of powdered baby milk. See *The Sunday Times,* London (26th April, 1981)."

2. The decline of imports of infant formula (IFI/TF) reported in the Results section may have been caused by changes in birth rates across the time periods. However, as can be seen in Table 3, the change in IFI/TF was unrelated to changes in birth rates over the test period for the 36 countries for which data were available.

3. Perhaps imports were influenced by changes in individual countries' economic conditions. As can be seen in Table 3, the decline in IFI/TF was found to be unrelated to changes in GDP and/or changes in foreign exchange available during the test period. Apparently, these economic conditions had no systematic influence on infant formula imports.

4. It may be that the decline in imports reflects increased local production. As mentioned previously, the manufacturers favored investments in production facilities in the larger countries. Therefore, we retested the hypotheses using a subset of the smallest countries (1979 population less than five million). As can be seen in Table 2, the decline in formula consumption (IFI/TF) is still statistically significant. Thus, increased local manufacturing does not offer adequate explanation.

5. Other marketing mix decisions, besides promotional practices, may have influenced consumption. However, promotion was the focus of the controversy, the manufacturers' remedial actions, and this study. Indeed, had the firms segmented their markets more carefully and distributed the product more narrowly, or had the product been sold in diluted form (as is done now in the United States), perhaps the negative consequences of formula sale would have been dramatically reduced. Unfortunately, no data are available with which to address such broader questions.

6. One reviewer suggests that infant formula is supplied as part of U.S. foreign aid, which will not show up in import data. Since the government sources we checked provided no information about infant formula as part of foreign aid, this last challenge to the validity of our results remains unanswered.

Indeed, still other challenges may be offered, but our evidence and results must be evaluated in the context of the difficulty of investigating the negative consequences

TABLE 3   Competing Explanations for the Change in Imports of Infant Formula as Measured by IFI/TF

$$\frac{(1976+1977+1978-1972-1973-1974)}{3}$$

Independent Variables	*Pearson Correlation Coefficients*
% Change in Birth Rates	
$\dfrac{\text{Births }(1976+1977+1978-1972-1973-1974)}{\text{Births }(1972+1973+1974)}$	.098[a] (N = 36)[b]
Source: *Demographic Yearbook of the United Nations*	
Change in GDP Index	
$\dfrac{\text{GDP index }(1976+1977+1978-1972-1973-1974)}{3}$	.048[a] (N = 59)[b]
Source: *International Financial Statistics*	
% Change in Available Foreign Exchange (deflated)	
$\dfrac{\text{Foreign exchange }(1976+1977+1978-1972-1973-1974)}{\text{Foreign exchange }(1972+1973+1974)}$	.081[a] (N = 66)[b]
Source: *International Financial Statistics*	

[a] Not statistically significant ($p < 0.10$).
[b] Sample sizes limited by data available.

of corporate behavior. Key, even conclusive, information *is* available in company records—promotion expenditures and sales histories—but companies are unwilling to share it (Post 1978). Until such data are made available for close and objective scrutiny, studies such as this one must suffice. Until companies provide evidence to the contrary, one must conclude that their promotion of infant formula led directly to increased consumption of the product in environments where its misuse led to sickness and death. Post (1978, p. 120) makes a similar comment regarding his research for the U.S. Senate hearings in 1978:

> Data relating to the infant-formula industry is difficult to acquire. Most information on sales volume, profits, market share of manufacturers, and even the manner in which firms do business is regularly denied researchers because of its proprietary nature. Published information is very limited in the United States, and even more scarce in developing nations. This void is frustrating to researchers such as myself; it also frustrates those who want to understand the magnitude of the problems on which these hearings are focused.

Implications for Managers and Policymakers

The results of this study suggest that advertising and promotion can influence consumer behavior in socially undesirable and unintended ways. Despite the good intentions of marketers, advertising can have negative consequences. As suggested in Figure 1, marketing strategies must be evaluated in view of the environment in which they will be executed. In the case of infant formula, promotion strategies designed for *industrialized* countries resulted in sickness and death for infants in *less developed* countries. The context of promotion, purchase, and product use must be taken into account by producers and distributors. Managers marketing products with potential usage problems should attempt to anticipate these and do careful research in test markets. Furthermore, market-ers should not ignore criticism from responsible sources but instead should thoroughly investigate their own culpability. Finally, as Nicosia and Mayer (1976) advocate, managers must measure and take responsibility for all the effects of their advertising and not just focus on sales.

To the extent that firms fail to recognize their responsibility, policymakers will take action. The World Health Organization's *International Code of Breastmilk Substitutes* (Anderson 1981) is the most recent example. The ban of cigarette advertising from U.S. television and the Federal Trade Commission's investigation of advertising of sugared cereals (leading to more stringent industry self-regulation) also come to mind. In a similar vein is the present controversy over beer and wine television commercials.

In this last case the arguments bear a striking resemblance to those which arose in the Nestlé controversy. The critics suggest that TV advertising increases overall con-sumption of alcoholic beverages and, in turn, alcoholism. Brewers and vintners counter that TV advertising does nothing more than serve to distribute market share (Hume 1985). Critics maintain that TV advertising influences underage drinking; advertisers argue that the ads are carefully targeted toward adults. Likewise, Nestlé argued that its advertising was aimed at the educated and high income consumers in developing countries, while their critics suggested that baby formula ads reached other segments. Finally, *60 Minutes* reporters asked teenage drinkers if TV advertising influenced them to drink, and they said no. Similarly, Nestlé cited the World Health Organization study (1979) wherein 23,000 mothers in nine developing countries were asked what induced them to stop breast-feeding. Not once was advertising mentioned. In both situations, one might ask why consumers would be expected to admit to, or even be conscious of, their response to commercial advertising.

Beer and wine advertisers may be operating under the assumption that because one part of the market can use the product safely, all consumers can. A similar assumption was made by the infant formula manufacturers. Just as Figure 1 shows that environmen-tal influences affect purchase and use of infant formula in developing nations, environ-mental influences may affect the purchase and use of alcoholic beverages by certain groups (for example, teenagers) such that a great potential for misuse (alcoholism, drunk driving) exists.

The similarities in the arguments indicate possible applications of our findings concerning infant formula to the case of beer and wine advertising. The latter may be influencing product consumption rather than simply brand selection, although the study for Anheuser-Busch reported by Hume (1985) concludes the contrary. Further research is needed to learn more about the relationship between promotion, product and brand choice, and product use. This is particularly true in cases where promotion may have undesirable effects on society as well as positive effects on sales.

References

Anderson, K. (1981), "The Battle of the Bottle," *Time* (June 1), p. 26.

Armstrong, J. (1985), "Ethics and the Infant Formula Controversy," a paper presented at the Pan-Pacific Conference: A Business, Economic and Technological Exchange, Seoul, Korea (May).

Beaver, B. and F. Silvester (1982), "The Gall in Mother's Milk: The Infant Formula Controversy and the WHO Marketing Code," *Journal of Advertising,* 1 (January-March), 1–10.

Benton, A., L. Huston, M. J. Janse, and T. D. McCollough (1978), "Infant Malnutrition, Breastfeeding and Infant Formulas in Developing Nations," testimony and supplementary testimony presented to the U.S. Senate Subcommittee on Health and Scientific Research of the Committee on Human Resources, May 23, Washington, DC.

Buzzell, R. D. and F. D. Wiersema (1981), "Modelling Changes in Market Share: A Cross-Sectional Analysis," *Strategic Management Journal,* 2 (January-March), 27–42.

Cateora, P. R. (1983), *International Marketing,* 5th ed., Homewood, IL: Irwin.

Cox, D. O. (1978), "Summary Statement of Abbott Laboratories on the Role of Prepared Infant Formulas in the Third World," and a follow-up letter to Senator Kennedy, both included as testimony and supplementary testimony presented to the U.S. Senate Subcommittee on Health and Scientific Research of the Committee on Human Resources, May 23, Washington, DC.

Farley, J. U., T. D. J. Louis, and S. K. Reddy (1980), "Joint 'Social Marketing' Promotion of a Weaning Food and a Contraceptive in Sri Lanka," *Journal of International Business Studies,* 2 (Winter), 73–80.

Feder, J. L. (1982), "On Exports and Economic Growth," *Journal of Development Economics,* 12 (February-April), 59–73.

Hume, S. (1985), "Study Snips at Ads' Ties to Beer Demand," *Advertising Age,* 56 (March 4), 18.

International Financial Statistics (1978), International Monetary Fund, Washington, DC.

James, J. (1983). *Consumer Choice in the Third World,* London: Macmillan.

Jelliffe, D. B. (1971): "Commerciogenic Malnutrition? Time for a Dialogue," *Food Technology,* 25 (February), 56.

McComas, M., G. Fookes, and G. Taucher (1983), "The Dilemma of Third World Nutrition," a pamphlet published by Nestlé S.A.

McGuinness, T. and K. Cowling (1975), "Advertising and the Aggregate Demand for Cigarettes," *European Economic Review,* 6 (July), 311–328.

Muller, M. (1975), *The Baby Killer,* 2d ed., London: War on Want.

Nestlé (1983), *The Nestlé Case,* published by the Nestlé Coordination Center for Nutrition, Inc., 1120 Connecticut Avenue, N.W., Suite 301, Washington, DC 20036.

——————— (1980), "The Story Behind the Issue: Infant Feeding in Developing Countries," a pamphlet published by the Nestlé Coordination Center for Nutrition, 1900 M Street, N.W., Suite 750, Washington, DC 20036.

Nicosia, M. and N. Mayer (1976), "Toward a Sociology of Consumption," *Journal of Consumer Research,* 3 (September), 65–75.

PAG (1972), "Protein Advisory Group, Statement No. 23 on Rational Promotion of Processed Foods," New York: PAG United Nations (July 18).

Pagan, R. D., Jr. (1986), "The Nestlé Boycott: Implications for Strategic Business Planning," *Journal of Business Strategy,* 6 (Spring), 12–14.

Post, J. E. (1978), "The International Infant Formula Industry," testimony and supplementary testimony presented to the U.S. Senate Subcommittee on Health and Scientific Research of the Committee on Human Resources, May 23, Washington, DC.

——————— (1985), "Assessing the Nestlé Boycott: Corporate Accountability and Human Rights," *California Management Review,* 27 (Winter), 113–131.

Salvatore, D. (1983), "A Simultaneous Equations Model of Trade and Development with Dynamic Policy Simulations," *KYKLOS,* 36 fasc. 1, 66–90.

Schudson, M. (1984), *Advertising, the Uneasy Persuasion,* New York: Basic Books.

Sethi, S. P., H. Etemad, and K. A. N. Luther (1985), "International Social Activism and Its Impact on Corporate Behavior—The Case of the Infant Formula Controversy," a paper presented at the Pan-Pacific Conference: A Business, Economic and Technological Exchange, Seoul, Korea (May).

_____ (1986), "New Sociopolitical Forces: The Globalization of Conflict," *Journal of Business Strategy,* 6 (Spring), 25–31.

Sethi, S. P., and J. E. Post (1979), "The Marketing of Infant Formula in Less Developed Countries: Public Consequences of Private Actions," *California Management Review,* 21 (Summer), 35–48.

Stafford, J. R. (1978), "Statement of Wyeth International, A Subsidiary of American Home Products Corporation," testimony and supplementary testimony presented to the U.S. Senate Subcommittee on Health and Scientific Research of the Committee on Human Resources, May 23, Washington, DC.

Stiegler, G. P. (1985), personal interview with Carnation Company Vice President for Asia/Pacific during 1974–1982.

United Nations (1983), *Demographic Yearbook of the United Nations,* New York: Department of Social Affairs, Statistical Office.

Weede, E. (1983), "The Impact of Democracy on Economic Growth: Some Evidence from Cross-National Analysis," *KYKLOS,* 36 fasc. 1, 21–39.

World Health Organization (1979), "Collaborative Study on Breast-feeding: Methods and Main Results of the First Phase of the Study—Preliminary Report, MCH/79.3," Geneva, Switzerland: World Health Organization.

World Trade Annual (1969–1979), *Supplement to the World Trade Annual,* vols. 1–3, New York: Walker and Company.

Comments on Gilly and Graham's "A Macroeconomic Study of the Effects of Promotion on the Consumption of Infant Formula in Developing Countries"

Jean J. Boddewyn.   *Jean J. Boddewyn is Professor of Marketing and International Business at Baruch College, City University of New York, New York.*

Mary Gilly and John Graham (1988) have had the courage to tackle the difficult problem of unraveling the macro relationships between the promotion and consumption of a controversial product—infant formula—in developing countries (LDCs). Much of what they report and discuss is relevant for that purpose or, at least, thought provoking. However, I believe there are basic theoretical and operational flaws in their conceptualization, modeling, and analysis which vitiate their overall conclusion, namely, that there is a causal link between the promotion and consumption of that product.

Unjustified Causal Statements

We all know the difficulty if not impossibility of proving cause and effect in social science research. There are too many variables and relationships—some of which we do not even suspect—to model, and data are insufficient to reach a causal condition in the case of complex phenomena such as the purchase and use of infant formula (IF) in LDCs.

Yet, from the start, Gilly and Graham use in their abstract (p. 21) such expressions as "resulted in" and "causal link between promotion and consumption." Furthermore, they state that "one must conclude that [the] promotion of infant formula led directly to increased consumption of the product in [LDC] environments" (p. 29). Elsewhere, they use more appropriate statements of probabilistic relationship: "Consumption of infant

The *Journal of Macromarketing* is published by the Business Research Division of the University of Colorado at Boulder. Reprinted with permission.

formula was found to be positively related to changes in industry promotional effort" (p. 28), and "advertising and promotion can influence consumer behavior" (p. 30). By then, however, the harm has been done to the extent that some foes of infant formula promotion as well as unwitting users of Gilly and Graham's research findings will quote them as having *proved* cause and effect between IF promotion, purchase, and consumption.

A Theoretical Model and Interpretation

Gilly and Graham do not rely on any explicit and generally accepted theories regarding (1) how advertising and other forms of promotion work, (2) the factors affecting the demand for particular product categories, such as infant formulas, and (3) buyer/consumer behavior, particularly in developing countries. It is not that they ignore relevant variables, but their choice does not readily fit into any theoretical framework, notwithstanding their model (Figure 1, p. 22) and the interesting consideration of "alternative explanations" on pp. 28–30.

As we know, anyone can throw variables together to find out whether they correlate. Sophisticated research, however, requires understanding *a priori* why it makes sense to relate them. I readily acknowledge that the dominant theories of advertising, economic demand, and buyer/consumer behavior are still incomplete and in a state of flux. Still, Gilly and Graham's text and bibliography do not reveal any profound consideration of whatever theories are available on these issues. Therefore, I will use various theoretical and methodological considerations to challenge their premises, research design, conclusions, and interpretations.

Specific Criticisms

First, their discussion of advertising theory is really limited to discussing whether it affects *brand* shares only, rather than overall *market* size. Besides, Gilly and Graham assume a simple stimulus-and-response model of how promotional efforts work. If women in developing countries see brand advertisements, receive company brochures, and are given free baby bottles and IF samples, then suddenly they are hooked on that product. My understanding of the current advertising theory literature is that it has moved away from a simplistic model of what advertising does *to* people to the more complex questions of what people do *with* advertising; what people use advertising *for* (Lannon 1986, p. RC-7). Just because marketing and advertising are more "actionable" than poverty and illiteracy (p. 24) does not *ipso facto* make the former "effective."

Second, there have been many discussions of whether advertising budgets are set as a percentage of *past* sales experience—in which case sales affect advertising expenditures—or are set in terms of *targeted* sales, in which case, at least, there is an assumption that advertising drives sales even though actual results cannot be guaranteed. Gilly and Graham really assume that increased sales *always* follow increased promotion expenditures, since their second and key hypothesis about consumption (pp. 23–24) uses as its key independent variable the level of promotion—more before 1975, less after 1975.

Altogether, it is as if one did not need to know promotion theory to engage in their type of research, which is largely limited to correlating various economic and demographic variables in some sort of a black box.

Third, they ignore the extensive economic and econometric literatures on the macro relationships between demand and advertising. Promotion does not operate in an economic, social, political, and cultural vacuum. As was discovered long ago, *if underlying conditions are favorable to an increase in demand for the product, the use of advertising tends to enhance and accelerate the rising trend of demand,* and vice versa (Borden 1942, pp. xxviii–xxix). In other words, *advertising does not initiate demand but can amplify it.*

Yet Gilly and Graham's second and central hypothesis ("consumption of infant formula is positively related to changes in promotional efforts" (pp. 23–24), their textual analysis, and their "causal" conclusions (see above) do not provide any investigation of "underlying conditions" for the demand for IF. I readily grant that their initial model (Figure 1, p. 22) lists 14 "environmental influences," such as urbanization, industrialization, income levels, birth rate, and attitudes and practices of the health care profession, but few of these variables are systematically investigated in the subsequent analysis. One might also observe that their model leaves out other apparently relevant variables, such as modernization, Westernization, and the second oil crisis of 1977–1978, which made the prices of IF increase considerably.

It is as if promotion had created demand all by itself, and their numerous citations from critics of the IF industry go in the same direction (for example, "the promotion of infant-formula products was rampant and unchecked before 1970," quoted on p. 22). Their alternative hypothesis ("consumption of infant formula is unrelated to changes in promotional efforts," p. 23) is equally as simplistic, a strawman easy to knock off. What is missing is an "in-between" hypothesis aimed at isolating promotion's effect from that of other variables; and their consideration of "alternative explanations" (pp. 28–29) is like a series of afterthoughts rather than part of an overall research design integrating a series of independent and moderating variables.

Fourth, Gilly and Graham erroneously assume that the demand for IF (and other breastmilk substitutes, really) is the same as the demand for all foods. For that matter, their key test and proof rest on a comparison of "infant-formula imports" and "[total] food imports" in 79 countries (p. 27). Yet, can one reasonably argue that, for example, the demand for *beer* is affected by the same factors as the demand for *all alcoholic beverages,* for *all drinks,* and for *all foods?* Of course not. Otherwise, we would lose all our rationales for market segmentation and product positioning, besides sacrificing common sense and experience.

The magnitudes involved also support the above point. IF imports in their Table 1 (p. 27) represent at best 2.1 percent of total food imports, so that one should not assume that such a small fragment is representative of all foods, a very heterogeneous group in any case, with each segment bound to be affected by very different combinations of supply and demand factors.

It is true that Gilly and Graham provide for some control factors, such as inflation and foreign exchange rates (the two are interrelated), but I think that such corrections are insufficient to address the fundamental heterogeneity of product categories and of their respective supplies and demands. Later on, their "alternative explanations" (pp. 28–30) introduce additional factors, such as public policy, economic conditions, foreign exchange availability, local production, other marketing mix variables, and foreign aid distribution of free IF. In some cases, the available information was insufficient to test the importance of these additional variables, and they cannot be blamed for it. Their Table 3 (p. 29), however, gives "not statistically significant" Pearson correlation coefficients regarding the relationships between IF imports and the respective changes in birth rates, GDP indices, and available foreign exchange, but their discussion of these additional factors (on p. 28) is so brief that I must confess I do not quite understand what they are testing and concluding.

Fifth, Gilly and Graham's justification for choosing 1975 as the "critical year" (p. 26) that separated a period of intense promotion by the IF industry from one of less intense promotion is questionable. They cite, in Exhibit 1 and on pp. 24–25, a variety of dated events to justify this choice. However, it is evident from these data that some industry curtailment of promotion had already taken place *before 1975* and that major promotional curtailments date from *later than 1978*. Why, then, leave out the post-1978 period (for which comparable statistics must have been obtainable), which witnessed major governmental controls and consumerist pressures? This later period would have provided a much more reliable testing period than 1976–1978 for measuring the effect of curtailed promotion on IF consumption.

More important still, in my opinion, is that the periods considered in their analysis (1972–1974 compared to 1976–1978) are far too short to test hypotheses in the case of an event—the infant formula controversy—that developed over a much longer time and culminated, so to speak, with the World Health Assembly approving the WHO code on the marketing of breastmilk substitutes in 1981. Gilly and Graham's only justification for comparing such short periods seems to be that no import data were available for 1971 so that only data from 1972 onward could be used. This, in turn, led to the precurtailment period for promotion being limited to 1972–1974 and the postcurtailment period to a comparable three-year span from 1976 to 1978. But was such symmetry essential to test their hypotheses? They could have used subsequent three-year periods to find out whether the rates of relative decline in imports had persisted.

Besides, my reading of the WHO (1979) study, which they cite, does not seem to justify the choice of 1975 as a critical year. The field work for this study was conducted in 1975–1977 in six LDCs, but only on p. 65 does the WHO report briefly refer to curtailed promotional activities through the mass media in four LDCs. Elsewhere, the general impression is that promotional activities were still high in these countries and—presumably—in other LDCs.

Sixth, Gilly and Graham are strangely silent about *infant formula imports still increasing in absolute terms after 1975* (from $107.4 million in 1974 to $148.4 million in 1978), although promotion had decreased. In other words, their conclusion is based on a decline in the *relative rate of increase* in IF imports after 1975. This leads them to claim that IF imports "might have reached $178 million, had manufacturers maintained their much criticized promotional practices through 1978" (p. 28). This last statement is purely conjectural and unprovable. It resembles the one used by some opponents of the tobacco industry to justify tobacco advertising bans (see Bjartveit and Lund 1987). They, too, draw imaginary dotted lines past the year of the ban to claim that the advertising ban succeeded in curtailing tobacco consumption because the latter *would* have been higher in the absence of such a ban. In fact, one can never know what would or could have happened.

Seventh, as was mentioned before, Gilly and Graham considered alternative explanations of the relative decline in the IF imports' rate of increase. However, they do not envisage the possibility of a product life cycle effect where the market reaches the maturity stage. Could the LDC markets have come to that point after 1975, to the extent that the pool of mothers (particularly urban and more affluent ones) likely to adopt IF in LDCs had reached its natural limit around that time on account of various "underlying conditions" (Borden 1942)? At the maturity stage of the cycle, promotional activities—whatever their overall size and rate of growth—tend to shift to battles for market share rather than to enhancing and accelerating the rising trend of demand.

Eighth, I believe that Gilly and Graham are too subjective in the interpretation of their findings, although we all commit that sin, since research is never value free. For example, they ignore evidence from the 1979 WHO report (which they quoted) about the real but limited effect of promotion on the LDC mothers' decisions to adopt IF. This WHO report (1979) is much subtler in its fundamental assumption and appraisal of promotion playing *some* role in fostering consumption: "The approach taken in the survey *assumes* that the adoption of bottle feeding by the mother is a function of an interplay between *a variety of factors,* and that *intensive* marketing of commercially prepared infant foods is *one* of these factors" (p. 58; emphasis added). (Notice, by the way, the mention of "intensive" marketing efforts in the WHO report for the 1975–1977 period, which challenges Gilly and Graham's characterization of 1976–1978 as a period of diminishing promotional activities.)

Besides, the WHO report states that "advice from husbands, friends *and from the media* was not commonly quoted in any country or group" (1979, p. 41; emphasis added). Gilly and Graham reject such contrary evidence by answering that "one might ask why consumers would be expected to admit to, or even be conscious of, their response to commercial advertising" (p. 30). I find this kind of answer baffling. Of course, if one accepts without question that there are "hidden persuaders" preying on "vulnerable consumers," their rebuttal makes sense. But that is a big "if" which I am not quite ready to swallow on faith when no empirical evidence is provided to buttress it. Their reply amounts to saying that we do not know how advertising works and consumers behave—but, then, why link promotion and consumption?

Similarly, to state, as Gilly and Graham do, that "until [information available in company records is] made available [by IF manufacturers] for close and objective scrutiny, studies such as this one must suffice [to prove that their promotion of infant formula in LDCs led directly to increased consumption]" (p. 29) is unfair and unscientific since one cannot prove a negative. They really want IF manufacturers to prove that promotion did *not* affect consumption, an impossible task!

Altogether, I think their case is not proved, *partly* because of the real methodological and statistical problems which they could not avoid, but *mainly* because of serious theoretical lacunas, analytical weaknesses, and partisan attitudes on their part. Ultimately, a rather tiny reed of debatable IF import evidence is all they could lean on to prove their point. That is not enough, in my opinion.

To quote Wickstrom (1979), who participated in the WHO study (1979) but also studied cigarette marketing in LDCs at about the same time: "All of this does not necessarily mean that there are no effects of advertising upon smoking, only maybe that the models are misspecified and the measurements techniques inadequate" (p. 9). Amen.

References

Bjartveit, Kjell and K. E. Lund (1987), "Smoking Control in Norway," Oslo, Norway: National Council on Smoking and Health, November.

Borden, N. H. (1942), *The Economic Effects of Advertising,* Chicago, IL: R. D. Irwin.

Gilly, Mary C. and John L. Graham (1988), "A Macroeconomic Study of the Effects of Promotion on the Consumption of Infant Formula in Developing Countries," *Journal of Macromarketing,* 8 (Spring), 21–31.

Lannon, Judie (1986), "New Techniques for Understanding Consumer Reactions to Advertising," *Journal of Advertising Research,* 26 (August–September), RC 6–9.

Wickström, Bo (1979), *Cigarette Marketing in the Third World,* Göteberg, Sweden: Department of Business Administration, Marketing Section, University of Gothenburg.

World Health Organization (WHO) (1979), "WHO Collaborative Study on Breastfeeding; Methods and Main Results of the First Phase of the Study-Preliminary Report, MCH/79.3," Geneva, Switzerland: WHO.

Comment on Infant Formula: Trees or Forest?

Bill Meade. *Bill Meade is a doctoral student at Michigan State University, East Lansing, Michigan.*

In "A Macroeconomic Study of the Effects of Promotion on the Consumption of Infant Formula in Developing Countries," Mary Gilly and John Graham (1988) set themselves the task of determining the relationship between promotion and sales. Like many other marketers in this debate, they have not focused on the crucial marketing point. Marketing affects quality of life and society negatively as well as positively, and when ineptly done has even killed people. Infant malnutrition, illness, and death are the essential problems in the formula controversy.

In *Advertising, The Uneasy Persuasion,* Schudson (1986, pp. 214–215) uses the concepts of "Capitalist Realism" and "Socialist Realism" to show how presenting "reality as it should be" can be used in persuasion. These stylized persuasive modes "simplify and typify" reality, creating a "characteristic abstractness." The infant formula debate has drifted into such an abstractness. The fixation on promotion made it depart the plane of reality where negative consequences occur and made it nonmarketing because solving the problem was forgotten in fighting the battle.

The requirements domain (the market, economic, physical, resource, and competitive requirements for success) (Bacon 1981) would have been a better place for this debate. Apparently, infants are harmed and die because formula is made with contaminated water and because formula is overly diluted (due to its high prices to relatively poor customers). In requirements terms, technical and economic failures caused these consequences. But this did not have to occur; good milk could have been made with bad water. Simple cold filtering *eliminates bacteria* from contaminated water. Solving the whole infant formula problem requires bacteria removal and lowering prices so that poor customers will not dilute it too much. Both water contamination and dilution are cost reduction problems. Discovering cost reduction to open up markets is near the marrow of marketing (see Levitt 1986, p. 155).

Rather than hoping for technology to be benign, marketers should assume marketing mixes will *always fail* in new cultures. For example, in LDCs each infant marketing mix variable precipitated unique responses. *Product* shortcomings apparently harmed babies

The *Journal of Macromarketing* is published by the Business Research Division of the University of Colorado at Boulder. Reprinted with permission.

in the "poor" and "bad water" segments. *Promotion* interacted with *place* (milk-nurse missionary sales people) and was too effective, exacerbating product design problems and providing the target for attacks on formula producers. *Price* probably contributed to death through too much dilution. In this case marketing produced profits and pestilence side by side. Taking markets for granted can have great social consequences. Gilly and Graham ignore this, trivializing its significance.

Marketing is about solving problems and creating/capturing value while doing so. Formula makers responded to their critics with claims that "promotion does not increase demand." This battlefield response to criticism deflected discussion away from solutions. The antiformula people may well have a "hidden agenda" against formula use, that is, they are against formula more than they are for babies, but such an agenda does not absolve formula suppliers from solving the mortality problem. The important lesson is that inept marketing can, and in this case did, catastrophically reduce quality of life for significant numbers of Third World mothers and babies.

The infant formula problem happened for lack of creative marketing mix development. When problems with formula surfaced, formula suppliers and antiformula people fell into a battlefield mentality, and creative solutions were never developed. When Gilly and Graham followed the traditional abstractness of the controversy, they overlooked the essential issue. Infant death is the crucial problem. It is a micromarketing problem with macromarketing consequences.

References

Bacon, Jr., Frank R. and Thomas W. Buter, Jr. (1981), *Planned Innovation,* Ann Arbor: Industrial Development Division, Institute of Science and Technology, University of Michigan.

Gilly, Mary C. and John L. Graham (1988), "A Macroeconomic Study of the Effects of Promotion on the Consumption of Infant Formula in Developing Countries," *Journal of Macromarketing,* 8 (Spring) 21–31.

Levitt, Theodore (1986), "Marketing Myopia," "What Ford Put First," in *The Marketing Imagination,* new and expanded edition, New York, The Free Press.

Schudson, Michael (1986), *Advertising, The Uneasy Persuasion,* New York, Basic Books.

Rejoinder to Comments by Boddewyn and Meade regarding "A Macroeconomic Study of the Effects of Promotion on the Consumption of Infant Formula in Developing Countries"

John L. Graham and Mary C. Gilly

We very much appreciate the hard work and careful thought put into the comments by J. J. Boddewyn and William Meade regarding our article, "A Macroeconomic Study of the Effects of Promotion on the Consumption of Infant Formula in Developing Countries" (1988). Because their criticisms are quite divergent (that is, Boddewyn suggests we have overstepped the bounds of quality social science, particularly pushing our interpretation too far, whereas Meade argues that we have not studied the most important problem), we will respond to them separately.

Response to the Comments of Jean J. Boddewyn

Ordinarily, we would just deal with the issues, but Boddewyn questioned, albeit subtly, our own source credibility by accusing us of "partisan attitudes" and characterizing our study as "too subjective" and not "value free" (1988, p. 43). We cannot argue that our study does not suffer from such limitations. Indeed, Merton (1968) and others caution that all scientific work is value laden, and it is the responsibility of scientists to try to take their own biases into account.

Boddewyn's criticism is that our study *proves* nothing. The failsafe position of the infant formula manufacturers, the tobacco producers, and the alcoholic beverage industry is that one can never *prove* that the sale of these products causes health problems. Attorneys worry about proof. The job of social scientists is to provide evidence, not to

The *Journal of Macromarketing* is published by the Business Research Division at the University of Colorado at Boulder. Reprinted with permission.

prove things. We mightily disapprove of Boddewyn's misleading out-of-context quotes which imply that we think otherwise. He describes our statements, "causal link between promotion and consumption" and "one must conclude that promotion of infant formula led directly to increased consumption of the product in [LDC] environments" as harmful. Yet, he left out key qualifiers on our part. The more complete quotes are "a causal link between promotion and consumption of the product *is supported by the data*" and "until companies provide evidence to the contrary, one must conclude that their promotion of infant formula led directly into increased consumption." Then he adds on page 43 that it would be "unfair and unscientific" to ask the companies to prove that their promotion did not lead to consumption.

Simply stated, Boddewyn's courtroom approach asks too much of any one study. Our question for him and the infant formula manufacturers is: "Do you have evidence to show that promotion does not have a causal effect on consumption?" If so, it should be put forward for scrutiny.

Finally, our own motivations for conducting the study are relevant. The two of us had a disagreement about the issue—our disparate *a priori* views are reflected in the hypotheses. We decided to settle the disagreement by seeing which view was supported by the data.

Boddewyn's Specific Criticisms

Initially, Boddewyn complains that our study lacks a foundation in "generally accepted theories" (p. 40). In a sense we agree. Rather than merely a generally accepted theory, our study rests on an axiom of marketing—promotion increases sales. The only people who disagree with this basic truth are those who have a stake in the disagreement, namely, the advertisers of alcoholic beverages, tobacco products, and infant formula producers. Indeed, a multibillion dollar advertising industry is built upon the axiom. We cannot argue that more complex theories of advertising's effects (for example, Lannon 1986) are not useful, but the parsimony of the axiom is compelling. Boddewyn's summary charge of "serious theoretical lacunas" (p. 43) is simply untrue.

Regarding theories of advertising's effects on consumer behavior in developing countries, we cite several studies in the original paper, all more relevant and recent than Boddewyn's key reliance on Borden (1942). We see no need for reviewing this well-trodden ground. And we will certainly not argue with Boddewyn's point that "advertising does not initiate demand but can *amplify* it" (p. 41). Webster defines amplify as "to make stronger"—precisely our finding!

Boddewyn's second point regards an assumption he assumes we made in the study, namely, that "increased sales always follow increased promotion" (p. 41). He implies that the relationship we discovered between promotion and consumption was due to the companies anticipating reduced demand and concomitantly cutting back promotional expenditures. Yet, in the voluminous literature regarding the controversy there is no evidence to support such a view. No one in the industry at that time talked about a potential decline in demand. Indeed, the comments and testimony of the manufacturers emphasized the expected growth in the market. Also, please notice the inconsistency in Boddewyn's statements. Here he allows the relationship between promotion and consumption but argues that the causal arrow is reversed. Later he attacks the relationship itself on several grounds.

Third, Boddewyn makes the easiest criticism of all—that our model is incomplete and does not consider *all* the relevant variables. All social science research is subject to this obvious criticism. We have examined relevant variables to the extent possible. Indeed, with support from the infant formula manufacturers we might specify and test more complex models of the phenomenon. We would be most pleased to have access to sales and advertising records of the companies involved.

In the fourth section of Boddewyn's criticism the inconsistencies of his own arguments again surface. Having complained about the incompleteness of our model, in this section he voices concern about our attempt to be more comprehensive through controlling for several kinds of exogenous economic factors. We cannot necessarily disagree with his comments here; however, we would have appreciated some actionable suggestions of *better* alternatives for controlling for exogenous factors.

Next, Boddewyn attacks our choice of 1975 as the key year of change of promotional practices in the industry. However, we feel the support for our choice is quite strong and well documented. He also argues that the three-year test periods we used in the analysis are too short to demonstrate the changes in demand we report. We wonder how long a period would satisfy him? Of the several colleagues reviewing our study, only he has found fault with the three-year test periods. Boddewyn also mentions that the infant formula controversy "culminated" in 1981. Others report that it is not over yet, that Nestlé's promotion of infant formula in less developed countries (Duncan 1988) and in the United States (Sanchez 1988) deserves renewed scrutiny.

In his sixth section Boddewyn takes issue with our suggestion that infant formula sales would have been even higher in 1978 had not the companies curtailed their promotional efforts. The reader will note that again he quotes us out of context, leaving off our qualifying remark, "*other things being equal.*" In his words, our statements are "purely conjectural and unprovable." Yes, better *proof* might be developed using some sort of field experiment wherein promotion levels are carried across regions. But hypothesis confirmation in such a study would be grisly indeed.

The seventh issue raised by Boddewyn regards a product life cycle effect as an alternative explanation. That is, perhaps infant formula reached the maturity stage in its product life cycle in less developed countries. Perhaps. However, nowhere in the literature, including the testimony of industry representatives, is such a leveling off of demand mentioned. Again, this is an area where industry supplied data may help answer questions.

Boddewyn's eighth specific comment accuses us of selectively quoting the 1979 World Health Organization report. He seems to ignore that Nestlé reprinted that particular section of the report in one of its own public relations brochures. We do applaud Boddewyn for pointing out that the report does describe "the intensive marketing of commercially prepared infant foods" as one of the causal factors influencing breast feeding behavior.

The last point is crucial. Throughout his criticism, Boddewyn implies that we attribute consumption of infant formula *solely* to its advertising and promotion. Yet, from the very beginning of our article, we present a quite comprehensive model of the factors influencing breast feeding behavior and consumption of infant formula. Granted, our data allow us to study only one part of the model. Our findings are consistent with the theory that promotion has a causal effect, but we *never* argue that promotion is the only factor.

Our findings support the theory that industry advertising and promotion can have a causal effect on primary demand for products. Boddewyn frequently cites the cigarette advertising controversy as being analogous to the issue examined in our study of infant formula marketing. Curiously, he stands silent on the most recent studies in the marketing literature which support the causal relationship between industry advertising and primary demand for cigarettes. (See Leeflang and Reuijl 1985; a careful reading of Holak and Reddy 1986.) Such other studies are quite important, because only through a body of research is the truth revealed. That is, it is always easy to attack a single study; limitations are unavoidable. But *consistent findings*, from a series of studies with different limitations and different researchers, are a bit more difficult to criticize convincingly. Boddewyn states: "Ultimately, a rather tiny reed of debatable [infant formula] import evidence is all they could lean on to prove their point" (p. 43). Rather, our study well represents the continuing accumulation of evidence that industry advertising and promotion increase primary demand for products.

Responses to the Comments of Meade

Contrary to Boddewyn, Meade does not criticize our theory or method; rather, he indicates that we defined the problem incorrectly. Meade claims we have ignored the fact that "taking markets for granted can have great social consequences" and that we "trivialize its [the problem's] significance" (1988, p. 44). We would argue that we were trying to address the problem by investigating how one component of marketing, promotion, had an effect on the sales of infant formula in developing countries. Meade advances, and we agree, that other elements of the marketing mix, such as distribution and price, also contributed to the infant formula problem. But if it were possible (as Meade implies) to design and conduct a study in which all marketing mix variables are included as the independent variables and "infant malnutrition, illness, and death" (p. 44) are measured as the dependent variables, we would certainly applaud such an effort.

Meade's claim that "solving the whole infant formula problem requires bacteria removal and lowering price so that poor customers will not dilute it too much" (p. 44) fails to consider other contributing factors, such as illiteracy and lack of education. Studying macromarketing problems, such as marketing's effects on society and quality of life, involves complex relationships like those represented in Figure 1 of our original paper.

Finally, we very much agree that infant death is the crucial problem. But lacking infant mortality information and data regarding other relevant contributing causes, we decided to study the variables we could access and at least make a contribution toward understanding this important macromarketing problem.

References

Boddewyn, Jean J. 1988, "Comments on Gilly and Graham's 'A Macroeconomic Study of the Effects of Promotion on the Consumption of Infant Formula in Developing Countries,' " *Journal of Macromarketing*, 8 (Fall), 40–43.

Borden, N. H. (1942), *The Economic Effects of Advertising*, Chicago: R. D. Irwin.

Duncan, Jaurie (1988), "Group Calls for Resumption of Nestle Boycott," *Los Angeles Times*, October 5, pp. 1 and 9.

Gilly, Mary C. and John L. Graham (1988), "A Macroeconomic Study of the Effects of Promotion on the Consumption of Infant Formula in Developing Countries," *Journal of Macromarketing*, 8 (Spring), 21–31.

Holak, Susan L. and Srinivas K. Reddy (1986), "Effects of a Television and Radio Advertising Ban: A Study of the Cigarette Industry," *Journal of Marketing*, 50 (October), 219–27.

Lannon, Judie (1986), "New Techniques for Understanding Consumer Reactions to Advertising," *Journal of Advertising Research*, 26 (August-September), PC 6–9.

Leeflang, Peter S. H. and Jan C. Reuijl (1985), "Advertising and Industry Sales: An Empirical Study of the West German Cigarette Market," *Journal of Marketing*, 49 (Fall), 92–98.

Meade, Bill (1988), "Comment on Infant Formula: Trees or Forest?" *Journal of Macromarketing*, 8 (Fall), 44–45.

Merton, Robert K. (1968), *Social Theory and Social Structure*, New York: The Free Press.

Sanchez, Jesus (1988), "Marketing to Moms," *Los Angeles Times* July 2, Section IV, pp. 1 and 4.

Adapting Ethical Decisions to a Global Marketplace

Kent Hodgson.

A smaller planet has put nations and peoples face-to-face as never before. Only now are we coming to grips with how intertwined our customs and values really are. They are as different yet proximate as camels loping by Abram tanks in the desert; mud-and-thatch huts only minutes away from million-dollar suburban homes; or foreign nationals graduating from Harvard Business School and returning to villages in Yemen or Panama, while their American counterparts interview with Xerox and Citicorp in Manhattan.

In part of Africa, a "family" celebration at the conclusion of a business deal—a party for which you are asked to pay—may well be a sign of friendship and lasting business relationships, not a personal payoff. "Grease" payments to customs officials in some countries may be part of their earning a living wage—not blackmail. In a large number of countries, custom, law and religion support the fact that women are denied personal and professional rights of equality.

Each of these practices is part of some group's ethical standards and affects business dealings between you and the group's members.

Each of these practices also represents a problem of differences—a conflict of values and norms among stakeholders—but not necessarily of right versus wrong, truth against falsehood or knowledge encountering ignorance. It is certainly not a question of our "good ethics" versus their "bad ethics." Such a view begs the integrity question, but more important, it risks destroying any sense of cooperation based on mutual trust and goodwill.

The real challenge is to bridge differences and value gaps, and hurdle our own perceived obstacles (see related story in *MR* April, page 42). In today's world, there is much to be accomplished and mutually gained through understanding and respect across cultural lines. The opportunities are there, but so is the clash of values and interests.

A basic step in finding practical solutions to cultural challenges in a global market is to answer two initial questions: First, do you accept the premise that most decisions involve both business and ethics? Second, are you an American businessperson or member of an organization that happens to do business overseas, or are you a global

138

businessperson or member of an organization that happens to have headquarters in the United States?

Your answer to the first question embodies a key philosophical commitment. An affirmative answer means adoption of primary working values and principles—like the health and welfare of customers—from which action decisions will be made. Your answer to the second question determines a key responsibility commitment; it makes other countries and peoples either valued stakeholder partners or just potential profit centers and resource sites.

Stakeholder Viewpoints

Another step toward better global decision making is to be aware of, and acknowledge, the clash among different cultures, values and principles. This acknowledgement is really a process of learning about other cultures without making business or moral judgments based solely on American customs and mores. You should know the historical, ethnic, cultural, political, legal and religious facts about a country or region, as these facts influence the way the people think, interact and do business. Then you should allow those facts to affect your thinking and acting.

Acknowledgment of the differences between peoples should also include a tolerance of diversity. Our values, beliefs, customs and ethics are not the only acceptable ones. Many nations have value systems that did not evolve from Graeco-Roman and Anglo-Saxon roots, which emphasize the rule of law. Americans easily forget how relatively young and unique the U.S. Constitution and Bill of Rights are. Indeed, most other systems were practiced for centuries before the United States existed.

The values and customs of other nations are not necessarily primitive, degraded or wrong because they are different from ours. Hence, they don't call for our immediate suspicion, distrust or condemnation. Until proved otherwise, they are only different—having evolved under distinct geographies, conditions and heritages.

By example, let's look at the practical problems of bribery and payoffs. Most foreign governments, including many well known for corruption, have enforced statutes against most forms of private payoff. Yet in some countries of Africa, ancient traditions take precedence over law. Payoffs have become the norm and are rooted in a "communal heritage," in which a community leader's wealth was shared with the community; those who hoarded were scorned. The Nigerian practice of "dash"—private pay for private service—traces back to trade in the form of gifts exchanged for labor.

American organizations frequently deal through foreign nationals who have been educated in the United States, know American business ways, but are very much a part of their own culture. They may hold seemingly conflicting values: some instilled in the West, others a part of their local tradition and life. They may see no conflict in negotiating along Western lines and then reverting to communal traditions when discussing more private remuneration. These people need not be labeled completely corrupt; rather, they are drawn by both indigenous and Western values. They may have American ideals of personal business enrichment and want to adhere to communal obligations at the same time.

Working with Your Principles—and Theirs

Awareness and acknowledgment of differences in values among regions should bring about changes in your thinking and initiatives.

Practices you view as questionable, illegal or simply exploitative may be revealed as local tradition, courtesy and even friendship. I'm not suggesting that you break or ignore your own country's laws or those of other nations. Nor am I condoning begging, blackmail or bribery. This would spell financial, legal and ethical trouble for you, your organization and possibly those of other countries. But you can take initiatives other than outright rejection of legitimate values different from yours on the one hand, or completely selling out your own values on the other.

You can capitalize on new and existing opportunities for business in the following general ways.

1. Become more sensitive to the customs, values and practices of other peoples, which they themselves view as moral, traditional, practical and effective.

2. Don't judge the business customs of others —when different from your own—as necessarily immoral, corrupt, primitive or unworkable. Assume they are legitimate and workable until proved otherwise.

3. Find legitimate ways to operate from their ethical and commercial points of view; do not demand that they operate only by your ground rules.

4. Avoid rationalizing borderline actions, which usually are justified by the following:

   • "This isn't *really* illegal or immoral."

   • "This is in the organization's and my best interest."

   • "We're safe; no one will find us out."

   • "The organization will condone this and protect me."

5. Refuse to do business when stakeholder options violate or seriously compromise laws or fundamental organizational values.

6. Conduct relationships and negotiations as openly and aboveboard as possible—including reports to stakeholders and public accountability.

7. Avoid purely legalistic but ethically questionable strategies, such as calling "agents" (who are accountable to employers) "distributors" (who are not).   —*K.H.*

If you are involved in business with Third World countries, you need to understand three widespread traditions that affect business transactions and added remunerations: the inner circle, future favors and the gift exchange.

Inner Circle

Communal societies divide people into two groups: Those with whom they have relationships, and those with whom they have none—the goal being group prosperity and protection. There are the "in" people and the "out" people. The "ins" are family; the "outs" are strangers. In East and West Africa, inner circles can be true relatives, comrades or persons of similar age or region. In China, they may be those who share the same dialect; in India, members of the same caste. These are not unlike the "old boy networks" in the United States. The effect in many of these countries is to restrict social and business dealings to those with whom the businessperson has safe, trusting relationships. Often that trust is forthcoming if Westerners willing to honor communal values become part of the inner circle.

Future Favors

The system of future favors operates within the inner circles. In Japan it is known as "inner duty," in Kenya, "inner relationship," and in the Philippines, "inner debt." In these traditions, the person obligated to another is expected to repay the favor sometime in the future. Some form of favor or service will repay the earlier debt; this repayment then places the grantor of the original favor under future obligation. Lifelong shifting obligations create relationships of trust and are the basis for doing business.

Gift Exchange

In many non-Western circles, the gift exchange tradition has evolved into a business tool: Gifts begin a process of future favors. They are an immediate sign of gratitude or hospitality, but upon acceptance, they generate an obligation that the recipient must someday repay.

Inner circles, future favors and gift exchanges exist in American society also, but they don't usually have the same sense of obligation—either in the present or in the future. Nor is there the same sense of "family" with ensuing trust or loyalty present. Rather, many Americans feel a sense of ethical wariness when the relationship seems to move beyond gratitude, courtesy or friendliness to even remotely suggest influence in decision making.

The Results System

Looking closely at the consequences of foreign practices rather than the actions themselves can clarify difficult situations. Gift giving is a good example. Solicitation of gifts has no place in U.S. business circles when it smacks of exploitation. This may be true in other countries too, but foreign colleagues often are at a loss to know how to initiate honorable, lasting relationships that form around business ventures—especially when Americans have little time for social amenities, are ignorant of local traditions or are wary of the exchange of gifts that creates obligations and trust.

Foreigners often take on the role of initial giver or may suggest that gift giving is the traditional way of entering the local business system. This role is viewed as a courteous and acceptable means of furthering business. You should look at the true purpose and legitimate consequences of such gift giving, considered in a local context other than your own.

An American company that exclusively manufactured and distributed medical devices for human implantation was asked for payment outside the contract; if it did not comply, it would lose the right to sell in a certain foreign country. The company had to weigh payment to certain nongovernmental parties against its business interests as well as the life-and-death need of hundreds of citizens who could not obtain the device by any other means. Weighing the good consequences of an action against a questionably ethical "means to the end" makes for a tough call. Yet a decision for remuneration in some form could well be the right one, given the importance of the devices versus an unwanted but unavoidable payment.

The Responsibility System

A promise to respond to important stakeholders in a spirit of cooperation also allows for new initiatives in doing business in foreign countries. Whereas directly granting requests for private monies exposes U.S. organizations to financial and legal threats, invoking the principle of responsibility to—but not for—other stakeholders makes alternate answers appropriate. Nonmonetary public service benefits could well replace payoffs and satisfy the needs of both sides, for instance.

I wonder if the specter of foreign payoffs and bribes doesn't sometimes blind American organizations to the fact that technical expertise, follow-up satisfaction and customer service also are powerful incentives to buy. Responsibility to the customer through quality, partnering and service is the name of the game today. It has top priority within the United States—why not overseas as well? While firmly rejecting direct private payoffs, you may counter with monies clearly directed at needed help to others not touched by the contracts themselves. Even if these funds make the foreign contacts richer, in the long run some portion of the wealth is often shared communally with many relatives and "mates."

In fact, Kenya and Indonesia have made such requests of U.S. companies. It is not uncommon for non-Western colleagues of American organizations to view requests for private monies as a way of helping themselves, but also as a means to aid larger groups and their nations.

Responsibility also may suggest that donations could be open contributions to build schools, hospitals, medical clinics or agricultural projects. Such donations could be directed to the provinces or villages of the foreign counterparts or colleagues. Donating services, tools or machine parts is another alternative to private payoffs. Tanzanian poaching patrols have been helped in this way by British companies, and Coca-Cola hired Egyptians to plant acres of orange trees. Both cases resulted in a needed political favor, increased local employment and goodwill.

The object, of course, is self-interest on both sides. But cooperation and goodwill are the responsible means. Public service, donations, employment, social progress and the use of local customs and traditions are far superior to bribes, misunderstanding, or simply walking away from mutual business opportunity and benefit.

America's Foreign Corrupt Practices Act of 1977 (FCPA) prohibits payments to foreign officials, political parties or candidates for the purpose of influencing an act or decision intended to obtain or retain business. Companies and their managers also are liable if they know, or had reason to know, that their agents used payments from a U.S. concern to pay foreign officials for a prohibited purpose.

Nowhere does the FCPA prohibit the use of funds to aid developing societies. You and your organization often can solve ethical/business dilemmas by turning potential private payoffs into public services. Such decisions then would be openly defensible and justifiable on ethical as well as legal grounds—a powerful argument.

Three-Step Process

Ultimately, you will want to apply the following process to issues or dilemmas posed in the global marketplace:

1. Examine the situation. Acknowledgment of the histories, customs and values of the people involved gives added insight into the critical facts of the situation. You will be better able to identify the key stakeholders, who may be more numerous than in the United States. Communal traditions, inner circle relationships, and other non-Western colleagues lengthen the list.

2. Establish the dilemma. Identify the working principles and norms that drive each of the stakeholder options (i.e., why they want their options chosen). Since foreign values and principles are likely to differ from those you quickly assign to American clients, this will help you focus the issue or dilemma.

With a more balanced acknowledgment of why foreigners hold certain values and "stakes" when approaching business, you will better understand their intentions. Projecting the outcomes of the stakeholders' options should then be closer to reality and less colored by your own values and principles.

Then you can attempt to determine the actions that stakeholders will take to produce the outcome they want. At this point, ask whether those actions, as means to the end, violate your own or organizational principles. You may see significant clashes of your principles, and your laws with theirs. But you also will find common values.

Awareness of their values and customs will help you judge more accurately and fairly whether the means they will use in fulfillment of their options are acceptable or unacceptable ground rules for you.

3. Evaluate the options. The key to value-based decision making is to choose an option for action that flows from business values and principles rooted responsibly in the Magnificent Seven General Principles (see box). Given your awareness of the similarities and differences in interpretation of these principles by other people, identify which principle is driving each stakeholder option, including your own.

Finally, compare the General Principles behind each option. Which is the most responsible principle in this situation? The answer to this question will come as a result of weighing the General Principles that drive all the options.

Moving Forward

Awareness and acknowledgment of differences, respect for traditions other than your own, changes in thinking and in initiatives, principled and responsible decisions flowing from a practical decision-making process—all these will help open the door to waiting opportunities.

The Magnificent Seven Principles

1. Dignity of Human Life

The lives of people are to be respected. Human beings, by the fact of their existence, have value and dignity. We may not act in ways that directly intend to harm an innocent person. Human beings have a right to live; we have an obligation to respect that right to life. Human life is to be preserved and treated as sacred.

2. Autonomy

All persons are intrinsically valuable and have the right to self-determination. We should act in ways that demonstrate each person's worth, dignity, and right to free choice. We have a right to act in ways that assert our own worth and legitimate needs. We should not use others as mere "things," or only as means to an end. Each person has an equal right to basic human liberty, compatible with a similar liberty for others.

3. Honest

The truth should be told to those who have a right to know it. Honesty is also known as integrity, truth-telling and honor. One should speak and act so as to reflect the reality of the situation. Speaking and acting should mirror the way things really are. There are times when others have the right to hear the truth from us; there are times when they do not.

4. Loyalty

Promises, contracts and commitments should be honored. Loyalty includes fidelity, promise keeping, maintaining the public trust, good citizenship, excellence in quality of work, reliability, commitment, and honoring just laws, rules and policies.One should honor and keep confidences, proprietary information and personal private information that is freely and willingly shared. People should fulfill written and verbal contracts and commitments. They should fulfill just rules, laws and policies.

5. Fairness

People should be treated justly. People have the right to be treated fairly, impartially and equitably. People also have the obligation to treat others fairly and justly. Everyone has the right to the necessities of life. Justice includes equal, unbiased treatment. Fairness tolerates diversity and accepts differences in people and their ideas. All employees have the right to fair treatment under work contracts, company policies and procedures, and the law.

6. Humaneness

This has two parts: Our actions ought to accomplish good; and we should avoid doing evil. We should do good to others and to ourselves. We should have concern for the well-being of others; usually, we show this concern in the form of compassion, kindness, serving and caring. We should act and speak in ways that benefit our valid self-interests and those of others. We must avoid actions that are evil.

7. The common good

Actions should accomplish the greatest good for the greatest number of people. One should act and speak in ways that benefit the welfare of the largest number of people, while trying to protect the rights of individuals.   —K.H.

It would be naive to think that all the differences and contradictions between our business and ethical systems can be overcome to the mutual satisfaction of all. Some differences will never be reconciled.

No country or its businesspeople should have to sell out to another. But Americans have not been sensitive and open enough to business and ethical systems other than our own. While different from yours and mine in many ways, the cultures and customs of other countries are not beyond a working spirit of what we both could call, in our own ways, cooperation and shared moral responsibility.

Understanding the Reasons for the Failure of U.S. Firms in Japan

Eduardo G. Camargo and Michitaka Saito. *Eduardo G. Camargo holds a Ph.D. in Marketing from Northwestern University and an MBA from Keio University, Tokyo. He has taught at the School of Business at the University of Southern California and is now Director of Strategy Development for RBS, Porto Alegre, Brazil. Michitaka Saito is an Associate Professor of Marketing at Keio University, Tokyo. At the time this article was written he was Visiting Associate Professor at the International Business Education and Research (IBEAR) Program, University of Southern California.*

Introduction

The purpose of this paper is to examine the reasons for the failure of U.S. firms in Japan from the point of view of the subjective experiences of executives involved in establishing and/or operating those enterprises. Alternative views on the reasons for failure emerge, but different definitions of failure make straightforward comparisons hard.

Reported here are interviews with both American and Japanese executives, in the United States and in Japan, as well as findings derived from the literature. Whenever possible, data on the respondent will be supplied, but often, to maintain candor, the source will not be mentioned. In most cases, the executive's position within the company's hierarchy, as well as the name of the company or industry it belongs to will be divulged.

In order to better assess the nature of the difficulties American companies in Japan face now, this research report will first examine the historical dimensions of foreign business interest in the Japanese market, as well as the different phases of Japanese economic development.

The Meaning of Failure

The understanding of U.S. company failure in Japan is complicated by the fact that the yardsticks used by the subsidiary or mother company tend to vary drastically. Also, headquarters and subsidiary personnel differ in defining an appropriate way to measure

The authors are thankful to the Japan International Trade and Investment Council for the funds made available for this research.

performance. As the American CEO of a Japanese subsidiary with annual sales of $40 million, manufacturing a steel-made industrial supply, said,

> My company's goal is 10 percent profit after tax. The Japanese tax rate is 55 percent, higher than in the States. It is easier to accomplish that kind of profit in the Unites States. Also, it seems that my headquarters don't understand that if you make that kind of money in Japan you are in trouble with your suppliers and customers, since they don't make that kind of money! Next time you go make a sale, they'll ask for a discount.

This executive said he would rather be measured by return on net assets. Showing lower profits to avoid client comparisons also affects the image of the hardships of doing business in Japan. An American investment banker in Tokyo said his company tries to shift profits back to U.S. headquarters every time a transaction is made within the company's New York and Tokyo offices:

> In the States the taxes are lower, and also we don't want to give the Japanese the impression we are making a lot of money here, since there is pressure for us to cut our commission. We have already changed our commission structure downward a few times and feel we can't keep going in that direction.

A manufacturer of office equipment with subsidiaries in over 15 countries and annual global sales of approximately $200 million decided that to compare the performance of its subsidiaries, it needed a common yardstick that could be used everywhere. The company chose subsidiary sales divided by subsidiary country GDP, a standard ratio that indicated its Japanese subsidiary was the worst performer. Clearly, this measure is problematic, since Japan has the world's second largest GDP. Some might say it is a good measure, since a large economic base should indicate the existence of a large market. But many other variables intervene. In the case of office equipment, it would be useful to control the GDP variable by a measure of average office size, for example. To managers familiar with Japan that would sound evident, but headquarters seemed more interested in finding a simple way of tracking performance in a comparative way than in paying attention to the specifics of each market.

Other companies use sales volume, a market share indicator, as the yardstick. If there is growth quarter after quarter on an annualized basis, the company is thought successful. But in Japan in the first years after start-up, a lot of time is devoted to developing business relationships, with the first sale occurring only—from the American viewpoint—after a long period of time. Sales growth may be a valid measure after several years, but not in the early stages. Even when the measure is appropriate, several executives said that success or failure must be concluded by comparison of the different competitors within the Japanese market instead of across the company's subsidiaries.

The final dimension of this problem is related to the depth of failure. In some cases failure occurs at the product-line level and in others at the company level. For example, overall IBM Japan is a success story, ranked by Japanese executives in a survey by *Shukan Daiamondo* as the 38th best company in Japan on the basis of all-around management ability. Nevertheless, its personal computer line has not done well, regardless of special efforts developed by the company in Japan, including IBM PC shops. In this case, a product line failure overshadows IBM's success in Japan and might be perceived as an example of foreign company failure in Japan.

Finally, failure often has no country-of-origin connotations. Failure is one outcome of any competitive environment and addresses an all-familiar concept in business: risk. Every year, at least 20,000 Japanese companies go bankrupt, besides those that close down. The Japanese business environment is fierce, and the measure of success and failure should be appropriate to the company's industry within Japan.

Foreign-Business Attitudes toward Japan and Japanese Economic Development

At the end of World War II Japan was a devastated country, and its rebuilding efforts started immediately. At that time, a window of opportunity was open to foreign enterprise, in that Japan needed support to acquire raw materials and products necessary for reconstruction. In this period, several companies were created, either by staff members of the Occupation forces or by other foreigners who had immigrated to Japan after the war. These enterprises became Japan's contact with the outside world. Due to the volume of business available, they had the opportunity to grow at a quick pace. Many of these companies are still successful today, having shifted their locus of interest as Japan moved from a position of importer of basic raw materials to importer of sophisticated consumer goods, such as caviar, and exporter of high-value-added products. These enterprises took advantage of Japan's need to obtain supplies.

At that time, many U.S. corporations preferred to concentrate their efforts in Western Europe for several reasons, including a stronger sense of affinity. Japan was not seen as a friend, and feelings of distrust dominated the facts about the potential of the Japanese market. The period up to the late 1950s was marked by lack of interest in and often intentional disregard of Japan. Companies that went to Japan in this period, such as Coca-Cola, had the opportunity to build their businesses from scratch, developing and implementing strategies as they saw fit. That early entry turned out to be an important tool, since competition was weakened and growth could be attained at a lower cost. The benefits of early entry are still being reaped; even today, Coca-Cola is the soft-drink market-share leader in Japan. Nevertheless, few companies attempted to penetrate the Japanese market at that point. Personal income could not justify high consumption of higher-priced consumer durables.

In the late 1950s and the 1960s, the Japanese government erected barriers of entry around strategic industries. A General Motors executive told us that although GM had been in Japan since before the war, "After the war we were told by the Japanese to leave." In order to enter the Japanese market, IBM was required to supply technology to fledgling Japanese computer companies.

The early 1960s saw the end of the reconstruction efforts. The domestic economy was operating fully, and the local market was starting to pick up, due to productivity gains and income distribution pressures (much as Korea has been doing in the past five years). Toward the late 1960s the Japanese economy was at full blast, with its major corporations anxious to enter foreign markets. At first, this effort was made through original equipment manufacturer (OEM) contracts, in which Japanese manufacturers supplied U.S. companies with products whose brands were owned by the client. Domestic competition was fierce but was mediated by an ever-growing demand.

It was in 1970 that the Osaka Expo launched Japan to the world, and the image of a technology-driven country was created. During this decade, tremendous growth occurred in the Japanese economy, with the first oil shock signaling that further opportunities would have to be searched for abroad. Foreign companies started to try to move into Japan in a more forceful manner, but without much success. These frustrated attempts were marked by the European Community report that referred to Japanese homes as "rabbit hutches," implying that there were plenty of opportunities in Japan for foreign businesses, as well as that the Japanese should pay more attention to their own market instead of trying to take over the world.

In the early 1980s, foreign frustration mounted, and both governments and companies produced lists of tariff and nontariff barriers created by Japan to keep foreign enterprise out. During this period, the Japan External Trade Organization created publications such as *Doing Business in Japan,* trying to teach foreigners the appropriate mores. The official view in Japan was that the market was not as closed as many thought; much of the issue was due to foreigners' inability to conduct business in a Japanese-like fashion.

Case stories were produced showing that there were many successful foreign companies in Japan. The Mainichi Shimbun published *Cracking the Japanese Market,* a set of 18 interviews with high-level executives of foreign-affiliated companies, including Proctor & Gamble, Warner-Lambert, Converse, Cross, Digital Equipment Co., Levi Strauss, Kentucky Fried Chicken, Wilson Sporting Goods, Continental Airlines, American Family Life Insurance, and the California Almond Growers Exchange, each with its own recipe on how to do well in the Japanese market. In this period, other American companies such as Sunkist, McDonald's, American Express, and Citibank were seen as successful enterprises. Work, Lord, and Bork Jr. (1987) published the success stories of Kodak, Goodyear, Brown-Forman (Jack Daniels), Texas Instruments, and Morgan Stanley. Not often mentioned but also operating in Japan were Nike, Visa, Wendy's, Victoria Station, Shakey's Pizza, Shaklee, Domino's Pizza, Arby's, Dunkin' Donuts, Winchell's, Tony Roma's, Upjohn, NCR, Mobil, and several others, some through licensing or franchising arrangements.

Several joint ventures also existed, among them Mitsubishi/Caterpillar, Fuji/Xerox, Hewlett-Packard/Yokogawa, Mitsubishi/Monsanto, and 7-Eleven/Ito-Yokado. Several medium-size American companies also existed, some with 100 percent foreign ownership, such as the General Binding Corp. Besides these operating enterprises there were cases of stock ownership, such as GM's participation in Suzuki and Ford's share of Mazda.

Nevertheless, frustration mounted during this period, and politicians exerted pressure on the Japanese government, since the U.S. trade deficit with Japan was growing year after year. The U.S. trade representative office was in permanent search of a "closed" market so that it could try to negotiate its opening. Tobacco, citrus fruit, beef, and rice were part of the battle at the agricultural end. At the high-tech end the fight was over telephone equipment, high-end hospital equipment, and supercomputers. In the service sector, the question was the construction and engineering market, including the battle over the construction of the new Kansai Airport in the Osaka area.

Some of these issues produced more results than others. In the tobacco case, foreign imports were allowed in higher volume at a lower price, and the channels of distribution were slowly allowed to carry those brands. At the same time, though, the Japanese government privatized the Tobacco and Salt Public Corp., creating the Japan Tobacco Corp., which developed strategies to enter the American cigarette market with its own Japanese brands. The same occurred in telephone equipment with the privatization of NTT (Nippon Telegraph & Telephone). The privatization strategy increased the flexibility of the companies, who were allowed not only to purchase or compete with foreign goods in Japan but also to compete or create associations with them abroad.

Most of these accomplishments may be explained by the fact that during the 1980s Japanese corporations wanted to further penetrate foreign markets, mostly consolidating their position in the United States and Europe. At the same time, the Japanese economy was fully developed, and the risks associated with the entry of world-class foreign competitors into Japan were relatively small. Diplomatically, it was to Japan's interest to open up so that friction with other countries would not shut out opportunities for Japanese multinationals. Retaliation and threats, including the 1988 Omnibus Trade and Competitiveness Act and its infamous Super 301, helped convey to Japan that opening up was the most acceptable policy.

Except for some agricultural and high-end high-tech products, the Japanese market became one of the most open in the world, with an express reduction of all tariff barriers. The agricultural products protection remained due to a strong alliance between the farmers and the ruling Liberal Democratic Party, which gets most of its votes from the countryside. On the high-tech front, protection existed to facilitate the development of world-class products in Japan by Japanese corporations.

The 1990s will probably see a further reduction in barriers, most of which will be nontariff in nature. U.S. companies' ability to enter and perform well in the Japanese market will depend more and more on their understanding of how Japan and the Japanese operate. The report will now turn to the major reasons for the failure of U.S. companies in Japan.

Reasons for the Failure of U.S. Firms in Japan

Considering the gradual opening of the Japanese market to foreign enterprise, and the concomitant reduction in trade barriers, the failure problem must be examined in a dynamic, multifaceted way. Over time, barriers seem to be changing in nature, and failure itself can be attributed to more than one source.

Most foreign failures in Japan can be related to two general sources: the company itself and the Japanese business environment. Usually both components operate simultaneously. Often, the complexity of failure is blurred by the biases and even hypocrisy of the parties involved, as well as by the press. The foreign companies that do well in Japan tend to be seen as paragons of management and strategic powerhouses. In contrast, when a foreign firm fails to enter or fails in the Japanese market, that failure is attributed to Japan-imposed barriers. Only now are a few enlightened U.S. executives starting to change their view on this issue. In the words of John Akers, chairman of IBM:

> Being successful in international markets has a lot more to do with fielding a strong team than it does with raising tariffs, restricting imports or imposing sanctions. . . . I'd wish we'd stop whining. (Jacobs 1989)

The understanding that the world market is not like the U.S. market, and that American executives deal with it as it is has been grasped by Western Digital Corp. president Roger Johnson:

> What we have here is a rapidly changing world economy that the United States has been very slow to respond to. What we need to do is recognize and preach and teach others that we are dealing in a world market. (Jacobs 1989)

Company-Driven Failure

Failures attributable to foreign corporations may be classified into before and after market entry. Before-market-entry failures are usually due to poor planning and a general lack of understanding of the Japanese business environment. After-market-entry failure is related to the inability to implement a strategy that sustains the organization. A detailed analysis of both types follows.

Before-Market-Entry Failure.   Five major issues are often mentioned by executives as crucial problems: inadequate planning, lack of market understanding, poor selection of executives, entry resistance, and poor association strategy.

Inadequate Planning.   Often the prevailing attitude of U.S. businessmen trying to enter the Japanese market is, "You don't change what's working." So they use assumptions that work well in the U.S. market. These executives believe they are good planners and good competitors and that harsh economic realities will wash away any cultural idiosyncrasies the Japanese might have. What escapes them is that the planning horizon in Japan is different; over there, a year is short term, and people often discuss 10-year business plans.

They also don't understand that Japan is the most competitive country in the world. You might not see that if you don't understand Japan, since competitive behavior is hidden by a veil of politeness. These American executives often believe in the power of money and think that with the right incentive they will get their way. Unfortunately, it is not often so. As a 12-year veteran in the shipping business said:

> We tried to do things in a different way. Instead of paying salaries and two bonuses a year to our Japanese staff, we decided to pay them a higher salary and no bonus. We were under the U.S. wisdom that we were helping them, since they would have more money earlier. Unfortunately it didn't work. They wanted to be paid like other Japanese employees are. The problem was compounded by the fact that we had to face the issue of cutting their salaries once we added bonuses. That didn't help morale, either.

Another executive, from the already mentioned manufacturer of industrial supplies, said that expectations of U.S. managers often don't work in Japan because Japanese employees behave in a way not easily understood:

Japanese employees are risk averse. They deliver what they promise, but they are too careful on what they promise. They believe that if something under their responsibility doesn't work they'll have to leave the company. I tell them, "No, responsibility is to learn from your mistakes and do better the next time."

The solution to this problem is to spend more time and effort in the planning stage, which will reduce aggravation and cost in the long term. Also, being open and curious about a different culture is crucial to creating a realistic plan. As Masami Atarashi (1989), president of Johnson & Johnson K. K., said,

Historically, American business executives have tended to have a very limited knowledge of Japan, its culture, people, business practices, and idiosyncrasies. This traces back to the fact that, until a few years ago, the United States represented as much as one-third or more of global GNP and could afford to be economically self-sufficient—and self-centered, too.

Lack of Market Understanding.   Often Americans believe that our product is great and everyone will readily accept it. The reality, though, is that American companies are distant from the Japanese market. A manufacturer of office equipment found that its successful line of products was seen in Japan as too big, heavy, cumbersome, and hard to operate. Japanese users wondered why the equipment was mechanical instead of electronic and why the manufacturer didn't bother thinking about the size of the average Japanese office. Users tended to stack piles of paper and folders over the machine in order to gain space, which precluded the equipment being used often, drastically reducing the after-market for supplies.

We also tend to think our product will be sold for the same price in Japan as in the United States, overlooking the fact that cost structure in Japan is different, due to both long channels of distribution and high rental costs. As the president of Johnson & Johnson K. K. exemplifies,

Sixty-five percent of all Johnson & Johnson products in terms of their yen value go to primary wholesalers, then retailers, and then consumers. Twenty-five percent go to primary wholesalers, secondary wholesalers, retailers, and then consumers. Ten percent go to primary wholesalers, secondary wholesalers, tertiary wholesalers, retailers, and then consumers. (Atarashi 1989)

Pre-entry market research would bring out the major aspects of the product that require adaptation to local needs.

Poor Executive Selection.   The quality of the relationship between headquarters and the Japanese subsidiary will determine the success of the operation, so executive selection both at home and abroad is crucial. First is the choice of the executive who will be in charge of the home-office position that will be directly responsible for the subsidiary's performance.

For the executive who will head the subsidiary, some experts recommend an American, while others recommend a Japanese. Historically, the person sent from headquarters to manage the Japanese operation is not the best prepared. Often, the choice is seen not as a reward but as a way of getting rid of somebody. Many firms that decide to hire a local Japanese executive end up in trouble because they never socialize him or her in the ways of headquarters. This reduces the executive's ability to work out compromises within the company that might have a positive impact in the Japanese market. The Japanese executive heading the subsidiary spends more time negotiating with his own headquarters than with clients.

The executive in charge at headquarters, usually a vice president for international operations, needs to be well versed in both headquarters networking and subsidiary sensitivity. In the case of Japan, where employees tend to remain with the same employer for many years or even their whole working life, the subsidiary CEO, if Japanese, tends to have longer tenure than his counterpart in the United States. This creates a whole set of unexpected problems, in the words of a U.S.-educated Japanese CEO of an American subsidiary in Tokyo:

> I have been in this company for 12 years, and in this period, I've had four different bosses. A new VP comes on board at headquarters; it takes him a year to develop an international plan; during the second year I receive the plan and prepare my team to implement it, which happens in the third year; in the fourth year, the VP either leaves or is let go, a new VP comes in, and the cycle starts all over again. In these 12 years we have done four cycles. You can imagine what this lack of stability and continuity does to employee morale in Japan. . . . we just can't be responsible for results that way.

The same problem is shared by the president of Johnson & Johnson K. K.:

> I know of an American consumer products company . . . that in the course of six years changed its president five times, all in reflection of its short-term picture. I know of another American consumer products firm that changed its president eight times in 15 years. The introduction of new blood is one thing, but too big an infusion can be a big mistake. (Atarashi 1989)

The issue here is to have an executive in Tokyo who is able to interface successfully with both headquarters and his local Japanese staff. The executive's nationality is much less important than an ability to speak both English and Japanese and exert influence at headquarters and subsidiary alike.

Entry Resistance.   A reluctance to invest in Japan mostly occurred in the first 20 years after World War II, the period when Japan's competitive environment was more vulnerable to strong foreign competitors. A prior executive at Carnation Co. told us that:

> Until the old man, the company founder, died, we had not gone to Japan. He had told us we could invest anywhere we wanted, but in Japan. With his death, his son took over, and changed that policy. By the time we got there was a bit too late. We tried to develop a relationship with Morinaga, and introduced a line of ice creams, but it never did well. We ended up scrapping that deal.

The problem here is war-related sentiment, and the solution usually lies in letting young executives take charge, since their perceptions of Japan are different.

Poor Association Strategy.   The final cause of before-market-entry failure is U.S. companies that decide to go the joint venture route unintentionally selecting an incompatible partner to operate in the Japanese market. Often the goals and long-term strategies of the two companies are different. For several years, General Foods tried to establish itself in Japan, but developing channels of distribution proved to be difficult—something Nestlé was better at. GF then decided to form a joint venture with Ajinomoto, the giant food company that early in the century invented monosodium glutamate (MSG). Thus AGF was formed. Things went well for a while, but then General Foods sold its share of AGF to Ajinomoto. Today it just licenses several brands, including Maxwell House instant coffee, to Ajinomoto. What started as a joint venture ended as a licensing arrangement.

The solution to this problem is to select a partner not only in terms of how it can contribute to the relationship today and in the future, but also based on the U.S. firm's long-term ability to maintain that relationship: Will it possess things the Japanese partner will want over the long term? Are there other projects the companies could work on together for mutual benefit? Is the Japanese partner much larger or does it possess something crucial for survival? Do I have anything as important to it to give in exchange?

Another issue here is the use of general trading companies as distributors or sole agents for Japan. This relates to the relative size of the market for the U.S. firm in Japan and the relative importance of its product line to the distributor. Often, the trading company discovers that the size of the business opportunity is relatively meager and doesn't allocate much talent to it. As a result, the American company's products end up with a minuscule market share.

After-Market-Entry Failure.   Once the subsidiary has been established in Japan, a new set of problems needs to be dealt with. These involve the company's ability to implement its strategy and the three Cs of survival in Japan: contribution, commitment, and compromise.

Poor Implementation of Strategy.   Often a sound and tested strategy, when implemented in a different environment, does not produce the expected results. Warner-Lambert markets its Schick razors in Japan through H. Hattori & Co., the owners/distributors of Seiko watches. This alternative channel of distribution has been so successful that Schick now has 70 percent of the safety razor market in Japan, with annual sales of $65 million. (Ginsberg 1984) Nevertheless, when it tried to introduce its Trident, Chiclets, Bubblicious, and other chewing gum to the Japanese, the strategy didn't work. The company decided to bypass its wholesalers because they had not been pushing the retailers hard enough. Once again, it didn't work. Labich (1986) offers an explanation:

> The change not only upset wholesalers but also created suspicion among retailers . . . Sales finally took off when Warner-Lambert came up with a Solomonic solution: its own salesmen solicit orders from retailers and then pass them back to the wholesalers. The company now has 17 percent of the Japanese gum market.

The same happened to Avon when it entered Japan in 1969. It tried to implement its U.S. sales strategy in Japan but learned that Japanese women feel uncomfortable knocking on the doors of strangers. The strategy was changed to women selling to their acquaintances, and 1975 sales reached approximately $175 million.

Often strategy is not as well defined in Japanese corporations as in the United States. Often strategies are not written; if they are, they are fuzzy compared to the American companies' documents. Very important in Japanese strategy is the constant, relentless effort of the sales force. Japanese sales reps often visit their clients daily and prospects maybe once a week. That behavior is maintained over time, and when a sales rep is promoted, he personally introduces his replacement to the client. The sales position is one of the first taken by fresh college graduates after their training period, and the best among them are selected to interface with clients. Since U.S. firms are not used to this type of sales approach and (as we will examine later) are unable to attract the best graduates, it becomes almost impossible to emulate the Japanese strategy.

Weak Contribution. One of the most important rules of the Japanese market (which many U. S. companies don't follow) is the need to make a strong contribution in terms of product, process, or distribution. Due to the highly competitive nature of the Japanese market, it is hard to do well with a me-too solution. IBM took new technology to Japan, Coca-Cola took a new business system in which independent bottlers would distribute the product, and McDonald's introduced a new way of producing quality hamburgers at a fast pace. Even Domino's Pizza, through its Japanese licensee, has combined a traditional Japanese food delivery system with a Western product.

It is important to develop a distinctive approach, even at the brand image level. At a second stage, the company must offer constant innovations, since competition will erase that innovative edge very soon. Denny's family restaurant chain entered the Japanese market through a licensing arrangement with Ito-Yokado. It has over 100 units in Japan, and it did extremely well initially. In an interview with Ginsberg (1984), Barry Krantz, Denny's marketing vice president, acknowledged that:

> For the first five years we were there, we saw uninterrupted and substantial growth. All of a sudden, there's competition. . . . Right now, one of them has a stronger menu, and the other has us beat on pricing.

Lack of Commitment. Another common problem faced by American companies in Japan is the difficulty of reassuring potential Japanese clients, suppliers, and employees that they are making a long-term commitment. It often escapes foreigners that Japan is a centuries-old society that already had a long business history by the time Christopher Columbus landed in America. This tradition, associated with the development and maintenance of personal relationships, handicaps foreign newcomers. The only way to countervail the status quo is by signaling commitment.

Commitment requires both time and money, although the former can be bought with the latter. That is even easier if the company has an established image back in the United States that the Japanese are familiar with. The issue of commitment affects foreign companies in every respect, even hiring. Normally, the best educated Japanese (those attending top private or national universities) prefer to join the top Japanese corporations. Some who have been exposed to the world early or have stronger individualistic personalities might consider joining a well-known foreign corporation. But most perceive a lack of long-term opportunity in foreign corporations. Most Japanese college graduates believe they will never be transferred to U.S. headquarters, so they can never become highly successful. Large organizations such as IBM Japan do not face this kind of problem, since they can provide ample growth opportunities. IBM Japan has signaled that it will provide such opportunities by appointing a Japanese president of the company. Japan's policy of almost zero unemployment makes it hard for foreign companies without a strong reputation to attract quality Japanese workers.

Potential clients will avoid disrupting old relationships that may go back a couple of generations. This is the toughest nut to crack, persuading potential clients to switch suppliers or even to put that relationship in jeopardy by switching part of an order to a new supplier. The same would happen if you wanted to manufacture in Japan and one of your local suppliers had a standing order with another client. In other words, what is necessary here is to "conquer your spot under the sun." This problem is so widespread it applies to foreign companies already established in Japan. Work, Lord and Bork Jr. (1987) make the point:

> The problem is that Eastman Kodak, in Japan for 90 years, had never committed itself to the Japanese market. The company had no direct marketing, no local manufacturing base and no resident manager. Its Tokyo staff of 25 relied instead on a complex system of local distributors. Visits from top executives in Rochester were rare.

Kodak decided to change that. In August 1984 it sent to Japan its director of planning, who quickly understood the need to convey that the company was in Japan to stay. Within a year (and with cash), Kodak bought out its 60-year distributor, bought 9.5 percent of a camera manufacturer in order to start production of its 35mm cameras, developed a joint venture with a local film-processing company, and built a four-story R&D facility. The staff was boosted to 140, a fivefold increase, and moved to offices with higher visibility. In 1987 Kodak hired 17 graduates from Japan's top engineering schools, who were offered long-term employment and stock options. With this strategy, Kodak increased market share by half in three years, from 10 percent to 15 percent.

The same kind of commitment test has been applied to U.S. firms, such as Brown-Forman and Goodyear, who were quick to understand the challenge. As Peter Rutledge, chairman of Brown-Forman International, says:

> You don't develop anything in Japan on a fast-turn basis. You nurture it and let it develop. (Work, Lord, and Bork Jr. 1987)

Goodyear, too, needed two full years in Japan before making its first sale.

A company can show commitment by transferring authority to the Japanese subsidiary, letting it make the decisions it believes are the best for the Japanese market, and giving it full budgetary support for a relatively longer period of time. A common way to show commitment is by renting prime office space. Due to the high cost involved and cash deposits required, potential employees, customers, and suppliers alike will perceive the company as a long-term player.

Inability to Compromise.   Often foreign companies in Japan don't understand the concept of not breaking your neighbor's rice bowl. Although competition in Japan is fierce, there is a sense of kinship among members of the same industry. This requires the company to belong to its industry trade association and to fulfill its obligations as agreed by the association members. The same is true for company-level and trade association-level relationships with the Japanese government in situations of consultation and guidance.

American companies in Japan often perceive some of these arrangements as collusive in nature, contradicting acceptable principles of business behavior and even U.S. legislation. But the required behavior in Japan includes being a good citizen, which means performing those activities. Some of them may merely fall into the gray area, such as Texas Instruments' consultation with the Ministry of International Trade and Industry (MITI) on semiconductor production targets.

Other practices, though, might be seen by Americans as downright unethical. Examples are the traditional kickbacks in the food industry to restaurant chefs (split with the staff) and agreement among large construction companies on which would win the next government project bidding. In fact, it is said that a well-known American institution in Tokyo found out its chef was receiving cash back from its food suppliers. When the institution fired the chef, nobody showed up for work the next day—cooks and waiters alike.

Some practices deemed unacceptable by Americans are common, group-sanctioned activities in other environments. A judgment call is required, and it becomes an ethical issue. The American company must either adapt to the local practice or conduct no business in Japan, because in the short term it would be impossible to change such an established practice. The point is that American inability to compromise with Japanese expectations can jeopardize business.

Environment-Driven Failure

Also contributing to the failure of U.S. firms in Japan is the environment in which business is done. Contextual barriers may be classified as visible or invisible.

Visible Barriers.   These barriers are imposed by the Japanese government to preclude the entry or successful expansion of foreign companies. They fall into three general categories: tariffs, quotas, and licenses.

Some industries, such as agriculture and mining, are still plagued by these barriers, since strong interest groups within Japan don't want a change in their status quo. On the other hand, many other countries also protect these kinds of economic activity.

Tariffs.   Duties used to be relatively high, but Japan has drastically reduced tariffs to levels in many cases lower than both the United States and Europe's. Overall, tariffs are not a major impediment to trade now, and the general belief is that they will come down even further. For example, Kodak's tariff for photographic paper and film is only 3.7 percent.

Quotas.   This type of visible barrier has also been lifted or reduced in most industries in the past five years. The U.S. trade representative office has of lately selected three areas in which it believes Japan is not a fair trader: forestry products, supercomputers, and satellites. Some other industries may face quotas designed to protect threatened Japanese industries, but the tendency is to reduce them at least to U.S. levels—although that might take some time.

Licenses and Certification.   This is the most fascinating of the visible barriers since very often it catches U.S. businesses by surprise. By some accounts, in order to open a business one may need to get 39 different licenses. As Jack Whitehouse, president of International Public Relations Co., said,

> It is very difficult for an American firm to succeed without acceptance of a bureaucrat there. . . . They need someone who can help them with the certifications, licensing and the maze of government control. (Jacobs 1989)

Often, domestic licensing also strongly affects U.S. business in Japan. For several years during the early 1980s, pressure mounted for the Japanese to allow a higher volume of foreign cigarettes into Japan and reduce taxes on them. Quotas were increased several-fold, and over a number of years, the price of foreign cigarettes moved down steadily. The interesting issue, though, is that the goal of the lobbying effort had been to obtain a higher quota. Once U.S. cigarettes started pouring into Japan, industry executives found out that their distribution had been limited to only 10 percent of the retail outlets; import volume would not make much of a difference if you couldn't distribute the product in a massive way. The trick was that tobacco shops needed a government license to sell foreign tobacco products, and only a minority of shops had been able to get one. Clearly, the next lobbying step was to increase the number of licenses or abolish the system, but time is a crucial strategic issue.

In the area of certification, similar problems have occurred. An executive who owns a Tokyo trading company told us he wanted to import automobile paint for the aftermarket. He found out the paint needed to be tested for conformity to Japanese standards. The procedure took approximately 60 days, and certification was granted. He proceeded to import the first shipment, but customs authorities denied entry. The executive produced the certification papers but was told that those were valid only for the color that had been tested; he needed to get the same certificate for each color of paint he was going to import. Through long-established connections he was finally able to get certification for all colors without having to duplicate the test.

American businesses must devote a great deal of time to acquiring information on all issues that might affect product delivery to the final customer, since the process has built-in snags. The same rules are valid for Japanese businesspeople, whose sole advantage is familiarity with the system.

Invisible Barriers.   These barriers are encountered by foreign businesspeople in areas that are not directly related to government regulation but affect the final outcome. These barriers tend to affect the superstructure of the business system instead of each individual company or industry. They include the Keiretsu structure, Tsusansho and Keidanren, differences in negotiation styles and goals, and incompatible economic structures.

Keiretsu Structure.   Japanese business groupings used to be very tight power structures in the prewar days, when they were referred to as *zaibatsu.* These have been abolished, but new, supposedly loose groups were formed after the war, most of which maintained their former identity and companies. These new groups, called *keiretsu,* are seen by foreign businesspeople as tight cliques whose goal is to help their member companies.

Keiretsus compete with each other, but many perceive preferential treatment vis-à-vis outside companies. The U.S. Treasury structural impediments initiative, appended to the Super 301 report, calls for discussions with the Japanese on the keiretsu, in which "... families of manufacturers and suppliers ... make it difficult for outsiders offering cheaper and better products to get a foot in the door" (*The Economist* 1989). An American executive in a keiretsu-controlled shipping company told us,

> There is no special treatment. The difference is that it is easier to be introduced to people. We need a ship sitting at the harbor at the right time. If so, with the right price, we will get the cargo. Otherwise, the cargo goes to a competitor.

Japan may need to make explicit efforts to avoid showing preferential treatment. Often, both companies belong to the same keiretsu and have been doing business for many years; it may be hard for a newcomer to break that relationship simply because the Japanese are reluctant to jeopardize established relations.

Tsusansho/Keidanren.

This relationship has probably contributed most to the term "Japan, Inc.," conveying the Japanese-style collaboration between business and government. Robert Galvin, the chairman of Motorola, in an interview to Heiman (1982), said,

> If Japan is permitted to continue to protect them [Japanese companies] against foreign competition, "they will appear superior—they will be stronger because of the collective effort of their country's society."

The Keidanren is the Federation of Economic Organizations, a trade association that encompasses approximately the 300 largest Japanese corporations, while Tsusansho is the Japanese word for MITI which is in charge of coining most of Japan's industrial policy and giving administrative guidance to troubled companies and industries, as well as to companies that embark on specially selected priority projects, including coordination with the Industrial Bank of Japan (and consequently with the Ministry of Finance). The Keidanren perceives its role as protecting the interests of Japanese big business.

Some believe that the relationship between Keidanren and MITI is too cozy, the cost being the exclusion of foreign businesses as well as smaller or new Japanese companies from the decision-making process. In fact, MITI's choice of future growth industries, the ones that will receive government funds for development, has been strongly affected by the Keidanren's interests.

Back in 1964, when it arrived in Japan, Texas Instruments planned to build a semiconductor plant. Work, Lord, and Bork Jr. (1987) write,

> TI came up against a Japanese government even more sensitive about foreign competition and investment in Japan than it is today. TI's proposed 100% ownership of the factory was rejected. Instead, ... [MITI] wanted to force TI into a joint-venture with Sony, a domestic company that would have majority control. Despite its objections, TI eventually acquiesced but only after the conflict had escalated.

Today, the same result might be reached in a somewhat different fashion, since it is reported that MITI's influence has diminished recently due to the lessened financial dependence felt by Japanese corporations. Nevertheless, in specific areas pinpointed for strategic development, MITI will probably exert influence to protect the interests of domestic industry.

Differences in Negotiation Styles and Goals.   This aspect affects business in a serious way, but its advantage is that it is somewhat under the control of businesspeople, since many of the behaviors can be mastered. The most difficult element is to conciliate one's own headquarters' interests with the Japanese way of doing things.

Part of the difference can be explained at the personality and sociological levels; the Japanese tending to be more introverted and group oriented, while the Americans tend towards extroversion and individualism. Also, Japanese come from a vertical, strongly hierarchical society, while Americans grow up in an environment that reinforces egalitarian values. These differences are confronted in buyer–seller relationships. The Japanese believe the buyer is hierarchically above the seller, while Americans tend to believe they are more side by side. A Japanese buyer expects the seller to defer completely to his demands, which Americans feel is unfair. This attitude frustrates Japanese buyers who tend to go back to their Japanese supplier. The problem is compounded by the fact that American buyers don't know how to behave like Japanese buyers often and end up getting a worse deal.

Other relevant differences in business-to-business negotiations are that Americans try to make a deal, while the Japanese try to establish a relationship. Americans feel the need to accomplish results in the short term, while the Japanese are long-term oriented. As Hugh Hamilton (1987) said,

> Foreign companies that want to succeed in Japan must be patient, persistent, flexible, and willing to invest time and effort.

Also, in a business relationship Americans tend to spend a lot of time in persuasion, as if convincing the other party that one has a good product would make him or her buy it. The Japanese prefer to spend most of their time exchanging product-relevant information.

These differences tend to increase stress and frustration, causing the negotiating parties to search for people who are more like themselves to negotiate with. By definition, this reduces the business opportunities available to American companies.

Incompatible Economic Structures.   The final contextual problem refers to the capabilities of the U.S. and Japanese economies to supply each other with goods and services needed by both. Although the balance of trade is highly favorable to Japan, at the rate of at least $10 billion per quarter for the past several years, no solution seems to exist. It has been argued that even if Japan extinguished all its visible and invisible barriers to trade, the trade deficit would shrink by one-third at most. It has also been said that if import restrictions on the items covered by the Super 301—supercomputers, satellites, and forestry products—were lifted, the trade gap would be reduced by merely $2 billion a year.

The only innovative solution was presented by Japan several years ago. It wanted to import oil from Alaska, since it would carry lower transportation charges than Arab oil does. The idea was met with disapproval by the United States, which wants to keep high oil reserves on national security grounds.

The economic structures of the two countries do not complement each other. Today the United States does not have raw materials, products, technologies, or services that could be sold to Japan at a high enough volume to compensate for Japan's exports to the United States. In other words, one reason for the failure of U.S. firms in Japan is that our economy (reflected in the collective of U.S. firms) doesn't have anything to offer the Japanese market that would serve as counterpart for its exports to us.

Conclusion

This paper has discussed the major reasons for failure of U.S. firms in Japan up to now. We covered both firm-related and environment-related causes for failure and believe that most failures are due to both sources.

It seems to us that both countries need to learn more about each other. Often, though, we end up teaching each other the wrong things, due to short-term political interests, hypocritical economic behavior, or sensationalism by the press.

It is clear that both societies think in different ways about their futures and what they want to accomplish. Nevertheless, our peoples and economies are more intertwined as times goes by, and it would be to mutual benefit if issues were handled with candor and openness.

It is our hope that this report has conveyed the major problems U.S. firms face in the Japanese market, from the perspective of their own experiences. Our goal was not to support or deny issues, but to try to cover the whole spectrum in the hope that the report will serve as a mechanism to reduce conflict between Japan and the United States. If U.S. firms use this report to help them better understand Japan before they try to penetrate that market, we believe fewer complaints about unfairness will be made in the future.

Japan has for the past several years been moving in the direction of an open society, and it will continue to move in that direction in the years to come. This is corroborated by a report from the U.S. Department of Commerce (1987) that said that "the market has never been more open to foreign goods, services and investment that it is today." Some protectionism may remain in some sensitive areas—those selected for Japan to become a world leader within 20 years or so—because of national priority, national security, or pride.

Overall, though, we expect an open market with low tariffs and quotas, as well as opportunities for foreign business expansion. If Americans do their homework, they will be able to succeed in Japan through their own efforts and be less dependent on joint ventures. This will give them more control over their operations, and enable them to move along the experience curve required to understand their Japanese competitors. Then they will be able to compete successfully with Japanese companies in the emerging global market.

References

Atarashi, Masami (1989), "Curing the Ills of the Overseas Subsidiary," *PHP Intersect,* January, 10–16.

Economist (1989), "Dialogue of the Deaf," June 10, 64–65.

Ginsberg, Stanley (1981), "Beating the Japanese in Japan," *Forbes,* April 27, 44–46.

Hamilton, Hugh A. (1987), "Marketing to the Japanese," *East Asian Executive Reports,* March, 19–20.

Heiman, Grover (1982), "Competing with the Japanese," *Nation's Business,* November, 46–48.

Jacobs, Chip (1989), "Stop Your Bellyaching and Start Selling to the Japanese," *Los Angeles Business Journal,* August 7, 35–40.

Japan External Trade Organization (1982), "Doing Business in Japan," JETRO Marketing Series 8, Tokyo: JETRO.

Labich, Kenneth (1986), "America's International Winners," *Fortune,* April 14, 34–45.

Mainichi Shimbun (1985), "Cracking the Japanese Market: The Experience of 18 Foreign Companies in Japan," Tokyo: Mainichi Newspapers.

Shukan Daiamondo (1983), "Leading Industries, Principal Executives Rated," August 13, in Japanese.

U.S. Department of Commerce (1987), "Marketing to Japan," *East Asian Executive Reports,* April, 12–16.

Work, Clemens P., Mary Lord, and Robert H. Bork, Jr. (1987), "How to Beat the Japanese," *U.S. News & World Report,* August 24, 38–44.

Buyer/Seller Relationships in Japan and Germany: An Interaction Approach

N. C. G. CAMPBELL. *Manchester Business School.*

Introduction

Germany and Japan are two countries with enviable records of success in economic growth and new technology. Firms from both countries have penetrated foreign markets, often with harsh consequences for the local companies. How do they achieve this success?

This article looks at the development and handling of relationships between suppliers and customers in both countries. Buyer/seller relationships are at the "heart" of the marketing and purchasing of industrial goods [1] and can be studied using the interaction approach, developed by the IMP* group [2]. This approach provides a framework for analysing buyer/seller relationships and thus for comparing the differences between Germany and Japan.

Such comparative marketing studies "can make an important contribution to the development of a theory of marketing systems" [3]. They can provide a stimulus for examining the universality or specificity of various marketing concepts, under different types and ranges of environmental factors and settings. They can help to refine or develop marketing concepts, and improve the methodologies used for comparison.

The interaction approach used by the IMP group and the results of their research were presented in Hakansson [2]. The project involved research with 300 companies in Sweden, France, Italy and the UK. The IMP researchers placed great emphasis on comparative analysis of how suppliers and customers in various product technologies and end-use industries handled their relationships in domestic and foreign markets. In addition, the researchers collected and analysed information from marketing and purchasing executives about their attitudes to buyers and suppliers in different countries [4]. This established the important influence on buyer/seller relationships of cultural differences.

*The International Marketing and Purchasing (IMP) Group comprised—France: Jean Paul Valla and Michel Perrin; Germany: Michael Kitschker; Italy: Ivan Snehota; Sweden: Jan Johanson; UK: Malcolm Cunningham, Peter Turnbull, David Ford, Elling Homse.

Reprinted with permission of MCP University Press from The *European Journal of Marketing,* Vol. 19, No. 2, © 1983 MCP University Press.

In contrast to the IMP research, which covered a wide variety of dissimilar industries, the results reported here are part of an ongoing study of trading relationships in the packaging industry. Only by restricting the study to one industry was it felt that comparisons could be made. The research started as a broad study of buyer/seller relationships in the German carton industry conducted with considerable help from Europak, a leading packaging supplier [5]. Part of the way through this study an opportunity arose to carry out interviews in the Japanese carton industry.

Since time was available only for a limited number of interviews they were concentrated in comparable market segments. Detergent cartons was one such market segment. A good knowledge of the relationships in this segment had been gained in Germany from interviews with the three leading customers (accounting for over 80 per cent of sales) and with Europak, one of the leading suppliers. In Japan, two of the three leading customers were interviewed (accounting for 44 per cent of sales) as well as the two leading suppliers (accounting for 47 per cent of purchases). In total, including detergent cartons, this study draws on eight interviews in Japan and 17 in Germany covering other consumer goods such as frozen foods, ice cream, sweets, biscuits, soap and petfoods. In both countries, the interviews represent a purposive rather than a random or representative sample. In most cases, the respondent was the senior marketing or purchasing executive with a knowledge of the relationships. The interviews were guided by a semi-structured questionnaire and the focus was buyer/seller relationships and an understanding of the purchasing and marketing strategies being employed. In addition to the field interviews, desk research took place and meetings were held with trade associations to establish the industry backgrounds.

In view of the limited scope this research is necessarily exploratory and descriptive rather than rigorously analytical. The article is divided into several sections. First, a brief explanation of the interaction approach is presented. The results of the research are then discussed with respect to the four groups of variables defined by the approach environment, interaction parties, the interaction process and the interaction atmosphere. Thereafter, the similarities and differences between the approach to handling relationships in Germany and Japan are summarised and their implications discussed.

Interaction Approach

The interaction approach developed by the IMP group is consistent with a number of observations which empirical studies indicate are important in industrial markets. Among the most important observations are, firstly, that both buyer and seller are active participants in the market. Each may engage in a search to find a suitable buyer or seller, each may prepare specifications of requirements or offerings, and each may attempt to manipulate or control the interaction process. Secondly, the relationship between buyer and seller is frequently long-term, close and involves a complex pattern of interaction. In addition to these and other empirical insights, the IMP group draws on prior theoretical work in the field of inter-organisation theory and on developments in microeconomic theory associated with the markets and hierarchies approach [6].

The interaction model, Figure 1, which is the outcome of these theoretical and empirical contributions, contains four groups of variables:

FIGURE 1

The Interaction Model

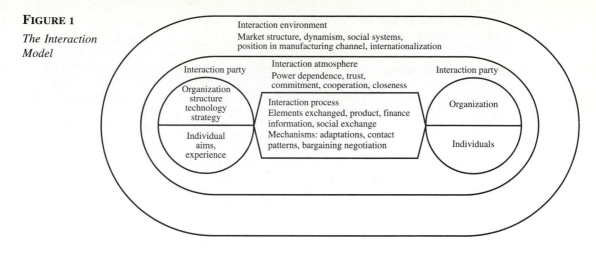

- Variables describing the environment within which the interaction takes place.
- Variables describing the parties involved, both as organisations and as individuals.
- Variables describing the elements and processes of interaction.
- Variables describing the atmosphere affecting and affected by the interaction.

To compare buyer/seller relationships in Japan and Germany, we look at the differences between these four groups of variables.

Comparing the Interaction Environments

The interaction between a buying and selling company cannot be analysed in isolation. It is subject to social, economic and political factors in the environment. In the comparison between Germany and Japan, three important features of the environment are explored—the structure of the markets, including differences in concentration, market shares and the extent of vertical integration; the "dynamism" of the markets; and the social systems in each country. The IMP group included two other facets of the environment—internationalisation, and position in the manufacturing channel. As regards position in the manufacturing channel there is clearly no difference since the same industry is being studied in each country. As regards internationalisation, while it is greater in Germany, the trade which crosses national frontiers is less than 10 per cent. For this reason it is not discussed further.

The framework, or descriptive model, in Figure 1 does not explicitly distinguish between the environment of the buyer and the seller. However, in this article we follow Homse [7] and compare the environment of packaging suppliers separately from the environment of the packaging customers (see Table 1).

The general picture emerging from Table 1 is that the environments are similar, although the Japanese industry is somewhat more fragmented and Japanese customers

TABLE 1   Interaction Environment:
Differences between Germany and Japan

Interaction Variables	Packaging Suppliers	Packaging Customers
Market Structure	Both industries are fragmented with the number of suppliers exceeding 1,000. In both countries the two leading companies have about 23 percent of the market. The rest of the industry is more fragmented in Japan (the top six suppliers have only 33.8 percent compared to 51.5 percent in Germany). Backward integration is slight in both countries.	Customers in both countries are very diverse. Backward integration is much more important in Germany than in Japan.
Dynamism	Both industries are experiencing low or negative growth. But Japanese industry is more dynamic. It is younger, more receptive to new systems, more active in modernising its production facilities and very competitive.	Comparisons are difficult because of the great variety of end-use markets. Probably dynamism is similar.
Social System	Relevant differences are the Japanese dislike of newcomers, tribal loyalties, and preference for close relationships.	Relevant differences are the Japanese dislike of newcomers, tribal loyalties, and preference for close relationships.

TABLE 2   Buying and Selling of Packaging for Detergents:
Market Structure Differences

	Japan	Germany
Customers		
Number of customers	7	5
Market share of top three (%)	80	90
Herfindahl Index	26	32
Suppliers		
Number of suppliers	5	10
Market share of top three (%)	69	77
Herfindahl Index	27	27

are less likely to have integrated backwards. For the detergent carton market Table 2 indicates very similar market structures.

A more detailed look at the "network" of trading relationships for the detergent carton market leads to the data in Table 3.

TABLE 3 Buying and Selling of Packaging for a Household Product: Customers' Spread of Purchases among Suppliers

	Customers	*S1*	*S2*	*S3*	*S4*	*S5*	*S6 & 7*
Japan	C1	—	50	—	50	—	
	C2	80	—	—	—	20	
	C3	30	30	40	—	—	
Germany	C1	In-house supplier					
	C2	—	—	15	25	40	20
	C3	80	20	—	—	—	—

Table 3 compares the way the top three customers in Germany and Japan have spread their purchases. The customers are represented by the symbols C1, C2 and C3. C1 has the highest market share, C2 the next highest and so on. In Germany, the leading company C1, which has 40 per cent of the market, used its own in-house supplier. In Japan, the leading company has 35 per cent of the market, but splits its business evenly between two suppliers S2 and S4. Despite the even split this company dominates the relationships with these two suppliers, requiring them to provide detailed cost data and insisting that they both supply at the same price.

The second supplier in Germany, C2, belongs to the same multinational group as C3 in the Japanese market. The parent company adopts a competitive approach to purchasing in all its world-wide operation. Thus, in both Germany and Japan this company spreads its purchases more widely than its main competitors. Finally, C3 in Germany and C2 in Japan follow similar strategies with their business split between two suppliers on an 80/20 basis.

Table 3 also illustrates a tendency in both markets towards "pairing." In Germany, each customer has its own suppliers and they do not trespass on each other's territories. This type of "network" structure provides some empirical evidence for Arndt's [8] concept of "domesticated" markets.

Dynamism in a market arises from the rate of technical change, the growth potential, and the intensity of competition. Clearly it is not possible to discuss the dynamism of all the different customer markets. Attention is, therefore, focused on the characteristics of the two supplier industries.

Both supplier industries are facing difficult trading conditions. In Japan, a decline in the consumption of paper-based packaging is predicted; in Germany, growth is likely to be zero or negative. Cost pressures and competition from other packaging materials are causing this decline. Japanese consumers buy larger quantities of specially packed items during the gift-giving seasons. In addition, the Japanese climate makes important demands on the packaging industry. In the winter, it is very cold and dry, while the summer is hot and humid. Thus, the requirements of consumers and climate make for exacting technical standards. In addition, the Japanese industry is active is bringing in new technology. (Mitsubishi has set up a special company just to import packaging technology.) Finally, in both the supplier and customer industries there is fierce competition between the leading companies. The two leading suppliers in Japan are like two tribes competing for the same territory. Rivalry and competition is intense which leads to aggressive modernisation of facilities. Rivalry also exists between the leading companies in Germany, but it is more muted; personal contacts exist between the industry leaders, and the trade association seeks to protect the larger companies from inroads by non-members.

Thus, although the growth rates are similar, the greater activity in technical development in Japan and the greater intensity of competition put Japanese packaging suppliers in a more dynamic environment than those in Germany.

A comprehensive discussion of differences in social systems is well beyond the scope of this article. Valuable insights into differences between East Asian and Western cultures are found in Hofheinz and Calder [9]. More detail on business and society in Japan is found in Richardson and Ueda [10]. Most commentators agree that the Japanese are more group minded than Westerners; that Confucian traditions have helped to mould a greater loyalty between the employee and his firm, leading to intensive rivalry between firms; and that intruders or newcomers are looked on with suspicion.

Comparing the Interacting Parties

The interaction model postulates that a buyer/seller relationship will depend on the technology, size, structure and strategy of each party as well as the aims and experience of the individuals involved.

Although this research is comparing the same markets in each country, it is clear that, even in a narrowly defined market segment, such as detergent cartons, Japanese buyers and sellers differ from their counterparts in Germany. While, in both countries, the carton suppliers and customers are large, substantial companies, many differences in size, structure, historical development and so on exist between them. Likewise, the aims and experience of the individual buyers and sellers are different. This research did not attempt to record all these differences, but rather it focused on differences between the strategies German and Japanese companies employed in handling their relationships. Two such differences emerged.

The first was the absence in the Japanese interviews of any evidence that a customer changed suppliers for organisational reasons. Whereas in Germany there were several examples of new suppliers being taken on because a salesman or buyer moved, or because of a take-over, no such examples were found in Japan. Of course, this may be due to the small number of responses in Japan as compared with Germany. On the other hand, it may reflect the fact that, on the whole, Japanese companies neither poach staff from competitors, nor make acquisitions.

Another difference was the way in which suppliers in Germany and Japan organised their sales teams. Suppliers in both countries have two problems to overcome. The first is whether to have separate salesforces for different packaging products: for example, separate salesforces for flexible packaging, carton packaging and plastic containers. The second problem is how to cope with problems of confidentiality when selling to customers who compete with each other. Different solutions were found in each country.

**TABLE 4   Interaction Processes and Atmosphere:
Differences between Germany and Japan**

Interaction Variables	Japan and Germany Compared
Content of information exchange	Japanese customers receive more detailed cost data from suppliers. In both countries, many customers warn existing suppliers when their prices are uncompetitive; however, information about technical improvements is treated confidentially.
Extent of personal contact patterns	Japanese salesmen visit more frequently than German salesmen. Japanese salesmen are more likely to visit customers' factories and have more access to marketing people than German counterparts.
Formality of information exchange	Germans prefer formal written agreements. Japanese operate without agreements.
Social exchange	Frequent entertainment of customers by suppliers is common in Japan and rare in Germany.
Closeness, commitment and trust	Japanese relationships tend to be closer and more trusting.

In Germany, Europak organises sales around product and market knowledge. Separate salesforces for each type of packaging are split into teams by end-use markets. For example, there is a sales team dealing with carton packaging to the frozen food industry. The specialist knowledge of such groups and their reputation for integrity have overcome the problems of confidentiality. In contrast, the two leading Japanese suppliers formed their sales teams by customer. Thus, each of the leading customers was served by a sales team which dealt with all that customer's packaging needs. Strict rules prevented sales teams, serving competing customers, from interchanging information.

Comparing Interaction Processes and Interaction Atmosphere

The interaction process can be divided between the elements exchanged (product, information, finance, and social exchange) and the mechanisms used, which involve adaptations, contact patterns and the manner in which negotiation and bargaining is conducted. All these elements have an effect on the atmosphere of the relationship; that is, the extent of commitment, trust and closeness which exists between the two parties.

In a comparative study of Western (Germany) and Eastern (Japan) markets, differences in the processes and atmosphere of relationships are to be expected. The way of handling relationships is different because the national cultures are so different. Table 4 makes some comparisons, in summary form.

In Japan, when there are negotiations over price increases, the customer receives detailed justifications of labour costs, raw material cost increases and changes in overheads. One customer even provides suppliers with a special form so that cost data from two suppliers are easily compared. The provision of such detailed cost data does not seem to occur in Germany.

In both Germany and Japan the customers keep a check on their suppliers' prices by doing their own cost calculations from known raw material prices, and by obtaining quotations from other sources. However, when the customer obtains a better quote he will normally warn his existing supplier before transferring his business to a new source. Whilst it was common to warn customers about price discrepancies, this was not the case with technical innovation. New ideas were treated as entirely confidential between customer and supplier. In one Japanese case, the customer worked with a supplier for 18 months on a new packaging material and, when it was perfected, he informed his existing supplier that, as from next month, he would receive no more orders. The same is true in Germany—technical developments between customer and supplier are treated more confidentially than price information.

In Japan, personal communication is more extensive. Japanese salesmen call on large customers at least once a week. Indeed, one customer commented that someone from his main supplier was likely to be somewhere in the building every day! In contrast, Europak, the German supplier, is centralising its sales staff in offices beside the factory many hundreds of miles from its key customers. There is daily telephone contact, but personal visits are less frequent.

As well as making more frequent visits to their counterparts in the buying departments. Japanese packaging salesmen are more likely to have access to the marketing department in the buying company and are more likely to visit the customer's factories. In Germany, most buyers hesitate to let their suppliers get too close, fearing that this could lead to overcharging.

The greater extent of personal contact in Japan may be one reason why Japanese relationships have fewer written agreements. In Japan, legal agreements are rarely used, whereas in Germany, they are much more common. In Germany, Europak had written agreements covering confidentiality and exclusivity wherever substantial developments took place.

In contrast, a Japanese biscuit company, and one of its major suppliers, developed a new concept for combining a biscuit finger and a chocolate dip in one package. The customer's exclusive use of this development was never written into a formal agreement. The relationship was such that neither side would seek an unfair advantage over the other.

Social exchange is a more important part of buyer/seller relationships in Japan than in Germany. Whereas, in Germany, buyers frequently do not wish to be entertained by their suppliers, the pattern is reversed in Japan. A supplier in Japan is partly judged on the frequency and quality of his entertainment. The entertainment is not expected to buy favours, but rather to enable the two sides to get to know each other better, and to understand each other's objectives so that, when problems do arise, they are quickly resolved. This frequent interchange does seem to foster closer and more trusting relationships.

The competitive strength of German and Japanese companies in many industrial markets makes a study of their marketing systems interesting and relevant. In industrial markets the central role of buyer/seller relationships is increasingly recognised, and the emphasis which the interaction approach gives to relationships makes it an appropriate research framework for this comparative study.

In both Germany and Japan the market structures (concentration and spread of market shares) are similar. In both countries, customers tend to warn existing suppliers

Variables	Compared with Germany, Japan Has…
Interaction environment	• less backward integration on the part of customers
	• fewer take-overs between suppliers
	• a more dynamic technical environment—the industry is younger, climatic conditions are different and consumers set high standards
	• a more harmonious, trusting social system
	• a more competitive business climate
Interaction parties	• selling departments organised in groups around individual customers
	• less movement of staff between companies
	• less willingness to change suppliers
Interaction processes and atmosphere	• more provision of cost data by supplier; greater analysis by the customer
	• more frequent and more extensive personal contacts during and out of office hours
	• fewer formal agreements and greater trust and commitment

about price discrepancies, while keeping quiet about differences in technology. Nevertheless, differences seemed to outweigh similarities as illustrated below.

These differences all seem to put emphasis on technically based competition. The lack of movement of staff between companies means that a supplier cannot poach salesmen to increase its sales. The general unwillingness to change suppliers and the insistence on checking the basis for price differences means that the strongest arguments are those based on genuine innovations. The extensive personal contacts, and the high degree of trust between buyer and seller, which, on European experience, might be expected to lead to institutionalised relationships, with each side taking the other for granted, seem to lead instead to a high level of service and a continued search for new ideas to benefit the customer.

No doubt the intensity of competition in Japan and the habit of making detailed checks on suppliers' costs prevent a cosy relationship from developing. The importance of innovation in obtaining new customers is illustrated by a remark from the sales manager of one of the two leading suppliers. "It is difficult," he said, "to get customers just from sales effort." Not only must a Japanese supplier regularly innovate to retain his existing customers, but he must also make major advances to have a chance of securing new customers. Could it be that the legendary Japanese interest in overseas technology results partly from this pressure? In the packaging industry, Mitsubishi has set up a special 40-strong department simply to scour the world for new ideas and bring them to Japan.

Undoubtedly, technical innovation is also an important basis for competition in Germany. Furthermore, the limited scope of this research can only suggest that the way buyer/seller relationships are conducted in Japan makes innovation an extremely important aspect.

If Japanese buyer/seller relationships are more innovative, what is the reason? Since the market structures are similar perhaps the differences result from differences in culture? We cannot answer this question definitely. However, it seems that the influence of climatic differences, of differences in customers' requirements and of many other unrecorded differences between interacting parties and individuals is slight compared to differences in social behaviour and ways of handling relationships, which stem from cultural differences.

References

1. Ford, D. I., "Introduction to Special Issue on Industrial Marketing," *European Journal of Marketing,* Vol. 14, No. 5/6, 1981, pp. 287–290.

2. Hakansson, H., *International Marketing and Purchasing of Industrial Goods: An Interaction Approach,* Chichester, John Wiley & Sons, 1982.

3. Wind, Y. and Douglas, S., "Comparative Methodology and Marketing Theory," in *Theoretical Developments in Marketing,* C. W. Lamb and P. M. Dunne (Eds.), Chicago, American Marketing Association, 1982.

4. Cunningham, M. T. and Turnbull, P. W., *International Marketing and Purchasing: A Survey among Marketing and Purchasing Executives in Five European Countries,* London, Macmillan, 1981.

5. Campbell, N. C. G., *Interaction Strategies for the Management of Buyer/Seller Relationships in Industrial Markets,* unpublished PhD Dissertation, University of Manchester, Institute of Science and Technology, Manchester, 1983.

6. Williamson, O. E., *Markets and Hierarchies,* New York, Free Press, 1975.

7. Homse, E., *An Interaction Approach to Marketing and Purchasing Strategy,* unpublished PhD Dissertation, University of Manchester, Institute of Science and Technology, Manchester, 1981.

8. Arndt, J., "Towards a Concept of Domesticated Markets," *Journal of Marketing,* Vol. 43, No. 4, 1979, pp. 69–75.

9. Hofheinz, R., Jr. and Calder, K. E., *The East Asia Edge,* New York, Basic Books, 1982.

10. Richardson, B. M. and Ueda, T., *Business and Society in Japan: Fundamentals for Businessmen,* New York, Praeger, 1981.

Who Owns the Twenty-First Century?

Lester C. Thurow. *Lester C. Thurow is dean of the MIT Sloan School of Management.*

In the United States, most of the last half century has been devoted to worrying about the Soviet Union. Democracy and capitalism faced off against dictatorship and communism. Suddenly, the threat disappeared. The Berlin Wall came down; East Germany and West Germany were united; democracy and capitalism arrived in the formerly communist countries of middle Europe and then in Eastern Europe. Democracy and capitalism had won.

In 1945 there were two military superpowers, the United States and the Soviet Union, and one economic superpower, the United States. In 1992 there is one military superpower, the United States, and there are three economic superpowers, the United States, Japan, and Europe (centered on Germany), jousting for economic supremacy. Without a pause, our national challenge has shifted from being military to being economic.

From everyone's perspective, replacing a military confrontation with an economic one is a step forward. No one gets killed; vast resources don't have to be devoted to negative-sum activities. The winner builds the world's best products and enjoys the world's highest standard of living. The loser gets to buy some of the world's best products—but not as many as the winner.

However, this shift in focus does create difficulties for the United States. Attempting to be both a military and an economic superpower is ambitious: it requires Spartan self-discipline. Both enterprises call for major investments in infrastructure, research and development, and education. Yet the United States is increasingly a consuming rather than an investing society. If it is to win the economic battle ahead, its investment and consumption patterns must change drastically.

A New Economic Game

Looking backward, historians will see the twentieth century as a century of niche competition and the twenty-first century as a century of head-to-head competition. In 1950 the United States had a per capita GNP four times that of Germany and fifteen

Reprinted from *Sloan Management Review,* Spring 1992, pp. 5–17, by permission of publisher. Copyright 1992 by the Sloan Management Review Association. All rights reserved.

times that of Japan. Imports from Germany and Japan did not seem to threaten the good jobs that Americans wanted, and America's exports did not threaten good jobs in Germany and Japan.

The 1990s is a very different time. In broad terms there are three relatively equal contenders—Japan, the European community, and the United States. Each country or region now wants the same industries to ensure that its citizens have the highest standards of living in the twenty-first century: micro-electronics, biotechnology, the new materials sciences, telecommunications, civilian aviation, robotics and machine tools, and computers and software.[1] Niche competition is win-win. Head-to-head competition is win-lose. Not everyone can control those seven key industries.

Individualistic vs. Communitarian Capitalism

The economic competition between communism and capitalism is over, but another competition between two forms of capitalism is underway. Using a distinction first made by George Lodge, a Harvard Business School professor, I believe that the individualistic, British-American form of capitalism is going to face off against the communitarian, German and Japanese variants of capitalism.[2]

America and Britain trumpet individual values: the brilliant entrepreneur, Nobel prize winners, large wage differentials, individual responsibility for skills, ease of firing and quitting, profit maximization, and hostile mergers and takeovers. In contrast, Germany and Japan trumpet communitarian values: business groups, social responsibility for skills, teamwork, firm loyalty, industry strategies, and active, growth-promoting industrial policies. Anglo-Saxon firms are profit maximizers; Japanese firms play a game that might better be known as "strategic conquest"—they are more focused on market share than on profit.

These different visions of capitalism have profound effects on everything from labor relations to public education.

New Sources of Strategic Advantage

Historically, individuals, firms, and countries became rich if they possessed more natural resources, were born rich and enjoyed the advantages of having more capital per person, employed superior technologies, or had more skills than their competitors. Putting some combination of these four factors together with reasonable management was the route to success.

New technologies and institutions are combining to substantially alter these four traditional sources of competitive advantage. Natural resources essentially drop out of the competitive equation. Being born rich becomes less of an advantage than it used to be. Technology gets turned upside down. New product technologies become secondary; new process technologies become primary. And in the twenty-first century the education and skills of the work force will be the dominant competitive weapon.

New Rules[3]

The GATT-Bretton Woods trading system that has governed international trade since the end of World War II is dead. It died not in failure, but as the normal end of a very successful life. Logically, a new Bretton Woods conference should now be underway. But politically it cannot be called. Such a conference can occur only if there is a dominant political power that can force everyone to agree. In 1944 the United States was such a power; today there is no such power.

The required economic changes cannot wait for the right political moment. As the Europeans negotiate the rules for their internal common market and decide how outsiders relate to that market, they will effectively if informally be writing the rules for world trade in the next century. Those who control the world's largest market get to write the rules. When the United States had the world's largest market, it wrote the rules.

The Europeans are writing rules for a system of managed trade and "quasi-trading blocks." The countries within any one block, such as Canada within the American market, will get special trading privileges not given to outsiders. I call these "quasi" blocks because, unlike the trading blocks of the 1930s, they will not attempt to reduce or eliminate trade between blocks; rather, they will attempt to manage it.

The sections that follow compare the strategic advantages and disadvantages each major player brings to this new economic game. In the final section, I propose a game plan for the United States.

The House of Europe: Catalyst for Change

Two events make Europe the focal point of attention in the 1990s.[4] In Western Europe at the stroke of midnight on 31 December, 1992, the European Community integrates, and with that integration it instantly becomes by far the world's largest economic market— 380 million people, now that the members of the European Free Trade Area have effectively been added to the 337 million inside the EC.[5] And in middle and Eastern Europe communism has dissolved and is being replaced by capitalism. In both Eastern and Western Europe something is being attempted that has never before been done—in the former, a move from central planning to a free market, and in the latter, a voluntary integration of a very large, linguistically heterogeneous market of former military enemies.

The rest of the world watches these events with some ambivalence. Third world countries note that the ex-communist countries have low wages, well-educated populations, and a convenient location next to the world's largest market. Any special access the ex-communist countries receive will effectively close Europe's market to mid- and low-income countries elsewhere in the world. Japan and America worry that economic integration will make it harder to sell their products in Europe—and they're right. When talking to each other, Europeans acknowledge that if they did not gain some special privileges relative to the rest of the world, there would be no reason to integrate. Realistically, outsiders have to face the fact that European integration will hurt them. It wouldn't work if it didn't.

The federation of Europe will take a long time, and progress will be erratic. It is easy to make a long list of difficult issues that will have to be resolved. The list could be used to argue that real European integration will never occur. But the formation of the House of Europe is now unstoppable. First, the opportunities to create an integrated

House of Europe are just too good to pass up. Second, the need to compete against the Americans and the Japanese in a global economy almost demands that the House of Europe be built. If it isn't, the individual countries will find themselves economically marginalized between two much bigger, more aggressive economies. Third, enough integration has now occurred to make withdrawal very difficult. Fourth, an internal dynamic has been established whereby each step forward essentially forces the participants to make further steps forward.

The development of a market economy in middle and Eastern Europe—and this economy's partial integration with Western Europe—is also fraught with difficulty and is far from inevitable. Yet strong links between the two Europes could be the key to the House of Europe's winning the economic war.

Will Europe Own the Twenty-First Century?

Europe was the slowest mover in the 1980s, but it starts the 1990s with the strongest strategic position on the world economic chess board. If Europe makes the right moves economically, it can become the dominant economic power in the twenty-first century, regardless of what Japan and the United States do. The moves are easy to see but very difficult to make.

If Europe can truly integrate the EC (337 million people) into one economy and gradually move to absorb the rest of Europe (more than 500 million people), it can put together an economy that no one else can match. Its 850 million people are the only group of that size in the world that are both well educated and not poor. Some of the countries that need to be added to the EC, such as Sweden, Norway, and Austria, are in fact some of the richest in the world.

Europe's major advantage is that almost everyone starts out well educated. The communists may not have been able to run good economies, but they ran some of the best K-12 educational systems on the face of the earth. Europe is the only region where one country (Germany) is a world leader in production and trade, and another country (the former Soviet Union) is a leader in high science. In many areas of theoretical science it leads the world. Germany's trade surplus in 1990 was the largest in the world; on a per capita basis it was almost three times that of Japan. A decade from now, when eastern Germany is fully integrated and up to western German productivity standards, Germany will be even more formidable. Germany's traditional markets, middle and Eastern Europe, are apt to be the fastest growing in the world in the early twenty-first century.

If the high science of the former Soviet Union and the production technologies of the German-speaking world are added to the design flair of Italy and France and a world-class London capital market efficiently directing funds to Europe's most productive areas, something unmatchable will have been created. The House of Europe could become a relatively self-contained, rapidly growing region that could sprint away from the rest of the pack.

Since the European countries represent both the communtarian and the individualistic strains of capitalism, the compromises necessary for Europe's integration could lead to a mixture of the best parts of each.

This does not mean, however, that Europe will win. It just means that it *can* win if it makes exactly the right moves. But doing so involves two major problems. The economies of Western Europe really have to integrate and that integration has to be quickly extended to middle and Eastern Europe. The ex-communist countries have to become successful market economies. Neither is an easy task. Both will require European citizens to make sacrifices today to create an economic juggernaut tomorrow. Western Europe will have to give large amounts of economic aid to the ex-communist countries in order to get capitalism started.

Ancient border and ethnic rivalries in both Eastern and Western Europe will have to be put aside. The English and the Germans will both have to become Europeans.

These obstacles aside, the House of Europe holds the strongest starting position.

Japan: The Challenge of Producer Economics

When facing American or European competition, Japanese firms always seem to win. Their market share always goes up, never down. Inexorably, they defeat the pride of American and European industry. Yet practices such as age-based seniority that don't take individual merit into account should make Japanese business firms inefficient. What are handicaps for other economies seem to be strengths for the Japanese.

Are they playing the same game but doing it better by working harder, saving more, and being smarter than everyone else? Or does their success spring from having organized a better system? Is Japan just better, or is it exceptional? If Japan is exceptional, and I believe it is, it will force major changes in how capitalism is played around the world.

Before we examine Japan's strategic position vis-à-vis America and Europe, we need to discuss the underpinnings of its form of capitalism.

Profit Maximization vs. Strategic Conquest

The profit-maximizing Anglo-Saxon business firm is based on the idea that more consumption and more leisure are the sole economic elements of human satisfaction. Higher productivity at work is desirable because it gives individuals higher incomes to buy more goods and the ability to obtain more leisure without sacrificing consumption.

This model is not wrong. Individualism and the desire for consumption and leisure are parts of human nature. However, they are not all of human nature. Individuals are also social builders who want to belong to empires that expand, and firms can be based on that need, too.

As social builders, individuals may rationally decide to have fewer consumption goods in their home so that they can have more production goods at work. To them, ownership of investment goods can generate just as much pride as ownership of consumption goods. A higher standard of living at work may be even more important than a higher standard of living at home. Such behavior is seen in American farmers, who often choose to have the fanciest tractor in the neighborhood, not the fanciest car. In the language of bumper stickers, humans may be born to shop, but they are also born to build. This desire to build generates what I will call Japanese "producer economics," to distinguish it from consumer economics.[6]

Producer-economics firms and profit-maximizing firms both want profits, but the role played by those profits is very different.[7] In the profit-maximizing firm, profits per se are the goal. In the empire-building firm, profits are a means to the end of a larger empire. The goal is market share. A profit-maximizing firm will devote its profits to individual consumption; an empire-building firm will devote its profits to investment in expanding its empire.

If one thinks of a continuum with profit-maximizing firms at one end and empire-building firms at the other, the exact placement of a nation's firms would be controversial, but the order of their positions is not. American firms are closer to the profit-maximizing end, and Japanese firms are closer to the empire-building end. German firms are on the empire-building end, although not so far along as the Japanese, whereas British firms are perhaps even further along the profit-maximizing continuum than American firms.

An economy interested in producer economics will organize itself to lower consumption and raise investment. Japan has systematically built a society to raise investment (plant and equipment, R&D, human skills) at the expense of individual-consumption privileges.

The system starts with company unions, the bonus system, and the annual spring wage offensive that holds down labor's share of national income. Japan's work force gets the lowest share of national income in the five leading industrial countries, and its share is falling. At the same time, the average Japanese worker enjoys an expense account that is generous when compared with that of American workers: consumption activities that contribute to team building at work are encouraged; consumption activities at home are discouraged.

With lower wages, more income is left to the corporation, but little of that income goes to the shareholders. The returns to external shareholders are limited to the capital gains that accrue from rising share prices. After paying wages, essentially everything is reinvested in future growth.

Firms that invest more must be willing to accept lower rates of return on their investments. Studies show that the returns on the investment required for American firms to invest in robotics are 50 percent higher than those of Japanese firms.[8] Many very successful firms in Japan (Honda, for example) have in fact made rates of return over the past two decades lower than they could have made by simply investing in government bonds.

To maximize the income going to businesses, consumer prices are held far above what would prevail in a free market. Relative to New York, the Tokyo consumer pays three times as much for rice, beef, and potatoes. Other aspects of the system force individual consumers to save a large portion of their incomes.

The system has worked. In the last five years of the 1980s, Japan invested 35.6 percent of its GNP, while the United States invested 17 percent.[9] If housing investments are left out (technically investment but actually consumption), the two-to-one investment gap becomes a three-to-one gap.

Interestingly, the Japanese see the American desire for profits as a major cause of America's weakness in international competition.[10] What they see as a weakness tells us something about what they see as a strength in themselves.

Japanese firms' emphasis on building market share is supported not only by their investment patterns but also by how they structure business groups, perceive various stakeholders, treat workers, view training and R&D, and structure national-level trade policies.

Business Groups.   To lengthen time horizons and accept a lower rate of return, impatient consumption-oriented stockholders must be controlled. The Japanese business groups, or *keiretsu,* have been organized to do that. They're organized into vertical groups made up of suppliers, producers, and retailers, and into horizontal groups make up of firms in different industries. Seventy-eight percent of the shares listed on the Tokyo stock exchange are owned by *keiretsu* members.[11] Because a majority of the shares of each member are owned by other members of the group, no member can be bought by outsiders. Each member is part operating company, part holding company, and part investment trust.[12]

Members gain not by being paid dividends but by getting and giving preferential treatment as suppliers and customers. Direct discrimination does not occur; the preferential treatment comes in the form of buyers and sellers willing to work together to ensure that the Japanese *keiretsu* supplier is in fact the best supplier. If the Japanese don't treat American firms equally when it comes to buying parts or selling parts in short supply, they are not being unfair. They are simply doing what everyone does—playing ball with the people on their team.

Countries that believe in producer economics make it easy to form business groups. Countries that believe in profit maximizing don't. In the United States, Japanese-style business groups are illegal under the antitrust laws.

Priority of Stakeholders.   If the executives of profit-maximizing firms are asked to state the order in which they serve various constituents, shareholders come first, with customers and employees a distant second and third. Most managers will argue that the sole purpose of the company is to maximize shareholder wealth. If Japanese firms are asked the same question, the order of duty is reversed: employees first, customers second, and shareholders third.[13]

Treatment of Labor.   The empire-building firm sees labor as a strategic asset to be nurtured;[14] the profit-maximizing firm does not. In the last two decades U.S. firms have reduced wages even as sales and profits were rising. Partly to force wages down, U.S. firms have rapidly moved to offshore production bases. Lower-wage part-time workers have replaced higher-wage full-time workers. Japanese firms did not move production abroad, nor did they move to part-time employment, to anywhere near the same extent. When a sample of Japanese firms was asked what they had done to reduce labor costs, only 2.6 percent listed discharging workers or employing part-time workers[15]

Studies show that when automation goes up in America, wages go down. In contrast, when automation rises in Japan, wages rise as well.[16] In Japan, these investments are used to enhance labor productivity rather than to replace skilled labor with unskilled labor, as happens in the United States. For U.S. firms, lower wages equal higher profits.

When it comes to training, very difficult expenditure patterns emerge in Japanese and U.S. firms, as well.[17] Americans invest less per worker and concentrate their investments heavily in management education. They invest less in general background skills and more in the narrow job skills required for the next task; that pattern is reversed in Japan.

Bonus systems are also different. The American system is keyed to rewarding individual performance, whereas the Japanese system is keyed to stimulating teamwork. Narrow profit centers are much more widely used in the United States than they are in either Japan or Europe. Quarterly profits in narrowly defined profit centers are the American way. In Japan, bonuses are not normally keyed to profitability but to the growth, productivity, and market share of the entire company. The U.S. system fits into a world view in which individuals are motivated solely by their income and group efforts are not important. The Japanese system fits into a world in which the group's output is the dominant factor in total production.

In keeping with consumption maximization, we would expect U.S. CEOs to be paid more than those running similar firms in the world of producer economics. And so they are.[18] In 1990 U.S. CEOs made 119 times as much as the average worker; Japanese CEOs made only 18 times as much as the average worker.[19] When Steve Ross, the CEO of Time Warner, pays himself $78 million and then lays off 600 people because of declining ad revenues, he is just practicing what Americans preach.

Cycles in Investment, R&D, and Training.   In the United States, private research and development spending falls in recessions and rises in booms.[20] In Europe and Japan, it does not. To an American firm, cutting R&D is a technique for maintaining profits during a period of declining sales. The same spending patterns exist in investment and training.

These different patterns are reflected in the respective accounting systems. In U.S. accounting conventions, since R&D is expensed, cutting R&D leads to higher bottom-line profits immediately. In Japan, where R&D is capitalized, it does not. Thus the Japanese accounting system discourages short-term behavior, and the American system encourages it.

Will Japan Own the Twenty-First Century?

If one looks at the last twenty years, one would have to consider Japan the betting favorite to win the economic honors in the next century. Japan's home market is the smallest of the three, but it has the advantage of a long, unified history. Cohesion and homogeneity give Japan an ability to focus that few others can rival. No single nation can organize better to march toward well thought out common goals. Japanese high school students come near the top in any international assessment of achievement, and the nation's ability to educate the bottom half of the high-school class is unmatched anywhere.

No nation is investing more in its future. Plant and equipment investment per employee is three times as high as in the United States and twice as high as in Europe; civilian R&D spending as a fraction of GNP is 50 percent above that of the United States, slightly above that of Germany, and far above that of Europe as a whole.

Japan's strength—its powerful, cohesive internal culture—is also its weakness. Japanese firms manage foreign workers well, but, to the extent that the twenty-first century requires firms to integrate managers and professionals from other cultures into a homogeneous team, it has a problem. Japan's traditions and language (which is hard to master) make it very difficult to integrate foreign managers and professionals as equals.

Another weakness is the lack of new product innovation. While every nation struggles to catch up some of the time, those that have become leaders also learn how to pioneer breakthroughs. Japan has yet to demonstrate this ability. If products have to be copied from abroad, Japan's own economic advance will be limited by the pace of its competitors' inventions.

Japanese success has been based on an export-led-economy, but that cannot be the route to success in the future. The rest of the world could tolerate Japan's growth so long as its exports were relatively small. But the country is now so large economically that the rest of the world cannot allow Japan's exports to rise and capture markets at the rate that Japan will need in order to continue to grow much faster than anyone else. The rest of the world will simply stop Japan from being an export-led economy by instituting overt restrictions, if necessary. So if Japan is to grow faster than anyone else in the twenty-first century, it has to find a way to do so while its exports grow more slowly than its GNP. Essentially, it must become an economy pulled ahead by its domestic demands rather than an economy pushed ahead by exports.

Japan's producer economics may be the smartest form of capitalism in the twenty-first century's economic game, but for the Japanese to win, some consumer economics will have to be grafted on. The ultimate owner of the twenty-first century will have to balance the drive to consume with the drive to build.

Japan comes into the competition with momentum on its side. It is growing faster and investing more in the future than anyone else.

The United States of America: The Great Wall Is Down

In the years after World War II, the United States was effectively living behind a wall built of five overwhelming advantages: it was the largest market, and it had the highest-skilled workers, the most money, the best technology, and the best managers in the world. Put these factors together, destroy the rest of the world in a major war, and the result is effortless economic superiority. However, both inside and outside these protective walls, changes were occurring. Americans did not notice and did not change their behavior.

As the rest of the world began to catch up with income levels in the United States, the relative size of the American market got smaller and smaller. Today America is technologically only average if one includes both product and process technologies. Our level of nonmilitary R&D investment is low relative to our competitors. Unless one believes that Americans are smarter than the Germans or the Japanese, today's spending levels will eventually lead to a secondary position for American science and engineering and to lower rates of productivity growth.[21]

The rest of the world noticed the payoff from America's system of mass education, copied it, and upped the ante. Comparative international exams reveal that Americans at all age levels know less than citizens in other advanced industrial countries. The older the secondary-school student, the larger the educational achievement gap. Those who graduate from college catch up with their foreign counterparts because most of the industrial world has not yet made the investments necessary to shift from elite to mass education at the university level. Yet relative to the rest of the world, we produce too few engineers and scientists. Much of this can be traced to bad math and science education in high school. But that is not an excuse for failing to insist that every college graduate be numerate—that is, mathematically literate.

For those who do not go on to college, a poor educational starting position is compounded by less on-the-job skill investment than their foreign counterparts receive.

Technically, the United States has not been the richest country in the world for some time, but its purchasing power is roughly equivalent to that of its competitors. However, because of America's private and public consumption levels, investments in education, R&D, and the infrastructure run well behind those of our competitors.

American management talent and experience are no longer clearly better than those in the rest of the world. If measured by outcomes—trade deficits and slow productivity growth—they are worse.

Will the United States Own the Twenty-First Century?

Having been rich longer than anyone else, the United States starts the twenty-first century with more real economic assets than anyone else. Technologically, it is seldom far behind and often far ahead. Its per capita income and average productivity are second to none. Its college-educated work force is the best in the world. Its domestic market is far larger than that of Japan and far more homogeneous than that of Europe.

But it squandered much of its starting advantage by allowing its educational system to atrophy, by allowing itself to run a high-consumption, low-investment society, and by incurring hugh international debts. No one is preparing less for the competition that lies ahead.

American investment is simply not world class. Plant and equipment investment is simply not world class. Plant and equipment investment per labor force member is half that of Germany, one third that of Japan.[22] Civilian R&D spending is 40 percent to 50 percent less than that of Germany or Japan. Physical infrastructure investments are half those of the late 1960s.

In the 1980s America's slow productivity growth was hidden by a rapidly growing labor force and an unused borrowing capacity that raised real standards of living higher than was warranted by productivity growth. In the 1990s, America's labor force will not grow rapidly, and its borrowing capacity is already close to full utilization. As a result, the unseen and unsolved problem of the 1980s, slow productivity growth, will move front and center in the 1990s. America's chances of owning the twenty-first century depend upon the answer to a simple question: Can it get its productivity growth rate up to the standards of its chief rivals?

Paradoxically, if America wants to have a world-class consumption standard of living in the twenty-first century, it will have to shift from being a high-consumption, low-investment society to being a high-investment, low-consumption society. To raise investment, consumption (public and private) must grow more slowly than output for an extended period of time so that investment (public and private) can rise as a fraction of GNP.

When it comes to workforce skills and education, the picture is mixed. The college-educated part of the work force is excellent. The part of the U.S. work force that does not go on to college, however, is not world class, and the part of the work force that does not graduate from high school (29 percent) is positively Third World when it comes to educational skills.

At the same time, the United States has some real cultural strengths. If Japan's culture makes it the country where foreigners find it hardest to participate as equals, American's culture makes it the country where outsiders can most easily become insiders. And Americans may not be great exporters, but they are the world's best when it comes to running offshore production facilities. If the sales of offshore production facilities had been treated as exports, the 1986 U.S trade deficit of $144 million would have become a trade surplus of $57 million.[23] Americans quickly turn offshore employees into successful American businesspeople.

In crises, such as Pearl Harbor, or in situations that can be made to look like crises, such as Sputnik, Americans respond magnificently. Clear problems get clear, clean, well-managed solutions. America is perfectly capable of claiming the twenty-first century for itself. America's problem is not winning—but rather forcing itself to notice that the game has changed and has to be played by new rules, using new strategies.

An American Game Plan

President Bush is fond of saying that the United States has "more will than wallet" when he discusses domestic issues. The truth, of course, is exactly the opposite. America's per capita real GNP is two and one-half times as large as it was when it began to finance the Marshall Plan, which rebuilt the world. America has a lot more wallet than will and could easily invest the sums necessary to give it a competitive economy.

But Americans are particularly resistant to changing their system because they tend to believe that they got it right the first time. When the American system fails, as of course it does from time to time, Americans don't look for system failures. They look for human devils who have mucked up a perfect system. Thus, instead of reforming America's financial system when it essentially collapsed at the end of the 1980s, Americans found devils (Mike Milken, Charles Keating, Neil Bush) who needed to be punished. Nothing was done to change the system.

While rebuilding America's systems will have to take tradition and culture into account, it will also require constructing something new. The sections that follow propose systemic changes in four key areas: savings and investment, education, business groups, and national strategy.

Savings and Investment

It does not take a deep understanding of economics to know that America cannot have a competitive productivity growth rate when it invests half as much as the Japanese and two-thirds as much as the Europeans. That would be possible only if Americans were substantially smarter than everyone else. From an economist's point of view, it is easy to restructure America to ensure greater investments. But all routes to that objective require someone, somewhere, to consume less. That won't happen until there are political leaders willing to talk realistically to the American people. I will return to the question of leadership shortly.

Step one is for Americans as individuals to quit borrowing to finance consumption purchases. Step two is for Americans as a group to quit running government deficits. Step three is to adopt a tax system with powerful incentives for saving and powerful disincentives for consumption. Step four is to establish strong incentives for private investment and larger government budgets for public investment. All of these steps point to the federal tax system as the place where America's consumption diet must be designed.

Americans believe they pay the highest taxes in the world, when in fact they are at the bottom of the industrial league—ranking twenty-fourth among twenty-four major industrial nations in terms of tax collections as a fraction of GNP. Every U.S. tax (income, payroll, property, and indirect) is far below those of the most of the developed world (see Table 1).[24] Simply raising taxes to eliminate the federal deficit would not be the end of the world. Americans would still be paying fewer taxes than their compatriots in most of the rest of the industrial world.

At the same time, there are real opportunities to cut spending. If fears of the Soviet Union more than doubled defense spending in the 1980s, the disappearance of the Soviet

---

TABLE 1 **Government Tax Collections as Percentage of GDP, 1990**

Country	Tax Rate	Country	Tax Rate
United States	30.0%	Germany	37.0%
Australia	30.0	Finland	37.2
Turkey	30.0	New Zealand	40.0
Japan	30.0	Italy	40.2
Switzerland	31.0	Austria	41.0
Greece	32.0	Luxembourg	41.5
Iceland	32.5	France	43.0
Spain	33.0	Belgium	45.0
Portugal	33.2	Holland	46.0
Canada	34.0	Norway	46.1
Britain	35.0	Denmark	47.5
Ireland	35.3	Sweden	58.0

SOURCE: Organization for Economic Cooperation and Development. Cited in *The Economist,* 21 September 1991, p. 123.

Union can more than halve defense spending in the 1990s. America does not need to spend more than 12 percent of its GNP on health care—one-third more than the next-highest-spending country.

Americans love to fight about government spending, but the real issue is not public versus private spending. The real issue is investment, public and private, versus consumption, public and private. America should set itself a goal to design a tax and expenditure system in which consumption, public and private, rises 1 percent per year less rapidly than the GNP.[25] If this were done for a decade, America would have world-class savings and investment at the end of the decade, and no one's consumption would have to fall—it would just grow slightly more slowly. One does not need to devastate the present to protect the future. One just needs to be concerned about the future.

A system to raise investment by 1 percent of GNP per year could be designed from either a liberal or a conservative perspective. My optimal system would include value-added taxes to encourage exports and discourage consumption.[26] To make this tax progressive, an offsetting income-tax credit would be established for the first $10,000 in consumption for a family of four. There would be tax-free savings accounts, but individuals would have to prove that they were adding to their savings accounts by reducing their consumption, not simply moving money from one account to another, as happened with IRAs. If tax rates were then raised on that fraction of income not saved (consumption), tax-free savings accounts would be a powerful vehicle. Savings would effectively be exempted from taxation, and this would turn America's progressive income tax into a progressive consumption tax.

My ideal system would also eliminate payroll taxes to encourage investment in human resources and eliminate the corporate income tax to stimulate physical investment.

As suggested by Senator D. Patrick Moynihan, the federal government would take the very large Social Security surplus out of its budget calculations and balance what remains. The necessary revenue for balancing would be raised with value-added and gasoline taxes.[27] If one includes existing state and local surpluses, such a strategy would double national savings.

Consumer and mortgage down payments would be raised to inhibit those who consume more than their income. Germany requires a 40 percent down payment on a house; Italy a 50 percent down payment. If Americans can get everything they want without saving, why should they save?

These suggestions reflect only my own preferences. America would have to design a system that could be supported by both liberals and conservatives, so that, as the political tides come and go, the tax system could continue to provide stable, long-run incentives for investment and growth.

This brings us back to the issue of leadership. Polls show that Americans are worried about their economic futures but confused as to why their incomes are falling relative to the rest of the world.[28] For many, economic failure is somehow linked with moral failure—crime in the streets, drugs, family breakdowns. They cannot make sense of the jumbled stew of economic and moral problems. They want to be led to a solution if the burdens are fairly shared across the population.

To sort out this stew of jumbled beliefs will require an American establishment that can articulate the demands of the future and that can suggest unselfish programs for responding to them. To do this, a U.S. president will have to unlearn what every politician, Republican and Democrat, has been taught by former President Reagan. He taught them one fact of political life: that in American politics, optimists beat pessimists. And then he did the real damage by redefining the word *optimism.* In the Reagan political dictionary, an optimist is someone who denies that America has any problems. To admit that it has fundamental problems is to be a pessimist and unfit for political office.

By this definition of optimism, President Kennedy was a pessimist when he admitted the Russians were ahead of America in space and had been growing faster economically in the 1950s. But at the time Americans thought of him as an optimist. He had solutions, and they worked. Americans got to the moon first, and productivity grew at record rates in the first half of the 1960s. Today, President Kennedy's advisers would warn against man-on-the moon speeches.

Americans cannot strengthen their economic team unless the president is first willing to tell them that the news from the economic battlefield is bad. In America, the existence of an establishment that works for the public good (instead of its own enrichment) depends on having a president willing to lead. America is not Japan, where an establishment among elite civil servants can keep the country on track, whatever the politicians do.

Skill Building

If the "British disease" is adversarial labor-management relations, the "American disease" is the belief that low wages solve all problems. When under competitive pressure, U.S. firms first go to the low-wage, nonunion parts of America and then on to a succession of countries with ever-lower wages. But the strategy seldom works. For a brief time lower wages lead to higher profits, but eventually others with even lower wages enter the business, prices fall, and the higher profits generated by lower wages vanish.

The search for the holy grail of high profitability lies in a relentless upscale drive in technology to ever-higher levels of productivity—and wages. Since rapid productivity growth is a moving target and therefore hard to copy, high long-term profits can be sustained with such a strategy. But to get the necessary human talent to employ new technologies, large skill investments have to be made and high wages have to be paid. Paradoxically, high wages leave firms with no choice but to go upscale in technology. High wages and high profits are not antithetical—they go together.[29]

To create the productivity that can justify high wages, American K-12 education will have to improve. The problem is not lack of information or studies.[30] The problem is generating action in a system with 15,000 independent local school boards whose incentives lie in other directions. To bring about the necessary reforms, a grand bargain needs to be struck.

In their part of the bargain, the taxpayers would agree to bring the wages of schoolteachers up to the levels found in Germany or Japan—$40,000–45,000 per year versus $30,000 in America.[31] When schools had a captive female labor supply, high-quality teachers could be hired without high wages. Today, quality and wages are directly linked. In a capitalistic society, if one wants skilled teachers in the classroom, one has to pay for them.

The teachers, for their part, would have to agree to world-scale work effort and efficiency. The school day would be lengthened by a couple of hours per day in high school, and the school year would be at least 220 days long. German teachers work 220–240 days, not the 180 days common in America.

Competitive wages would force Americans to spend more, but not a lot more. America now spends 4.1 percent of GNP on K-12 education. Germany spends 4.6 percent, and Japan, 4.8 percent.[32]

Another part of the bargain is to set a quality standard for the noncollege bound. Here the high-wage business community in each state should write an achievement test that would cover what they think high-school graduates need to know to work at America's best firms. Local school boards could continue to graduate whomever they please, but those students who had passed this "business achievement test" would have their diploma so stamped. (This would be one way around the excessive power held by America's 15,000 local school boards.)

In addition, communities would agree to quit using schools as a dumping ground for social problems that cannot be solved elsewhere. The frontlines of the war on crime, drugs, teenage pregnancy, or housing desegregation should be established elsewhere. Better nutrition, drivers' training, and sports are secondary. The energy of our school systems should be focused on education, period.

Better schools are just the beginning. American firms do not invest as much in training as firms abroad, and what they do invest is much more heavily concentrated on professional and managerial workers.[33] "Following Joe around," the American system of on-the-job training simply isn't a system.

A number of avenues exist for increasing the skills of the average worker. One possibility is to pass the American equivalent of the French law that requires business firms to invest 1 percent of their sales in training. Firms must pay a tax on this amount but can deduct their internal training costs. Since all firms have to pay for training, they might as well train.

Business Groups[34]

In today's world economy, where American businesses must match up with the business groups of Germany and Japan, U.S. firms need to be able to form the same strategic alliances, the same self-help societies, and the same joint strategies for conquering world markets. To give them the necessary weapons, America's laws and regulations must be drastically overhauled.

American finance should be put in an institutional straight-jacket so that it cannot succeed unless American industry succeeds. Key to this is changing the financial regulations that prevent American banks and other financial institutions from becoming merchant banks—financial institutions that own and control industrial corporations or are owned by them.

Today's laws draw too sharp a distinction between loans and equity. To avoid the appearance of conflict of interest, executives from banks, insurance companies, and other lenders are not supposed to be financially involved participants. But that flies in the face of reason. It is precisely the institutions that provide major long-term loans to companies that should take an active role in the strategic direction of those companies. They should be interested directors, not outsiders. To bring this about, long-term loans should carry voting rights.

Allowing financial institutions to take stakes in industrial companies, or the reverse, will over time lead to the formation of business groups that are equivalent to those that now exist in Germany and Japan. These groups are simply necessary in today's world.[35] A framework of mutual support is needed not only to make raiding difficult, but also to give directors, who represent real owners, the clout to fire bad managers.

In reformulating banking and antitrust laws, conglomerate groups or vertical supplier-customer groups, such as those in Japan, should be permitted.[36] What should be prohibited are the single-industry groups that J.P. Morgan sometimes organized, where almost the entire steel industry would be organized into one company. The latter leads to monopoly; the former leads to more competition.

Since stockholders will have access to inside information, the new laws should see to it that all institutional or individual dominant stockholders are locked in to their investments. Anyone who owns a dominant position in any company—say, 20 percent or more—should be forced to give the public one day's advance notice of the intention to sell any shares. Such notice would almost inevitably trigger a general rush to sell that stock before the major investor could, leaving the investor to sell at much reduced prices. Locked-in investors would think long and hard before trying to bail out of a company in trouble. Instead, they would have a major incentive to minister to the sick company, designing the strategies necessary to return it to health.

To reinforce the distinction between traders and investors, the voting rights of equity shares should rise over time. Major investors subject to the 20 percent rule would become instant owners, but others would gain full voting rights only over a period of time. Stock traders could still be traders, getting rich by buying and selling shares, but those who want to be short-term traders would be separated from those who want to be long-term owners.

While the tyranny of the quarterly profit statement as a deterrent to good management is probably exaggerated, it should be repealed as a symbol. Japan has gradually moved from quarterly to half-year to annual reports. Nothing has been lost. The same should be done in the United States. Managers should not be placed in a position in which, if they incur expenses this quarter to make future prospects better, they will be penalized with falling stock prices.

In any reformulation of the rules governing America's industrial structure, one central goal must be kept in mind. Put real capitalists back in the driver's seat of the American corporation. Then lock them in so that they have no choice but to improve their firms and hence the nation's productivity and competitiveness.

National Strategy

It is the official U.S. position that no economic strategy at the national level is needed—and that such policies simply don't work. But this belief is increasingly untenable if one looks at the industries that have been lost, such as robots, or the industries under threat, such as aircraft manufacturing.

The key difference between the United States and the rest of the industrial world is not the existence of protection. About 25 percent, double what was true twenty years ago, of all U.S. imports are now affected by nontariff trade barriers.[37] International businesspeople see Japan as the world's most unfair trading nation, but they see the United States as the third most unfair (behind Japan and Korea).[38] But these barriers add up to, as the Japanese say, a "loser-driven" industrial policy—the product of random political lobbying to gain protection for dying industries.[39] The rest of the world's industrial policies involve strategic thinking and are winner driven.

The results show. Although a big decline in the dollar's value reduced the Japan-U.S. trade deficit, the high-tech, high-wage part of the trade deficit is expanding.[40] America depends increasingly on low-wage, low-tech, commodity exports to balance its trading accounts.

In the real world—the world of falling real wages, stagnant productivity growth, and a growing high-wage trade deficit—defensive industrial policies are unavoidable. Such policies are not designed to help American corporations; they are simply part of a general strategic growth policy designed to help the American people. In fact, public investments to gain sustainable advantage should be limited to investments staying in America, such as investments in skills or the domestic infrastructure.

Beyond such investments, the search for strategic advantage abroad now revolves around process R&D investments. In Japan, MITI has shifted from foreign exchange and capital allocations strategies toward pushing key technologies. The Europeans have set up an alphabet soup of cooperative R&D projects designed to do the same thing. While the details differ, the basic organizational structures are the same.

The strategies are industry led; groups of companies, not government civil servants, propose the technologies that should be pushed. Governments never provide more than 50 percent of the total funding. Companies have to put together their own consortia so that the government is not subsidizing a special favorite. The idea is to magnify private funds with public funds, not to publicly finance R&D. The projects have finite lifetimes and clearly stated objectives. The purpose is never to advance knowledge for its own sake. The bureaucracy that makes the funding decisions can be very small because the firms themselves are making the basic decisions when they decide whether to risk their own money.

Economic analysis show that there are gains to be made with strategic trade policies, especially in industries with increasing returns. If government aid drives technology faster, everyone is a winner in the long run.

An Empirical Experiment

A decade ago it was possible to argue that America could solve its problems by moving to a more vigorous form of traditional, Anglo-Saxon capitalism. Both Mrs. Thatcher and President Reagan were elected on such platforms. Both emphasized the role of the individual in economic performance. Government enterprises were privatized in Britain. American income taxes were dramatically lowered.

Both experiments are now more than a decade old. Neither succeeded. In the United Kingdom, unemployment is higher than when Mrs. Thatcher took office, and the country continues its slow drift down the list of the world's richest countries.[41] In the United States, productivity growth was negative in the two years before Reagan took office and in the two years after he left office.[42] What was a small trade surplus became a large trade deficit.

The countries that are outperforming America in international trade—Germany and Japan—do not have less government or more motivated citizens. They are countries noted for their careful organization of teams—teams that involve workers and managers, suppliers and customers, government and business. Teamwork has been an important part of American history—wagon trains conquered the West, for example, and teamwork put the U.S. on the moon. But American mythology passes it over and instead extols the individual—Rambo and the Lone Ranger. Only national mythology stands between Americans and the construction of successful economic teams.

Systematic benchmarking reveals that the United States does not have to undergo a period of blood, sweat, and tears to regain its productive edge. Much of what has to be done, such as building a better K-12 education system, would make America a better place to live. Consumption, both public and private, just has to grow more slowly than the GNP. It doesn't have to fall.

While the necessary solutions would impose small burdens on the present, the failure to adopt these small solutions will impose major burdens on the future.

The American problem is not the severity of the necessary solutions. America's tough problem is realizing that there are problems to be solved. Without that realization, nothing can be done.

References

1. Nomuran Research Institute American, "New Directions in Corporate Management and the Capital Market," 1990, p. 1.

2. G.C. Lodge, *Perestroika for America* (Boston: Harvard Business School Press, 1991), pp. 15–16.

3. This section is drawn from ideas in L. Tyson and L.C. Thurow, "The Economic Black Hole," *Foreign Policy,* Summer 1987, p. 3.

4. U.S. Congress, Joint Economic Committee, *Bibliography on Europe in 1992,* prepared by Hunter Monroe, 26 April 1989.

5. EC Delegation to the United States, *A Guide to the European Community* (Brussels: EC, 1991).

6. See L.C. Thurow, "Producer Economics," *IRRA 41st Proceedings,* 1989, p. 9; J.L. Baxter, *Social and Psychological Foundations of Economic Analysis* (New York: Harvester Wheatsheaf, 1988); and M.A. Lutz and K. Lux, *Humanistic Economics* (New York: The Bootstrap Press, 1988).

7. A.H. Amsden, "East Asia's Challenge to Standard Economics," *American Prospect,* Summer 1990, p. 71.

8. E. Mansfield, "Technological Change in Robotics: Japan and the United States" (Philadelphia: University of Pennsylvania, Working Paper), p. 12.

9. *Fortune,* 30 July 1990, p. 109.

10. S. Yamamoto, "Japan's Trade Lead: Blame Profit-Hungry American Firms," *Brookings Review,* Winter 1989–1990, p. 14.

11. C. Rapoport, "Why Japan Keeps on Winning," *Fortune,* 15 July 1991, p. 85; *Economist,* 16 February 1991, p. 75.

12. "The Giants that Refuse to Die," *Economist,* attributed to Tom Hill of SG Warburg, 1 June 1991, p. 72.

13. M. Yamazaki, "The Impact of Japanese Culture on Management," in *The Management Challenge: Japanese Views,* ed. L.C. Thurow (Cambridge: MIT Press, 1986), p. 31.

14. J.C. Abegglen and G. Stalk, Jr., *Kaisha, The Japanese Corporation: How Marketing, Money, and Manpower Strategy, Not Management Style, Make the Japanese World Pace Setters* (New York: Basic Books, 1984).

15. K. Hirose, "Corporate Thinking in Japan and the U.S.," *Journal of Japanese Trade and Industry* 4 (1989).

16. D.E. Westney, "Sociological Approaches to the Pacific Region," in *The Pacific Region: Challenges to Policy and Theory,* American Academy of Political and Social Science, September 1989, p. 27.

17. MIT Committee on Productivity, *Made in America* (Cambridge: MIT Press, 1989), p. 81.

19. L. Mishel and D.M. Frankel, *The State of Working America,* 1990–1991 (Washington, D.C.: Economic Policy Institute, 1991), p. 121.

20. National Science Foundation, R&D Expenditures (Washington, D.C.: GPO, 1990), pp. 1–20.

21. U.S. Department of Labor, *The Impact of Research and Development on Productivity Growth,* Bulletin 2331, September 1989.

22. *Fortune,* 30 July 1990, p. 109.

23. D. Julius, *Global Companies and Public Policy* (London: Royal Institute of International Affairs, 1990).

24. *Economist,* 20 September 1989, p. 105.

25. Committee on America's Future, *An "Investment Economics" for the Year 2000* (Washington, D.C.: Rebuild America Coalition, 1988).

26. L.C. Thurow, "VAT the Least Bad of Taxes," *Newsday,* 9 March 1986.

27. L.C. Thurow, *Zero Sum Solution* (New York: Simon and Schuster, 1985).

28. D. Yankelovich, "The Competitiveness Conundrum," *The American Enterprise,* September–October 1990, p. 43 and 45; Public Agenda Foundation, "Public Misperceptions" (New York: Public Agenda Foundation, Working Paper, 1990), Chart A.

29. Commission on the Skills of the Work Force, *America's Choice: High Skills or Low Wages,* 1990, ch. 5.

30. The following contains more than 5,000 pages of briefing papers on educational problems: Commission on Workforce Quality and Labor Market Efficiency, *Investing in People,* September 1989 (Washington, D.C.: The Commission, September 1989).

31. "U.S. Sets Priorities," *International Herald Tribune,* 17 February 1988, p. 9.

32. M.E. Rasell and L. Mishel, "Shortchanging Education" (Washington, D.C.: Economic Policy Institute, 1990).

33. *Made in America* (1989), p. 81.

34. This section is drawn from ideas in L. Thurow, "Let's Put Capitalists Back into Capitalism," *Sloan Management Review,* Fall 1988, p. 67–71.

35. Commission on Workforce Quality and Labor Market Efficiency (September 1989).

36. "Keiretsu: What They Are Doing, Where They Are Heading," *Tokyo Business Today,* September 1990; "Mitsubishi and Daimler-Benz Start Collaboration," *Tokyo Business Today,* November 1990.

37. "Mercantilists in Houston," *Economist,* 7 July 1990, p. 13.

38. W. Dullforce, "Japan Viewed as World's Most Unfair Trading Nation," *Financial Times,* 13 March 1990, p. 20.

39. *Journal of Japanese Trade & Industry,* No. 4, 1988, p. 15; and "Fiddling while U.S. Industry Burns," *Rebuild America,* February 1990.

40. C.H. Farnsworth, "U.S. Is Asked to Review Japan Trade," *New York Times,* 25 March 1991, p. 14.

41. National Institute of Economic and Social Research, *National Institute Economic Review,* November 1979, p. 23, and May 1991, p. 23.

42. *Economic Report of the President,* 1991.

Political Risk and Political Loss for Foreign Investment

Llewellyn D. Howell.   *Llewellyn D. Howell is Chairman, Department of International Studies, American Graduate School of International Management, Glendale, AZ 85306.*

Political Risk

The term "political risk" refers to the possibility that political decisions, events, or conditions in a country will affect the business climate in such a way that investors will lose money or not make as much money as they expected when the investment was made. Despite the fact that many in the academic field of political science do not immediately recognize the term "political risk" and do not associate it with their own regular pursuits, it is one of the oldest areas of political analysis and has been practiced by corporations and traders for hundreds, if not thousands, of years. It is a critical interface between the world of politics and that of economics (see Brewer, 1985:3–12). Political risk exists for both domestic investors and foreign investors and many of the techniques for assessment of risk are the same for both of them. Many of the responses to risk are different for them, however. Political risk assessments usually come in the form of a letter grade or numerical score for a country as a whole, with text support for the grade or score and its method of derivation. Investors use this grade as advice. It could be advice to avoid investing in certain countries. Choices are seldom this drastic and the investors then go on to utilize the ratings in negotiations. Negotiations would continue in many cases because risk also implies opportunity. Other investors might have left the field; the investor can guard against risk; risk may constitute a gamble and, as with gambling anywhere, high risk might mean high gain. As an example of negotiating opportunity, if the rating is poor, the investor might ask for a longer tax-free status than is otherwise granted in exchange for bringing capital to a dangerous situation. Whichever way the risk assessments are used, we see in political risk assessment a direct application of social scientific analytical outcomes to the business world where the costs and benefits are measurable in real dollar terms.

Political risk, as a field, has gone through an evolution over the past several decades. In the 1960s, confiscation, expropriation, and nationalization became critical concerns for companies with foreign operations and newly independent states managed their lack

The International Executive, Vol. 34(6) 485–498 (November/December 1992). © 1992 John Wiley & Sons, Inc. Reprinted by permission of John Wiley & Sons, Inc.

of capital by simply taking it (see Haendal, 1979:71–90). The field became considerably more complex after the 1979 fall of the Shah of Iran, when questions of political stability were added to the variables already being examined (Fry, 1983:57–60). Rummel and Heenan (1978:68–72) described the extant approaches as attempts to deal with political uncertainty and noted the variety of methods of trying to determine risk. They proposed a method of converting uncertainty into probability terms, using the term "risk" as a "mechanism for the objective evaluation of foreign investment climates." F. Theodore Haner had already developed the Business Environment Risk Information (BERI) Index as a quantitative guide to risk ratings, and William Coplin and Michael O'Leary began in 1979 what was to become the highly developed Political Risk Services (PRS) evaluation system. The variety of approaches were widely utilized by investors in the 1980s and continue to be highly popular as foreign investment burgeons in the aftermath of the Cold War's end.

Given the direct and immediate impact of the analyses, the importance of closely examining both the theory and method of a risk assessment approach is critical. Poor theory (or method) could result in ratings which are inaccurate and, in turn, not only cost the investor money but also do damage to a political system that does not receive investment or that has to make many concessions to foreign-owned corporations. In order to measure or even "assess" accuracy, the analyst must have data on losses due to political or social causes. Such data is difficult to obtain and is in short supply. Nevertheless, it must be obtainable or we must continue to take risk assessments at simple face value. Below we examine one case of a risk projection with a preliminary attempt to match the projections against actual outcomes.

Applied Risk Assessment: The *Economist* Method

There are a variety of circumstances under which political risk is assessed. Individual corporations assess risk using their own personnel and resources. Independent risk assessment corporations, such as Political Risk Services (PRS) or Business Environment Risk Information (BERI), regularly produce reports on 80–100 countries for corporations that do not have their own internal capability. A third and much more widely consumed method of producing analyses is that employed by several respected periodical publications, such as *Fortune* magazine and *The Economist*. Such publications are important in the risk analysis business because of both their readership and their professional character. They have also provided data that is in the public domain and which is useful in setting the groundwork for a contemporary analysis.

In 1986, *The Economist* (1986:25–38) produced a risk analysis under the title "Countries in Trouble." Its unnamed writers explained the method of analysis in three pages, with one table summarizing the results. While the explanation was brief, the method parallels those used by other risk analysts and can be interpreted in terms common to social science. While we may not entirely agree with the method established—indeed, some of it is not fully described and theoretical underpinnings are not even mentioned—it is a method that is concise, clear, and reflective of the thinking that is prevalent among businessmen who ultimately will make decisions about whether or not to take political risks with their investments. It does not break risk down into industry categories, as does Political Risk Services (Direct Investment, Finance, and Export), but it does address critical political and social variables that are primary in the attention spectrum of overburdened business executives.

Briefly, the article presents a list of factors that it describes as economic, political, and social (political and social are combined here as "political"); provides a scheme for weighing their individual impact and relative roles (measures of "risk" contribution); and offers a method for combining the risk scores and ranking them in such a way as to advise the reader of useful directions to take in investment ("analysis"). This study focuses only on losses due to political factors, and therefore does not consider the economic variables.

The Economist does confuse the issue somewhat by frequent use of the term "instability" instead of political or social risk. This is the first of many theory issues that require attention. While concerns about stability are common enough, conceptually stability—especially in the short term—is not what *The Economist* is talking about nor what investors are really interested in. For example, *The Economist* gives importance to the degree of authoritarianism in a system as a negative factor. That is, they assign more negative weight to more authoritarianism. But historically, authoritarian rule has been both characterized and justified as necessary for contributing to stability. The scaling system presented by *The Economist* weighs authoritarianism in the converse way, linking increased levels of authoritarianism with increased instability. This inconsistency would be problematic if the concern were "instability" rather than "political risk." Since political risk assessments are explicitly projections over an expected life of an invest-ment and not just the short term, the stability that might be induced by authoritarian rule is obviously not the primary concern here. Short-term stability under an authoritarian leader might simply be masking a greater discontent that ultimately (i.e., within the life of an investment) would result in political violence against an oppressive ruler. It is not appropriate, therefore, to equate instability with political risk. Instability may well be a separate variable that will bear on short-term political risk, but it was not one of those included in the study by *The Economist*. This analysis focuses explicitly on the political and social variables specified by *The Economist* so that this assessment will parallel theirs.

The Economist's method appears to be simple but, in fact, is relatively complex. An index of risk was created based on 100 points. Of those 100 points, 33 were attributed to economic factors, 50 to politics, and 17 to "society." How these divisions between sets of variables were made is not explained in the text, but reportedly were contributed by editors and reporters.

For each of the three areas, specific variables were selected that the writers felt reflected that particular domain. Among economic factors, *The Economist* selected "Falling GDP per person," "High inflation," "Capital flight," "High and rising foreign debt," "Decline in food production per person," and "Raw materials as a high percent-age of exports." While no explanation was provided of why these variables were selected or others (such as level of employment) were not, the variables chosen make sense from both a business and common sense perspective. This is another point, however, where underlying theory should have directed choices but apparently did not.

The set of political and social variables was selected via the same process. A brief discussion of *The Economist's* variables and their relative weights is necessary to understand how their advisory listing of attractive and unattractive investment environments was derived.

Social and Political Variables in Risk

The Economist chose six political variables worth a total of 50 points in weight and four social variables worth 17 points to represent the origins of what is generally called "political risk." They are described briefly below.

Bad Neighbors (three negative points). *The Economist* recognized the situational context as being a critical political variable. They argued that being near any superpower almost automatically meant trouble in that superpowers tend to control their peripheries, often with the use of force. Trouble spots are those with a history of being "disturbed" or with historically continuous violence. They cite the Middle East and South Africa as examples. The important implication of the inclusion of this variable is that domestic political environments are inextricably linked with regional and international systems and, no matter what their internal policies or conditions, the success of investment will depend on activities that may be outside the direct control of governments in the investment state.

Authoritarianism (seven points). Whether totalitarian or authoritarian, the lack of democracy in a state forbodes ill. The text of *The Economist's* description is somewhat murky on this point, recognizing that totalitarians, such as Fidel Castro, can use iron-fisted control to maintain a tolerable investment climate, but the data table labels the variable "how authoritarian" and assesses the countries that way. As indicated above, we agree with the latter operationalization and provided 1990 evaluations on the same basis: even rigid totalitarian control is only a temporary holding pattern; disruption and probably violence will seeth underneath.

Staleness (five points). The argument is that a leader needs about five years to get his or her bearings and a grip on the situation, but that after ten years he begins to get detached and stale. Complacency accompanies entrenchment, along with its siblings corruption, disdain, and delay.

Illegitimacy (nine points). Legitimacy implies an uncoerced and positive acceptance on the part of the population of a state. Political risk is a function of the gap between acceptability and a government's persistence in power. It is important to note here that legitimacy, in the sense used here, is a condition as perceived by those directly ruled, not by outsiders. Israel's legitimacy is a function of how its citizens feel about it, not the way the Islamic world sees it.

Generals in Power (six points).   In response to instability or the lack of competent civilian authority (or the military's perception of competent), military authorities often step in and take control themselves. *The Economist* argues that most military men do not know how to govern nor how to step aside gracefully. Simply as a matter of their own competence, they usually govern like they run their own military establishments. Since there is little in the way of democracy within the military, little shows in military-run regimes and such rigidity tends to breed dissent.

War/Armed Insurrection (20 points).   War, the most impactful of any of the variables selected, clearly penetrates the investment picture in a number of ways. Apart from the obvious destruction of physical plant, war disrupts the economy and brings about losses in a number of other ways. Raw goods and supplies are delayed or diverted to war use. Workers are drafted or simply prevented from getting to production facilities. Products are commanded to be altered to support war efforts instead of export. War has many ways of disrupting the economy, and therefore limiting the profitability or even retention of investment by foreign corporations. It should be noted that the Overseas Private Investment Corporation (OPIC) counts War and Civil Strife as two of their categories of sources of loss, rather than ingredients in a situation that later result in loss. This is not entirely inconsistent with what *The Economist* does. For *The Economist's* study, the war variable can be viewed as an indicator of probable past or ongoing loss, which naturally should be factored into calculations about what the future holds. To be consistent, though, a revised scheme should include a past history of inconvertability and expropriation in calculations of future risk. The current method does not.

Urbanization Pace (three points).   When the urbanization process is too rapid, or is too concentrated on a single city, a number of problems accompany the shift. These include "idleness and crime," an expansion of the drug trade, and economic irregularities, such as in the pricing of food. It is not the fact of urbanization itself but rather the nature of the process and its effect on the society that threatens the foreign investor.

Islamic Fundamentalism (four points).   *The Economist* argues that there was never much political fervor in Hinduism or Buddhism and that Christianity is a spent force. But, they continue, Muslim radicals could still change the world and where they are strong, the risk to investors is high, especially when the investors are foreign and not Muslim. There is certainly something of importance here and many observers focus on Muslim radicals as a key to the nature of the investment climate. But several questions must be dealt with in other studies on the question of political risk. First does "Islamic Fundamentalism" equal "Muslim radicals"? Many argue that there is more than a finite difference. Second, is it in fact true that other religious fundamentalists are as impotent as *The Economist* claims? Events in November of 1990 in India where Hindu fundamentalists were instrumental in bringing down the government of Prime Minister V. P. Singh would seem to indicate that religious fundamentalists of various types remain potent in political environments. In the Middle East context, a strong case can be made that Jewish fundamentalism in Israel has had a significant impact on the Israeli government's posture such that investors are at risk in ensuing strife. In any case, to parallel *The Economist*'s study, we have assessed Islamic fundamentalism in particular, which makes sense in the Middle East context in any case.

Corruption (six points).   Corruption exists everywhere. U.S. federal department scandals at the end of the Reagan administration and Savings and Loan problems into 1991 reflect its impact in the United States. But, in some cases, it has gotten out of hand. Corruption can distort the economy in ways that the best of investor awareness or even power cannot accommodate.

Ethnic Tension (four points).   Ethnic, religious, and racial tension provide an environment in which simple industry does not suffice. It may redirect government attention, invoke restrictions on investors (hiring one group and not the other), restrict labor resources, or result in open conflict. Governments may fall on the basis of its convolutions. Its presence detracts from normal functioning of political processes, which are almost always necessary for normal economic processes.

Many questions remain about the theoretical underpinnings of this set of variables and their weights. Subsequent studies will examine them more closely. In the meantime, *The Economist's* results have been widely distributed. Their scores for the political and societal variables—which fall together under the category of "political risk"—are presented in Table 1.

The Economist's Results, 1986

The Economist did not explain who generated its scores or exactly how they were created. It is necessary to assume that they were compiled from contributions by their own staff. While there is disagreement with many of the particular scores that were assigned, at least one study with a separate set of assessments, done shortly after the results were published, resulted in very similar scores and rankings for a subset of the countries (see Howell, 1989).

Table 1 includes the political and social risk scores for all 50 of the countries covered in the original study. The selection of variables generally seems to make sense to area specialists and most of them recur in the single replication that has thus far been reported (Howell, 1989). The weights may similarly be challenged, but for the initial part of this study they have been retained both because of the precedent and because of their heuristic value.

To test the capability of *The Economist's* model, researchers at the American Graduate School of International Management and at American University created a "loss" indicator for the period following the assessment (1987–91) by *The Economist,* The measure was scaled on a basis of 0–10 using information drawn from OPIC, from "Foreign Economic Trends," and from corporate reports or interviews. A measure of loss due to political reasons was needed to test the model and the theory, in this case employing multiple correlation and regression. It is important to emphasize that political risk only assesses likelihood of loss due to the political situation in a country, not those losses due to economic conditions or simply to business practice. To provide a feel for

TABLE 1   *The Economist* 1986 Political Risk Evaluations

	Neig.	Auth.	Stal.	Ille.	Gene.	War	Urba.	Isla.	Corr.	Ethn.	Totl.
Brazil	0	2	1	2	0	2	0	0	2	2	11
Venezuela	1	2	0	1	2	3	1	0	1	0	11
Portugal	0	2	0	1	1	5	1	0	1	1	12
Hong Kong	3	2	0	5	0	1	3	0	1	0	15
Greece	2	2	0	0	2	3	2	0	4	0	15
China	3	3	1	2	1	4	0	0	2	1	17
Singapore	0	5	5	3	0	0	3	0	0	2	18
Uruguay	0	3	2	4	2	3	2	0	2	0	18
Argentina	0	4	2	0	4	5	1	0	2	0	18
Algeria	1	4	3	2	0	4	0	2	2	1	19
Ecuador	1	3	2	3	2	5	1	0	3	0	20
Malaysia	1	4	0	4	0	5	1	1	3	4	23
South Korea	3	3	0	4	5	6	1	0	1	0	23
Colombia	0	0	0	2	1	10	1	0	6	3	23
Taiwan	3	4	4	4	2	3	0	0	1	3	24
India	2	2	3	2	0	7	0	0	5	4	25
Turkey	3	4	1	3	4	8	0	1	2	2	28
Bolivia	0	5	3	4	3	5	1	0	6	1	28
Mexico	3	5	5	4	0	5	1	0	5	1	29
Poland	3	4	5	5	5	4	0	0	3	1	30
Tanzania	2	6	5	3	1	5	1	0	6	1	30
Peru	0	5	0	4	3	12	1	0	4	2	31
Morocco	2	5	3	3	2	9	1	3	2	1	31
Tunisia	2	5	5	3	2	5	1	3	4	1	31
Sri Lanka	0	3	0	6	2	15	0	0	1	4	31
Saudi Arabia	3	7	5	5	2	3	0	3	3	1	32
Kenya	1	5	3	4	2	7	2	0	6	3	33
Bangladesh	0	5	3	5	5	5	1	1	6	2	33
Burma	1	5	5	3	3	10	0	0	4	2	33
Thailand	3	3	2	3	6	10	2	0	3	1	33
Guatemala	2	3	2	3	2	14	1	0	4	3	34
Zimbabwe	3	4	2	5	2	10	1	0	3	4	34
Yugoslavia	3	5	5	5	3	5	0	1	3	4	34
Philippines	0	3	4	4	3	10	1	2	4	3	34
Zambia	3	6	5	4	3	7	1	0	5	2	36
Zaire	2	6	5	5	3	7	0	0	6	3	37
Egypt	3	3	2	5	4	8	1	4	5	2	37
Ghana	0	5	2	5	6	7	1	1	6	4	37
Pakistan	3	4	3	4	4	7	0	4	5	3	37
South Africa	3	4	3	7	3	12	0	0	2	4	38
Chile	0	7	4	9	6	10	1	0	3	1	41
Nigeria	0	6	3	5	6	9	0	3	6	4	42
Vietnam	3	4	5	4	6	15	0	0	3	2	42
Indonesia	1	6	5	5	5	8	0	3	6	3	42
El Salvador	3	4	1	5	4	17	0	0	5	3	42
Sudan	3	5	3	4	3	16	1	3	5	4	47
Uganda	1	5	4	6	6	15	2	1	6	4	50
Iran	3	6	2	5	2	20	1	4	6	3	52
Ethiopia	2	6	3	6	6	17	1	1	6	4	52
Iraq	3	6	4	5	5	20	2	2	6	4	57

what constitutes a political loss, the Overseas Private Investment Corporation (OPIC, *Investment Insurance Handbook*) compensates its insured (i.e., those who take out political risk insurance in three major categories: (1) *inconvertibility*—active or passive denial of access to foreign exchange; (2) *expropriation*—nationalization or other uncompensated seizures of properties or operations of the foreign enterprise; and (3) *political violence*—losses resulting from violent acts undertaken with the primary objective of achieving a political objective. Losses from political violence are divided into "war damage" and "civil strife."

Although OPIC payment could constitute a measure of "political loss," OPIC only insures American firms and its insurance does not cover all forms of political loss, such as that due to ruthlessness of rulers or corruption. A broader measure was therefore needed. For example, in November of 1991, four engineers that had been kidnapped in Colombia were freed after their company reportedly paid between $800,000 and $1 million. Such costs, while entirely due to the political situation in the country, are not recoverable from OPIC, and therefore are not tabulated under this one existing loss tabulation system. Because of the deteriorating political and military situation in Burma, Thai Airlines flights to Rangoon have flown only minimally occupied. Considerable revenue has been lost, similarly without compensation. How can such losses be incorporated in a measured indicator?

For 33 of the countries, the researchers conducted interviews with businessmen and government officials in Washington, DC, sought written reports on possible corporate losses in these countries, and consulted with OPIC on reports to them and insurance payments for losses incurred by U.S. investors. Based on these reports, and after two reviews, the researchers assigned a value to each of the 33 countries on a scale of 0–10, where 0 meant no losses to foreign investors being reported, then ranging up to 10 for total loss of all investment. These loss scores were then correlated against each individual political or social variable as determined by *The Economist*. The loss scores were also correlated with the total summary score for all risk (16 variables), the political and social total score alone (ten variables), and the economic risk variables alone (six variables).

As the model in Figure 1 implies, the risk projection—if it in fact has appropriate theoretical underpinnings and accurate data—should correlate with subsequent losses. Even if theory and data were perfect, there might be less than a perfect correlation due to the fact that exogenous variables can always intervene, and also because knowledge of the risk assessment can be incorporated into planning by either the investor or the government of the country into which the investment is flowing. But if the theory and data are appropriate, there should be at least some significant correlation between the projection and actual losses in the following five-year period. This, however, was not the case.

Although the researchers looked specifically for losses that were related to political events or social conditions alone (i.e., not due to economic reasons), the correlation (Pearson's r) between the total of the weighted sociopolitical variables and the loss indicated was only .10 ($p = .29$). For the overall score, combining the economic, political and social variables, the correlation was somewhat improved but a still poor .17 ($p = .167$). The best projection of the "political and social" losses came from the economic variables taken by themselves. Here the correlation was .25 ($p = .078$), still not a large correlation and not significant.

FIGURE 1

*The
Economist's
1986 political
risk model*

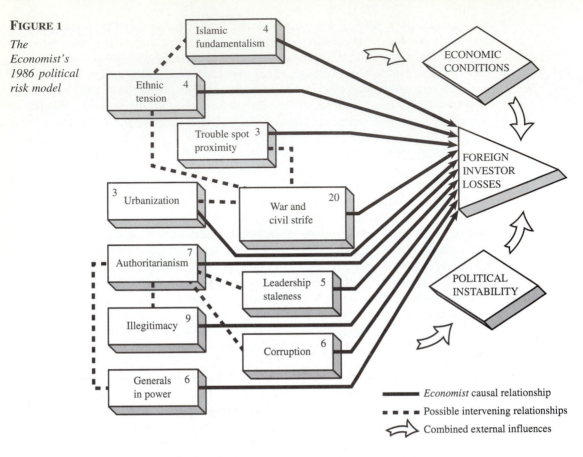

The largest correlation between any of the predictor variables and subsequent losses was with "Strife and war," which correlated with losses at .29 ($p = .049$). Each of the remaining variables correlated at less than .16 and none were significant.

The dependent variable (losses) clearly requires a more detailed assessment itself, although the researchers replicated their studies once and expressed confidence in their figures. As yet another replication of this exercise at the American Graduate School of International Management demonstrated, however, firms are reluctant to give out details of their losses, have not kept or have never had solid loss figures, do not distinguish between political and other types of losses if they are not insured by OPIC, and otherwise have not expected to be asked about this kind of hard loss data.

There is some evidence, however, that the problem does not lie simply with the dependent variable. A 1986 study using a loss variable constructed from OPIC insurance payments data and the Department of Commerce's "Foreign Economic Trends and Their Implications for the United States" (Howell, 1986), sources are used in this study, showed that there was predictability in the 18-month and five-year projections put forth by another political risk assessment enterprise using a different model and quite different variables.

TABLE 2   **Pearson Correlations**

Predictor Variables	Losses
Bad neighbor	$r = .12$
	$p = .25$
Authoritarianism	$r = .07$
	$p = .36$
Staleness	$r = -.12$
	$p = .26$
Illegitimacy	$r = .04$
	$p = .41$
Generals in power	$r = .05$
	$p = .40$
Strife/warfare	$r = .29$
	$p = .05$
Urbanization	$r = -.16$
	$p = .28$
Islamic fundamentalism	$r = -.11$
	$p = .28$
Corruption	$r = .09$
	$p = .31$
Ethnic confrontation	$r = .07$
	$p = .34$

Several other approaches to the problem of noncorrespondence should also be tried. Both the weights of the independent variables and the inclusion of the particular ten chosen by *The Economist* can be challenged. It may also be that fewer variables selected on the basis of factor-analyzed groupings or just more explicit theory would be appropriate. What we do have at this point is some evidence that the projections offered by *The Economist* in its 1986 study—although interesting and potentially useful—were not useful to its readers.

The approach to political risk analysis employed by *The Economist* still has value for a variety of reasons. It is clear and appealing. It is transparent; in contrast to more academic approaches to analysis, its method is openly presented and therefore easily replicated—something that is much needed for most analyses, including those presented in the major academic journals. By inviting criticism and evaluation of theory and method, *The Economist's* article provides a significant contribution to the field of political risk analysis. More than virtually every other subfield of political science, political risk analysis directly and immediately affects both the firms that employ it and the national economies that depend on investors. A risk projection that is far off base, because of poor theory or poor data or poor analytical methods, can easily result in losses themselves and become a contributor to the very phenomenon they are trying to observe. Underlying theory, in particular, has been widely neglected in the assessment of political risk analyses. This certainly should not be the case. The absence of solid data on politically related losses to businesses compounds the analytical problems and leaves the investor without a basis for determining the accuracy of political risk projections. Such theory, method, and data problems undermine the credibility of potential risk analysis and deserve and require directed attention.

References

Brewer, Thomas L. (1985) "Politics, Risks, and International Business," in Thomas L. Brewer (Ed.), *Political Risks in International Business: New Directions for Research Management, and Public Policy,* New York: Praeger Publishers, 3–12.

"Countries in Trouble" (December 20, 1986) *The Economist,* 25–28,

Fry, Earl H. (1983) *The Politics of International Investment,* New York: McGraw-Hill.

Haendel, Dan (1979) *Foreign Investments and the Management of Political Risk,* Boulder, CO: Westview Press.

Howell, Llewellyn D. (1986) "Area Specialists and Expert Data: The Human Factor in Political Risk Analysis," in Jerry Rogers, (Ed.), *Global Risk Assessments, Book 2,* Riverside, CA: GRA, Inc., 47–84.

Howell, Llewellyn D. (November 18, 1989) "Political Risk Analysis Inside-Out: A Malaysian Perspective on Malaysia," Paper presented at the Academy of International Business (AIB) Conference, Singapore.

OPIC (n.d.) *Investment Insurance Handbook,* Washington, DC: Overseas Private Investment Corporation.

OPIC (n.d.) *1990 Report,* Washington, DC.

OPIC (September 30, 1990) "Insurance Claims Experience to Date: OPIC and its Predecessor Agency," Washington, DC: OPIC.

Rummel, Rudolf J. and Heenan, David A. (January–February 1978) "How Multinationals Analyze Political Risk," *Harvard Business Review,* 67–76.

The Legal Environment

Law alludes to a compendium of rules of conduct or practices established and enforced by governmental authority, legislation, or community custom in a region, state, or nation. For the international marketer, a basic understanding of four legal systems is essential; common law, code law, Muslim law, and the legal systems of the member republics of the former USSR. Each is different philosophically and in practice.

This section contains four important contributions. The first covers key aspects of intellectual property piracy and protection. The design and trade dress of products, their trademarks, and packaging are widely copied by international counterfeiters around the world. What can be done to stem the tide of this multibillion dollar impingement? It documents government and private sector initiatives to redress such wrongdoing. Worldwide patent protection is equally important for the international marketer. An insightful paper on the important differences between Japanese patent law system and that of the United States and European nations documents the difficulty of protecting oneself in Japan. The goal of Western nations' patent laws is to protect product uniqueness from infringement by others and thereby reward innovators. By contrast, the goal of the Japanese patent system is to encourage the spread of technology among competitors.

The next paper documents the nature and importance of 20 key nontariff barriers that adversely affect firms seeking to penetrate foreign markets. Entry strategies to be considered by small business owner/managers are included in this contribution.

The scope of international bribery is the final topic in the section. Has the passage by the United States of the Foreign Corrupt Practices Act, which forbids American companies from making payments to foreign officials in order to obtain a competitive advantage, placed our firms at a disadvantage? Lobbyists for American industry answer in the affirmative. Research studies by others suggest that this fear is exaggerated. Decide for yourself. Keep in mind that lubrication payments to lower-level personnel or officials to expedite the normal performance of legal work are now permitted under the Foreign Corrupt Practices Act. But recall also that in certain European countries, bribes can be deducted from business tax returns as a legitimate expense. That same practice is not permitted in the United States.

Rip-Off

Warren Strugatch.

Sitting in their boxes on the shelf of an upscale Parisian toy store, the Sindy dolls manufactured by Hasbro's French subsidiary seem a perfectly innocuous gift item to the prosperous young matrons and doting aunts shopping for gifts on a recent morning. The genteel calm is shattered suddenly when several gendarmes file into the store, take the proprietor aside and begin yanking the dolls off the shelves. That afternoon, criminal charges are filed against a senior executive of Hasbro SA.

Such toy wars represent small skirmishes in a growing battle between US manufacturers and their allies against those who would steal the fruits of their intellectual labor. This toy store-dragnet began when Mattel complained to French police that arch-rival Hasbro Europe had created Sindy—sold only in Europe—as a knock-off of Mattel's legendary Barbie doll. The cops came in because that's how you pursue copyright infringement in France, says Mattel copyright enforcer Viki McBroom.

Sales of Sindy to would-be Barbie buyers not only siphon away revenues unfairly, but also erode Mattel's image, according to McBroom. "We get letters from parents who bought Sindy," she says. "The leg broke off and they blame us. They send us broken toys in the mail, and say it's a faulty product and want us to reimburse them. It damages Mattel's reputation and, as an infringing product, we want it off the shelves."

One thing is clear: Piracy did not die off with Long John Silver. According to government estimates, US manufacturers lose $60 billion a year because foreign companies or individuals poach on American brainpower. Yet international copyright law transcends simplistic jingoism: Sometimes it's US companies that are vilified as copycats. Compounding the problem are conflicting international intellectual property laws and the lack of agreement on what constitutes a proprietary idea. Says Hasbro general counsel Donald Robbins: "Mattel thinks they have the rights to blonde hair and blue eyes. Obviously, we think they don't."

Americans indeed poach on one another, both here and overseas. But more often the Skull and Crossbones is hoisted over foreign vessels. Piracy is increasingly recognized as a trade barrier no less vicious than rice quotas, licensing restrictions, and protectionist duties. And the Bush Administration is moving to hold governments responsible when US intellectual property is plundered by their nationals. The leverage is trade sanctions.

This spring, US Trade Representative Carla Hills pushed the envelope by citing the three most notorious IPR violators—China, India, and Thailand—under the so-called

Reprinted from *World Trade,* August/September 1991.

Special 301 measure. The measure, a section of US trade law amended by the Omnibus Trade and Competitiveness Act of 1988, allows the three countries six months to improve IPR legislation and enforcement practices or face serious trade sanctions. It was the first time the measure has been used; most assuredly it will not be the last.

"We have widespread recognition of the importance of IPR issues for the first time in my career, and that goes back 30 years," says Larry W. Evans, director of the patent and license department at BP America, and former president of the Licensing Executives Society. "It is recognized that the US is still the creator of most of the basic intellectual property in the world. As such we are the chief victims of piracy. We are beginning to attack these issues diligently in proportion to the extraordinary losses occurring overseas ever year."

Extraordinary, indeed. According to the International Intellectual Property Alliance (IIPA), a Washington coalition representing over 1,600 companies in publishing, recording, films, and business technology, piracy losses in the so-called core copyright industries in 11 "problem countries" cost the US economy over $1.3 billion in 1988, the most recent year surveyed. Worst offender, says IIPA: The People's Republic of China.

The core copyright industries are sound recordings, book publishing, film production, computer software, and music publishing. Other victims: Pharmaceuticals, toys, apparel, textiles, luggage, and personal computers. Just about anything you can copyright, patent, trademark or license is being knocked off, copied, dubbed, cloned, and sold. To bury all their loot, today's international pirates would need a desert island the size of Greenland.

Losses aren't limited to overseas sales. Millions of products manufactured abroad without permission are imported into this country where they typically underprice the bona fide originals. Most of it is distributed to discount retailers, which undermines market positioning. Disgruntled customers blame the wrong party, when the counterfeit goods disappoint, further blighting sales.

The victims of piracy include some of the standard-bearers of corporate America, as well as thousands of inventors, designers, songwriters and recording artists who have never worn a business suit (nor a droopy bow tie) in their lives. In May, five software biggies, including Lotus Development Corp. and Microsoft Inc., filed criminal charges in Korea against unlicensed users. At the same time the music industry was continuing its efforts to halt sales of bootlegged product both here and abroad, claiming it was protecting the proverbial little guy no less than such megastars as Madonna and Springsteen.

Most audiocassette and compact disc piracy involves international pop hitmakers, but the industry's more marginal players are hardly exempt. Take the Bodeans, up-and-coming rockets whose tapes and CDs you can find at both your local music outlet or on your next trip to Bangkok. Too many lost sales to the gray market, and the Bodeans are history. Says Charles Sanders, staff attorney for the National Music Publishers Association: "It's not just money out of Madonna's pocket. The songwriter doesn't get royalties, and the mid-level artist might sell 250,000 copies while another 250,000 are pirated. The songwriter will have to take a day job, and the artist will get dropped from the label."

Pirating isn't limited to product. If you're planning to sell overseas using a trademark or servicemark, expect that sooner or later you'll confront that scourge of marketers, the trademark extortionist. This rogue will try to register your mark in his country, then sell your own mark back to you. James A. Amos, Jr., international licensing manager for the Dallas-based I Can't Believe It's Yogurt chain, had just cracked his first overseas market, Great Britain, when he got a ransom letter for UK rights to the ICBIY mark. Amos, however, had registered the mark in advance, and tossed the letter. His next market, Thailand, featured a similar welcome. This time Amos merely shrugged off the demands: In Thailand such niceties hardly matter. The lesson: "Each country is different. But you absolutely can't let piracy deter you."

The Japanese, predictably, put their own spin on this. Inventors of manufacturing processes are particularly vulnerable in Japan—thanks to a patent system favoring the Japanese corporation and stifling the small technology developer. When US-based Fusion System Inc. filed a Japanese patent for a microwave-charged lamp with a manufacturing application, Mitsubishi Corp. quickly surrounded the patent with numerous similar patents, in effect smothering the original.

"It's called patent flooding," snarls William K. Krist, vice-president for international affairs for the American Electronic Association. "A company like Mitsubishi will pull stuff out of physics textbooks and file two or three hundred patents around yours. You've got to refute each one of those, and that takes forever." Even if "forever" lasts only several years, the technology's cutting edge has dulled.

A final insult added to injury: Patentholders must sometimes defend themselves against lawsuits when counterfeits cause damages or injuries. Mattel import-export manager Fermin Cuzo observes that counterfeiters rarely follow the industry's safety standards. That raises the liability issue and forces some companies to prove they did not manufacture the bogus stuff. In the early '80s Monsanto Corp. fought in court to prove the rice presticide that failed to protect an entire Taiwanese rice crop one year was a copyright infringement and not a Monsanto product. They were successful, but at great expense.

For all the skullduggery out there, the majority of the world's nations do indeed recognize IPR. Those that don't rarely escape the corrective actions of industry collectives and the US government. The threat of trade sanctions is no paper tiger. Industry insiders laud Carla Hills' evident willingness to play hardball, sending the message loud and clear to foreign governments that they better shape up. Other messages, delivered more privately, have targeted lesser offenders in the Pac Rim, as well as violators in Africa, the Middle East, and South America. Sometimes the exigencies of foreign policy blunt these efforts, however; nobody is going after Saudi Arabia, number-two trampler of US intellectual property rights.

China, number one on the pirate list, is a different story. It's probably no coincidence that as trade with the PRC has tilted dramatically in China's favor—it is today our second-biggest deficit trading partner—Beijing's treatment of US intellectual property has become a hot political issue. The big US loser here is the publishing industry. An intensive campaign by the Association of American Publishers (AAP), once hailed as a prototype for Americans eager to nurture respect for intellectual property rights overseas, has ended up remaindered and shredded, a victim of Chinese intransigence and sovereign arrogance.

Chapter One started several years ago, when the AAP hosted a lengthy US visit by a Chinese delegation studying intellectual property rights in anticipation of drafting new

PATENT TRENDS

First to Invent? Or First to File?

One problem for US intellectual property holders: We don't play by the same set of rules as everyone else. Outside the Philippines, we are isolated in following a system known as first-to-invent. The rest of the world follows first-to-file. In the US, an inventor must prove he was first to come up with the idea; elsewhere, whoever files first gets the patent. The two systems are incompatible because of what's known as the absolute novelty requirement. That means that if word gets out in Asia, say, about a new widget, the fellow who invented that widget but did not file a patent loses ownership claims in that market.

Word gets out because an inventor makes the rounds to promote his or her gadget to potential corporate customers. Why not file first and then get out and make the promotional rounds? Simple: Filing for patent protection costs money.

"You want to assess the value of your technology before spending maybe $100,000 on filing expenses," observes patent expert Walter J. Steinkraus, an attorney with the Minneapolis firm of Vidas & Arrett. To write and file a case in the US costs up to $7,000; add the cost of translations and filing in every country in the world that represents a potential market and the wisdom of Steinkraus' advice becomes clear.

The Geneva-based World International Property Organization is said to be considering a compromise that would allow US inventors a grace period of a year. During that year, they could promote their ideas and still be able to file for ownership. Ultimately, however, full harmonization is inevitable. And that means that the US will probably have to accept the first-to-file system, says BP America's Larry W. Evans.

legislation. AAP staffers tutored the bureaucrats in the intricacies and philosophy of US copyright law. There were nods, polite smiles, and handshakes all around. Unlike most foreign students, the Chinese went home with the school's library, in this case an extensive collection of legal volumes given them by their hosts. Once home, they indeed advised their leaders in Beijing—but certainly not in the way the AAP had in mind. The new policy leaves US books as vulnerable to infringement as ever. Fumes Carol Risher, an AAP official who doubles as IIPA executive director: "The Chinese played around for years and then passed a domestic copyright law but did not take steps to ensure protection for foreign works. I call it 'wanton piracy.'"

Japan is another problem area, although efforts to disengage piracy from Japanese business-as-usual are predictably frustrating. The Fusion-Mitsubishi quarrel is the flashpoint of this debate. Former International Trade Commissioner Paula Stern, now a trade consultant in Washington and advisor to Fusion, agrees the Mitsubishi patents would certainly have been disallowed under US law. Japan, however, is not the US. "The rules of the road are different" in Japan and elsewhere, she observes. Her advice to global-minded manufacturers: "Learn the rules."

That's what Symbol Technologies did. In 1987, Symbol, the world leader in bar-code data scanners, took a Japanese company to US Federal court, charging patent infringement. Last year, the Bohemia, NY-based company won that case against Opto Electronics Co., Ltd. of Japan and its US subsidiary, Opticon of Orangeburg, NY. At issue were sales in the US of various hand-held laser scanners made in Japan.

The rule seems simple: Find a foreign partner who knows its home market better than you do. Less than a year after the Federal court decision, Symbol announced a comprehensive long-term technology agreement aimed at the Japan market. Symbol's partner is Olympus Optical Co., Ltd. of Tokyo, the $1.5-billion company famous for its cameras and related products. The joint venture company, Olympus-Symbol Inc., will be licensed by Symbol Technologies to sell and support bar-code data products in Asia. Initially, the products will be manufactured and supplied to the joint venture company by Symbol Technologies in the US. Once the know-how is transferred from Symbol, Olympus will design and manufacture—and protect—them in Japan.

Efforts by Washington and leading trade associations have yielded remarkable success in certain countries, most notably Singapore. Once the undisputed world capital of piracy, by the early '80s Singapore was increasingly isolated from technological innovations and faced the loss of favorable trade status. Its government clamped down on piracy, but hard. Losses in the core US copyright industries dropped from $358 million in 1984 to only $10 million in 1988, the IIPA reports. Similar improvements were registered in Taiwan and Indonesia, and to a lesser extent Korea.

"Why these countries are changing is a good question," says Kate Hotchkiss, Asian expert at the Minnesota Trade Office. "International scrutiny is one reason. These countries do substantial trade all over the world, and they know this is one area in which they did not have a good reputation. They knew they needed to improve, and they are improving. But it's a slow process."

Battling the pirates is easier from our own shores. Under controversial Section 337 of the Tariff Act, Customs can inspect shipments suspected of containing unlicensed imports and detain what seems unlicensed. Often they work on tips from staff attorneys and trade group officials. The complainant must post a bond worth 120 percent of the shipment's values, which is non-refundable if the goods prove legitimate. The Recording Industry Association of America even maintains a hotline so sources can snitch on bootleggers (call 1-800-BAD-BEAT). CDs are hot now; last year more than 152,000 were confiscated internationally, 40 percent of them by Customs. Don't expect to find Horowitz or Coleman Hawkins discs among them. Says RIAA attorney Steven D'Onofrio: "If you want to know what's being bootlegged, just check the Top 40 list."

The idea behind 337 is to enable small companies to protect their licenses. Says John Peterson, of Neville, Peterson & Williams law firm in New York: "If your trademark or copyright is registered correctly, Customs will stop a shipment if the consignee is not someone licensed to accept it. It's a step even a very small company can take without incurring major expense."

Utilizing Section 337 is no day at the beach, however. At Applause Inc., which buys and transfers licensing agreements for dozens of trademarked gift items, staff attorney Harold Kyle contends that the price of a sound licensing import program is eternal vigilance. Licensed to import merchandise bearing the likenesses of the California Raisins—remember them?—Kyle kept busy watching 60 copyrights when the trend peaked. Kyle kept in frequent contact with Customs agents at local ports in efforts to catch the merchandise before it reached the distribution chain. The effort, he says, was successful.

Nor is Section 337 without its critics. Some complain that Double-Three-Seven is a license to kill competition. At least one lawsuit has been filed by a small importer seeking to prohibit the RIAA from consulting to Customs. "A private organization advising a government agency as to what may or may not be counterfeit strikes me as a large competitor of mine advising the government as to whether my imports are counterfeit or not," says Wes Oishi, a Los Angeles importer who is not involved in that lawsuit. It would be better, he says, if Customs agents understood the products passing through the ports, and made their own decision. "If you're in charge of commodity in the record business, you should know the difference between the Beatles and Liberace," he says. "Often Customs agents don't."

Customs cannot inspect every container, of course, even with help from 337. Apparel merchandisers yearn to keep knock-offs, imported and domestic alike, out of discount outlets, a graveyard for upscale products. "Knock-offs happen whenever you have an attractive 'mark,'" says Antonio R. Sarabia, a staff lawyer with Guess? Inc. "You can't just let it go. We patrol swap meets and flea markets throughout the country, really throughout the world, to locate vendors selling mock merchandise. The vendors usually surrender the merchandise without fuss," he says.

While counterfeit products are at times indistinguishable from the real McCoy, just as often the manufacturer's haste to get the product out of the shop produces the biggest guffaws in what is otherwise a rather somber profession. When IPR types let their hair down these days, they often tell the story of the new candy knock-off selling throughout China. It's called W&Ws. The slogan promises: "Melts your mouth, not your hands."

Ouch.

Non-Tariff Barriers and Entry Strategy Alternatives: Strategic Marketing Implications

Earl Naumann and Douglas J. Lincoln.   *Dr. Naumann is associate professor of marketing at Boise State University. His current research areas include a variety of international marketing issues. He has conducted numerous international research projects in the Pacific Rim. Dr. Lincoln is professor of marketing and chairman, Department of Marketing and Finance, Boise State University. He has conducted numerous research projects involving small business.*

Currently, the U.S. export market is dominated by large companies and multinational corporations. Kathawaba, Judd, Montipallil, and Weinrich (1989) state that only 10 percent of the total U.S. export business is conducted by small business despite the fact that foreign markets may offer the smaller firm solid opportunities for long-term growth and profitability. Furthermore, involvement in international business is not typically a formal objective flowing from the strategic thought processes of most U.S. small businesses. Instead, initial attempts to export are often stimulated by an inquiry from a potential customer located in a specific foreign country (Suzman and Wortzel 1984, Piercy 1981). Graham and Meloan (1986) found that 86 percent of the firms in their study initiated exporting as a result of these foreign inquiries and only 17 percent of the firms indicated that any significant research was completed before exporting began. Johnston and Czinkota (1985) had similar findings in their study of three industries. Only 38 percent, 50 percent, and 53 percent of the firms in each industry actively sought their first foreign order; conversely, between 47 percent and 62 percent of these firms received their first order on an unsolicited basis. Thus, despite the potential for sales growth and the existence of numerous government and private sector support programs, it appears that the majority of American small businesses begin exporting because someone overseas seeks them and/or their product, not because of a planned marketing strategy to enter a foreign market. Ironically, very few small businesses attempting to compete domestically would admit that they can be successful by waiting for customers to come to them. It may be just as illogical to expect high levels of international marketing success by taking this reactive approach.

Although small businesses can seemingly achieve some success in exporting by waiting for foreign customers to contact them on an unsolicited basis, the more

---

Reprinted from the *Journal of Small Business Management*, April 1991, pp. 60–70.

successful exporters probably pursue a focused, planned approach that clearly identifies foreign target markets and adapts their current domestic strategy when and where necessary (Dawson 1985, Kaynak et al. 1987, Namiki 1988). While a well organized, planned entrance into international markets will enhance the probability of success as well as the level of success (e.g., sales or profit volumes), many obstacles and challenges are likely to be encountered. These obstacles originate from sources both internal and external to the firm.

Non-tariff barriers (NTBs) constitute a complex set of constraints that can frustrate and thwart the small business's international efforts. Recent literature has suggested that NTBs may now be the major obstacle faced by firms attempting to enter foreign markets (Czinkota, Rivoli, and Ronkainen 1989; Jeannet and Hennessey 1988).

The purpose of this article is to provide an analysis of the NTBs most likely to be encountered by small businesses and to suggest strategies that can be used to overcome these constraints to international trade. NTBs are thus viewed as "restraints" to the small business international marketing efforts that can require business strategy changes in order to adapt to market differences.

Non-Tariff Barriers

Non-tariff barriers did not seriously affect trade flows until the mid-1960s (Baldwin 1970). Prior to that time, tariffs (e.g., financial surcharges) were the dominant means of distorting world trade flows to the benefit of a particular host country. However, the success of the General Agreement on Tariffs and Trade (GATT) rounds has resulted in relatively low tariff levels (averaging between 4 and 7 percent) among industrialized countries. As tariff protection has diminished, non-tariff protection has emerged as a difficult, challenging constraint and may now be the most significant trade distorting mechanism (Ray and Marvel 1984). While a free, unconstrained flow of world trade is a theoretical economic ideal, political realities make protectionism a persistent fact of life. Thus, small businesses entering international trade markets must be familiar with the pervasiveness of NTBs. Any encounter with NTBs can spell instant failure for the small business not cognizant of the implications. Simply stated, NTBs provide a challenge not typically encountered in the smaller firm's domestic markets.

NTBs may be defined as "government laws, regulations, policies, or practices that either protect domestic producers from foreign competition or artificially stimulate exports of particular domestic products" (*Foreign Trade Barriers* 1987). For all practical purposes, this definition is normally broadened to include private sector business practices, such as monopolistic or oligopolistic industrial structures (e.g., closed distribution systems) that effectively preclude foreign access to domestic markets or restrain competition with domestic organizations. This broader definition is used here, and includes both public and private sector practices that distort trade flows.

Types of Non-Tariff Barriers

While NTBs are acknowledged to be important trade distorting mechanisms, few studies have addressed their strategic implications for either large or small businesses. Several

---

TABLE 1   20 Common NTBs

1. Import quotas
2. Minimum import pricing
3. Marketing or advertising restrictions
4. Restrictive transportation requirements
5. Port of entry taxes or levies
6. Import licensing requirements
7. Complex customs procedures
8. Product quality or technical standards
9. Arbitrary product classification
10. Safety and health requirements
11. Packaging and labeling requirements
12. Low cost government financing and subsidies
13. Local content regulations
14. Rebate of domestic taxes to exporters
15. Discriminatory government procurement contracts
16. Required countertrade
17. Voluntary export restraints
18. Domestic monetary restrictions
19. Volatile exchange rates
20. Lack of access to suitable market channels

---

studies have categorized NTBs in some manner (Cao 1980, Onkvisit and Shaw 1988, Ray 1981, Ray and Marvel 1984). Other studies have provided comprehensive lists of possible NTBs (Organization for Economic Cooperation and Development 1985, United Nations Conference on Trade and Development 1983). Moreover, other studies have provided insight into the NTBs that may influence a particular product (Monke and Taylor 1985) or a particular industry (Food and Agriculture Organization 1986). However, these studies generally focus on international trade policy issues and neglect the strategic implications for businesses.

The remainder of this section will provide a brief discussion of each of the 20 NTBs presented in Table 1. These 20, based on our review of the literature, appear to be those most likely to be encountered by U.S. small businesses that are initiating international trade efforts. It is important to note that NTBs are not applied uniformly from country to country or even among different industries in a given country. Hence, the following discussion is intended to be *illustrative* of the most common types of NTBs; in specific situations, other NTBs not addressed here could be quite important.

Import quotas are fairly straightforward quantitative restrictions on imports and may be expressed as individual units imported or as a total value of imports. Since quotas are commonly imposed on an annual basis, this type of NTB has the effect of forcing imports into the first part of the year as foreign competitors rush to capture domestic share before the quota is reached and all imports cease. This NTB has implications for inventory levels (i.e., stock build up), timing of promotional efforts (i.e., early in the year), and financing and credit strategies (arranging inventory financing).

Minimum import pricing is intended to provide a pricing floor which is pegged in some manner to the domestic price structure. Depending upon the required price level, this can effectively increase the domestic firm's gross profit margin and shift its marketing strategy emphasis to non-price elements. This may be a significant strategic barrier for small businesses with generic or commodity products where product differentiation is difficult or impossible to achieve.

Marketing or advertising restrictions are placed on the types of products that can be advertised, the types of advertising claims allowed, and ads which name competing products (i.e., comparative advertising). Small businesses whose domestic promotional strategies rely on such approaches may find creating customer awareness very difficult in foreign markets.

Restrictive transportation requirements may include pallet size, container size, and material handling limitations. Also, many less developed countries (LDCs) simply lack a reliable domestic transportation infrastructure. China offers an excellent example of this NTB.

Port-of-entry taxes or levies are sometimes placed on imports flowing through a country's ports of entry. The original purpose of this NTB was to generate a user-based tax to help defray infrastructure development costs for airports as well as port facilities. However, these taxes often endure well past the time necessary to offset the original capital cost and are often higher than operating costs would indicate. These NTBs may vary from port of entry to port of entry in the same country. As with many other NTBs, a small business looking into foreign markets must assess the impact of these taxes on their anticipated margins, price competitiveness, and overall financing goals.

Import licensing requirements can take one of two forms. First, the right to import certain types of products can be limited through the allocation of import licenses, restricting the number of foreign competitors in a given industry. Thus, a late market entrant would be excluded from that country. Second, import licenses may be unlimited, but the process of obtaining the license is difficult. Due to bureaucratic delays, it may take a year or more to obtain the right to import products. Thus, a strategic window could close before a firm would be able to respond to a market opportunity. Without a foreign agent or partner who "knows the system," a small business may be excluded from such markets.

Customs procedures, while uniformly applied, may be an NTB through sheer complexity. Without the help of foreign-based expertise, the American small business may experience great difficulty in overcoming this NTB.

Product quality or technical standards for determining a product's quality level are not uniform from country to country and product testing performed in one country may be of little or no value in another country. Thus, the product testing for many products must be done in those foreign countries due to the unacceptability of foreign data. Also, product adaptation may be necessary to meet unique technical requirements.

Arbitrary product classification refers to the sometimes unpredictable manner in which a foreign country classifies the small business's product(s). A given product's classification, which can be highly subjective, affects its duty status. In some cases, the small business may be able to change its classification to a more advantageous position by altering its packaging or other informational programs.

Safety and health requirements can be an obstacle, as many countries have unique product content requirements not found elsewhere. Again, product changes for the small business represent one of the costliest changes and may therefore suggest a "no-go" entry decision.

Packaging and labeling are typically unique for each country. This NTB requires that inventory be maintained separately for each destination country and carries with it significantly increased finished product inventory levels.

Low-cost government financing or direct government subsidies to domestic firms indicates the relationship between government and business in many foreign countries is much closer and more symbiotic than in the U.S. This often results in the government, either directly or indirectly, providing loans at very favorable rates to its domestic businesses. This pattern is particularly prevalent in the "planned" economies of the Pacific Rim.

Local content regulations are typically expressed as a minimum percentage of a product's total value added that must be produced in a host country to avoid high tariffs. This can be satisfied through acquisition of component parts, product assembly, or finish work and is intended to provide a degree of domestic employment.

Rebates of domestic taxes to exporters are often found in countries with a heavy export reliance. Commonly, a portion of value added taxes are rebated or credited to domestic producers based on the total value of exports. This has the effect of reducing the marginal cost associated with the level of production that is exported. Another commonly rebated tax is the import duty on items such as component parts intended for further re-export. Somewhat less common is the rebating of tariffs on imported equipment and machinery, if the equipment or machinery is used to support an export directed product. The small firm that exports to such a country may actually pay the import tax while the domestic firm receives the rebate.

Discriminatory government procurement contracts are one of the oldest and most common NTBs. This NTB reflects the desire to spend public funds in the domestic economy. Examples of this NTB can be found in almost every country (e.g., U.S. Government purchases), and the large volume of public expenditures in the industrialized economies make the economic impact of this NTB significant. Bidding deadlines are also often sufficiently short to make it difficult for foreign small businesses to effectively respond.

Required countertrade is an NTB found primarily in developing countries and less developed countries. The intent is to boost domestic exports while maintaining an even balance of trade. A small business will have to carefully assess whether or not it can use and/or effectively market products that it would receive as part of a countertrade arrangement.

Voluntary export restraints (VER), sometimes referred to as "orderly market arrangements," are "gentlemen's agreements" among countries that limit the level of product flows in international trade. The internal allocation of exports is typically fixed on a base year, and market share becomes fixed at that level. This implies that "growing" countries or firms are at a disadvantage while the industry leader is at a distinct advantage. Looking from the opposite side, small businesses "late" into a market would be precluded from exporting to a country enforcing a VER.

Domestic monetary restrictions, particularly those in the less developed or newly industrialized countries, impose limitations on the expatriation (removal) of profits from their country. This effectively forces profits to be reinvested domestically. Tight controls on cash transactions are also imposed in many countries, thus dictating cash management strategy.

Exchange rates between industrialized countries are often allowed to float within targeted ranges while exchange rates in less developed countries are more volatile. Large differences in relative exchange rates may result in a competitive delivered cost position in one country and a prohibitively high delivered cost in another country. The small business manager must anticipate exchange fluctuations and deal with this NTB just as larger organizations do.

Lack of access to suitable marketing channels occurs in many of the Pacific Rim countries that are "planned" economies requiring close coordination between government and industry. The frequent result of this coordination is the development of industries that are controlled by relatively few firms. If a U.S. small business attempts to export to such a situation, it must deal with one of the dominant firms or be shut out of the desired market.

NTB Summary

The NTBs discussed above appear to be the more important ones that may occur in many foreign markets. However, there are numerous other NTBs that can be significant obstacles in specific situations. Additionally, NTBs are rarely applied individually. Rather, they are often used in combination so that the effective level of protectionism can be quite high. In some cases, the quantity and severity of a foreign country's NTBs may be such that the small business's entry into the market is not economically viable. However, in other cases, the costs are not as large, and knowledge of NTBs suggests to the small business *why* and *how* their current (domestic) business/marketing strategy should be altered to achieve international success.

Entry Strategies

Once small business owners/managers decide to engage in international trade, they must decide how they are going to enter foreign markets. The alternative approaches are referred to as entry strategies. It has been noted that closed markets (i.e., those with a high level of tariffs and/or NTBs) are the biggest challenge to firms entering international trade (Jeannet and Hennessey 1988). However, the level of protectionism encountered may be influenced by a firm's choice of entry strategies. The entry strategies of direct and indirect exporting usually face more barriers than other strategies such as joint ventures, foreign licensing, or direct investment. Since exporting countries or firms gain more benefits (profits, wages, employment, etc.) than importing countries or firms (lower prices, increased variety), many countries may discriminate against imports. Those same countries may be very encouraging for joint ventures or licensing agreements, however. Therefore, the selection of an entry strategy should be directly related to the level and nature of protectionism likely to be encountered. Thus, the choice of an entry strategy should "flow" from knowledge about specific NTBs that will be encountered. The following sections will review the various entry strategies that a small business might pursue in relation to obstacles presented by the NTBs discussed previously.

Indirect exporting involves using a middleman to handle exporting activities. The most common types of middlemen are export brokers and manufacturing export agents who develop expertise in particular countries. These individuals develop a network of contacts in a given country and gain experience in penetrating foreign markets. Thus, they become quite familiar with the various NTBs in a country and are often knowledge-able about whether or not one can circumvent trade constraints, and if so, how. By operating on a commission basis, these middlemen represent only variable costs for the exporter. Unfortunately the use of indirect exporters typically results in the small business gaining very little direct knowledge about how NTBs affect its success. Thus, a small business that shifts from an indirect to direct marketing exporting approach to seek more profits often does so without the aid of this significant experience. A small business that finds success in indirect exporting may only learn that foreign demand for its products exists in a given country. However, it may never be fully cognizant of how or why certain NTBs affect its strategy and related success or failure.

Direct exporting typically requires that the small business assume responsibility for all the activities necessary to deliver its product(s) to a foreign market. Such a business might hire specialized firms to assist in fulfilling various tasks, but the ultimate responsibility rests with the exporter. Due to the higher level of involvement, small businesses gain experience in international trade very quickly. A working, first-hand knowledge of NTBs is a major benefit of direct exporting. However, much international trade experience is unique to a given country. Therefore, specific NTB knowledge may not be transferable to other foreign markets. One study of small business exporters indicated that each exporter was exporting to an average of nine countries (Kedia and Chhokar 1985). If this is typical of all small business exporters, much managerial commitment and many resources will be necessary to become familiar with the unique environment in each country.

Licensing allows a foreign firm to produce and/or market product(s) in return for an initial fee and a royalty on each unit sold. License agreements may include patents, copyrights, production and technical expertise, etc. The license agreement normally specifies geographical and time horizon agreements. This entry strategy requires little initial cash investment by the domestic small business, but it does require careful research in identifying the possible foreign firms(s) to license. Foreign licensing can provide additional cash flow to defray product development costs and effectively extend product life cycles. A possible limitation of foreign licensing is the emergence of the foreign licensee as a competitor in other markets. Also, countries with currency restric-tions make the repatriation of royalty earnings difficult. The small business may also have to buy products for export in the host country, import the products to the United States, and sell the product to realize the royalty earnings (that is, it may have to countertrade).

Franchising is essentially an advanced form of licensing that results in a much higher level of control by the franchisor. The franchisor typically provides marketing programs, training, managerial support, and operations policies and guidelines. As with licensing, franchising usually requires a foreign firm to pay an initial franchise fee and subsequent royalties with little direct foreign investment required by the franchisor. The problems of franchise selection, product adaptation, and repatriation of royalty fees are the primary constraints.

Joint ventures typically involve equity infusions from both the host country small business firm and the foreign firm. To be successful, both partners must have goal congruity and clearly defined responsibility. Often the host country partner will maintain operating control. Joint ventures often are intended to circumvent protectionistic barriers due to import restraints or restrictions on foreign business ownership. The problems with cultural differences, divergent goals, and disputes over control and responsibility are the major difficulties in joint venture relationships. These relationships, to be successful, require a substantial amount of research and information seeking. Many small businesses lack the resources and commitment to fully develop meaningful joint ventures.

Wholly owned subsidiaries usually involve larger multinational corporations pursuing a direct investment strategy. A more recent type of international strategy (strategic alliances) occurs when two firms agree to share resources and expertise. While both of these strategies are common among larger firms, they are typically beyond the resources of most small businesses. Therefore, smaller firms are unlikely to use these strategies.

Implications

The selection of an entry strategy is a result of both internal and external analysis. The internal analysis focuses on resources that a small business has at its disposal and management's willingness to commit resources to international marketing efforts. If a firm has a limited resource base, it may lack the ability to make a long-term investment to penetrate a foreign market through internal efforts. In this situation, pursuing indirect exporting through the use of export agents or brokers may be the most appropriate entry strategy. Similarly, a small business that has excess productive capacity may be looking for a short-term market to reduce inventory. This situation would also favor the indirect exporting strategy. Conversely, if a firm anticipates significant potential in foreign markets, possesses sufficient resources, and is committed to a strategic focus on international markets, a direct exporting or joint venture entry strategy may be more appropriate. However, such a strategy may take years to implement and require significant managerial commitment and financial resources. Thus, the longer term a firm's commitment to international marketing is, the more appropriate the more complex entry strategies.

The external analysis consists of identifying market potential, evaluating the competitive situation, and assessing the environment for international trade. The focus of this article was on the environmental constraints of diverse protectionistic measures exemplified by non-tariff barriers (NTBs), but the foreign competitors also influence the international trade decision and are quite important. The small business considering international trade must gather considerable data to make effective "go/no-go" and "how to" decisions.

Assuming that a small business decides to conduct research on the international trade opportunities and obstacles prior to developing an entry strategy, the first step must be information acquisition. Sources of information are diverse and variable from state to state and from country to country. Table 2 presents a summary of sources commonly available. Due to the geographical diversity, these types of organizations may not exist in all states, or they may be supplemented by other organizations in some states. However, the sources will provide the starting point for information acquisition.

TABLE 2   Sources of Information on Non-Tariff Barriers

State or Local	Other U.S. Sources
Other small business exporters (international business directories)	World Trade Center
	Industry trade associations
Commercial banks (international divisions)	Foreign Credit Insurance Association
State department of commerce	Foreign embassies or consulates
Export development councils	
Export management companies	Overseas Sources
Export trading companies	State trade development offices
Colleges and universities (center for international business)	U.S. Foreign Commercial Service
	U.S. embassies or consulates
	U.S. Chamber of Commerce
Federal Government	Importers' associations
U.S. Department of Commerce	Foreign banks
U.S. International Trade Administration	Consulting firms (marketing, accounting, management, etc.)
U.S. Small Business Administration	
U.S. Department of State	Trade fairs
Export–Import Bank	Foreign government agencies (i.e., JETRO in Japan, Hong Kong Trade Development Council in Hong Kong)
Office of U.S. Trade Representatives	
	Import brokers, agents
	Foreign trading companies

Many of the foreign organizations fulfill a somewhat different role than their U.S. equivalents. For example, banks play a more active trade development role in many foreign countries than in the U.S. Accounting firms provide a diverse array of services overseas, much broader than found in the U.S. Thus, business people seeking information should not be restricted by their perceptions of what services will be available. The original role of the Japanese External Trade Organization (JETRO) was to encourage and facilitate Japanese exports. However, the current primary role of JETRO is to facilitate imports into Japan. Therefore, JETRO now provides extensive data bases on market potential in Japan.

When evaluating the array of entry strategies, it is essential for a small business to take a long-term perspective. Some marketing mix variables, such as pricing and promotion, can be changed very quickly, but other mix variables, such as product features and channels of distribution, are much more costly to change. Since selection of an entry strategy is, at least, an implicit selection of a distribution channel, a small business must carefully consider its long-term international business goals. If the long-term goal is to establish a permanent presence in foreign markets, then investing the time and money to pursue direct exporting would probably be justified. Due to a greater level of managerial control, direct exporting also holds more sales and profit potential over the long term. Conversely, if a small business is simply experimenting with exporting to reduce inventory or to determine if foreign demand exists, then an indirect exporting strategy, which requires less commitment, may be more appropriate. Knowledge of NTBs should dramatically aid the small business in assessing this risk/return tradeoff.

Conclusion

International trade is often viewed as a complex, high-risk activity for small businesses. It is interesting (but not surprising) to note that small businesses involved in exporting have consistently more favorable attitudes toward exporting than firms not engaged in exporting (Kedia and Chhokar 1985, Johnston and Czinkota 1985, Cavusgil and Nevin 1981). Thus, negative perceptions of exporting may be a significant deterrent to initiating export efforts.

If closed markets are the biggest challenge to international trade, as suggested by Jeannet and Hennessey (1988), then studying the level of protectionism must be a major part of market analysis. With the decreasing level of tariffs and increased use of NTBs instead as trade distorting measures, the study of NTBs in a particular country of interest seems to be a critical starting point for the small business contemplating business in foreign markets.

A major determinant of success in international business is managerial commitment to international activities (Cavusgil and Nevin 1981). To overcome the array of important NTBs found in foreign markets, a small business must be strongly committed to international trade. This is likely to be reflected in an aggressive, opportunistic approach to international efforts and will clearly require a long-term commitment and a well-designed strategy. Specifically, overcoming NTBs requires a well-organized effort that extends over a period of several years. Furthermore, the choice of entry strategies (exporting, foreign direct investment, joint ventures, acquisition, mergers, etc.) must reflect the relative importance of NTBs as an environmental constraint in a given country. Overlooking the importance of this environmental constraint can lead to failure of a small business's attempt to enter international markets.

References

Baldwin, Robert E. (1970), "Non-Tariff Distortions of International Trade," Washington, D.C.: The Brookings Institute.

Cao, A.D. (1980), "Non-Tariff Barriers to U.S. Manufactured Exports," *Columbia Journal of World Business* (Summer) 93–102.

Cavusgil, Tamer, and J. R. Nevin (1981), "International Determinants of Export Marketing Behavior: An Empirical Investigation," *Journal of Marketing Research* 18 (1), 114–119.

Czinkota, Michael R., Pietra Rivoli, and Ilkka A. Ronkainen (1989), *International Business.* New York: Dryden Press.

Dawson, Leslie M. (1985), "Marketing to Less Developed Countries," *Journal of Small Business Management* 23 (4), 13–19.

Food and Agriculture Organization (1986), "Trade in Forest Products: A Study of the Barriers Faced by Developing Countries," Rome.

Foreign Trade Barriers (1987), Office of the United States Trade Representative, United States Department of Commerce.

Graham, John L., and Taylor W. Meloan (1986), "Preparing the Exporting Entrepreneur," *Journal of Marketing Education* (Spring), 11–20.

Jeannet, Jean-Pierre, and Hubert D. Hennessey (1988), *International Marketing Management Strategies and Cases,* Boston: Houghton Mifflin, 54–58.

Johnston, Wesley, and Michael R. Czinkota (1985), "Export Attitudes of Industrial Manufacturers," *Industrial Marketing Management* 14, 123–132.

Kathawaba, Y., R. Judd, M. Montipallil, and M. Weinrich (1989), "Exporting Practices and Problems of Illinois Firms," *Journal of Small Business Management* 27 (1), 53–59.

Kaynak, Erdener, Pervez N. Ghauri, Torbjorn Olofsson-Brendenlow (1987), "Export Behavior of Small Swedish Firms," *Journal of Small Business Management* 25 (2), 26–32.

Kedia, Ben L., and Jagdeep Chhokar (1985), "The Impact of Managerial Attitudes on Export Behavior," *American Journal of Small Business* (Fall), 7–16.

Monke, Eric A., and Lester D. Taylor (1985), "International Trade Constraints and Commodity Market Models: An Application to the Cotton Market," *The Review of Economics and Statistics* 67 (3), 98–107.

Namiki, Nobuaki (1988), "Export Strategy for Small Business," *Journal of Small Management* 26 (2), 32–37.

Onkvisit, Sak, and John Shaw (1988), "Marketing Barriers in International Trade," *Business Horizons* (May–June) 64–72.

Organization for Economic Development (1985), "Costs and Benefits of Protectionism," Paris: OECD, 9–24.

Piercy, Nigel (1981), "British Export Market Selection and Pricing," *Industrial Marketing Management* 10, 287–297.

Ray, Edward J. (1981), "The Determinants of Tariff and Non-Tariff Barriers to Trade in the United States and Abroad," *The Review of Economics and Statistics* 63 (May), 161–168.

Ray, Edward J., and Howard P. Marvel (1984), "The Pattern of Protection in the Industrialized World," *Review of Economics and Statistics* (August), 452–458.

Suzman, C.L., and L.H. Wortzel (1984), "Technology Profiles and Export Marketing Strategies," *Journal of Business Research* 12, 183–194.

United Nations Conference on Trade and Development (1983), "Protectionism, Trade Relations, and Structural Adjustment," UNCTAD-274 (January).

On the Take

There are parallels between bribery and nuclear weapons. A bribe can win a contract, just as a nuclear bomb can win a war. But to offer bribes and to make nuclear weapons invites rivals to do the same. When all companies bribe, none is sure of winning the contract, but each must pay so as not to be outdone. As bribers bid against each other, the cost rises; bribery's effectiveness does not. All companies—and the countries whose officials are corrupted—would gain from an agreement to scrap bribes.

In 1975 the United Nations began work on an international ban on bribery. Progress is even slower than on arms control. Frustration has bred an urge for unilateralism; but here the nuclear comparison stops. Unilateral nuclear disarmament would hardly serve the interests of a country like the United States. But America is bribery's unilateralist, and its experience indicates that renouncing bribery need not damage the fortunes of a country's businessmen.

In 1977 America passed the Foreign Corrupt Practices Act, which forbids American companies from making payments to foreign officials. Companies are liable to a fine of $1m for each violation; individuals to a fine of $10,000 and five years in jail. Prison terms are the more powerful half of the deterrent, since the potential revenues from some bribes make a $1m fine look like loose change. The Pemex scandal in the 1970s, in which Mexico's national oil company received bribes from a Texan businessman, involved contracts worth $293m.

After the anti-bribery legislation was passed, American businessmen complained that they were losing orders to Japanese and European competitors for whom bribery was sometimes not merely legal but tax free, since it could be counted as a business expense. Business lobbyists have repeatedly demanded that the act be repealed or diluted, citing the country's $150 billion trade deficit as a reason for urgent action.

America's law suffers from being vague. It does not, for instance, forbid "facilitating payments" to government employees "whose duties are essentially ministerial or clerical." Only a handful of companies have been prosecuted under the Foreign Corrupt Practices Act. But though the act has its faults, damage to American exports is apparently not one of them.

Studies by Mr. John Graham of the University of Southern California and Mr. Mark McKean of the University of California at Irvine suggest that the businessmen's cries of pain are exaggerated. Using information from American embassies in 51 countries that together account for four-fifths of America's exports, Mr. Graham divides the countries into two groups: one where bribery is endemic, the other where it is not. He then checks the embassies' impressions against American press reports of bribery, which broadly

Virtue Rewarded

	US share of imports of corrupt countries, %	US share of imports of uncorrupt countries, %
1977	17.5	13.8
1978	17.8	13.6
1979	18.6	12.9
1980	18.6	13.7
1981	19.1	14.8
1982	18.9	14.8
1983	18.7	14.6
1984	18.2	14.4

SOURCE: John Graham and Mark McKean.

confirm the corrupt/noncorrupt classification. He has found that in the eight years after the Foreign Corrupt Practices Act was passed, America's share of the imports of corrupt countries actually grew as fast as its share of the imports of non-corrupt ones (see table). His findings are convincing even though, over the period studied, a few of the baddies may have become goodies (and vice versa).

Shady Folk in Sunny Places

The need to pay bribes to win business is, it seems, overestimated. Bribes are awkward to distribute: it is not always clear in a foreign country who should be bribed, or with how much. "Commissions" are sometimes not passed on. Sometimes they are, but the enriched official then awards the contract on the basis of merit. Costs are incurred and risks are run for uncertain benefits. As well as being expensive, bribes can be embarrassing if exposed. Many man-hours are therefore spent fudging accounts and keeping things quiet. Low prices and high quality are often an easier way to win contracts.

The success of the Foreign Corrupt Practices Act ought to have encouraged other governments to copy America's virtuous example. None has: nearly all countries have laws against the bribing of their own officials, but only America forbids the bribing of other people's. Despite the evidence from America, bribery is still thought of as a necessary part of doing business in the third world. Anthropologists' studies of gift-giving are wheeled in to show that bribery is part of the culture of many poor countries: non-bribers are presented as cultural imperialists as well as naive businessmen. The way share-ownership is becoming more international is cited as another reason for business managers to bribe freely: whatever their personal moral scruples, they should not impose them on shareholders to whom such morals might be alien.

Such attitudes once prevailed in America, too. Lockheed, an American aircraft manufacturer, admitted in 1975 that it had paid out $22m in bribes since 1970; but it protested that: "Such payments . . . are in keeping with business practices in many foreign countries." Yet the Lockheed scandal—along with the humiliating revelations of corrupt political practices that came with the Chilean-ITT and Watergate hearings—helped to bring about a change of mood among America's politicians, even if not among its businessmen.

In 1977 the Senate was told that the Securities and Exchange Commission had discovered that more than 300 American companies had paid bribes abroad. The image both of American government and of American business was suffering, and so were America's relations with friendly foreign governments. Lockheed's bribes to Mr. Kakuei Tanaka when he was Japan's prime minister in 1972–74 led to his arrest in 1976 and a protracted trial that has still not been completed. The Senate report also made a point that has grown with the fashion for *laisser-faire* economics. A free-market economy is based on competition—which corruption subverts.

The report's result was the Foreign Corrupt Practices Act. Far from being patronizing, the act's proponents argued, it enforced American compliance with other countries' anti-corruption laws. Even Saudi Arabia, renowned for the lush bribing that goes on there, has anti-corruption legislation on its books. Indeed, it may often be developing countries' standards that are brought down by multinational firms, rather than the other way round.

Innocents Abroad

Two researchers from the University of Western Ontario, Mr. Henry Lane and Mr. Donald Simpson, argue that foreign businessmen on brief visits to Africa presume corruption too easily, and so make it worse. If they fail to win a contract, they prefer to believe that the rivals won with larger bribes than that their own products were not up to scratch. Once sown, rumours of corruption spread quickly among the expatriates of an African capital. This leaves westerners with the impression that they have little choice but to bribe; the rumours are self-fulfilling.

The style of western business also encourages bribery. Executives from head office spend fleeting days in a poor country's capital. Few know their way about, or understand the workings of the cumbersome local bureaucracy. The foreignness of foreign cities makes it hard to resist the speakers of excellent English who hang around the hotel bars: a westerner gets conned, and quickly spreads the news that the city is corrupt. Alternatively, his lack of time makes him impatient with local bureaucratic rules. The simplest solution, so it seems, is to cut through the rules with bribes.

Mr. Lane and Mr. Simpson base their views on private talks with officials and businessmen. None, for obvious reasons, wants to be named, so the theories cannot be checked. But they fit with Mr. Graham's conclusions. First, the moral justification for bribery abroad—that it is part of local custom—is sometimes spurious. Second, the business justification does not stand up either: since bribery is not expected of foreign firms, contracts can be won without it. Yet European governments show no signs of heeding such research and legislating against bribery abroad.

Their mistakes need not be repeated by European companies, which could also learn from their counterparts in the United States. More and more American companies are telling their employees to act ethically as well as profitably. Managers have three standard weapons in their armoury. Company codes of practice lay down general ethical guidelines. These are fleshed out with training courses, based mainly on case studies. Then there are ways of catching offenders by encouraging colleagues to report them. One is to create an ethics ombudsman to whom employees may report anonymously. Another is IBM's "skip level" management reporting, whereby everybody spends periods working directly for his boss's boss, and so has a choice of two familiar superiors to report to.

According to the Ethics Research Centre, a Washington-based research group, 73% of America's largest 500 companies had codes of ethics in 1979; by 1988 the figure had risen to 85% of the 2,000 biggest. In 1980 only 3% of the companies surveyed had ethics training for their managers; now 35% do. In 1985 the centre knew of no company that had an ethics ombudsman; by 1987 more than one in ten had created the post.

Most American business courses now include a training course in ethics. At Harvard nearly a quarter of the business-school students opt for the ethics course. More European business schools are also starting to teach business ethics. Last year an umbrella body, the European Business Ethics Network, was set up in Brussels.

Down to Self-Defence

Yet the fight against corruption remains a peculiarly American concern. The Europeans and Japanese (whose own country is pretty corrupt) hurt themselves by their complacency, but they hurt developing nations more. In the end it is up to poor countries to defend themselves from foreigners' corruption—as well as from their own.

Sheer poverty makes this hard to do. By 1900 Britain had beaten the worst of its corruption. But in 1900 the average Briton had a yearly income (GDP per person in today's price) of $4,000—more than ten times that of the average person in the developing world today. Britain had acquired a middle class, whose belief in reward for hard work was the antithesis of corruption. Few of today's poor countries have a sizable middle class; the rest are sat upon by elites accustomed to acquiring money through inheritance and other gifts.

Poverty goes with a weak state, which makes corruption worse. If the state cannot enforce laws, nobody will respect it. Disrespect quickly breeds disloyalty among civil servants: corruption seems eminently sensible, since it involves robbing from the state in order to give to relatives and friends who provide the security that the state is too feeble to deliver. Thus impoverished, the state's strength diminishes further; the rival authority of the clan is consolidated.

Though hampered by their poverty, developing countries can dent the worst of their corruption. The first step is to **admit corruption exists.** It hides behind respectable masks. Mexican policemen ask for "tips." Middlemen in business deals demand "consultancy fees" and "commissions." A favourite trick in Pakistan is for the post-office teller to be out of stamps. Terribly sorry, but there happens to be a street vendor just outside the post office who sells them—at a premium. Not everybody guesses that half the premium goes to the teller.

It is also necessary to admit it is damaging. The Mexican policeman gets the national minimum wage (a bit over $3 a day), so it may seem natural that he should supplement his pay. The bribes accepted by an official before he awards a government contract do not necessarily distort competition among rival tenderers: sometimes, all are accompanied by a similar bribe, which serves as an entry fee. Equally, a judge may offer the plaintiff with justice on his side the first chance to make a "contribution." For businessmen, a modest bribe may seem an efficient way to secure a licence quickly.

Even these apparently mild examples of corruption are harmful. Mexican policeman refuse to investigate crimes reported by those who cannot afford to pay the tip: access to public services, which should be equal, is thus restricted to the better off. While refusing to investigate crimes that do not pay, the Mexican police assiduously tackle non-crimes that do: innocent motorists are stopped to extract a bribe.

The poor and innocent suffer, but there is wider damage too. The tip for a quickly issued licence encourages officials to invent new licences. The tangle of lucrative redtape strangles would-be entrepreneurs—and the economy suffers. The state's venality diminishes its standing in the eyes of its citizens. No sane Mexican respects the police. South Africa's supposedly independent homelands are made all the more despicable because their rulers are thieves.

By weakening the state, corruption can even promote—or at least provide the excuse for—political violence, as when Nigeria's President Shehu Shagari was deposed in 1984. Honest regimes, by contrast, are generally strong enough to get even their unpopular policies accepted. Ghana's Flight-Lieutenant Jerry Rawlings, who overthrew his civilian predecessors because of their corruption, has imposed an awesome dose of economic austerity on his people, but still survives in power.

Once corruption's harmfulness is acknowledged, **train civil servants to spot and stop it.** The polite silence that surrounds corruption often blocks the passing on of useful tips on how to tackle it. The story is told of an engineer responsible for an irrigation system in India. The rich farmers in the area bribed a local politician, who in turn ordered the irrigation engineer to divert water from poor farms to rich ones. The engineer agreed to do as he was told, so long as the politician would speak his order into the engineer's tape recorder: whereupon the politician backed down. If this was made a case study for trainee water engineers, India's water might be better managed.

As well as instructing the virtuous on how to beat corruption, training should explain to the not-so-virtuous why corruption is so damaging. It may not be a bad idea to explain the benefits to a country of an honest civil service, much as student lawyers learn some jurisprudence. The same goes for businessmen. Some Latin countries—Mexico, Chile—are making ethics training part of their business-school curriculums, which should make businessmen aware of the harm that corruption does to the economy, and to the standards of their firms.

Next, let **journalists and other snoops** help in exposing corruption. It is not enough for governments to break their silence on the subject; general openness is essential for having corruption discussed. In the Soviet Union, parts of which are pretty poor, Mr. Mikhail Gorbachev is allowing more press freedom than before partly in order to expose the corruption that festered under the secretive rule of Leonid Brezhnev.

Greater openness is the first step towards increased accountability. Mr. Gorbachev also wants some party officials to be exposed to elections, so that they can be judged on the records that *glasnost* has made known. Elections are one good way of holding people to account. Another is the separation of powers. Independent executives, judiciaries and legislatures can keep tabs on each other.

Even strong and open states have difficulty retaining civil servants' loyalty, so the wise ones **reduce bureaucrats' discretion:** fewer licences will mean fewer bribes. In famously corrupt Indonesia, the government's economic-reform programme includes the burning of red tape. To build a hotel only one licence is now required; once, an entrepreneur needed 33.

In particular, do away with economic controls that create black markets. If the state fixes the exchange rate artificially high, foreign currency will be scarce, and distributing it will be the task of bureaucrats. Bribes will flow, because businessmen who need to import spare parts will pay generously for dollars or import quotas. The same happens when state food-marketing boards force farmers to sell their crops at artificially low prices: farmers are encouraged to bribe the board's officials to overlook their grain, and then to bribe customs officials to allow it across the border into a country where it will fetch more. Five years ago Ugandan coffee could be sold in Kenya for ten times its domestic price.

Slimming down the state will make possible the next corruption-beating move that is **sometimes** needed: **pay public employees more,** so that they no longer depend on "tips." The Indonesian government is likely to find its anti-corruption policies damaged by the freeze it has put on civil servants' pay. It may do wonders for Indonesia's budget, but it will probably encourage civil servants to find pay of their own. Along with better training, better pay will improve morale. The more pride that officials take in working for their governments, the less likely they are to subvert them by accepting bribes.

Another way to raise the professional moral of bureaucrats is to make the civil service **meritocratic.** Competitive entry examinations and promotion on merit helped diminish corruption in nineteenth-century England. In Mexico today, the relatively high professional standards of the Finance Ministry, Bank of Mexico and Foreign Ministry go with their relatively clean reputations. The Indian civil service has competitive examinations but, in some states at least, civil-service jobs are known by the size of bribe needed to obtain them. So long as that persists, those who do the jobs will see them as an instrument of plunder, not as a chance to serve the state.

Tolerated, corruption spreads easily. The civil servant who buys his job will reimburse himself corruptly. In the Philippines corruption has even infected the body investigating corruption under the country's deposed ruler, Mr. Ferdinand Marcos. Because it is so hard to beat, and because all societies and institutions develop taboos against snitching on colleagues, corruption is too often met with defeatism or indulgence. That is an unkindness to bureaucracies and businessmen, whether poor or rich.

Bribery in International Business: Whose Problem Is It?

Henry W. Lane and Donald G. Simpson. *Henry W. Lane is Associate Professor of Organizational Behavior at the School of Business Administration, The University of Western Ontario, London, Ontario. He is at present Director of the Centre for International Business Studies. His most important publication is:* Managing Large Research and Development Programs *(with Rodney Beddows and Paul R. Lawrence), (State University of New York Press, Albany, 1981). Donald G. Simpson is Associate Professor at the University of Western Ontario. He is at present Associate of the Centre for International Business Studies. He was formerly Associate Director of Social Sciences Division at the International Development Research Centre, Ottawa, Canada, and Executive Director of the Office of International Programs, University of Western Ontario.*

Introduction

No discussion of problems in international business seems complete without reference to familiar complaints about the questionable business practices North American executives encounter in foreign countries, particularly developing nations. Beliefs about the pervasiveness of dishonesty and the necessity of engaging in such practices as bribery vary widely however, and these differences often lead to vigorous discussions that generate more heat than light. Pragmatists or "realists" may take the attitude that "international business is a rough game and no place for the naive idealist or the fainthearted. Your competitors use bribes and unless you are willing to meet this standard, competitive practice you will lose business and, ultimately, jobs for workers at home. Besides, it is an accepted business practice in those countries, and when you are in Rome you have to do as the Romans do." "Moralists," on the other hand, believe that cultural relativity is no excuse for unethical behavior. "As Canadians or Americans we should uphold our legal and ethical standards anywhere in the world; and any good American or Canadian knows that bribery, by any euphemism, is unethical and wrong. Bribery increases a product's cost and often is used to secure import licenses for products that no longer can be sold in the developed world. Such corrupting practices also contribute to the moral disintegration of individuals and eventually societies."

The foregoing comments represent extreme polar positions but we are not using these stereotypes to create a 'straw-man' or false dichotomy about attitudes toward

Reprinted by permission of Kluwer Academic Publishers from the *Journal of Business Ethics*, 1984, pp. 35–42, © 1984 by Kluwer Academic Publishers.

practices like bribery. These extreme viewpoints, or minor variations of them, will be encountered frequently as one meets executives who have experience in developing countries. Some 'realists' and 'moralists' undoubtedly are firm believers in their positions, but many other executives probably gravitate toward one of the poles because they have not found a realistic alternative approach to thinking about the issue of bribery, never mind finding an answer to the problem.

The impetus for this article came from discussions with executives and government officials in Canada and in some developing nations about whether a North American company could conduct business successfully in developing countries without engaging in what would be considered unethical or illegal practices. It was apparent from these talks that the question was an important one and of concern to business executives, but not much practical, relevant information existed on the issue. There was consensus on two points: first, there are a lot of myths surrounding the issue of pay-offs and, second, if anyone had some insights into the problem, executives would appreciate hearing them.

In this article we would like to share what we have learned about the issue during the two years we have been promoting business (licensing agreements, management contracts, joint ventures) between Canada and African companies. Our intention is not to present a comprehensive treatment of the subject of bribery nor a treatise on ethical behavior. Our intention is to present a practical discussion of some dimensions of the problem based on our experience, discussions and, in some cases investigation of specific incidents.

The Problem Is Multi-faceted

It can be misleading to talk about bribery in global terms without considering some situational specifics such as country, type of business and company. Our discussions with businessmen indicate that the pay-off problem is more prevalent in some countries than in others. Executives with extensive experience probably could rank countries on a scale reflecting the seriousness of the problem. Also, some industries are probably more susceptible to pay-off requests than others. Large construction projects, turn-key capital projects, and large commodity or equipment contracts are likely to be most vulnerable because the scale of the venture may permit the easy disguise of pay-offs, and because an individual, or small group of people, may be in a strategic position to approve or disapprove the project. These projects or contracts are undoubtedly obvious targets also because the stakes are high, the competition vigorous and the possibility that some competitors may engage in payoffs increased. Finally, some companies may be more vulnerable due to a relative lack of bargaining power or because they have no policies to guide them in these situations. If the product or technology is unique, or clearly superior, and it is needed, the company is in a relatively strong position to resist the pressure. Similarly, those firms with effective operational policies against pay-offs are in a position of strength. Many senior executives have stated, with pride, that their companies have reputations for not making pay-offs and, therefore, are not asked for them. These were executives of large, successful firms that also had chosen not to work in some countries where they could not operate comfortably. These executives often backed up their claims with specific examples in which they walked away from apparently lucrative deals where a pay-off was a requirement.

Two other elements of the situational context of a pay-off situation that vary are the subtlety of the demand and the amount of money involved. All pay-off situations are not straightforward and unambiguous, which may make a clear response more difficult. Consider for example the case of a company that was encouraged to change its evaluation of bids for a large construction project. Some host country agencies were embarrassed by the evaluation results since Company *X*, from the country providing significant financing for the project, was ranked a distant third. The agencies sought a re-evaluation on questionable technicalities. The changes were considered but the ranking remained the same. At this point pressure began to build. Phone calls were made berating the firm for delaying the project and hinting that the large follow-on contract, for which it had the inside track, was in jeopardy. No one ever said make Company *X* the winner or you lose the follow-on.

Although no money was to change hands, this situation was similar to a pay-off request in that the company was being asked to alter its standard of acceptable business practices for an implied future benefit. The interpretation of the 'request,' the response, and the consequences, were left entirely to the company's management. Refusal to change may mean losing a big contract, but giving in does not guarantee the follow-on and you leave the company vulnerable to further demands. In ambiguous situations factors such as corporate policies and the company's financial strength and its need for the contract enter into the decision. In this case the company had firm beliefs about what constituted professional standards and did not desperately need the follow-on contract. Although it refused to change, another company might find itself in a dilemma, give in to the pressure, and rationalize its behavior.

Finally, pay-offs range in size from the small payments that may help getting through customs without a hassle up to the multi-million dollar bribes that make headlines and embarass governments. The pay-off situations we discuss in this article are more significant than the former, but much smaller and far less dramatic than the latter. These middle-range pay-offs (tens of thousands of dollars) may pose a problem for corporations. They are too big to be ignored but possibly not big enough to be referred to corporate headquarters unless the firm has clear guidelines on the subject. Regional executives or lower level managers may be deciding whether or not these 'facilitating payments' are just another cost of doing business in the developing world.

On the Outside Looking In (The North American Perspective)

"It's a corrupt, pay-off society. The problem has spread to all levels. On the face it looks good, but underneath it's rotten." Comments such as these are often made by expatriate businessmen and government officials alike. The North American executive may arrive in a Third World country with a stereotype of corrupt officials and is presented with the foregoing analysis by people-on-the-spot who, he feels, should know the situation best. His fears are confirmed.

This scenario may be familiar to some readers. It is very real to us because we have gone through that process. Two cases provide examples of the stories a businessman may likely be told in support of the dismal analysis.

The New Venture: Company *Y,* a wholly-owned subsidiary of a European multinational, wished to manufacture a new product for export. Government permission was required and Company *Y* submitted the necessary applications. Sometime later one of Company *Y*'s executives (a local national) informed the Managing Director that the application was approved and the consultant's fee must be paid. The Managing Director knew nothing about a consultant or such a fee. The executive took his boss to a meeting with the consultant—a government official who sat on the application review committee. Both the consultant and the executive claimed to remember the initial meeting at which agreement was reached on the $10,000 fee. A few days later the Managing Director attended a cocktail party at the home of a high ranking official in the same agency. This official recommended that the fee be paid. The Managing Director decided against paying the fee and the project ran into unexpected delays. At this point the Managing Director asked the parent company's legal department for help. Besides the delay, the situation was creating a problem between the Managing Director and his executives as well as affecting the rest of the company. He initially advised against payment but after watching the company suffer, acquiesced with the approval of the parent company. The fee was re-negotiated downward and the consultant paid. What was the result? Nothing! The project was not approved.

The Big Sale: Company *Z,* which sold expensive equipment, established a relationship with a well placed government official on the first trip to the country. This official, and some other nationals, assured Company *Z* representatives that they would have no trouble getting the contract. On leaving the country, Company *Z* representatives had a letter of intent to purchase the equipment. On the second trip Company *Z* representatives brought the detailed technical specifications for a certain department head to approve. The department head refused to approve the specifications and further efforts to have the government honour its promise failed. The deal fell through. Company *Z*'s analysis of the situation, which became common knowledge in business and government circles, was that a competitor paid the department head to approve its equipment and that the government reneged on its obligation to purchase Company *Z* equipment.

While in the country, the visiting executive may even have met Company *Z*'s agent in the 'Big Sale,' who confirms the story. Corruption is rampant, and in the particular case of the 'Big Sale' he claims to know that the department head received the money and from whom. The case is closed! An honest North American company cannot function in this environment—or so its seems.

On the Inside Looking Out (The Developing Country's Perspective)

During his visit the executive may have met only a few nationals selected by his company or government representatives. He probably has not discussed bribery with them because of its sensitive nature. If the businessmen and the officials he met were dishonest, they would not admit it; if they were honest he probably felt they would resent the discussion. Also, he may not have had enough time to establish the type of relationship in which the subject could be discussed frankly. It is almost certain that he did not speak with the people in the government agencies who allegedly took the pay-offs. What would he say if he did meet them? And more than likely he would not be able to get an appointment with them if he did want to pursue the matter further. So the executive is convinced that corruption is widespread having heard only one side of the horror stories.

Had the visitor been able to investigate the viewpoints of the nationals what might he have heard? "I would like to find a person from the developed world that I can trust. You people brought corruption here. We learned the concept from you. You want to win all the time, and you are impatient so you bribe. You offer bribes to the local people and complain that business is impossible without bribing."

Comments like these are made by local businessmen and government officials alike. If the visiting executive heard these comments he would be confused and would wonder whether or not these people were talking about the same country. Although skeptical, his confidence in the accuracy of his initial assessment would have been called into question. Had he been able to stay longer in the country, he might have met an old friend who knew the department head who allegedly was paid-off in the Big Sale. His friend would have made arrangements for the visitor to hear the other side of the story.

The Big Sale Re-visited: After the representatives of Company Z received what they described as a letter of intent to purchase the equipment they returned home. On the second visit they had to deal with the department head to receive his approval for the technical specifications.

At the meeting they told the department head that he need not worry about the details and just sign-off on the necessary documents. If he had any questions regarding the equipment he could inspect it in two weeks time in their home country. The department head's initial responses were: (1) he would not rubber stamp anything, and (2) how could this complex equipment which was supposedly being custom made for his country's needs be inspected in two weeks when he had not yet approved the specifications.

As he reviewed the specifications he noticed a significant technical error and brought it to the attention of Company Z's representative. They became upset with this 'interference' and inferred that they would use their connections in high places to ensure his compliance. When asked again to sign the documents he refused, and the company reps left, saying that they would have him removed from his job.

After this meeting the Premier of the country became involved and asked the company officials to appear before him. They arrived with the Premier's nephew for a meeting with the Premier and his top advisors. The Premier told his nephew that he had no business being there and directed him to leave. The company officials then had to face the Premier and his advisors alone.

The Premier asked if the company had a contract and that if it had, it would be honoured. The company had to admit that it had no contract. As far as the Premier was concerned the issue was settled.

However, the case was not closed for the Company Z representatives. They felt they had been promised the deal and that the department had reneged. They felt that someone had paid-off the department head and they were quite bitter. In discussions with their local embassy officials and with government officials at home they presented their analysis of the situation. The result was strained relations and the department head got a reputation for being dishonest.

Well, the other side of the story certainly has different implications about whose behaviour may be considered questionable. The situation is now very confusing. Is the department head honest or not? The executive's friend has known the department head for a long time and strongly believes he is honest; and some other expatriate government officials have basically corroborated the department head's perception of the matter. But the businessmen and government officials who first told the story seemed reputable and honest. Who should be believed? As the visiting executive has learned, you have to decide on the truth for yourself.

Patterns of Behaviour

The preceding vignettes illustrate our position that bribery and corruption is a problem for North American and Third World businessmen alike. We also have observed two recurring behavioural patterns in these real, but disguised, situations. The first is the predisposition of the North American businessman to accept the premise that bribery is the way of life in the developing world and a necessity in business transactions. The second behavioural pattern occurs in situations where payments are requested and made.

We believe that many executives visit Third World countries with an expectation to learn that bribery is a problem. This attitude likely stems from a number of sources. First, in many cases it may be true. In some countries it may be impossible to complete a transaction without a bribe and the horror stories about the widespread disappearance of honesty are valid. However, in some instances the expectations are conditioned by the 'conventional wisdom' available in international business circles. This conventional wisdom develops from situations like the ones we have described. As these situations are passed from individual to individual accuracy may diminish and facts be forgotten. This is not done intentionally but happens since it is rare that the story tellers have the complete story or all the facts. Unverified stories of bribery and corruption circulate through the business and government communities and often become accepted as true and factual. The obvious solution, and difficulty, is learning how to distinguish fact from fiction.

Another factor influencing initial expectations are the unfavourable impressions of developing countries and their citizens that are picked up from the media. Often only the sensational, and negative, news items from these countries are reported in North America. We learn of bombings, attacks on journalists and tourists, alleged (and real) coup d'etats, and major scandals. These 'current events' and the 'conventional wisdom' combined with an executive's probable lack of knowledge of the history, culture, legal systems or economic conditions of a country all contribute to the development of unfavourable stereotypes that predispose the executive toward readily accepting reports that confirm his already drawn conclusions: all Latin American or African countries, for example, are the same and corruption is to be expected.

The stories that constitute 'evidence' of corruption may be tales of bribery like the 'New Venture' or the 'Big Sale,' or they may take other forms. The story we have heard most often has the 'protect yourself from your local partner' theme. It goes like this: "If you are going to invest in this country, particularly in a joint venture, you have to find a way to protect yourself from your partner. He is likely to strip all the company's assets and leave you nothing but a skeleton. Just look what happened to Company *A*."

On hearing the 'evidence,' particularly from expatriates in the foreign country, a visiting businessman most likely accepts it without further investigation. He has forgotten the old adage about there being two sides to every story. His conclusions and conviction are most likely based on incomplete and biased data.

Is there another viewpoint? Certainly! Many nationals have expressed it to us: "The Europeans and North Americans have been taking advantage of us for decades, even centuries. The multi-nationals establish a joint venture and then strip the local company bare through transfer pricing, management fees and royalties based on a percentage of sales rather than profits. They have no interest in the profitability of the company or its long-term development."

The situation is ironic. Some local investors are desperately looking for an honest North American executive whom they can trust at the same time the North American is searching for them. Our experience indicates that this search process is neither straight-forward nor easy. And while the search continues, if it does, it is difficult for the North American to maintain a perspective on the situation and remember that there are locals who may share his values and who are equally concerned about unethical and illegal practices.

In summary, we would characterize the first observed pattern of behavior as a preparedness to accept 'evidence' of corruption and the simultaneous failure to examine critically the 'evidence' or its source.

The second behavioral pattern appears in the actual pay-off process. The request very likely comes from a low- or middle-level bureaucrat who says that his boss must be paid for the project to be approved or for the sale to be finalized. Alternatively, it may be your agent who is providing similar counsel. In either case you are really not certain who is making the demand.

Next, the pay-off is made. You give your contact the money, but you never really know where it goes.

Your expectations are obvious. You have approached this transaction from a perspective of economic rationality. You have provided a benefit and expect one in return. The project will be approved or the sale consummated.

The results, however, may be very different than expected. As in the case of the 'New Venture,' nothing may happen. The only outcome is indignation, anger, and perhaps the loss of a significant amount of money. Now is the time for action, but what recourse do you have? Can you complain? You may be guilty of bribing a government official. And, you certainly are reluctant to admit that you have been duped. Since your direct options are limited, your primary action may be to spread the word: "This is a corrupt, pay-off society."

Why Does It Happen?

There are numerous explanations for corruption in developing nations. First and most obvious is that some people are simply dishonest. A less pejorative explanation is that the cost of living in these countries may be high and salaries low. Very often a wage earner must provide for a large extended family. The businessman is viewed opportunistically as a potential source of extra income to improve the standard of living. Finally, some nationals may believe strongly that they have a right to share some of the wealth controlled by multi-national corporations.

Besides being familiar to many readers, these explanations all share another common characteristic. They all focus on 'the other person'—the local national. Accepting that there may be some truth in the previous explanations, let us, however, turn our focus to the visiting North American to see what we find. We could find a greedy, dishonest expatriate hoping to make a killing. But, let us give him the same benefit of the doubt we have accorded to the local nationals so far.

On closer examination we may find a situation in which the North American executive is vulnerable. He has entered an action vacuum and is at a serious disadvantage. His lack of knowledge of systems and procedures, laws, institutions, and the people can put him in a dependent position. Unfamiliarity with the system and/or people makes effective, alternative action such as he could take at home difficult. A strong relationship with a reputable national could help significantly in this situation. Quite often the national knows how to fight the system and who to call in order to put pressure on the corrupt individual. This potential resource should not be dismissed lightly. Although the most powerful and experienced MNC's may also be able to apply this pressure, most of us must be realistic and recognize that no matter how important we think we are we may not be among the handful of foreigners that can shake the local institutions.

Time also can be a factor. Often the lack of time spent in the country either to establish relationships or to give the executive the opportunity to fight the system contributes to the problem. Because the North American businessman believes that time is money and that his time, in particular, is very valuable, he operates on a tight schedule with little leeway for unanticipated delays. The pay-off appears to be a cost-effective solution. In summary the executive might not have the time, knowledge, or contacts to fight back and sees no alternative other than pay or lose the deal.

Some Real Barriers

If, as we think, there are many honest businessmen in North America and in the developing world looking for mutually profitable arrangements and for reliable, honest partners, why is it difficult for them to find each other? We believe a significant reason is the inability of both sides to overcome two interrelated barriers—time and trust.

Trust is a critical commodity for business success in developing countries. The North American going to invest in a country far from home needs to believe he will not be cheated out of his assets. The national has to believe that a joint venture, for example, will be more than a mechanism for the North American to get rich at his expense. But, even before the venture is established, trust may be essential if the perspective partners are ever to meet. This may require the recommendation of a third party respected by both sides.

Establishing good relationships with the right people requires an investment of time, money and energy. An unwillingness of either party to make this investment is often interpreted as a lack of sincerity or interest. The executive trying to do business in four countries in a week (the 'five-day wonder') is still all too common a sight. Similarly the successful local businessman may have an equally hectic international travel schedule. Both complain that if the other was really serious he would find time to meet. Who should give in? In our opinion the onus is on whichever party is visiting to build into his schedule the necessary time to work on building a relationship or to find a trusted intermediary. Also both parties must be realistic about the elapsed time required to establish a good relationship and negotiate a mutually satisfactory deal. This will involve multiple trips by each party to the other's country and could easily take 12 to 18 months.

The Cost of Bribery

The most quantifiable costs are the financial ones. The cost of the 'service' is known. The costs of not bribing are also quantifiable: the time and money that must be invested in long term business development in the country, or the value of the lost business. However, there are other costs that must be considered.

1. You may set a precedent and establish that you and/or your company are susceptible to pay-off demands.

2. You may create an element in your organization that believes pay-offs are standard operating procedure and over which you may eventually lose control.

3. You or your agents may begin using bribery and corruption as a personally nonthreatening, convenient excuse to dismiss failure. You may not address some organizational problems of adapting to doing business in the developing world.

4. There are also personal costs. Ultimately you will have to accept responsibility for your decisions and action and those of your subordinates. At a minimum it may involve embarrassment, psychological suffering and a loss of reputation. More extreme consequences include the loss of your job and jail sentences.

Conclusion

It is clear that bribery can be a problem for the international executive. Assuming you do not want to participate in the practice, how can you cope with the problem?

1. Do not ignore the issue. Do as many North American companies have done. Spend time thinking about the tradeoffs and your position prior to the situation arising.

2. After thinking through the issue establish a corporate policy. We would caution, however, that for any policy to be effective, it must reflect values that are important to the company's senior executives. The policy must also be used. Window dressing will not work.

3. Do not be too quick to accept the 'conventional wisdom.' Examine critically the stories of bribery and the source of the stories. Ask for details. Try to find out the other side of the story and make enquiries of a variety of sources.

4. Protect yourself by learning about the local culture and by establishing trusting relationships with well-respected local businessmen and government officials.

5. Do not contribute to the enlargement of myths by circulating unsubstantiated stories.

Finally, we would offer the advice that when in Rome do as the *better* Romans do. But, we would add, do not underestimate the time, effort, and expense it may take to find the better Romans and establish a relationship with them.

Acknowledgment

For the past two and one-half years the authors have been engaged in a project to promote Canadian business ventures in the developing world. The authors wish to acknowledge the support of the Plan for Excellence and the Centre for International Business Studies at Western's Business School and the Industrial Cooperation Division of the Canadian International Development Agency.

Marketing Around the World: Similarities and Differences

This section consists of an eclectic mix of papers documenting the demographic, economic, and political aspects of emerging markets that are targets of opportunity for American marketers in the 1990s.

This first article is a report card summary of the potential for business in each of the republics in the Commonwealth of Independence States, the former USSR. An accompanying piece provides an insightful view of Soviet negotiation protocols, goals and likely length. Commercial success in the CIS republics requires understanding of their negotiating styles.

The Islamic nations of the world are enumerated in the next article, along with a review of requirements of the Muslim religion and the resultant marketing implications for international business executives. The authors predict growing opportunities for international marketers in Muslim nations, which are experiencing an emerging middle class along with a significant number of Western-educated students returning to their homelands.

A companion piece provides invaluable guidelines for marketers to Third World countries. While most less-developed nations are too small to be important market targets by themselves, the authors contend that their combined wealth and potential are significant to Western marketers.

Doing Business with the Soviet Republics

How Republics Make the Grade

The Soviet Union is breaking up. The Baltics have claimed their independence. The other republics are taking charge of their economies. If you're thinking of doing business in that vast land, which of the 15 Soviet republics would be most welcoming for U.S. companies?

USA TODAY asked Michael Claudon, president of the Geonomics Institute in Middlebury, Vt., to work with us to develop an investment report card for the 15 republics.

Claudon's criteria for grading:

- Living standards. "Higher incomes imply faster market growth once reforms take hold," Claudon says.
- Capacity for earning hard currency. Because Soviet rubles are worthless to U.S. companies, many businesses want to find or make products that can be exported from the Soviet Union to Western nations.
- Government posture toward market reforms.
- Conversion of defense plants to civilian use. The change will drain local economies. Conversions will take time and money and will mean plants must close, then reopen with fewer workers, leaving many former workers of the overstaffed factories unemployed.
- Mix of industry. Consumer goods and energy are potentially the fastest-growing.
- Amount of business contact with the West in the past.

The republics were graded on a curve, comparing them with one another, not to the outside world. Otherwise, the Baltics would rate on par with Mexico.

One thing to keep in mind: The Soviets have lied about their economic figures for so long, no one is sure of such things as gross national product. Consider the numbers as relative guides.

Reprinted by permission of *USA TODAY* newspaper, September 30, 1991, pp. 6B and 7B. Copyright © 1991, USA Today.

Report Card

Each republic's grade reflects its overall potential for business.

Republic	Grade	Republic	Grade
Estonia	A	Moldavia	C
Latvia	A	Armenia	C–
Lithuania	A–	Uzbekistan	D
Ukraine	A–	Azerbaijan	D
Russia	B+	Turkmenistan	D–
Georgia	B–	Kirghizia	D–
Kazakhstan	C+	Tadzhikistan	D–
Byelorussia	C		

SOURCE: Geonomics Institute.

Geonomics is a not-for-profit group that has worked closely with Soviet leaders and U.S. businesspeople to help promote economic reform in the Soviet Union.

Business travel: Getting to Moscow isn't too tough. Getting to Ashkhabad, in Turkmenistan, or Irkutsk, in Siberia, can be another matter entirely. Some basics:

- The flight. A Pan Am-Aeroflot joint venture flies nonstop to Moscow from New York or Washington, D.C. The flight takes about nine hours. European carriers such as Lufthansa will get you from the USA to Moscow with one or two stops. That's where the fun begins. Often, the only way to get to a remote Soviet city is to make a connection in Moscow. But when you land at Moscow's international airport, you have to go to a different airport to fly to a domestic destination. If you want to fly to a republic to the south or east, the airport is an hour's drive away. Some of the European carriers will fly from Western Europe directly into Soviet cities such as Kiev or Minsk, an option worth checking out.

- The visa. The Baltics have taken control of their visas. You can get a visa on arrival when you land at the airport. For the rest of the Soviet Union, visas still are being issued by the Soviet Embassy in Washington. You need an invitation from a Soviet to get a business visa, which can take up to two weeks. Tourist visas can take much longer.

- The money. It's confusing, but rubles are worth different amounts at different times. You can only change money at official locations in the Soviet Union, where you usually will get the tourist rate—1 ruble for about 3 U.S. cents. But restaurants, shops and hotels that take only hard currency list prices in rubles, then convert at the commercial exchange rate of 1 ruble for $1.60. Keep U.S. currency—small bills—on hand. It can work magic on taxi drivers and just about anyone else in the Soviet Union.

- Fitful phones. Expect the worst when it comes to communications. All international calls must go through Moscow. There are just 91 circuits between Moscow and the USA. AT&T is asking to activate 42 more. AT&T plans to begin direct service to Armenia next month. When available, one of the best ways to communicate with Soviets is by facsimile machine. Faxes are abundant in Riga, Tallinn, Vilnius, Leningrad and Moscow but rare elsewhere.

- Talking business. If you want to impress your host, try these Russian business phrases:

  Ocheen priyatna bilo s'vami rabochatz. (It's a pleasure to be able to do business with you.)

  Bolshoi spaseebo. (Thank you very much.)

  Skolyaka eta sto-eet? (How much is it?)

  Mozhna priglaseetya vass na abyet? (May I invite you to lunch?)

Five Ranked Best among the Lot

Estonia

"An excellent transportation system and highly developed consumer-goods manufacturing sector are complemented by a highly educated populace having longstanding ties to Finland and a strong Western orientation. They welcome Western investment and are prepared to accommodate special needs."

GNP: $10 billion.

Population: 1.6 million.

Per capita GNP: $6,240.

Major city: Tallinn (capital, 478,000).

Ethnic groups: 65% Estonian, 28% Russian.

Languages: Estonian, Russian.

Climate: Moderate.

Infrastructure: Good internal roads, railroads; ports on the Baltic; connections to Leningrad, Helsinki; Moscow is 1½ hours away by air; technology and phones are among the best in the Soviet Union, though international connections still must be made through Moscow.

Agriculture: A net food exporter; major products are dairy, cattle, pigs, grain, potatoes.

Industry: Electronics industry makes computers, electric motors and measuring instruments. It also is a major furniture-making center.

Registered joint ventures: 104.

Lodging: In Tallinn, the Viru, a large, basic foreign-tourist hotel; the Tallinn, older but less hectic.

History: Founded by Danes and ruled in turn by Germans, Swedes and Russians. It was independent from 1918 to 1940, when annexed by Stalin in pact with Hitler. Proclaimed independence after Aug. 19 coup failed.

Current situation: After recently claiming independence, it has been passing strong laws toward a market economy. New laws allow property ownership and give Soviet-seized property back to former owners or heirs. Some will get securities equal to the value of the property. Privatization of industry has begun, giving Estonians preference, though foreigners may buy firms using hard currency. Food prices were freed, and prices doubled.

Leader: President Arnold Ruutel.

Investment opportunities: Furniture, electronics (especially electric motors at Volta plant in Tallinn), consumer goods, garment industry.

Latvia

"Latvians are of average education and strong Western orientation who enjoy a high standard of living. They are well-versed in details of international commerce and have developed ties in Austria and Sweden."

GNP: $18.2 billion.

Population: 2.7 million.

Per capita GNP: $6,740.

Major city: Riga (capital, 1 million).

Ethnic groups: 54% Latvian, 33% Russian.

Languages: Latvian, Russian.

Climate: Moderate.

Infrastructure: Excellent road and rail transport; ice-free Riga port is second only to Leningrad's; Moscow is 1½ hours away by air; technology and phones are excellent by Soviet standards.

Agriculture: A minor role in the economy. Main products: potatoes, grain, eggs, dairy.

Industry: Major electric-products industry, making telephone switches and electric buses and railway cars. Made half of Soviet motorcycles, 20% of radios. Also biotech, textiles, chemicals. Has few raw materials.

Registered joint ventures: 39.

Lodging: In Riga, the Latvia, busy, basic but only hotel set up for foreigners.

History: Long held by various European forces, it was part of Russia from 1800 to 1918, when it proclaimed independence. Annexed by Stalin in 1940 in pact with Hitler. Proclaimed independence after Aug. 19 Soviet coup failed.

Current situation: Having newly claimed independence, it is making moves toward privatization of land and business. Hasn't gone as far as other Baltics in freeing prices and allowing market forces. Still squabbling with Moscow over what factories and infrastructure left in Latvia belong to Soviets and what Latvia can claim.

Leader: President Anatoly Gorbunovs.

Investment opportunities: Railway-car, motorcycle plants; biotech; electronics and scientific equipment; food processing; synthetic-fiber manufacturing.

Lithuania

"Well-educated and pro-Western, their transition to a thriving market economy will be aided by the strong and financially successful Lithuanian population in the U.S., which is now eagerly investing in the country."

GNP: $21.8 billion.

Population: 3.7 million.

Per capita GNP: $5,880.

Major city: Vilnius (capital, 566,000).

Ethnic groups: 80% Lithuanian, 9% Russian, 7% Polish.

Languages: Lithuanian, Russian.

Climate: Moderate.

Infrastructure: Good internal roads, railroads; ports on the Baltic with connections to Leningrad, Helsinki; Moscow is 1½ hours away by air; technology and phones are excellent by Soviet standards.

Agriculture: Grain, potatoes, beef cattle, pigs, poultry; relatively productive.

Industry: Well-developed electronics industry making computers, industrial robots, TVs and stereos; shipyards along the Baltic coast; wood products such as furniture and building materials; amber. Big drawback: few indigenous raw materials.

Registered joint ventures: 18.

Lodging: In Vilnius, Lietuva, one of the Soviet Union's best hotels; also the Astoriya.

History: The Grand Duchy of Lithuania united with Poland to create a large state in 1410, but it soon fell to Russia. Independent from 1918 to 1940, when it fell to Stalin as part of a secret pact with Hitler. From March 1990, it had been the most vociferous republic calling for independence from Moscow.

Current situation: Newly independent, the republic has been racing toward a market economy. Since early this year, it has been freeing prices, which has led to rampant inflation, readying businesses and property for privatization and squabbling with the Soviet government over what belongs to the Soviets and what belongs to Lithuania. Likely will introduce its own currency—perhaps the first republic to do so.

Leader: President Vytautas Landsbergis.

Investment opportunities: Precision machine tools, consumer electronics, amber.

Ukraine

"The Ukraine combines a broad industrial base, substantial mineral deposits and a rich agricultural sector. It is outdistancing its rival republics in its efforts to convert defense plants to civilian industry. But Deutsche Bank gave the Ukrainians a failing grade on businessmindedness."

GNP: $243 billion.

Population: 51.7 million.

Per capita GNP; $4,700.

Major cities: Kiev (capital, 2.6 million), Kharkov (1.6 million).

Ethnic groups: 74% Ukrainian, 21% Russian.

Languages: Ukrainian, Russian.

Climate: Moderate, Mediterranean.

Infrastructure: Decent roads, railroads, links to Eastern Europe; Moscow is about one hour away by air; technology, phones are fair, worse in countryside.

Agriculture: Strongest in the Soviet Union. Contributes 46% of Soviet output; grows wheat, corn, tobacco, vegetables; 24% of Soviet beef cattle.

Industry: Made 12% of Soviet refrigerators, 32% of TVs, 23% of canned goods, 20% of chemicals. Biggest Soviet producer of computer processors and peripherals. Mines coal, oil, gas.

Registered joint ventures: 99.

Lodging: In Kiev, Dniepro, centrally located, best for business but small, often booked up. Others in Kiev: Lybid, Rus, In Kharkov, Intourist, Mir.

History: For centuries a part of the Russian empire. Peter the Great smashed an independence rebellion in 1709. In 1919, Lenin had to put down an independence movement. The 1986 Chernobyl nuclear accident left northern parts contaminated.

Current situation: Made limited breakaway moves before the coup—such as declaring that all state enterprises would come under Ukrainian control. But stayed communist until coup dissolved. Pressing for self-determination and a market economy but will keep economic ties to union.

Leader: President Leonid Kravchuk.

Investment opportunities: Farm equipment, computers, tourism, food processing.

Russia

"The hub of the U.S.S.R., Russia is actively trying to attract Western investment by establishing free trade and special economic zones in Leningrad and on Sakhalin Island. But it was rated as unbusinessminded and is burdened by the conversion of 460 defense plants to civil enterprises."

GNP: $854 billion.

Population: 147.4 million.

Per capita GNP: $5,810.

Major cities: Moscow (capital, 9 million), Leningrad (5 million), Novosibirsk (1.4 million).

Ethnic groups: 83% Russian, 4% Tartar.

Language: Russian.

Climate: Ranges from moderate in the south to arctic. Moscow's is similar to that of Calgary, Alberta.

Infrastructure: Moscow has the nation's busiest and best international airport. Decent roads and rail links extend from Moscow to major cities. Land travel is nearly impossible in much of the countryside, especially Siberia. Technology, phones are decent in Moscow, fair to poor in most of the rest of the republic,worst in the far north and east.

Agriculture: The republic's 15 million people employed in agriculture produced half the nation's grain and potatoes and 43% of other vegetables.

Industry: Heavy industry and raw materials dominate. Russia made half of the Soviet Union's steel, most of its cars, 60% of its cement, 63% of its electricity, 84% of its paper. Siberia has a wealth of resources—half of the world's coal and natural gas, more oil reserves than Saudi Arabia, one-fifth of the world's gold.

Registered joint ventures: 1,072.

Lodging: In Moscow, the Savoy is best set up for Western businesspeople but hard to get into. Try the Radisson, National, Mezhdunorodnaya or Rossia. In Leningrad, the Astoria, newly restored. In Novosibirsk, Intourist.

History: The Kiev Rus, a Viking people, dominated much of what is now Russia by 1054. Borders and leaders shifted until the czars pushed to the Pacific and down through the Ural Mountains by the 1700s. The heart of the 1917 revolution, Russia spread its control throughout the Soviet Union and Eastern Europe after World War II.

Current situation: Russia will be the powerhouse and catalyst behind any confederation of Soviet republics. Its leaders are pressing for a market economy, private property and strong legal framework for business, but those moves are only in beginning stages.

Leaders: Boris Yeltsin, president (popularly elected); Alexander Rutskoi, vice president; Anatoli Sobchak, Leningrad mayor.

Investment opportunities: Consulting, accounting and other business services; telecommunications; consumer products; tourism; medicine.

The Other Ten Republics and Their Market Niches

Georgia

"Though it has a relatively well-developed industrial structure, excellent agricultural sector and perhaps the most businessminded people of the Soviet Union, Georgia's low degree of self-sufficiency in industrial and consumer goods makes it particularly vulnerable to a breakdown of interrepublic trade."

GNP: $23.8 billion.

Population: 5.4 million.

Per capita GNP: $4,410.

Major city: Tbilisi (capital, 1.2 million).

Ethnic groups: 69% Georgian, 9% Armenian, 7% Russian.

Languages: Georgian, Russian.

Climate: Mild, Mediterranean on Black Sea coast.

Infrastructure: Good to fair roads and railways; Moscow is two hours away by air; technology and phones are fair to poor.

Agriculture: Hugely successful in grapes, citrus fruits, tea and spices. Georgian wine is popular throughout the Soviet Union.

Industry: Mostly food production—wineries, breweries, canneries. Mining, trucks and tractors. A tourism industry thrives on the Black Sea coast.

Registered joint ventures: 41.

Lodging: Tbilisi—the Iveria, modern, basic, swimming pool on roof; the Tbilisi, opened in 1914, city center, more elegant.**Current situation:** Ethnic unrest and battles between political factions dominate Georgian life. Likely will stay in a confederation of Soviet states. Economic reform moving slowly. Some food rationing is in place despite the republic's agricultural output. Signed one of the first interrepublic economic agreements, trading Georgian food for Azerbaijani oil.

Leader: President Zviad Gamsakhurdia, under pressure to step down.

Investment opportunities: Tractor production, tourism (on Black Sea), wine, food products.

Kazakhstan

"Blessed with potentially lucrative oil fields and huge deposits of rare minerals and led by charismatic, pro-Western leader, Kazakhstan is still unlikely to attract significant Western investment. Its population is relatively uneducated and divided into 100 nationalities that are unlikely to agree on common reform policies."

GNP: $60.3 billion.

Population: 16.2 million.

Per capita GNP: $3,720.

Major city: Alma-Ata (capital, 1.1 million).

Ethnic groups: 36% Kazakh, 41% Russian.

Languages: Russian, Kazakh.

Climate: Dry continental; half the republic is desert.

Infrastructure: Land travel nearly impossible—poor roads, difficult terrain and many off-limit areas (Soviet space launches and nuclear tests are done here). By air, Alma-Ata is five hours from Moscow. Technology and phones are poor.

Agriculture: Successful grain, tobacco, fruit, cotton growing; important meat exporter.

Industry: Abundant minerals, coal, oil and gas. Well-developed primary industry: iron, steel, chemicals, electricity.

Registered joint ventures: 10.

Lodging: In Alma-Ata, the Otrar or the Zhetysu in city center. Both are basic and offer international calling.

Current situation: Government has moved swiftly to pass several economic measures—allowing private ownership of housing and setting foreign-trade priorities. But there's still a long way to go. Consumer-goods industry is underdeveloped. Strongly pushing for the confederation. Kazakhstan likely would be an economic force in the new nation.

Leaders: President Nursultan Nazarbayev, emerging as one of the strongest leaders in the Soviet Union.

Investment opportunities: Oil, gas and mineral mining.

Byelorussia

"While blessed with well-educated people, close proximity to Europe and relative self-sufficiency in industrial goods, the republic is burdened with low-quality textile, food, machinery and consumer-goods (radios, TVs, computers, watches) industries. It is poor in natural resources and has limited hard-currency earning capacity. Commercial ventures will likely service Byelorussia from neighboring Russia."

GNP: $60.8 billion.

Population: 10.2 million.

Per capita GNP: $5,960.

Major city: Minsk (capital, 1.5 million).

Ethnic groups: 79% Byelorussia, 12% Russian.

Languages: Byelorussian, Russian.

Climate: Moderate.

Infrastructure: Roads are moderate to poor, but there are good rail links to Berlin, Warsaw and Moscow. Kiev, Leningrad and Moscow each is a one-hour flight away; the Baltics are even closer. Technology and phones are fair to poor.

Agriculture: Grew 20% of Soviet potatoes, 30% of flax.

Industry: Heavy auto and agricultural-machinery industries (made 20% of Soviet motorcycles, 15% of tractors); refrigerators, machine tools (14% of Soviet total).

Registered joint ventures: 27.

Lodging: In Minsk, the Yubileynaya—comfortable, modern, city center; the Planeta—further out, more hectic.

Current situation: Will stay part of a confederation of republics. Continuing political battles have meant that economic reforms are scattered and ineffective. There are limited moves to free prices and make farms private. The 1986 Chernobyl nuclear accident has left parts of southern Byelorussia heavily contaminated.

Leader: Stanislav S. Shushkevich, first deputy chairman of the Byelorussia Parliament.

Investment opportunities: Food products; truck and tractor manufacturing.

Moldavia

"Moldavia is close to Western Europe, has an excellent infrastructure by Soviet standards and has highly productive fruit, vegetable, wine and tobacco industries—which have excellent hard-currency earning capacity. Manufacturing-investment opportunities are scarce. Industrial base is limited to small-scale manufacturing of appliances, TVs, farm machinery and electric transformers."

GNP: $16.5 billion.

Population: 4.3 million.

Per capita GNP: $3,830.

Major city: Kishinev (capital, 663,000).

Ethnic groups: 64% Moldavian, 14% Ukrainian, 13% Russian.

Languages: Moldavian, Russian.

Climate: Warm, equable.

Infrastructure: Better than elsewhere in the Soviet Union. Good road and rail links to Kiev, Romania and Odessa on the Black Sea. Technology and phones are fair to poor.

Agriculture: Favorable climate for vegetables, tobacco, grapes for wine.

Industry: Mostly food processing and some light industry.

Registered joint ventures: 14.

Lodging: Kishinev—the Intourist and Kishinev in city center; the Motel Strugurash a bit farther out.

Current situation: Likely will join the confederation but keep close links with neighboring Romania with an eye toward eventual reunification (Moldavia was part of Romania until the Soviet Union annexed it in 1940). Moving surprisingly fast on economic reform, freeing some prices this month and beginning an aggressive step-by-step program to privatize land and businesses.

Leader: Prime Minister Valeriu Muravsky.

Investment opportunities: Food, wine, tobacco production, possibly small-scale consumer products such as TVs, appliances.

Armenia

"Its strength is its population's free-enterprise orientation and a well-developed infrastructure. But its machine-building and chemical industries are unlikely to earn hard currency soon. Its people are poorly educated, and ethnic conflicts dim its attraction."

GNP: $15.5 billion.

Population: 3.3 million.

Per capita GNP: $4,710.

Major city: Yerevan (capital, 1.2 million).

Ethnic groups: 90% Armenian, 5% Azerbaijani.

Languages: Armenian, Russian, Azerbaijan.

Climate: Continental, hot.

Infrastructure: Better than elsewhere in the Soviet Union, though most mountainous regions are impassable by land. Links to neighboring Turkey. Three hours to Moscow by air. Technology, phones are poor.

Agriculture: The mountainous country isn't good for farming. Crops include grain, potatoes and grapes.

Industry: Machine tools, foundry equipment, plastics, footwear and textile, notably woven carpets. Major deposits of copper, zinc, aluminum.

Registered joint ventures: 10.

Lodging: Yerevan—the Ani, central but bland; the Armenia, central but bland.

Current situation: Likely will stay in a confederation of republics. Armenia and Azerbaijan agreed recently to a cease fire in ethnic conflicts. Still, Armenia feels vulnerable to Azerbaijan to the east and ancient enemy Turkey to the west. Privatization has been erratic and laws continue to be revised, but the republic seems to be moving quickly to sell or give land and small businesses back to its people.

Leader: President Levon Ter-Petrosyan.

Investment opportunities: Metals, carpets, textiles.

Uzbekistan

"Uzbekistan is the world's third-largest cotton producer, offering a relatively strong investment attraction for textile firms. But its environment has been devastated by irrigation and fertilization. The Aral Sea has shrunk 40%. Pervasive pesticide and chemical pollution of drinking water worries Westerners. The cost of cleanup of its water is estimated at 25 billion rubles."

GNP: $54.7 billion.

Population: 19.9 million.

Per capita GNP: $2,750.

Major city: Tashkent (capital, 2.1 million).

Ethnic groups: 69% Uzbek, 11% Russian.

Languages: Uzbek, Russian.

Climate: Continental, extreme temperatures.

Infrastructure: Fair to poor roads and railways. Tashkent is four hours by air from Moscow. Technology, phones are poor.

Agriculture: 9% arable land, cotton is chief crop.

Industry: Natural gas, chemicals.

Registered joint ventures: 11.

Lodging: In Tashkent, the Uzbekistan, relatively well-appointed but no business services. Other hotels are far inferior.

Current situation: Troubled by ethnic, social, political unrest. Too little food, raging inflation and one of the lowest-paid workforces in the Soviet Union. Limited moves toward a market economy. Likely will stay in confederation.

Leader: President Islam Karimov.

Investment opportunities: Cotton, textiles, natural gas.

Azerbaijan

"The republic has poorly developed industry and infrastructure, and its people suffer from low education levels. But its raw materials' hard-currency earnings capacity is substantial."

GNP: $26.3 billion.

Population: 7 million.

Per capita GNP: $3,750.

Major city: Baku (capital, 1.7 million).

Ethnic groups: 78% Azerbaijani, 8% Armenian, 8% Russian.

Languages: Azerbaijani, Russian, Armenian.

Climate: Continental, mild in Baku.

Infrastructure: Poor roads and railways; flights to Moscow take three hours; technology, phones are poor.

Agriculture: Weak and menaced by droughts; cotton, grain, sheep.

Industry: Most of the economy is oil-based. Azerbaijan has one of the richest oil fields in the world, still largely untapped. It refines oil and makes petrochemicals and has been the Soviet Union's major producer of oil-drilling equipment.

Registered joint ventures: 10.

Lodging: Baku—the Moskva, best in town for business, city center; Intourist, standard but near sea front.

Current situation: Probably will stay in the confederation, but popular movements call for uniting with neighboring Iran. Signed a cease fire with Armenia in ethnic conflicts. Stronger ties with United States than most republics because of its oil. A number of U.S. oil executives and government officials have visited, and several oil companies are seeking joint ventures—most notably Chevron. Few economic reforms.

Leader: President Ayaz Mutalibov.

Investment opportunities: Oil production, oil-field equipment.

Turkmenistan

"The republic is renowned for its fine carpets, Turkoman horses and Karakul sheep. The people have shown little appetite for economic reform."

GNP: $11.8 billion.

Population: 3.5 million.

Per capita GNP: $3,370.

Major city: Ashkhabad (capital, 398,000).

Ethnic groups: 68% Turkoman, 13% Russian.

Languages: Turkoman, Russian.

Climate: Extreme temperatures, 90% is desert.

Infrastructure: Poor roads; Ashkhabad is on the Transcaspian rail line linking the Caspian Sea to Uzbekistan; Moscow is 3½ hours away by air; technology and phones are poor.

Agriculture: 2% arable land; main crop is cotton.

Industry: Oil and gas production, salt.

Registered joint ventures: One.

Lodging: In Ashkhabad, the Ashkhabad hotel—basic with no business services but two good restaurants.

Current situation: Mostly quiet since the Aug. 19 coup attempt. Little political or economic reform. President issued list of items that can't be privately owned—including weapons, drugs and printing equipment. Likely will join confederation.

Leader: President Saparmurad Niyazov.

Investment opportunities: Natural-gas production, carpets, cotton and textiles.

Kirghizia

"Its poor transportation system and earthquake exposure make the republic an unlikely investment destination for Westerners. Its industry is relatively undeveloped and its population is less educated and businessminded than in other republics."

GNP: $13 billion.

Population: 4.3 million.

Per capita GNP: $3,030.

Major city: Frunze (capital, 630,000).

Ethnic groups: 48% Kirghiz, 26% Russian.

Languages: Kirghiz, Russian.

Climate: Continental, dry, half of mountainous republic 10,000 feet above sea level.

Infrastructure: Poor roads and railways; Moscow is three hours away by air; technology and phones are poor.

Agriculture: 7% arable land; potatoes, vegetables, cotton; beekeeping; mostly livestock breeding—sheep, goats, yaks.

Industry: Metallurgy, coal, oil and gas production, tourism (health spas).

Registered joint ventures: Two.

Lodging: In Frunze, the Ala Tau, three floors, no elevators, spartan.

Current situation: Ethnic tensions, land shortages and poverty are the rule. The government has passed market-reform laws and is seeking foreign investment, but that's made little difference to Kirghizia's sorry economy. Likely will stay in the confederation.

Leader: President Askar Akyayev.

Investment opportunities: Oil, coal and gas, tourism, wool.

Tadzhikistan

"Perhaps the republic's most notable characteristic is that it contains Communism Peak, at 24,590 feet the highest point in the Soviet Union. Interest in doing business is scarce."

GNP: $11.9 billion.

Population: 5.1 million.

Per capita GNP: $2,340.

Major city: Dushanbe (capital, 582,000).

Ethnic groups: 59% Tadzhik, 23% Uzbek, 10% Russian.

Languages: Tadzhikan, Russian, Uzbek.

Climate: From subtropical in regions to harsh in Pamir Mountains.

Infrastructure: Very poor roads and railways; Moscow is about four hours away by air; technology and phones are poor.

Agriculture: 6% arable land; grain, cotton, sheep, cattle, yaks.

Industry: Textiles, carpet weaving, metal mining and processing.

Registered joint ventures: One.

Lodging: In Dushanbe, the Tadzhikistan.

Current Situation: The only republic where the Communist Party has reclaimed leadership. The republic is mired in unemployment and poverty and has made little economic reform. Likely will stay in the confederation but seek ties with nearby Iran.

Leader: Rakhman Nabiyev, president until Oct. 27 elections.

Investment opportunities: Carpets, wool, hydroelectric power.

Sources for This Report

Information on the republics and business travel was prepared from the following sources:

1. Geonomics Institute, Middlebury, Vt.
2. Deutsche Bank reports available through Trans-Atlantic Futures, Washington, D.C.
3. PlanEcon, Washington, D.C.
4. *U.S.S.R.: The Economist Business Traveller's Guides* (Prentice Hall, $19.95).
5. *Commersant,* a Soviet business weekly available through Refco Group, Chicago ($265 a year).
6. *Berlitz Russian for Travellers* ($5.95).
7. Intourist, the Soviet tourism enterprise, New York.
8. *Doing Business in the Union of Soviet Socialist Republics,* Price Waterhouse, New York.
9. *Meltdown: Inside the Soviet Economy,* Paul Craig Roberts and Karen LaFollette (Cato Institute, $9.95).
10. *The HarperCollins Business Guide to Moscow* (HarperCollins, $9.95).

Nobody's Grandfather Was a Merchant: Understanding the Soviet Commercial Negotiation Process and Style

Mahesh N. Rajan and John L. Graham. *Mahesh N. Rajan is a Ph.D. candidate in Business Policy/International Business in the Graduate School of Management at the University of California, Irvine. He has also consulted with several firms in India and in the U.S. John L. Graham is a Professor of International Business and Marketing in the Graduate School of Management at the University of California, Irvine. He is the author (with Yoshihiro Sano) of* Smart Bargaining: Doing Business with the Japanese *and has published in the* Harvard Business Review, *the* Columbia Journal of World Business, *the* Journal of Higher Education, *the* Los Angeles Times, *and* The New York Times.

It looked strange indeed. There were two Americans with their sleeves rolled up bargaining with three Japanese sitting stiffly, and the conversation was dubbed into Russian. Instead of *yes* or *hai,* it was *da* and so on. The videotapes were part of two-day seminars the second author was delivering to groups of Soviet enterprise managers in Moscow in 1989. The programs had two goals. The first was to learn about Soviet negotiation styles by directly observing Soviet behavior in simulated commercial negotiations. The second goal was to help familiarize the Soviets with the American and Japanese negotiation styles, since both groups are important investors in the evolving Soviet market system. Our research and experiences in Moscow confirm that American managers dealing with Soviets today and in the future will need what Tolstoy referred to as: "The strongest of all warriors . . . time and patience."[1]

We very much appreciate the helpful comments and suggestions of the outside reviewers. We would also like to acknowledge the editorial assistance and help of Ms. Greta Brooks of the Graduate School of Management, University of California, Irvine, in preparing this manuscript. This study was made possible by a grant from the Marketing Science Institute, Cambridge, MA. We are, however, solely responsible for the views contained within.

Background

Hardly a day passes without some mention in the popular media of the dramatic changes taking place in the Soviet Union and Eastern Europe. Though much uncertainty surrounds his own future, Mikhail Gorbachev's campaigns of *perestroika* (restructuring) and *glasnost* (openness) have greatly transformed the nature and core of global politics. Consequentially, the world has witnessed such radical events as the tearing down of the Berlin Wall and the reunification of the two Germanies, freely elected noncommunist governments in Poland and Czechoslovakia, the bloody overthrow and execution of Rumania's hard-line dictator, and the disbanding of Bulgaria's once highly feared secret police.

Speculation is no longer necessary about whether these changes mark the beginning of an irreversible process. These changes signal a shift in ideology and also herald economic opportunities for American and Western firms in hitherto closed, totalitarian nations. Dissension within COMECON, the 40-year-old system which once controlled trade in Eastern bloc countries, has caused it to lose power and subsequently has sent member countries scurrying to find new sources of capital and technology. Of these countries, the Soviet Union, because of its geographic and economic immensity, probably interests American firms the most as a potential market.

Unfortunately, economic relations between the U.S. and the Soviet Union have been overshadowed and influenced by their political discourses. Clearly, the U.S. government's historical practice of ad hoc trade policies to either help or harm the Soviets (depending on the current U.S. perspective) is a well-documented testimony to this. In the last few decades, this unfortunate condition is reflected in the fact that there is far more English language literature dealing with formal state-to-state negotiations between the Soviet Union and the U.S. than there is on *commercial trade negotiations* between the two. Corporate America suffers from a paucity of knowledge about Soviet culture and the logic of Soviet negotiation processes, coupled with a general suspicion and skepticism of the Soviets rooted in the heightened political conflicts of the past seventy years. Ideologically driven by stereotypical images of their counterparts, American business executives generally find negotiations with the Soviets tedious and cumbersome, and such negative experiences further fuel fallacious thoughts and actions. Given the ideological differences between the U.S. and the Soviets, as well as the fragile existence of economic trade between the two, it is not surprising that Americans lag behind Europeans and Japanese in venturing into business in the Soviet Union. As their respective views shift to be less confrontational, however, new opportunities for cooperation may emerge. Frustrations may be lowered, business endeavors facilitated, and economic ties strengthened as both sides gain insights into one another's cultures and the logic of their negotiation styles.

Our own studies investigated similarities and, more importantly, differences in the processes and outcomes of negotiations in the U.S. and the Soviet Union. For instance, in both cultures a cooperative and interpersonal approach tended to lead to higher satisfaction for the partners—a critical factor for establishing long-term business relationships. However, a problem-solving approach yielded higher profits for individual negotiators among the Americans, but a similar approach among the Soviets resulted in lower profits. Thus, the cooperative approach may yield positive results when used by Americans in negotiations with their fellow countrymen, but it may not work in the same way with Soviet negotiators. Conversely, a competitive or distributive approach which tends to work among Soviets may not achieve comparable results with American business executives. Based on our most recent studies, these differences appear to be crucial and fundamental, hence they must be acknowledged and examined to develop normative models of negotiations for the two countries. For negotiations to be successful, both sides must be cognizant and sensitive to how their differences can precipitate problems.

A point of caution—the kind of Soviet negotiator you will be sitting across from may be quite different from even last year. Until recently, only officials from Foreign Trade Organizations (FTOs) participated in commercial negotiations with Western firms. Though representatives and managers of Soviet state enterprises were allowed to be present at such meetings, foreign trade (i.e., imports and exports) was under the exclusive control of the few dozen FTOs. However, since April 1988, more than 5,000 Soviet state enterprises have applied for direct trading rights—meaning Western managers can now call on Soviet buyers and sellers directly, thus avoiding the previous bureaucratic channels. Additionally, provinces such as Russia and Lithuania are threatening to conduct trade autonomously and outside of the Union of the Soviet Republic.

Moreover, most of the previous literature on the Soviet negotiation style is based upon observation of political negotiators and to a lesser extent FTO personnel. However, several scholars have suggested that very basic driving forces influence traits and behaviors of Soviet negotiators across all negotiation situations—commercial, political and arms reduction talks.[2] This point is best articulated by Beliaev, Mullen, and Punnett, who state:

> All individual or collective actions of Soviet negotiators are overwhelmingly influenced by the state and the state ideology. The emphasis on individual behavior, which is culturally "in the blood" of Americans, leads to a tendency for them to underestimate the pervasiveness of the Soviet state in the consciousness and behavior of every Soviet person. It is necessary to realize that the Soviet people take virtually no step, in their public or private lives, which does not depend on the state.[3]

Therefore, in our discussion of the Soviet negotiation process and style, relevant material from the literature regarding arms and political negotiations is also considered.

Finally, though dramatic changes have been taking place in the structure of the Soviet economy, it certainly does not mean that the Soviet Union is on the verge of becoming a normal market economy. While commitment to the party or state ideology may be on the wane, we feel that it will be perhaps generations before such fundamental values can be eradicated, if at all, from the culture and lifestyle of the Soviet people. Hence, institutional controls (such as price-fixing) and nonprofit-maximizing goals will remain, thereby influencing Soviet and American negotiators to respond differently to economic stimuli.

The Soviet Negotiation Process

Lengthy

Negotiations involving Soviets can last for a few years before an agreement is reached. Indeed, McDonald's of Canada first started talking to the Soviets in 1976. The primary reason for long, drawn-out negotiations is that often they are divided into two sequential stages: technical and commercial. The technical stage may or may not include the end-user and spans issues such as technical requirements, product specifications, and technology considerations. Only after its successful completion, which can take a year, will the Soviets discuss the financial aspects of the deal. Then the commercial stage, often involving representatives from the Foreign Trade Organizations and from Soviet financial institutions, generally takes a like amount of time. There are other factors which also slow down the negotiation process: overlapping and conflicting ministerial divisions, multiple layers of decision making, centralized planning, tenuous lines of internal communication, and intense specialization (which results in no one individual having complete information or authority). Further, the Soviets may prolong the technical negotiation stage to acquire as much knowledge of Western technology as possible. Finally, they, like managers in most foreign countries, may also deliberately dally to gain concessions by taking advantage of the renowned "eagerness" and "impatience" of the Americans. Alternatively, the Soviets can hasten negotiation processes when the object of the negotiations has a high priority to them or when they are the seller.

Location

Connected closely with timing is location. And there's simply no ideal place to negotiate with a Soviet, at least from the standpoint of the typically impatient American. For example, we know of one American firm whose managers travelled to the south of France (a neutral location) to close negotiations with a Soviet customer on a multimillion-dollar natural gas pipeline equipment deal. The Soviets arrived and, true to their reputation, refused to budge on any provision. The American negotiation team was quite discouraged until it occurred to them that the Soviets weren't in a hurry for several reasons. Negotiation tactics, yes, but the Soviets were also simply enjoying their stay on the Mediterranean. So the Americans, with wary permission from their headquarters, decided to slow things down themselves. The two sides would meet at 10 a.m., quickly decide that nothing could be resolved, then agree to meet the next morning at 10 a.m. Then both sides would hit the golf links or the beach or get some paperwork done. This routine went on for one, two, three weeks. Finally, in the fourth week, the Soviet side began making substantial concessions. The Soviets were not in a position to return to Moscow without a signed contract after a month in southern France!

So, if you bring the Soviets to the U.S. or to a neutral location, they'll take their time. However, negotiating in Moscow is also a bad option. At this writing, the living conditions for visiting foreign executives are among the worst in the world. Americans will be even more impatient than in other foreign cities because Soviet accommodations lack the "creature comforts" typically available at the local Hilton. Moreover, in

Moscow, the dearth of secure communication facilities makes negotiation processes very difficult. Perhaps the tongue-in-cheek comment about Reykjavic being the ideal location for a U.S./ Soviet summit has some truth in it—"Nobody *enjoys* visiting Iceland."

Difficult

Characteristically, Americans and Soviets have different priorities and ideological orientations, making negotiations between them arduous. Americans primarily are concerned with bottom-line profits and personal gains, while Soviets are more apt to be driven by ideological goals and collective gain for their organizations. Many Soviets may be unfamiliar with Western management concepts and practices: "the word *market* has no equivalent in Russian language"[4] and "some Soviet managers are even hazy about the meaning of the word *profit*"[5] [emphases added]. In fact, the chairman of the Central Council of Trade Unions in the Soviet Union states that the Soviet "people discuss the market without even knowing what it is. We know more about space research than we do market research."[6] This knowledge gap tends to further aggravate American business executives. Moreover, the Soviets view negotiations as tests of potential suppliers and, hence, intentionally complicate and prolong them, believing that companies which survive such ordeals are likely to be better partners than firms which drop out of the talks. Finally, Americans often find the Soviets' insistence on favorable credit terms exasperating, which contributes to the overall difficulties of negotiations.

Countertrade Issues

Issues of countertrade play such a significant role in the negotiation processes that they warrant separate mention. Nonmonetary compensation schemes are explored by the Soviets for all but the highest priority items. The countertrade arrangements they propose can range from simple barter to highly complex product buy-backs and three-party switching agreements. In the wrap-up of negotiations, after agreements have already been reached regarding such things as price, quantity, and time frames, the Soviets propose such countertrade. Besides being concerned with the inconvertibility of the ruble, the Soviets are driven by two other motives. First, countertrade allows them to conserve their much treasured, relatively limited hard currency reserves. Second, but of more importance, it helps them penetrate foreign markets without having to develop marketing skills and with no outlay for distribution facilities. Thus it should not be surprising that Soviets prefer to deal with firms which are agreeable to countertrade transactions. They probably assume that direct exporting will become easier once world markets become accustomed to Soviet products. If the opposite party insists on a cash-only method of payment and if there are no alternative suppliers or forms of agreement, the Soviets will introduce countertrade proposals as bargaining tools to gain additional concessions.

Generalized Warranties and Written Contracts

Soviet buyers attempt to get the most generalized warranty agreement possible from the seller. Hence, they downplay American concerns about liabilities arising from non-specific warranties and unforeseen contingencies such as Act of God *(force majeure)* provisions. However, they have been known to hold the other party responsible for delays or failures even when the factors for non-compliance were beyond that party's control. Business executives who do not specifically spell out in writing the terms of responsibility and liability in the warranty section of their agreements will be rudely awakened by how boldly the Soviets attempt to exploit the vagueness of the agreement. All contracts between American firms and Soviets are generally governed by Soviet law, which does not recognize oral agreements as binding, so business deals are not consummated until all concerned parties have signed the documents. Written contracts then supersede all previous unwritten agreements and implicit assumptions, which explains why Soviet negotiators introduce countertrade issues so late in the process. Further, the Soviets insist on writing down every other aspect of the transaction—things taken for granted in Western nations such as verbal confirmations of receipt of goods and telephone reorders—except the warranty section.

Peculiar Twists

When negotiations have been conducted in the Soviet Union, they have been marked by Soviet acts which Americans have generally found both unusual and disconcerting, to say the least: long-scheduled meetings were canceled; agenda and venue were changed frequently; large orders were mentioned casually and just as casually denied; negotiation leaders were switched without informing the Americans. Americans who have dealt with the Soviets are divided on whether such Soviet actions are deliberate and hence unfair tactics, or if such developments are system-related and therefore not only inevitable, but also legitimate. This issue continues to be a controversial debate as neither claim has been definitively proved. It behooves U.S. business executives, however, to be alert to and prepared for such peculiar developments.

Protocol/Symbolism

Soviets are so sensitive to protocol issues that, in addition to preferring that concerned parties deal directly rather than through intermediaries, they usually appoint negotiators comparable in position to the other party's representatives. They seem to gauge a firm's sincerity about doing business with them by the rank and status of the firm's negotiator and interpret simple acts (such as frequent trips to the Soviet Union by top executives, the opening of offices in the Soviet Union, and participation in trade fairs and exhibits in or sponsored by the Soviet Union) as symbolic representations of friendship and as acknowledgment of the worthiness of the Soviet market. Rival bidders have found that the firm which spends the most time, effort, and money wooing the Soviets often emerges from negotiations with the written contract.

Continuity

Perhaps the most remarkable aspect of the negotiation process is the Soviets' perspective of continuity. Because they prefer to do business with those with whom they have satisfactorily interacted in the past, the Soviet negotiators pay extra attention to a firm's reputation and capabilities during the first encounter. Successful initial contracts may pave the way for even more profitable future ventures as the Soviets become more cooperative and trusting of their foreign business partners and eventually voluntarily mitigate some of the hazards their partners find so thwarting.

The Soviet Negotiation Style

Secretive

Perhaps Winston Churchill put it best: "I cannot forecast to you the action of Russia. It is a riddle wrapped in a mystery inside an enigma."[7] The Soviet penchant for secrecy becomes apparent immediately to negotiators from other cultures, especially from Western nations. Isolation from and distrust of the rest of the world generally lead the Soviets to reveal very little information about themselves or their motives to outsiders. From an organizational and administrative perspective, in a bureaucratic monolith such as the Soviet Union, officials become tight-lipped because information is a source of power and upward mobility and is guarded jealously.

Risk-Averse

Soviet negotiators' fears of being reprimanded and/ or removed from privileged positions for unsuccessful and unfavorable contracts force them to have a basically conservative outlook and behavior. Moreover, the fundamentally deterministic nature of the (still largely) centralized planning system of the Soviet Union, with its history of ideological blindness to capitalistic management theories, encourages Soviet negotiators to be extremely wary of overstepping official bounds in their interactions with Western managers.

Detail-Oriented

The complexity of the Soviet bureaucracy, combined with the Soviets' risk-averse nature, forces their negotiators to pay great attention to even trivial and extraneous details. Also, to win the approval of their superiors, Soviet negotiators must be sure that they have not overlooked the minutest of details. In fact, it is said that such attention to detail is expected from Soviet negotiators as evidence of their integrity and commitment to the socialist ideology. Therefore, on several occasions Soviet negotiators have been known to expend a great deal of time and effort negotiating the picayune details in the "fine print" of contracts after generally agreeing to ventures worth millions of dollars.

Unsympathetic

The Soviets are known to interpret the terms of a contract literally and will brook no excuses from the other side for delays or failures to meet contractual obligations. There have been a few instances in the past when American firms have been penalized by the Soviets for non-performance even though the factors causing non-compliance were directly controlled by the Soviets. American business executives should make sure that they take nothing for granted and that all conditions which determine the fulfillment of their obligations are specified in writing. Though they are irritated by the Soviet negotiators' dogged attention to detail, seldom do American business executives realize that their own interests are protected and enhanced by the highly detailed agreements that result from such negotiations.

Uncompromising

Perhaps the most conspicuous aspect of Soviet negotiators at the bargaining table is their uncompromising attitude. Scholars as well as American business executives have frequently described them as tough, hard, confrontational, inflexible, competitive, stubborn, and rigid. Their behavior is said to reflect either the rigidity of their organizational structures, their ideologies, their culture, or some combination of the three.

Economic plans drawn up by the upper echelons of Soviet bureaucracy generally leave little authority or room for Soviet representatives, who are usually from the lower and middle levels of the organization, to maneuver at the negotiation table.

From an ideological standpoint, the Soviets view the negotiation process as neither a means of achieving higher profits for their organization nor as a vehicle for furthering personal goals—unlike Americans. Instead, to the Soviets the negotiation process represents an opportunity for "right" (their world view) to succeed over "wrong" (the American perspective); thus they assume inflexible, uncompromising, conflictual stances.

According to two experts on the Soviet Union, Vladimir and Victorina Lefebvre, Americans and Soviets are governed culturally by two different "ethical systems."[8] Western cultures are dominated by an ethical system in which the behavior of individuals who seek compromises to resolve conflicts with their adversaries is considered positive. However, Soviets are governed by a different ethical system in which it is positive for individuals to create new conflicts with adversaries and to exacerbate existing ones. The Lefebvres further contend that the very word "deal" itself has negative associations in the Russian language, because anyone seeking compromises is considered cowardly, weak, and unworthy. After observing the interactions of Soviet schoolchildren with Western tourists near the Kremlin, Professor Weigand commented that a "single stick of Juicy Fruit will get a foreigner a small piece of colored ribbon, but a whole package—*after some tough bargaining*—can win a bronze-like medal of Marx and Lenin."[9] His observation of children seems to corroborate the Lefebvres' theory that such rigidity on the part of the Soviet negotiators in their interaction with outsiders may be a product of the Soviet culture and thus may actually be a national trait, rather than due solely to bureaucratic and ideological forces.

Indeed, based upon our own studies of the Soviet negotiation style, they seem to by nature take a much different approach to commercial negotiations. Perhaps Alexander Arefiev, CEO of INFORCOM (an important Soviet management development firm), puts it best: "My biggest problem is convincing my Soviet clients to take a cooperative approach with Westerners." That is, by nature, Soviet executives will take a competitive or adversarial approach in negotiations with Americans, Creative, win-win solutions don't fit the Soviet psyche well. So cooperation and commitment to open and honest information exchange must be imbued.

Professor Oleg Vihansky, head of Moscow State University's Department of Management, provides a deeper cultural explanation where he contrasts the Soviets' approach to business partnerships with that of the Japanese. He suggests that the Japanese are the best at searching for creative bargaining solutions—making the pie bigger before it is divided. Traditionally, Soviets see negotiations as more a zero-sum activity—they tend to worry about how the pie is to be divided with little thought to increasing its size. Rooted deep in the Soviet psyche is the idea that one person's success is *always* at the expense of someone else.

One aspect of our studies of negotiation styles around the world directly supports Professor Vihansky's analysis. Not only have Americans and Soviets participated in our negotiation simulations, so have almost 800 businesspeople from twelve other cultures. (Of course, materials were translated in each case and bargainers used their own native languages.) The simulation allows for creative bargaining solutions—it is not a zero-sum game; the "pie" can be made bigger via cooperative negotiation strategies. As Vihansky would predict, the Japanese have been the best of all the cultural groups at making the pie big, that is, at maximizing joint profits. The bargaining solutions achieved by the Americans were near the average for all fourteen groups. The Soviet outcomes were quite close to the bottom, a finding which confirms and clarifies the picture that Soviets are, *by nature,* uncompromising.

Finally, we mentioned in an earlier section that Soviet managers are "hazy about the meaning of the word profit." The Soviet word *pribyl* (meaning "for profits") implies exploitation; that is, profits are always at someone else's expense. Alternatively, the English term *profits* can imply exploitation but also often implies creativity. Indeed, this difference between the two languages in meanings of the term *profits* is a reflection of the more fundamental differences in the two social and commercial systems. When you say "profits," your Soviet counterpart thinks "exploitation," not "creativity."

Manipulative

As most commercial negotiations with Soviets take place in the Soviet Union, the Soviets can and do manipulate negotiation processes in order to gain better terms for themselves. Three of the more popular techniques employed by the Soviets as tools of bargaining leverage are described as follows:

- They will negotiate the price at the initial stages of the process under the pretext of placing a large order. Once they have wrangled the best possible price from the suppliers, the Soviets will then, in addition to bringing up countertrade demands, require either additional concessions (such as service contracts or personnel training programs) or reduce the volume of their purchases while demanding the previously agreed upon price.
- "Whipsawing" is another favorite manipulative technique of the Soviets, wherein they carry on negotiations with several competing firms simultaneously. They then use selective information from their interaction with one firm in their negotiations with another, pitting the rival firms against each other, thus obtaining the most self-serving contract. On occasion, in not-too-subtle demonstrations of their relatively superior bargaining position, the Soviets have made arrangements for executives from rival firms to stay at the same hotel at the same time.

- An unknown Soviet bureaucrat will enter the room during actual negotiations and fly into a rage at the other side for treating the Soviet negotiators with disrespect and distrust. Expecting the American negotiators to be unnerved by this "tirade," the Soviets will then indicate a willingness to *forgive* the Americans in exchange for additional concessions.

While many American business executives would consider such acts by the Soviets unethical and unprofessional, these techniques may appear perfectly rational and legitimate in the eyes of the Soviets.[10] Given that different "ethical systems" govern the two cultures, such a difference of opinion should be regarded as neither surprising nor unusual. Based on their empirical study of Soviet emigrants' and middle-class Americans' responses to several hypothetical situations, the Lefebvres concluded that while "the majority of former Soviet citizens consider it acceptable to use bad means to achieve good goals . . . the majority of Americans disagree with this."[11] Our own more recent comparisons of American and Soviet managers attitudes strongly confirm the Lefebvres' findings.

Loyal

Though most of the previously discussed material presents the Soviets in an adversarial and combative light, the authors certainly do not mean to imply nor to advocate that American firms should avoid the Soviet market. The Soviet Union is a highly desirable and potentially profitable market, as has been proved by the experiences of firms such as Occidental Petroleum and Pepsico. However, the development and nurturing of personal relationships with the Soviet negotiators are critical prerequisites to establishing good business relationships with the Soviets. The Soviet emphasis on interpersonal relationships and its effect on the outcome of negotiations is perhaps rivalled by only a few cultures, if any. Organizational constraints, ideologically driven fear and suspicion of outsiders (especially of Americans), and a fundamentally risk-averse nature make it absolutely imperative for the Soviet negotiators to sign contracts only with firms (and executives) they feel they can depend upon. Personal relationships based on mutual respect and understanding, combined with a history of satisfactory business transactions, are crucial for successful ventures with the Soviets. Efforts on the part of the American executives to acknowledge and gratify these requisites are rewarded with trust and loyalty by the Soviets, thereby perpetuating the Soviet preference for "continuity" in their commercial transactions with foreign firms.

Reliable

Given the overall difficulty and frustrating nature of the Soviet negotiation process and style, a surprising characteristic of the Soviets is that until 1990 they were extremely reliable and always honored their contractual commitments. Even more impressive was the impeccable record that the Soviets have had, until now, in fulfilling their financial obligations, to the extent that some American suppliers with their Western customers were equally prompt and conscientious in their payments. Last year in Moscow, John Minneman, Chase Manhattan's vice president/representative in the USSR, told us about his Soviet banking counterparts: "They're sophisticated and tough, but they never lie and always pay on time." An observation by another expert on international trade succinctly sums up the nature of the Soviet negotiation process and style: "Although the Soviets drive a very hard bargain in contract negotiations, they will abide faithfully by its provisions, and expect the other party to do the same. They have an excellent record in honoring their financial commitments."[12]

However, the picture of the Soviets as reliable fiscally has become somewhat clouded in recent months. Several Western concerns have reported slow payments by Soviet customers. State-backed transactions at this point are not the problem, but some Soviet enterprise and foreign trade organizations (FTOs) are having trouble meeting current obligations and *are not* being bailed out by the Bank of Foreign Economic Affairs as was customary in the past. No one has yet defaulted,[13] but some American firms have stopped shipping to Soviet clients. In fact, most Western analysts blamed the problem on confusion caused by the reshuffling of Soviet officials as part of President Gorbachev's *perestroika* and *glasnost* programs. However, one top-ranking Soviet official, addressing a symposium in the United States, allayed Western concerns about the Soviets defaulting on their payments by stating that "we do pay our bills, and we don't rob from Peter to pay Paul."[14] Moreover, the Soviet Union has begun depositing large amounts of gold with Western banks as collateral for loans; and to help cover overdue bills abroad, it is also drawing on Moscow's hard currency reserves and setting up an internal collection agency.[15] These corrective measures, taken by the Soviets to restore and protect their once excellent credit rating, should provide incentive and reassurance to foreign firms seeking new or increased trade opportunities. However, Americans must clearly recognize that in the long run, as free enterprise comes to the USSR, so will concomitant business failures and defaults.

Some Tips for American Managers

In interacting with the Soviets, besides profiting by a general awareness of the culture and the complex bureaucratic governance structure of the Soviet Union and their effects on the negotiations, American business executives may find it beneficial to adopt the following strategies.

Be Cautious

While tremendous changes are taking place with respect a huge array of opportunities for American firms, the risk and uncertainty surrounding *perestroika* cannot be ignored nor trivialized. Mikhail Gorbachev is a charismatic leader who definitely has set the wheels of change in motion, but whether these reforms will last and lead to greater economic standards, only time will tell. Investing large amounts of capital and technology in a society governed by such a different ideological and political structure is perilous, as painfully illustrated in China last year. The fact that trade with socialist countries is subject to government intervention based on the political climates, *particularly of the U.S.,* warrants a cautionary approach to the Soviet market.

Be Open-Minded

American managers need to find ways to shed biases rooted in decades of selective and politically motivated information and images of the Soviet Union. These images hinder objective evaluation of the viability of the Soviet market and make negotiations with the Soviets formidable. They also increase the chances of American firms losing out to more impartial competitors. In the long run, emphatically ruling out the viability of the Soviet market on the basis of ideological considerations may not be good business. Remember, the Soviets prefer dealing with long-known business partners.

There are no Dun and Bradstreet services for the Soviet Union. The only way to size up a potential partner is by relying on a network of acquaintances that you have established through a corporate presence in the country. You must take the time to *learn* the market and the people—there's just no quick way.

Be Culturally Sensitive

Centuries of isolation and oppression have not only instilled a general fear and suspicion of outsiders, but also have forced the Soviets to rely solely on their cultural roots for the inner strength and ardor that typifies them. In spite of such onerous backgrounds, the Soviet people are an exceptionally proud and patriotic people. So much are they influenced by and committed to national and collective interests that they almost always relegate personal gain and welfare to a secondary status in their thoughts and behaviors. They appreciate and respect foreigners who are knowledgeable of and empathetic to their historical and cultural origins. Further, acquiring such knowledge not only helps American business executives understand Soviet citizens, but also helps them make the adjustments necessary for successful business relationships with them.

Unlike citizens in other countries, Soviets have no collective memory of free enterprise. In Eastern Europe and even the People's Republic of China and North Korea, young people have grandfathers who were merchants before World War II. Not so in the Soviet Union—the communist tradition goes back to 1917, so no Soviet's grandfather was a merchant.

Be Patient

Any visitor to the Soviet Union, on business or as a tourist, immediately is aware of the incredible complexity and size of the Soviet bureaucracy. The assorted restrictions set by the monolithic and hierarchical administrative structure on Soviet negotiators force them to behave in ways that frustrate American executives. Additionally, current changes in the governance structure have removed the exclusivity of the well-trained and highly skilled FTO officials in dealings/negotiations with foreign corporations. Hence, state enterprise managers and middle-level officials who are unaware of Western management concepts have been thrust into negotiation settings, making these situations painful and slow for both parties. A key point for Westerners sitting at the table with Soviets to remember: Be both cognizant and patient with the traditional Soviet approach; "help" your partners learn to look for ways to make the commercial pie bigger for both sides—it's simply not their natural style. Even if the longevity and arduousness of the negotiations are of a deliberate nature, American executives can, by exhibiting atypical patience, pave the way not only in initial contracts, but also in opening up future profitable opportunities.

Exchange Views about Negotiation Processes

Caution is suggested here. One Soviet executive told us that what bothers him most about Americans is their arrogance. He said that "Americans take a teaching approach" while "Japanese listen cordially." While it is true that Soviets are willing to learn directly about the American free enterprise system in management seminars, they may resent being "taught" by their business partners. In negotiations, we recommend an information exchange or mutual teaching approach. It is all right to say, "This is the way things work where I come from," only if you've first asked how things work in the USSR.

During your get-acquainted meetings or dinners, you may want to ask your counterpart how negotiations typically proceed in the Soviet Union. That is, you might verify the information we provide here about the Soviet negotiation style and process. Tell them this is what you have been reading about the Soviet approach, and then ask, "What do you think of Rajan and Graham's ideas?"

Then you will be in a position to say things like, "In the West we try to be creative in business negotiations by exchanging information freely—we try to make the pie bigger before we cut it up." Show an interest in their system and its transformations *before* you begin giving advice. And get these things straightened out before you begin your specific task-related discussions.

Be Flexible

A rigid adherence to planned strategies and goals may not be the best negotiation stance for American firms in the Soviet Union. One area of negotiations where flexibility and a willingness to consider other options are particularly important is the area of credit and payment provisions. Though American managers are indoctrinated by the free market and their corporate structural orientations to have a "hard-currency-transaction-only" attitude, it is not profitable to apply this in negotiating with the Soviet Union. Professor Yoffie observed that "in a buyer's market countertrade can be especially important. When price, technology, and quality are comparable, willingness to countertrade often separates winners from losers."[16] Therefore, American managers, if they wish to compete successfully for the Soviet market with Japanese and European competitors (who have accepted non-monetary compensation agreements somewhat more enthusiastically), need to consider seriously the opportunities of trade without money.

Hopefully, other American firms and their executives can learn something from the Pepsico example. Obviously, Pepsico Inc. is quite satisfied with its long-standing countertrade arrangements with the Soviets—Pepsi-Cola bartered for Stolichnaya vodka and scrap iron from moth-balled Soviet battleships. They have recently agreed to a dramatic expansion of their operations in the USSR, including continuing provisions for countertrade.

Right now most American managers seem to suffer badly from what we call "allassophobia," or "fear of countertrade."[17] Recently, we had lunch with an executive of a local high-tech firm who was about to depart for the Soviet Union. We asked him how he planned to handle his Soviet customer's probable countertrade proposals. His response was a classic display of acute allassophobia: "We won't do countertrade. Our company has a policy against it." Within ten days of our luncheon, a major competitor announced being awarded that very bid, and, of course, the deal included countertrade provisions.

Allassophobia is a serious malady which impairs American firms not only in Soviet trade but also in world trade generally. Despite the fact that 20 to 30 percent of world trade is financed via countertrade, American financial institutions ignore its key importance. Alan Shapiro reserved only three pages for a discussion of countertrade options in his very popular textbook on international finance. The number crunchers on Wall Street fear what they cannot easily measure, thus countertrade is ignored in textbooks and consequently eschewed in American board rooms. The key lesson here is that avoiding countertrade as a matter of corporate policy, as so many U.S. companies do, accomplishes nothing more than tying the hands of your negotiators. Certainly your Japanese and European competitors do not suffer from allassophobia.

Finally, countertrade may be another way to hedge against potential hard currency payment problems. Who can predict the availability of hard currency in the USSR? As we mentioned, recent signals suggest that the USSR may be reaching the limit of its currency reserves. Thus, countertrade deals should be examined and considered, because they may be the most attractive options in the future.

Have a Long-Term Orientation

In any nation burdened with a stagnant or declining economy and lacking the internal capability to develop its own untapped potential, investments take a long period to come to fruition, if they mature at all. Though they are somewhat inappropriate, the characteristically short-term concerns of corporate America may succeed to some extent in other countries with private sector industries. In a non-market economy like the Soviet Union, however, the probabilities of ventures with such orientations succeeding are rather infinitesimal. The Soviets (and the other Eastern European countries) desperately need and are looking for Western firms that are willing to invest in critical industries in their country, transfer much needed technology, train their labor force and managers, accept noncash and/or lower cash payments, and play an invaluable overall role in helping them reform and develop the Soviet economy. While initially these adjustments may be rather difficult, the subsequent goodwill of the Soviet people and favored access to the tremendous potential of the Soviet market would be the rewards for American corporations that make the transition.

West Germans and South Koreans, in addition to the Japanese, are taking the necessary long-term approach to the Soviet market. Consider the comments of Alfred Herrhausen, former CEO of Germany's biggest bank, regarding Deutsche Bank's investments in the USSR: "It will take at least two generations. One generation is necessary to be willing to introduce freedom, but it will take the next to figure out how to make economic use of its benefits."[18] Also, the fact that both West Germany and South Korea have either announced or are considering loans to the Soviet Union attests to the long-term orientations of these two countries.[19] Recently, Korea's Daewoo Motor Company gave a Soviet ministry fifty automobiles—a $250,000 or so investment towards future sales and goodwill.

Moreover, while many Western firms have halted shipments to the Soviet Union in response to the unusual delays in payments, the Japanese have taken a different approach. Several major Japanese trading houses, while continuing deliveries to the Soviet Union, have submitted export insurance claim notices to their government. (According to some analysts, the Japanese companies' low profile on this problem is intentional as they don't want to harm future trade prospects.) "They're being cautious," said Kazuko Motomura, an official with the Institute for Soviet and East European Economic Studies (a research organization set up by traders who do business with Eastern Europe). "But they're also thinking about the promising possibilities of the market in the future."[20]

Nissho-Iwsai (a major trading company), despite notifying the Japanese government about delays in Soviet payments for its steel and chemical products, confirmed that it still intended to participate in a consortium that is involved in a 38 billion yen ($239.4 million) project to build three compressor plants in the USSR. "We think that the Soviet Union will definitely make the payment," said Tetsuya Ouishi, an official in Nissho-Iwsai's public relations division.[21]

Finally, take a ride up the elevator at the World Trade Center (Sovin Center) in Moscow sometime, There you'll find offices of Chase Manhattan (17th floor) and Bank of America (16th floor), the latter with no executive permanently in Moscow at this writing. But on the way up, the elevator will undoubtedly be crowded with Japanese in blue suits, a few of whom will exit at the Mitsubishi floor, then the Mitsui and Sumitomo floors, and so on.

Conclusions

The pace and nature of change in the Soviet Union are such that many American perceptions and opinions of the Soviets, and perhaps some of the contents of this article, have become and are becoming increasingly obsolete. While it certainly is not an exhaustive account, we hope the above discussion provides American business executives a general insight into the Soviet negotiation process and style. If this article does nothing more than create an awareness among American managers of several key issues which contribute to the difficulties of negotiating with the Soviets and of appropriate and possible adaptations which may lead to many profitable ventures in the Soviet Union, we consider its purpose achieved. In spite of the many obstacles, economic trade will be enhanced if Americans gain a better understanding of the Soviet peoples' history and culture. Also, the ambassadorial efforts of business leaders like Armand Hammer and James Giffen are indeed commendable and should be encouraged. Other events are encouraging: the formation of the American Trade Consortium by six major corporations (including Chevron and Kodak) and its signing of an agreement with the Soviet Foreign Economic Consortium; the recent signing of a trade pact by officials from both countries which could lead to trade worth about $15 billion; and the passing of the "private property" law by the Soviet legislature in March 1990. Hopefully, these are milestones, not merely token symbolic representations, and depict the foundations of greater and more stable economic cooperation between these two great nations. In his address to the ninth annual meeting of the USSR Trade and Economic Council, President Gorbachev pointed out that "if we are to have genuinely stable and enduring relationships capable of ensuring a lasting peace, they should be based, among other things, on well-developed business relations."[22]

Without exception, the Soviets and Americans we talked to emphasized the necessity in U.S.–Soviet trade for developing *personal* relationships, relationships which persist beyond political change and ideological differences. Indeed, such personal relationships can cause political change. If American business leaders wish to influence Soviet politics, they might—instead of contributing to the political campaigns of favorite Republicans or Democrats in the U.S.—invest in business partnerships in the Soviet Union. Incentives for peace can best be created if Americans and Soviets understand one another on a personal basis. Indeed, Kipling's lines remain quite pertinent today:

> Oh, East is East, and West is West, and never the twain shall meet,
> 'Til Earth and Sky stand presently at God's great Judgment Seat;
> But there is neither East nor West, border, nor breed, nor birth,
> When two strong men stand face to face, though they come from the ends of the earth![23]

References

1. Leo Tolstoy, *War and Peace,* book X, chapter 16.

2. Leon Sloss and Scott M. Davis, "The Pursuit of Power and Influence through Negotiation," in Hans Binnendijk, ed., *National Negotiation Styles* (Washington, D.C.: Center for the Study of Foreign Affairs, Foreign Service Institute, U.S. State Department, 1987); Andreas Von Czege, "Soviet Negotiating Tactics in Trade with the West," *Soviet and European Trade,* 19 (Spring 1983): 32–54.

3. Edward Beliaev, Thomas P. Mullen, and Betty Jane Punnett, "Understanding the Cultural Environment: U.S.–U.S.S.R. Trade Negotiations," *California Management Review* (Winter 1985), pp. 100–112.

4. John J. Pialka, "Soviet Bottom Line Is That Few People Know What One Is," *The Wall Street Journal,* April 15, 1989, p. A13.

5. Peter Gumbel, "Western Money, Technology, Fall on Infertile Soviet Soil," *The Wall Street Journal,* December 1, 1989, p. A16.

6. "Soviet Market Reform Will Be Put to Voters," *Los Angeles Times,* May 24, 1990, p. A1. The reader should note that languages adapt to reflect changing cultures. In Russian there has always been a word for a place where goods are bought and sold—*rynok.* However, its meaning is quite narrow compared to the English "market." Indeed, the English term can be either a noun (as in a place) or a verb (as in an activity). Victorina Lefebvre tells us that only during the last year have the Soviets directly adopted the term "marketing" when they mean the activity in the Western sense.

7. Winston Churchill, radio broadcast, October 1, 1939.

8. Vladimir A. Lefebvre and Victorina D. Lefebvre, *Soviet Ways of Conflict Resolution and International Negotiations,* vols. 1 and 2 (Irvine, CA: School of Social Sciences, University of California, Irvine, 1986); Victorina D. Lefebvre, *Ethical Features of the Normative Hero in Soviet Children's Literature of the 1960s–70s,* Studies of Cognitive Sciences, 20, School of Social Sciences, University of California, Irvine, CA, 1983.

9. Robert E. Weigand, "International Trade Without Money," *Harvard Business Review* (November/ December 1977), p. 28.

10. The reader will note that in their popular book on negotiation, *Getting to Yes,* Roger Fisher and William Ury specifically warn about Americans taking such approaches.

11. Lefebvre and Lefebvre, op. cit.

12. Sondra Snowdon, *The Global Edge: How Your Company Can Win in the International Marketplace* (New York, NY: Simon and Schuster, 1986), p. 376.

13. Laurie Hays and Peter Gumbel, "Soviet Concerns Falling Behind in Paying Bills," *The Wall Street Journal,* March 6, 1990, p. 1.

14. "Plan on Paying Overdue Bills Set by Soviets," *The Wall Street Journal,* May 23, 1990, p. A20.

15. Neil Behrmann, "Soviets Deposit Gold in Western Banks as Collateral for Easing Cash Squeeze," *The Wall Street Journal,* June 4, 1990, p. A3.

16. David B. Yoffie, "Profiting from Countertrade," *Harvard Business Review* (May/June 1984), p. 9.

17. Theodore Brunner (Director of *Thesaurus Linguae Graece,* a data bank of ancient Greek tests at the University of California, Irvine) helped coin the term by combining the ancient Greek words *allassein* (to barter) and *phobia* (fear).

18. Daniel Burnstein, *Los Angeles Times,* December 3, 1989.

19. "A Loan from South Korea," *The Wall Street Journal,* June 1, 1990, p. A12; and Ferdinand Protzman, "Bonn to Prop Up Kremlin Reforms with $3 Billion Loan Guarantee," *New York Times,* June 23, 1990, p. A1.

20. "Japanese Traders Informing Tokyo Soviet Bills Unpaid," *The Wall Street Journal,* May 2, 1990, p. A11.

21. Ibid.

22. Mikhail S. Gorbachev, "Remarks on U.S.–U.S.S.R. Trade," *Harvard Business Review* (May/June 1986), p. 56.

23. Rudyard Kipling, "The Ballad of East and West," 1889.

Marketing in Islamic Countries: A Viewpoint

Mushtaq Luqmani, Zahir A. Quraeshi, and Linda Delene. *Western Michigan University, Kalamazoo, Michigan.*

Recent global developments have had a profound effect on the dynamics of world trade. A new international economic order is being forged, bringing with it new demands and pressures on world markets. Many of the changes can be attributed to the growing influence of Islamic countries.

Islam has about 767 million followers, constituting about 20 percent of the world's population (see Exhibit 1). In sheer numbers, the Islamic nations account for a large and growing group of markets. Many are rich in resources, and their wealth has multiplied rapidly in a short time. More significant is the growing trend in many Islamic countries toward transcending national boundaries and unifying Muslims into a common "brotherhood." If this goal is to be achieved, even partially, a consequence would be a politico-economic entity that could significantly alter the patterns of world trade. An emerging Islamic community could provide important market opportunities and challenges to global marketers.

This article will discuss the implications of these developments for marketing in Muslim countries and will focus on countries attempting to industrialize with an Islamic environment.

For many outsiders, Islam often evokes images of a strongly anticapitalist and antiprogressive religion. In order to participate effectively in the opportunities (and challenges) of marketing in Islamic countries, the global businessperson must first dispel some commonly held stereotypes.

Islam has more in common with the rest of the world than most people believe. Central to Islamic thinking is the right of every individual, Muslim or non-Muslim, man or woman, to own property. This is consonant with the capitalist view. Similarly, the importance of trade and business has always been recognized. The prophet Muhammad was himself a successful businessman.

There are some differences between the Islamic and the Western philosophies of doing business. Yet, these vary more in degree than in substance. One difference is in the definition of profit levels. In Islam, "excessive" profit is viewed as tantamount to exploitation. This is contrary to capitalist views, which hold that high profit levels or

Reprinted from *MSU Business Topics*, Summer 1980.

EXHIBIT 1 The Islamic Populace, Estimates for 1979

I: Population Is 90 Percent or More Muslim

Countries	In Millions	Percentage of Total Population	Countries	In Millions	Percentage of Total Population
Afghanistan	20.3	99	Morocco	18.8	95
Algeria	18.5	97	Pakistan	76.6	97
Bahrain	.3	91	Oman	.9	100
Djibouti	.2	94	Qatar	.2	100
Egypt	36.9	91	Saudi Arabia	9.5	95
Gambia	.5	90	Somalia	3.5	99
Jordan	2.8	93	Tunisia	6.3	92
Kuwait	1.2	93	Turkey	43.4	98
Indonesia	135.9	90	United Arab Emirates	.6	92
Iran	34.5	98	Yemen Arab Republic	7.2	99
Iraq	12.1	95	Yemen, People's		
Libya	2.7	98	Democratic Republic	1.7	90
Maldives	.1	100	Total	434.8	
Mauritania	1.4	96			

II: Population Is 50 to 89 Percent Muslim

Countries	In Millions	Percentage of Total Population	Countries	In Millions	Percentage of Total Population
Albania	1.9	70	Mali	3.8	60
Bangladesh	73.6	85	Niger	4.3	85
Brunei	.1	60	Senegal	4.5	82
Chad	2.2	50	Sudan	12.4	72
Comoro Is.	.3	80	Syria	7.3	87
Guinea	3.2	65	Total	115.2	
Lebanon	1.6	51			

III: Population Is Less than 50 Percent Muslim

Countries	In Millions	Percentage of Total Population	Countries	In Millions	Percentage of Total Population
Benin	.5	16	Mauritius	.2	17
Bulgaria	1.0	11	Mongolia	.2	10
Burma	1.3	4	Mozambique	1.0	10
Cameroon	1.2	15	Nigeria	33.2	47
Central African			Philippines	2.4	5
Empire	.1	5	Sierra Leone	1.0	30
China	18.0	2	Singapore	.4	15
Cyprus	.1	18	Sri Lanka	1.2	8
Ethiopia	12.2	40	Tanzania	4.1	24
Ghana	2.0	19	Thailand	1.9	4
Guinea-Bissau	.2	30	Togo	.2	7
India	75.0	12	Uganda	.8	6
Israel	.3	8	Upper Volta	1.4	22
Ivory Coast	1.4	25	U.S.S.R.	41.9	16
Kenya	1.4	9	Yugoslavia	4.2	19
Liberia	.3	15	Zaire	.6	2
Madagascar	.6	7	Total	216.9	
Malawi	.8	15			
Malaysia	5.8	44	Total Islamic population: 766.4		

NOTE: The percentage of Muslims in the total population in 1979 was assumed to be the same as in 1978 and was extracted from *Muslim Peoples, A World Ethnographic Survey*, Richard V. Weeks, ed. (Westport, Conn.: Greenwood Press, 1978). Population estimates taken from *Information Please Almanac*, Atlas and Yearbook, 34th ed. (N.Y.: Simon & Schuster, 1980), pp. 110–11.

return on investment indicate efficiency in the use of resources. The intent in Islam is toward moderation, to share wealth with those less fortunate. Individuals are responsible for the well-being of the community. The concept of sharing wealth is manifested in one form through *zakaat,* an annual tax of 2.5 percent levied upon individuals and used for the collective benefit. Usury is forbidden. Generally, banks in fundamentalist Islamic countries take equity in financing ventures, sharing resultant profits (and losses).

In some Islamic countries that have tried industrialization and modernization policies, discontent with the results has been interpreted as antiprogressive. While recently acquired oil wealth has brought about the means to modernize, it also has created conflict regarding the appropriate patterns of progress. The question, of course, is what constitutes progress. If it means the development of school systems, hospitals, and agriculture, Islamic countries would welcome modernization. If progress means only a shallow imitation of Western life-styles at the expense of respected Islamic cultural traditions, it will be unwelcome. For example, Islam prohibits alcohol consumption (and any form of intoxication). Although perceived by some in the West as adherence to a primitive and outdated code, it should be recognized that the prohibition is believed to prevent many social problems.

The perception of the Western impact on cultural mores and traditions has led Islamic countries to be highly selective in borrowing ideas from the West and accepting concepts of progress and development. Consider Iran, where efforts to industrialize rapidly led to a migration of rural workers to urban centers with the consequent neglect of the agricultural sector. One outcome was that the majority of Iran's population (who did not enjoy the bounties of oil wealth) experienced the devastating effect of inflation in the price of food, housing, and other necessities. In reaction, there has been a mistrust of the industrialization that would have been a natural consequence in any developing nation—Islamic or non-Islamic.

One common stereotype is that a Muslim is fatalistic. While a devout Muslim believes that one's fate is preordained, this does not mean one has foreknowledge of that fate. Islam encourages initiative and respects those who strive to better themselves. However, if the outcome of a particular undertaking is not successful, one is expected to accept it pragmatically and cope with the situation realistically.

Similarly, when a marketing manager in an Islamic country is asked if sales goals for the year will be met, the reply may be "Inshallah" (if God wills). Much has been made of this attitude, which has been interpreted to mean the manager is fatalistic. Starting a new venture, a Muslim may say "Bismillah" (begin in the name of God). These are common forms of religious expression that should *not* be interpreted to mean that the speaker is fatalistic.

Marketing in an Islamic Framework

A typical Islamic view of progress is that industrialization and modernization should occur in a coherent, organized manner, joining the goal of economic development with an appreciation of the social and cultural context in which it occurs. More than a religion, Islam is a way of life with prescribed codes of everyday conduct. These sanctions and codes permeate the social, cultural, civil, and political fabric of all Islamic nations. Presently, most of these countries are in a state of flux as a result of four forces:

1. Islamic religious fundamentals—major Quranic principles and precepts:
2. Islamic cultural values—those values resulting from the historical experiences and development of the religion and traditions practiced by the prophet Muhammad;
3. Regional/local cultures—the effect of other cultures on the Islamic populace, for example, Buddhist influence on Muslims in Thailand;
4. Political nationalism—for example, Arabic nationalist movements.

Since the intent of this article is to identify marketing opportunities within the Islamic framework, only the first two influences will be discussed. From this discussion, generalizations can be made for many Islamic nations, and an overall market and trade perspective is provided. The implications for marketing are contained in Exhibit 2, which shows that consumers sensitive to Islamic fundamentals exhibit different purchase behavior in response to market factors than do other world consumers.

Market Demands

Apart from marketing opportunities that exist as a result of religious and cultural influences, there are those that are the result of world pressures and the rapidly changing wealth of Islamic countries. To identify market opportunities within the latter context is an arduous task, because many of these countries have different market characteristics, growth rates, and amounts of financial, human, and natural resources. Recognizing these constraints, the aim here is to make a broad overall assessment. The general premise is that, apart from some dissimilarities, these markets have in common a unifying religion, a well-defined set of cultural values and traditions, and the goal of economic development. The focus will be on two major goods categories, consumer and industrial.

Consumer Markets

Opportunities for international marketers seem promising in countries with a rapidly developing middle class and a high proportion of Western-educated students returning to their homelands. A growing middle class generates demand for products and services in market categories where international marketers have traditionally had more experience. Included are a range of products from nutritious and more hygienically packaged foods to various kinds of household furnishings, appliances, and entertainment-oriented products. Also, an increasing proportion of the middle class is educated and therefore likely to accept the introduction of new products, including those currently marketed in industrialized countries. Western-educated students returning home tend to have consumption habits similar to those in the West. These returnees influence the consumption patterns of the rapidly forming middle class. Countries such as Saudi Arabia and Nigeria serve as good examples. Both have a rapidly expanding middle-class base and a sizeable Western-educated elite primarily responsible for the introduction and rapid acceptance of Western-oriented products and styles in home furnishings, tableware, appliances, and furniture. A list of consumer goods with market potential in this type of Islamic nation is provided in Exhibit 3. It should be cautioned that the demand for these products will be moderated by Islamic influences within each of these countries.

EXHIBIT 2 Marketing in an Islamic Framework

Elements	*Implications for Marketing*
I. Fundamental Islamic concepts	
A. Unity. (Concept of centrality, oneness of God, harmony in life.)	Product standardization, mass media techniques, central balance, unity in advertising copy and layout, strong brand loyalties, a smaller evoked size set, loyalty to company, opportunities for brand-extension strategies.
B. Legitimacy. (Fair dealings, reasonable level of profits.)	Less formal product warranties, need for institutional advertising and/or advocacy advertising, especially by foreign firms, and a switch from profit maximizing to a profit satisficing strategy.
C. Zakaat. (2.5 percent per annum compulsory tax binding on all classified as "not poor.")	Use of "excessive" profits, if any, for charitable acts, corporate donations for charity, institutional advertising.
D. Usury. (Cannot charge interest on loans. A general interpretation of this law defines "excessive interest" charged on loans as not permissible.)	Avoid direct use of credit as a marketing tool; establish a consumer policy of paying cash for low-value products; for high-value products, offer discounts for cash payments and raise prices of products on an installment basis; sometimes possible to conduct interest transactions between local/foreign firm in other non-Islamic countries; banks in some Islamic countries take equity in financing ventures, sharing resultant profits (and losses).
E. Supremacy of human life. (Compared to other forms of life objects, human life is of supreme importance.)	Pet food and/or products less important; avoid use of statues, busts—interpreted as forms of idolatry; symbols in advertising and/or promotion should reflect high human values; use floral designs and artwork in advertising as representation of aesthetic values.
F. Community. (All Muslims should strive to achieve universal brotherhood —with allegiance to the "one God." One way of expressing community is the required pilgrimage to Mecca for all Muslims at least once in their lifetime, if able to do so.)	Formation of an Islamic Economic Community—development of an "Islamic consumer" served with Islamic-oriented products and services, for example, "kosher" meat packages, gifts exchanged at Muslim festivals, and so forth; development of community services—need for marketing or nonprofit organizations and skills.
G. Equality of peoples.	Participative communication systems; roles and authority structures may be rigidly defined, but accessibility at any level relatively easy.
H. Abstinence. (During the month of Ramadan, Muslims are required to fast without food or drink from the first streak of dawn to sunset—a reminder to those who are more fortunate to be kind to the less fortunate and as an exercise in self-control.)	Products that are nutritious, cool, and digested easily can be formulated for Sehr and Iftar (beginning and end of the fast).
Consumption of alcohol and pork is forbidden; so is gambling.	Opportunities for developing nonalcoholic items and beverages (for example, soft drinks, ice cream, milk shakes, fruit juices) and nonchance social games, such as Scrabble; food products should use vegetable or beef shortening.
I. Environmentalism. (The universe created by God was pure. Consequently, the land, air, and water should be held as sacred elements.)	Anticipate environmental, antipollution acts; opportunities for companies involved in maintaining a clean environment; easier acceptance of pollution-control devices in the community (for example, recent efforts in Turkey have been well received by the local communities).
J. Worship. (Five times a day; timing of prayers varies.)	Need to take into account the variability and shift in prayer timings in planning sales calls, work schedules, business hours, customer traffic, and so forth.

(continued)

EXHIBIT 2   (concluded)

Elements	Implications for Marketing
II. Islamic Culture	
A. Obligation to family and tribal traditions.	Importance of respected members in the family or tribe as opinion leaders; word-of-mouth communication, customer referrals may be critical; social or clan allegiances, affiliations, and associations may be possible surrogates for reference groups; advertising home-oriented products stressing family roles may be highly effective, for example, electronic games.
B. Obligations toward parents are sacred.	The image of functional products could be enhanced with advertisements that stress parental advice or approval; even with children's products, there should be less emphasis on children as decision makers.
C. Obligation to extend hospitality to both insiders and outsiders.	Product designs that are symbols of hospitality, outwardly open in expression; rate of new-product acceptance may be accelerated and eased by appeals based on community.
D. Obligation to conform to codes of sexual conduct and social interaction. These may include the following:	
1. Modest dress for women in public.	More colorful clothing and accessories are worn by women at home; so promotion of products for use in private homes could be more intimate—such audiences could be reached effectively through women's magazines; avoid use of immodest exposure and sexual implications in public settings.
2. Separation of male and female audiences (in some cases).	Access to female consumers can often be gained only through women as selling agents, salespersons, catalogs, home demonstrations, and women's specialty shops.
E. Obligations to religious occasions. (For example, there are two major religious observances that are celebrated—Eid-ul-Fitr, Eid-ul-Adha.)	Tied to purchase of new shoes, clothing, sweets, and preparation of food items for family reunions, Muslim gatherings. There has been a practice of giving money in place of gifts. Increasingly, however, a shift is taking place to more gift-giving; due to lunar calendar, dates are not fixed.

Industrial Markets

The term *industrial markets* here refers to goods and services that either are used in or facilitate future production of goods and services such as major capital equipment, component parts, and process and raw materials. Overall, the goal of most Islamic nations has been to create a prosperous, educated society using advanced technology while retaining the codes and precepts of Islam. Many have set aside huge capital-expenditure budgets to improve living standards and to gain economic self-sufficiency. It is estimated that the oil-producing Islamic countries plan to spend over $300 billion within the next five years for industrial development projects alone. These countries presently account for about 10 percent of imports from the free world. Second only to the industrialized West, this high share of imports is greater than that of the Latin American nations, other African or Asian countries, and the Eastern European bloc. The United States is still the largest exporter to Islamic countries, with an estimated 18 percent share of the total in 1978, although Germany and Japan, with about 13 to 14 percent each, are rapidly increasing their share of exports. Presently, imports by Islamic countries account

EXHIBIT 3 **Consumer Market Opportunities in Islamic Countries with a Rapidly Growing Western-Educated Middle Class**

Product Categories	Current Demand[a]	Potential Demand[b]
Electrical appliances	★	
Home furnishing and decorative pieces		★
Household furniture	★	
Modified kitchen utensils	★	
Appliances, gadgetry, and basic tools	★	
Clothing (for men—Western dress shirts, pants; for women—long dresses, scarves)	★	
Shoes	★	
Perfumed toiletries	★	
Automobiles with maximum options	★	
Home-care products (furniture polish, wax, window cleaners)		★
Health products (vitamins)		★
Novelty gift items (utility or status-oriented)	★	
Hobbies and leisure games (video games)	★	
Hobbies and leisure games for outdoors		★
Nonfood baby items	★	
Processed foods		★

[a]Current demand means a reasonably good-sized market presently exists for these products, for example, in Saudi Arabia, Algeria, Indonesia.

[b]Potential demand means that changes in attitudes or awareness levels will have to be developed before demand increases sufficiently to justify a market base, for example, in Malaysia, Egypt, and, to some extent, Pakistan.

for a substantial percentage of total U.S. exports for several commodities (see Exhibit 4). The present export strength of the United States in certain industries also promises a strong on-going demand for replacement parts and services.

The potential size of these export markets, a major portion of which is for industrial products, coupled with the firm resolve of most Islamic governments to develop their country's industrial base, means that substantial opportunities are present and growing. These cover a wide spectrum of activities from strengthening the infrastructure (utilities, communications, transportation, materials handling, heavy-equipment leasing, sewage treatment systems, and prefabricated housing and commercial buildings) to developing resource-related industries (petrochemicals, polyethylene plants, cooling equipment, basic chemicals, and so forth), with diversification into such areas as food processing and pharmaceuticals plants for the purpose of future manufacturing and economic self-sufficiency.

Since different Islamic countries have different needs and resources for industrial development, classification is useful in order to assess market opportunities. All can be categorized as developing countries. Within this context, two basic factors can be used for further classification: (1) natural resource wealth—countries are classified as resource-rich; potential resource-rich, or resource-poor; and (2) present indigenous devel-

EXHIBIT 4 Major Industrial Products Exported by the United States with 20 Percent or More Accounted for by Islamic Markets (1978)

Type of Product/Commodity	Exports to Islamic Countries[a] (in Millions of Dollars)	Percentage of Total Exports
Motor buses	71.3	66.2
Cast-iron pipes and tubes	30.7	60.7
Finished structural parts and structures (iron and steel)	233.8	55.6
Household refrigerators and freezers[b]	85.3	55.2
Generator sets, engine-driven	228.4	54.6
Builders' woodwork and prefabricated buildings	45.3	52.3
Wire cable (iron, steel, copper, and aluminum)	45.3	50.0
Finished structural parts and structures (aluminum)	64.3	48.4
Nonpiston engines	88.5	48.4
Air-conditioning machinery and parts	300.0	42.9
Trailers and intermodal containers	68.8	41.0
Insulated electrical conductors (cable)	157.5	40.4
Manufacturers of mineral materials	27.8	40.0
Measuring and dispensing pumps, liquids elevation	49.5	35.6
Radio transceivers and transmitters	92.7	35.6
Building materials of asphalt, asbestos, cement	10.1	32.9
Electric transformers	37.0	32.0
Steam and other vapor-generating boilers	10.6	29.8
Telecommunications, telephone, telegraph equipment and parts	193.6	29.0
Iron or steel tube and pipe fittings	61.2	28.2
Furniture and parts[b]	72.9	25.2
Lighting fixtures, lamps, and parts[b]	34.8	23.4
Air and gas compressors	106.5	23.2
Parts of construction and mining machinery	486.0	22.8
Electric motors and generators	59.2	22.3
Mineral insulating materials	8.4	22.0
Construction and mining machinery	210.4	21.9
Parts and attachments for pumps	63.4	21.9
Trucks	348.8	21.8
Parts of television, radio, and sound-reproduction equipment	224.0	21.7
Filtering and purifying equipment and parts	115.0	21.3
Expanded metal (iron, steel, copper and aluminum)	5.0	20.6
Caps, cocks, and valves	118.9	20.0
Lifting, loading, and conveying machines	204.3	20.0
Parts for steam-generating boilers	28.1	20.0

[a] Small shipments not included in the calculations.

[b] Although a portion of these products represent final consumer demand, eventual parts replacements and services fall within the industrial demand category and therefore are included.

SOURCE: U.S. Bureau of the Census, *U.S. Exports, Schedule E Commodity Groupings by World Areas,* Report FT450, Annual 1978.

EXHIBIT 5   Classification of Major Islamic Countries

| | Industrial Base | |
Resources	*Relatively Strong*	*Relatively Weak*
Rich	Group I—Algeria, Indonesia, Iran, and Iraq	Group II—Saudi Arabia, Nigeria, Libya, Gulf States, United Arab Emirates
Potentially rich	None	Group III—Sudan, Morocco, Senegal, Somalia, Malaysia
Poor	Group IV—Turkey, Egypt, Lebanon, Jordan, Pakistan, Tunisia, Syria	Group V—North and South Yemen, Bangladesh, Chad, Mali, Afghanistan, Gambia, Niger

opment base—countries are classified as having a relatively strong development base or a relatively weak one. Here, a strong development base refers to the presence of trained managers and technocrats, a semiskilled labor force, and an "adequate" infrastructure. Exhibit 5 illustrates such a classification of major Islamic countries.

Countries that are both resource-rich and have a strong developmental base (Exhibit 5, Group I) offer broad consumer and industrial marketing opportunities. Other resource-rich countries (Group II) can overcome the drawback of a weak indigenous industrial base through massive technical assistance from outside sources, particularly from the West. Such countries are also able to import skilled workers and technicians in large numbers. Saudi Arabia and Nigeria fall into this category.

Group I and II countries that aspire to catch up technologically with the advanced industrial nations first need to develop basic technologies, for example, in chemicals and metal and alloy processing. Since many of these nations possess a desirable combination of extensive capital, energy resources, and moderate labor skills (local or imported), they should be able to develop basic technologies that require high inputs of energy and capital. Products such as agricultural chemicals, synthetic fibers, plastics, and resins can be produced for the domestic market as well as for export to other Islamic and less developed countries. With both energy advantages and the ability to purchase new technology, these countries can compete effectively in world markets. Beyond exports, joint ventures with international marketers could provide a lucrative return in the future to all parties.

In addition, a number of Group I and II countries will be looking toward expanding beyond basic technology. An area of natural expansion would be related intermediate processes that can be energy-intensive in application. Examples are the use of petrochemical technology to develop plastics, synthetic rubber, metal alloys, welding, and pulp and paper industries. These could lead to other forms of industrial growth, such as manufacture of container boxes, basic tooling, light electrical machinery, assembly factories, building materials, and pharmaceuticals.

It is conceivable that some currently imported products, based on relatively stable technologies, would be gradually replaced by domestic production. Examples are cables, insulating materials, asbestos, glass, lubricating oils and greases, electric motors, and filtering and purifying equipment. Long-term dependence on these products as continuing exports should be viewed with caution, and major U.S. exporters should consider the feasibility of establishing joint manufacturing ventures.

Certain countries that have future resource potential but now have a weak indigenous base (Group III) will be able to exploit these resources, given outside assistance and some time. Presently, they can facilitate the development of potential resources by serving as a source of supply for Group I countries. For example, the Sudan, with its rich agricultural base, could receive infusions of capital from nonfood-producing Islamic nations and, thus, further its own technological transition.

Among resource-poor countries with a strong indigenous base (Group IV), many have large populations that ordinarily create a national consumer market, one prerequisite for industrial development. At the same time, their relatively higher population growth rates negate any productivity gains. A key factor in development of these countries is deceleration of population growth. If Group IV nations continue to provide semiskilled labor to other Islamic countries, their development will be facilitated, and there would still be cheap labor at home. It is conceivable that such a labor force could serve in the production of high-demand, intermediate-technology products for Group I and II countries. Moreover, within Group IV nations the need remains for technology that is affordable yet appropriate. The sale of somewhat less sophisticated, used industrial equipment, modified for greater labor input, may be the answer (for example, in textile manufacture).

Group V countries have neither the resources nor the indigenous base to participate or serve in an effective commercial market system. Unless major findings of scarce resources are made, these countries presently lack any visible economic base for development.

All groups in Exhibit 5 are ideal targets for government projects that strive to establish economic status and credibility; examples include steel, cement, highways, and buildings. Again, the level of sophistication would depend upon each country's ability to pay for the technology.

International marketers should also be sensitive to the increasing interdependence among the Islamic countries, due partly to religious reasons and partly to their proximity. In particular, international marketers should not ignore the inevitable link between some of the oil-rich, nonfood-producing countries and the capital-poor, food-producing regions. Egypt, Pakistan, and the Sudan are acquiring importance as food suppliers for the Middle Eastern nations. Although these markets may now be small compared to world standards, future rewards are potentially great. Serious consideration should be given to the establishment of agribusiness ventures within some of these food-producing Islamic countries. Moreover, it may be advantageous for international marketers to locate in labor-surplus areas in order to produce labor-intensive goods for export to other Islamic countries.

Conclusion

The marketing potential of Islamic countries was discussed here with special reference to international marketers. Greatest advantage can be taken of this potential within the context of a more comprehensive, balanced understanding of Islamic principles and culture. This can occur only if current political problems, such as those in Iran, are kept in perspective.

Market opportunities were identified and discussed in three major categories: (1) products and markets that are essentially Islamic in nature; (2) consumer markets influenced by a population with a growing middle class and Western-educated segment; and (3) an industrial base that thrives on the resource capabilities and needs of Islamic countries and their growing interdependence on one another and the industrialized West.

The context for these marketing opportunities is complicated by the presence of problems common to many developing nations; for example, bureaucratic mismanagement and inefficiencies, bribery and corruption, and undefined competitive environment, and political uncertainties. With these and other similar factors in mind it still seems that the existing market opportunities are plentiful and the potential rewards promising. Moreover, the establishment of an "Islamic common market" may be viable in the foreseeable future. With the possibility of such significant developments, marketers who become involved early in key market and product areas will benefit the most. It is an understatement that international businesses continue to view Islamic markets as primitive and underdeveloped. These areas are ripe for penetration, and the innovative marketer can reap substantial benefits.

Marketing to the Third World Countries

Osman Atac and S. Tamer Cavusgil.

For various reasons, trade with the Third World can be quite problematic. First, the market potential in each individual country is small, which leads to high selling costs as a proportion of sales. For example, U.S. exports to the Third World exceeded one billion dollars for many countries during 1983, whereas exports to Japan and EEC countries were $22 billion and $42 billion, respectively, in the same year. Most developing countries tend to have unstable markets with very little or no published information available about trends. This discourages western firms that need to plan future sales and production. In addition, most non-commodity type imports to these countries are basically job-order, requiring special planning and custom-made production, thus increasing manufacturing costs.

Furthermore, negotiations with a Third World country usually take more time and require more information, which not only increases the cost of sales but also increases business risks. In addition, most Third World countries do not have stable political regimes. It is not a rare event that a business deal ends up with no agreement because of a change in administration, policies, or personnel. Add to these problems the pain and agony of dealing with a totally different culture, and one no longer wonders why the literature finds the subject unattractive; for it is full of problems for which there may not be any ready solutions.

The fact remains, however, that Third World markets are lucrative markets for most exporters. The purpose of this article is to examine the appropriate marketing strategies, especially for non-commodity industrial goods and projects, for the Third World, especially to the low to medium income countries. A marketing approach for selling to such countries is presented. This discussion is followed by operational recommendations for the international marketer.

Reprinted from *Singapore Marketing Review, 1990,* by permission of the *Asian Journal of Marketing;* and from *International Marketing Strategy,* edited by Thorelli, Chapter 20, pp. 261–77, 1991, Elsevier Science, Ltd., Pergamon Imprint, Oxford, England.

Third World as a Market Segment: The Significance of Developing Country Markets in World Trade

While each individual Third World market may be too small to be a target market, with most of them quite poor, their combined wealth is impressive due to the large number of Third World countries. According to World Bank classifications, there are 148 Third World, 6 oil capital-surplus, 20 industrialized, and 12 centrally planned countries.

For example, in 1980, 38% of the total exports of the U.S. were imported by the Third World. The share of world trade accounted for by the Third World is constantly increasing. Exports of manufactured goods from developing countries climbed from $4 billion in 1965 to $39 billion in 1976. Although East Asia alone clearly dominates the export of manufacturers, Latin America, South Asia, the Middle East, and sub-Saharan Africa increased exports as well.

Third World countries are diverse in culture, stage of economic development, and size. However, they possess certain similar economic and marketing characteristics that may be critical for the exporting company. If the Third World is to be targeted as a special market segment, marketing strategies should be based on such similarities. After examining some of these similarities, operational recommendations and a marketing approach will be discussed.

Most U.S. companies are accustomed to marketing in a buyers' market with numerous, diffused buyers and little or no government interference. Markets in the Third World, on the other hand, are characterized by: (1) a sellers' market where individual consumer concerns are not crucial; (2) a concentrated market where most direct selling strategies require modification; and (3) direct and close involvement of government with business.

Although some of the Third World countries such as Turkey, Malaysia, and Chile, who once followed protectionist economic policies, are liberalizing their economies for a variety for reasons, most are still far from becoming open market economies. Even in consumer goods, most Third World markets are still best characterized as sellers' markets.

There are various reasons for this. First domestic markets are small, both in terms of absolute size and purchasing power. This leads to natural monopolies where the production (or imports) of a single entrepreneur becomes more efficient than many. Even with the absence of import restrictions, competition for a share of the domestic market is accompanied by a relatively low return—discouraging new entries. Second, wholesale distribution in most of the Third World is controlled by the manufacturers/importers, thus creating a formidable barrier for entry. A new entrant may soon discover that, although its product is superior to the products of competitors, the existing channel is not willing to distribute it unless excessively compensated. In addition, establishing new channels of distribution is extremely expensive, if not impossible.

Wholesalers tend to control the retailers in terms of their product portfolios and financing agreements. Most wholesalers and traders carry a monopoly on a portfolio of high-margin items that are attractive to the retailers. In the absence of fair trade regulations and antitrust laws, these wholesalers are in a position of dictating the product mix to the retailers. This is especially true in the regional distribution of many products. These market imperfections result in highly controlled markets where the buyer purchases whatever goods are available. The power of the "natural" monopolies in most cases is unchallenged because of their traditional ties with the government and with one another. There is geographical concentration as well. In Turkey, some 60% of the manufacturing is realized in five of the 67 provinces. Of the 40 million people in Egypt, more than one fourth lives in or around Cairo.

Government involvement is more than regulatory. First, the inability of the private sector to accumulate the capital required for investments leads governments to be directly involved in the production of goods and services in the so-called State Economic Enterprises (SEEs). Some of the other reasons for the active economic role played by the governments of the Third World include the maintenance of economic security and the development of externalities, such as creating employment or subsidizing a sector. Although privatization of government controlled enterprises is under way in most Third World and Western European countries, the share of SEEs in most Third World economies is quite substantial. In Brazil, the government still controls more than 75% of postal services, telecommunications, electricity, gas, railway, oil production, coal, and steel industries. In India, in addition to these industries, the shipbuilding industry and the airways are controlled by the State. In Turkey, SEEs control more than 55% of the manufacturing industry—ranging from textiles and ceramics to steel.

Beyond the direct involvement of government in the economy through ownership of economic enterprises, there is also the indirect involvement through centralized economic planning. Government intervention in most cases increases concentration in these economies in the sense that business deals are not made with individual buyers, but with bureaucrats of various government offices. It is common practice for the international marketer to start sales calls with civil servants at the Capitol City instead of the actual buyer. Like the old adage, "All roads lead to Rome," in the case of Third World countries, all deals go to the government at one point or another. The process of marketing to the Third World based on these generalities is illustrated in Figure 1.

Phases in the Marketing Process

The marketing process suggested in Figure 1 is typical of the experience which would be encountered by a firm in selling to both private and government sectors in the Third World. Most of the experiences are related to cases where a non-commodity type product or a project is offered. Each phase is discussed below in detail.

Phase One: Scanning. Most aggressive firms develop and maintain sophisticated marketing intelligence systems to monitor global sales opportunities. Internal sources are traveling managers, subsidiary managers, and overseas representatives. External sources are the Agency for International Development and corresponding organizations in other industrial countries, World Bank, embassies, international banks, industry organizations, and other firms in the industry. Many publications exist, including *Worldwide Projects,* which is a particularly helpful source.

Often it is too late for an exporter to sell to the Third World once the sales opportunity is published/publicized. For that reason, intelligence about sales opportuni-

FIGURE 1

The process of marketing to developing countries

Phase 1
Scanning

Market surveillance to learn about forthcoming projects

Phase 2
The approach

Presentation of critical information to buyer in order to increase awareness and to influence writing of technical specifications

Phase 3
Competitive bidding

Preparation and submission of bid

Phase 4
Negotiations

Technical and economic evaluation of bids; informal and formal meetings concluding in a final bidding

Phase 5
Completion

Carrying out the project activity, typically involving construction, training, and service

Phase 6
Follow-up

Monitoring project performance and cultivating "spin-off" sales

ties must be alert to the early signs, in additional to the aforementioned more traditional sources of information. One such course is the country development plans. Unlike their Western counterparts, most Third World buyers must comply with an annual economic plan and its yearly implementation programs. Development plans differ in detail and direction from country to country. Nevertheless, although they are called "advisory" for political reasons, most plans are sufficiently directive. Understanding the process of plan preparation and familiarity with the plan itself is one of the first steps in successful marketing to the Third World.

> A U.S. manufacturer of power plants lost a sizeable market niche in a European country when this country changed its power plant specifications from oil to coal in their five year development plan (see example II below for reasons). The U.S. company was capable of offering both types of power plants. But once the plan was out, competitors were already ahead in establishing contracts. The U.S. company did not have a chance although they had been doing business in that country for almost two decades.

It is through the planning process that most Third World governments announce their import and investment priorities. Industrial-sectoral programs are usually integral parts of development plans. These too, are important documents for market planning for the international marketer. In many countries, plans change with governments. Therefore, the international marketer must also be familiar with the programs of powerful political parties where the policy guidelines for the annual plans can be found.

Sometimes certain sectors may be left outside of the scope of annual plans or the plan may not be directive. In this case the situation is not much different. Given the insufficient capital accumulation in these countries, almost all private and government enterprises are forced to operate with high financial leverage. Most financing originates from: (a) private-state owned banks and (b) direct/indirect government subsidies. The government subsidies, such as tax rebates and low interest credits, are more directive than the plan in most cases. Without such incentives, it is almost impossible to realize an investment in many of the Third World countries. Therefore, even in the sectors that appear to be not regulated by plans, government interference and control is quite dramatic.

Obviously, the task of following plans, programs, and party policies can be quite cumbersome for the international marketer. This is why international marketers use overseas representatives or agents to stay abreast of sales opportunities. These agents are usually local business people who work on a commission-on-sales basis. As natives, local business people are in a better position to identify sales opportunities and can provide invaluable services during lengthy sales negotiations.

There are two types of representatives, exclusive and non-exclusive. An exclusive representative earns commissions regardless of the role in sales. As the only representative in that country, whether involved with the sales or not, the exclusive representative is compensated. A non-exclusive representative is compensated only when personally making a sale.

Several considerations are relevant to selecting a representative. First, since non-exclusive representatives do not get paid unless a sale is made, they may attempt to represent as many companies as possible to increase revenues. The international marketer should be careful in selecting a representative to avoid a conflict of interest. Second, most representatives essentially run "one-man show" operations. Even if there is a professional manager running office operations, there always is a majority shareholder, or a family, who is actually known to the locals as the owner. The personal history and reputation of this person is extremely important. A representative's business is a business of reputation and contact. A check on the history and degree of success of the representative with other clients is always advisable. Relevant experience of the repre-sentative is also important.

> A U.S. company had supplied power plants to a Near Eastern country successfully for sixteen years and was represented by a very shrewd and capable representative. The country was contemplating changing the specifications from oil to coal under the pressure of increasing oil prices. The representative, however, had no contacts or experience in coal fueled power plants and was known as an oil fueled power plant expert. Therefore, he was neither approached by nor was he informed of the change by the client. When the specifications were finally changed from oil to coal, the U.S. company was not prepared.

Finally, corruption is a reality in most of the Third World. The international marketer, without the help and commitment of an exclusive representative, would be in a very difficult position when confronted with such a situation. Representatives, being familiar with the culture and people, could be beneficial under such circumstances. When a top manager of a Canadian nuclear power plant was negotiating a potential deal a payoff of $100,000 was mentioned. In reality, the actual amount asked was only $25,000.

Phase Two: The Approach.   Once the opportunity for a specific project is identified, the marketer must approach the buyer with relevant information and attempt to influence the writing of tender specifications, which usually take the form of a *feasibility report*. A marketer's aim at this stage is to present information and, if possible, monitor the specifications.

> The feasibility reports, like the annual plans, contain information when published that is practically useless to the international marketer. A U.S. company started building its market in Turkey which has traditionally been ordering 150 MegaWatt power plants. Two years prior to bidding, the U.S. corporation working with the middle level technocrats managed to convince the client to order 300 Mega Watt plants. When the feasibility reports were prepared and the bids were invited, the U.S. corporation had no competitors.

Therefore, an important aspect of the marketing effort is to use the *first mover* advantages. A marketer that can beat competitors in supplying relevant information to a buyer will have a head start in the selling process.

These *tie-up strategies* are usually based on: (a) a technical solution to the buyer's problem, (b) social linkages between the buyer and seller, (c) financial linkages in terms of provisions for financing, and (d) other informational linkages. These linkages are illustrated in Figure 2. Creation of first mover advantage can be likened to a spinning of a web so that the buyer is enclosed in the net while the competitors are locked out. Growing interdependence between the buyer and seller, strengthened through the four types of linkages, should be a facilitating factor in successful bidding. Japanese compa-nies, for example, are known to frequently invite the top managers of the potential overseas partners and buyers to Japan for a tour of their facilities. Efforts of this sort can make the difference between successful and unsuccessful sales in Third World markets.

The local exclusive representatives usually lack necessary technical know-how. In addition, they cannot make commitments on behalf of the foreign vendor. Therefore, when the prospective project idea warrants it, a team from the vendor must be in direct

FIGURE 2

*Strengthening
buyer–seller
linkages*

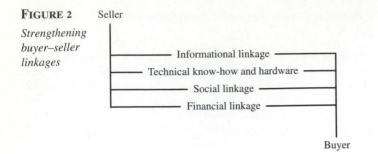

Seller

Informational linkage

Technical know-how and hardware

Social linkage

Financial linkage

Buyer

contact with the potential client during the preparation of the feasibility study. One way of accomplishing this is to have *ad hoc* project teams for Third World markets. The *ad hoc* project staff must be organized quickly in order to avoid missed sales opportunities.

When feasibility reports are prepared by outside consultants, these consultants must be treated as the client. It is always a good idea to keep a mailing list of technical personnel in private, government, educational, and consulting organizations, establishing regular contacts with them.

For large-scale projects, it is not unlikely to find an international consulting firm to be assigned to the preparation of the feasibility report. In fact, for large scale projects which are financed by the transnational financial markets, a feasibility report prepared by an international consulting company is usually a loan requirement. The use of a consulting firm hardly guarantees a better report. Since most international consultants are unfamiliar with the market, they may overlook major factors or rely on incomplete information. Furthermore, political and business considerations force international consultants to act as mediators in most cases. Rarely will a consulting firm be willing to make radical suggestions, since in most Third World countries, almost all decisions, especially related to large investment/import projects, result in power struggles and political controversy. In almost all cases, international consultants employ a local company/person as their counterpart. Both the international consultant and their counterparts must be closely monitored during the preparation of the feasibility report.

Phase Three: Competitive Bidding. In most cases, once the feasibility report is written, a tender is published and competitive bids are invited from a list of selected vendors. Needless to say, a company must be on the mailing list to get the tender, which is the job of the local representative. Usually tenders are purchased for a nominal fee. Competitive bidding can be open or closed, with closed being the norm. In open competitive bidding, firms bid down in an auction, whereas in closed bids, firms turn in their offers in sealed envelopes and bids are opened all at the same time. Communication during the open competitive bidding sessions is crucial since time is extremely limited and millions are at stake.

For large-scale projects, the technical terms and conditions will be followed by a so-called "Administrative Terms and Conditions" (ATC). Various legal, financial, and administrative issues are also spelled out and procurement procedures are revealed. Due to its expensive nature, a critical decision at this stage relates to how much time and other resources should be invested in the preparation of the bid.

In most Third World countries, government or SEE buying is regulated by law. This is actually helpful to the vendor since the organizational buying process and the authority and responsibility of each unit are clearly described. The regulations related to government procurements state how the requisitions are to be placed, who will have decision-making authority, and how the decision will be implemented. The international marketer must become familiar with these regulations. Unfortunately, almost all regulations carry an exemption clause. Using this clause, the SEE or the government agency may exempt itself from the regulations, especially as related to the conditions specifying the terms under which the bids are to be awarded. Often these terms award the contract to the lowest bidder, and in many cases bind the buyer to award the contract, even if there are no acceptable offers.

In the case of privately owned concerns in the Third World, there usually are no guidelines related to procurement. Organizational structures of the corporation are usually centralized. Shares of even the largest corporations are controlled by either individuals or families. This is actually helpful to the foreign vendor to identify the decision-makers.

Phase Four: Negotiations.   Once the bids are submitted, they are evaluated by the buyer from both a technical and economic perspective. In large scale projects, typically the bids are short listed and a few vendors are invited for further discussions, which usually mark the beginning of lengthy negotiations. These meetings provide opportunities for the marketer to present additional explanations and details. As such, they can be crucial in terms of their impact on the selection of a bid.

Finding the right person to negotiate in the government of SEEs, however, may be difficult. International marketers may be surprised to discover that they have to talk to a dozen people from different echelons and divisions of an agency or agencies without knowing the actual decision-maker(s). Some agency personnel will pretend to be the real decision-maker. Inside information from the local representative will provide valuable guidelines in such instances.

Some international marketers concentrate their efforts on the person who appears to be the final decision-maker and neglect or even avoid the others in the process. In Third World countries this strategy is likely to backfire. Bureaucrats in lower levels of the hierarchy are generally intolerant of being bypassed.

> A sales opportunity was lost by a U.S. firm because of an oversight. The contract was seen as a sure bet. Corporate executives were told by the Minister of Industry and other top level officials that an $80 million textile machinery renewal project sponsored by the World Bank was going to be awarded and that the U.S. bid was the most attractive. However, at the last minute, an "expert" in the state planning organization claimed "inappropriate technology," and convinced the Ministry of Finance, who was negotiating the financing of the contract, not to award the contract.

The Third World drives a hard bargain in most cases. Through bilateral and multilateral agreements, Third World buyers try to improve their bargaining position. Application of uniform import taxes, pooling of commodity imports, and cartel type agreements are not rare. Pooling of import purchases for commodity production such as fertilizers and tractors from the multinational corporations is one example of such agreements.

More frequently, the bargaining power of Third World buyers will be affected by the military and economic agreement with the governments of the suppliers. Usually, such agreements weaken their bargaining positions. It would be a mistake, however, to use this point as a bargaining strategy. It should be remembered that, unlike the Eastern bloc, the Western countries do not act as a uniform front, especially on matters of business. Having an alliance with the West does not mean much to a Third World country when it comes to business negotiations. Furthermore, for a Third World buyer it does not make any difference whether the supplier is a Japanese, Canadian, German or American firm. If forced, they may go to another Western supplier and still keep their commitments. Political alliances are best kept out of the business deals.

Most Third World countries lack the necessary financial resources, especially in terms of foreign exchange. For most large scale imports, 100% financing by the seller is now a common practice. Tight international money markets and low credit ratings of many Third World countries force them to look for the best terms of payments. Increasing international competition places the Third World in a position where they can drive a hard bargain. Japanese firms, for instance, are quite successful in negotiations because they provide a complete package including low interest financing. Limitations in certain products/processes may be overcome by strengths in financial terms.

> Australian and Dutch competitors get 30% to 70% of their overseas marketing costs subsidized through direct government reimbursement known as a bounty. An Australian dredge builder used this 20% bounty to overcome a 10% price disadvantage and won a contract in Africa against a U.S. company.

Balance of payments continues to be a serious problem for most Third World countries. Therefore, an opportunity to improve the importing country's payments enhances the bargaining power of the seller. Even in countries where there are no balance of payments problems, many Third World buyers are not technically but financially minded.

> An Arizona based company manufacturing prefabricated housing units, after spending years in negotiations, failed to capture a niche in the Saudi market. Although the company's products were of much superior quality to those offered by the competition, numerous presentations seemed to have failed in convincing the buyers. A New York based consulting organization suggested a change in the marketing approach. Instead of lengthy technical presentations, the company presented very simple financial analyses to the prospective clients. The results were very successful.

Most Third World countries are trying new channels and suppliers. The increasing aggressiveness of the Eastern bloc in international markets provides additional bargaining power for them. Many U.S. firms are at a disadvantage in this respect, especially with regard to supplies, parts, and raw material requirements. U.S. manufacturers often limit the options of buyers, which, in addition to being managerially unattractive to the buyers, also creates psychological resistance. Many successful bidders include alternative sources for parts and suppliers as a standard document.

A Turkish company was planning to buy a deep sea fishing vessel. The U.S. bid submitted was superior in quality and was acceptable in price. However, the Soviet bid specified that the parts for the vessel could be obtained from any Soviet [bloc] country or from the West. The U.S. corporation demanded that the parts could only be bought from them. The contract was awarded to the Soviets.

Negotiations can take a long time. The bidder should be prepared for an adequate time and patience allotment. Sometimes the information requested by the buyer may seem endless. There are various reasons for this, in addition to the well publicized cultural differences. At times, the bidders supply the buyers with conflicting information. Thus, the Third World buyer gets confused and keeps demanding more and more information.

A country which was a large consumer of refined salt decided to become self sufficient in salt. A project based on solar evaporated salt pans was offered. A feasibility study paid by the government stated that evaporating ocean water in boilers is a more attractive alternative, although requiring a much higher initial cost. The government was confused and asked for more information. After more than a year, negotiations were still continuing.

Also, when the buyer is at a disadvantage, the bidder requests certain conditions to guarantee a certain level of profitability. These conditions range from monopoly rights to tax holidays, including a host of other bargaining elements such as a special tariff on competitive imports, duty relief on raw materials, anti-dumping control, currency convertibility, and repatriation privileges. The Third World buyer may demand more information to justify the demands of the seller.

A surgical dressings manufacturer agreed to invest in a Third World country in exchange for a monopoly equal to 80% of current imports. The government asked the company to justify its position. After a year of negotiations, the government officials were still not convinced.

Distasteful and unethical as it may be, lubrication or grease payments are a way of life in most Third World countries. The international marketer should be prepared to take a position on such issues and make this position known to representative from the outset. In certain countries, one must go through intermediaries who are close to the government. Their commissions, usually about 10%, are paid almost automatically. Although such payment is considered a bribe by U.S. standards and the Foreign Corrupt Practices Act, to them it is payment for services. Local representatives will be in a position to advise the international marketer in such matters.

When technology is relatively simple and available, buyers play one seller against another to get better terms. Some of the alternatives offered may be simple and therefore inexpensive. It is tempting for a buyer to procure such machinery and technology, or play inexpensive offers against more modern and expensive ones. In this case, the seller can point out that simple technology is usually single-purpose, whereas modern technology is flexible. The old adage that one should not put all the eggs in one basket is extremely relevant for the Third World. Hundreds of millions of dollars worth of investments in the Third World are idle or closed because of inflexible manufacturing systems, changing world markets, and economic conditions. Custom made, flexible designs will have a considerable advantage in the bargaining process.

Ability of the supplier to utilize local resources is an additional feature which is attractive to most Third World buyers. Especially in the case of government purchases, the seller who can demonstrate that the offer creates additional jobs and added value will have better bargaining power. The ratio of the cost of the goods imported to the prices of the final product is an important consideration in the bargaining process. In many cases, the share of imports in the total cost of the manufactured or processed goods is considerable. This makes it very difficult for the Third World country to pass it on to the end user, domestic or international.

Buyers who are servicing local markets are not seriously concerned about the quality of the final product. For instance, in aluminum die-casting, Italy may be preferred as a source of supply because of its low price. However, the silicon content of such raw material is low and the metal is basically recycled and therefore less durable. Nevertheless, buyers may be willing to sacrifice quality for price. If there is a price disadvantage, emphasizing quality is not likely to increase the bargaining strength of the seller. The seller should try to provide similar quality at lower prices. It should be noted that top quality is not always the best for many Third World countries. Many times inexperienced representatives of sellers express their surprise when told about the prices of competitors. It is only then that they examine the offers and note quality differences, which leads them into an effort to build a case around quality which is usually fruitless. Therefore, the international marketer should be ready to compete against low as well as high quality.

In many cases where the procurement of the developing country is related to export oriented programs, any assistance that can be extended in the distribution of the final product will strengthen the bargaining position of the seller. Often, Third World countries are unable to market what they produce because they cannot penetrate the international channels of distribution. The seller who has some control over such channels or who can secure the cooperation of a trading company or broker will have considerable bargaining power in the negotiation.

Finally, an important element which strengthens the bargaining power of the seller is the managerial expertise and flexibility that can be provided in the post-investment operations.

> A U.S. construction company building a military complex in Saudi Arabia almost failed to meet the deadline if it had not been for the flexibility of the site manager. A change in construction specifications was required due to a mistake on the part of the client represented by a high level military officer. The bomb site selected by this offer covered a historic caravan route that had been in use for centuries. The contract did not cover the expenses of the U.S. firm that would result from the change. The representative of the client did not want the embarrassment of asking for additional funds from the Saudi Government, but did not want to assume the cost. The representative of the company manipulated certain excavation figures and accommodated the Saudi representative by changing the bomb site without incurring any additional expenses. The project was completed on time as well.

Turnkey agreements are no longer attractive to many Third World countries. There are various reasons for this. First, they feel that they do not have the managerial expertise needed to successfully run the investment. Second, even though the operations can be handled, marketing becomes a problem. Third, and most importantly, Third World countries feel they are sold inappropriate or outdated technology. As a solution, *turnkey-plus* operations, or Build, Own, and Operate Models, are favored by many Third World countries. In this kind of an agreement the host guarantees to buy all or most of the output of the investment. The seller is asked to provide a turnkey investment and then operate it, also providing the managerial expertise needed. After a specific period, the host guarantees to buy the seller out. This way the buyer tries to put the burden of choosing the right kind of investment on the seller. The risk for the seller is naturally greater with such an agreement, thus strengthening the seller's bargaining power.

Phase Five: Completion. Once a certain supplier is selected, the supplier then delivers, installs, and initiates different components of the project. Typically, a temporary organization is formed to complete the assignment. Most projects in Third World countries involve a combination of construction, training of personnel, project management, and service. Any one of these can be used as bargaining chips during negotiations.

> Many countries offer direct grants to the buyers when equipment is bought from that country. For example, a training grant to China totaling $1.5 million from Holland was very influential in the client's decision to choose a Dutch manufacturer over a U.S. contender.

One of the most critical problems for the exporter can be the financial guarantees in this phase. Once the contract is signed, many Third World countries usually insist that the seller buy insurance from them to protect Third World insurance revenues. The rates can be as much as 200% higher and most policies obtained are quite restrictive. For further protection, sellers can hire a skilled international broker and buy DIC (Differences in Conditions) insurance in New York or London which would become effective if the local policy is inadequate.

Phase Six: Follow-up. Successful completion of a sale usually generates a considerable amount of spin-off sales. Opportunities exist for selling service contracts, parts, peripheral equipment, and software. Of course, it is desirable to maintain contact with the consumer to ensure satisfaction and to learn about developing projects.

Conclusion

In the light of the recent pressures to globalize marketing operations, the previously neglected Third World markets gain importance. It is a misconception that Third World markets are unorganized and chaotic. On the contrary, the buying process is usually more formalized in many respects. The fact that Third World markets are more concentrated and that the government is an integral part of most processes provides opportunities for the international marketer. Most buying is done by organizations, either private or government operated. Markets are basically sellers' markets. Most purchases are based on some sort of a feasibility plan compatible with a macro economic country development plan. Marketing plans can be built on these purchasing patterns.

TABLE 1   Guidelines for Marketing to Third World Countries

1. Follow the development plans, yearly programs, government programs and programs of political parties closely. These are easily accessible.
2. Familiarize yourself with the government incentives for investments. These will determine future demand.
3. Select a good exclusive local representative. Make sure that he does not represent your competitors, that he has an area of specialization and that he is reliable.
4. Familiarize yourself with the process of preparing a feasibility report.
5. Provide technical know-how during the preparation of the technical specifications.
6. Keep in close contact with domestic and international consulting organizations who may be preparing technical specifications or feasibility reports. Keep in touch with the local technocrats and engineers. They are small in number and easily accessible. They will determine what will be bought.
7. Establish friendly relations with potential buyers even if they are not buying now. It is an inexpensive but very effective public relations effort.
8. Familiarize yourself with the regulations related to government and State Economic Enterprise procurements. Note that the governmental agencies do not have to follow such regulations at all times.
9. Find the "Lion" in each organization. In each organization one or two people will have the "final say." Make sure that you know who they are, but never ignore others who are involved.
10. Familiarize yourself with the international agreements of the country. Do not use political-military alliances as a part of your sales strategy.
11. Offer a complete deal. Be ready to finance your own sales.
12. Certain issues prove efficient in negotiating sales. The ability of your offer to improve the balance of payments, create employment, add value, utilize local resources, countertrade, decrease import dependence, increase the international options of the county both in terms of buying and selling in the future, and improve the flexibility of the operations are examples.
13. Be ready to deal with bribery. Use your local representative and stay out of it.
14. Get ready for a turnkey-plus operations agreement.

Experience in working with Third World customers has generated a battery of useful principles for the Western business executive. These are summarized in Table 1. Although they are by no means rigid rules, these guidelines can assist the executive in successfully cultivating business in the Third World and in managing relationships with Third World customers.

It should be recognized that putting these suggestions to work requires teamwork on the part of the seller. A team that includes managerial and technical expertise will be needed. International selling to the Third World is not solely the job of a sales representative. A mistake unfortunately made by many companies is to send a sales representative and expect that representative to close the sale. Given the competitive nature of global markets, appropriate marketing strategies promise considerable rewards in the Third World market.

PART THREE

INTERNATIONAL AND GLOBAL MANAGEMENT AND STRATEGY

Strategic Issues in Marketing

The first companion piece on Japanese versus German marketing traditions and strategies reveals that the Japanese are more price oriented in their desire for market share than are the Germans. In Germany there is often tension between engineers and marketing managers, which is less likely in Japan. In advertising, the Germans tend to emphasize product features and attributes, while the Japanese focus on product usage and imagery.

The requirements for joint venture success and the reasons joint ventures can fail are summarized in the concluding piece of this section. Assessing joint venture partners and managing such relationships successfully are important aspects of this contribution.

A Structural Comparison of Japanese and German Marketing Strategies

Hans Günther Meissner. *Professor-Doktor Hans Günther Meissner holds the Chair of Marketing at the University of Dortmund. He has special expertise in international marketing and the intercultural aspects of marketing. The present article is based on his immediate knowledge of Japanese companies in Japan, Germany and other markets. He co-operates with Japanese colleagues in the field of economic and social sciences and is an informed observer of Japanese marketing strategies in world markets.*

Introduction

The growth in world trade to which Japan has so substantially contributed represents a major structural element of our time. This growth has, together with the technical and economic developments in the world, led to a situation of increasing rivalry between Japan and the Federal Republic of Germany. This has become particularly clear in the U.S. market, for example, in the iron and steel sector, motor vehicles, recreational electronic apparatus, camera and, increasingly, in specialized machinery. Japan has, however, become an important competitor of German companies not only in third markets, but also in the Federal Republic of Germany itself. On the other hand German companies, in common with companies from the U.S.A. and other Western countries, are confronted with the difficulty of obtaining a larger share of the market in Japan. This results in Japan's achievement of a very high balance of payments surplus, and in consideration being given by the world to counter measures against Japanese export activities.

Various reasons are brought forward to explain Japan's climb to being one of the world's leading trading nations. In particular, reference is made to the current strength of the rate of exchange for the dollar, which creates a specific competitive advantage for Japanese manufacturers and also for the exporters of other countries in the American market. Furthermore, the high work morale of the Japanese labor force plays an important role, as does the particular competence of Japanese industry in certain industrial areas, such as the recreational electronics sector, in which Japanese companies have reached a leading position in the world. Attention has also been drawn to the co-ordination of commercial policy activities in Japan by the Ministry of International Trade and Industry (MITI), which give particular impetus to the Japanese export

Source: The *Irish Marketing Review,* Spring 1986, Mercury Publications, Ltd., 37 Main St., Donnybrook, Dublin 4, Ireland. Reprinted with permission.

offensive. Behind the efforts of Japanese companies to increase their share of the world market there stands also the political will of the Japanese government to extend its world economic influence and to safeguard it in the long term.

In addition to these situational, political and economic-structural factors there are also special features of Japanese marketing strategies, which have smoothed the way for the world triumph of Japanese companies and are safeguarding it with success. The international competitiveness of Japanese companies is certainly connected with the policy of the MITI, and it has been assisted through developments in world exchange rates. The protracted success in world trade has, however, also been achieved by the development of appropriate marketing strategies by Japanese companies, by use of which these firms have risen to international prominence.

There has grown up in the meantime an extensive literature on the peculiarities of Japanese management covering, among others, the following topics: decision-making with the aid of the Ringi system, the special Kanban distribution system, the tight, almost familial binding of Japanese workers to their companies, coupled with the system of life-long employment in the large companies and the loyalty of the companies to the Japanese government, supported by formal ties and, even more strongly, by informal ties. The peculiarities of Japanese marketing as an essential prerequisite for international marketing success—and simultaneously as one of the factors in the difficulties foreign companies experience in obtaining larger shares of the market in Japan—have not hitherto been examined in a systematic manner.

The German Marketing Tradition

In order to understand the differences between German and Japanese marketing strategies one must keep in mind that the American idea of marketing was confronted with different contexts in Japan and in the Federal Republic of Germany, and that there have therefore formed in these two countries clearly distinct understandings of marketing in theory and in practice. In these two countries there have developed different basic patterns (paradigms) to explain and to understand marketing activities. In the Federal Republic of Germany the process of synchronization between products and consumption has been particularly influenced by the *craftsman's tradition.*

Even international German concerns, which are today of world importance, arose from small craft-oriented companies. This specific tradition, with its pride in the craftsman's efficiency and with its relationship to comprehensible and controlled conditions of the market and of competition, continues to work today in many of the marketing concepts of German firms. Thus, for example, advertising law in the Federal Republic of Germany is more detailed and carefully ordered than is the case in any other country, in order to ensure at all costs that competition through advertising is carried out within an orderly framework, just as the guilds in the Middle Ages took care that competition was orderly. Quite apart from the fact that the Federal Republic of Germany surpasses all Western industrial nations in the control of advertising, there are, in addition to the legal control of advertising, even further voluntary self-restricting codes within industry, for example, those imposed by the rule of the *Markenverband* (Trade-Marks Union) and by the *Deutscher Werberat* (German Advertising Council).[1]

We find an analogous regulating tendency in the legal controls on shop closing times or on special sales. The interesting thing about these regulations is that product competition is *not,* primarily, carried on at the level of communication and by sales promotion activities, but rather that such competition is restricted to price and achievement. However, the tradition of craft management works towards the prevention of open price competition. Competition is therefore concentrated on the *quality of production,* which corresponds to the craftsman's tradition of efficiency.

Product orientation represents the central marketing focus of a large number of German companies. This product orientation is thoroughly approved by the consumers or the buyers of these products. The quality guarantee of the products and the competitive quality consequently play a greater role than, for example, competition in prices.

Product orientation, coupled with guarantees of quality, has become the decisive factor in the international competitiveness of German companies and the international success of German firms arises above all from the combination of a quality-conscious product policy with a customer-oriented service policy.

Of relevance also is the fact that the communication policy of German companies is much more strongly marked by personal communication than by the strategic utilization of mass communications, which is necessary in order to reach anonymous mass markets. Mass communication is judged by many companies as well as by consumers often skeptically and sometimes disparagingly. The American influence in marketing is associated in the Federal Republic of Germany precisely with mass communication. The marketing identity of Germany companies is marked, on the other hand, by pride in technical efficiency and by the intensity of personal attention to customers.

The Japanese Marketing Tradition

Industrial development in Japan took a completely different course. It was marked by transference, by the transfer of techniques and forms of behavior from other countries to Japan. The adoption of Western technologies since the opening of Japan by the Meiji rulers followed the pattern that had already been set by the reception of Chinese culture in Japan.[2] Furthermore, industrialization in Japan was not connected with the rise of a new class, as was the case in Europe, where the nobility was ousted from its position of leadership by the successful businessmen and engineers. In Japan it was the ruling Samurai elite which, with the support of the Imperial House, carried out the transfer of Western technologies and production methods to Japan. This transfer process requires two different forms of behavior, first, an extremely marked *adaptive capacity* for new technologies and new forms of behavior, thought patterns and operative strategies and, second, the ability to *preserve one's own identity,* so that one does not lose oneself in this process of transfer and perhaps lose one's own cultural identity. Accommodation to Western technology and retention of traditional Japanese identity are the two sides of the industrialization process in Japan. We find in Japan, to the confusion of many foreign visitors, the coexistence of extremely modern and future-oriented strategies (based on western models) and the tendency to maintain the traditional Japanese way of life and identity. This is apparent in the organization of Japanese firms, which are so structured that the members can feel as if they are in a family, and in that the decision processes are so organized by the Ringi system that all members of the organization can keep face even in extreme conflict situations.

Marketing strategies in the international Japanese concerns are also stamped by this double ability of accommodation and of the retention of identity. This has made Japanese companies successful, particularly in those cases where it was a question of the successful adoption of Western technologies, for example, in the iron and steel industry, in ship-building, and in the textile industry. The importance of the preservation of identity shows its consequence for marketing in the efforts of Japanese companies to follow a strategy which harmonizes with the traditions of Japan. The idea of orderly marketing governs in many areas the competition policy of the Japanese government, and at the same time, the marketing strategies of Japanese companies. From this standpoint one can understand, too, the readiness of the Japanese government to enter into self-limiting agreements so that the international efficiency of Japanese companies will not be endangered by the protective measures of foreign governments. In this situation one sees the characteristic combination of adaptability and retention of identity. Both adaptability and the retention of identity are qualities which bear a rather strong passive stamp, and which also make it difficult for Japanese companies or employees to cope actively with the problems faced by foreign buyers.

For this reason, international Japanese competitiveness is much more strongly characterized by price competition than is the case with German firms. This specific Japanese marketing orientation has led to the situation where the international efficiency of Japanese companies is to be found precisely in those products in which the transfer capability is especially marked. This holds true, for example, in the photography industry, the hi-fi industry, ship-building and the car industry. These four areas are characterized by the fact that the product idea is determined by the transfer concept. And it is just in the mastering of transfer processes that the idea of Zen Buddhism comes into its own, according to which the way is more important than the goal, as becomes particularly evident in, for example, the tea ceremony. The way is important, whereas the goal is relativized, just as in an advertisement of a Japanese firm in Los Angeles following the Olympic Games: "United States won the Gold, Fuji took the pictures." German marketing strategy is directed towards solving the problems of the buyer or of the customer. Japanese marketing strategy aims at producing, in co-operation with the customer, a feeling of harmony and mental equilibrium. German marketing seeks dialogue and will even, under certain circumstances, make allowance for conflict with the customer. Japanese marketing aims at a harmonious agreement with the customer and is at pains to avoid open conflict.

German companies are to a large extent marked by the tradition of the craftsman and Japanese companies by the Samurai tradition. In the following section we will investigate how this basic orientation works itself out in the practice of marketing in the national and international business of German and Japanese firms.

The Practice of Marketing

Marketing strategies are differentiated with reference to price policy, product policy and promotion policy.[3] In promotion strategies there are differences between decisions about sales promotion and advertising decisions. In view of the particular importance of advertising in the explanation of differences between Japanese and German marketing strategies the topic is explored in some detail below.

Because of the Japanese tendency to adopt foreign technologies, within the framework of transferability and simultaneous preservation of identity, Japanese *product policy* is more open to innovations, even if these innovations have not themselves been developed in Japan. This may be seen in the adoptions in microelectronics, a field developed by American companies, or also in the adoption of the Wankel engine, which was developed by a German company. German companies have much greater difficulty in developing technical innovations and in pushing them through in their own organizations, and then in the market subsequently. The orientation towards tradition of German companies intensifies the tendency to cling too long to those products which, indeed, may produce great returns for the moment (cash cows), instead of promoting risky new developments, whose market success is still uncertain. A failure also leads to personal consequences for those who bear the responsibility for such decisions.

The principle of personal responsibility, which is an important component of the German legal and cultural system, does not encourage spontaneous and enthusiastic coping with innovations. The socially safeguarded system in Japanese companies favors the taking-up of innovations, and the organization of Japanese companies also makes it easier to overcome possible failures internally. It is precisely in foreign trade that German companies have as a competitive advantage their readiness to deal with the specific problems of a buyer and to offer him a solution to his problem according to the principle of the "the tailored suit." This is particularly true in the case of large construction jobs, but it also holds good in broad areas of German mechanical engineering, as well as in the electrical and chemical industries. This focus on dialogue and the readiness of German companies to discuss matters with their foreign counterparts exert a positive influence on international competitiveness.

When the transfer process between Japan and the foreign customer encounters difficulty, Japanese firms concentrate their marketing strategies on *price policy*. In this the big companies pursue long-term goals, and also take quite long periods of loss into account, in order to conquer a market. For example, it took about ten years for the Japanese car companies to achieve their market breakthrough into Europe. The acceptance of losses in the run-up years is, however, only possible for big companies, which find possibilities of balancing this in other markets. From this arises the necessity for Japanese companies to merge or to co-operate with friendly companies. Medium-sized German companies defend their independence and in order to do so they must follow a price policy which safeguards their existence. Long run-up losses or failures in the market cannot be borne for long by German medium-sized companies or even large companies, unless these want to risk their continued existence. To this extent German companies are much more closely oriented to the goal of guaranteed profitability, whereas Japanese companies are more strongly interested in processes of expansion and development, from which a profit may follow later.

A further important difference between German and Japanese marketing is to be found in the fact that—precisely in view of the product orientation of German marketing—there is in many German companies a certain tension between the engineers and the businessmen. This occasionally leads to a disintegration of marketing strategies in German companies, i.e., the production policy is not co-ordinated with the price and promotion policy. The advertising department leads a relatively independent life and is more or less detached from the technically oriented company management. This form of disjointed marketing leads to a certain naivety in the marketing efforts of some German companies. Japanese marketing strategies, in keeping with the typical form of Japanese company management, are more strongly integrated and show a high degree of sensitivity. Accordingly, the relative naivety of Germany marketing strategies can be contrasted with the pronounced sensitivity of Japanese ones.

This naivety also shows itself in the short-term perspective of the price strategies of German companies, which tend to be guided by tactical or operational factors, in order to meet costs and profitability in the current financial period, whereas Japanese companies follow a long-term price strategy, which is intended to ensure the market success of Japanese companies in the long term. German companies are more inclined to follow a strategy of skimming-off in their international price policy, while Japanese companies follow a strategy of penetration. The skimming-off strategy brings the companies short-term gains, but it makes it difficult to secure large shares of the market in the longer term. The Japanese strategy takes run-up losses into account, in order to achieve the greatest possible shares of the market in the long term. Of course, it is precisely Japanese pricing policy which is also producing resistance to the market conquering strategy of Japanese companies, a resistance which is forming at present in the U.S.A. and in European countries.

In international promotion strategy, Japanese companies clearly emphasize the creation of their own *marketing channels,* both to avoid conflicts in the marketing channel and to influence the transfer processes between Japanese producers and foreign consumers in the Japanese interest. This has led, for example, to the development of the Japanese colony in Düsseldorf. This has the result that Japanese products have a distinctive Japanese identity. Germany companies are much more open in the structuring of their marketing channels, and make decisions about them according to more short-term commercial considerations. Therefore they set up their own divisions only in those markets where a sufficient market volume is guaranteed, and in other countries, where there are only sporadic sales, they rely on agents.

Japanese companies also make much greater use of market research, in order to secure their long term position in foreign markets, while German companies rely more strongly on their experience or the experience of their divisions, and especially on personal contacts, which are made on foreign visits or at trade fairs. German international marketing carries, above all, a personal stamp, whereas the burden of Japanese international marketing is borne to a very much greater extent by the organization of the companies or by the institutions for trade promotions, for example, the Japan Export Trade Organization (JETRO).

The Importance of Advertising

Both the Federal Republic of Germany and Japan show advertising expenditure taking up an increasing share of the Gross National Product (GNP). The ZAW (ZAW: Central

Committee of the Advertising Industry, Bonn) gives net advertising turnover for the year 1984 in the Federal Republic of Germany as 15 thousand million DM. This represents an increase over the previous year of 5.7%. The GNP of the Federal Republic of Germany has annually increased by only 4.6%.[4] At this level, direct advertising expenditure in the Federal Republic of Germany lies at under 1% of GNP, whereas for example, advertising expenditure in the U.S.A. amounts to over 2% of GNP. Japan is on a comparable level with the Federal Republic of Germany. There too, advertising costs run at about 1% of GNP.[5]

The differences between the Federal Republic of Germany and Japan result in particular from the difference in significance which the individual media have for the communication process in each society, as well as from the culturally differentiated structures of advertising in the two countries. Japan is characterized by the fact that television and the daily newspapers compete with each other as media of advertising, and are more or less equally important. In Japan, 31.3% of the money spent on advertising goes to the daily newspapers and 35.4% to television. Besides this, only outdoor and direct advertising play an important role.[6] Advertising in the Federal Republic of Germany is dominated by the daily newspapers and the general periodicals. 39.8% is spent on the daily newspapers, 17.8% on general periodicals, and television advertising accounts for 9%, about the same as advertising in specialized journals. Direct and outdoor advertising have a share of 15%.[7]

As advertising in Japan is dominated by the media of television and daily newspapers, it acquires a rather fleeting, transitory character, all the more so as it is directed towards a public which is little differentiated. It employs much more strongly emotional appeals than is the case with German advertising. The instrument of advertising in the Federal Republic of Germany is particularly strongly influenced by the daily newspapers, and this facilitates regional differentiations. Advertising is also carried out through general periodicals, with their target group focus, and through specialized journals which are directed towards a select specialist public. The structure of advertising in the Federal Republic of Germany is more strongly subject-matter oriented and informative, while at the same time German advertising is also regulated in an intensive manner, especially with respect to misleading advertising and comparative advertising. This basic type of factual and informative advertising has positive results for the advertising efforts of Germany's industry, particularly in the international sector. The heavy goods sector which predominates in the export trade employs this style of advertising.

The significance of personal communication, which characterizes the marketing strategy of many German companies, is highlighted by the preference for international fairs as channels of communication. From the point of view of advertising, the whole aim in taking part in a fair is to make up the display stand in such a manner that it is seen by as many customers as possible from both home and abroad, so that these customers might be drawn into intensive consultative discussions. In these attention is expressly drawn to particular technical efficiency and to individual problem-solving capacity. The advertising structure has only a door-opening function, that is, it enables personal communication.

Japanese companies also have in the international sector a different expectation of their advertising. Advertising is supposed to speak for itself, that is, for both the product and the company, and is with its strong emotional appeal supposed to bring the customer or interested party into such a mental state that he is positively receptive to a Japanese product and its producer. Emotional preparedness for a purchasing act is produced directly. Any residual buyer resistance is then dismantled by means of price concession. The readiness, and also the ability, to enter into a detailed factual discussion with the buyer or customer are not present in many cases. In addition to this there are often difficulties of language in communication. Further, the particular organizational structure of Japanese companies makes it difficult for their employees to pass on comprehensive information in an individual conversation with a customer. The Japanese model of decision-making in a group process would in such a case require a fairly large number of colleagues to come together in a conference, in order to discuss technical or commercial details with foreign customers. The advertising appeal aims to establish a positive atmosphere, which binds customer and company to a system of give and take in mutual understanding.

This binding into an exchange process is a priority target for Japanese advertising and it presents itself as a marketing instrument which permits in its functional practice only limited comparison with other Western industrial nations.

The differences in advertising style may be illustrated by advertisements of Lufthansa and of Japan Airlines. In a series of advertisements Lufthansa gives priority to technical information, and places the technical quality of its fleet and the maintenance of equipment in the foreground. For Lufthansa, an essential advertising claim is the punctuality of its services. It does not advertise flying with comfort but advertises safety, dependability. In advertisements of Japan Airlines stress is put on comfort on board, and on the experience of flying, in accordance with the old Zen tradition that the way is as important as the goal. Japan Airlines also places its advertising in the tradition of Japanese culture, for example, in the tea ceremony or in Japanese painting.

In German advertising the product and the product philosophy stand in the center of the advertising claims, whereas in Japanese advertising the consumer and his feel for life are in the center.

Particularities of Consumer Behaviour

The differences in marketing strategies of German and Japanese companies are closely related to the particularities of consumer behaviour in the two countries. Economic development in the Federal Republic of Germany from the milieu of the craftsman and the farmer led to all the techniques of marketing being used in a relatively robust manner by companies. In Japan industrial development was led by the nobility, whose manner of behaviour had been stamped for centuries by cultural refinement. This basic principle was also carried into economic behaviour. Japanese investment and consumer behaviour is characterized by a very high degree of sensitivity. It is a question here of a culture particularly characterized by "weak signals." In Japan it is not permissible to display personal wealth by demonstrative consumption, and the constant requirements of harmony in society lead also to a situation in which it is more important for consumers to be part of this society than to mark themselves off from it by conspicuous behaviour. In the

Federal Republic of Germany, on the other hand, consumer behaviour is achievement-oriented, and both particular social position and the self-esteem of the person are emphasized and underlined by consumer and behaviour patterns.

Particular social and cultural traditions lead in the two countries to different forms of consumer behaviour. This requires of German companies an adjustment in marketing strategies in dealing with Japan. This adjustment has been highly successful for some individual German producers, particularly when they have worked very closely with Japanese advertising and market research firms. The situation in Japan requires particularly sensitive tuning to particular Japanese conditions. A linear transfer to Japan of marketing strategies such as have been practiced with success in the Federal Republic of Germany and other countries of the world would, with a high degree of probability, lead to failure there. The difficulties, which many German and also many American companies have encountered in attempting to capture a larger share of the market in Japan, are connected in many cases with the firms' being insufficiently sensitive to the particularities of the Japanese environment.

But it is an imperative too for Japanese firms to adjust themselves to the particular conditions of the market in Germany and in other European countries. Japanese companies have practiced this systematically and, in individual cases, successfully. The ability to absorb individual elements from other cultures, which has played a role time and time again in Japanese history, allows Japanese companies to adjust themselves relatively quickly and precisely to the particular conditions of the Federal Republic of Germany and of Europe.[8] Typical of the marketing policy of Japanese companies in the German market is, in particular, the high advertising intensity, which is proportionately greater than the share of the market actually won by Japanese sellers. Foreign companies in Japan would have to develop as high an investment in advertising, in order to win higher shares in the market there and to secure this market in the long term.

Consumer behaviour in Japan is particularly characterized by the significance of the middle class. The middle class marks both Japanese business and Japanese society. Consumer behaviour in the Federal Republic of Germany, as in Europe, is on the other hand, much more strongly differentiated and stretches from the "Jet Set" to the "New Poor." In German consumer behaviour the middle class does play an important role, but often in the form of the upwardly ambitious middle class.

This development is directly connected with political events in Europe. In Japan there exists, admittedly, the upwardly ambitious middle class pattern, but in a rather discrete form. There is an increasing tendency to change life-style and to separate from the traditions of parents. But these developments take place with a high degree of sensitivity, and they do not place the basic consensus of Japanese society in question. Owing to the great homogeneity of Japanese culture, there are hardly any differences between town and country, or between individual regions.

In Japan *business* and retail trade function as transmitters of the models of consumption to Japanese society, models which are in the West largely transmitted by branded articles and by the advertising for branded articles. Commercial companies in the Federal Republic of Germany are at pains to satisfy the special wishes and also the changing tastes of consumers. In the West, the consumers have attained a position of importance, often even a position of predominance in the commercial decision-making and co-ordinating process. In Japan on the other hand the consumers experience more strongly their dependence on the economic and social system, and it is precisely through this that they gain their Japanese identity and their well-tailored social consciousness.

In Japan housewives play an essential role in the consumer spectrum. The Japanese family is normally so organized that consumer decisions are made by housewives, even decisions about investments or the purchase of real estate. In the Federal Republic of Germany both consumer and investment decisions are generally made as family decisions, especially in the case of "high-involvement" products. The non-working wives of the leading executives of Japanese banks, of industry and of government form something like the "new class" in Japan. The consumer climate and the behavioural patterns in Japan increasingly follow their preconceptions. In the Federal Republic of Germany consumer behaviour is more strongly influenced by youth. In their first working years, so long as they have not set up a household, young people have available to them a relatively high, freely disposable income. The consumer culture is strongly oriented towards the requirements of this group, particularly in the sectors of sports gear, travel or fashion. Up to now, there has been no comparable influence of youth on the consumer climate in Japan.

All in all, there has formed in Japan a pattern of consumer behaviour which could be described paradoxically as Calvinistic consumer behaviour, that is, the rejection of extravagant and especially of provocative consumption, in order to live in harmony with society. Consumer behaviour is influenced by the social desires to belong and to identify with Japanese society. The society of the Federal Republic of Germany has largely freed itself from Calvinistic precepts, even if there is, precisely among young people, a new movement concerned with the rejection of consumption. Consumption is seen in Germany as an expression of personality which serves to fulfill conscious wishes and also, to some extent, those which are unconscious, up to the point where it gives rise to a bad conscience. Consumer behaviour in West Germany is much more strongly oriented towards a goal and not so much towards enjoyment during consumption. Goal-oriented consumer behaviour aims to bring about change in the personality and create respect in the peer group, as well as positively influencing self-esteem. These aims are served by, for example, fashion, jewelry or long-distance travel.

These peculiarities of consumer behaviour work back on the structure of marketing in the two countries and on the respective strategies which are followed by companies. West Germany is characterized by a greater dynamic, which aims at change and growth, whereas marketing in Japan is directed towards adjustment and transfer, although it is precisely thereby that the growth of Japanese business is achieved. The differentiation of consumer behaviour in West Germany leads to the necessity of identifying and differentiating target groups in marketing. The more intensively markets are segmented, the smaller the relevant target markets become, so that the companies increasingly direct their attention to opening up additional markets abroad or to expanding existing export markets. The outstanding marketing strategy is *niche marketing,* the addressing of highly differentiated target groups.

Japanese marketing is much more strongly *mass marketing,* which does not differentiate according to individual target groups, which uses the media of mass communication, especially television and the daily newspapers, and becomes the domain of big business. Japanese companies experience difficulties in finding their feet in the niche philosophy of the European markets and in identifying target groups. Conversely it is difficult for German companies to find a niche in the Japanese mass market in which they can operate successfully. They are most likely to succeed with products which exhibit outstanding technological quality.

Comparison of Marketing Strategies

The particularities of marketing and of consumer behaviour may be systematized in the following matrix—a comparison which serves to identify tendencies and orders of influence. The differentiation undertaken will not be provable in every individual case as there is a series of exceptions to this basic scheme. Further, in matching the marketing strategies of companies not the least influence felt will be the all-encroaching American one. Nevertheless, this matrix should fulfil its purpose of making clear the structural differences between German and Japanese marketing. It is only the perception of such difficulties which will enable companies to match their marketing strategies to the relevant environment and thus create the conceptual preconditions for their market success in Japan or in West Germany.

Development Perspectives of Marketing

Both marketing strategies as well as consumer behaviour are negatively influenced by developments in the U.S.A. From this standpoint, we see the function of the U.S.A. as a model to be followed acting itself out in West Germany and Japan, not least in the dominating influence of American marketing theory on marketing models and marketing concepts. In both countries there run largely parallel processes tending towards the stronger integration of these countries into the world economy. This trend will continue

Dimension	Japan	Federal Republic of Germany
Principles and preconditions	Transfer concept Identity Consensus	Product concepts Pluralism Competition
Marketing strategies	Mass marketing Media conscious Software concept Sensitive Emotional	Niche marketing Contact-oriented Hardware concept Robust Analytical
Consumer and investor behaviour	Middle Class Adjustment Housewife decision Role of business	Climber Independence Family decision Influence of branded articles

in intensified form against a background of relatively small home markets confronted with the requirement of mass production, and because of the necessity to develop innovations which are directed towards the world market in its entirety. Therefore the common ground for the development of the marketing strategies of the two countries will grow greater, and it is to be expected that a certain process of mutual adjustment and learning will take place. We may expect to see German advertising become more sensitive and Japanese advertising more robust, and that German marketing strategies will take ideas of transfer more into account, while Japanese market strategies will become more strongly product-oriented.

This matching-up process will take place first of all in German companies in Japan and in Japanese companies in West Germany. The instrument of mutual tie-up of capital in the context of foreign investment or of other forms of co-operation will promote this process. Nevertheless, the cultural differences and varying traditions, which have marked the development of the two countries, will remain. In the future, too, there will be clear differences in the marketing strategies of these two countries. The differences in these marketing strategies present a challenge both to the companies and to advertising agencies and business consultants. It is through the particularities of the instruments of marketing that the German or Japanese identities of products and firms emerge.

In addition to this necessary differentiating of marketing strategies, companies which are active on a world scale will increasingly feel the need to develop a world-wide identity and to establish it in the market. Such a world-wide identity represents for many firms today an important precondition for the guaranteeing of their international market success. To this extent, for example, German companies in Japan will find themselves in a position where they will not only have to adjust themselves to Japanese forms of consumer behaviour, but will at the same time have to underline their typically German identity, in order to be successful in Japan. Also, Japanese companies will have to take care not to lose their identity in other countries but to adjust themselves nevertheless to local market conditions. For this situation marketing managers in both West Germany and Japan will have to develop a new, highly sensitive consciousness. Their marketing decisions will have to take into account, in increasing and in appropriate manner, the results which will emerge from these strategies for the perception of their companies on the world market.

References

1. See Zentralausschuss der Werbewirtschaft (ZAW), *Werbung, '84,* Bonn, 1984, pp. 18–25.

2. Edwin O. Reischauer, *Japan Past and Present,* 3rd edition, Tokyo, 1976, p. 16 ff.

3. See Philip Kotler, *Marketing Management,* 4th edition, Stuttgart, 1984, *passim.*

4. See Zentralausschuss der Werbewirtschaft (ZAW), *Werbung, '85,* Bonn, 1984, p. 11.

5. Nikkei Advertising Research Institute, *Japan's Market and Advertising,* Tokyo, 1983, p. 5.

6. *Ibid.,* p. 6.

7. See ZAW, *op. cit.,* p. 11.

8. See Erfolg macht hungrig—Worauf das Marketing japanischer Unternehmen zielt in *Absatzwirtschaft,* No. 3, 1985, 52 ff.
   Source: "Japanische and Deutsche Marketingstrategien—Ein struktureller Vergleich," in *Mitteilungen der Bundesstelle fur Aussenhandels information,* Köln, November 1985. *Translation:* Noel Deeney.

Why Joint Ventures Fail

Kathryn Rudie Harrigan. *Kathryn Harrigan is Associate Professor at the Graduate School of Business of Columbia University.*

Joint ventures are in fashion again, and many firms throughout the world are rushing to find partners. Even skeptical managers are being swept up by the contagious belief that joint ventures and other forms of corporate marriage will solve their firms' problems with a handshake and the stroke of a pen. Managers hope that by teaming up with partners that offer strengths which their own firms lack, the result will be a stronger competitive posture in the markets they hope to serve.

Strategic alliances are, in fact, as difficult to sustain and nurture as marriages. The difficulties of making joint ventures succeed cause many managers to throw up their hands in despair. Yet the benefits provided by joint ventures and other forms of cooperative strategy frequently make them well worth the extra effort of learning how to cope with the complexities of shared ownership and shared decision-making.

Joint Ventures Defined

"Joint ventures" are owned by two or more sponsoring firms that share resources and skills to create new entities. Examples include International Himont (Montedison and Hercules), NUMMI (General Motors and Toyota), and General Numeric (Siemens and Fujitsu). In such ventures, owners contribute resources, personnel, technology and market access; they share in the returns from their venture's operations through equity ownership; and share decision-making responsibility for their venture's day-to-day operations as well. (Note that minority investments involve shared equity, but they do not have the shared decision-making feature of strategic alliances—whether such alliances involve equity ownership of the venture or not—that are the focus of this article.)

Firms also cooperate through non-equity ventures, including cooperative agreements, research and development partnerships, cross-production, cross-licensing and cross-marketing agreements, and joint bidding activities. Although they may not create a

Reprinted from the *Euro-Asia Business Review,* July 1987. Used with permission from the Euro-Asia Centre, Boulevard de Constance, 77309 Fontainebleau Cedex, France. This article is based on materials contained in K.R. Harrigan, *Strategies for Joint Ventures.* Lexington, MA: Lexington Books, 1985, and K.R. Harrigan, *Managing for Joint Venture Success.* Lexington, MA: Lexington Books, 1986. Permission to use this material is gratefully acknowledged. Research support from the Strategy Research Center, Columbia University, and suggestions from its Chairman, William H. Newman, are also gratefully acknowledged.

separate organizational entity, many of the problems I have seen that prevent managers from effectively exploiting the advantages of strategic alliances apply to non-equity forms of venture as well as to joint ventures.

Joint ventures have been a commonplace way of doing business for decades in industries like offshore oil and gas exploration, petrochemicals, mining, metals processing and electronic components. Cooperative strategies have often been required in strategic industries (like aerospace) or as the price of admission into some countries' markets.

Now joint ventures (and other forms of strategic alliance) have become popular as a strategy option in a wide variety of troubled industries, such as communications services, pharmaceuticals and medical products, steel, precision controls and robotics, financial services, entertainment programming and programming packaging, among others, where cooperation has less of a track record.

The Cooperative Strategy Option

More firms are embracing strategic alliances in their home markets now because the requirements for successful competition have become more demanding. As Table 1 suggests, domestic joint ventures are becoming more widespread now due to: (1) economic deregulation, (2) increasingly rapid rates of technological change (hence shorter product lives), (3) larger capital requirements (to undertake risky new projects and develop new processes), (4) entry by new firms (that are supported by their respective governments), (5) industry and economic maturation in the United States, Europe, and Japan, (6) improved communications and computational power, and (7) globalization in industries where competition was previously constrained by geographic boundaries.

Joint ventures will become particularly important in markets where industry boundaries are blurring between formerly disparate activities. For example, when the capabilities of information processing and data transmission technologies link old activities in new ways and products are redefined to encompass a wider scope of activity, firms may see partners to supplement the skills they lack in-house, especially if they fear being left behind as a promising marketplace develops.

Joint Venture Dynamics

Terms of the formal (and informal) agreements creating joint ventures may change over time, as Table 2 indicates, due to (1) changes in the venture's industry (and success requirements therein) and the effectiveness of the venture's strategy for serving its industry, (2) changes in the sponsoring firms' needs for joint activity with their current partner under the agreement's current terms, and (3) changes in the pattern of autonomous activity or close owner-venture coordination needed for the venture's competitive success. Although the terms of a joint venture agreement are modified (or the venture is terminated) when the arrangement has fulfilled its purpose, many such ventures are ended before completing their task due to problems among sponsoring firms, managerial problems within the venture itself, or problems in the relationship between owners and their ventures.

TABLE 1   **Motivations for Joint Venture Formation**

A.   Internal Uses

1. Cost and risk sharing (uncertainty reduction)
2. Obtain resources where there is no market
3. Obtain financing to supplement firm's debt capacity
4. Share output of large minimum efficient scale plants
    a. Avoid wasteful duplication of facilities
    b. Utilize by-products, processes
    c. Shared brands, distribution channels, wide product lines, and so forth
5. Intelligence: obtain window on new technologies and customers
    a. Superior information exchange
    b. Technological personnel interactions
6. Innovative managerial practices
    a. Superior management systems
    b. Improved communications among strategic business units
7. Retain entrepreneurial employees

B.   Competitive Uses (Strengthen Current Strategic Positions)

1. Influence industry structure's evolution
    a. Pioneer development of new industries
    b. Reduce competitive volatility
    c. Rationalize mature industries
2. Preempt competitors ("first-mover" advantages)
    a. Gain rapid access to better customers
    b. Capacity expansion or vertical integration
    c. Acquisition of advantageous terms, resources
    d. Coalition with best partners
3. Defensive response to blurring industry boundaries and globalization
    a. Ease political tensions (overcome trade barriers)
    b. Gain access to global networks
4. Creation of more effective competitors
    a. Hybrid's possessing owners' strengths
    b. Fewer, more efficient firms
    c. Buffer dissimilar partners

C.   Strategic Use (Augment Strategic Position)

1. Creation and exploration of synergies
2. Technology (or other skills) transfer
    a. Toehold entry into new markets, products, or skills
    b. Rationalization (or divestiture) of investment
    c. Leverage-related owners' skills for new uses

My insights concerning why strategic alliances never fulfilled their promise were obtained from interviews in the United States with a variety of experienced managers. (See Appendix 1 for details of the study.)

Managers suggested that joint ventures are most likely to fail because:

(1) the market for the venture's product disappears,

(2) what is thought to be good technology from one partner (or whatever the contribution is to be) does not prove to be as good as is expected,

TABLE 2   Joint Venture Change Forces

The stability of a joint venture agreement (and timing of changes in its terms) depends upon:

1. Changes in the venture's industry (and success requirements therein)
2. Effectiveness of joint venture's competitive strategy
3. Changes in partners' relative bargaining power vis-á-vis each other
4. Changes in owners' strategic missions
5. Changes in importance of the joint venture to owners
6. Changes in venture's need for autonomous activities
7. Changes in patterns of owner-venture coordination needed for competitive success

(3) partners cannot get along,

(4) partners simply renege on promises to deliver on their part of the agreement,

(5) venture managers from disparate partners cannot work together,

(6) managers within the venture cannot work with managers within sponsoring firms,

(7) owners that are to contribute information or resources to their venture cannot get their personnel down the line to deliver what has been promised, or

(8) other reasons destroy partner's cooperative spirits.

These same managers also offered some hope for the future use of strategic alliances because many of them believed that there is an experience curve in using joint ventures in the sense that as managers better understand what works, they are more eager to replicate their successes and they become more skillful at doing so.

Joint Ventures and Competitive Success Requirements

Competitive stakes increased in the 1980s as many firms tried to assimilate information-processing, telecommunications and other competitive skills. Because no firm could develop the many technologies they needed in-house or afford to fund all of the projects needed to remain competitive on several fronts, they looked to joint ventures as a means to cope with their industries' changing success requirements.

Many firms in the 26 industries I examined did obtain easier access to expertise and to distribution outlets through joint ventures, and results suggest that few firms could have moved as quickly in securing market share if they had to develop the assets enjoyed by their joint ventures on their own. By pooling facilities, firms are able to keep their costs low until their internally-generated sales volumes reach the critical mass that justifies having their own plant, equipment, sales force and other facilities.

But results also suggest that there are limits to the widespread efficacy of joint ventures, and firms must adjust their cooperative strategies to the special problems of particular competitive environments. In particular, learning to work together in joint ventures can slow down the speed with which firms move into promising markets or respond to competitors' manoeuvres. Cumbersome agreements can be deadly in volatile competitive environments because some market opportunities evaporate within months if they are not exploited quickly. High technology products, in particular, often need rapid market penetration in order to place them into distribution channels and into consumers' hands before products become obsolete or can be copied by others.

Embryonic Industries

In embryonic industries, for example, where great uncertainty looms concerning which marketing approaches will prove most successful or which technological standards customers will embrace, successful firms form more liaisons—each of shorter duration—than in better-established industries. Astute managers adopt less binding partnership terms in order to avoid entanglements that might prove to be wrong later. Moreover, experienced firms do not work through ventures exclusively with any particular partner for long in environments of high uncertainty.

Some managers have even concluded that ventures in embryonic industries should not be bound by arrangements involving shared equity. Instead, their firms create non-equity entities on a project-by-project basis in highly-changeable environments. They do so because when partners' interest change, their joint ventures must end in a non-disruptive fashion as firms move on to their next dancing partners. To facilitate easy transitions, agreements are formed for only a few months at a time, and proceed on a handshake rather than a voluminous legal document.

Shorter Product Lives

It becomes especially important to have access to international market linkages within industries where technology (or product design) changes rapidly, yet must be compatible with devices in operation throughout the globe. Firms find it increasingly expensive to reach key markets within global industries quickly when the half-life of a technology is very short because firms can scarcely recoup their development costs by going it alone.

This expense explains, in part, why so many joint ventures, cross-marketing contracts, cooperative agreements and minority investments were made in the pharmaceutical industry in the early 1980s; firms sought products to enter new therapeutic categories and market access to reach more customers with existing products before their source of competitive advantage had expired.

Stable Industry Environments

Joint ventures are more likely to result when partners join forces in the early stages of industry maturity, when technology changes less rapidly and when product standards have at last been established. As demand uncertainty lessens, concerning the nature of customer tastes, price sensitivities, product features and other market traits, and as firms become more concerned with how to forge effective strategies to satisfy demand, they begin to seek the talents of accomplished partners and form joint ventures of greater scope and longevity.

Much of the criticism that is levelled against joint venture strategies fails to recognize that different cooperative strategies—of differing durations and involving different types of progeny— are best used in industries of different ages and infrastructure stability. Where there is still great uncertainty concerning the efficacy of technologies, customers' tastes and other structural traits that can affect profit-making opportunities within an industry, effective managers keep their firms' joint activities informal and brief. When their industries mature, as more competitors enter and technological standards are better accepted, managers forge fewer joint ventures per firm, and each venture encompasses a larger-sized investment or broader market scope, as in the petrochemical, communications equipment and home video entertainment industries. Thus, managers are more likely to be disappointed in their ventures if they try to make them overly-formal or inflexible too early in an industry's development.

Solving Technological Problems

Although few firms engage in partnerships in basic R&D or other areas that are highly-sensitive to their strategic postures, ventures to exploit knowledge in new applications or markets thrive in mature economies.

Technological prowess is the key to attaining competitive advantage when technologies (1) change frequently, (2) are highly risky, and (3) require extremely high creativity in design or precision in manufacturing. Joint ventures permit firms to hedge their bets concerning competing standards and keep abreast of other innovations while sharing in development costs.

Cooperation is a fundamental structural trait of many high technology industries, yet licenses and informal agreements are more commonplace than shared-equity joint ventures. Difficulties in managing owner-venture relationships, and in particular transferring knowledge and skills, explains part of the shortfall in joint venture activity in high technology industries. Their inability to collaborate effectively with partners' personnel also explains, in part, why joint ventures seldom realize their promise in solving technological problems.

A Spider's Web of Ventures

Success within industries requires firms to forge many, parallel ventures in a pattern like a spider's web (with themselves at the hub). When firms must move quickly to exploit a transitory advantage, partners are needed that offer attractive solutions for particular customer problems. Few stand-alone ventures result from these marriages, and like the musical chairs pairing of the electronic components industry, no firm is expected to solve all problems alone.

A willingness to dance with several partners allows firms to move faster in responding to changes in market demands than exclusive arrangements of longer durations. Part of their flexibility in using a spider's web of agreements arises from the informality of these alliances. (A caution: this very practice comes back to haunt firms that engage in spider's webs of ventures without telling their existing Japanese partners since it is interpreted as a loss of confidence in the existing partner's abilities.)

Loose alliances—personal service contracts, OEM vendor agreements or other arm's length arrangements—are preferred by managers when dealing with highly dissimilar partners, entrepreneurs and other situations where managers feel uncomfortable about forming joint ventures. Examples where this approach is preferred include creative people who want an equity participation but do not want a salary nor to be part of a corporate monolith. Results suggest that the national origins of partners matter less to venture success than whether partners are of similar asset size and venturing experience. Most importantly, successful partnerships agree on the venture's priorities—they share similar values—regardless of their national origins.

Managing Partnerships

Good partners should be prized because managers will return to them with increasing frequency to create new ventures in the future. Yet despite their apparent worth, opportunities to create advantageous joint ventures are often missed because (1) managers are unwilling to pay deference to differences in corporate cultures, and (2) firms will not be open with potential partners during the negotiating process.

If managers cannot discuss cooperation in an open and flexible way, the strain that an inarticulate and narrow negotiating team places on any venture that results can reduce severely the joint venture's chances of realizing its full promise. Although the venture's management team may overcome this false start and find a way to work together, sponsoring firms will always be uneasy if they started their relationship awkwardly and cannot provide adequately for their true expectations concerning the venture when they negotiate its terms.

Negotiating an Agreement

Individuals with hidden agendas make joint ventures fail. It is more important for potential partners to talk through everything of importance to them—even if it means that the ultimate agreement is very different from the original venture concept—than it is to become bogged down in financial details. If care is taken in finding good partners and letting the proposed arrangement work its way through both firms' organizations, the deal can eventually be done with great enthusiasm on both sides.

Experience Pays.   The results of my US-based research indicate that successful and experienced venture sponsors prefer to work with equally experienced partners. Their objective in choosing a joint venture partner is to find one that complements their firm's strengths. The more experienced the partner, the more realistic his expectations about joint ventures, and the more willing he is for a little give and take to occur in hammering out a satisfactory joint venture compromise.

Move Cautiously.   Unsatisfied managers suggested, in retrospect, that poor matches are made when negotiating teams devote too much attention to questions of who will control the venture's technology and what the financial arrangements will be, while too little attention is devoted to questions of how partners' relationships will be managed. This is not to suggest that attention should not be directed also to details concerning financial arrangements, technology, transfer or other issues concerning sponsoring firms' assets. But rather, it cautions managers not to confine their negotiating teams to lawyers who will not have bottom line responsibility for making the venture work.

Build on Success.   Managers that take a cautious approach—a little project, then another one if the first experience is a good one—are more satisfied with the use of joint ventures than those who move too fast or not carefully enough in forming alliances. The incremental approach to negotiations enables managers to keep adding to the complexity or breadth of things that they trust a partner to do on the basis of previous experience. The incremental approach also keeps their expectations for a particular partner lower and enables managers to be more analytical in assessing why a particular venture did not work out.

Assessing Partners

The promised advantages of cooperation are not always realized though this is rarely acknowledged. If stock prices enjoy speculative gains when joint ventures are announced (especially those concerning technology transfers), valuation errors are never admitted to outsiders later. If there are start-up problems or partners' contributions are not as promised, these realities are often masked by the apparent delight of investors that small firms are betting their technological positions (by allying with big firms) or that big firms that were doing nothing impressive in a particular line of research have found a promising way to catch up.

Do Your Homework.   Therefore, it is necessary for managers to be well informed on the value of technologies before discussing joint ventures because it is easy to become perplexed in discussions of risky and unproven technological approaches. The most successful technological joint ventures are formed by firms that have each done considerable R&D work on the problem prior to their collaboration. With such preparations, managers know whether a joint venture is technically appropriate and commercially viable.

Test Potential Partners.   If managers are uneasy with their counterparts, they can learn more about potential partners in many ways. Cautious managers favor a step-by-step relationship when forming a joint venture with new partners. They suggest giving potential partners a proposal and some issues to study. If the firm's managers return for negotiations with suggestions and can articulate their firm's concerns on the critical points of the venture, a small project is warranted. If that cooperation works out, another joint venture is formed.

Build Consensus.   The managers of one successful firm with several joint ventures to its credit take a very deliberate approach towards the formation of their firm's joint ventures. They identify the need for a partnership. They search methodically throughout the globe for the best possible partners, by interviewing the customers they hope their joint venture will serve, by interviewing research institutes and any other experts with knowledge concerning where the technologies they seek might be obtained.

Managers develop a list of potential partners and screen them. They approach several partners simultaneously to discuss the venture and judge which candidate will be the best partner for the venture in question. Managers insist on a long engagement period where executives and operating managers on both sides move slowly to consensus on how to operate their venture. When the marriage is finally consummated, the venture receives everything needed to run as a stand-alone entity. Subsequent interventions by sponsoring firms in their venture's operating decisions are minimal because the resulting management team closely reflects the values of its owners.

Partner Disharmony.   Partners must understand their venture's activities and trust its management team well enough to avoid becoming a source of irritation to the joint venture relationship. Schisms occurred frequently in partnerships where managers from sponsoring firms doubted (or did not like) what they were told but did not understand the venture well enough to alleviate their doubts. Although it is difficult to avoid friction between owners and overly-enthusiastic venture managers, care is needed in negotiating the venture to ensure that partners obtain adequate information to evaluate its performance.

Managing Jointly-Owned Ventures

Managers within sponsoring firms sometimes believe erroneously that they can set up joint ventures and let them run themselves. They overlook the importance of their choices concerning which managers to place in charge of the venture's operations, how to evaluate the venture's performance and how to transfer knowledge between owner and venture. The venture's management team must possess both diplomatic skills and entrepreneurial aggressiveness in order to balance the need to represent each owner's viewpoint fairly to its partners against the need to make the venture an economic success. Results suggest that if managers want the venture to succeed badly enough, they find a way to work together—regardless of their origins.

Joint Venture Management Style

Joint ventures can fail if the wrong executives are chosen to lead them. Sponsoring firms cannot tap their managers' entrepreneurial tendencies if joint ventures become personnel dumping grounds or if supervising managers drive out risk-taking zeal through their control system demands. In one disastrous venture, high-performing managers were removed from joint venture assignments soon after the first honeymoon was over. In this company, burnt-out, low potential or politically-embarrassing managers were sent to joint ventures, and the venture's requests for assistance were treated accordingly. Rather than make joint ventures a convenient parking place for senior executives awaiting retirement, firms can make them a reward for enterprising managers, if they want the venture to succeed.

Joint venture managers must be skilled in diplomacy in order to capture the support of the managers within sponsoring firms, but they should also be detached from loyalties to any particular owner in decision-making. To combat the problem of split loyalties in their venture's managers, some firms close the "revolving door" back to their organizations and hire outsiders—with loyalties to no owner—to lead the venture and staff critical jobs. Managers representing each owner are still placed in the venture to coordinate the venture's activities with those of its owners, but they need not have line responsibility.

The Changeling

Sponsoring firms must be prepared for their venture's success. That means funding must be provided to exploit opportunities that may develop for the joint venture, and if owners cannot provide the cash needed for new opportunities, their venture must approach the capital markets in its own right to obtain funding. Withholding the means for success will sap the venture managers' spirits. Moreover, managers within sponsoring firms must recognize that the interests of the venture may diverge from their own.

In many cases, the venture is an underdog. Its rag-tag managers receive little respect because they are the "black sheep" of their respective firms. The pressures venture managers feel from their respective owners often drive them together in their efforts to make the venture succeed, especially if there is no possibility of returning to their previous corporate positions. Venture managers will become champions for their organization and will expect the venture to be rewarded for its successes like any other business unit. If the venture's team becomes so successful at working together that the venture out-performs wholly-owned units and competes for their resources, managerial jealousies within sponsoring firms may result and these animosities must be diffused.

Managing Owner-Venture Relationships

The preceding section has raised the problems created by overly-zealous venture managers that want more autonomy than managers within sponsoring firms are willing to sanction. Boisterous managers are less of a problem if they can be given control over the resources needed for their competitive success and allowed to operate autonomously. Problems, arise, however, in managing owner-venture relationships effectively when close coordination between them is needed. Industry differences can suggest how quickly ventures should evolve from loose cooperation to partnerships to stand-alone entities (if at all). Some relationships retrogress, as in the example of Xerox pulling Rank-Xerox more closely under its control as competition intensified and profit margins thinned, while others allow the venture more autonomy over time.

Joint ventures offer a unique management problem due to their shared-ownership nature: decision-making is cumbersome within a joint venture. This problem becomes especially germane when sponsoring firms hope to create synergies through their joint ventures because resource-sharing requires close coordination in order to be successful. Yet managers within sponsoring firms often become frustrated when negotiations with other owners are needed to change output allocations, for example.

Managers often take out their frustrations with the joint venture form of cooperation on the venture's management team. Unfortunately, their resentment can draw the venture closer when its managers need greater autonomy to compete effectively, or their anger may cut off the venture's managers when greater coordination between owner and venture is needed. If the linkages owners employ to monitor and influence their venture's activities are inappropriate, they can destroy the opportunities to realize synergies or transfer knowledge for which the venture was created.

Creating Synergies

If synergies are to be created through joint ventures, they will accrue from vertical relationships or from sharing resources. But these relationships may require managers to evaluate joint venture performance differently than they would evaluate that of wholly-owned, stand-alone business units. For example, a joint venture need not have any downstream facilities, provided it is not penalized for its failure to sell outputs that are not consumed by its owners.

If owners rely too heavily on the products, services and innovations supplied by their joint venture, they cut themselves off from a way of evaluating whether their venture is obsolete. If joint ventures are restricted from dealing with outsiders—by right-of-first refusal arrangements or outright prohibition—they may become overly-reliant on their owners when they should instead be providing them with intelligence about competitive conditions. An appropriate balance must be found.

Sharing Knowledge

One of the side benefits of working together in joint ventures is the cross-pollination process whereby ideas are shared among research, manufacturing or marketing personnel and transferred to owners' organizations. Some firms consciously try to encourage technological bleedthrough. Bleedthrough is knowledge (not covered by formal agreements) that is gained by working with partners on joint ventures. Successful sponsors of joint ventures develop a system for managing relationships between owner and venture to ensure that knowledge of work methods, managerial practices and technology is returned to them and readily accepted by their in-house research organizations. Some sponsoring firms run parallel research experiments in their wholly-owned laboratories or move scientists and the other technical people through the joint venture and back to their wholly-owned laboratories to disseminate information.

Other firms ensure that the knowledge gained through exposure to partners in joint ventures is diffused back to owner laboratories through meticulous programs of repatriation. At the group level, for example, firms hold annual technical meetings where engineering managers and leading R&D scientists gather divisional engineering and R&D personnel for an interchange of information and ideas.

At the corporate level, top technical officers coordinate the use of technology developed in-house in joint ventures with other divisions or with outsiders, as well as technology that is received from others—through licenses or joint ventures—that might be useful in some other part of the company. Some firms use an integrated sales force and marketing organization that sells products from all divisions, regardless of their ownership status.

Evaluating Joint Ventures

Joint venture termination need not suggest that a venture has failed. Even well-informed and well-managed joint ventures must end some day because the necessity that once spurred a venture's creation will not exist forever in evolving competitive markets. Moreover, the tensions of shared decision-making encourage one partner to buy out the others. Finally, human resource development policies that rotate managers to differing assignments can accelerate a joint venture's demise if the sponsoring firms' management teams change so dramatically that the new personnel can no longer recall the logic that once stimulated the venture's creation. Consequently, these managers are more likely to terminate joint ventures that they do not understand rather than nurture them.

From the examples and discussion above, it is evident that joint ventures go awry because they are far more complex to manage than many firms have recognized. They can go awry when partners forget their purpose, when owners become inflexible concerning how they use their ventures, when venture managers forget their role in sponsoring firms' strategies, or when other factors upset their delicate balance. Joint ventures have a high mortality rate and do not last long in most industries. But their short life-cycles do not suggest that joint ventures cannot be effective in attaining their objectives.

The outlook and skills needed to master joint ventures are still alien to most managers, and many executives deny their firms' needs for cooperative strategies because they do not believe that the benefits of joint ventures justify the efforts needed to run them effectively. But the success rate for joint venture in mature economies is improving as more firms apply creative solutions to their old ideas concerning what joint ventures can do, how long ventures must last, who must be in charge, and what each partner should bring to the party.

A balanced assessment of the value of cooperative strategies should suggest that these skills are well worth learning, particularly if joint ventures will become increasingly important as a means of keeping abreast of competition. Joint ventures are a way to manage transitions; they are an intermediate step on the way to something else. Joint ventures should always offer greater opportunities for profitability because there are greater scale economies, integration economies, and other cost savings from pooled resources that can reduce the total cost of doing business. From a wealth-creating owner's perspective, the well-managed joint venture should always offer an opportunity to improve upon what firms can do alone.

Joint ventures (and other forms of cooperation) are an important change in the way that firms do business. They require a different approach to management by virtue of their complexity. If managed skillfully, joint ventures can offer sponsoring firms wider range of strategic flexibility than they can hope to develop by going it alone.

Appendix I

Research Methodology for Studying Joint Ventures

Target firms were selected from announcements of joint ventures and non-equity cooperative agreements contained in *Mergers & Acquisitions* and from a special compilation of joint ventures contained in the *Funk & Scott Index of Corporate Change.* Questionnaires requesting details of these announcements were mailed to 2,094 sponsoring firms, yielding 884 usable responses, of which 492 (or 55 per cent) concerned joint ventures.

Information concerning competitive conditions at the time of the joint venture's announcement (and thereafter) was gathered from archival sources that included annual reports, other financial disclosure documents, trade journals and trade association publications, and government documents.

Background papers were prepared for 26 industries, and experienced executives within them were interviewed. Information concerning joint venture formation, operation and termination was refined through 444 field interviews and telephone conversations. Results were corroborated through additional interviews, follow-up letters, and revisions to the background papers and interview transcripts. Data were gathered for statistical analyses from 197 of the 492 respondents with experience in using joint ventures.

Marketing Organization and Personnel

In today's complex world, it is impossible to have a truly effective universal global manager. That is the thesis of the initial paper in this section, "What Is a Global Manager?" The authors argue that three groups of specialists are required in global companies: business managers, country managers, and functional managers. At corporate headquarters, top executives coordinate the complex interactions between the three groups.

"Global Competitors: Some Criteria for Success" summarizes the core characteristics of successful global competitors. The author delineates 10 key elements of effective competitors. Success requires the formulation of an integrated worldwide business strategy supported by major investments, the utilization of technological innovation from world sources, deployment of high-quality professional managers, and close review of the nuances of political change in markets where they compete.

In recent years women have been pursuing graduate management education in increasing numbers. As part of their professional careers, these women exhibit growing interest in international business experiences. While the United States is arguably one of the most assertively egalitarian nations in the world, professional women have encountered major barriers in being selected for international assignments.

"Women: World-Class Managers for Global Competition" documents the scope of these barriers with mail survey data plus personal interviews with women expatriates who were interviewed while on assignment in Asia and after returning to North America. Overwhelmingly, these expatriates characterized their overseas experiences as successful despite the reluctance of their firms to post them abroad. The authors believe that women have social and communication skills that qualify them as prime candidates for international assignments. The gender of these professional managers should not be a deterrent to success.

What Is a Global Manager?

Christopher A. Bartlett and Sumantra Ghoshal. *Chistopher A. Bartlett is a professor at the Harvard Business School and chairman of the International Senior Management Program there. Sumantra Ghoshal is a professor and Digital Equipment Research Fellow at INSEAD in Fountainebleau, France. Recent books by Bartlett and Goshal include* Managing Across Borders: The Transnational Solution *(Harvard Business School Press, 1989) and* Transnational Management: Text, Cases, and Readings in Cross-Border Management *(Irwin, 1992).*

In the early stages of its drive overseas, Corning Glass hired an American ex-ambassador to head up its international division. He had excellent contacts in the governments of many nations and could converse in several languages, but he was less familiar with Corning and its businesses. In contrast, ITT decided to set up a massive educational program to "globalize" all managers responsible for its worldwide telecommunications business—in essence, to replace its national specialists with global generalists.

Corning and ITT eventually realized they had taken wrong turns. Like many other companies organizing for worldwide operations in recent years, they found that an elite of jet-setters was often difficult to integrate into the corporate mainstream; nor did they need an international team of big-picture overseers to the exclusion of focused experts.

Success in today's international climate—a far cry from only a decade ago—demands highly specialized yet closely linked groups of global business managers, country or regional managers, and worldwide functional managers. This kind of organization characterizes a *transnational* rather than an old-line multinational, international, or global company. Transnationals integrate assets, resources, and diverse people in operating units around the world. Through a flexible management process, in which business, country, and functional managers form a triad of different perspectives that balance one another, transnational companies can build three strategic capabilities:

- global-scale efficiency and competitiveness;
- national-level responsiveness and flexibility; and
- cross-market capacity to leverage learning on a worldwide basis.

While traditional organizations, structured along product or geographic lines, can hone one or another of these capabilities, they cannot cope with the challenge of all three at once. But an emerging group of transnational companies has begun to transform the classic hierarchy of headquarters–subsidiary relationships into an integrated network of specialized yet interdependent units. For many, the greatest constraint in creating such an organization is a severe shortage of executives with the skills, knowledge, and sophistication to operate in a more tightly linked and less classically hierarchical network.

In fact, in the volatile world of transnational corporations, there is no such thing as a universal global manager. Rather, there are three groups of specialists: business managers, country managers, and functional managers. And there are the top executives at corporate headquarters, the leaders who manage the complex interactions between the three—and can identify and develop the talented executives a successful transnational requires.

To build such talent, top management must understand the strategic importance of each specialist. The careers of Leif Johansson of Electrolux, Howard Gottlieb of NEC, and Wahib Zaki of Proctor & Gamble vividly exemplify the specialized yet interdependent roles the three types of global managers play.

The Business Manager: Strategist + Architect + Coordinator

Global business or product-division managers have one overriding responsibility: to further the company's global-scale efficiency and competitiveness. This task requires not only the perspective to recognize opportunities and risks across national and functional boundaries but also the skill to coordinate activities and link capabilities across those barriers. The global business managers' overall goal is to capture the full benefit of integrated worldwide operations.

To be effective, the three roles at the core of a business manager's job are to serve as the strategist for his or her organization, the architect of its worldwide asset and resource configuration, and the coordinator of transactions across national borders. Leif Johansson, now president of Electrolux, the Swedish-based company, played all three roles successfully in his earlier position as head of the household appliance division.

In 1983, when 32-year-old Johansson assumed responsibility for the division, he took over a business that had been built up through more than 100 acquisitions over the previous eight years. By the late 1980s, Electrolux's portfolio included more than 20 brands sold in some 40 countries, with acquisitions continuing throughout the decade. Zanussi, for example, the big Italian manufacturer acquired by Electrolux in 1984, had built a strong market presence based on its reputation for innovation in household and commercial appliances. In addition, Arthur Martin in France and Zoppas in Norway had strong local brand positions but limited innovative capability.

As a result of these acquisitions, Electrolux had accumulated a patchwork quilt of companies, each with a different product portfolio, market position, and competitive situation. Johansson soon recognized the need for an overall strategy to coordinate and integrate his dispersed operations.

Talks with national marketing managers quickly convinced him that dropping local brands and standardizing around a few high-volume regional and global products would be unwise. He agreed with the local managers that their national brands were vital to maintaining consumer loyalty, distribution leverage, and competitive flexibility in markets that they saw fragmenting into more and more segments. But Johansson also understood the views of his division staff members, who pointed to the many similarities in product characteristics and consumer needs in the various markets. The division staff was certain Electrolux could use this advantage to cut across markets and increase competitiveness.

Johansson led a strategy review with a task force of product-division staff and national marketing managers. While the task force confirmed the marketing managers' notion of growing segmentation, its broader perspective enabled Johansson to see a convergence of segments across national markets. Their closer analysis also refined management's understanding of local market needs, concluding that consumers perceived "localness" mainly in terms of how a product was sold (distribution through local channels, promotion in local media, use of local brand names) instead of how it was designed or what features it offered.

From this analysis, Johansson fashioned a product-market strategy that identified two full-line regional brands to be promoted and supported in all European markets. He positioned the Electrolux brand to respond to the cross-market segment for high prestige (customers characterized as "conservatives"), while the Zanussi brand would fill the segment where innovative products were key (for "trendsetters").

The local brands were clustered in the other two market segments pinpointed in the analysis: "yuppies" ("young and aggressive" urban professionals) and "environmentalists" ("warm and friendly" people interested in basic-value products). The new strategy provided Electrolux with localized brands that responded to the needs of these consumer groups. At the same time, the company captured the efficiencies possible by standardizing the basic chassis and components of these local-brand products, turning them out in high volume in specialized regional plants.

So, by tracking product and market trends across borders, Leif Johansson captured valuable global-scale efficiencies while reaping the benefits of a flexible response to national market fragmentation. What's more, though he took on the leadership role as a strategist, Johansson never assumed he alone had the understanding or the ability to form a global appliance strategy; he relied heavily on both corporate and local managers. Indeed, Johansson continued to solicit guidance on strategy through a council of country managers called the 1992 Group and through a set of product councils made up of functional managers.

In fact, the global business manager's responsibility for the distribution of crucial assets and resources is closely tied to shaping an integrated strategy. While he or she often relies on the input of regional and functional heads, the business manager is still the architect who usually initiates and leads the debate on where major plants, technical centers, and sales offices should be located—and which facilities should be closed.

The obvious political delicacy of such debates is not the only factor that makes simple economic analysis inadequate. Within every operating unit there exists a pool of skills and capabilities that may have taken a lot of time and investment to build up. The global business manager has to achieve the most efficient distribution of assets and resources while protecting and leveraging the competence at hand. Electrolux's household appliance division had more than 200 plants and a bewildering array of technical centers and development groups in many countries. It was clear to Johansson that he had to rationalize this infrastructure.

He began by setting a policy for the household appliance division that would avoid concentration of facilities in one country or region, even in its Scandinavian home base. At the same time, Johansson wanted to specialize the division's development and manufacturing infrastructure on a "one product, one facility" basis. He was determined to allocate important development and manufacturing tasks to each of the company's major markets. In trying to optimize robustness and flexibility in the long term rather than minimize short-term costs, Johansson recognized that a specialized yet dispersed system would be less vulnerable to exchange-rate fluctuations and political uncertainties. This setup also tapped local managerial and technical resources, thereby reducing dependence on the small pool of skilled labor and management in Sweden.

Instead of closing old plants, Johansson insisted on upgrading and tailoring existing facilities, whenever possible. In addition to averting political fallout and organizational trauma, Electrolux would then retain valuable know-how and bypass the startup problems of building from scratch. An outstanding example of this approach is Zanussi's Porcia plant in Italy, which Electrolux turned into the world's largest washing machine plant. After a massive $150-million investment, the Porcia plant now produces 1.5 million units a year.

Although acquisition-fueled growth often leads to redundancy and overcapacity, it can also bring new resources and strengths. Instead of wiping out the division's diversity through homogenization or centralization, Johansson decided to leverage it by matching each unit's responsibilities with its particular competence. Because of the Scandinavian flair for modular design, he assigned the integrated kitchen-system business to Electrolux's Swedish and Finnish units. He acknowledged Porcia's experience in component production by consolidating design and production of compressors there. Johansson's reshaping of assets and resources not only enhanced scale economies and operational flexibility but also boosted morale by giving operating units the opportunity to leverage their distinctive competences beyond their local markets.

Newly developed business strategies obviously need coordination. In practice, the specialization of assets and resources swells the flow of products and components among national units, requiring a firm hand to synchronize and control that flow. For organizations whose operations have become more dispersed and specialized at the same time that their strategies have become more connected and integrated, coordination across borders is a tough challenge. Business managers must fashion a repertoire of approaches and tools, from simple centralized control to management of exceptions identified through formal policies to indirect management via informal communication channels.

Leif Johansson coordinated product flow—across his 35 national sales units and 29 regional sourcing facilities—by establishing broad sourcing policies and transfer-pricing ranges that set limits but left negotiations to internal suppliers and customers. For instance, each sales unit could negotiate a transfer price with its internal source for a certain product in a set range that was usually valid for a year. If the negotiations moved outside that range, the companies had to check with headquarters. As a coordinator, Johansson led the deliberations that defined the logic and philosophy of the parameters; but he stepped back and let individual unit managers run their own organizations, except when a matter went beyond policy limits.

In contrast, coordination of business strategy in Johansson's division was managed through teams that cut across the formal hierarchy. Instead of centralizing, he relied on managers to share the responsibility for monitoring implementation and resolving problems through teams. To protect the image and positioning of his regional brands—Electrolux and Zanussi—he set up a brand-coordination group for each. Group members came from the sales companies in key countries, and the chairperson was a corporate marketing executive. Both groups were responsible for building a coherent, pan-European strategy for the brand they represented.

To rationalize the various product strategies across Europe, Johansson created product-line boards to oversee these strategies and to exploit any synergies. Each product line had its own board made up of the corporate product-line manager, who was chair, and his or her product managers. The Quattro 500 refrigerator-freezer, which was designed in Italy, built in Finland, and marketed in Sweden, was one example of how these boards could successfully integrate product strategy.

In addition, the 1992 Group periodically reviewed the division's overall results, kept an eye on its manufacturing and marketing infrastructure, and supervised major development programs and investment projects. Capturing the symbolic value of 1992 in its name, the group was chaired by Johansson himself and included business managers from Italy, the United Kingdom, Spain, the United States, France, Switzerland, and Sweden.

Indeed, coordination probably takes up more of the global business manager's time than any other aspect of the job. This role requires that a manager have great administrative and interpersonal skills to ensure that coordination and integration don't deteriorate into heavy-handed control.

Many traditional multinational companies have made the mistake of automatically anointing their home country product-division managers with the title of global business manager. Sophisticated transnational companies, however, have long since separated the notions of coordination and centralization, looking for business leadership from their best units, wherever they may be located. For example, Asea Brown Boveri, the Swiss-headquartered electrical engineering corporation, has tried to leverage the strengths of its operating companies and exploit their location in critical markets by putting its business managers wherever strategic and organizational dimensions coincide. In Asea Brown Boveri's power-transmission business, the manager for switch gear is located in Sweden, the manager for power transformers is in Germany, the manager for distribution transformers is in Norway, and the manager for electric metering is in the United States.

Even well-established multinationals with a tradition of tight central control are changing their tack. The head of IBM's telecommunications business recently moved her division headquarters to London, not only to situate the command center closer to the booming European market for computer networking but also "to give us a different perspective on all our markets."

The Country Manager: Sensor + Builder + Contributor

The building blocks for most worldwide companies are their national subsidiaries. If the global business manager's main objective is to achieve global-scale efficiency and competitiveness, the national subsidiary manager's is to be sensitive and responsive to the local market. Country managers play the pivotal role not only in meeting local customer needs but also in satisfying the host government's requirements and defending their company's market positions against local and external competitors.

The need for local flexibility often puts the country manager in conflict with the global business manager. But in a successful transnational like Electrolux, negotiation can resolve these differences. In this era of intense competition around the world, companies cannot afford to permit a subsidiary manager to defend parochial interests as "king of the country."

Nor should headquarters allow national subsidiaries to become the battleground for corporate holy wars fought in the name of globalization. In many companies, their national subsidiaries are hothouses of entrepreneurship and innovation—homes for valuable resources and capabilities that must be nurtured, not constrained or cut off. The subsidiaries of Philips, for one, have consistently led product development: in television, the company's first color TV was developed in Canada, the first stereo model in Australia, and the first teletext in the United Kingdom. Unilever's national subsidiaries have also been innovative in product-marketing strategy: Germany created the campaign for Snuggle (a fabric softener); Finland developed Timotei (an herbal shampoo); and South Africa launched Impulse (a body perfume).

In fact, effective country managers play three vital roles: the sensor and interpreter of local opportunities and threats, the builder of local resources and capabilities, and the contributor to and active participant in global strategy. Howard Gottlieb's experience as general manager of NEC's switching-systems subsidiary in the United States illustrates the importance of all three tasks.

As a sensor, the country manager must be good at gathering and sifting information, interpreting the implications, and predicting a range of feasible outcomes. More important, this manager has the difficult task of conveying the importance of such intelligence to people higher up, especially those whose perceptions may be dimmed by distance or even ethnocentric bias. Today, when information gathered locally increasingly applies to other regions or even globally, communicating effectively is crucial. Consumer trends in one country often spread to another; technologies developed in a leading-edge environment can have global significance; a competitor's local market testing may signal a wider strategy; and national legislative initiatives in areas like deregulation and environmental protection tend to spill across borders.

Gottlieb's contribution to NEC's understanding of changes in the telecommunications market demonstrates how a good sensor can connect local intelligence with global strategy. In the late 1980s, Gottlieb was assigned to build the U.S. market for NEAX 61, a widely acclaimed digital telecom switch designed by the parent company in Japan. Although it was technologically sophisticated, early sales didn't meet expectations.

His local-market background and contacts led Gottlieb to a quick diagnosis of the problem. NEC had designed the switch to meet the needs of NTT, the Japanese telephone monopoly, and it lacked many features U.S. customers wanted. For one thing, its software didn't incorporate the protocol conversions necessary for distributing revenues among the many U.S. companies that might handle a single long-distance phone call. Nor could the switch handle revenue-enhancing features like "call waiting" and "call forwarding," which were vital high-margin items in the competitive, deregulated American market.

In translating the needs of his U.S. division to the parent company NEC, Gottlieb had a formidable task. To convince his superiors in Japan that redesigning NEAX 61 was necessary, he had to bridge two cultures and penetrate the subtleties of the parent company's Japanese-dominated management processes. And he had to instill a sense of urgency in several corporate management groups, varying his pitches to appeal to the interests of each. For instance, Gottlieb convinced the engineering department that the NEAX 61 switch had been underdesigned for the U.S. market and the marketing department that time was short because the Bell operating companies were calling for quotes.

A transnational's greater access to the scarcest of all corporate resources, human capability, is a definite advantage when compared with strictly local companies—or old-line multinationals, for that matter. Scores of companies like IBM, Merck, and Procter & Gamble have recognized the value of harvesting advanced (and often less expensive) scientific expertise by upgrading local development labs into global centers of technical excellence.

Other companies have built up and leveraged their overseas human resources in different ways. Cummins Engine, for example, has set up its highly skilled but surprisingly low-cost Indian engineering group as a worldwide drafting resource; American Airlines's Barbados operation does much of the corporate clerical work; and Becton Dickinson, a large hospital supply company, has given its Belgian subsidiary pan-European responsibility for managing distribution and logistics.

Indeed, the burden of identifying, developing, and leveraging such national resources and capabilities falls on country managers. Howard Gottlieb, after convincing Tokyo that the United States would be an important market for NEC's global digital-switch design, persuaded headquarters to permit his new engineering group to take part early on in the product development of the next generation switch—the NEAX 61 E. He sent teams of engineers to Japan to work with the original designers; and, to verify his engineers' judgments, Gottlieb invited the designers to visit his customers in the United States. These exchanges not only raised the sensitivity of NEC's Japan-based engineers to U.S. market needs but also significantly increased their respect for their American colleagues. Equally important, the U.S. unit's morale rose.

As a builder, Gottlieb used this mutual confidence as the foundation for creating a software-development capability that would become a big corporate asset. Skilled software engineers, very scarce in Japan, were widely available in the United States. Gottlieb's first move was to put together a small software team to support local projects. Though its resources were limited, the group turned out a number of innovations, including a remote software-patching capability that later became part of the 61 E switch design. The credibility he won at headquarters allowed Gottlieb to expand his design engineering group from 10 to more than 50 people within two years, supporting developments not only in North America but also eventually in Asia.

In many transnationals, access to strategically important information—and control over strategically important assets—has catapulted country managers into a much more central role. As links to local markets, they are no longer mere implementers of programs and policies shaped at headquarters; many have gained some influence over the way their organizations make important strategic and operational decisions. In most of today's truly transnational companies, country managers and their chief local subordinates often participate in new product-development committees, product-marketing task forces, and global-strategy conferences. Even at the once impenetrable annual top management meetings, national subsidiary managers may present their views and defend their interests before senior corporate and domestic executives—a scenario that would have been unthinkable even a decade ago.

Of course, the historic position of most national units of worldwide companies has been that of the implementer of strategy from headquarters. Because the parent company's accepted objectives are the outcome of discussion and negotiation involving numerous units, divisions, and national subsidiaries, sometimes a country manager must carry out a strategy that directly conflicts with what he or she has lobbied for in vain.

But a diverse and dispersed worldwide organization, with subsidiaries that control many of the vital development, production, and marketing resources, can no longer allow the time-honored "king of the country" to decide how, when, and even whether his or her national unit will implement a particular strategic initiative. The decision made by the North American subsidiary of Philips to outsource its VCRs from a Japanese competitor rather than the parent company is one of the most notorious instances of how a local "king" can undermine global strategy.

At NEC, Howard Gottlieb spent about 60% of his time on customer relations and probing the market and about 30% managing the Tokyo interface. His ability to understand and interpret the global strategic implications of U.S. market needs—and the software-development group he built from scratch—allowed him to take part in NEC's ongoing strategy debate. As a result, Gottlieb changed his division's role from implementer of corporate strategy to active contributor in designing that strategy.

The Functional Manager: Scanner + Cross-Pollinator + Champion

While global business managers and country managers have come into their own, functional specialists have yet to gain the recognition due them in many traditional multinational companies. Relegated to support-staff roles, excluded from important meetings, and even dismissed as unnecessary overhead, functional managers are often given little chance to participate in, let alone contribute to, the corporate mainstream's global activity. In some cases, top management has allowed staff functions to become a warehouse for corporate misfits or a graveyard for managerial has-beens. Yet at a time when information, knowledge, and expertise have become more specialized, an organization can gain huge benefits by linking its technical, manufacturing, marketing, human resources, and financial experts worldwide.

Given that today's transnationals face the strategic challenge of resolving the conflicts implicit in achieving global competitiveness, national responsiveness, and worldwide learning, business and country managers must take primary responsibility for the first two capabilities. But the third is the functional manager's province.

Building an organization that can use learning to create and spread innovations requires the skill to transfer specialized knowledge while also connecting scarce resources and capabilities across national borders. To achieve this important objective, functional managers must scan for specialized information worldwide, "cross-pollinate" leading-edge knowledge and best practice, and champion innovations that may offer transnational opportunities and applications.

Most innovation starts, of course, when managers perceive a particular opportunity or market threat, such as an emerging consumer trend, a revolutionary technological development, a bold competitive move, or a pending government regulation. When any of these flags pops up around the world, it may seem unimportant to corporate headquarters if viewed in isolation. But when a functional manager acts as a scanner, with the expertise and perspective to detect trends and move knowledge across boundaries, he or she can transform piecemeal information into strategic intelligence.

In sophisticated transnationals, senior functional executives serve as linchpins, connecting their areas of specialization throughout the organization. Using informal networks, they create channels for communicating specialized information and repositories for proprietary knowledge. Through such links, Electrolux marketing managers first identified the emergence of cross-market segments and NEC's technical managers were alerted to the shift from analog to digital switching technology.

In the same manner, Wahib Zaki of Procter & Gamble's European operations disapproved of P&G's high-walled organizational structures, which isolated and insulated the technical development carried out in each subsidiary's lab. When Zaki became head of R&D in Europe, he decided to break down some walls. In his new job, he was ideally placed to become a scanner and cross-pollinator. He formed European technical teams and ran a series of conferences in which like-minded experts from various countries could exchange information and build informal communication networks.

Still, Zaki needed more ammunition to combat the isolation, defensiveness, and "not invented here" attitude in each research center. He distributed staff among the European technical center in Brussels and the development groups of P&G's subsidiaries. He used his staff teams to help clarify the particular role of each national technical manager and to specialize activities that had been duplicated on a country-by-country basis with little transfer of accumulated knowledge.

In response to competitive threats from rivals Unilever, Henkel, and Colgate-Palmolive—and to a perceived consumer trend—P&G's European headquarters asked the Brussels-based research center to develop a new liquid laundry detergent. By that time, Zaki had on hand a technical team that had built up relationships among its members so that it formed a close-knit network of intelligence and product expertise.

The team drew the product profile necessary for healthy sales in multiple markets with diverse needs. In several European markets, powdered detergents contained enzymes to break down protein-based stains, and the new liquid detergent would have to accomplish the same thing. In some markets, a bleach substitute was important; in others, hard water presented the toughest challenge; while in several countries, environmental concerns limited the use of phosphates. Moreover, the new detergent had to be effective in large-capacity, top-loading machines, as well as in the small front-loading machines common in Europe.

Zaki's team developed a method that made enzymes stable in liquid form (a new technique that was later patented), a bleach substitute effective at low temperatures, a fatty acid that yielded good water-softening performance without phosphates, and a suds-suppressant that worked in front-loading machines (so bubbles wouldn't ooze out the door). By integrating resources and expertise, Zaki cross-pollinated best practice for a new product.

The R&D group was so successful that the European headquarters adopted the use of teams for its management of the new brand launch. P&G's first European brand team pooled the knowledge and expertise of brand managers from seven subsidiaries to draft a launch program and marketing strategy for the new liquid detergent Vizir, which ensured its triumphant rollout in seven countries in six months. P&G's homework enabled it to come up with a product that responded to European needs, while Colgate-Palmolive was forced to withdraw its liquid detergent brand, Axion—which had been designed in the United States and wasn't tailored for Europe—after an 18-month market test.

As a reward for his performance in Europe, Wahib Zaki was transferred to Procter & Gamble's Cincinnati corporate headquarters as a senior vice president of R&D. He found that researchers there were working on improved builders (the ingredients that break down dirt) for a new liquid laundry detergent to be launched in the United States. In addition, the international technology-coordination group was working the P&G's Japanese subsidiary to formulate a liquid detergent surfactant (the ingredient that removes greasy stains) that would be effective in the cold-water washes common in Japanese households, where laundry is often done in used bath water. Neither group had shared its findings or new ideas with the other, and neither had incorporated the numerous breakthroughs represented by Vizir—despite the evidence that consumer needs, market trends, competitive challenges, and regulatory requirements were all spreading across national borders.

Playing the role of champion, Zaki decided to use this development process to demonstrate the benefits of coordinating P&G's sensitivity and responsiveness to diverse consumer needs around the world. He formed a team drawn from three technical groups (one in Brussels and two in the United States) to turn out a world liquid laundry detergent. The team analyzed the trends, generated product specifications, and brought together dispersed technical knowledge and expertise, which culminated in one of Procter & Gamble's most successful product launches ever. Sold as Liquid Tide in the United States, Liquid Cheer in Japan, and Liquid Ariel in Europe, the product was P&G's first rollout on such a global scale.

As Zaki continued to strengthen cross-border technology links through other projects, Procter & Gamble gradually converted its far-flung sensing and response resources into an integrated learning organization. By scanning for new developments, cross-pollinating best practice, and championing innovations with transnational applications, Wahib Zaki, a superlative functional manager, helped create an organization that could both develop demonstrably better new products and roll them out at a rapid pace around the world.

The Corporate Manager: Leader + Talent Scout + Developer

Clearly, there is no single model for the global manager. Neither the old-line international specialist nor the most recent global generalist can cope with the complexities of cross-border strategies. Indeed, the dynamism of today's marketplace calls for managers with diverse skills. Responsibility for worldwide operations belongs to senior business, country, and functional executives who focus on the intense interchanges and subtle negotiations required. In contrast, those in middle management and front-line jobs need well-defined responsibilities, a clear understanding of their oganization's transnational mission, and a sense of accountability—but few of the distractions senior negotiators must shoulder.

Meanwhile, corporate managers integrate these many levels of responsibility, playing perhaps the most vital role in transnational management. The corporate manager not only leads in the broadest sense; he or she also identifies and develops talented business, country, and functional managers—and balances the negotiations among the three. It's up to corporate managers to promote strong managerial specialists like Johansson, Gottlieb, and Zaki, those individuals who can translate company strategy into effective operations around the world.

Successful corporate managers like Floris Maljers, co-chairman of Unilever, have made the recruitment, training, and development of promising executives a top priority. By the 1980s, with Maljers as chairman, Unilever had a clear policy of rotating managers through various jobs and moving them around the world, especially early in their careers. Unilever was one of the first transnationals to have a strong pool of specialized yet interdependent senior managers, drawn from throughout its diverse organization.

But while most companies require only a few truly transnational managers to implement cross-border strategies, the particular qualities necessary for such positions remain in short supply. According to Maljers, it is this limitation in human resources—*not* unreliable or inadequate sources of capital—that has become the biggest constraint in most globalization efforts.

Locating such individuals is difficult under any circumstances, but corporate managers greatly improve the odds when their search broadens from a focus on home-country managers to incorporate the worldwide pool of executives in their organization. Because transnationals operate in many countries, they have access to a wide range of managerial talent. Yet such access—like information on local market trends or consumer needs that should cross organizational boundaries—is often an underexploited assets.

As a first step, senior executives can identify those in the organization with the potential for developing the skills and perspectives demanded of global managers. Such individuals must have a broad, nonparochial view of the company and its operations yet a deep understanding of their own business, country, or functional tasks. Obviously even many otherwise talented managers in an organization aren't capable of such a combination of flexibility and commitment to specific interests, especially when it comes to cross-border coordination and integration. Top management may have to track the careers of promising executives over a number of years before deciding whether to give them senior responsibilities. At Unilever, for example, the company maintains four development lists that indicate both the level of each manager and his or her potential. The progress of managers on the top "A1" list is tracked by Unilever's Special Committee, which includes the two chairmen.

Once corporate managers identify the talent, they have the duty to develop it. They must provide opportunities for achievement that allow business, country, and functional managers to handle negotiations in a worldwide context. A company's ability to identify individuals with potential, legitimize their diversity, and integrate them into the organization's corporate decisions is the single clearest indicator that the corporate leader is a true global manager—and that the company itself is a true transnational.

Global Competitors: Some Criteria for Success

James F. Bolt. *James F. Bolt is founder and president of Executive Development Associates, a consulting firm based in Westport, Conn., that specializes in the development of customized executive education programs. This paper was developed for use in an executive education program designed for a Fortune 200-sized firm aimed at preparing its executives for global competition.*

No set of criteria has ever been developed to assess what makes a corporation a successful global competitor. No magic formula or convenient road map for the international executive exists. That conclusion, reached after conversations with experts at academic and research organizations, is hardly surprising. No two global competitors are alike. The combinations of management styles, products, markets, strategies, countries, plants, and myriad other factors are virtually limitless. What works for one corporation might be disastrous for another. Some years ago, Pieter Kuin, then vice-chancellor of the International Academy of Management and a past president of Unilever, N.V., wrote in the *Harvard Business Review* that "the magic of multinational management lies not so much in perfection of methods or excellence of men as in developing *respect* for other nationalities and cultures and for the *determination* to succeed in foreign markets."[1] This observation is as valid today is it was more than a decade ago.

Yet, some broad criteria, the ones most-often cited as necessary for a successful global competitor and most-often evident in large corporations that have succeeded in the global business arena, can be isolated. These criteria can be broken, somewhat arbitrarily, into ten separate statements.

1. Successful global competitors perceive themselves as multinational, understand that perception's implications for their business, and are led by a management that is comfortable in the world arena.

If there is one key criterion for successful global competitors, it is this one. In virtually all corporations, global success is dependent on a corporate leadership that sees the world as a global village. Successful leaders all seem to understand that there are two distinct breeds of multinational corporations—the multi-domestic corporation and the truly global corporation.

The multi-domestic company pursues different strategies in each of its foreign markets. Each overseas subsidiary is essentially autonomous. In this type of arrangement, "a company's management tries to operate effectively across a series of worldwide positions with diverse product requirements, growth rates, competitive environments and political risks. The company prefers that local managers do whatever is necessary to succeed in R&D, production, marketing, and distribution, but holds them responsible for results."[2]

In effect, the company competes with local competitors on a market-by-market basis. Many successful American companies operate this way. Procter & Gamble in household products, Honeywell in controls, Alcoa in aluminum, and General Foods in consumer foods, for example.

The global company, on the other hand, pits its entire resources against its competition in a highly integrated way. Foreign subsidiaries and divisions are largely interdependent in both operations and strategy. Says one expert:

> In a global business, management competes worldwide against a small number of other multinationals in the world market. Strategy is centralized, and various aspects of operations are decentralized or centralized as economics and effectiveness dictate. The company seeks to respond to particular local market needs, while avoiding a compromise of efficiency of the overall global system.[3]

Many multinationals are moving in this direction. Those who have already arrived include IBM in computers; Caterpillar in large construction equipment; Timex, Seiko and Citizen in watches; and General Electric, Siemens, and Mitsubishi in heavy electrical equipment.

The important thing is that successful global competitors have carefully considered the difference between multi-domestic and global. Corporate leadership can show that it is serious by making sure that someone at the top is knowledgeable about and comfortable in the world arena. A Conference Board study some years ago found that the companies with foreign operations doing well invariably were led by chief executive officers who were "uncommonly well read, well traveled and took a very broad view of the world and the role of business in that world."[4]

2. Successful global competitions develop an integrated and innovative global strategy that makes it very difficult and costly for other companies to compete.

Perhaps the best evidence for this criterion was amassed by Thomas Hout, Vice President of the Boston Consulting Group; Michael E. Porter, professor at the Harvard Business School; and Eileen Rudden, Manager of the Boston Consulting Group's Boston office.[5]

The three authors argue that most successful global competitors "perceive competition as global and formulate strategy on an integrated worldwide basis." They develop "a strategic innovation to change the rules of the competitive game in its particular industry. The innovation acts as a lever to support the development of an integrated global system." The authors cite three cases to illustrate this point—Caterpillar, whose strategic innovation was in manufacturing; L. M. Ericsson, of Sweden, whose breakthrough was in technology; and Honda, where the innovative strategic thrust was in marketing.

The common denominator is that each of these highly successful global competitors altered the dynamics of its industry and pulled away from the other major players. Caterpillar achieved economies of scale through commonality of design. The competition could not match Caterpillar in either costs or profits. Consequently, the competition could not make the large investments required to catch up.

Ericsson, by developing a unique modular technology, created a cost advantage. Its global strategy turned electronics from a threat to Ericsson into a barrier to its competitors.

Honda unlocked the potential for economies of scale in production, marketing, and distribution through aggressive marketing. The only thing left for the competition was the small-volume specialty market.

In each case, there existed within the industry the potential for a worldwide system of products and markets. A company with an integrated global strategy (something all three companies had) could exploit that situation, which these three did.

3. Successful global competitors aggressively and effectively implement their worldwide strategy, and they back it with large investments.

That leads conveniently to our third criterion for success on the global stage: the determination and the ability to back the strategy with substantial long-term investments. The Caterpillar experience is a case in point. Caterpillar is the only Western company that matches its major competitor, Komatsu, in capital spending per employee. In fact, Caterpillar's overall capital spending is more than three times that of its Japanese competitor. And Caterpillar does not divert resources into other businesses or otherwise dissipate its financial advantage. With almost single-minded purpose, it pumps huge proportions of its profits back into its base business and dares the competition to try to match it.[6]

In *Competitive Strategy: Techniques for Analyzing Industries and Competitors,* Michael E. Porter points out that successful global competitors not only are willing to invest heavily, but (perhaps even more important) they are also willing to wait long periods of time before these investments pay off.[7] Porter adds that implementing such strategies takes time. The result, he says, can be major investment projects with zero or even a negative return on investment for periods that would be thought unacceptable a few years ago.

A case in point is the experience of Xerox Corporation. In the mid-1970s, the company's Japanese subsidiary, Fuji Xerox, fell on hard times. The oil shock hurt

Japan's economy severely. Ricoh introduced a highly successful line of inexpensive, low-volume copiers. Xerox sales in the Far East plummeted, and the partnership reached a crossroads.

Had Xerox considered Fuji Xerox to be a basically Japanese subsidiary doing business only in that part of the world, it probably would have opted to scale back operations. But Xerox took a global approach, realizing that the partnership could be a powerful weapon in its worldwide battle with the Japanese. The company made large investments in technology, product development, and manufacturing capacity.

Although the investment did not become profitable for five years, it has since paid for itself many times over. Fuji Xerox is now the leader in its market. More important, Fuji Xerox supplies low-volume copiers for Xerox to market in much of the world—including the United States.[8]

4. Successful global competitors understand that technological innovation is no longer confined to the United States, and they have developed systems for tapping technological innovation abroad.

Another key factor in the battle for supremacy in international markets is technological innovation. In the late 1950s, more than 80 percent of the world's major innovations came from the United States. That percentage has steadily declined, and today less than half of the world's innovations can legitimately lay claim to the "made in America" slogan.[9]

How do the more successful global competitors respond to challenges on the worldwide technological front? Robert Ronstadt, associate professor of management at Babson College, and Robert J. Kramer, project director at Business International Corporation, sought to find answers in their landmark study three years ago. Their analysis was based on interviews with more than 50 American, European, and Japanese managers of multinationals, a mail survey of 240 corporations around the world, and data covering more than 100 foreign-based R&D investments.[10]

Their data suggests that those companies who have done well in the international technological arena do some or all of the following:

- **Scanning and monitoring.** This includes reading journals and patent reports; meeting with foreign scientists and technical experts through conferences and seminars, and serving on advisory panels and study teams sponsored by the government and professional associations.

- **Connections with academia and research organizations.** Successful global enterprises actively pursue work-related projects with foreign academics, and they often make these associations with faculty members formal by using consulting agreements.

- **Programs to increase the company's visibility.** Many technological bonanzas go to companies with the right reputation. One common method of attracting attention is providing information to computer data banks that facilitate communication between prospective purchasers and vendors.

- **Cooperative research projects.** Many successful global enterprises enter into research projects with each other to broaden their contacts, reduce expenses, diminish the risk for each partner, or forestall the market entry of a competitor.

- **Acquiring or merging with foreign companies that have extensive innovative capabilities.** The two researchers found that the acquired company's innovative capability is not the primary reason for the merger. Nevertheless, significant technology may be acquired that can enhance an organization's ability to innovate abroad.

- **Acquisition of external technology by licensing.** A corporation may license in a technological innovation from another country, license out its own technology to others in the hope of getting access to improvements made by the licensee, or exchange its technology for another company's by cross-licensing.

Ronstadt and Kramer emphasize that "company owned R&D labs located overseas provide the best opportunities for managers to internationalize their scanning operations and obtain foreign innovations or new technology. . . . U.S. multinationals have spent untold time and money establishing extensive operations and resources abroad. The time has come for greater utilization of these resources—not just as sales outlets for domestic or foreign products but as sources of innovation in technology and management that will aid in the resurgence of U.S. industry and the world economy."[11]

5. Successful global competitors operate as though the world were one large market, not a series of individual countries.

Daniel J. Boorstin characterizes our age as driven by "the Republic of technology whose supreme law . . . is convergence, the tendency for everything to become more like everything else."[12] In business, this trend has pushed markets toward global commonality. Successful global competitors have embraced the new phenomenon; they now sell standardized products in similar ways across increasingly larger portions of the planet.

Writing in the *Harvard Business Review,* Theodore Levitt says:

> The transforming winds whipped up by the proletarianization of communication and travel enter every crevice of life. Commercially, nothing confirms this as much as the success of McDonald's from the Champs Elysees to the Ginza, of Coca-Cola in Bahrain and Pepsi-Cola in Moscow.[13]

The implications for all global competitors—consumer-goods producers and high-technology companies—are profound. American corporations, in particular, have built their success largely on giving their customers *precisely* what they say they want, even if that means higher costs. That philosophy has led many corporations to overreact to different national and regional tastes, preferences, and needs. There is powerful new evidence that this road is doomed to failure. Lynn W. Phillips, Dae Chang, and Robert D. Buzzell, in their as yet unpublished Harvard Business School working paper, document that this notion of being all things to all people dramatically drives cost up and quality down.[14]

Successful global competitors, on the other hand, have remembered Henry Ford and the Model T. They stress simplification and standardization. Much of the success of the Japanese is based on this approach. It is significant that Japanese companies operate almost entirely without the kinds of marketing departments and market research so prevalent in the West. John F. Welch, Jr., the chairman of General Electric, puts it this way: "The Japanese have discovered the one great thing all markets have in common—

an overwhelming desire for dependable, world-standard modernity in all things, at aggressively low prices."[15]

This new reality is difficult for many American managers to comprehend. It runs counter to the methods that they have been taught and that have proved successful in the past. But companies that do not adapt to the new global realities lose to those that do adapt.

"Corporations geared to this new reality," according to Levitt, "benefit from enormous economies of scale in production, distribution, marketing, and management. By translating these benefits into reduced world prices, they can decimate competitors that still live in the disabling grip of old assumptions about how the world works."[16]

6. Successful global competitors have developed an organizational structure that is well thought out and unique.

Of all the subjects our research covered, the question of organization was the most vexing. There is simply no clear answer. If one examines the organization charts of most global competitors, it becomes clear that "there is no one way in which international companies organize their domestic and foreign activities."[17]

Most United States-based multinationals have at one time or another established international divisions to manage their overseas operations. As they grew, these same companies also sprouted several product-oriented divisions at home. In many cases, the result was a structural conflict between the geographic orientation of the international division and the product orientation of the domestic operations.

It is not surprising, therefore, that the international division has proved to be a transitory organization for many global competitors. As growth mushroomed in these companies, many of them abandoned their international divisions as such. J. William Widing, Jr., one-time vice president of Harbridge House, has identified three alternative structures that are most often used:

- Worldwide product divisions, each responsible for selling its own products throughout the world.
- Divisions responsible for all products sold within a certain geographic area.
- A matrix consisting of either of these arrangements with a centralized functional staff, or a combination of area operations and worldwide product management.[18]

The literature on organization and multinationals is extensive. Much of it is opinion and conjecture. Still, some broad guidelines do emerge. Among them are the following:

- Corporations using the worldwide-product-division structure have grown about 50 percent faster than those using the area-division structure. Whether there is a cause-and-effect relationship is debatable, but there seems to be at least a preference for worldwide product divisions in situations involving rapid growth.
- The greater the diversity of product lines, the more likely it is that an American company will manage its foreign business through worldwide product divisions.
- The availability and depth of management resources is also important. The international division provides the easiest way to concentrate scarce managerial expertise for international operations. Worldwide product divisions provide the widest scope and latitude for individual decision making and risk taking. A geographic structure requires a large number of broad-gauged managers with considerable general management experience.

- Geographic divisions can concentrate most efficiently on developing close relationships with national and local governments. Worldwide product divisions do not fare as well in this regard.

- Although the relative cost of operation varies, the matrix form tends to be the most expensive. It focuses extra attention on functional considerations and thus requires more staff personnel. Area divisions usually have the leanest staffs and, therefore, the lowest operating costs.

These and other guidelines are just that. "Organizational structure and reporting relationships present subtle problems for a global strategy," according to Hout, Porter, and Rudden. "Effective strategy control argues for a central product-line organization. Effective local responsiveness argues for a geographic organization with local autonomy. A global strategy argues for a product-line organization that has the ultimate authority, because without it the company cannot gain system-wide benefits. Nevertheless, the company still must balance product and area needs. In short, there is no simple solution."[19]

Echoing this sentiment, Levitt writes that "there is no one reliably right answer—no one formula by which to get it. . . . What works well for one company or one place may fail for another in precisely the same place, depending on the capabilities, histories, regulations, resources, and even the cultures of both."[20]

7. Successful global competitors have a system that keeps them informed of political changes abroad and the implications for their business.

The world in which multinationals must operate is fraught with risk. Says Thomas A. Shreeve, a political analyst with the United States Department of State and a research associate at the Harvard Business School, "A new political party in power—or the new head of an old governing coalition—can easily decide to change the fundamentals for operating and investing by altering the regulation of licensing, for example, or so changing foreign equity restrictions, local participation requirements, or the basis of corporate taxation."[21]

Most successful global competitors have some system that attempts to read the winds of political change. As early as 1969, Gulf Oil formed an international policy analysis unit to keep senior executives apprised of political developments on a daily

Reproduced with permission from General Motors Corp.

basis. Dow Chemical, General Motors, IBM, most large banks, and virtually all oil companies have people dedicated exclusively to political analysis.

But few multinational corporations seem satisfied with the way their systems function. Part of the problem is that most systems are designed to track dramatic events, such as the overthrow of a government or the taking of hostages. These types of events do not need to be monitored because they quickly become public knowledge, and because once they happen there is little the corporation can do. Corporations need systems that pay attention to small details that, when pieced together, provide advance information of what is likely to happen.

8. Successful global competitors recognize the need to make their management team international and have a system in place to accomplish the goal.
Most senior executives in large multinational corporations profess their commitment to bringing foreign managers into their inner circles. Yet, when one looks at the hierarchies of large global competitors, "the gap between their stated aims to have truly multinational executive personnel and the practice of actually having them is great. . . . And in the face of pressures from without and from within, it is becoming obvious that solving this human problem incurred in developing MNCs will be critical to the success of the enterprise in question."[22]

The crux of the problem seems to be a matter of attitude, not policy. For example, in determining who will receive incentive compensation, who will get a foreign assignment or who has high management potential, the home-country executive is likely to rely on his own perception of who is the most competent and trustworthy, his compatriot down the hall or a foreigner thousands of miles away who he rarely sees. Given that choice, a variety of cultural and social biases often dictate the selection.[23]

Not surprisingly, then, most multinationals have a poor track record in integrating their management teams. One survey of 150 of the largest global competitors found that barely 1 percent of the senior headquarters positions were filled by foreign nationals, despite the fact that the average income generated by overseas operations was at least 20 percent of the companies' total income.[24]

Another survey found that "executives we questioned in several successful companies closely associate paying greater attention to foreign nationals with improvement of corporate performance."[25] This same study, which was conducted by Howard V. Perlmutter, chairman of the Multinational Enterprise Unit at the Wharton School of Business, and Daniel A. Heenan, then vice president for manpower planning and development at First National City Bank, identified four critical areas which need attention.

The first is headquarters and foreign service assignments. As one observer puts it: "They all love to talk about the Brazilian in London and the Indian in Belgium. But all that talk is for public consumption . . . the ultimate responsibilities still lie with the Americans." Those who have broken this pattern usually have done so with a two-pronged approach: a manpower-resource planning system that is dedicated to identifying and moving people across national boundaries, and a company godfather who is responsible for a handful of senior foreign executives. This role is normally reserved "for a person of considerable stature and influence in headquarters whose role is to ensure that people on overseas assignments are neither forgotten nor allowed to neglect the

growth of their functional skills."[26] IBM is the most-often-cited example of this two-pronged approach.

The second critical area that needs to be addressed is compensation. Even today, only a handful of global competitors maintain truly multinational compensation programs for their managers. In many instances, foreigners with identical credentials and jobs receive one-half to one-third the total compensation package of their American counterparts. One expert explains the problem this way: "Without pay practices that offer equal monetary incentives for all managers, companies run the risk of not attracting and retaining high quality professionals."[27]

A third key area is managerial inventories. The manpower lists from which candidates are assigned to key overseas and headquarters positions tend to be exclusive. While American expatriate managers are invariably included in these worldwide inventories, foreign nationals are not. If the manpower-planning lists contain only Americans, it should not be surprising that only Americans are found in prime international positions.

The fourth key area is performance-appraisal techniques. The Perlmutter–Heenan study found that the most successful global competitors had "adopted a worldwide performance appraisal system that assesses a manager's functional and administrative abilities plus his skills to operate in a global setting. The MNC executives we talked with suggest blending the best evaluative techniques from all over the world."[28]

Our research indicated that many multinationals who now have relatively good foreign representation among their senior executives began that process by placing a foreign manager in the hierarchy of personnel. That person tends to act as a catalyst and conscience when key operating assignments open up.

9. Successful global competitors give their outside directors an active role in the affairs of the company.

More and more multinationals are appointing local nationals to their foreign subsidiaries' boards of directors. Much of this trend is in response to foreign legislation that demands it. But the more sophisticated and successful global competitors realize that "the outside director who is also a citizen of the host country can play an important role in developing an atmosphere of trust in which they will be able to operate with a reasonable degree of freedom."[29]

Writing in the *Harvard Business Review,* Samuel C. Johnson and Richard M. Thomson offer some sage advice: "The chief executive of the MNC should not delegate to others the selection of outside directors and the invitation to serve. His personal involvement will indicate the significance he ascribes to the position."[30]

Tasks the outside board members perform that are most often considered positive contributions include the following:

- Becoming familiar with the operation of the business and keeping abreast of local economic, legal, and political developments, so he or she can anticipate changes affecting business not only in his or her home country, but in the entire region or continent as well.

- Making certain that the subsidiary follows objectives and policies established by the parent and communicated to him or her through memoranda and discussions with the corporation's officers.
- Counseling the parent company regarding local compensation standards, trade-union regulations, and other personnel matters.
- Periodically appraising the performance of the subsidiary's management (primarily through review of its financial reports).
- Counseling the subsidiary's management on its relations with financial institutions, governmental bodies, and the public.
- Offering advice and counsel on broad political and social trends that may have a significant impact on long-range planning.
- Helping to insure that the subsidiary behaves as a responsible member of the community.

Successful global competitors seem to have two things in common in their use of local nationals on their boards of directors. First, they are selected by the chief executive officer and have his confidence, support, and trust. Second, they are not just figureheads. They are effective contributors. Says one source: "If he (the outside director) is doing his job properly, he will have his hands full. The onus is on him to be vigorous and informed. The responsibility of the parent company is to listen and react."[31]

10. Successful global competitors are well-managed.

This may seem self-evident, but it bears mention. It would be foolhardy to think that a corporation could successfully expand beyond its own national borders if its domestic management house was not in order.

There are numerous ways, of course, to assess a corporation's management effectiveness—not the least of which are healthy financial statements that show relative freedom from debt and consistent revenue and profit growth. We have elected to include here for the basis of discussion the eight attributes which best-selling authors Thomas J. Peters and Robert H. Waterman, Jr. used in *In Search of Excellence.* They are:

- **A bias for action.** While these companies may be analytical in their approach to decision making, they are not paralyzed.
- **Close to the customer.** They learn from the people they serve. Many of the innovative companies got their best product ideas from customers. That comes from listening, intently and regularly.
- **Autonomy and entrepreneurship.** The innovative companies develop many leaders and many innovators throughout the organization.
- **Productivity through people.** Excellent companies treat the rank and file as the root of quality and productivity gain. They do not have we/they labor attitudes.
- **Hands-on, value driven.** The basic philosophy of an organization has far more to do with its achievements then do technological or economic resources.
- **Stick to the knitting.** The odds for excellent performance strongly favor those companies that stay reasonably close to business they know.

- **Simple form, lean staff.** The underlying structural forms in the excellent companies are elegantly simple. Top-level staffs are lean; it is not uncommon to find a corporate staff of fewer than 100 people running multi-billion-dollar enterprises.
- **Simultaneous loose-tight properties.** The excellent companies are both centralized and decentralized.[32]

Any corporation seeking to expand globally would do well to ask itself how well it measures up to the Peters–Waterman criteria for excellence. At the very least, they provide some useful food for thought.

As we said at the outset, these ten criteria for global successful competitiveness are somewhat arbitrary. Each reader could probably add to the list or refine it. Nevertheless, any corporation seeking to expand globally can help itself succeed by taking inventory against these ten criteria.

References

1. Pieter Kuin, "The Magic of Multinational Management," *Harvard Business Review,* November–December 1972, p. 89.

2. Thomas Hout, Michael E. Porter, and Eileen Rudden, "How Global Companies Win out," *Harvard Business Review,* September–October, 1982, p. 103.

3. Hout, Porter, and Rudden (see note 2).

4. *Organization and Central of International Operations* (New York: The Conference Board, 1978), p. 8.

5. Hout, Porter, and Rudden (see note 2), pp. 98–108.

6. Hout, Porter, and Rudden (see note 2).

7. Michael E. Porter, *Competitive Strategy: Techniques for Analyzing Industries and Competitors* (New York: Free Press, 1980).

8. Jeff Kennard, "An American Expatriate's View of Japanese Business," *Agenda: A Journal for Xerox Managers,* March 1983, pp. 4–10.

9. Robert Ronstadt and Robert J. Kramer. "Getting the Most Out of Innovation Abroad," *Harvard Business Review,* March–April 1982, p. 94.

10. Ronstadt and Kramer (see note 9), pp. 94–99.

11. Ronstadt and Kramer (see note 9), p. 99.

12. Daniel J. Boorstin, *The Americans,* (New York: Random House, 1973), p. 284.

13. Theodore Levitt, "The Globalization of Markets," *Harvard Business Review,* May–June 1983, p. 93.

14. Lynn W. Phillips, Dae Chang, and Robert D. Buzzell, "Product Quality: Cost Production and Business Performance—A Test of Some Key Hypotheses," *Harvard Business School Working Paper No. 83–13.*

15. John F. Welch, Jr., *Speech to the Foreign Policy Association,* New York City, November 28, 1983.

16. Levitt (see note 13), p. 92.

17. Joseph La Palombara and Stephen Blank, *Multinational Corporations in Comparative Perspective* (New York: The Conference Board, 1979).

18. J. William Widing, Jr., "Reorganizing Your Worldwide Business," *Harvard Business Review,* May–June 1973, p. 156.

19. Hout, Porter, and Rudden (see note 2), p. 107.

20. Levitt (see note 13), p. 100.

21. Thomas W. Shreeve, "Be Prepared for Political Changes Abroad," *Harvard Business Review,* July–August 1984, p. 111.

22. Howard V. Perlmutter and David A. Heenan, "How Multinational Should Your Top Managers Be?" *Harvard Business Review,* November–December 1974, p. 123.

23. Howard V. Perlmutter, "The Tortuous Evolution of the Multinational Corporation," *Columbia Journal of World Business,* January–February 1969, p. 9.

24. Perlmutter and Heenan (see note 22), p. 124.

25. Perlmutter and Heenan (see note 22), p. 124.

26. David A. Heenan, "The Corporate Expatriate," *Columbia Journal of World Business,* May–June 1970, p. 49.

27. David Young, "Fair Compensation for Expatriates," *Harvard Business Review,* July–August 1973, p. 117.

28. Perlmutter and Heenan (see note 22), p. 130.

29. *The Changing Role of the International Executive,* The Conference Board, SBP No. 119, p. 18.

30. Samuel C. Johnson and Richard M. Thomson, "Active Role for Outside Directors of Foreign Subsidiaries," *Harvard Business Review,* September–October 1974, p. 14.

31. Johnson and Thomson (see note 30), p. 14.

32. Thomas J. Peters and Robert H. Waterman, Jr., *In Search of Excellence* (New York: Harper & Row, 1982), pp. 89–318.

Women: World-Class Managers for Global Competition

Mariann Jelinek and Nancy J. Adler. *Mariann Jelinek is associate professor of management policy at the Weatherhead School of Management, Case Western Reserve University, where she was tenured in 1987. Previously she held appointments at the State University of New York-Albany, McGill University, The Amos Tuck School at Dartmouth College, Worcester Polytechnic Institute, and Bentley College. She was educated at the University of California at Berkeley, where she received her Ph.D., and at Harvard Business School, where she earned her DBA.*

Dr. Jelinek's teaching assignments include policy and advanced manufacturing technology and corporate strategy, and her research and consultation interests center on the effective management of innovation, strategic change, and manufacturing technology. The author of six books, including Institutionalizing Innovation *(Praeger, 1979), and more than 20 articles (among them "Plan for Economies of Scope," an article with Joel Goldhar, which appeared in the* Harvard Business Review*), Professor Jelinek's latest book* Patterns of Innovation *(with C. B. Schoonhoven), which deals with the management of high-technology firms, will be published by Basil Blackwell.*

Nancy J. Adler is a professor of organization behavior and cross-cultural management at McGill University. Her research focuses on international transition issues (entry, cultural shock, adaptation, and re-entry), managing in multinational environments (including negotiation, culturally synergistic problem solving, and team building) and, most recently, on women in international management. She has consulted to corporations and government organizations on projects in Asia, Africa, North and South America, and Europe. Dr. Adler has written numerous articles on cross-cultural management and produced a film on the role of the spouse in international moves, entitled A Portable Life. *Her book,* International Dimensions of Organizational Behavior, *was published in late 1987.*

It is no secret that business faces an environment radically different from that of even a few years ago, the result of increasingly global competition. The Commerce Department estimated in 1984 that in U.S. domestic markets some 70% of firms faced "significant foreign competition," up from only 25% a decade previously. By 1987, the chairman of

This paper draws extensively on research reported in Nancy J. Adler's "Pacific Basin Managers: A *Gaijin*, Not a Woman." *Human Resource Management* 26:2 (Summer 1987), pp. 169–192. The interested reader may find a more complete account of the research there; reprints may be ordered from John Wiley & Sons, Periodicals Division Reprints, 605 Third Avenue, New York, NY 10158; (212) 692-6025.

EXHIBIT 1   Focus on Competition

When Focus of Competition Is:

Local or Regional	National	Export sales	Sourcing or manufacturing abroad	Global business arena

Managerial Focus Is:

Home country focus		←	→	Global focus

Managerial Relations Tend to:

Depend on own views, own resources, "Lone Ranger"		←	→	Depend on a variety or views, others' resources "team spirit"

Personnel Policy Emphasizes:

Home country personnel policy	Some expatriates	Some foreign nationals	Multicultural and multinational personnel policy
	←	→	

Thus North American companies in locally oriented competition tend to focus on the home country, with managers generally depending on their own resources and home country personnel. In contrast, a firm sourcing or manufacturing abroad is much more likely to have an international focus and to have moved toward seeing a variety of views and others' resources as essential to team-spirited management, deliberately using multicultural personnel.

---

the Foreign Trade Council estimated the figure to be 80%. In 1984, U.S. exports to markets abroad accounted for 12.5% of the GNP; by comparison, Japan's 1984 exports were 16.5% of its GNP.[1] Global competition is serious, it is pervasive, and it is here to stay.

More stringent competition is an important result of this global economy. (See Exhibit 1.) Because markets are increasingly interconnected, "world-class standards" are quickly becoming the norm. New products developed in one market are soon visible in markets around the world, as initial producers use their advantage, forcing competitors to meet the challenge or lose market share. Product life-cycle has been reduced by 75%. Product development and worldwide marketing are becoming almost simultaneous. For example, recent developments in superconductivity, initially demonstrated in Zurich, were quickly replicated in The People's Republic of China, the United States, Japan, and in Europe. Similarly, U.S. automobile customers quickly learned to demand improved quality from U.S. automakers, once the Japanese autos had demonstrated it. Standards for price, performance, and quality have been permanently altered worldwide.

New Competitive Strategies

The problem for Americans, who historically have enjoyed the luxury of a large and generally protected domestic market, is how to respond to all these changes. Global competition means much more than sending excess domestic production abroad. Today, many formerly eager markets are contested by well-entrenched locals or by competing foreign companies. The new competition does not involve simply sales abroad, or even foreign competitors here and abroad. Rather, its varied faces are likely to include the following circumstances—none of them typical for most business even a few years ago:

- Extensive on-going operations within foreign countries. This means a vastly increased demand for sophisticated, multiculturally adept managers. Foreign operations and markets are neither temporary or trivial, but essential for long-term survival.

- Strategic management across cultures. Global management necessitates working in numerous countries at once. Yet what works at home, or in one foreign country, may not work in another. Cultural norms and expectations differ. Sensitivity and finesse must be brought to bear on strategic intentions, to transliterate them sensibly. In many cases a straight translation probably will not do, whether of a product name or the more complicated matters of market attack, strategic intent, or mission.

- More foreign personnel throughout the company. Foreign personnel are both necessary and valuable to a firm seeking to penetrate global markets. Even within the United States a broadly pluralistic personnel pool with substantial ethnic identity—most notably Hispanic and Asian, but others as well—belies the mythical "melting pot" image of prior decades. Effectively managing multicultural organization dynamics is a prerequisite for success today and tomorrow, not merely an indulgent gesture or a legal requirement.

- More joint ventures and strategic alliances to gain access to new technology, new markets or processes, and to share costs and lower risk. Indeed, not only are U.S. firms increasingly becoming involved in joint ventures with foreign firms, but more and more the U.S. firm is not the dominant partner. Today, "we" often need "them" as much as or more than "they" need "us." Thus, cross-cultural management is becoming increasingly critical to success—even survival.

Each of these new competitive strategies demands new skills. Improved ability to communicate across profound differences in approach and expectations, assumptions and beliefs—to say nothing of languages—is key. Because culturally based beliefs, perceptions, expectations, assumptions, and behaviors are deeply held, they are especially sensitive issues, requiring exceptional tact. (See Exhibit 2.)

In short, managing globally calls upon an array of cross-cultural skills not readily at hand for most American managers, and not widely taught in most American business schools. To address these nontraditional problems we suggest a nontraditional resource: women managers. Our case is not based on altruism, nor equal opportunity under the law, nor even fairness, although all of these should be mentioned. Our case is based on the pragmatic self-interest of firms facing a challenging global environment.

But can women make it, especially in foreign cultures that presumably do not consider women men's equals? Won't they be ignored, mistreated, or intimidated? Shouldn't we respect foreign countries' cultural norms—even if they appear discrimina-

---

EXHIBIT 2   Some Alternative Values Orientations

	Culture A	*Culture B*	*Culture C*
Individuals seen as:	Good	Both good and evil	Evil
World is:	To be conquered	Lived with in harmony	To be endured
Human relations center on:	Individuals	Extended groups	Hierarchical groups
Time orientation:	Future	Present	Past
Action basis is:	Free will and facts	Cultural or social norms	Biological or theological

Adapted from ideas in Nancy J. Adler and Mariann Jelinek, "Is 'Organization Culture' Culture Bound?", *Human Resource Management* 25:1 (Spring 1986), 73–90; as based on F. Kluckhohn and F.L. Strodbeck, *Variations in Values Orientations* (Evanston, IL: Row, Peterson, 1969).

---

tory to us? And do American women managers really want to take on this challenge? These are valid concerns, and an emerging body of research suggests some surprising answers. We will look at the special skills women bring to the new global competition and at the results women are achieving abroad, particularly in the fastest growing market in the world, the Pacific Rim. The conclusions may surprise you at first. However, upon reflection, they are utterly comprehensible and point to a powerful resource for a sustainable competitive advantage not readily available or duplicable in other cultures.

A Nontraditional (but Increasingly Valuable) Resource

All cultures differentiate male and female roles, expecting males to behave in certain ways, females in others; anticipating that men will fill certain roles, and women others. In many cultures, including America's, the traditional female role supports many attitudes and behaviors contradictory to those defined as managerial. This has been one of the key barriers to women's entry into managerial careers in the U.S. domestic arena: it operates both in terms of self-selection and differential difficulty.

After two decades of women's liberation movements and despite legislation and education, women remain different from men, even in the United States, arguably one of the most assertively egalitarian countries in the world. Men are still typically raised to be more aggressive and independent; women are still typically raised to be social and more communal.[2] Of course, there have been visible changes in sex roles and norms in North America as elsewhere in the world. There is also substantial debate over how much of the difference in behaviors can be attributed to biology and how much to acculturation factors. Nevertheless, in general, men still tend to be more aggressive than women.[3]

Melvyn Konner makes a strong argument that male aggression has biological roots in puberty, but that thereafter, greater aggression may be a learned and socially reinforced pattern. He notes that males commit the vast majority of violent crimes in every known society. Women, whose biochemistry does not initially encourage aggression at puberty, according to Konner, tend to evolve behavior patterns that emphasize sensitivity, communication skills, community, inclusion, and relationships.[4]

Research on sex roles and managerial characteristics has tended to reinforce the rather limited view of management skills and leadership most of us have acquired, a view identifying leadership with power and potency with adversarial control. In study after study, undergraduates, MBAs, and managers (male and female) in the United States have tended to identify stereotypically "masculine" (aggressive) characteristics as managerial and stereotypically "feminine" (cooperative and communicative) characteristics as unmanagerial.[5]

Yet American women now make up about half the U.S. workforce, and occupy over a quarter (27.9%) of all managerial and administrative positions,[6] although as late as the mid-1980s they represented only 5% of top executives.[7] In international management, women are rarer still, less than 3%.[8] Yet their achievements call into question some widely held beliefs about women and about management. Their unconventional achievements suggest a resource difficult for others to match.

Women Abroad

American women have been pursuing graduate education in management in increasing numbers, now accounting for about 50% of the enrollment at some large state schools and about a third of the enrollment at the most prestigious private schools. More and more are developing an interest in international postings. It would be surprising if they did not, as international business is so clearly "where the action is" in many companies today. To investigate the role of North American women as expatriate managers, Adler undertook a four-part study. In the first part, 686 Canadian and American firms were surveyed to identify the number of women sent abroad. Of 13,338 expatriates, 402 or 3% were female.[9] Other parts of the study sought to explain why so few North American women work abroad. The second part of the study surveyed 1,129 graduating MBAs from seven management schools in the United States, Canada, and Europe. Overall, 84% said they would like an international assignment at some point in their career; there were no significant differences between males and females.[10] While there may have been a difference in the past, today's male and female MBAs appear equally interested in international work and expatriate positions.

One need not depend on opinion or assumptions for assessing women's performance internationally; there are documentary research results. In the working world, women are beginning to be assigned abroad. In another part of the study a survey of 60 major North American multinationals revealed that over half (54%) of the companies were hesitant to post women overseas. This is almost four times as many as were hesitant to select women for domestic assignments (14%). Almost three-quarters of the personnel vice-presidents and managers believed that foreigners are prejudiced against female managers (73%), and that prejudice could render women ineffective in international assignments. Seventy percent believed that women in dual-career marriages would be reluctant to accept a foreign assignment, if not totally disinterested. For certain locations, the personnel executives expressed concern about women's physical safety, hazards involved in traveling in underdeveloped countries and, especially for single women, isolation and potential loneliness.[11] These findings agreed with those of a survey of 100 top managers in *Fortune 500* firms operating overseas: The majority believed that women face overwhelming resistance when seeking management positions in the international division of U.S. firms.[12]

No Welcome Mat?

There is certainly evidence to suggest that women are discriminated against as managers worldwide; women managers in foreign cultures are very rare indeed.[13] In many societies, local women are systematically excluded from managerial roles. Japan offers an excellent case in point; there are almost no Japanese women managers higher than clerical supervisors, especially in large, multinational corporations. In general, Japanese society expects women to work until marriage, quit to raise children, and return, as needed, to low-level and part-time positions after age 40. In Japan, the workplace remains a male domain.[14] Similarly, while women from prominent families in the Philippines can hold influential positions in political and economic life, overall only 2.7% of working women hold administrative or managerial positions in business or government.[15] The picture is similar in India, where women are constitutionally equal to men, but are culturally defined as primarily responsible for the home and children. Women have fared somewhat better in Singapore, where government policy and a booming economy between 1980 and 1983 helped raise women to 17.8% of managerial and administrative positions, up from 7% in 1980.[16] Only recently, and as yet rarely, do women fill managerial positions in these countries.[17]

Women in International Management

Clearly, it is the cultures of these foreign countries that perpetuate this scarcity of indigenous female managers in most Asian countries. If so, how can North American companies successfully send female managers to Japan, Korea, Hong Kong, the Philippines, the People's Republic of China, Singapore, Thailand, India, Pakistan, Malaysia, or Indonesia? Is the experience of these countries' women—most specifically their relative absence from managerial ranks—the best predictor of what expatriate women's experiences will be?

Research results suggest that local women's experience is not a good predictor of North American women's reception, experiences or success in Pacific Rim countries.[18] Indeed, it seems that North American predictions confuse the noun "woman" with the adjective "female," as in "female manager." The research disconfirms a set of North American assumptions predicting how Asians would treat North American female managers based on the North Americans' beliefs concerning Asians' treatment of Asian women. Confusing? Yes. Fundamentally important? Also yes. The problem with these assumptions, and the conclusions they lead to, is that they have been proved wrong.

Fifty-two female expatriate managers were interviewed while on assignment in Asia or after returning from Asia to North America as part of the larger study described earlier. Because of multiple foreign postings, the 52 women represented 61 Asian assignments. The greatest number were posted in Hong Kong (34%), followed by Japan (25%), Singapore (16%), the Philippines and Australia (5% each), Indonesia and Thailand (4% each), and at least one each in Korea, India, Taiwan, and the People's Republic of China. Since most of the women held regional responsibility, they worked throughout Asia, rather than just in their country of foreign residence. The majority of the women were posted abroad by financial institutions (71%), while the others were sent by publishing, petroleum, advertising, film distribution, retail food, electronic appliances, pharmaceuticals, office equipment, sporting goods, and soaps and cosmetics firms, and service industries (including accounting, law, executive search, and computers).

On average, the women's expatriate assignments lasted two and a half years, ranging from six months to six years. Salaries in 1983, before benefits, varied from US $27,000 to US $54,000 and averaged US $34,500. The women supervised from zero to 25 subordinates, with the average being 4.6. Titles and levels varied considerably; some held very junior positions (such as trainee and assistant account manager), while others held quite senior positions (including one regional vice-president). In no case did a female expatriate hold her company's number-one position in any region or country.

The Expatriate Experience

These expatriates were pioneers. In the majority of cases, the female expatriates were "firsts," with only 10% having followed another woman into her international position. Of the 90% who were first, almost a quarter (22%) represented the first female manager the firm had ever expatriated anywhere; 14% were the first women sent by their firms to Asia, 25% were the first sent to the country in question, and 20% were the first women abroad in their specific job. Clearly, neither the women nor their companies had the luxury of role models; there were no previous patterns to follow. With the exception of a few major New York-based financial institutions, both women expatriates and their firms found themselves experimenting, with no ready guides for action or for estimating the likelihood of success.

The companies decided to send women managers to Asia only after a process that might be described as "education." In more than four out of five cases (83%), it was the woman herself who initially introduced the idea of an international assignment to her boss and company. For only six women (11%) had the company first suggested it, while in the remaining three cases (6%) the suggestion was mutual.

The women used a number of strategies to "educate" their companies. Many women explored the possibility of an expatriate assignment during their initial job interview, and simply turned down firms that were totally against the idea. In other cases, women informally introduced the idea to their bosses and continued to mention it "at appropriate moments" until the assignment finally materialized. A few women formally applied for a number of expatriate positions before finally being selected. Some women described themselves as having specifically planned for international careers, primarily by attempting to be in the right place at the right time. For example, one woman predicted that Hong Kong would be her firm's next major business center and arranged to assume responsibility for the Hong Kong desk in New York, leaving the rest of Asia to a male colleague. The strategy paid off: within a year the company sent her, rather than her male colleague, to Hong Kong.

Overall, the women described themselves as having had to encourage their companies and their bosses to consider the possibility of expatriating women in general and themselves in particular. In most cases, they confronted and overcame numerous instances of corporate resistance prior to being sent. For example:

> **(Malaysia)** *"Management assumed that women don't have the physical stamina to survive in the tropics. They claimed I couldn't hack it."*
>
> **(Thailand)** *"My company didn't want to send a woman to 'that horrible part of the world.' They think Bangkok is an excellent place to send single men, but not a woman. They said they would have trouble getting a work permit, which wasn't true."*
>
> **(Japan and Hong Kong)** *"Everyone was more or less curious if it would work. My American boss tried to advise me, 'Don't be upset if it's difficult in Japan and Korea.' The American male manager in Tokyo was also hesitant. Finally the Chinese boss in Hong Kong said, 'We have to try.'"*
>
> **(Japan)** *"Although I was the best qualified, I was not offered the position in Japan until the senior Japanese manager in Tokyo said, 'We are very flexible in Japan'; then they sent me."*

In some instances, the women faced severe company resistance. Their companies sent them abroad only after all potential male candidates for the post had turned it down.

> **(Thailand)** *"Every advance in responsibility is because the Americans had no choice. I've never been chosen over someone else."*
>
> **(Japan)** *"They never would have considered me. But then the financial manager in Tokyo had a heart attack and they had to send someone. So they sent me, on a month's notice, as a temporary until they could find a man to fill the permanent position. It worked out and I stayed."*
>
> **(Hong Kong)** *"After offering me the job, they hesitated. 'Could a woman work with the Chinese?' So my job was defined as temporary, a one-year position to train a Chinese man to replace me. I succeeded and became permanent."*

This cautiousness and reluctance are particularly interesting because they tend to create an unfortunate self-fulfilling prophecy. As a number of women reported, if the company is not convinced you will succeed (and therefore offers you a temporary position rather than a permanent slot, for instance), this will communicate the company's lack of confidence to foreign colleagues and clients as a lack of commitment. Foreigners will then mirror the home company's behavior, also failing to take the temporary representative seriously. Assignments can become substantially more difficult. As one woman in Indonesia put it, "It is very important to clients that I am permanent. It increases trust, and that's crucial."

Outcomes Abroad: Did It Work?

Ninety-seven percent of the North American women described their experiences as successful, despite the difficulties and the reluctance on the part of their firms. While their descriptions were strictly subjective, a number of objective indicators suggest that most assignments did, in fact, succeed. For example, most firms decided to send another woman abroad after experimenting with their first female expatriate. In addition, many companies offered the pioneer woman a second international assignment upon completion of the first. In only two cases did women describe failures: one in Australia and one in Singapore. The Australian experience was the woman's second posting abroad, preceded by a successful Latin American assignment and followed by an equally successful post in Singapore. The second woman's failure in Singapore was her only overseas assignment to date.

Advantages

Perhaps most astonishing was that, above and beyond their descriptions of success, almost half the women (42%) reported that being female served more as an advantage than a disadvantage in their foreign managerial positions. Sixteen percent found being female to have both positive and negative effects, and another 22% saw it as irrelevant or neutral. Only one woman in five found the professional impact of gender to be primarily negative abroad.

The women reported numerous professional advantages to being female. Most frequently, they described the advantage of being highly visible. Foreign clients were curious about them, wanted to meet them, and remembered them after the first meeting. It was therefore somewhat easier for the women than for their male colleagues to gain access to foreign clients' time and attention. Examples of this high visibility included:

> **(Japan)** *"It's the visibility as an expat, and even more as a woman. I stick in their minds. I know I've gotten more business than my two male colleagues. They are extra interested in me."*

> **(Thailand)** *"Being a woman is never a detriment. They remembered me better. Fantastic for a marketing position. It's better working with Asians than with the Dutch, British, or Americans."*

> **(India and Pakistan)** *"In India and Pakistan, being a woman helps for marketing and client contact. I got in to see customers because they had never seen a female banker before. . . . Having a female banker adds value for the client."*

Visibility was not the only advantage. The women also described the advantages of good interpersonal skills and their observation that men could talk more easily about a wider range of topics with women than with other men. This ease of interchange was especially important in cross-cultural situations, where difficulties of nuance and opportunities for miscommunication abound. The women's ease was unforced and quite sincere, since it springs from fundamental socialization patterns. For example:

> **(Indonesia)** *"I often take advantage of being a woman. I'm more supportive than my male colleagues. . . . Clients relax and talk more. And 50% of my effectiveness is based on volunteered information."*

> **(Korea)** *"Women are better at treating men sensitively, and they just like you. One of my Korean clients told me, 'I really enjoyed the lunch and working with you.' "*

> **(Japan)** *"Women are better at putting people at ease. It's easier for a woman to convince a man . . . The traditional woman's role . . . inspires confidence and trust, there's less suspicion, and I'm not threatening. They assumed I must be good if I was sent. They became friends."*

In addition, many of the expatriates described a higher status accorded them in Asia. That status was not denied them as foreign female managers; on the contrary, they often felt that they received special treatment not accorded their male colleagues. Clearly, it was always salient that they were women, but being women did not appear to prohibit them from operating effectively as managers. Moreover, most of the women claimed benefits from a "halo effect." Most of their foreign colleagues and clients had never worked with a female expatriate manager. At the same time, the foreign community was highly aware of how unusual it was for North American firms to send female managers to Asia. Thus, the Asians tended to assume that the women would not have been sent unless they were the best. Therefore, they expected them to be "very, very good."

The problems the women did experience were most often with their home companies rather than their Asian clients. For instance, after obtaining a foreign assignment, some women experienced limits to their opportunities and job scope imposed from back home. More than half the female expatriates described difficulties in persuading their home companies to give them latitude equivalent to that given their male colleagues, especially initially. Some companies, out of concern for the women's safety, limited their travel (and thus their role and often their effectiveness), excluding very remote, rural, and underdeveloped areas.

Other companies made postings temporary, or shorter than the standard male assignment of two to three years. This temporary status was often an important detriment: One Tokyo banker warned potential foreign competitors,

> *"Don't go to Japan unless you're ready to make a long-term commitment in both time and money. It takes many, many years."*[19]

Business relationships and the effective development of "comfort levels" center on personal relationships and reliability over the long haul, especially in Japan, but also in many other "slow clock" cultures that focus on the long term.[20] It takes time to build relationships, and time to learn the culture. The contrast to the infamous American emphasis on "fast tracks" and quarterly results could not be more stark.

Managing foreign clients' and colleagues' initial expectations was a key hurdle for many of the women. Since most Asians had previously never met a North American woman in a managerial position, there was considerable curiosity and ambiguity about her status, level of expertise, authority, and responsibility—and therefore the appropriate form of address and demeanor to be used with her. In these situations, male colleagues' reactions were important. Initial client conversations were often directed at male colleagues, rather than at the newly arrived female manager. Senior male colleagues, particularly from the head office, became important in redirecting the focus of early discussions toward the woman. If well done, smooth, on-going work relationships were quickly established.

Woman as *Gaijin*

Throughout the interviews, one pattern emerged persistently. First and foremost, foreigners are seen as *foreigners*. Like their male colleagues, the female expatriates are categorized as *gaijin* (foreigners) above all, and not locals. Foreign female managers are not expected to act like local women. Thus, the rules governing the behavior of local women, potentially limiting their access to management and managerial responsibilities, do not apply to the expatriate women. The freedom of action this identification carries is substantial.

> **(Japan)** *"The Japanese are very smart: they can tell that I am not Japanese, and they do not expect me to act as a Japanese woman. They will allow and condone behavior from foreign women which would be absolutely unacceptable from their own women."*

As Ranae Hyer, a Tokyo-based vice-president of personnel to the Bank of America's Asia Division said, "Being a foreigner is so weird to the Japanese that the marginal impact of being a woman is nothing. If I were a Japanese woman, I couldn't be doing what I'm doing here. But they know perfectly well that I'm not."[21]

Ultimately, of course, the firm's product or service and the woman herself must be acceptable in business terms. Simply sending a female will not carry an inadequate product or too-costly services:

> **(Hong Kong)** *"There are many expat and foreign women in top positions here. If you are good at what you do, they accept you. One Chinese woman told me, 'Americans are always watching you. One mistake and you are done. Chinese take a while to accept you and then stop testing you.'"*

> **(Hong Kong)** *"It doesn't make any difference if you are blue, green, purple or a frog. If you have the best product at the best price, they'll buy."*

Nevertheless, the incremental advantages of easier communication and visibility, greater facility at relationships *per se,* and greater trust and openness often allow a female expatriate to enjoy significant pluses in a highly competitive atmosphere. Perhaps even more important, women's advantage in succeeding abroad draws on characteristics that have traditionally been a fundamental part of the female role in many cultures—their greater sensitivity, communication skills, and ability to establish rapport. Women need not buy into the competitive game. They can subtly shift the interaction out of the power and dominance modes so typical of business interchange—and so highly dysfunctional in cross-cultural relations—into the sort of cooperative, collaborative modes becoming increasingly important today.

Global competition is a tough game, and "world class" standards are a genuine challenge. Our opponents are worthy foes, strong competitors with numerous advantages. Foreign firms now control state-of-the-art technology, producing top-quality, low-cost products and services that respond quickly and effectively to worldwide clients' rapidly changing needs. Moreover, they often enjoy lower costs for capital and personnel, concerted government support and, in some cases, nontariff, cultural barriers to foreign firms' entry into their domestic markets and long-established relationships with other foreign nations. These advantages must be overcome if North American firms are to prosper in the future. Yet the traditional image of business as warfare and the character of the relationships based on it are increasingly dysfunctional. New modes of "collaborative competition" require traditionally "female" skills. The new competition is so challenging that only the best can stay in the game; we need all the advantages we can muster—including full usage of the best of our resources, male and female.

Alliances and Cooperative Competition

In business from automobiles to semiconductors, insurance and financial services to brokering and steel, competition is very often a matter not only of global enterprise but of collaboration with other firms, foreign as well as domestic. Collaborative competition succeeds by making common cause, by cooperation rather than the independence so typical of North American business behavior. Alliances may be essential to navigating the intricacies of, for instance, nontariff barriers to entering the Japanese market; making the connections required to do business in foreign lands; and especially sharing the increasingly substantial investment required to develop new technologies. Global operations require coordinated activities across the whole spectrum of business activity, not merely sales or marketing. Success rests upon relationships, including those at the most senior executive levels—relationships made far more difficult by cultural differences.

Among the more important differences between North America and the cultures of the Pacific Rim, South America, the Middle East, Africa, and most of Europe are the different cultural "clocks" and norms, particularly regarding the depth and strength of relationships *per se:*

> *"In Germany, your product is most important to your success; in Japan, it is the human relationships you build. Without them, you will not succeed." (Manager of a trading company)[22]*
>
> *"The Japanese don't want people who do a good job but have a bad attitude." (Japanese CEO, automobile industry)[23]*
>
> *". . . strict adherence to personal loyalty is at the core of Japanese concern for people rather than for principles."[24]*

The Bottom Line

In a highly competitive world, especially one generating new norms of business behavior that are counterintuitive to past practice, only the most canny organizations will prosper. Where many competitors form alliances and cooperative ventures, firms that cannot or will not, will operate at a significant disadvantage. They will have to struggle along, "reinventing the wheel" with each new culture.

The sorts of collaborative alliance we have described go far beyond selling or buying abroad. They encompass a broad spectrum of joint activities and common endeavors united by a common thread: the need to negotiate, communicate, cooperate closely over an extended period of time, and build enduring professional relationships across significant intercultural barriers. Such relationships are a very serious matter in other cultures, where longevity and trust accrue together and where the nuances of communication can make or break a deal.

Often, simply because so much of "business" is, in the context of other cultures, really a "relationship," it may be invisible to those North Americans most intent on "business, first and last," and most impatient with "socializing." In many other cultures, what we may see as purely social is for them a crucial testing process—to discover whether a relationship can be created that might be the foundation for doing business. Failure to invest the time and energy needed to build the relationship may well doom any attempt to establish a business arrangement. Without a firm basis of trust, cross-cultural suspicion will find many reasons to feel insulted or challenged by a "rude" foreigner. Failure to comprehend that friendship may have important strategic consequences is equal folly.

Within such a context, women represent a significantly underutilized resource. With good management school credentials and business performance, women are a readily trainable, highly useful source of talent—and the international arena suggests a particularly apt new application for the relationship skills still more highly developed among women than among men today. We believe that women are perfect candidates for expatriate positions and international careers both because they perform so well and because their skills are the skills of the future.

Of course, there are men who are sensitive and skilled in communication; and of course there are women who are insensitive. In general, however, it is women who tend to possess greater sensitivity and relationship skills. Does this mean that these skills cannot be taught to males? On the contrary: the socialization process most women experience is, indeed, a form of "teaching."

Women who are successful abroad can provide role models and coaching for their male colleagues. This means that the women will have to be seen as resources, consulted and relied upon for their special expertise. Business school curricula can also help. Both specialized coursework and cross-cultural elements in all courses can highlight the importance of the international arena. Organizational behavior, organizational development, international management, and cross-cultural experiential activities can all present far broader perspectives than the standard BBA or MBA work focused completely on United States business practices.

American business already faces a global marketplace and global competition. This world is too small and too interconnected for "Lone Ranger" business practices; no single view encompasses all of its reality, and intolerance is a luxury we cannot afford. Traditional U.S. business approaches to competition as battle, which build arm's length business relationships on this basis, seem very risky indeed. Alliances, cooperative efforts, joint ventures, collaborations, and even business more or less as usual but carried out across cultural lines, can be facilitated by skills traditionally thought of as "female."

Global competition is a tough league, so challenging that we must employ all our skills and advantages, and the best of our people. We believe women possess a crucial advantage in social relationship and communication skills. Increasingly, the best of our male managers too will be working to acquire and hone important skills formerly seen as "female"—those centering on relationships, communication, and social sensitivity.

References

1. Discussions of competition are widespread in the business press and current management literature. See, for instance, Thomas J. Peters' "Competition and Compassion," *California Management Review,* 28(4),

Summer 1986, pp. 11–26. Several sources for comparison figures on the U.S. economy and those of our trading partners can be found in Lester Thurow's *The Zero Sum Solution.* New York: Simon and Schuster, 1985; and Bruce Merrifield, U.S. Department of Labor, cited in Lester Thurow's "Why We Can't Have a Wholly Service Economy," *Technology Review,* March 1985.

　　For a thought-provoking look at some of the changes, see also Thomas J. Peters, "A World Turned Upside Down," *Academy of Management Executive,* 1(3), August 1987, 231–242.

2. Carol Gilligan, *In a Different Voice.* Cambridge, MA: Harvard University Press, 1982.

3. See "Women, Men and Leadership: A Critical Review of Assumptions, Practices and Change in the Industrialized Nations," by Jeff Hearn and P. Wendy Parkin, *International Studies of Management & Organization,* v. 16 (Fall-Winter 1986), pp. 33–60, for a useful discussion from a thoughtfully international perspective.

4. Melvyn Konner, *The Tangled Wing: Biological Constraints on the Human Spirit,* New York: Harper Colophon, 1982.

5. Gary N. Powell and D. Anthony Butterfield, "The 'Good Manager': Masculine or Androgynous?" *Academy of Management Journal,* 22: 2 (1979), pp. 395–403.

6. U. S. Department of Labor, 1982.

7. A. Trafford, R. Avery, J. Thornton, J. Carey, J. Galloway, and A. Sanoff, "She's Come a Long Way—Or Has She?" *U.S. News and World Report,* August 6, 1984, 44–51.

8. Nancy J. Adler, "Women in International Management: Where Are They?" *California Management Review,* 26(4), Summer 1984, 78–89.

9. See Footnote 8 above.

10. See Nancy J. Adler's "Do MBAs Want International Careers?" *International Journal of Intercultural Relations,* 10(3), 1986, 277–300; and "Women Do Not Want International Careers and Other Myths About International Management," *Organizational Dynamics,* 13(2), Autumn 1984, 66–79.

11. Nancy J. Adler, "Expecting International Success: Female Managers Overseas," *Columbia Journal of World Business,* 19(3), Fall 1984, 79–85.

12. N. Thal and P. Cateora, "Opportunities for Women in International Business," *Business Horizons,* 22(6), December 1979, 21–27.

13. There are a number of useful resources for information on women in Japanese management, including the following: Tracy Dahlby, "In Japan, Women Don't Climb the Corporate Ladder," *New York Times,* September 18, 1977; M.M. Osako, "Dilemmas of Japanese Professional Women," *Social Problems,* 26, 1978, 15–25; Marguerite Kaminski and Judith Paiz, "Japanese Women in Management: Where Are They?" *Human Resource Management,* 23(3), Fall 1984, 277–292; and Patricia G. Stinhoff and Kazuko Tanaka, "Women Managers in Japan," *International Studies of Management and Organization,* 17(3–4), Fall-Winter 1987, 108–132. Reprinted in Nancy J. Adler and Dafna N. Israeli (Eds.) *Women in Management Worldwide.* Armonk, NY: M. E. Sharpe, 1988.

14. Blas F. Ople, "Working Managers, Elites," *The Human Spectrum of Development.* Manila, the Philippines: Institute for Labor and Management, 1981.

15. Audrey Chan, "Women Managers in Singapore: Citizens for Tomorrow's Economy," in Nancy J. Adler and Dafna N. Israeli (Eds.) *Women in Management Worldwide.* Armonk, NY: M. E. Sharpe, 1988.

16. Nancy J. Adler (Ed.) *Women in Management Worldwide,* special issue of *International Studies of Management and Organization,* 17(3–4). Fall-Winter 1987; and Nancy J. Adler and Dafna N. Israeli (Eds.) *Women in Management Worldwide.* Armonk, NY: M. E. Sharpe, 1988.

17. Nancy J. Adler, "Pacific Basin Managers: A *Gaijin,* Not a Woman," *Human Resource Management,* 26(2), Summer 1987, 169–192.

18. Eric Morgenthaler, "Women of the World: More U.S. Firms Put Females in Key Posts in Foreign Cultures," *Wall Street Journal,* March 16, 1978, 1, 27.

19. Edward T. Hall and Mildred Reed Hall, *Hidden Differences: Doing Business with the Japanese.* Garden City, NY: Anchor Press/Doubleday, 1987.

20. See Footnote 12 above.

21. See Footnote 15 above.

22. See Footnote 16 above.

23. See Footnote 16 above.

24. Mark Zimmerman, *How to Do Business with the Japanese.* New York: Random House, 1985.

PART FOUR

INTERNATIONAL AND GLOBAL MARKETING OPERATIONS

Products and Services

The opening article in this section posits a product positioning framework which enables an international marketer to evaluate how the stereotyping of different nations affects a given position. Stereotyping is interpreted as a way of thinking about people and products from a country that colors beliefs about them. German, American, and Japanese cars are utilized by the authors in this product positioning and perceptual mapping study.

In *Product Development the Japanese Way,* the authors note that the Japanese utilize an incrementalist view of product development that emphasizes continuous technology-rooted improvements in order to make successful products even better for customers. They use the marketplace as an R&D laboratory to gain insights from customers about how to enhance products and services on an ongoing basis.

The key characteristics of services—inseparability, intangibility, perishability, and heterogeneity—make successful international marketing of them much more difficult than for either consumer or industrial goods. The marketing problems associated with these four major characteristics are explored by the author of the third paper in this section. The pressure brought by the United States to reduce tariff and nontariff barriers in services marketing during the recent round of GATT negotiations is a timely aspect of this paper, along with a review of managerial issues in international services marketing.

Marketing Satellites Internationally is a unique commissioned paper on an aspect of international business that has been neglected in marketing literature. It covers the commercial, political, economic, and countertrade characteristics of the international outreach of American technology.

A R T I C L E   3 0

International Product Positioning

Johny K. Johansson and Hans B. Thorelli. *Johny K. Johansson is a Professor in the Department of Marketing and International Business at the Graduate School of Business Administration, University of Washington. Dr. Johansson received his doctorate from the University of California at Berkeley, and currently serves on the editorial boards of both the* Journal of Marketing Research *and the* International Marketing Review. *His recent research includes Japanese companies and their marketing strategies. Hans B. Thorelli is the E. W. Kelley Professor of Business Administration at Indiana University and a Fellow of the Academy of International Business. He led the team which developed the International Operations Simulation (INTOP) at the University of Chicago, and has directed or codirected several research projects in consumer information research and marketplace experience as well as consumer policy in various industrialized and developing nations.*

Introduction

This paper presents a decision model for positioning products in markets abroad. It draws on empirical findings in the international marketing literature which show that a product's country-of-origin and associated stereotypes play an important role in buyer perception and evaluations (Bilkey and Nes, 1982). Since perceptual influences from country stereotyping have the effect of introducing systematic shifts as well as random noise in individuals' beliefs about a product (see Erickson, Johansson and Chao, 1984), the country-of-origin factors directly affect where a product is positioned in consumers' perceptual maps of the product space.

The international product positioning approach proposed here makes it possible to evaluate explicitly how different countries' stereotyping affects a given position. The suggested procedure identifies the means by which the international marketer can measure the relative disadvantage or advantage a product possesses compared to those of competitors from other countries. In the proposed framework, overcoming a relative disadvantage requires a temporary price reduction or some other special inducement. Employing the concept of "efficient choices," the article shows how one can compute the amount by which price has to be reduced to overcome a deficient position.

Thanks for helpful comments are due Professors M. Tamura and T. Kagono and their colleagues at Kobe University, to Professor K. Ikegami and his colleagues at Rissho University in Tokyo and to Bruce Buchanan, Avijit Ghosh, and Robert Shoemaker at New York University. The data collection was supported by funds from the Pacific Rim Project at the Graduate School of Business Administration, University of Washington.
Journal of International Business Studies, Fall 1985.

363

International Perceptual Maps

Product Positioning

The starting point behind the international positioning concept is the notion that an evoked set of products can be described as different bundles of attributes which are capable of generating a stream of benefits to the buyer and user. As part of the targeting of specific market segments the marketer will attempt to develop these attributes so that the benefits generated match the special requirements of that segment. This is a product design problem that involves not only the functional characteristics of the offering but also features such as the packaging, the brand name, and the styling. This design task is generally called "product positioning." Since in the final analysis what matters is the buyer's perception of the benefit-generating attributes, not the "actual" attributes scores (a "fast" car is one that is perceived to be fast, for example, not simply one that possesses good acceleration figures), product positioning is the activity by which a desirable "position in the mind of the customer" is created for the product (Ries and Trout, 1981).

Viewed in a multi-dimensional space (commonly denoted the "perceptual space" or "product space"), a product can be graphically represented as a point defined by its attribute scores. Other products are represented by other points. If the points are close, the products have similar attribute scores and are thus fair substitutes. The further away a point is from another, the less the direct competition tends to be (since they differ

FIGURE 1

Automobile space map with preference vector (United States)

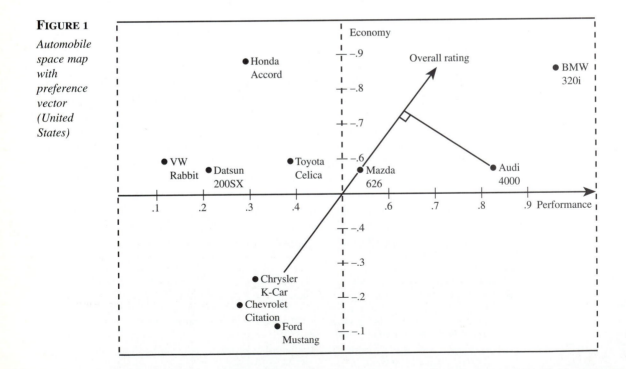

considerably on the salient attributes). The location of a product's point in this product space is its "position." An example of a positioning map is given in Figure 1.

The product space map of automobiles given in the figure is based on American respondents' perception of ten car makes.[1] The positions shown in the map were derived using factor analysis to first reduce an original set of twelve attributes into a more manageable two dimensions and then plot the position using the factor scores of the cars on the two significant factors.

The figure also exhibits the overall rating vector for the automobiles in the U.S. market. This depicts the direction in which the desirability of a car increases, regardless of price. The vector was derived from the respondents' answers to an overall rating question for each car, regressing these on the cars' scores on the two dimensions across all respondents (on the procedure, see Urban and Hauser, 1980, pp. 197–204 and 243–48). By projecting each car's position on to the vector through a perpendicular line (such as the one from Audi) it is possible to identify the top choices in the market segment. Among these respondents, the most desirable cars are the BMW, the Audi and the Accord, while the Citation and the Mustang are tied for last place.

The most advantageous position for the producer is one that yields the highest rating among the target segment. Whether this is a feasible position or not depends mainly on the company's specific production and marketing capabilities (whether customers can be convinced, for example). If the Ford company is able to manufacture the kind of car that can beat the BMW, it should at least consider this option, since this particular group of people seems to favor that type of car. Alternatively, the Ford cars might be aimed at another target segment, or they will have to score better on attributes not accounted for in the product space map. Ford could offer superior service, bank credit, or other "augmenting" benefits which might be instrumental in making the customer buy its car.

The chief inducement to buy a "low-position" (in the sense that it does not represent a top choice in its market segment) product is the *price* paid. From a positioning viewpoint, a low price is the factor which allows less than top brands to be successful in a market. By the same token, the greater the differentials between a top choice like the BMW and its nearest competitor (the Audi 4000 in Figure 1), the greater the price premium that buyers are willing to pay for the BMW. The distance between the brands on the preference vector (where the perpendicular lines fall) is a measure of the degree of price discretion a company can exercise.

The names of the axes, "Performance" and "Economy," are based on the underlying belief scores from the respondents across all the attributes. These are depicted in Figure 2, which is derived from the factor loadings employed in developing the product space (see Urban and Hauser, 1980, pp. 197–99). The direction of the vectors shows which of the two axes reflects more of each attribute (a car's score on an attribute vector can as before be identified by a perpendicular projection). The length of the vectors conveys the degree of importance that the attribute has in determining the space. For example, "color" is not a very important attribute in this product space but "driving comfort" is, and for these cars the ratings of "color" and of "driving comfort" follow the same pattern. For both attributes, BMW rates highest, followed by the Audi, with VW Rabbit and Chevrolet Citation both showing low scores.

The twelve attributes as reflected in the vectors in Figure 2 make it possible to interpret what underlies the low ratings of the American cars. They are apparently seen

FIGURE 2

*Interpreting
the space axes
(United States)*

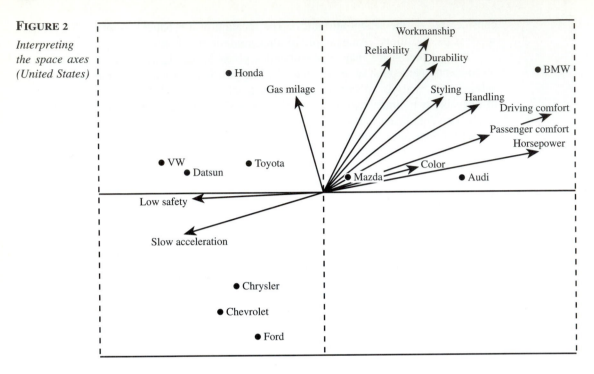

as possessing no attractive features, scoring high only on undesirable attributes such as
"low safety" and generally scoring low on desirable features (especially reliability,
workmanship and durability). Repositioning these cars to make them competitive with
the Japanese models shown might involve more work than can be economically justified.
It might simply be better to offer considerable price discounts; how large those discounts
need to be is discussed in detail below.

Using the attribute vectors to give names to the two axes, it seemed reasonable to
call the horizontal axis "Performance" and the vertical axis "Economy." The first
dimension reflects the driving characteristics (including handling and acceleration) of the
vehicles, the second the usage costs (gas mileage, repairs and depreciation) of the cars.

Country Stereotyping

There are numerous causes of misperceptions of a given product, many lodging in the
unique perceptual biases and selectivity of each individual. There are also factors which
create shared misperceptions among larger segments of a population. One such common
source of misperception in international markets is country stereotyping. There is much
evidence that people in one country tend to have common notions about people in other
countries, and also that these stereotypical evaluations carry over into the realm of
product evaluations (for a recent review, see Bilkey and Nes, 1982). Since these
stereotypes are shared among many people, the international marketer has to take them
into account when positioning the product abroad.

FIGURE 3

Misperceptions:
Actual positions
(squares) versus
perceived
(United States)

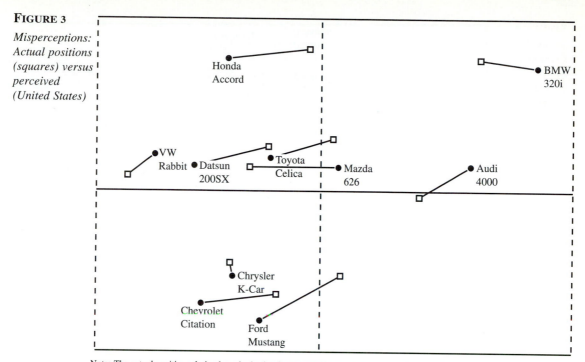

Note: The actual positions derived on the basis of auto magazines and *Consumer Reports* ratings.

What do we mean by "country stereotyping"? In the present context it can be interpreted as a way of thinking about people and products from a country which is "biased" and "colors" our beliefs about them. In the multi-attribute case, the biases show up on the belief ratings people give a foreign brand. Since automobiles represent one case where there are at least some attributes with objectively correct scores available (gas mileage, acceleration, repair records, etc.), some of the biases in the product space map of Figure 1 can be identified. The resulting map of misperceptions is shown in Figure 3. In calculating the "actual" positions, the completely subjective "styling" and "color" attributes were simply set at their mean values for each model across all respondents, while the other true scores were assembled from *Consumer Reports* and auto magazines. Even though these "true" scores also suffer from subjectivity and potential country-of-origin bias, the extensive use of standardized tests and equipment makes *CR* ratings more objective than individuals' own ratings (Maynes, 1976, Chapter 5).

As can be seen in Figure 3, the misperceptions do not actually change the space map drastically, although most cars suffer from some degree of "incorrect" positioning. When interpreting the general tendency evidenced in the map it is necessary to keep in mind the fact that a position more to the northeast is preferable, one towards the southwest leading to lower ratings. Thus, it is clear that these respondents tend to overrate the German cars (the BMW, the Audi, and even the U.S.-built V.W.) while underrating the American and the Japanese cars (the one exception being the slightly

FIGURE 4

*Automobile
space map
with
preference
vector (Japan)*

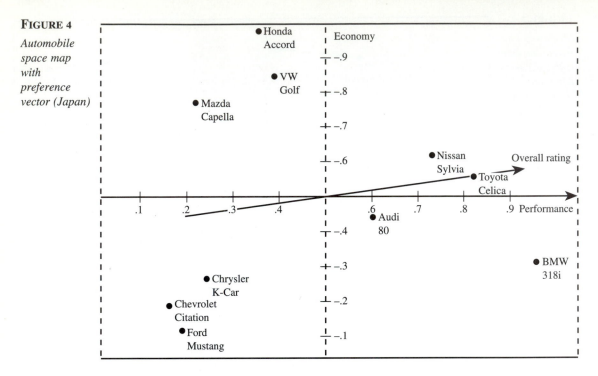

overrated Mazda). Judging from the attributes depicted in Figure 2, the German cars are rated *too* high on driving comfort, handling and acceleration, while the Japanese and American cars are rated *too* low on these factors.

Differences across Countries

The stereotyping of products with a given country-of-origin is generally different across nations (see e.g., Bilkey and Nes, 1982: *Reader's Digest,* 1963). To show how international differences in stereotyping affect the positioning of a product, it is instructive to look at the product space for the automobiles included in Figures 1–3, but for a set of Japanese respondents chosen to match the American cars sampled, see the Appendix.

The product space among the Japanese differs to some extent from the one generated from the United States market (see Figure 4). The anchoring of the three American makes is similar to the early graph, but the directions of the preference vectors have been changed and with them the position of the other makes. BMW is again the car most highly rated but now the Toyota and the Nissan Sylvia (as the Datsun 200SX is known in Japan) are close. Another noteworthy feature of the space map is the relatively large distance between the Toyota and Nissan makes on the one hand and the other two Japanese cars, Honda and Mazda, on the other.

To interpret the space axes, we again turn to the vector projections of the attributes (Figure 5). A comparison with the corresponding figure for the U.S. sample (Figure 2) reveals that the space is largely a rotated version of the previous one. There are some minor differences in the exact attribute locations (the safety vector is here below the acceleration vector, for example) but otherwise the spaces have very similar interpreta-

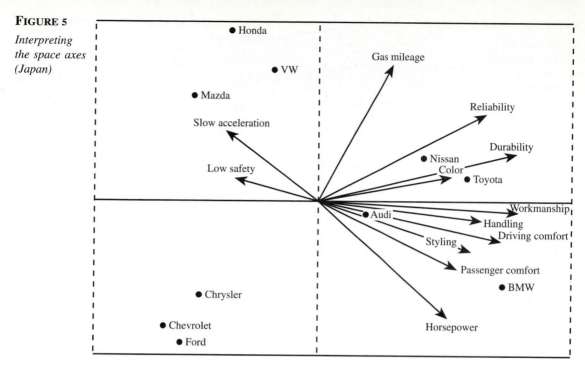

FIGURE 5

Interpreting the space axes (Japan)

tions. The horizontal axis can again be labeled "Performance" and the vertical "Economy." For the Japanese, however, the "Performance" and the "Economy" aspects of the cars seem to be closer together than for the Americans. The attributes are clustered around the horizontal axis, with gas mileage closest to the vertical axis.

As for the actual positions of the cars among the Japanese, we see from the map in Figure 6 that the split between Nissan and Toyota on the one hand and Mazda and Honda on the other seems partly due to misperceptions. It might be that the large shares for the Nissan and Toyota models in the Japanese market confer upon these cars an unwarranted positioning, much closer to the German cars than to their quite similar Japanese compatriots, at least on the attributes incorporated into this map (cf. the similar results reported by Nagashima, 1970). In other respects the misperceptions are quite similar to the ones evinced by the respondents from the United States. The German cars are overrated, while the American cars are generally underrated (viewing a shift from west to east in the map as desirable because of the direction of the rating vector depicted in Figure 4).

Efficient Choices

The Efficient Frontier

One managerial issue in international positioning is the extent to which the misperceptions due to country stereotyping affect the chances that the product will be purchased.

FIGURE 6

*Misperceptions:
Actual positions
(squares) versus
perceived
(Japan)*

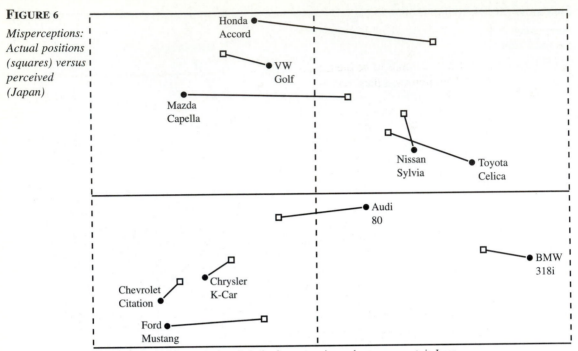

Note: The actual positions derived on the basis of auto magazines and company reports in Japan.

The direction of the biases has already been identified. But to see whether the effect is serious on the final purchases, it becomes necessary also to introduce the *prices* at which these alternatives are made available. An "inferior" (i.e., lowly evaluated) product might still be preferred if its price is very low.

The set of "efficient" choices comprises those evoked alternatives which provide a benefit per dollar others cannot match. These "dominant" choices are located on an "efficient frontier" in the space. They are identified by a calculation which divides each product's factor scores by the relevant price so as to arrive at a "benefit per dollar" figure (for a full discussion of this approach, see Hauser and Gaskin, 1983). The new scores for the two dimensions of the space are then used to develop a new space and position for each car. The relevant prices are given in Table 1, from which the perceived prices (multiplied by 0.0001 for scaling purposes) were used to compute the efficient choices for the American respondents (Figure 7) and the Japanese respondents (Figure 8).

In the figures the choices positioned in the upper northeast corner generally dominate those in the lower part of the quadrant (because of the way the preference vectors were projected in Figures 1 and 4). For example, in Figure 7, the Honda Accord provides more benefit per dollar than the VW Rabbit both in terms of "Performance/$" and "Economy/$." The VW is "dominated" by Accord. The other (less efficient) cars do not offer sufficient benefits per dollar to be competitive with any brand positioned to the northeast of it.

TABLE 1   Dollar Prices*

| Car Model | U.S. Base Price | | | Japanese Base Price | |
	Actual	Perceived		Actual	Perceived
Honda Accord	$ 8,085	$7,620		$ 5,280	$ 5,215
Datsun 200SX	7,839	7,674	Nissan Sylvia	6,520	7,513
Mazda 626	8,245	8,394	Mazda Capella	4,600	5,751
Toyota Celica	8,244	8,711		6,560	7,959
Ford Mustang	7,153	7,016		15,640	11,874
Chevrolet Citation	6,650	6,859		13,120	11,721
Plymouth K-Car	6,858	7,555		15,400	12,536
VW Rabbit	6,849	7,269	VW Golf	8,280	8,140
Audi 4000	11,065	9,411	Audi 80	16,200	11,331
BMW 320i	13,290	11,620	BMW 318i	15,680	13,414

*The Japanese yen has been converted at 250 to the dollar. The *actual* prices reflect the "blue book" prices in the two countries in the spring of 1982. There are of course various levels of discounts offered from these prices, so the *perceived* prices are not necessarily incorrect. In particular, the lower prices perceived for foreign cars in Japan (although still high) are probably due to a "gray market" in unauthorized imports.

FIGURE 7

Efficient choices (U.S.)

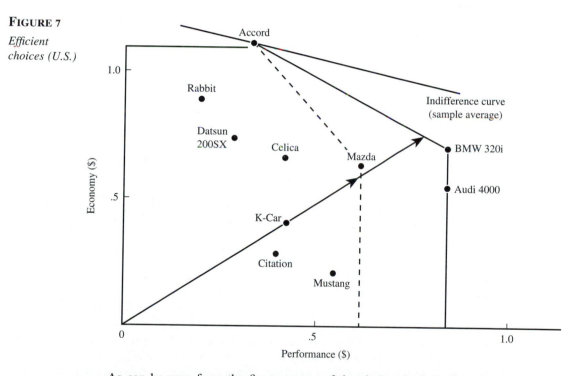

As can be seen from the figures, most of the choices included are dominated by a minority of the cars at this aggregate level. The efficient cars for the Americans, for example, consist of the Honda Accord, the BMW, and the Audi. The other cars cannot offer sufficient benefits per dollar to be competitive in the aggregate, although there may well be niches of customers who perceive the cars differently from the average depicted in the figure.

FIGURE 8

Efficient choices (Japan)

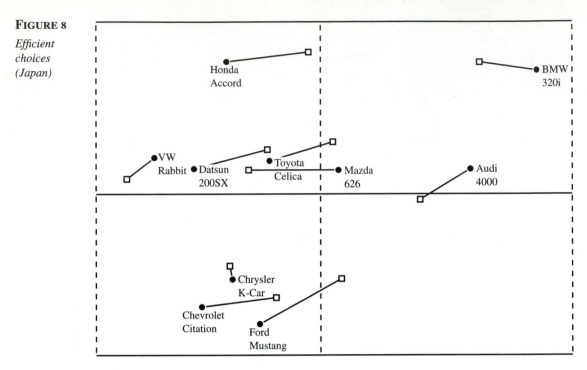

"Efficient" Choices

Generally speaking, the actual choice from among the proffered alternatives will be drawn from the efficient frontier members, based on the customer's preference curve and budget constraint. The preferences can be depicted as indifference curves in the space, based on the importance that the buyer assigns to the component attributes (the ratios of the reported or fitted importance weights can be used—see Hauser and Shugan, 1983). Two such indifference curves based on the fitted preference functions in Figures 1 and 4 are drawn in Figures 7 and 8, respectively.

Apart from the possibility that individuals show different perceptions (and thus differing efficient frontiers) from the aggregate, a dominated car could still be chosen by some customers. One typical reason why this happens relates to the actual size of the outlay and the consumer's budget constraint. For example, the BMW might provide a very efficient mix of benefits per dollar, but the total outlay involved in purchasing the car might still prohibit some respondents from buying it. The reader can see from Figure 7 that once the BMW and the Audi are removed from the frontier, a car like Mazda will become efficient and possibly preferred. When applying the international positioning framework it becomes important to identify not only the products in the evoked set and the preferences, but also what purchases are feasible under the customer's budget constraints.

A third reason why "non-efficient" cars might be chosen is that the space attributes are not sufficient to cover all the relevant non-price factors that enter the buying decision. Among these one must include special promotional deals, cents-off, Chrysler's recent $500 rebate, credit availability and interest rates charged, service and warranty offers, etc. Among these intervening variables is sometimes a country-of-origin normative bias, e.g., the desire to "buy American" or "support Japan."

The Role of Price Reduction

The proposed framework can be used to compute how much of an added inducement is necessary for a product to become "efficient." Take, for example, the K-Car in Figure 7. In order for it to beat the Mazda, its closest competitor on the constrained frontier, the K-Car needs a shift in position in a northeasterly direction. This shift can be accomplished by a reduction in the price of the K-Car of slightly more than $2,000.

The computations required to arrive at this figure are carried out under the assumption that a price reduction will not change the perceptions of the product (i.e., there should be not adverse quality impact). Such an assumption is usually tenable only to the extent that the price reduction is temporary.

If a price decrease involves no perceptual change, its mix of attribute scores will stay the same. A decrease in price will simply shift the car outwards from the origin; an increase will move it towards the origin. This "fixed proportions" case is graphically represented in the efficient space by a vector projected from the origin through the car's present position.

The vector of the K-Car is indicated in Figure 7 for the American subsample. As can be seen, the vector intersects the constrained efficient frontier just to the south of the Mazda car. This means that a price decrease that makes the K-Car competitive in the market will generally position it against the Mazda (although one could expect that potential buyers of the Toyota and the BMW might also be tempted, judging from Figure 7).

The last step in the analysis is then to compute the required price discount that will move the K-Car onto the frontier. Projecting the vector out until the frontier is reached, it is easy to read the point of intersection off from the graph. Using the "Economy" dimension, we see that the K-Car has to reach a value of approximately .50 to be competitive with the Mazda. (Only one dimension needs to be used, since the other is given by the fixed-proportion requirement.) Since the K-Car's existing "Economy" score from the perceptual space (Figure 1) is about .26, the requisite new price X is generated by the following equation:

$$.26/X = .50, \quad \text{or} \quad X = .52$$

Re-scaling to actual dollars, the selling price of the K-Car needs to be $5,200 to make it efficient. The perceived price at the time of the study was $7,555. The required discount is therefore[2]

$$\$7,555 - \$5,200 = \$2,355$$

It is, of course, also possible to carry out the same calculations for the Japanese sample. Using the graphs in Figures 4 and 8 to do just that, the requisite new price is much lower (about $2,400, a stark contrast to the actual price of $15,400—see Table 1). This extreme value, based on the perceptions of these particular Japanese respondents, reflects the kind of competitive disadvantage the U.S. cars suffer in the Japanese market. Remember again, however, that there might well be some individuals within the market with different ratings for the cars than the average ones employed here—and that also there might be omitted attributes which affect the attractiveness of the U.S. cars particularly strongly (one example would be "status"). Also, the relatively large differences between the actual prices in Table 1 and the perceived prices (used here) would lead one to suspect that the actual size of required discount could vary a great deal among individuals.

Summary Discussion

Competitive (Dis)Advantages

The framework of international product positioning presented in this paper bears a direct relationship to the identification of the firm-specific and country-specific advantages of the firm as discussed in the theory of the multinational enterprise. Quite generally, the position differences in the perceptual maps represent firm-specific advantages (FSAs) as perceived by the consumers in the marketplace. The differences can be related directly to the required price premiums or discounts necessary to make two alternative products of equal value to the buyer. This price differential will be reflected in actual prices, especially when the market is reasonably efficient so that competing alternatives are well known to the buyers.

Whether the individual firm will be able to provide the requisite price discounts over an extended period of time hinges directly on its cost situation and the possibly negative effects a low price might have on the brand image. Where the FSAs are lodged in factors which generate low cost per unit, a less desirable product from a positioning viewpoint might still be on the efficient frontier because of its lower price. The product is a best seller simply because of superior cost figures enabling the price to be kept low (a "low-cost" strategy). Alternatively, the particular attribute mix provided through a given offering might be such as to place the alternative on the efficient frontier of at least some segment (a "niche" in the market).

The misperceptions evidenced in these perceptual maps are generally due to image factors such as brand name and country-of-origin stereotypes and are thus examples of both firm-specific and country-specific advantages. This means that country stereotyping can at times represent quite a considerable price disadvantage in a market. Because of this, the multinational marketer might well consider the possibility of shifting production in such a fashion as to exploit the existence of country-specific advantages. The current vogue of establishing joint ventures with the Japanese automakers can be viewed as one such attempt, where a positive country-of-origin association is substituted for a negative one.[3]

Since country stereotypes can change considerably over time (*vide* the Japanese example), such "tricks" can be expected to work only in the short run. In the long run, the international marketer needs to offer a product which exhibits sufficiently strong FSAs to place it on the efficient frontier of at least some segment of the market. The viable options are those where either the product attributes are superior and present an opportunity for a premium price, or where the firm has a low-cost advantage and can push its product onto the efficient frontier by way of a lower price. The low price option suffers from the threat of low-cost producers starting elsewhere (the product life cycle argument), and also from the difficulty of maintaining a desirable positioning with high customer loyalty. For many companies, the option of developing a superior product priced so as to be one of the efficient choices and targeted so as to become the preferred choice among at least a niche in the market will be the most viable alternative in the longer term. It is in this strategic decision process that the international positioning framework presented will be most useful.

APPENDIX
Data Collection

The illustration of the proposed method draws on a comparative study of American and Japanese respondents' evaluation of automobiles. Cars were a natural choice since in both countries there is a large number of foreign makes available, and although specifications differ from country to country, many of the makes are quite similar in different countries.

The sampling was guided by the fact that students at several Japanese universities could be accessed. To ensure comparability, this sampling frame was matched with a corresponding group in the U.S. The number of respondents on the U.S. side amounted to 70 graduate students at a West Coast university. The Japanese sample comprised a total of 82 usable returns, from 6 different universities in Japan (around Tokyo and Kobe). These students were both graduate and undergraduate and belonged in the majority of cases to the motor clubs so common at Japanese universities. This stratagem proved necessary to eliminate the relatively large number of students without driver's licenses. (For further information concerning sample characteristics the reader is referred to Johansson, Douglas and Nonaka, 1985.)

The ten car models and twelve attributes selected (after two pilot studies) were the following (Japanese names in parenthesis where different)

The "true" attribute values were collected from secondary sources (car magazines and *Consumer Reports*) and supplemented by base price figures collected from each country.

Car Models	Attributes
Honda Accord	
Datsun 200SX (Nissan Sylvia)	Handling
Mazda 626 (Mazda Capella)	Horsepower
Toyota Celica	Acceleration
	Gas mileage
	Safety
Ford Mustang	Driving comfort
Chevrolet Citation	Passenger comfort
Plymouth K-Car	Reliability
	Durability
VW Rabbit (VW Golf)	Workmanship
Audi 4000 (Audi 80)	Styling
BMW 320i (BMW 318i)	Color selection

The layout of the questionnaire followed the standard multi-attribute format, with questions of belief ratings for the ten cars on each attribute followed by a rating of the importance of the attributes. The overall ratings then followed, after which familiarity with each model was assessed. The questionnaire ended with a few questions concerning background variables.

The Japanese version of the questionnaire was translated into English using the standard method of re-translating into English for spotting errors (Douglas and Craig, 1983, Chapter 7). Some rewording of questions was necessary to accommodate the more polite approach common among Japanese, but otherwise the translation was quite literal.

Notes

1. For a description of the data used in the illustrations, see Appendix. The scaling of the axes is ordinal and based on the factor scores.

2. The same figure is arrived at by checking dimension two, "Performance," Lowering price to $5,200 moves the position of the K-Car along the horizontal axis to .33/.52 or .63 (the .33 is the score of the K-Car on the performance axis in Figure 1). At .63 in Figure 7, the K-Car moves exactly the distance required to intersect the frontier just south of the Mazda while staying on the projected vector from the origin. The fixed proportion requirement is satisfied, since .26/.33 is .50/.63 approximately, allowing for rounding errors. If the misperception of the price of the K-Car could be corrected, the required discount is lowered to $6,858 − $5,200, or $1,658, since $6,858 is the blue book price (see Table 1).

3. Not that all such ventures are based upon this "imaginary" basis. Most of the rationale behind them is probably derived from the infeasibility of actually producing the requisite attribute bundle within the existing country. Nevertheless, there is a component of country-of-origin imagery in several of these joint ventures, as exemplified by Chrysler's Dodge Colt, "built by Mitsubishi."

References

Bilkey, W. J. and E. Nes (1982), "Country-of-Origin Effects on Product Evaluations," *Journal of International Business Studies,* 1 (Spring-Summer), 89–99.

Douglas, Susan P. and Samuel C. Craig (1983). *International Marketing Research.* Englewood Cliffs, N.J.: Prentice Hall.

Erickson, G. M., J. K. Johansson and P. Chao (1984), "Image Variables in Multi-Attribute Product Evaluations: County-of-Origin Effects," *Journal of Consumer Research,* Vol. 11 (September), 694–699.

Hauser, J. R. and R. Gaskin (1983), "Defensive Strategy: Application and Predictive Test of Consumer Model," Working Paper No. 1404-83, The Marketing Center, Sloan School of Management, M.I.T. (April).

———— and S. M. Shugan (1983), "Defensive Marketing Strategies," *Marketing Science,* Vol. 2, No. 4, Fall.

Johansson, J. K., S. P. Douglas and I. Nonaka (1985), "Assessing the Impact of Country-of-Origin on Product Evaluations: A New Methodological Perspective," *Journal of Marketing Research,* XXII, November (forthcoming).

Maynes, E. Scott (1976), *Decisionmaking for Consumers: An Introduction to Consumer Economics,* New York: Macmillan.

Nag, Amal (1984), "Chrysler Tests Consumer Reaction to Mexican-Made Cars Sold in U.S.," *The Wall Street Journal,* July 23, Section 2.

Nagashima, A. (1970), "A Comparison of Japanese and U.S. Attitudes toward Foreign Products," *Journal of Marketing,* Vol. 34, January, pp 68–74.

Reader's Digest Corporation (1963), *European Common Market and Britain,* New York.

Ries, A. and J. Trout (1981), *Positioning: The Battle for Your Mind,* New York: McGraw Hill.

Urban, G. L. and J. R. Hauser (1980), *Design and Marketing of New Products,* Englewood Cliffs, N.J.: Prentice Hall.

Product Development the Japanese Way

Michael R. Czinkota and Masaaki Kotabe

The decade of the 1980s saw a great surge in the global market success of Japan. Increasingly, there has been talk about the beginning of the Japanese century and the emergence of an overpowering Japanese economy.

Policymakers have responded to these visions by expressing concern about the trade competitiveness of the United States and taking actions designed to break down real or perceived trade barriers. Competitiveness, however, is driven and maintained to a large degree by individual firms and their marketing efforts. A quick review of the successes and inroads achieved by Japanese products confirms this perspective.

Japanese firms have been successful in established industries in which U.S. firms were once thought invincible, as well as in newly developing industries. They have been able not only to capture third-country market share from the U.S. competition but also to obtain major footholds in the U.S. domestic market. They supplied almost 20 percent of U.S. imports in 1989 and achieved their surplus in trade in manufactured goods on the basis of both high-technology and non-high-technology products.

As a result, U.S. producers' domestic market share for color televisions has dropped from 90 percent in 1970 to less than 10 percent today, and the domestic share of semiconductor production has declined from 89 percent to 60 percent. Even more startling are the developments in the newly emerging high-definition television (HDTV) technology, which harbors the promise of a new electronic age. Several Japanese electronics giants have developed HDTV technology commercially. U.S. producers, which previously balked at the idea of such technology because they did not see a ready market for it, are now seeking shelter behind standard-setting rules by the U.S. Government.

In spite of the expenditure of vast funds on research and development (R&D), a number of U.S. products do not seem to be able to perform sufficiently well in the marketplace. Yankee ingenuity once referred to the ability of U.S. firms to successfully imitate and improve on foreign technology.

For example, the British discovered and developed penicillin, but it was a small U.S. company, Pfizer, which improved on the fermentation process and became the world's

Reprinted from *The Journal of Business Strategy* (November–December 1990). Permission granted by Faulkner & Gray, 11 Penn Plaza, New York, NY 10001.

foremost manufacturer of penicillin. The Germans developed the first jet engine, but it was two American companies, Boeing and Douglas, that improved on the technology and eventually dominated the jet airplane market.

Yankee ingenuity seems to have vanished and reemerged in the form of Japanese marketing techniques, which appear to see what many others do not recognize and often are right on target in identifying market needs. Perhaps it is time that U.S. firms rediscover their former talents in order to compete with renewed vigor in the global market.

Incrementalism vs. the Giant Leap

Technology researchers argue that the natural sequence of industrial developments comprises imitation (manufacturing process learning), followed by more innovations. In other words, continual improvements in manufacturing processes enable a firm not only to maintain product innovation-based competitiveness but also to improve its innovative abilities in the future. Failed innovators, in turn, lack the continual improvement of their products subject to a market-oriented focus.

During the postwar period, Japanese firms relied heavily on licensed U.S. and European technology for product development. Product quality was improved through heavy investment in manufacturing processes with the goal of garnering differential advantage over foreign competitors. Continued major investment in R&D earmarked for product innovation heralded the technological maturation within Japanese firms, where the quality and productivity levels began to match or even surpass those of the original licensor.

U.S.-style product innovation has placed major emphasis on pure research, which would allegedly result in "giant leap" product innovations as the source of competitive advantage. By comparison, incremental improvements in products and manufacturing processes were neglected and relegated to applied research. As Peter Drucker has argued, however, research success may very well require the end of the nineteenth-century demarcation between pure and applied research. Increasingly, a minor change in machining may require pure research into the structure of matter, while creating a totally new product may involve only careful reevaluation of a problem so that already well-known concepts can be applied to its solution.

By contrast, the Japanese incrementalist view of product development emphasizes continual technological improvement aimed at making an already successful product even better for customers. Take the case of Japanese very-large-scale integration (VLSI) technology. The origin of VLSI technology was the transistor. Recognizing consumers' unsatisfied need to tune in their favorite music anywhere at any time, Sony introduced small portable transistor radios in 1955. Other Japanese companies quickly followed suit. There was quick market acceptance of the product worldwide.

Mass production made it possible to lower the cost and improve the quality of the product. In a short time, Japan reached a technological level at par with, and soon surpassing, that of the United States in transistor technology. As the age of integrated circuits (ICs) began, compact electronic calculators using this emerging technology boosted the growth of Japan's IC industry. The IC evolved into the large-scale integration (LSI) and now into VLSI.

These emerging technologies are used in consumer products, including personal computers, Japanese-language word processors, video cassette recorders (VCRs), compact disk players, and HDTVs. Many electronics products have sold in extremely large volumes, a fact which has subsequently made ongoing investment in production possible, as well as further technological development. Incremental improvements in IC technology have made it possible for Japanese firms to improve continually on a variety of products. In the end, emerging products such as HDTV are truly different from what they used to be both in form and concept.

This incremental technological improvement is not limited to high-tech industries. Steel making is considered a mature or declining industry in most developed countries. However, Japanese steel makers are still moving toward higher levels of technological sophistication, for example by developing a vibration-damping steel sheet (i.e., two steel sheets sandwiching a very thin plastic film).

It is a small technological improvement that has a wide range of possible applications. Due to the growing popularity of quiet washing machines in Japan, this steel sheet has been used successfully as the outer panel of washing machines and is increasingly finding its way into other noise-reducing applications, such as roofing, flooring, and automotive parts.

The Marketplace as R&D Lab

Due to the incrementalist product-development approach, Japanese firms have also been able to increase the speed of new product introductions, meet the competitive demands of a rapidly changing marketplace, and capture market share. Japanese firms adopt emerging technologies first in existing products to satisfy customer needs better than their competitors. This affords an opportunity to gain experience, debug technological glitches, reduce costs, boost performance, and adapt designs to customer use.

In other words, the marketplace becomes a virtual R&D laboratory for Japanese firms to gain production and marketing experience as well as to perfect technology. This requires close contact with customers, whose inputs help Japanese firms improve their products on an ongoing basis.

In the process, they introduce newer products one after another. Year after year, Japanese firms unveil not-entirely-new products that keep getting better, more reliable, and less expensive. For example, Philips marketed the first practical VCR in 1972, three years before Japanese competitors did. However, Philips took seven years to replace the first-generation VCR with the all-new V2000, while late-coming Japanese manufacturers launched an onslaught of no fewer than three generations of improved VCRs in this five-year period.

The continuous introduction of "newer" products also brings greater likelihood of market success. Ideal products often require a giant leap in technology and product development and are subject to a higher risk of consumer rejection. Not only does the Japanese approach of incrementalism allow for continual improvement and a stream of new products, but it also permits quicker consumer adoption. Consumers are likely to accept improved products more rapidly than they accept very different products, since the former are more compatible with the existing patterns of product use and life-style.

Japanese firms also display a willingness to take the progress achieved through incrementalism and develop a new market approach around it. An excellent example is provided by the strategies used by different Japanese automobile manufacturers. After decades of honing refinements in their products, these firms, within a short period of time, developed the Infiniti, Lexus, and Acura brands, which were substantially different in the consumer's mind from existing cars.

Each of these new brands was introduced to the market through an entirely new distribution system. Even though pundits had argued that in the automotive sector the time for new brands was over, let alone the likelihood of success for new channels, the approach chosen seems to be crowned by greater success than the more traditional acquisition route taken by Ford (Jaguar) or General Motors (Saab).

Market research is a key ingredient for successful ongoing development of newer products. The goal is to provide customers with more "value" in the products they purchase. Product value is determined by cost and quality factors. In the United States, cost reduction and quality improvements are too often thought to be contradictory objectives, particularly when quality is perceived to be measured mainly by choice of materials or engineering tolerances.

Japanese firms, by contrast, see cost reduction and quality improvement as parallel objectives that go in tandem. The word *Keihakutansho* epitomizes the efforts of Japanese firms to create value by simultaneously lowering cost and increasing quality. *Keihaku-tansho* literally means "lighter, slimmer, shorter, and smaller" and thus implies less expensive and more useful products that are economical in purchase, use, and maintenance.

Furthermore, Japanese perceptions consider quality in a product to be generated as well by the contextual usage of the product. If a product "fits" better for a given usage or usage condition, it delivers better quality. That is why Japanese firms always try to emphasize both the "high tech" and the "high touch" dimension in their product innovations.

The recent market success of Sony's black-and-white TV set illustrates this point. Conventional market research failed to show that a market existed for such products in the United States. However, by studying the contextual usage of TV sets, Sony found that in addition to a family's main color TV set, Americans wanted a small portable TV to use in their backyards or to take away with them on weekends.

How Does Japanese Market Research Differ?

U.S. market researchers, after developing an insulated staff function of their own, have grown enamored of hard data. By processing information from many people and applying sophisticated data manipulations, statistical significance is sought and, more often than not, found.

Toru Nishikawa,[1] marketing manager at Hitachi, summarizes the general Japanese attitude toward such so-called scientific market research. He provides five reasons against relying too much on a general survey of consumers for new-product development:

1. **Indifference.** Careless random sampling causes mistaken judgment, since some people are indifferent toward the product in question.
2. **Absence of responsibility.** The consumer is most sincere when spending, but not when talking.
3. **Conservative attitudes.** Ordinary consumers are conservative and tend to react negatively to a new product.
4. **Vanity.** It is human nature to exaggerate and put on a good appearance.
5. **Insufficient information.** The research results depend on the information about product characteristics given to survey participants.

Japanese firms prefer more "down to earth" methods of information gathering. Johansson and Nonaka[2] illustrate the benefit of using context-specific market information based on a mix of soft data (e.g., brand and product managers' visits to dealers and other members of the distribution channels) and hard data (e.g., shipments, inventory levels, and retail sales). Such context-specific market information is directly relevant to consumer attitudes about the product or to the manner in which buyers have used or will use specific products.

Several things stand out in Japanese new-product development (or in their continual product improvements). First, Japanese new-product development involves context-specific market research as well as ongoing sales research. Second, some of the widely observed idiosyncrasies of the Japanese distribution system serve as major research input factors. For example, when a manufacturer dispatches his own sales personnel to leading department stores, not only are business relationships strengthened, but a direct mechanism for observation and feedback is developed as well.

Third, significant effort is expended on developing data, be it through point-of-sale computer scanners or the issuance of discount cards to customers, which also carry electronically embedded consumer profiles. Fourth, engineers and product designers carry out much of the context-specific research.

Toyota recently sent a group of its engineers and designers to southern California to nonchalantly "observe" how women get into and operate their cars. They found that women with long fingernails have trouble opening the door and operating various knobs on the dashboard. Toyota engineers and designers were able to "understand" the women's plight and redraw some of their automobile exterior and interior designs.

City, another highly acclaimed small Honda car, was conceived in a similar manner. Honda dispatched several engineers and designers on the City project team to Europe to "look around" for a suitable product concept for City. Based on the Mini-Cooper, a small British car developed decades ago, the Honda project team designed a "short and tall" car, which defied the prevailing idea that a car should be long and low.

Yet, hands-on market research by the very people who design and engineer a prototype model is not necessarily unique to Japanese firms. Successful U.S. companies also have a similar history. For example, the Boeing 737 was introduced about twenty years ago to compete with McDonnell-Douglas's DC-9. However, DC-9s were a somewhat superior plane; they had been introduced three years before the Boeing 737 and were faster.

Witnessing a growing market potential in Third World countries, Boeing sent a group of engineers to those countries to "observe" the idiosyncrasies of Third World aviation. These engineers found that many runways were too short to accommodate jet planes. Boeing subsequently redesigned the wings, added low-pressure tires to prevent bouncing on shorter landings, and redesigned the engines for quicker takeoff. As a result of these changes, the Boeing 737 has become the best-selling commercial jet in history.

Hands-on market research does not negate the importance of conventional market research, emphasizing quantity of data and statistical significance. In developing the ProMavica professional still video system, which, unlike conventional 35mm still cameras, records images on a two-inch-square floppy disk, Sony did extensive market research involving a mail survey, personal and telephone interviews, and on-site tests to elicit user response to the product during its development. What was unique was that the ProMavica task force included both engineers and sales/marketing representatives from Sony's medical systems and broadcast units. Sony's engineers gained insights from talking with prospects as much as did their marketing peers, and they incorporated user comments into product modifications.

It is clear that engineers and designers, people who are usually detached from market research, *can* and *should* also engage in context-specific market research side by side with professional market researchers. After all, these engineers and designers are the ones who convert market information into products.

Some Recommendations

Clearly, U.S. new-product development and market research are sophisticated and successful. Yet, in order to improve competitiveness further, several aspects of Japanese activities could be considered by U.S. firms.

First, the incrementalist approach to product development appears to offer advantages in the areas of costs, speed, learning, and consumer acceptance. Second, such an approach requires a continuous understanding of current and changing customer needs and of the shortcomings of one's own products and those of the competition. In order to achieve such understanding, market research is essential.

In order for such research to be successful, the contextual usage and usage conditions of products need to be investigated and, once found, acted upon. While extremely useful in their own right, hard data alone are not the answer. This type of information often provides only limited insights into these contextual conditions.

It is therefore important to include soft information based on down-to-earth market observation. Since the ability to recognize dimensions of context is not uniquely confined to market researchers, it is important to fully include product managers, designers, and engineers in the research process.

Marketing research should not be a "staff" function performed only by professional market researchers, but rather a "line" function executed by all participants in the product development process. Not only will such an approach permit the discovery of more knowledge, but it will also immediately achieve the transformation of gleaned market data into information that is disseminated and applied throughout the entire organization.

References

1. Nishikawa, "New Product Planning at Hitachi," 22 *Long Range Planning*, 20–24 (1989).

2. Johansson and Nonaka, "Marketing Research the Japanese Way," 65 *Harvard Business Review,* 16–22 (1987).

Marketing Services Internationally: Barriers and Management Strategies

Lee D. Dahringer. *Lee D. Dahringer is Dean of the College of Business Administration at Butler University. Dr. Dahringer teaches and writes in the areas of international marketing, marketing strategies, and macromarketing. His papers have been presented at conferences and published in journals in the United States, Europe, India, Australia, and Latin America. He is co-author of* International Marketing: A Global Perspective, *which was published in 1990. Dr. Dahringer received his Doctor of Business Administration from the University of Colorado at Boulder, his M.B.A. from the University of Missouri at Columbia, and his undergraduate degree from Western Kentucky University.*

Introduction

The importance of services in the world economy is evidenced by the fact that they contribute an average of more than 60 percent to the gross national product of all industrial nations. About 50 percent of middle-income countries' and almost one-third of low-income countries' gross national product can be attributed to services.[11]. Socialist countries appear to average close to 30 percent of their national income from services.* In total, services account for some 25 percent of world trade.

The special characteristics commonly ascribed to services—inseparability, intangibility, perishability, and heterogeneity—make successful marketing of services more difficult than that for physical goods (see Figure 1 for a more complete description) and so a different type of marketing is needed.[11] Inseparability, for example, means the producer of the service becomes part of the total service, as the bank teller becomes part of the banking experience. Further, inseparability means that production and consumption of a service occur simultaneously, not sequentially. Intangibility means that services cannot be lifted, transported, felt, or seen. Thus service quality is more difficult to assess than is quality for goods. Supply-and-demand balancing becomes more difficult since services cannot be stored. And prices are more difficult to set, since customers find it difficult to determine a price-value relationship. Perishability relates to the ephemeral nature of services. Either they are available and consumed somewhat simultaneously, or they are

---

* For example, a warranty may be sold separately or as part of a total product package. If embodied or linked to the product, it would be treated as a physical product transaction in national accounts and is subject to current GATT guidelines.

Reprinted by permission of MCB University Press from *The Journal of Services Marketing,* Summer 1991, pp. 5–16, © 1991 MCB University Press.

FIGURE 1

Unique service features and resulting marketing problems

Unique Service Features	Resulting Marketing Problems
Intangibility	1. Services cannot be stored. 2. Services cannot be protected through patents. 3. Services cannot be readily displayed or communicated. 4. Prices are difficult to set.
Inseparability	1. Consumer involved in production. 2. Other consumers involved in production. 3. Centralized mass production of services difficult.
Perishability	1. Services cannot be inventoried.
Heterogeneity	1. Standardization and quality control difficult to achieve.

FIGURE 2

Scale of (in)tangibility

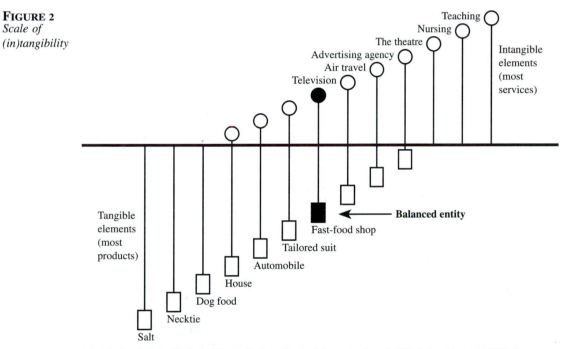

Adapted from G. Lynn Shostack, "How to Design a Service," *European Journal of Marketing,* 16, no. 1 (1982), 52.

lost. As a result, they cannot be inventoried for use after production. Finally, services have the quality of heterogeneity, meaning they are never the same from one consumption experience to another. A haircut, even if provided by the same stylist at the same hour on the same day of the week, will be different from the previous one. Thus standardization of the service product and, hence, quality control, is difficult to achieve. Service marketers are considerably challenged to manage service characteristics to allow services to be marketed successfully across national boundaries.

TABLE 1   **World Services Trade**

	Total Exports	Total Imports	Net Services	Imports as Percent of Total World Imports	Exports as Percent of Total World Imports
United States	138.7	120.5	18.2	16.3	21.5
France	54.5	47.7	6.8	6.5	8.5
United Kingdom	47.2	37.8	9.4	5.1	7.3
West Germany	45.7	40.7	−5.1	6.9	7.1
Japan	41.2	48.7	−7.6	6.6	6.4
Belgium–Luxembourg	30.3	28.4	1.9	3.8	4.7
Italy	25.6	23.6	2.0	3.2	4.0
Netherlands	23.2	22.9	0.3	3.1	3.6
Saudi Arabia	17.2	44.1	−26.9	6.0	2.7
Switzerland	17.2	10.1	7.0	1.4	2.7
Spain	13.7	8.6	4.1	1.2	2.1
Canada	12.1	27.1	−15.0	3.7	1.9
Austria	10.9	8.1	2.8	1.1	1.7
Singapore	9.2	5.7	3.5	0.8	1.4
Norway	8.6	10.0	−1.3	1.4	1.3
Mexico	8.1	17.1	−9.0	2.3	1.3
Sweden	7.9	10.4	−2.5	1.4	1.2
Australia	5.2	12.1	−6.9	1.6	0.8
Brazil	3.1	16.0	−12.9	2.2	0.5
Argentina	1.8	8.1	−6.3	1.1	0.3

In reality, all products combine tangible (usually called "goods") and intangible (usually called "services") dimensions. Figure 2 illustrates this range of tangibility which goods and services possess.[6]. But, while salt is highly tangible and physical, it is marketed as possessing an intangible dimension, "reliability," as witnessed in the Morton Salt slogan "When it rains, it pours." At the other extreme of the spectrum, teaching—imparting knowledge—is highly intangible, but educators frequently use physical symbols (diplomas, tests, books, classroom design) to provide a physical reassurance of the presence of the product. Similarly, lawyers and doctors take care in decorating their offices to project quality assurance through the symbols used in decorating. This article will focus on what are traditionally called services, those products that are intangible dominant, roughly from midrange of the spectrum illustrated in Figure 2 to the highly intangible end.

The future of international marketing of services is very promising. (The current level of nations' involvement in international marketing of services is illustrated in Table 1.) As one signal of growth, GATT (General Agreement on Trade and Tariffs) talks were recently expanded to include services as products in its efforts to lower barriers to trade. This formal recognition of services, in addition to the 20 to 30 percent growth in international service sales each year,[1]. signals an ever increased importance for services in world trade.

Barriers to the International Marketing of Services

Barriers to the international marketing of services are due largely to the close cultural relationships between a society and the services offered in that society. Thus they are more restrictive than barriers for the marketing of goods.[8]. Banking, insurance, telecommunications, and aviation tend to have more trade barriers than other service industries. For example, in the early 1980s an average of 22 barriers per country were imposed on service industries in European Community (EC) countries, and most restrictions focused on these four industries.[3].

Barriers to international marketing for services include tariff and non-tariff barriers. The latter include bilateral and multilateral country agreements, buy national policies, prohibited employment of foreigners, distance, direct competition from government, scarce factors of production, and restrictions on service buyers (see Table 2).

The lowering of tariff or non-tariff barriers to service marketing between nations is usually negotiated on a bilateral basis. For example, the office of the U.S. Trade Representative has reached an agreement with the Korean government that will increase U.S. corporate participation in the Korean insurance market, helping U.S. firms to gain market presence. India also has been cited under "Super 301" for similar barriers but so far has failed to lower its tariffs.

Some barrier-lowering plans are negotiated multilaterally. The most visible example is the various agreements among the country partners known as the European Community. Scheduled for complete economic integration in 1992, this market represents considerable opportunities for service organizations. For example, banks and financial services providers are now actively engaged in EC mergers and acquisitions in order to have a complete market presence by 1992.

Sources and the GATT

The General Agreement on Tariffs and Trade (GATT) talks represent an important multilateral approach toward reducing barriers to marketing in services. The United States, in particular, brought pressure to include services under the GATT framework. This lobbying effort was begun at the GATT Ministerial Meeting of 1982, and formally proposed at the Full GATT meeting at Punta del Este in 1986.

Developing countries have generally been opposed to such an expansion of GATT. They fear that their infant industries in high technology and other services would be eliminated by foreign competition if there were no barriers to service marketing. Developing countries also take the position that demands made by industrialized countries that they open up markets to services are one-way demands, because no concession is made which would help the economies of the developing countries. Further, critics of such a proposal argue that since the United States already dominates the world market in services, it would be the chief beneficiary of trade liberalization.[2].

Still other critics argue that because of unreliable international data on trading of services, it is premature to put service negotiations on the GATT agenda. A similar argument is that the types of service exports most likely to rise if market access is improved through GATT involvement would have only a modest effect on U.S. exports.

An argument for the inclusion of services within the GATT framework, beyond their increased importance in international trade, is the concept of indirect services. The link between indirect services embodied in goods† and international marketing of goods implies that barriers to international marketing and competition for services spill over to act as non-tariff barriers to competition in goods.[4]

Outside GATT, specific industries such as international air transport and shipping have specific conventions and agreements which govern them. And while telecommunications is dealt with in some agreements, the issue is largely based on technical issues or regulations and not barriers to marketing. Therefore, if there is to be a systematic, worldwide approach to lowering tariff barriers to service trade, it will probably have to be through the GATT framework.

The application of GATT to services faces problems in several specific GATT articles and codes. A discussion of a few of these issues may help illustrate the difficulties and also reveal some trade barriers that inhibit the global free flow of services. For example, under GATT guidelines, concessions to one trading partner are extended to all GATT contracting parties. Applying this code of *Most-Favored-Nation-Treatment* to services may have to be done on a conditional basis, particularly because developing countries are sensitive to protecting their infant industries.

Another GATT guideline is that of *National Treatment,* whereby imported products once cleared at the border are treated the same as any national firm's products. Currently, international banks are allowed to enter the U.S. market, but are not allowed to pursue consumer or "retail" accounts. If National Treatment were enacted, a question arises whether or not foreign firms established in the United States would be favored since they already have some market presence. If so, this would be to the detriment of entering firms.

Barriers at the Border is another important GATT principle. When barriers to marketing goods are imposed, they should be done at the border. Most obstacles to marketing services, however, do not lie at the border; rather they are cultural dimensions which impact through society. Applying this dimension of GATT may prove problematic for services. However, given the general movement of the world economy toward increased economic integration and free trade, it might be expected that after rather complex and long term discussions, the GATT framework will indeed be expanded to include services.

Tariff Barriers

Both tariff and non-tariff barriers to the international marketing of services exist as illustrated in Table 2, but the tariff barriers compared to non-tariff are relatively straightforward and transparent. Import taxes on imported services or contracts result in higher prices necessarily being charged by foreign providers. Higher user fees paid by foreign buyers have a similar impact, decreasing demand for international services.

---

† International trade data are more difficult to obtain and analyze because of reporting and accounting differences for socialist nations. Therefore, these estimates are more difficult to make than for industrialized nations, who follow a relatively standardized procedure.

TABLE 2   **Barriers to International Marketing of Services**

Type	Example	Impact
Tariff	Tax on imported advertising	Discriminates against foreign agencies
	Tax on computer service contracts	Prices international service providers higher than domestic which stand alone
	Higher fees for university students from outside the country	Decreases foreign student enrollment
Nontariff		
Bilateral and multilateral country agreements	GATT multilateral lowering of barriers	Increases international market potential and competition
	U.S. Korean Insurance	Lowers barriers to entry for U.S. companies
Buy national policies	U.S. government buying training services from only U.S. companies	Discriminates against foreign suppliers
Prohibit employment of foreigners	Canadian priority to citizens for available jobs	May prevent suppliers from going to buyers
Distance	International business education	Economies of bringing supplier to buyer, buyer to supplier, or both moving to a third location
Direct government competition	Indonesian monopoly on telecommunications	Must market services to government
Scarce factors of production	Lack of trained medical workers in Biafra	Limits production of services
Restrictions on service buyers or sellers	North Korea limited the number of tourists allowed to enter and exit the country	Limits the restricted industry

Non-Tariff Barriers

Non-tariff barriers such as those listed in Table 2 prove particularly problematic for international marketing managers of services.

Buy national policies are encountered in the international marketing of services as well as products. The effect is the same for both. Any policy that provides implicit or explicit preference for a domestic supplier makes it more difficult for an international competitor.

Another non-tariff barrier is *prohibition against employment of foreign nationals.* Professionals in service industries such as management consulting or medical care may be limited through such prohibitions. Such a barrier effectively prevents trading across national boundaries in cases where the provider goes to the buyer. It also has a negative impact on those services where either the provider or the buyer may move. For example, regulation of services designed to protect consumers is common in national markets. In the United States, in order to be classified as a "Certified Public Accountant," one must hold a degree in accounting from a recognized U.S. school of business and pass a national, standard exam. While this requirement is an attempt to ensure that only competent accounting services are offered to the market, it also has the effect of discriminating against foreign trained accountants, thus restricting the service seller.

Distance between markets is another non-tariff barrier to services. While this is also a problem for physical goods, improvements in transportation and logistics have eased the tasks of storing, inventorying, and transporting goods. For perishable, inseparable services, however, distance means greater expense in the movement of the supplier, buyer, or both to the transaction point. For example, an international business school based outside Paris must decide whether it is more cost efficient and more educationally effective to have a guest lecturer come to France to conduct a two-week seminar, or to take the students to the professor. The answer depends not only upon the financial implications, but also on the objectives of the organization and the needs of the students.

In many nations, *direct competition from government* serves as a barrier to the marketing of services. Governments often act as providers of goods and, almost always, of services. Often the government holds a monopoly on a service, such as the Dutch or Indonesian government monopoly on telecommunications. In those cases, market access is blocked to a foreign service organization, except through the establishment of a strategic partnership with the government. Another problem is that governments typically price their services to domestic users at less than cost; therefore a competing service organization faces market expectations of a below-cost price.

Scarce factors of production present another non-tariff challenge to the international service marketing manager. Since services are inseparable, they normally are labor-intensive (a competent service provider must interact directly and often one-on-one with the customer). For example, surgery cannot be performed without a doctor. Similarly, a first-class tourist resort cannot be run without well-trained, experienced management and other qualified personnel. Because of labor intensity, the demand for services may increase faster than an organization's capacity to fill that demand. This constrains domestic as well as international providers of services. Because of such limitations on labor, properly selecting partners for joint ventures, franchising, licensing, or strategic partnerships (the most popular forms of market entry for services) is even more critically important for service organizations than for physical-good companies.

Finally, *restrictions on service buyer movements* negatively affect international service marketing. Limiting tourist travel or the number of foreign flights allowed into or out of a country, for example, obviously limits the tourism industry. Students may be admitted on a quota basis or medical patients may be allowed into a country only for specific treatments. Any such limitations affect the marketing of services in cases where buyers go to providers or where both buyers and providers are mobile.

Managing the International Marketing of Services

Organizations that have successfully crossed national boundaries with services are numerous. Educational services, entertainment, medical care, fast food, and various business services are only some of the areas in which service firms profitably serve foreign markets. For example, as of 1988 *The Phantom of the Opera* was playing in London, New York, and Tokyo, and *Cats* was being produced in 16 countries.

Multinational transportation firms, such as Delta Airlines or British Caledonian, advertising agencies such as Dentsu or Ogilvy & Mather, and entertainment providers from Bruce Springsteen to Pavarotti all provide their services in a variety of national markets. Still, the international marketing of services presents special problems. Following are some guidelines which should improve the international services marketer's activities.

Embodying

One way around tariff and non-tariff barriers to services is to embody (include) services in physical goods, that is, move the total product toward the more tangible dominant domain mentioned in Figure 2. Doing this permits the import or export of services through the merchandise flow, where barriers are lower. For example, Yves St. Laurent extends his designing services (creating a "style") by embodying them in dresses sold through leading retailers throughout the world. Providers of computer maintenance contracts may be faced with restrictions on providing that service in specific markets, so they may attempt to embody the service through a joint venture with a country. Thus, when their partner imports a computer, they also import a service contract as part of the purchase agreement. The service contract may thus be subject to controls that apply to the computer itself—often less severe barriers than are applied to services marketed alone. The decision of whether to embody a service within a good or to market the service directly is determined by the magnitude of the barriers to marketing the service compared to that of the embodied good.

Employing Technology

The introduction of new technologies such as computer systems, software, and communication systems has had a considerable impact on international services marketing. In particular, the use of technology to aid in the design and delivery of services, and to serve as a method of getting around barriers to marketing, has been substantial.[5,9]

Communications and computer technologies are eliminating distance as a barrier to the marketing of many services. Travel agents can make global reservations quickly. Traders in equity or capital markets, linked by satellite, can instantaneously transfer funds from one country to another. Technology links stockbrokers and other investor advisement services to permit the 24-hour trading of stocks and bonds in markets around the world, as evidenced by the globally shared stock market crash in October 1987. Similarly, global broadcast images permit broadcasting or entertainment programs worldwide. Also the future should provide access to checking accounts through a global network of automated teller machines (ATMs).

Another approach to circumnavigating barriers to international marketing is through technology transfer, readily moving technology to another nation's market even if it is difficult to market products that incorporate that technology. For example, a licensing agreement can transfer to another nation the capacity to produce products that depend upon a given technology. Following such an approach, an advertising agency with a superior media buying computer program, if barred from entering a nation's market by a local regulation, could license the media buying technology to an existing firm within that market. In effect, technology transfer substitutes for the direct export of the service.

Customizing

Because services are heterogeneous, they can be customized. Markets with sufficient discretionary income either will go to the service that most closely delivers the set of desired benefits, or will pay a high price to bring that service to them. For the finest in high fashion, wealthy shoppers may fly to Paris to buy personally fitted clothes from Yves St. Laurent. Or a hairdresser who has international fame may be flown to the homes of rich clients to help prepare them for important engagements.

The strategy of customization is allowing U.S. insurance companies to enter the Korean market, since government negotiations broke down the artificial barriers to entry. U.S. firms aggressively designed life insurance policies that fit Korean customer's needs, thus penetrating the market quickly. In this way, marketing managers make their product fit market demands by creating benefit packages that result in a unique total product. Such a strategy also might include strong support services (pre- and post-sales) to help transfer technological services and goods.[7]. For example, the industrial market often demands complete service support for computer hardware and software.

Superior Management Systems

Superior management systems also aid in the marketing of a service in another national market. One high-growth international market entry form for services is strategic alliances, in particular, franchising. Superior management systems permit the service organization to deal more effectively with the service characteristic of heterogeneity. And internationally, providing a high, consistent level of service quality translates into a strong competitive advantage. Despite the high proportion of GNP provided by service sectors in all developed countries in general, the level of service quality is below the market's expectations. The advantage of franchising, either domestically or internationally, is that it permits a partnership (strategic alliance) between a locally knowledgeable participant and the mother organization, which supplies control systems that ensure consistent quality. Hyatt Hotels, for example, have management contracts in almost every country because of their ability to standardize, at a high level, the quality of service provided to business travelers and tourists. Similarly, S.A.S. Airlines is noted for its superior management systems, which results in its "moments of truth" leading to satisfied customers.

Superior Service Quality

Providing superior service quality, whether through improved management systems, unique providers, customizing, or investing in personnel, helps to ensure international market success. Higher quality at market prices is always a competitive advantage whether the product is a good or a service. Particularly in service industries where the domestic market has been slow to invest in improving the quality of services provided, a foreign corporation may have a competitive edge. Domino's, for example, has been successful in its entry into Europe because other pizza shops did not provide home delivery, or if they did, not as well. Japanese department stores are entering other national markets, in part because their upper management is convinced that they will be able to provide superior customer service.

Macro-Marketing

Ultimately the right to do business in a given nation, and the opportunity to apply any of the previously discussed management strategies, are dependent upon that country's government granting permission. The recent passage of the "Super 301" bill in the United States is an example of what many American marketers of both services and goods have been calling for. The bill's avowed purpose is to arm the American government with the power to impose retaliatory tariffs against countries it believes to be discriminating against U.S. marketers. This bill is an example of macromarketing, the concern and intervention of marketers at the policy level in order to influence the environments which, in the short-term, establish the parameters of marketing management. As GATT and bilateral negotiations progress, international service marketers may well need to be increasingly involved in policy matters in order to open markets, adjust for foreign government subsidies to competitors, and ensure equitable treatment before international bodies.

Summary

There can be little doubt that the international market represents considerable challenge and opportunities for service marketers in the 1990s. Before success can be achieved, however, the barriers to successful international marketing of services need to be understood.

International service marketers have a wide variety of management strategies from which to choose. The proper choice is basically a function of which barrier is being faced. The barriers and their related strategic choices are listed in Table 3. Tariff barriers are essentially responded to through embodying, superior management systems, and macromarketing. Embodying, for example, may permit the service marketer to bundle the tariff-blocked service with a low-tariff physical good. Superior management systems, especially through a strategic alliance, permit the international service marketer to, in effect, become a domestic marketer, avoiding tariff discrimination. Macromarketing is undertaken with the objective of eliminating the discriminatory tariff totally.

Since non-tariff barriers are wider ranging than tariff ones, the strategic range of choices is also wider. Bilateral and multilateral country agreements, for example, are responded to through macromarketing in a manner similar to tariff barriers. Buy-national policies are responded to through superior management systems to gain a domestic partner, or through customizing and superior service quality to gain a value-added position which overcomes nationalistic purchasing policies. When employment of foreigners is prohibited, embodying or bundling of products may be employed to transfer the service skills into a bundle of goods which includes the services. Or, technology may be employed to transfer the service elements across national boundaries without transferring the person(s) who generated those services.

TABLE 3   **International Marketing Strategies for Barriers to Marketing**

Type	International Marketing Strategy
Tariff	Embodying
	Superior management systems
	Macromarketing
Nontariff	
Bilateral and multilateral country agreements	Macromarketing
Buy national policies	Superior management systems
	Customizing
	Superior service quality
Prohibit employment of foreigners	Embodying
	Employ technology
Distance	Customizing
	Employ technology
Direct government competition	Customizing
	Superior management systems
	Superior service quality
Scarce factors of production	Employ technology
	Embodying
	Superior management systems
Restrictions on service buyers or sellers	Embodying
	Customizing
	Employ technology
	Superior management systems

If the barrier is distance, the service may be customized (raising value, which lowers the distance "cost") or employing the technology, which effectively lowers the distance, such as through electronic communications systems among international stock markets. Direct government competition barriers may be dealt with by customizing, again adding value to position the service as unique, as well as by superior management systems, which manage the service process better than the government can. Additionally, superior service quality may add high value to aid in positioning the service as unique, and thus, of value to the market since the government can't provide an equal quality service package.

The barrier of scarce factors of production can be responded to through employing technology, embodying, or superior management systems. Technology for services can substitute for scarce or high-priced labor, just as it does for goods. Embodying allows the more efficient use of scarce production resources, in effect circumventing the service characteristic of inseparability. Superior management systems permit the more efficient and effective use of scarce resources no matter what industry.

Finally, restrictions on service buyers or sellers is countered through the strategies of embodying, customizing employing technology, superior management systems and superior service quality. Embodying is used to bundle the service with a good that will have greater mobility than service buyers or sellers. Value-added through customizing will entice service buyers to find ways around restrictions placed on them. Employing technology may allow the provider of the service to transfer the service without actually traveling to the buyer. Superior management systems will allow the organization to move inside the market, gaining the advantages of being a "domestic" firm while maintaining its superior, internationally gained service quality and management systems. Superior service quality may generate such high demand that restrictions are lifted.

The characteristics of services that pose marketing problems domestically are even more problematic internationally. Service marketers, however, by applying the management approaches detailed in this article, can deal with those problems and increase their global competitiveness. Given the increased international nature of suppliers, competitors, and markets, service marketers must evaluate these approaches carefully and adopt those that provide their firms with an international competitive edge. Doing so now increases the probability of future success. Failure to do so now almost certainly ensures the service firm of failure.

References

1. Aronson, J. D., and P. F. Cowhey. *Trade in Services: A Case for Open Markets.* Washington, D.C.: American Enterprise Institute, 1984.

2. Bhagwati, J., "International Transactions in Services from a Developing Country Perspective," *World Bank Symposium on Developing Countries' Interests and International Transactions in Services,* July 1987.

3. Fong, P. E., and M. Sundberg, "ASEAN-EEC Trade in Services: An Overview," in J. Waelbroek, P. Praet, and H. C. Ruger, eds., *ASEAN-EEC Trade in Services: ASEAN Economic Research Unit,* ISEAS, 1985, pp. 48–49.

4. McCullouch, R., *International Competition in Services* (NBER Working Paper No. 2235, pp. 11–12). Cambridge, MA: National Bureau of Economic Research, 1987.

5. Quinn, J. B., "The Development of International Business in Australian Banks," *Australian Banker,* April 1988, pp. 42–45.

6. Rushton, Angela M., and David J. Carson, "The Marketing of Services: Managing the Intangibles," *European Journal of Marketing,* 19, no. 3 (1985) 19–40.

7. Samli, A. C., and R. Kosenko, "Support Service Is the Key for Technology Transfer to China," *Industrial Marketing Management,* April 1982, pp. 95–103.

8. "Services Also Feeling the Sting of Global Barriers." *Marketing News,* February 13, 1987, p. 1.

9. Tucker, K., "Traded Services, Regulated Markets, and Technological Change," in J. F. Brotchie, P. Hall, and P. W. Newton, eds., *The Spatial Impact of Technological Change.* London: Croon Helm Publishers, 1987, pp. 104–107.

10. Tucker, K., and M. Sundberg, *Services in ASEAN-Australian Trade* (ASEAN-Australia Economic Papers No. 2). Kuala Lumpur & Canberra: ASEAN-Australia Joint Research Project, 1983, p. 7.

11. Zeithaml, Valerie A., A. Parasuraman, and Leonard L. Berry, "Problems and Strategies in Services Marketing," *Journal of Marketing,* Spring 1985, pp. 33–48.

Marketing Satellites Internationally: Export/Import Issues

Bruce Leeds. *Bruce Leeds is manager of export/import operations for Hughes Aircraft.*

My review of Hughes satellite export/imports begins in the late 1970s, when the market for communication satellites really started to expand. Hughes began working on several contract proposals to build satellites. It decided to create a series of satellites that shared common hardware and other elements, which could then be modified to the specifications of a variety of customers. Hughes called this product the HS 376 line.

The first foreign customer for the HS 376 was Telesat Canada, which wanted to buy two satellites. We sold them two satellites initially and two more later—all HS 376s that shared hardware and structural elements. However, there was a major string attached: we had to spend a substantial portion of the contract price on Canadian goods and services. As a result, Hughes had to place tens of millions of dollars worth of business with Canadian suppliers. One can meet only so much of that offset requirement by flying on Air Canada and staying at Canadian hotels. We had to seek out things that Canadians could make for us. Hughes discovered key companies in Canada that had the capability of making spacecraft components and helped them produce these parts. Engineers were sent to teach Canadians how to make components. The Canadians were making parts that went into Canadian satellites they called Anik, an Eskimo word meaning *friend.*

But just making parts for the Canadian satellites would not take care of all of the offset. Hughes had contemplated building several of the 376 series. Each time we sold a 376 satellite to a customer, we would go back to the same Canadian suppliers for parts. Subsequently, the Canadians were building parts not just for the Anik satellites that we were selling to the Canadian customer but for all of the satellites in this series.

Two satellites in the series were called Westar and were made for Western Union, which had decided to get out of the telegraph and telex business since it was no longer doing well. It wanted to market satellite communication services instead. Western Union ordered a couple of satellites from Hughes. Two more were ordered by Indonesia. The Indonesians called theirs Palapa, for a phoenix type of mythological bird. In building these satellites for both Western Union and the Indonesians, we were able to use Canadian parts. At that time, payment of a duty was required on all items imported from

---

Provided expressly for this publication.

Canada. Now the Canada–U.S. Free Trade Agreement makes such transactions largely (but not entirely) free of duty.

The Customs tariff schedule has several thousand listings. Under each commodity number it specifies a duty rate. At that time, items that came from Canada carried the same duty rate as those from Japan or West Germany or wherever—there was no difference. Now we have special Canadian rates. If you look up "parts of satellites" in this book, there is no duty. You might think, "Oh, good, we can import these parts from Canada for free." Except that customs has an interpretive rule that if there is a more specific classification for the item being imported, then you must place it under the more specific category.

How that works can be illustrated in the importation of automobile parts. For example, you might import three items that go on cars—a fender, a windshield, and a carburetor. What duty rates will be imposed on those three items? Well, there is a category in the customs tariff that says "parts of motor vehicles." But a windshield is laminated glass, and the customs book lists "laminated glass for automobiles," which has a higher duty rate. That's where you have to classify the windshield. There is no listing in the customs tariff for a carburetor. Instead there are listings for parts of motor vehicles and parts for internal combustion engines. The interpretation is that engine parts are more specific than parts of automobiles. Only the fenders are classified as parts of motor vehicles.

We've imported one of the key components of the satellite, a traveling wave tube (TWT). It's a microwave electronic tube that takes a weak radio signal and makes it strong again. This is what makes the transmission of Voyager pictures from the outer planets possible. Hughes is a developer of the traveling wave tube and imports some of the TWTs to go into the satellites. Are they duty free because they are parts of satellites? No. The listing in the customs tariff for "electronic tubes" attaches a 4.2 percent duty.

TWTs are about a foot long and 1 1/2 inches around. The minimum price is about $100,000. I've seen them cost as much as $250,000 each, and we are building satellites that require as many as 48. If you take a traveling wave tube and attach a power supply to it, it becomes a traveling wave tube amplifier (TWTA), which is used to amplify a radio signal. There is another category in the tariff for "parts of radio transmission and reception apparatus," and it has a 5.9 percent duty. Only when the traveling wave tube amplifier is installed on an electronic shelf or bus unit, which is the heart of the spacecraft, does it become free to import since customs has no more specific classification.

The Westar and Palapa satellites were built using the Canadian parts we paid duty on. They were then sent down to Florida and loaded on the space shuttle, which took them into space. The space shuttle takes a satellite up about 200 miles, above most of the atmosphere and gravity, and releases it. From this altitude the satellite uses its own rocket motor to pull it an additional 22,000 miles about the Earth. These satellites are called geosynchronous; if one is orbited far enough away from the earth above the equator, the force carrying the satellite out and the gravity pulling it back equalize. The geosynchronous orbit enables the satellite to stay in one spot. Since its location is constant, radio signals beamed at it will be successful in making contact every time.

These two satellites were launched on consecutive days on a shuttle mission. The rocket motors failed to ignite or ignited improperly, and the two satellites were put into useless orbits. Both had been insured by Lloyds of London. The two customers, the government of Indonesia and Western Union, collected on the insurance policies, and Lloyds of London was now the owner of two satellites in useless orbits. It was proposed that a shuttle be sent up to bring the satellites them back to earth. Lloyds of London was willing to try, so a year later it paid NASA to recover the two satellites.

Customs has a program going back to 1789 called drawback. If a duty is paid on an import, but you use the imported product to make something else using U.S. labor and then export the end product, you can claim a refund on the duty originally paid. The idea is to encourage exports by refunding the duty paid on imported material. Imported material goes into the satellite, the satellite goes down to Florida, and the shuttle takes it into space. Customs considers a launch into orbit an export for drawback purposes. When the shuttle took the two satellites up, we filed claims for refunds of duty. The drawback claim total for the two was roughly $300,000.

When the shuttle went out to recover the satellites, the coverage was a TV spectacular. The news showed the astronauts floating around in their spacesuits, capturing the satellites and putting them in the shuttle bay. The customs employee who had handled drawback claims watched the news and called to say, "Aren't those the same two satellites you filed drawback claims on?" When I said yes, he replied, "On one of them I know we've already paid you, so we're expecting you to return the money. As for the other one, although we're processing the refund right now, we are going to stop payment."

I composed a three-page letter citing legal precedents about ships sinking at sea and similar disasters to justify our right to the refunds. I concluded, "Under Customs rules regarding imported merchandise, the owner of the goods is responsible for entry and duty payment. The owner is Lloyds of London. Here is the name and address of their agent in the United States. Collect from them and give us our refund." The customs official retired the very next month and neglected to stop payment on the second check. Customs never did ask for the money back that we had already received.

Lloyds of London still owned two satellites, but what could it do with them? It gave Hughes a contract to refurbish them and began seeking new customers. The Palapa satellite was eventually sold back to the Indonesians.

Lloyds eventually sold Westar to a consortium based in Hong Kong called AsiaSat. This consortium comprised British, Hong Kong, and Chinese investors. It renamed the satellite AsiaSat.

In the satellite industry, a customer normally contracts with a company such as Hughes or Loral to build a spacecraft and then contracts with another party to build a launch vehicle. When NASA gave up the commercial launch business, other companies filled the void. The major constructors in the United States are Martin-Marietta, McDonnell Douglas, and General Dynamics. The Europeans have a consortium called Arianespace whose members are various European aerospace and electronics companies. Their launch vehicle, the Ariane, is launched from French Guiana in South America.

The customer, in this instance AsiaSat, normally selects the launch vehicle. It may contract with one of the U.S. launch vehicle manufacturers or with Arianespace for a rocket. The Soviet-built Proton rocket is low cost and has a good reliability record, but the U.S. government will not grant an export license to send a satellite to Russia. The Chinese have a rocket called the Long March that was originally of Russian design. The Russians taught the Chinese how to build it as an ICBM, and the Chinese modified it into a launch vehicle. The Long March was a very good rocket with a high success rate. It was very effective at placing Chinese satellites into orbit, but by the late 1980s, no one other than the Chinese had ever used it for that purpose.

AsiaSat requested to have its satellite launched on the Long March rocket. Our relations with China had improved greatly by the time of the Reagan/Bush administrations. The U.S. administration hinted to AsiaSat and Hughes that if they applied for an export license to send the satellite to China for launch on the Long March rocket, it might be approved. So Hughes applied for a license to export the AsiaSat satellite to China for launch on the Long March and it was approved.

The Tianamen Square massacre occurred as we were making our initial preparations to send the satellite to China for launch. That put a stop to everything. The U.S. government suspended all export licenses to China, and our relations with China were in jeopardy. However, our Washington office was told to continue with the plan to ship the satellite to China for launch on the Long March.

It is not an easy task to ship a satellite and all of the accompanying equipment to China—especially when it has never been done before. A 747 freighter must be chartered at considerable expense. Certain items cannot be placed on a 747 freighter because no airline will accept them. That includes the hydrazine satellite fuel, which is highly toxic, and a variety of other dangerous items that must be transported by ocean freight.

Several export licenses and extensive planning are involved in preparing the shipments for a project of this magnitude. We were coordinating all of the arrangements to make this transaction happen—with no export license. Every time we would inquire about whether we had an export license, we were told to continue with the preparations and not to worry because the license would be coming. Time wound down to the end of 1989. The date for the ocean freight shipment of chemicals going to China was set for the first week of January 1990. The date for the 747 charter departure to China was mid-February. The Christmas holiday was closing in and we still didn't have an export license, yet we were continuing with our plans. One week before the ship with the chemicals was to sail, the export license arrived. Permission for it had come all the way from the White House.

One week before the 747 charter was ready to take off, I received a call from the Department of Commerce in Washington, D.C. The State Department grants export licenses, or did in those days, for items such as satellites and rocket motors. The Commerce Department licenses items such as test equipment. We obtained a State Department license to cover everything being sent to China, but Commerce objected because it had not been consulted about this groundbreaking project. We had obtained a license for one x-ray machine from Commerce, but it apparently felt this was not enough involvement on its behalf. I was called to Washington on 24 hours' notice to explain to the Commerce Department what we had done. This was five days before the charter was to leave. We had to apply for five Commerce licenses, which were approved in only three days. The day before the charter left, the Commerce licenses arrived.

What went to China? First there was the ship with hydrazine and alcohol. It traveled from Long Beach to Guangzhou (formerly Canton). The launch site in China is located in the interior, in a town called Xichang in southern Shihuan province. Xichang is at least 1,500 miles from Guangzhou or any major port. To transport the chemicals from Guangzhou to the launch site in Xichang, we asked the Chinese for assistance. They said they would ship it by rail. It took three weeks to get from Guangzhou to the launch site.

On board the 747 charter we planned to load the spacecraft itself, plus a solid fuel rocket motor. But we encountered problems when it came time to set up the charter. First we went out for bids. For security purposes, the government said it had to be a U.S. flag carrier. We selected Federal Express, formerly called Flying Tigers. The satellite was to be flown into a Chinese military airbase that had never seen a 747 freighter before. Federal Express wanted assurances regarding safety and information detailing the radar and air traffic control systems at the airport, the runway dimensions, and what the runway was made of. We gave the Chinese the list of questions from Federal Express. They simply answered, "Tell them they can land here, we'll take care of everything." Federal Express said, "Sorry, no deal. If you can't tell us about the airport, we're not flying. And if we're not flying, the satellite doesn't go." This was a very prestigious project for the Chinese. It was a matter of national honor to have a foreign satellite launched on their rocket. So I quickly received a seven-page fax from China with everything you'd ever want to know about that airport.

We weren't out of the woods yet. Two other problems cropped up. When we researched landing the plane in Xichang, unloading it, and taking the satellite 30 kilometers to the launch site, there was a problem with unloading the cargo from the side door of the 747 freighter. The door is approximately two stories off the ground. A K-loader, which works like a scissors jack, must be used to unload the plane. The container is rolled onto it, lowered, and then rolled onto the back of a truck. The only K-loaders in China were at Beijing Airport, so the Chinese had to transport one by railroad to be there at Xichang when the plane was scheduled to land. The second problem was that you don't put a satellite on just any kind of truck. It has to be an air-suspension truck that provides a very smooth ride to avoid damage to the electronics. In all of China, there was only one air-suspension truck. The Chinese guaranteed that it would be there on that day—and it was. During the 30-kilometer trip to the launch site we encountered a low bridge. Since the truck could not fit under the bridge, the Chinese army dynamited the bridge.

So we had the airplane, with the satellite and the rocket motor on board along with test equipment, frozen steaks, a Weber barbecue, and charcoal briquettes for our team. The briquettes were almost an issue; the airline had considered them hazardous cargo and could not have taken them. But the rules were changed in January 1990, and we managed to get the briquettes aboard. A Department of Transportation permit is necessary before putting hazardous goods on board an airplane. The permit is a prerequisite because after takeoff out of Los Angeles the plane flies over U.S. territory for a few miles, so it falls under U.S. jurisdiction.

About two weeks before the charter, we had learned of other hazardous material going to China. These included ETA lines, which are similar to fuses. There were also solvents that our security people use for fingerprinting and creating badges. In addition to these was an electric forklift using car batteries which, of course, are full of acid. The DOT would not permit any of these items on a 747 freighter. What could we do instead? There were plenty of air cargo planes going to Tokyo. But from Tokyo to Beijing, Japan Airlines had one 747 freighter a month. We looked up the schedule and it said, "as required." I called up our representative with Japan Airlines and found that the next flight was scheduled for the following week. We dashed out at the last minute, gathered up all of the cargo, and got it on the plane to Tokyo. It went from there to Beijing and arrived in Beijing on the first day of Chinese New Year.

In China the entire country shuts down for a week for the New Year. This fact created unexpected problems for us. Under the terms of the security arrangements for this project, the shipment had to be accompanied by a U.S. national at all times. We had one U.S. citizen accompanying it, who was to stay in Beijing with the shipment for one week. We began investigating to determine where we could store this equipment in Beijing where it would be under U.S. surveillance for 24 hours a day. The last resort was to put it in our employee's hotel room. We had checked with General Motors since it has an office in Beijing, but that office is staffed by Chinese nationals. We pulled some political strings the day before everything arrived, and the U.S. Embassy in Beijing took the whole shipment. The explosive bolts and the fuses and the forklift all sat there under Marine guard for a week. After Chinese New Year, everything was shipped to Xichang.

The 747 freighter arrived on schedule in Xichang, a town in rural China that had seldom seen Americans before. They had certainly never seen anything like our shipment. It was like a national holiday when it arrived. I was told that the entire 30-kilometer route, from the airport to the launch site, was completely lined with people, as if for a parade. When the locals saw the trucks coming down the road, they knew it was the biggest thing that had happened to them in a very long time. Our people were treated like celebrities and were followed around town.

Food was a problem in that part of China. Culinary and sanitary standards were not the same as in the United States. The Chinese had promised a chef from one of the biggest hotels in Hong Kong for us. When our crew arrived, they had a cook from the local hotel in Xichang. He lasted three days before they fired him and found another cook, who left after three more days. Eventually they got a cook from the provincial capital in Chengdu. The Hughes people showed him how to cook for American tastes. I understand that the first time he prepared a pork chop correctly, they gave him a standing ovation.

Two further challenges associated with the charter were the customs clearance in China and navigation. Fortunately the United States and China had an agreement covering this project. When the 747 arrived in Beijing in the early morning, a Chinese Customs officer came on board, and under the terms of the agreement he was not allowed to see the cargo at all. We showed him some perfunctory paperwork, he signed off, and away we went.

In parts of China, modern air traffic control systems do not exist. Navigation is primarily done by sight. For the flight from Beijing to Xichang, a Chinese navigator sat up in the cabin with his charts and maps and helped direct the plane.

Making subsequent food shipments to China was also challenging. You've heard of the Berlin Airlift; we had the Xichang Airlift. We shipped food ranging from frozen steaks to ice cream to six-packs of Coors beer. How do you keep steaks frozen while in transit? You pack them in dry ice. But dry ice is considered hazardous by the airlines, and it evaporates in 72 hours. A couple of times we had to re-ice everything in Hong Kong.

The launch was almost anticlimactic, because it went extremely well. The Hughes technical people said it was one of the most successful launches they had ever seen. They were pleased with how well the Chinese rocket worked.

After that, everything came back. There's what I call Newton's law of export/import: whatever goes out comes back. In this case it was all of the leftover equipment. We sent one of our people to China to document everything. The personal effects of the launch crew were the most troublesome items to bring back. Customs pounced on them. When everything was documented and ready, we chartered another 747 to bring it all back.

Now you might think that everything that was exported is duty free when it comes back. We had some test equipment made in Japan, other test equipment made in Switzerland, and instruments made in Taiwan. We also had a VCR and a television set that were made in Japan. Under normal rules we must pay duty on all foreign-made items. Even though they had been imported before, when they re-entered the United States, duty had to be paid again. On board the return charter, along with the test equipment and all of the other material returning from China, was one 20-foot container containing 20 bicycles and three rickshaws. The Hughes people had discovered that you could get a very high-quality bicycle in Xichang for $50. The regular cargo cleared in one day, but the bicycles and rickshaws took three weeks.

Later we built two satellites for Australia called Optus and launched them both in China. The first was scheduled to launch on April 15th, 1992. The satellite was mounted on the rocket and the rocket motor ignited, but as soon as it did, it shut down. This was actually a very good thing, because the rocket monitor detected a problem with the motor. Since it didn't use solid fuel boosters, the rocket remained sitting on the launch pad belching smoke. Six months later, it was launched successfully.

A critical issue was whether the smoke and chemicals from the failed launch pad incident had contaminated the solar cells on the satellite. Hughes sent out technicians with cotton swabs and alcohol who wiped down the cells and put the swabs in little sealed vials. In two years, the rules on hazardous cargo had tightened up so much that we couldn't ship the cotton swabs home on a passenger plane; they had to come back on a cargo plane. So our people came back and the cotton swabs arrived in the United States a week later.

In December 1992, Hughes launched the second Optus satellite in China. That one successfully lifted off. But 48 seconds into the launch, for reasons still not fully understood, the satellite exploded, scattering debris all over the Chinese countryside. I understand that the Chinese paid the local farmers 39¢ a pound to bring in pieces of the satellite. We left a 20-foot container in China, which Hughes personnel filled with satellite debris. Hughes conducted an investigation similar to an FAA investigation for a plane crash. It reassembled the pieces to discover what happened, but the specific cause for the failed mission has yet to be determined.

We brought back the shipment of scrap satellite debris for failure analysis. What value do you place on satellite debris and what duty rate does it take? We declared it as scrap aluminum, which is free of duty. When we sent the satellite to China for launch, we received a $300,000 duty refund. Normally, if the satellite returns, we are required to pay back the refund. However, we're not importing a satellite, we're importing scrap aluminum, so we were able to keep our money on export and didn't pay anything on import.

Marketing satellites is a fascinating industry. One must plan but also improvise.

Promotional Strategies

The authors of the initial article in this section, *Global Ads Say It with Pictures,* believe that marketers of virtually all products can create effective advertisements based on universal concepts communicated via strong visual images. Marketers need to visualize concepts for products—not the products themselves—that can be globally presented.

A companion piece summarizes key oral and written communication principles for the international marketer contemplating expansion in nations with high-context and low-context cultures. Adherence to the suggested principles should increase the effectiveness of U.S. executives, especially in the high-context cultures of Latin America, the Middle East, and Asia.

Effective promotion of quality products and services is required for commercial success in both the United States and Japan. For many companies, personal selling is the key, so proper management of the sales force is crucial in both countries. The third contribution in this section explores similarities and differences of salesperson motivation and management in these two major markets. An examination of sales force recruitment, training, compensation, and retention within both countries is included, along with guidelines for successful sales force management.

The concluding contribution explores the scope of training and indoctrination that Japanese managers receive before an assignment to the United States. Formal training is minimal since the new arrival to the United States is often assigned to someone who already knows the ropes. This approach, combined with presentations from returnees to Japan and seminars on Western business methods and culture, constitutes the formal education. In general, Japanese executives learn on the job through trial and error.

Global Ads Say It with Pictures

Marc Bourgery and George Guimaraes. *Marc Bourgery is vice chairman, Groupe FCA!. George Guimaraes is chairman and CEO, Bloom FCA!.*

In 1984, the advertising world was galvanized when Harvard professor and marketing guru Ted Levitt announced that global marketing was here—and here to stay. Leaps in technology and communications, he argued, had made this the time to market products on a global plane. Advertising agencies, he said, would need to align themselves globally, like their clients, to sell a "one sight—one sound" message. After all, he said, if Marlboro and Coca-Cola could do it, why not every product and service? Human emotion was the same the world over, he reasoned, and could be appealed to cross-culturally in the pursuit of marketing efficiency.

Almost ten years later, there's a lot of evidence to suggest Levitt is right. Mass media are, spanning the globe: MTV has crossed borders successfully, communicating strong fashion, music, and design messages. Cable News Network (CNN) is *the* worldwide news vehicle, and *The Price Is Right* seems to play as well in Trentino, Italy, as it does in Peoria, Ill. Brands like Chivas scotch, Dove soap, and IBM have made a global mark. And just as competitors like Japanese Sony, American AT&T, and Dutch Phillips are now teaming up across borders to develop the latest technologies, ad agencies have attempted to follow suit by achieving global mass through mergers and global, integrated approaches to communication.

Why then, is there still so much controversy brewing about global advertising? The controversy stems from a lack of understanding of the true essence of communication. Marketers need to focus on how to determine whether concepts for products—not the products themselves—will cross borders. Because the world has evolved into a visual culture, marketers must become as skillful in influencing people's attitudes, feelings, and behavior through the right visual imagery as they have been through language.

Visual imagery is one of the most efficient ways of transcending all language barriers, whether these barriers lie between different languages or "intralingually"—between different interpretations of meaning within the same language. Basing your ads on a strong visual image can also help you keep your messages consistent globally. No one, for instance, would advise McDonald's to advertise as fast food in Europe and the United States, and then to advertise in Russia as luxurious dining.

Reprinted from the *Journal of European Business,* May/June 1993. Permission granted by Faulkner & Gray, 11 Penn Plaza, New York, NY 10001.

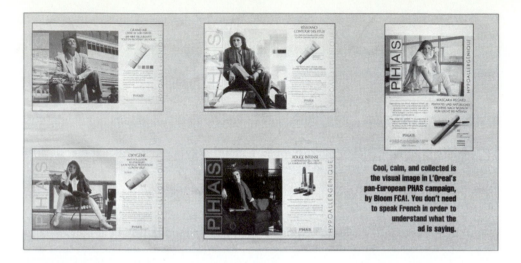

Cool, calm, and collected is the visual image in L'Oreal's pan-European PHAS campaign, by Bloom FCA! You don't need to speak French in order to understand what the ad is saying.

Advertising agencies today are trying to create a "visual esperanto": a universal language that will make global advertising possible for virtually any product or service. The new visual esperanto is based on the idea that visual imagery is more powerful and precise than verbal description (which leaves too much room for personal interpretation). Moreover, all people can comprehend the messages of visual imagery.

Advertising professionals no longer need to be traditional market researchers—corporate marketing professionals are sophisticated enough. Instead, the ad agency's role is to find solutions to communications problems that extend beyond language. This means acting out the message using all available marketing and communications channels.

Smooth as Silk

Consider an ad by Bloom FCA! for Silk Cut cigarettes. The print ad, which appears on billboards and in publications throughout Europe, features a pair of scissors cutting through silk. Because the image describes the cigarette's name, it reinforces name recognition—if you remember the image, you'll probably remember the name when you go to the store. The image also avoids the problems many current cigarette ads have faced: The ad doesn't depict a person, so antismoking advocates cannot blame the producers for targeting a specific age, sex, or race. It also does not depict a lifestyle—as do cigarette ads that imply smokers will be sexier, healthier, or more active if they puff on the particular brand. The ad doesn't depend on any words, and the visual image—silk—is understood by people everywhere as smooth and elegant—and those are the qualities, the ad implies, of Silk Cut cigarettes.

Portrait Planning

To create the appropriate visual image for your ad, start thinking in pictures as soon as possible. Instead of writing a statement of brand identity, visualize it. Then draw, photograph, or videotape what you've visualized. In other words, create a visual portrait of the personality of a brand. This portrait goes well beyond the typical written brand personality statement. It also keeps a brand's advertising consistent across countries.

Consider an ad, shown here, that used a visual portrait to market PHAS, a line of L'Oreal cosmetics. The visual image in the ad—that of a confident, independent, modern woman on the move—captures the product's personality, or brand identity. The text opposite the photo is almost irrelevant—it is the visual image that sells the product.

Through PHAS' personality portrait, L'Oreal has been able to build brand extensions with similar mood, tone, and image. The portrait also allowed PHAS to go beyond the one-product-equals-one-brand idea of marketing. PHAS has been so successful, in fact, that new product development, launches, advertising, promotions, public relations efforts, and direct marketing efforts have been closely tied to the PHAS personality and image. The advertising concept drives all marketing efforts for the brand. Without varying the message, the PHAS image appears in more than eight countries. The campaign has had a strong, positive impact on L'Oreal's bottom line.

Hitting a Moving Target

Settling on the right visual image for your ad is a little like trying to hit a moving target. As times change, words conjure up different visual images, and images convey different meanings.

Before you settle on a visual image, brainstorm about what messages that image sends to you and how the media have used that image recently. This is what Bloom FCA! calls "the context analysis," a non-traditional research method that allows you to predict emerging consumer influences by evaluating the editorial messages (print, television, movies) reaching consumers over a certain time period and across a spectrum of Western cultures. Context analysis acknowledges and builds on the fact that the media are the predominant forces influencing how consumers think, feel, and react to the world.

For example, take the word "exotic," a strong descriptor frequently used in advertising strategies. Analyzing the context reveals that the visual images associated with this single word have changed in a very short period of time—and so has its meaning.

"Exotic," a few years ago, was often portrayed in images of desolate, white, beautiful beaches—the Western consumer's dream destination. Today, however, when articles and ads refer to the exotic, they show a close-up of a tribal villager from Africa or the inside of a hut in the Andes mountains. This reflects the consumer of the 1990s' desire for first-hand experience of the unexploited world.

Take another example, "ecological." This is an important marketing concept today. Unfortunately, too many companies continue to send ecological messages akin to "save the planet," an idea that has worn itself thin. Marketers, instead, should depict ecology as a sound economic and industrial issue.

Context analysis is merely sensing the kinds of changes that shape the consumer experience. The marketer, however, has the ongoing task of fitting any concept into the consumer's life or "conceptual world." It is vital to depict brand identity visually instead

Worth a Thousand Words in Any Language

Here are a few ads American companies have recently launched successfully in Europe. Each of them depends on strong visual images.

This Apple Computer TV ad entitled "Powerbook Duo" shows a pair of hands closing up Apple's Powerbook, a laptop computer, to fit neatly inside a Macintosh. "The ad is very simple, yet powerful. The camera is always on the computers and keeps the audience aware at all times of the inventiveness of this product," says Kurt Haiman, president of the Art Director's Club of New York.

Ford's "Beauty with Inner Strength" TV ad for its new European car Mondeo uses special effects to highlight the car's distinctive elements both inside and outside. It features a skeleton car, specially built to represent the "inner strength" of Mondeo, merging with a specially-built "metalshell" car, which represents Mondeo's "beauty." Special effects fuse the car's two components. The commercial was launched in 13 European countries in March. Initial reaction to Mondeo has been outstanding throughout Europe, particularly in the U.K. where it has been awarded the 1993 What a Car! Car of the Year Award.

Jeans are an all-American product, so Lee Jeans looked for a well-known American symbol to associate with its jeans. Lee found what it was looking for in the twin towers of the World Trade Center, which, in "The Jeans That Built America" commercial, fill the two legs of a giant pair of Lee Jeans. "With all the miniaturization and special effects, this ad was a major production, but worth every penny of every detail the concept portrays," says Kurt Haiman.

Part of American Express' "Portraits" campaign, a series of celebrity photographs by Annie Leibovitz, "John Cleese in a Red Dress" won a Gold Award at the International Advertising Film Festival in Cannes in June 1992. Is it that people everywhere find a man dressed as a woman funny, or is it that they like to see the British let their hair down?

of in writing so that both marketer and advertiser agree on it. This makes sure that "exotic" says "exotic" to the creative director in the same way it will convey the idea to the brand manager and the consumer.

Skipping Breakfast

In a recent interview, *The Wall Street Journal* asked Ted Levitt about how to advertise orange juice. Although orange juice is a universal product, its marketers could not, in its global advertising, depict a family quaffing juice for breakfast because "the French don't drink it for breakfast." Levitt's response was, "Maybe a happy family at breakfast isn't the right metaphor."

In fact, while juice at breakfast may not work well in France, elsewhere it might not work at all—some cultures don't even have breakfast at all. Marketers should think of juice in terms of its main benefits: it quenches your thirst and it's healthy—especially when compared to most carbonated beverages. As most Western consumers are becoming more and more health-conscious, using a health-related image to advertise orange juice might be more appropriate than using a family at breakfast.

Levitt's point is that global advertising is indeed possible, it just takes the right approach to communicate an idea that's consistent and relevant.

By uncovering and visualizing meaningful concepts common from country to country and culture to culture, marketers can execute global campaigns for virtually any product or service. This includes food, beverages, travel—any of the categories traditionally labeled as too dependent on cultural sensitivities to be advertised globally using one concept.

Marketers and advertising agencies are constantly trying to discover new ways of reaching the consumer through message and media. The trick is discovering how people assimilate information and how they feel—not how they think. That means generating excitement and action through visual communications so that consumers, no matter where they are, understand your product and buy it.

International Communication: An Executive Primer

Ronald E. Dulek, John S. Fielden, and John S. Hill. *Ronald E. Dulek is a professor and chair of management and marketing. John S. Fielden is university professor of management communications, and John S. Hill is an associate professor of international business, all at the College of Commerce and Business Administration, The University of Alabama, Tuscaloosa.*

Euphoria frequently turns to paranoia when domestic executives face their first overseas assignment. Disturbing memories come pressing to the fore:

• A college anthropology professor gleefully pointing out that thousands of languages (and even more thousands of dialects) exist in the world;

• A semester or two of a foreign language that was hated, never mastered, and is now well forgotten;

• A once-hilarious book documenting the communications blunders American businesspeople apparently make every time they set foot on foreign soil (Ricks 1983).

These and a variety of other doleful thoughts cause now-wary executives to wonder how they—or anyone—could even begin to cope with thousands of different cultures and languages involved in international business. And there is ample evidence that coping with those cultures and languages is necessary.

Fact 1: By the year 2000, experts have predicted that multinational corporations will control approximately half the world's assets. So even if you are not now working for one of these companies, the odds are high that you will be—or that you will be interacting and communicating with other people who work for "foreign" companies.

Fact 2: Today English dominates the international business scene. But it is blind provincialism to believe that English will continue to be used everywhere for all occasions. Even today an ever-increasing number of foreign countries are demanding that contracts be drawn and negotiations be conducted only in the language of that area.

Fact 3: Sad but true, U.S. businesspeople have the lowest foreign language proficiency of any major trading nation. Despite accreditation association pressure, U.S. business schools do not emphasize foreign languages, and students traditionally avoid them.

Reprinted from *Business Horizons*, January–February 1991, pp. 20–25. Copyright © 1991 by the Foundation for the School of Business at Indiana University. Used with permission.

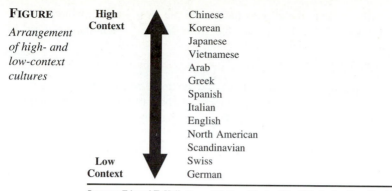

FIGURE

Arrangement of high- and low-context cultures

High Context

Low Context

Chinese
Korean
Japanese
Vietnamese
Arab
Greek
Spanish
Italian
English
North American
Scandinavian
Swiss
German

SOURCE: Edward T. Hall, *Beyond Culture* (Garden City, NY: Anchor Press/Doubleday, 1976), and "How Cultures Collide," *Psychology Today,* July 1976, pp. 67–74.

Fortunately, some generalizations will help U.S. businesspeople communicate more effectively internationally. These generalizations derive from a seemingly simple division of cultures into two polar types, which Edward T. Hall (1976) named high- and low-context societies.

Cultures (see the figure) were divided by Hall into those in which:

1. The social context surrounding a negotiation counts as nothing; all that count are the actual written agreements. These cultures he called low-context; and

2. The social context that surrounds a formal, written document is far more important than the written, legal documentation. These he called high-context cultures.

Low-Context Cultures

In low-context cultures (from the German to the North American) what counts is primarily what has been written in contractual form and sanctified by lawyers on both sides. The social context in which the agreement has been forged has no legal standing and hence, does not count.

High-Context Cultures

Just the reverse is true about very high-context cultures (from the Chinese to the Arab). These cultures are historically oral cultures; what a person says in writing is held to be much less important that who that person is, his or her status (or rank) in society, and his or her general reputation. The social context in which an agreement has been made counts for at least as much as, and usually far more than, the written agreement. Therefore, in high-context cultures the process of forging a business relationship is as important as, if not more important than, the written details of the actual deal.

Applying Context to International Communications

Knowledge of where a particular culture falls in the high- and low-context spectrum gives businesspeople valuable clues about how to communicate with people from different cultures. In this article, these clues have been put in the form of three sets of specific "dos" and "don'ts" for businesspeople to remember when they engage in international communication:

1. Conversational principles—those that should be remembered in all aspects of communication, ranging from informal luncheon chats to boardroom meetings.
2. Presentation principles—those applicable when making oral presentations to a foreign group.
3. Writing principles—those to remember when exchanging written information internationally.

Conversational Principle #1: Recognize that many high-context cultures need to know as much as possible about you and the company you represent. Always remember when you are in Latin America, Asia, and parts of Western Europe that even the most seemingly casual, insignificant conversations have a level of significance far beyond that dictated by the content being discussed. Conversations about your family, your company, or current events are used to "warm up relationships," just as one might warm a car engine on a cold day. You should also give your hosts insights into you as a person and recognize their need to find out what makes you "tick." Americans are not used to talking openly about personal or family intimacies; yet overseas, once the trust "bond" has been established, there are in many cases few things foreigners will not talk about.

The best approach to high-context negotiation, then, is to acknowledge that you and your company are under close scrutiny. You should take pains to provide your prospective Japanese or Arab client with as much information as possible about you and the company you represent. It is often best to provide information before you visit or entertain visitors from high-context cultures. Americans, it is said, like "to meet and get to know you." Persons from high-context societies often prefer "to get to know about you first and then meet you." Copies of your résumé as well as those of other people who hold important positions in your organization, documents, pamphlets, or annual reports that provide details about your company's history, other pieces of information detailing you and your colleagues' personal interests—all can be forwarded to associates in high-context cultures before your visit begins.

Conversational Principle #2: Speak slowly, clearly, and simply. Avoid jargon, slang, clichés, and idiomatic usage. When foreigners learn English, they learn a "correct" version of formal English. When they listen to Americans (or Britons, or Australians) lapsing into slang or idiom, they become confused. We must realize that even an everyday expression such as "Let's get rolling" or "I'm all ears" can be perplexing if the foreigner tries to translate it literally. Imagine foreigners having to translate a simple English idiom such as "So long" into their language. Also, sayings such as "first among equals" and "last but not least" are often untranslatable because, even when translated correctly, they appear illogical and contradictory.

Conversational Principle #3: Sprinkle your conversation with at least some words and phrases in the language of your listeners.   It is regarded as "good manners" to make at least an attempt to learn a few phrases in your host's language. This shows that you have made a good faith effort to learn something about the other person's language—and, by implication, his or her culture and background.

All of us have seen how statesmen regularly make use of their partial knowledge of another country's language when they visit that country. If the President of the United States visits Mexico and says in Spanish, *"¡Hola! ¡Me gusta estar aqui!"* the audience cheers wildly. We have all seen the care Popes have taken to deliver at least part of their sermons in the native language of the country visited.

Conversational Principle #4: Be careful about what your body language and your tone of voice communicate.   When listeners cannot follow what is being said, they will pay far greater attention to body language. And if they do understand English, they will look for contradictions between what is said and how it is said. If the words carry a message that is not reinforced by concomitant bodily expressions, either confusion results, or the listener may conclude that the speaker is not being sincere. When people say to foreigners, "I'm very pleased to meet you," but say so in a bland monotone and an expressionless face, this contradiction between words and action may convince the listeners that the speakers are not at all pleased to meet them. They may immediately wonder how much of what else is said will be truly sincere.

Many of our hackneyed expressions can actually undermine our credibility. In the U.S., someone asks us, "How are you doing?" Regardless of how we actually are doing, we usually answer something on the order of, "Fine, fine." However, when a question like this is asked abroad, Americans should fully expect to receive a sincere answer that may include detailed reasons as to why the respondent is feeling either great or terrible. If after inviting this response we register impatience, foreigners have every right to believe that they have been deliberately made to look foolish, although they may not really understand what was foolish about it.

Tone of voice also plays an important role when communicating internationally. There are vast cultural differences at play here: notice, for example, how softly people from most Asian cultures speak. Americans often seem loud and aggressive in negotiations and vigorous in arguments. And negotiations in Latin American, Greek, Italian, and Central European countries are far louder, often including heated, arm-waving exchanges of opinion that rarely mean anything personal.

Loud oral communications in Asia or the Middle East, however, are socially unacceptable. There is a Japanese saying that "The nail that sticks out will always be beaten." Disruptive elements such as loud or argumentative voices, waving of arms, and exaggerated hand gestures are all frowned upon.

Presentation Principle #1: Respect many foreign audiences' desire for greater formality of presentation.   Different cultures have varying ideas about what constitutes an effective oral presentation. Americans generally like presentations that seem natural and spontaneous, not "canned" or overly rehearsed. Most other countries, both high- and low-context cultures, expect more formality. "Natural" presentations, it is thought, give the impression that the speaker has not respected the audience sufficiently. Speakers who write on blackboards or on transparencies inadvertently give the impression that the presentation is not important enough for them to have prepared proper sets of visual aids prior to the actual presentation.

Also, efforts to customize what you present, as opposed to giving an off-the-shelf generalized presentation, will be appreciated.

Presentation Principle #2: Allow for differences in behavior of foreign audiences. U.S. presenters must not be "thrown off" by seemingly odd behavior of an overseas audience. Japanese audiences, for example, usually sit and nod their heads (which means they understand, not that they agree) and say nothing. However, on some occasions, they may start frenzied talking among themselves. Or, in open discussions, they may suddenly become evasive. What this usually means is that something that has been said is disturbing to them. At this point, presenters should take heed; get off that topic and go on to something else until they can find out, either directly from the audience or through a go-between, what the problem is.

To Americans, "looking people in the eye" is a sign that mutual respect has been established. U.S. businesspeople traveling overseas are often disappointed by their inability to establish eye contact. This is true especially in superior/subordinate relationships, but is also true in presentation to members of cultures where staring is considered "brash and insolent." Hence, in such countries, audiences will not seem attentive because they will spend most of the time staring down at the floor. It is hard for Americans to realize that this usually means the audience is showing respect, not inattention.

Presentation Principle #3: Have patience; design your presentation's length, completeness, and "interruptability" with the audience's culture in mind. Americans are impatient and are used to fast-paced, efficient presentations. Most foreigners, with the probable exceptions of Germans and the Swiss, prefer slower, more deliberate efforts. In situations where interpreters are used, the pace is automatically slowed. When the presentation is in English and there is no interpreter, a speaker must go very slowly. Be patient also in allowing those who raise questions to have time to search for the precise English word they need. Signs of impatience will be unfavorably received, and the presenter will be downgraded for not showing proper respect and courtesy.

Audiences in high-context cultures, such as Japanese, Latin American, and Arabic audiences, expect a presentation to be in short, separate segments that allow time for questions and digestion of what has been presented. This is wise because many high-context people communicate in what is referred to as "loops"; they will mix circuitous, irrelevant (by American standards) conversations with short dashes of information that go directly to the point. Because they are not as time- or efficiency-oriented, Arabs, for example, prefer presentations that allow frequent deviations from the major business topic. This allows them to relax for a while, after which they will be ready to loop back and listen intently to further discussions. These interruptions can prove wearing even to those who are experienced in international dealings. Yet companies whose presenters are the most patient, tolerant and, in their audience's eyes, "mature" will get the contracts. Impatience in these circumstances is interpreted as childish; the prevailing attitude is, "Who wants to do business with children when there are adults around?"

Presentation Principle #4: Match rank and age of presenter to rank and age of important members of foreign audiences.   In many American companies, meritocracy is dominant and fairly young executives rise rapidly to powerful positions early in their career. In high-context cultures, however, age (or seniority) is a major indicator of status. Therefore, sending young executives, regardless of their rank, to negotiate important contracts with businesspeople in high-context cultures can be a disaster. In those cultures, wisdom is associated with age, a throwback to the days when wisdom was assured through years of experience, when knowledge was passed on by elders, not by books or data sets. Hence a young presenter is unlikely to command the same respect as would an older, more seasoned executive. Sending a young hotshot may even invite interpretation that the American company does not take the foreign venture seriously enough to send in its "first team."

Writing Principle #1: Only in low-context cultures where communication efficiency is highly prized should you organize your communication so that its central point is directly and immediately stated.   The higher the context of a culture is, the more we should question whether we should write terse, concise, "bottom-line" communications to persons in that culture. In cultures where language is used not so much to document as to reveal the personal qualities of the individuals and their companies, written communications may need at times to be longer, more elaborate, more personally revealing, and less focused on getting the job at hand completed with dispatch.

But, oddly enough, just the reverse is frequently true. People from high-context cultures may settle for written business agreements that are extremely short and bottom-lined, in some cases merely stating the bare bones of the agreement. The reason for such brevity is that the parties to the agreement have already spent a great amount of time circuitously finding out about each other's integrity. Thus, when both parties are assured of each other's trustworthiness, a brief written statement for the record may be all that is required for this transaction and perhaps those that follow.

U.S. executives should also realize that if a formal, American-style contract is drawn up, the high-context partners will not read it in detail. They will assume that no one would be so crass as to conceal anything in the fine print. While this knowledge might tempt unscrupulous companies to slip in provisions favorable to themselves, one can be sure that succumbing to such a temptation will guarantee that their company will never again do business, not only with the company that was cheated, but probably not even with any other companies in that country.

There is another factor influencing whether communications should be bottom-lined. In international writing, hierarchial power differences between readers and writers affect the organization of messages even more than they do in the U.S. In Malaysia, for example, government bureaucrats bottom-line almost everything they write "down" to the citizenry (analogous to the imperial or bureaucratic "command"). But a businessperson writing "up," asking governmental permission for some action, is expected to be circuitous to the greatest possible extent. The longer the letter, the more "respect" it shows. Moreover, the businessperson is expected to include many long paragraphs praising the bureaucrat (or more subtly, the bureaucrat's administration) in the most lavish terms. This "respect" is necessary because high-context cultures usually have definite social divisions, and there are appropriate sets of verbal behavior depending upon whether one is speaking to another who is higher or lower in the social order.

But remember, not all cultures are high-context. Low-context cultures such as German, North American, Swiss, and Scandinavian prefer business messages to be very direct, even to the point of being terse.

Writing Principle #2: Adapt your style of writing to the preferences of the culture to which your readers belong.   The culture in which a piece of writing takes place clearly affects the style in which messages are expected to be written. In high-context cultures, there is a marked emphasis on politeness and decorum. Even communications going down in an organization will be phrased in polite and respectful ways and will appear to have less force attached to them. There will be differences in how instructions are given. Where there are close business relations between sender and receiver, great care is taken to observe social writing etiquette that to Americans seems vague and obscure. Underlings are asked to "consider" doing certain things and completion of a task may be "requested, if at all possible." These give the appearance that the recipient of the request has at least the option of refusing to do what is asked (although in reality, there is no such option). As result, what is to be avoided are forceful imperatives such as "Do this!" or "Do that!" A much greater reliance should be placed on a more passive, subtle style.

There are cultural differences and expectations about how formally one should write. In high-context countries much informal written communication takes place. Information is often exchanged through informal personal notes written at the bottom of documents. In high-context cultures there is far less need for subordinates to file CYA memos for the record (a person who does so will be thought of as insecure and as calling unnecessary attention to his or her activities). In such cultures writers do not have to document everything formally because they will not be held personally responsible if something goes wrong. Responsibility will be taken by the top of the organization. The subordinate need not fear being the "fall guy" for a mishap. If mistakes are made in the Middle East, Asia, or some parts of Europe, the person at the top will resign, regardless of whether he or she had anything personally to do with the blunder. In the U.S., responsibility flows all too often to the lowest organizational levels.

Not all cultures prize our flat, objective, "Business English" style of writing. Some cultures exhibit styles of writing that are quite colorful compared with English. Arabic, for example, is a poetic language filled with exaggerations, colorful adjectives, and metaphors. Arabs do not react, as English readers might, with shock or surprise at such colorful writing. Such language is just their normal way of expressing ideas. Compared with English, the Latin languages also delight in colorful verbal turns of phrase. Hence, when Americans write in English to members of these cultures, they need not be so hidebound in their expression as they are in standard English.

But many low-context cultures prefer just the reverse. Germans, for example, avoid colorful exaggeration and hyperbole in their writing, believing that people from other cultures (even Americans) exaggerate, abuse superlatives such as "most," "best," and "newest," and demonstrate egocentrism by overusing the personal pronouns "I" and "my." A passive, impersonal style is therefore best in communications with low-context cultures.

Writing Principle #3: Don't count on nonnative readers being able to understand English in all its subtleties and technicalities. Therefore, whenever possible enclose a translation in the recipient's language.   If writers are unsure about a foreign reader's ability to understand English, even when it is written as simply and unidiomatically as possible, then they should include a translation. Doing so will often better guarantee a response. Readers with limited command of English may simply not respond because (a) they do not know whether the unreadable communication is worth the cost of hiring a translator or (b) they may not want to admit publicly that they really don't understand English. Enclosing a translation into the reader's language will not be taken as an insult; instead it will be regarded as helpful and a diplomatic courtesy.

This primer will not make Armand Hammers out of ordinary domestic-variety executives. What it can do, however, is increase U.S. managerial effectiveness, especially in the high-context cultures of Latin American, the Middle East, and Asia. By avoiding cultural *faux pas* and by being sensitive to the needs of other cultures, participants in international business meetings and negotiations can better focus on the real issues in a more relaxed atmosphere. This should enhance the probabilities of successful outcomes, and plant the seeds from which international business relationships can be successful both at the corporate and the all-important personal level.

References

Culturegram Series, Brigham Young University, David M. Kennedy Center for International Studies.

Ronald E. Dulek and John S. Fielden, *Principles of Business Communication* (New York: Macmillan, 1990).

John S. Fielden and Ronald E. Dulek, "How to Use Bottom-Line Writing in Corporate Communications," *Business Horizons,* July–August 1984, pp. 24–30.

Edward T. Hall, *Beyond Culture* (Garden City, N.Y.: Anchor Press/Doubleday, 1976).

Edward T. Hall, "How Cultures Collide," *Psychology Today,* July 1976, pp. 67–74.

David A. Ricks, *Big Business Blunders: Mistakes in Multinational Marketing* (Homewood, Ill.: Dow Jones-Irwin, 1983).

ARTICLE 36

Managing Your Sales Force in Japan and the U.S.

John L. Graham, Shigeru Ichikawa, and Yao Apasu. *John L. Graham is Professor of Marketing at the Graduate School of Management, University of California, Irvine. Shigeru Ichikawa is Professor in the School of Commerce of Chukyo University in Nagoya. Yao Apasu is Assistant Professor of Marketing in the School of Business of Florida International University in Miami.*

Globalization of Competition

The globalization of competition is perhaps the most fundamental challenge facing multinational firms in the 1980s. The strength of firms specializing in domestic markets is being eroded as participation in the two largest markets in the world, Japan and the United States, becomes a competitive necessity. Increasingly domestic success and world-wide success are determined by penetration of these two key markets.

And it is no longer just enough to produce competitive products for these two markets. Efficient and effective *promotion* of quality products often makes the difference between success and disaster in both markets and for most companies personal selling is the key. Thus, sales force management is a crucial task in both countries.

What are the similarities and differences between managing salespeople in Japan and the United States? A recent survey of salespeople and their managers in America and Japan explored this question. Both the US and Japanese firms were large multinationals producing primarily electronic products, and more than 150 salespeople were included in each sample.

Unanticipated Similarities

The popular view of management in Japan and the United States holds that careful consideration must be given to the substantial differences in motives of employees in each country. Even the Japanese government has suggested that Japanese workers value economic well being far more than their American or European counterparts.[1] Our study of the values of salespeople in each country proved the opposite.

Euro-Asia Business Review, January 1987. Reprinted with permission from The Euro-Asia Centre, Boulevard de Constance, 77309 Fontainebleu Cedex, France.

TABLE 1   The Salespeople Were Asked to: 'Distribute 100 points among the Rewards in Terms of their Importance to You.'

Rewards	Relative Importance (mean)	
	Japanese	*Americans*
Job security	18.5	17.6
Promotion	13.7	14.9
Merit increase in pay	24.7	26.2
Feeling of worthwhile accomplishment	18.5	18.2
Social recognition (sales club awards)	8.1	5.2
Personal growth and development	16.6	17.8

When asked to rate the importance of eighteen different life goals, both the Japanese and the American sales representatives rated 'family security' as their number one priority and 'happiness' as number two. Moreover, there was no meaningful difference in their ratings of 'freedom': the Americans rated it as number three and the Japanese number five.

The similarities were even more striking when it came to job related rewards (see Table 1). Both the Japanese and American sales representatives valued a merit increase in pay most highly. The only real difference related to social recognition: the Americans considered sales club awards, etc., to be substantially less important than their Japanese counterparts.

The values and goals of sales representatives do not appear to differ much from one side of the Pacific to the other. This suggests that the tools used to motivate sales performance should also be similar. However, most companies selling in the two markets have adopted sales management practices tailored to the external business environment rather than the internal motivations of individual sales representatives in each country.

Employment Practices

The life-time employment practices of the major Japanese firms are well known. Of equal renown is the high employee turnover common in America. These disparate approaches to firm/employee relations are deeply ingrained into individual values and company policies in each country. And this basic difference in the two business systems translates into significant differences in sales force management practices.

Recruiting

In the United States new employees come from two main sources. Many American firms recruit sales representatives straight out of school (universities and colleges), and provide training in sales techniques. Many other firms 'buy' experienced sales representatives from other companies—often competitors or customers. Additionally, hiring practices of individual American firms often vary over time; that is, college recruits may be emphasized one year and 'buying experience' may be emphasized the next. The expected tenure of a new college sales recruit ranges between two and three years in the United States.

TABLE 2   The Sample of Sales Representatives and Managers

Demographic Characteristics		Japanese (N = 175)	Americans (N = 153)
Age	Under 20	—	—
	20–29	26%	21%
	30–39	72%	38%
	40–49	2%	14%
	50 or older	—	27%
Education	High school graduate	46%	2%
	Some college	1%	34%
	College graduate	53%	40%
	Some postgraduate	—	17%
	Graduate degree	—	7%
Income	Under $20,000	9%	2%
	$20,000–$29,000	41%	40%
	$30,000–$39,000	39%	42%
	$40,000–$49,000	9%	10%
	$50,000 and over	2%	6%
Tenure with company (mean)		9.0 years	8.7 years
Percent with previous sales experience		18%	64%
Number of representatives supervised (mean)		5.5	7.9

In Japan college graduates join large companies for life and job hopping, while not unheard of, is not at all common. Employers use a wide variety of tactics to keep employees including brow-beating, begging, and even appealing to families and neighbours. Moreover, employees are afraid of the stigma attached to switching jobs. So Japanese employers' college recruiting practices are incredibly intense and far more resources (both money and time) are spent on them than is the case in the United States. The pressure on the recruits is tremendous—they are obliged to make a life-time decision at age 21!

These differences are reflected in our data. Sixty-four percent of the American sales representatives had previous sales experience; in contrast, only eighteen percent of the Japanese reported working for another company. Hiring experienced people in Japan is thus not impossible, but much more difficult than in the United States.

Training and Organizational Culture

Because hiring experienced people is less common than in Japan, managers must invest more in training their sales representatives. Since employees are wedded to their companies, managers are almost certain to reap the rewards of such investments. Indeed, during the last fifteen years Japanese firms have sent more the 10,000 employees through American MBA programmes—an investment of approximately US$50,000 per person (two years expenses and lost productivity).

Japanese firms have achieved great rewards through this investment—huge market shares in the US market. American companies have done nothing comparable. And now companies in Taiwan and Korea are following the Japanese example, sending their employees to study the American market in American business schools.

Organizational culture and commitment is strongly promoted in Japanese firms, an approach that American companies have recently begun to imitate. However, examples of successful implementation of this approach are few and far between in the States.

Our study suggested an explanation: the value systems of American sales representatives and their managers displayed a much greater variance than those of the Japanese. The value systems of the Japanese were more homogeneous and consequently the corporate culture is stronger than amongst Americans.

Compensation

Another important difference in sales management practices has to do with compensation and monetary incentives. Most American firms use some combination of salary and commission to motivate sales representatives. The ratio between the two components often varies from year to year, depending on management policy and environmental changes. In contrast, straight salary is much more frequently the practice in Japanese firms.

Both Japanese and American firms also include bonuses as part of compensation packages, however, the bonuses are determined in different ways. For American sales representatives they are based primarily on *individual* performance—meeting quotas, etc.; for Japanese sales representatives they are based on *company* performance. Typically the labour union negotiates with the management of the company for a yearly bonus (a percentage of salary or wages) to be paid semi-annually. The sales representatives of the Japanese firm all receive an identical semi-annual percentage bonus to their salaries, regardless of individual performance.

It should be noted that some large Japanese companies, often subsidiaries of American companies, do provide compensation schemes with high commission components. Indeed, National Cash Register has pioneered commission selling in Japan, and IBM and some other Japanese firms have followed their example. However, this is the exception, not the rule in Japan.

Employee Satisfaction and Retention

Given the strong organizational culture in Japanese firms, one would expect Japanese sales representatives to be more satisfied with their jobs than their American counterparts. Surprisingly this is not the case. Indeed, the American sales representatives in our study were more satisfied with pay, opportunities for promotion, everyday duties, fellow workers, and customers than were the Japanese sales representatives. Further, the Japanese salespeople reported greater propensities to leave the firm.

In the United States employees who are extremely dissatisfied with their jobs leave the company. In Japan, they stay, for all the reasons stated earlier. So Japanese managers must deal with a small cohort of extremely dissatisfied workers, where their American counterparts have no such problem.

Research Method

American Group

Data was collected from a survey conducted in a division of a large American multinational electronics firm. The firm's products are highly technical and are often designed to meet consumer specifications. Its 153 salespeople are required to be flexible and sensitive to customer needs. They are problem solvers and likely to experience conflicting demands from their customers and their firm.

The questionnaires were sent through the company's mailing system with a cover letter indicating the purpose of the study and who was conducting it. The salespeople were assured of the complete anonymity of their responses. They were asked not to sign their names and were to send their responses directly to the investigators.

Japanese Group

The Japanese firm, like the American firm, is a large multinational manufacturing and selling a diverse line of electronic products. A sample of 175 was drawn consisting of experienced sales representatives attending a corporate training programme. The researcher administered the questionnaire during a scheduled session of the programme. The sales managers of the 175 representatives were mailed the sales manager questionnaire.

Management Implications

Guidelines for Successful Sales-Force Management

Foreign firms trying to enter the Japanese market face substantial barriers to establishing a high quality sales force. The major, well established firms have an insurmountable advantage in recruiting the better college graduates. And once they go to work for the established firms, they simply don't leave. So, firms new to the Japanese market are best advised to consider a joint venture or some sort of distribution agreement to obtain the requisite sales force.

In Japan, once a sales force has been established, firms can expect to invest more in training and organizational culture building activities than in the United States. Because of the loyalty of Japanese employees, sales managers can expect to reap the long-term rewards associated with such investments.

Although notable exceptions exist, the primary means of motivating Japanese sales representatives will be by encouraging their commitment to the firm.

Japanese representatives are subject to closer supervision than Americans. The mean number of representatives supervised by managers was less than six in Japan and almost eight in the United States.

Individual financial incentives apparently can work in Japan, but this is not common practice. Whereas financial compensation is the key factor in sales force management in the United States. A new firm in the United States can establish a sales force with relative ease, given the ability to buy experienced sales representatives from competitors, customers, or other associate firms. And once the experienced sales force has been established, individual incentive programmes and compensation packages can be designed to efficiently control the activities of sales representatives. This generally allows for looser supervision than in Japan.

Finally, managers of Japanese sales forces must contend with motivating a small contingent of dissatisfied and unproductive representatives. In the United States such employees would either quit or be fired. This puts pressure on management to work at retaining their staff.

Reference

1. "Youth See Life," *Focus Japan* (December 1978), p. 9.

Assignment USA: The Japanese Solution

Mauricio Lorence.   *Mauricio Lorence is a freelance writer based in Brooklyn, N.Y.*

Given the stereotypes we normally associate with Japanese businesspeople—rites, robots, routines, regimentation, and rigorous standards—you might also think they're prone to minutely-thought-out training programs, especially when the prize is a plum overseas assignment.

Well, think again.

Fujitsu, as typical a Japanese company as you're likely to find operating in the U.S., stresses job flexibility and an expectation of comprehensive judgment that goes beyond job manuals and explicit instructions from superiors. Believe it or not, this accurately describes the attitude of Japanese corporations toward the use of training manuals and management theories in the workplace.

As John Massey, marketing supervisor at Marubeni American Corp., an import/ export firm dealing in diversified foodstuffs, explains it, the only specific training the Japanese manager slated for an assignment overseas gets is a language course. Other than that, little is done to prepare the Japanese businessperson for American culture or business practices. In fact, it's generally assumed that most are already very familiar with American mores by virtue of the sheer fascination among the Japanese for just about everything American.

Even for those managers still wet behind the ears, Japanese companies resort to a more personalized training technique that many American businesspeople will find familiar—mentoring.

A new arrival is often "assigned" to someone in the company who already knows the ropes and spends the requisite time squiring and explaining. This method—sometimes combined with talks given by returnees to Tokyo for their colleagues back at headquarters and visiting lecturers hired especially for the task—seems to constitute the sum total of "formal" education regarding the ways of Western business culture.

Sales Marketing Management, October 1992.

Maximizing the Minimum

According to Massey, "The Japanese mentality seems to lean more toward the lines of strict on-the-job training. Basically, they'll put you in a job and your training is done by making mistakes and by learning. So as far as any formal training for positions, my understanding is that regardless of your background and past history, it all goes out the door. The training is done during your assignment." In other words, minimalism is the main message.

But if training isn't a primary factor in determining which Japanese managers get those key U.S. assignments, then what is? Besides being able to master the requisite language skills (no small challenge, considering the remoteness of most Asian languages to English 101), a choice employee will probably already be working at company headquarters. In most Japanese corporations, overseas assignments are awarded to promising candidates twice during their business lives, during which time they usually complete three to five stints in the U.S. The first assignments usually take place when managers are in their late twenties or early thirties, the second when they're in their late thirties, according to Massey.

All of this coming and going isn't without its disadvantages, of course. One American employee in a Japanese metals trading company (who asked not to be identified and is referred to as D.T. in this article) has this to say about the rotation of managers from Japan: "I've always said that by the time you break them in, they're gone. Breaking in takes two or three years and they're normally only here for five. It's almost like having children. You teach them, you nurture them, you tell them, 'You may say it that way in Japan, but if you talk to an American customer [like that], they're going to hang up on you.' But once they click in and you know they can make it in the real world, they go back to Japan. They you have to start all over again, and you're dealing with a different personality each time."

Formal training, as practiced by most American firms, is virtually nonexistent; it's supplanted instead by hands-on marketplace experience. At Marubeni, says Massey, training for high-profile positions in the New York or London office "is quite simply decided by upper management at our headquarters. It doesn't really have much to do with your past experience. More often than not, it's someone who has been covering that market. If we're selling in any particular market at a particular time in our career, we have knowledge of that market. We probably travel there a number of times for business. The same thing applies to the Japanese—just by working in the marketplace from Japan and traveling on business trips once in awhile, they get a fair understanding."

Not unexpectedly, service-oriented companies do seem to offer a bit more "formal training" for their salespeople—but less by training courses or manuals than by a set of company principles and policies with which employees are indoctrinated before they ever get here.

Customer satisfaction, according to Toshio Shiohata, president of Hitachi Cable America, is one of those abiding principles. Shiohata points to Mitsubishi, as well as to his own company, as examples. "American consumers," he says, "place more emphasis on the after-service, and Mitsubishi is perceived as having more to offer in that respect.

Customer satisfaction isn't just making the car or even selling the car to the customer. It's making sure that repairs are made in a neat and timely way. I think that's the difference between American and Japanese policies—how deeply customer satisfaction is thought about and valued. The consumer is the ruler in America, the [ultimate] judge."

An enthusiastic advocate of a global economy, Shiohata points out that "consumers are international" and the Japanese have to be "technical and managerial magicians in order to make the Japanese economy work. We have to squeeze people because we have nothing. God only gave us people. We have to import everything. So we have to produce something fancy that people will love to buy. The borderless economy is here. Who cares [if it's] made in Japan or the USA or in Canada? I want to buy a product that satisfies me the most. Nationality should be forgotten." And if Shiohata's predictions of a future "world tax" may seem doubtful to some, what's not at all in doubt is that in his vision of the business world—and in that of his employees—the customer is king.

The Prized Plateau

The business of getting to the prized plateau—that much-sought-after American assignment—is an arduous process. Japanese employees work for a long period of time in the "mother company"—the first seven or eight years or so of employment—"basically without [a] promotion," says Massey. Even then, Massey suggests, the ultimate decision by upper management is, more often than not, a political one.

Al Kusuda, senior vice president of Minolta Corp. in New Jersey, has lived 12 years in the U.S. but doesn't necessarily share Massey's view. Although he admits that you can find politics on both sides of the Pacific, in Japan selection for overseas jobs is mainly the result of reams of minutely detailed annual evaluations that are written for every employee throughout his company life. According to Kusuda, employees are rated not only on performance but on their attitude as well: "Through this kind of appraisal process, personnel, as well as management, will know who has the qualities to manage the company in the States."

Kusuda also points out that a career in Japan takes on a different configuration than in the States. For one thing, it's a more fluid affair, one in which employees identify more with a specific company rather than a particular job. The Japanese system involves changing departments and positions every few years *within* a company, and Japanese employers are firm believers in a hands-on, on-the-job, trial-and-error training approach in all areas. In a workplace built on hiring the young, offering lifetime employment, and depending on long-term employee loyalty, it's a practice that generally pays off handsomely, since employers have little fear that their minions will pick up stakes and swear their allegiance elsewhere.

As Kusuda explains: "We believe that by doing the actual work, you'll learn much more quickly, and we consider experience very important. Most managers who come from Japan don't receive any special training other than language. Of course, many personally do research to learn the differences in [American] society and the business environment. They can receive information on that through their predecessors who have worked in the States and through books. Of course we talk about it and read about it, but we don't go through special management training because we don't consider that to be necessary."

The Business of Sales

Most candidates for overseas posts have usually worked in a company's import/export or foreign division, so they're familiar with international trade prior to their departure for another country. Most speak English, but few have had any sales training or direct sales experience. "There just aren't that many people who come from Japan to sell or to become a salesperson," says Kusuda. "Most come over here in an administrative or sales management capacity. However, when I came to the States, whenever I had to discuss business issues with dealers or customers, I would go out with our American salespeople. It was sort of like walking with a cane. It's a kind of on-the-job training. You can learn quite quickly just by putting yourself in the field and going out with the salespeople."

For the Japanese, any fundamentals of sales and marketing are learned in college or high school and during the first few years at the company, where the practical application of those fundamentals constitutes the basic training course. Up-and-coming managers eventually go through all the divisions to familiarize themselves with all facets of the company so that when they're put in sales and marketing they already have a well-rounded background. Thus, for most businesspeople in Japan, the closest thing to a corporate training manual is the "how-to" section at the nearest bookstore. Other than that, there are consultants who offer their services to train executives for overseas duty, if this is deemed appropriate.

But make no mistake, the transition from doing business in Japan to doing business in the United States is viewed as both challenging and difficult. Cultural differences between the two societies affect negotiations and are plainly reflected in two very different sets of attitudes.

The Japanese, for example, tend to adopt a give-and-take approach, while Americans are far more direct in putting their needs and desires on the table and bypassing the casual opening banter that's typical of a Japanese business meeting. Despite their competitiveness, the Japanese often perceive American business practices to be highly aggressive. The Americans, on the other hand, view their Japanese colleagues as alternatively plodding and passive—to say nothing of frustrating.

Yoshikazu Hanawa of Nissan Motor Co. was quoted last year in *Automotive News* as saying, "We were told that Japan way was slow and inefficient, and we had to do business like Americans did or we wouldn't keep up." During his five-year stint at the company's plant in Smyrna, Ga., the two factions—American and Japanese—were frequently at odds because of differing opinions on the business of doing business. One of the main issues was the Japanese tendency toward compromise, a stance that most American businesspeople find impossible to embrace. "The Americans felt frustrated all day," Hanawa says. "But so did the Japanese."

Others have felt the same frustrations. D.T. recalls her dealings with a Japanese supervisor who used to say to her, "Please treat me more gently," when she would yell at him. "And I was trying to get him to harden up so that he could yell back at a customer if necessary," she explains.

Still, business ethics on both sides of the cultural coin can be of the dog-eat-dog variety, as evidenced by the spate of resignations, apologies, and corporate shakeups coming out of Japan of late. Massey thinks Japanese industries "are more organized, and collusion tends to be present more [there] then is generally found in U.S. businesses." In fact, there are some American businesspeople who hold to the theory that *keiretsu* (the Japanese system of long-standing relationships between suppliers and customers) and collusion are joined at the hip.

Many Japanese executives, on the other hand, don't perceive all that much of a difference between the ethics of the two countries. Al Kusuda, for example, expresses the opinion that the main difference lies in respective attitudes toward money. "People in the States seem to be more aware of the importance of money and have the drive to earn more money," Kusuda says. "Salespeople [in the U.S.] seem to have that drive more strongly than their Japanese counterparts. Most American salespeople work on commission, but in Japan, most of our salespeople are salaried. They may receive a bonus or bonuses, but they don't receive commissions. It's a different system."

Kusuda also recalls a story he read in a Japanese newspaper about a young salesman who was feted by his company because he finally landed an order from a company he'd called on 72 times. The report didn't mention, however, whether the company gave him a bonus or not.

As for whether the lack of formal sales training makes the Japanese less successful than their American counterparts, Kusuda sees the two running more or less neck-and-neck—but with distinctly different motivations. For the Japanese, for instance, "Success is not directly related to money or more income," he says. "In Japan, it's much more likely to be related to company recognition, self-esteem, promotion, and long-term security."

Settling on a Strategy

One area in which Japanese sales and marketing executives may be vulnerable is in their tendency to view markets as homogeneous. "People in Japan regard the U.S. as [a single entity]," says Kusuda. "They know there are many different ethnic groups here, but they don't think that different tactics are needed to approach different groups. They know there are many different races and that some difference in marketing techniques may be needed, but they don't address that specifically." This may be because the Japanese live in a quasi-homogeneous society where aliens—even those of Japanese decent—are few and largely ignored. Coping with the nuances of a multiethnic population, therefore, may simply not be indigenous to the Japanese psyche.

Instead, all those who were interviewed for this article felt that the sine qua non of Japanese salesmanship was essentially embodied in one word: quality. And marketing's job is to promise and deliver just that: quality—with an extra dollop of backup service where appropriate. "Quality is a very important issue, regardless of who the customer is," says Kusuda. "American consumers want the best quality, and they expect the best quality of the manufacturer. Americans buy Japanese cars because they seem to have a much better service record than American-made cars. Thus, cars, as well as other Japanese products, are perceived to be better in quality.

But do the Japanese care more about quality than Americans? "I don't think so," says Kusuda. "Higher quality comes from competition. In Japan, competition is especially keen where both prices and specifications are the same, so the better quality you have, the more sales you make. For that, each manufacturer will really try to put the very best quality into his products so he can make a strong showing compared to the competition. Of course, in the States, I know they're also doing that, but the competition may not be as keen. As you know, a long time ago, Japanese products were considered inferior: 'Made in Japan' meant something that breaks soon. So we had to do something to change that perception and the way to do that was to put in higher quality."

When asked if there was one thing the Japanese still have some trouble with, Kusuda cited pricing. "Japan is perhaps a competitor in quality, but now it's losing its competitiveness because of price. Everything has become very expensive. Japanese cars are pricier than American cars. Sooner or later, Japan is going to have to do something about pricing, or [Japanese automobiles] will soon be beyond our reach."

And while there are certain similarities in how each country looks at sales and marketing, there are some major differences as well. Take selling techniques, for instance. "Of course, in Japan, we have certain methods and steps that are similar to the American system," says Kusuda, "but we have a more personal approach. [In Japan], if you're liked by the buyer or a prospect, you're likely to get the sale. Personal contact and a personal approach are very, very important, rather than any theoretical selling approach. That's the major difference."

Given all this, perhaps it's time we amended our view of the Japanese approach to business to include the following terminology: personal, polite, patient, persistent, painstaking attention, and a seat-of-the-pants approach to training. Indeed, once you delve beyond the initial stereotypes, you find that these are the true principles behind Japanese sales concepts and practices.

And if you still have any doubts, just ask that salesperson who made 72 calls to get the order.

Pricing Issues

It is difficult to generalize about export pricing. Consequently, little has been written to assist a decision maker. The author of the first paper in this section has posited six key variables that influence export pricing: the nature of the product or industry, the locus of production, the system of distribution, the locale and environment of the target market, American government laws and regulations, and the attitudes of a firm's management about pricing. The paper includes a nine-step decision framework for export pricing.

The use of countertrade as an export strategy is the second piece in this sequence. It documents the counterpurchase, barter, offset, and coproduction arrangements that make possible many of the megadeals in international business today. A companion piece documents Pepsico's $3-billion deal in the former Soviet Union. It is a fascinating case history. Pepsico hoped to double its soft-drink sales in the Soviet Union and Pizza Hut restaurants in major cities. To finance this dramatic expansion, Pepsico planned to increase sales of Russian vodka abroad and also to lease or sell Soviet-built ships around the world. When the Soviet Union collapsed, the deal unraveled. Pepsico has persevered and may be able to continue with a revised plan.

Unraveling the Mystique of Export Pricing

S. Tamer Cavusgil. *S. Tamer Cavusgil is a professor of marketing and international business and director of the International Business Development Program at Michigan State University, East Lansing. Among his previous contributions to* Business Horizons *is "Guidelines for Export Market Research," published in the November–December 1985 issue.*

In recent years, hundreds of U.S. companies have become involved in international business. The initial foreign activity is typically exporting. Perhaps the most puzzling part of international business for these firms is making pricing decisions.

What role should pricing play in the exporting company's marketing efforts? Can pricing be used as an effective marketing tool? Or would that practice expose the firm to unnecessary risks? What considerations affect the choice between incremental and full-cost pricing strategies? What approach should management take when setting export prices? How can the firm cope with escalations in international prices? What strategies are appropriate when a strong currency impairs overseas competitiveness? These are only a few of the many questions international marketing managers must answer.

Export pricing is a complex issue, and simple decision rules are often inadequate. The complexity lies in the large number of variables that affect international pricing decisions and the uncertainty surrounding them. These variables can be classified as either internal or external to the organization. The internal group includes corporate goals, desire for control over prices, approach to costing, and degree of company internationalization. The external group includes competitive pressures, demand levels, legal and government regulations, general economic conditions, and exchange rates.

Despite export pricing's importance and complexity, very little empirical research has been conducted that might give managers norms to follow.[1] This article attempts to illuminate this important area of international marketing management. The overall purpose is to provide a better understanding of export pricing issues and to identify propositions that can be tested by more definitive, large-scale surveys, as well as to generate findings and implications useful to export managers.

Personal interviews, two to three hours in length, were conducted with one or more executives at each of 24 firms. Most of the firms studied were exporters of industrial or specialized products. The typical firm employed about 500 persons. Background information about each firm was collected with the use of a structured questionnaire either prior to or during the interview. All firms were located in the Midwestern United States.

Pricing Literature

Price is the only marketing variable that generates revenue. Top marketing executives call pricing the most critical pressure point of the 1980s.[2] Recently, with accelerating technological advances, shorter product life cycles, and increasing input costs, price changes have become more common. Despite these developments, academic research on pricing has been modest at best.[3]

The neglect of international pricing is even more serious.[4] Intracorporate (transfer) pricing issues received attention during the 1970s, when study of multinational corporations (MNCs) was intense, but other pricing topics remain relatively unexplored.[5]

Other studies have focused on pricing practices under floating exchange rates,[6] location of pricing authority within MNCs,[7] price leadership of MNCs,[8] multinational pricing in developing countries,[9] and uniform pricing.[10] Several studies have had a regional/industry focus. One found a relatively high degree of export price discrimination among industrial firms in Northern England.[11] Another compared the pricing practices of chemical and construction industries in South Africa.[12] A third, on the other hand, studied price-setting processes among industrial firms in the French market.[13]

This last study is particularly important, because it represents an effort to systematically describe and compare the processes used by firms to set prices. Through in-depth analyses of price decisions made by companies, the authors were able to develop flowcharts as well as indices of similarity, participation, and activity. They contend that decision-process methodology can help people gain insights into the dynamic activities of firms. The decision-making model for export pricing discussed in this article employs a similar approach.

The discussion here focuses on three major issues. First, those factors which have a bearing on export pricing are examined, and each factor's relevance is illustrated with company examples. The next section reveals that companies appear to follow one of three export pricing strategies. Finally, a decision framework for export pricing is offered.

Factors in Export Pricing

Export pricing is not a topic that lends itself easily to generalization. As with domestic pricing, any consideration of policies for setting export prices must first address the unique nature of the individual firm. Company philosophy, corporate culture, product offerings, and operating environment all have a significant impact on the creation of pricing policy. In addition, export marketers face unique constraints in each market destination.

The interaction of the internal and external environments gives rise to distinct—yet predictable—pricing constraints in different markets. These to a large extent determine export price strategy. For example, negotiation is normally required in the Middle East, so Regal Ware, a producer of kitchen appliances and cookware, uses a higher list price in such markets to leave a margin for discretion. But D. W. Witter, a manufacturer of grain storage and handling equipment, doesn't make price concessions in the Middle East. Witter is convinced that once a price becomes negotiable, the Middle Eastern buyer will expect and demand future concessions, making future negotiations interminable.

In Algeria, the interest rate is limited by the government. To counter this one company, a manufacturer of mining and construction equipment, builds the additional cost of capital into the price.

Six variables have important influences on export pricing. They are:

1. Nature of the product/industry;
2. Location of the production facility;
3. Chosen system of distribution;
4. Location and environment of the foreign market;
5. U.S. government regulations; and
6. Attitude of the firm's management.

A brief discussion of each factor is presented below.

Nature of the Product/Industry

A specialized product, or one with a technological edge, gives the firm flexibility. There are few competitors in such cases. In many markets there is no local production of the product, government-imposed import barriers are minimal, and importing firms all face similar price-escalation factors. Under such circumstances, firms are able to remain competitive with little adjustment in price strategy. Firms with a technological edge, such as the Burdick Corporation (hospital equipment) and Nicolet Instruments (scientific instruments), enjoy similar advantages, but both experience greater service requirements and longer production and sales lead times.

A relatively low level of price competition usually leads to administered prices and a static role for pricing in the export marketing mix. Over the years, however, as price competition evolves and technological advantages shrink, specialized and highly technical firms must make more market-based exceptions to their uniform export pricing strategies.

Many firms' export pricing strategies are also influenced by industry-specific factors, such as drastic fluctuations in the price of raw materials and predatory pricing practices by foreign competitors (most notably the Japanese). The presence of such factors demands greater flexibility in export pricing at some companies: Ray-O-Vac adjusts export prices frequently according to current silver prices. Other companies negotiate fixed-price agreements with suppliers prior to making a contract bid.

Location of Production Facility

Many U.S. companies produce exported products only in the United States. These U.S. exporters are unable to shift manufacturing to locations that make economic sense.

Purely domestic companies are tied to conditions prevailing in the home market, in this case in the U.S.

Those companies with production or assembly facilities abroad, often closer to foreign customers, have additional flexibility in overseas markets. These companies find it easier to respond to fluctuations in foreign exchange. Cummins Engine, for example, supplies Latin American customers with U.S. production when the U.S. dollar is weak. When the dollar is relatively strong, U.K. plants assume greater importance.

A number of factors may have impeded the global competitiveness of U.S. manufacturers in recent years. These include lagging productivity in many sectors of the economy and, until recently, reluctance to seek global sources of supply for materials, parts, and components. Also, strong unions and a high standard of living in the U.S. have contributed to higher labor costs. Naturally, these comparative disadvantages are reflected in the quotations submitted to overseas buyers.

Chosen System of Distribution

The channels of export distribution a company uses dictate much in export pricing. For example, subsidiary relationships offer greater control over final prices, first-hand knowledge of market conditions, and the ability to adjust prices rapidly. With independent distributors, control usually extends only to the landed price received by the exporter. As one might expect, many of the executives interviewed spoke of the difficulty of maintaining price levels. These firms report that distributors may mark up prices substantially—up to 200 percent in some cases.

When a firm initiates exporting through independent distributors, many new pricing considerations arise. Significant administrative costs stem from the selection of foreign distributors and the maintenance of harmonious relationships. Discount policies for intermediaries must be established. Also, the costs of exporting (promotion, freight service, and so forth) must be assigned to either the intermediaries or the manufacturer. To minimize the administrative, research, and travel expenses involved in switching to direct exporting, most firms use a relatively uniform export pricing strategy across different markets. Gross margins are then increased to account for additional levels of distribution. In other cases, companies establish prices on a case-by-case basis.

The use of manufacturers' representatives offers greater price control to the exporter, but this method is used less frequently. Finally, sales to end users may involve negotiation or, in the case of selling to governmental agencies, protracted purchasing decisions. List prices are not used in these circumstances.

Firms often attempt to establish more direct channels of distribution to reach their customers in overseas markets. By reducing the number of intermediaries between the manufacturer and the customer, they offset the adverse effects of *international price escalation*. Excessive escalation of prices is a problem encountered by most exporters. Aside from shorter distribution channels, the firms studied had developed other strategies to cope with price escalation. These alternatives are listed in Figure 1.

Location and Environment of the Foreign Market

The climate conditions of a market may necessitate product modification. For example, a producer of soft-drink equipment must treat its products against rust corrosion in tropical

FIGURE 1   Strategic Options to Deal with Price Escalation

- Shortening channels of distribution by reducing number of intermediaries or engaging in company-sponsored distribution. Fewer intermediaries would also have the effect of minimizing value added taxes.

- Reducing cost to overseas customers by eliminating costly features from the product, lowering overall product quality, or offering a stripped-down model.

- Shipping and assembling components in foreign markets. Popularity of the Free Trade Zones in Hong Kong, Panama or the Caribbean Basin is due to companies' desire to minimize price escalation.

- Modifying the product to bring it into a different, lower-tariff classification. The Microbattery division of Ray-O-Vac Corporation, for example, ships bulk to foreign marketing companies who then repackage. Another company, through consultations with local distributors, places products in "proper" import classifications. Proper wording is used for initial import registration to qualify for lower duties.

- Lowering the new price (landed price) to reduce tariffs and other charges by the importing country. This can be accomplished through the application of marginal cost pricing or by allowing discounts to distributors. Nicolet Instruments, a producer of scientific instruments, for example, compensates its distributors for the cost of installation and service. Western Publishing Company compensates its distributors for the differences in import duties between book and nonbook exports.

- Going into overseas production and sourcing in order to remain competitive in the foreign markets. Dairy Equipment Company located in Wisconsin, for example, supplies the European market with bulk coolers made at its Danish plant as a way of reducing freight costs.

markets. Another company, an agribusiness concern, must take into account climate, soil conditions, and the country's infrastructure before making any bid. Economic factors, such as inflation, exchange-rate fluctuations, and price controls, may hinder market entry and effectiveness.[14] These factors, especially the value of U.S. currency in foreign markets, are a major concern to most of the firms interviewed. Consequently, several companies have introduced temporary compensating adjustments as part of their pricing strategies. The unusually strong value of the U.S. dollar during the first half of the 1980s was a significant factor in pricing strategy.

Since currency fluctuations are cyclical, exporters who find themselves blessed with a price advantage when their currency is undervalued must carry an extra burden when their currency is overvalued. Committed exporters must be creative, pursuing different strategies during different periods. Appropriate strategies practiced by the firms studied are outlined in Figure 2.

It must be noted that, while exporters can implement some of these strategies quickly, others require a long-term response. For example, the decision to manufacture overseas is often a part of a deliberate and long-term plan for most companies. And while some strategies can be used by any exporter, others, such as countertrade and speculative currency trading, are limited to use by the larger, more experienced exporters. In fact, most managers interviewed said that high-risk propositions such as countertrade deals should be used only by multinational companies.

The cultural environment and business practices of the foreign market also play a large role in export pricing. Some countries abhor negotiation, others expect it. As previously noted, D. W. Witter has successfully overcome the expectation of price negotiation in the Middle East market. In some markets, a subtle barrier to foreign imports is erected in the form of procurement practices which favor domestic companies.

FIGURE 2 Exporter Strategies under Varying Currency Conditions

When Domestic Currency Is WEAK	*When Domestic Currency Is STRONG ....*
• Stress price benefits	• Engage in nonprice competition by improving quality, delivery and aftersale service
• Expand product line and add more costly features	• Improve productivity and engage in vigorous cost reduction
• Shift sourcing and manufacturing to domestic market	• Shift sourcing and manufacturing overseas
• Exploit export opportunities in all markets	• Give priority to exports to relatively strong-currency countries
• Conduct conventional cash-for-goods trade	• Deal in countertrade with weak-currency countries
• Use full-costing approach, but use marginal-cost pricing to penetrate new/competitive markets	• Trim profit margins and use marginal-cost pricing
• Speed repatriation of foreign-earned income and collections	• Keep the foreign-earned income in host country, slow collections
• Minimize expenditures in local, host country currency	• Maximize expenditures in local, host country currency
• Buy needed services (advertising, insurance, transportation, etc.) in domestic market	• Buy needed services abroad and pay for them in local currencies
• Minimize local borrowing	• Borrow money needed for expansion in local market
• Bill foreign customers in domestic currency	• Bill foreign customers in their own currency

U.S. Government Regulations

Government policy also affects export pricing strategy. While the majority of the firms interviewed are not directly affected by U.S. pricing regulations, they feel that U.S. regulations such as the Foreign Corrupt Practices Act put them at a significant competitive disadvantage. One company often receives "requests" by overseas customers to add over $100,000 to the contract price and make appropriate arrangements to transfer the money to private accounts abroad. Interestingly, such requests are sometimes openly made. Submission to demands for "grease payments" appears to be the only option if businesses want to compete in certain countries.

Attitude of the Firm's Management

Many U.S. firms still view exporting as an extension of the domestic sales effort, and export pricing policy is established accordingly. Smaller companies whose top management concerns itself mostly with domestic matters have major problems setting export prices. Price determination of export sales is often based on a full-costing approach. The preference for cost-based pricing over market-oriented pricing reflects the relative importance given to profits and market share. This is particularly notable with firms that are unconcerned with market share and require that every quote meet their profit expectations. Other companies are more concerned with selling one product line at any price, even below cost, and reap longer-term benefits from the sale of follow-up consumables and spare parts. Producers of expensive industrial equipment, scientific instruments, and medical equipment fall into this category.

Alternative Approaches to Pricing

Firms typically choose one of three approaches to pricing. These can be called the rigid cost-plus, flexible cost-plus, and dynamic incremental pricing strategies.

Rigid Cost-Plus Strategy

The complexity of export pricing has caused many managers to cling to a rigid cost-plus pricing strategy in an effort to secure profitability. This strategy establishes the foreign list price by adding international customer costs and a gross margin to domestic manufacturing costs. The final cost to the customer includes administrative and R&D overhead costs, transportation, insurance, packaging, marketing, documentation, and customs charges, as well as the profit margins for both the distributor and the manufacturer. Although this type of pricing ensures margins, the final price may be so high that it keeps the firm from being competitive in major foreign markets.

Nevertheless, cost-plus pricing appears to be the most dominant strategy among American firms. Approximately 70 percent of the sampled firms used this strategy. Over half of the firms using a cost-plus strategy adhered to it rigidly, with no exceptions. This approach may be typical of other exporting firms in the U.S. The following company examples illustrate the popularity of the rigid cost-plus pricing approach.

Autotrol is a Wisconsin manufacturer of water treatment and control equipment. The firm employs about 80 people, and exports account for about 60 percent of its estimated $14 million annual sales. Principal markets include Western Europe, Japan, Australia, New Zealand, and Venezuela. Autotrol sets export prices 3 percent to 4 percent higher than domestic prices to cover the additional costs. Such costs include foreign advertising, foreign travel, and all costs incurred when shipping the product from the factory to the foreign distributor. The firm has successfully exported for the past 15 years by using a rigid cost-plus strategy.

Chillicothe Metal Co. is a solely owned manufacturer of generator sets, pump packages, engine enclosures, controls, and spare parts. The firm has recently lost a significant portion of its foreign business. Sales dropped from $5 million in 1982 to $3 million in 1984, and the current employment of 40 is down from its 1982 high of 100. The company had successfully exported for more than 15 years, but current exports are down 40 percent from the 1982 level. Principal foreign markets are the Middle East, North Africa, and the Far East. The company adheres to a rigid cost-plus pricing strategy that includes a built-in margin ranging from 5 percent to 15 percent. However, the president has recently taken efforts to control costs, extend credit, and reduce margins for cash-in advance customers in an attempt to counter the effects of the slow business cycle.

Dairy Equipment Co. produces milk machines, bulk coolers, and other high-quality equipment for the dairy industry. The company's annual sales are about $40 million, with current employment at 400. Although the company has exported continuously over the past decade, export earnings have become negligible. This has been caused by a significant drop in sales in the company's primary foreign market—West Germany. Gross profit has remained the company's primary export goal, but the rigid cost-plus pricing strategy has not yet proved to be effective. The company has always sought equal profitability from foreign sales, although fierce competition in some markets has forced it to consider lower profit margins. The company's export pricing policy remains a static element of the marketing mix.

These examples demonstrate that a rigid cost-plus pricing strategy may or may not be effective. They also imply that just because a strategy has been successful in the past, there is no guarantee that it will be successful in the future. Competitive pressures often force firms to reevaluate their pricing decisions and consider new alternatives.

Flexible Cost-Plus Strategy

One such alternative is a flexible cost-plus strategy. This is also the most logical strategy for companies that are in the process of moving away from their traditionally rigid pricing policies.

Flexible cost-plus price strategy is identical to the rigid strategy in establishing list prices. Flexible strategy, however, allows for price variations in special circumstances. For example, discounts may be granted, depending on the customer, the size of the order, or the intensity of competition. Although discounts occasionally are granted on a case-by-case basis, the primary objective of flexible cost-plus pricing is profit. Thus, pricing is still a static element of the marketing mix. The following cases are good examples of companies that use a flexible cost-plus pricing strategy.

Baughman, a division of Fuqua Industries, manufactures steel grain-storage silos and related equipment. The company currently employs about 125 people, and annual sales are around $6 million. The company has traditionally exported about 30 percent of its sales over the past ten years, but recently exports have grown to over 50 percent of annual sales. Baughman's products are of high quality, and pricing has not often been an active element in the marketing mix. The firm's export sales terms consist of an irrevocable confirmed letter of credit in U.S. currency with no provisions for fluctuating exchange rates. Export and domestic prices are identical before exporting costs are added. However, Baughman will make concessions to this policy to secure strategically important sales.

Nicolet Instrument Corporation designs, manufactures, and markets electronic instruments that are used in science, medicine, industry, and engineering. The firm employs more than 500 people and has annual sales of over $85 million. Exports account for about 42 percent of total sales, and the firm has been exporting for the past ten years. Major foreign markets include Japan, West Germany, France, Canada, England, Mexico, Sweden, and the Netherlands. Foreign and domestic prices are calculated according to full cost. Since Nicolet has held a technological edge, it has not been affected by competition in foreign markets. However, the competitive gap has been slowly closing, and the company now varies from administered prices more frequently.

Badger Meter manufactures and sells industrial liquid meters. The company employs 700 people, and its annual sales are estimated at $60 million. The company has sold internationally for more than 50 years, but export sales only account for 9 percent of total sales. Major markets include Europe, Canada, Taiwan, and the Philippines. The company owns a production facility in Mexico and has licensees in Ecuador and Peru. Cost-based list prices are used for both domestic and foreign markets. Although prices usually remain fixed, the company has, at times, offered special discounts to regain market share or to offset unfavorable exchange rates.

Flexible pricing strategies are useful to counter competitive pressures or exchange-rate fluctuations. They help firms stay competitive in certain markets without disrupting the entire pricing strategy. However, if competitive pressures persist and technology gaps continue to close, the company could face losing its export market. This is when a company may consider the third alternative.

Dynamic Incremental Strategy

The dynamic incremental pricing strategy was used by approximately 30 percent of the firms studied. Most firms using this strategy had sales well over $50 million with exports ranging from 20 to 65 percent of total sales. In the dynamic incremental strategy, prices are set by subtracting fixed costs for plants, R&D, and domestic overhead from cost-plus figures. In addition, domestic marketing and promotion costs are also disregarded.

This strategy is based on the assumption that fixed and variable domestic costs are incurred regardless of export sales. Therefore, only variable and international customer costs need to be recovered on exported products. This makes it possible for a company to maintain profit margins while selling its exported products at prices below U.S. list. It is also assumed that unused production capacity exists and that the exported products could not be otherwise sold at full cost. Companies can thus lower their prices and be competitive in markets that may otherwise be prohibitive to enter or penetrate. The following examples illustrate this strategy.

Flo-Con Systems, a subsidiary of Masco Inc., manufactures high-quality and sophisticated flow-control valves for molten-steel-pouring applications. The company employs 500 people and has sales between $50 and $60 million, of which 25 percent result from exports. A plant located in Canada produces final products, and an additional plant in Mexico is being considered. Flo-Con finds the nature of its markets very competitive. The firm's export prices are based on competitive prices in the local market. Management is often forced to temporarily overlook costs and margins to remain competitive and secure orders.

Ray-O-Vac, a producer of batteries and other consumer goods, has been exporting successfully for over 30 years. Its Micro Power Division employs 250 and has estimated annual sales of $100 million. The major products in this division include batteries for hearing aids and watches. Exports account for 20 percent of total business, and major markets include Europe, Far East, and Japan. These markets are entered through wholly owned subsidiaries strategically located around the world. Each subsidiary may be treated as a cost or profit center depending upon the market circumstances. Competitive pressures demand flexible pricing, and discounts are often granted to gain market share or secure OEM business. Branch managers may adjust prices on a day-to-day basis to counter exchange-rate fluctuations. Export pricing is a very active ingredient in the firm's marketing mix.

Econ-O-Cloth is an independent manufacturer of optical polishing cloths and a wholesaler of related goods. Although the company has traditionally exported around 25 percent of its sales volume, this figure has slipped to around 5 percent over the past five years. Major markets include Canada, Mexico, and Western Europe. Econ-O-Cloth reduced export margins to compensate for the strong dollar in the early 1980s, and it considers pricing an active instrument for achieving marketing objectives. The firm continually monitors the foreign environment and at times modifies its prices and products to blend with foreign consumer demands. Econ-O-Cloth has been squeezed hard by competition, and it is still waiting for its dynamic pricing strategy to pay off.

The above examples demonstrate that pricing strategies are complex and that no single strategy suits a firm at all times. There is no guarantee that pricing strategies that work successfully today will continue to do so in the future. Many traditionally successful exporters have recently experienced sales downturns in their foreign markets. One can only speculate on whether a change of pricing strategies could have prevented these downturns. Also, it is not known to what extent other factors (poor market intelligence, weak distribution networks, no product modifications when they were needed, slow delivery, or poor image) were responsible.

The uncertainties of international business make it difficult for executives to select the pricing strategy that is best for their firm. As a result, most firms use the rigid cost-plus strategy until external pressures force them to reconsider. This strategy makes managers feel secure, and it is frequently used when a firm enters the export market. As competition and other external variables grow more intense, however, the firm typically makes exceptions to its pricing policy, moving from rigid to flexible cost-plus pricing. Few firms have attempted to price their export products according to the dynamic conditions of the marketplace. For these firms, the dynamic incremental strategy is usually required, and prices may change frequently in response to competition, the prevailing exchange rate, and other variables.

Most exporting firms appear to establish their pricing policies reactively, changing only when external pressures force the issue. In working this way, however, these firms lose valuable sales and market share during the transition period. Although this strategy may be defensible, three types of lags may result in irreversible damage. The recognition lag is the amount of time between an actual change in the environment and a company's recognition of that change. Reaction lag is the amount of time between the company's recognition of the problem and its decision to react to it. Finally, effectiveness lag is the amount of time needed to implement the decision.

One might conclude that if executives were proactive in their pricing strategy, they might avoid many of the headaches associated with exporting. But how can executives be sure which pricing policy is best for their firms? Considering all the variables that affect price, it is reasonable to assume that different pricing policies should exist for different markets. Furthermore, considering the volatility of foreign markets, one would suspect that these policies should be continuously reviewed and updated. It is not surprising, then, that most executives resort to setting their pricing policies reactively.

A Decision Framework for Export Pricing

Most companies lack a systematic procedure for setting and revising export prices. The absence of a formal decision-making procedure that incorporates and weighs relevant variables has led to the development of the framework described here. It is not intended to replace management judgment, since the business executive is usually in the best position to assess the suitability of various strategies and policies, but simply to provide a systematic framework for arriving at export pricing decisions.

FIGURE 3   Decision Process for Export Price Determination

Verify export market potential

⬇

Estimate target price range: floor, ceiling, and expected prices

⬇

Determine company sales potential at given prices

⬇

Analyze import, distribution and transaction barriers

⬇

Examine corporate goals and preference for pricing strategy

⬇

Select suitable pricing strategy:
1. Rigid cost-plus
2. Flexible cost-plus
3. Dynamic incremental

⬇

Check consistency with current price setting

⬇

Implementation: Select tactics, distributor prices, and end user prices

⬇

Monitor export market performance and make adjustments as necessary

---

Figure 3 illustrates the steps involved in a formal export price determination process. A brief description of each step is presented below.

Verification of Market Potential

The first step in the analysis gives firm information on the market potential in specific countries. The company can identify market potential for its products by using both formal and informal sources. Formal sources include market-research firms, the U.S. Department of Commerce, banks, and other agencies that provide information on foreign countries. Informal sources include trade shows, local distributors, international trade journals, and business contacts.[15] During this process, those countries that do not demonstrate adequate market potential are dropped from the list of possible markets.

Estimating Target Price Range

Once it is determined that a market has sufficient potential, the firm observes the price ranges of substitute or competitive products in the local market to find its target price range. This consists of three prices:

• The floor price, that price at which the firm breaks even;

• The ceiling price, the highest price the market is likely to bear for the product; and

• The expected price, the price at which the firm would most likely be competitive.

Estimating Sales Potential

Assuming that a high enough level of sales potential exists to warrant market entry, management then identifies the size and concentration of customer segments, projected consumption patterns, competitive pressures, and the expectations of local distributors and agents. The landed cost and the cost of local distribution are estimated. The potential sales volume is assessed for each of the three price levels, taking into account the price elasticity of demand.

Analyze Special Import, Distribution, or Transaction Barriers

If adequate sales potential exists, management then assesses any special import barriers not accounted for in its earlier efforts. These barriers include quotas, tariffs and other taxes, anti-dumping, price-maintenance, currency-exchange, and other governmental regulations that affect the cost of doing business in that country. In addition, internal distribution barriers must also be assessed. Lengthy distribution channels, high margins, and inadequate dealer commitment may present difficulties for the exporter. Finally, currency supply, payment terms, and financing availability should be reviewed. Is it customary for prices to be negotiable? Do customers expect certain credit or payment terms? Once again, sales potential, market share, and profitability should be analyzed in light of the above information in order to confirm the desirability of market entry.

Corporate Goals and Preference for Pricing

After deciding on a target market, some companies may not wish to consider anything but full-cost pricing (either rigid or flexible cost-plus). If desired margins can be achieved, this pricing policy can be implemented. If, however, the desired margins cannot be achieved, the firm can either abort market entry or resort to some form of marginal costing approach. If the firm's management is willing to consider pricing strategies that focus on market rather than profit objectives, it may continue the analysis with a systematic identification of the optimal pricing strategy.

Systematic Selection of Appropriate Pricing Strategy

The company needs to arrive at a strategy choice by systematically considering all relevant variables. Management faces a basic choice between a dynamic incremental pricing strategy and a cost-plus pricing strategy (either rigid or flexible). Dynamic incremental pricing implies a marginal costing approach, while cost-plus pricing implies full costing.

Figure 4 identifies 15 criteria that help management make choices between the two pricing strategies. Some criteria are derived from the general environment of the firm, while others are unique to the specific export opportunity being considered. Management

FIGURE 4 Criteria Relevant to the Choice between Full and Marginal Costing

Conditions Favoring Marginal Costing/ Aggressive Pricing	Criteria	Conditions Favoring Full Costing/ Passive Pricing
A. Firm-Specific Criteria		
Low	Extent of product differentiation	High
Committed	Corporate stance toward exporting	Half-hearted
Long term	Management desire for recovering export overhead	Short term
Sufficient	Company financial resources to sustain initial losses	Insufficient
Wide	Domestic gross margins	Narrow
High	Need for long-term capacity utilization	Low
High	Opportunity to benefit from economies of scale	Low
B. Situation-Specific Criteria		
Substantial	Growth potential of export market	Negligible
High	Potential for follow-up sales	Low
Continuous	Nature of export opportunity	One-time
High	End-user price sensitivity	Low
High	Competitive intensity	Low
Likely	Opportunity to drive out competition	Unlikely
Favorable	Terms of sale and financing	Unfavorable
Low	Exchange rate risk	High
Low	Cost of internal distribution, service and promotion	High

may choose to weigh each group, as well as individual criteria, in arriving at a choice. Figure 4 spells out the conditions that call for incremental pricing.

Checking Consistency with Current Pricing

If a firm is already in the targeted market, the recommended pricing strategy should be compared to the strategy currently in place. If deviations exist, they should be explained and justified. If they cannot be justified, the firm should seriously consider adopting the recommended pricing strategy in order to achieve marketing goals more effectively. It is also important to check for consistency of export pricing policies across export markets to minimize any conflicts (such as inter-market shipping by competing middlemen).

Implementation

The exporter will determine specific prices for distributors and end users, in accordance with the recommended pricing strategy, and decide on specific pricing tactics. A strategy may fail in a specific market if execution is not effective or if reaction to change is slow. For example, distributors may vary their margins as a response to price changes. Similarly, distributors may hold a large inventory of products at the old price, creating a lag before the new pricing policy actually becomes effective.

Monitoring

Exchange rates can be one of the more volatile variables in international business, especially in developing countries. These rates should be monitored continuously, and the effect of their changes on pricing policy should be evaluated. Variables such as competition, regulations, and price sensitivity can be monitored periodically. As these variables change, the firm can adjust its pricing strategy appropriately. The proposed decision process, therefore, provides a proactive means of establishing pricing policies.

A major implication of this analysis is that no export pricing strategy will fit all of a company's products and markets. International pricing issues are extremely complex, and pricing decisions are fueled by many variables. It is important that the company establish a systematic and periodic approach in selecting a pricing policy. The approach should account for both internal and external variables affecting the firm's export efforts. This framework for export pricing is one such approach. Executives may wish to modify the model in order to better blend it with their firms' perspectives.

A second implication is that many U.S. firms may be overlooking lucrative foreign markets because of their strict adherence to the full-cost pricing approach. Furthermore, this rigid practice may hinder effective market penetration in existing foreign markets. A complete reassessment of the firm's market-share objectives may be needed. Committed exporters will allocate the resources needed to accomplish this task if it becomes necessary.

Finally, there is no guarantee that those pricing policies that are suitable today will work in the future. Changing business trends, exchange rates, consumer preferences, and competition are only a few of the variables that have caught successful exporters off guard. Therefore, a method for monitoring changes in the pricing policy variables should be established. The most volatile variables, such as exchange rates and competitive transaction prices, should be monitored more frequently. Once again, committed exporters will recognize the need for this and allocate the appropriate resources to establish an adequate monitoring system.

Although no best pricing strategy exists, most American firms have adhered to a full-cost approach, often disregarding conditions that are particular to their targeted foreign market. Many companies have abandoned lucrative foreign markets because of seemingly unattractive potentials. Other firms have relinquished sales and market share to local or more aggressive foreign competitors. The full-cost approach is a major deterrent to improving the exports of American businesses.

The establishment of international pricing policies is a dynamic process. Success with one strategy does not guarantee that the same strategy will continue to work. Many companies react passively when global changes make their traditional pricing policies obsolete. Such companies are usually forced to either abandon the market or adapt their pricing strategy to the new conditions. The lag times associated with recognition, reaction, and effectiveness can cause an irreversible deterioration in a company's sales, profits, and market share in the foreign country.

A proactive stance on establishing pricing strategy can often reduce or eliminate these lags, enhancing the firm's flexibility and responsiveness to changing business conditions. To develop a proactive stance, businesses need to establish systematic methods to monitor and evaluate the variables associated with an international pricing policy. Firms that are committed to international business will quickly recognize this and allocate resources accordingly.

The guidelines and decision process discussed in this article have been derived from the experience of exporting firms. Such an empirically-based approach to developing managerial guidelines is appropriate, given the current dearth of export pricing literature. Insights obtained from the field can rip away the shroud of mystery that surrounds export pricing decisions. At the same time, it should be noted that the managerial guidelines offered here are appropriate for a given set of conditions. The seasoned executive will realize that these recommendations are not substitutes for good business judgment. The proposed strategies may need minor modifications to better reflect a company's perspectives and constraints on international pricing.

References

1. Vern Terpstra, "Suggestions for Research Themes and Publications," *Journal of International Business Studies,* Spring/Summer 1983, pp. 9–10.

2. "Pricing Competition Is Shaping Up as 84's Top Marketing Pressure Point," *Marketing News,* November 11, 1983, p. 1.

3. Vithala R. Rao, "Pricing Research in Marketing: The State of the Art," *Journal of Business,* January 1984, pp. 539–559.

4. See: James C. Baker and John K. Ryans, Jr., "Some Aspects of International Pricing: A Neglected Area of Management Policy," *Management Decision,* Summer 1973, pp. 177–182; S. Tamer Cavusgil and John R. Nevin, "State-of-the-Art in International Marketing: An Assessment," in B. M. Enis and K. J. Roering, eds., *Review of Marketing 1981* (Chicago: American Marketing Association), pp. 195–216; and Terpstra (see note 1).

5. See: Jeffrey S. Arpan, "Mutinational Firm Pricing in International Markets," *Sloan Management Review,* Winter 1973, pp. 1–9; M. Edgar Barrett, "Case of the Tangled Transfer Price," *Harvard Business Review,* May-June 1977, p. 21; Seung H. Kim and Stephen W. Miller, "Constituents of the International Transfer Pricing Decision," *Columbia Journal of World Business,* Spring 1979, pp. 69–77.

6. Llewellyn Clague and Rena Grossfield, "Exporting Pricing in a Floating Rate World," *Columbia Journal of World Business,* Winter 1974, pp. 17–22.

7. Baker and Ryans (see note 4).

8. Donald J. Lecraw, "Pricing Strategies of Transnational Corporations," *Asia Pacific Journal of Management,* January 1984, pp. 112–119.

9. Nathaniel H. Left, "Multinational Corporate Pricing Strategy in Developing Countries," *Journal of International Business Studies,* Fall 1975, pp. 55–64.

10. Peter R. Kressler, "Is Uniform Pricing Desirable in Multinational Markets?" *Akron Business and Economic Review,* Winter 1971.

11. Nigel Piercy, "British Export Market Selection and Pricing," *Industrial Marketing Management,* October 1981, pp. 287–297.

12. Russell Abratt and Leyland F. Pitt, "Pricing Practices in Two Industries," *Industrial Marketing Management,* 14:301–306.

13. John U. Farley, James M. Hulbert and David Weistein, "Price Setting and Volume Planning by Two European Industrial Companies: A Study and Comparison of Decision Processes," *Journal of Marketing,* Winter 1980, pp. 46–54.

14. Victor H. Frank, Jr., "Living with Price Controls Abroad," *Harvard Business Review,* March–April 1984, pp. 137–142.

15. S. Tamer Cavusgil, "Guidelines for Export Market Research," *Business Horizons,* November–December 1985, pp. 27–33.

Countertrade as an Export Strategy

Matt Schaffer. *Matt Schaffer is the author of* Winning the Countertrade Wars: New Export Strategies for America, *published by John Wiley & Sons in 1989. He is President of D.M. Schaffer Corporation of Sandpoint, Idaho, and Washington, D.C., an investment banking firm that does countertrade export consulting and merger and acquisition work for larger companies.*

The Christmas 1989 revolution in Romania and the U.S. invasion to Panama, when considered together, depict a U.S. dilemma. The United States has more than adequate military power to rescue a potentially troubled regime close to home. Yet, the United States has few economic tools as a government to assist Romania and its Eastern European neighbors now that they are becoming free.

For example, a U.S. trading company could establish barter and counterpurchase agreements with this emerging part of the world. (Romania could buy U.S. products and pay in cash if a company, in advance, agrees to buy its products.)

There is no U.S. Government trading company in the general sense, while Japan, West Germany, and other European countries have many such companies in their private sectors.

The United States has also severely cut back on its U.S. export–import bank loans; there are hardly any funds for making bank loans and guarantees to Eastern Europe. These loans might enable these countries to buy U.S. exports to speed their development. In the 1990s, it appears that Japan and Europe are better positioned than the United States to trade with Eastern Europe, the Soviet Union, and many Third World countries.

With their nonconvertible currencies, Eastern Europe and the Soviet Union, along with many other countries, use various forms of countertrade. The United States has gotten into the countertrade business reluctantly.

The United States pretends that countertrade does not exist, when much of the world trades this way. U.S. companies do a better job, often without the government support that is available in Europe and Japan. A few U.S. companies, such as General Motors, General Electric (GE), Monsanto, Coca-Cola, Pepsico, and Combustion Engineering, have established trading companies or units that are countertrade to increase sales.

Many U.S. companies, however, still do not use countertrade. And when a major transaction is in the works, even the best-prepared U.S. company must turn to a foreign trading company to market the products that are accepted in the countertrade. In its

Reprinted from the *Journal of Business Strategy,* May/June 1990, pp. 33–38. Permission granted by Faulkner & Gray, 11 Penn Plaza, New York, NY 10001.

recent $100 million sale of radar equipment to Jordan in exchange for phosphate, Westinghouse relied on the Japanese trading giant Mitsubishi to sell the mineral through its network.

This transaction illustrates the theory behind modern countertrade. It takes the idea that a product can be substituted for money in part of the transaction and adds a crucial idea: the concept of linked trading or mandated reciprocity.

Types of Countertrade

There are several types of countertrade arrangements, including the following:

Counterpurchase

In 1983, Rockwell used the counterpurchase technique to win a hotly contested sale to Zimbabwe of an $8 million printing press. A key element of Rockwell's successful bid was the offer of 100 percent counterpurchase.

Rockwell Trading Company offered to buy $8 million of ferrochrome and nickel, knowing that Zimbabwe has these minerals in oversupply. This agreement to purchase or "counterpurchase" the minerals and export them elsewhere was linked to the basic sales agreement calling for Zimbabwe to pay Rockwell cash for the printing press—cash financed with favorable credit from Great Britain's export credit agency, ECGD. Rockwell sourced or produced the press in Great Britain expressly to secure this favorable financing since U.S. Export–Import Bank loans were not available.

U.S.-based Rockwell developed this counterpurchase and financing strategy for a very simple reason. Its French competitor, Harris, had already been awarded the sale, thanks to a heavily subsidized French loan, which required no down payment, a twenty-year repayment, and 4 percent interest. However, Zimbabwe had not signed the contract and promptly rewarded it to Rockwell after receiving the U.S. company's new offer.

Counterpurchase has been picked up more formally by the countries of Eastern Europe and by several countries in Latin America, including Mexico, Venezuela, and Colombia, which makes it national policy. In counterpurchase, the products traded are not a substitution for money but a catalyst for the creation and release of hard currency. Counterpurchase, like countertrade, flourishes where money or hard currency is scarce.

Barter

While pure barter is rare in modern countertrade, barterlike transactions occur very often.

In 1981, GE resorted to this approach when U.S. Eximbank financing was withdrawn after production on a turbine generator for Romania had already begun. Rather than take a loss on start-up costs already committed, GE agreed to accept Romanian chemicals, metals, steel, rebar, and nails on a credit basis as payment over several years. GE founded its own trading company within two years to turn these items into cash and to handle the trade finance arrangements on individual transactions.

Offsets

In 1975, offset became popular among European countries with NATO's purchase of F-16 aircraft from General Dynamics and with the Swiss purchase of Northrop's F-5. A key feature of the F-16 sale was a coproduction agreement, which set up a production facility in the Netherlands for this state-of-the-art fighter plane. The Swiss added to the coproduction idea by convincing Northrop to export manufactured products from Switzerland (mainly machine tools and electronic components).

Today, offset is requested in nearly all major U.S. military exports; it is spreading beyond the military area into such fields as telecommunications and commercial aircraft.

Offset may involve a complex set of commitments requested from the company seeking to win an export sale. In its 1984 sale of 160 F-16s to Turkey, worth $4.2 billion in 1983 dollars, General Dynamics offered an offset package including (1) coproduction, (2) technology transfer, (3) the export of miscellaneous Turkish products (called indirect offsets), and (4) electronic and military components (called direct offsets because they are more directly related to the F-16 program).

Countries often place a higher value on direct rather than indirect offsets because the related exports tend to strengthen their own domestic defense industry. Thus, when Great Britain and France bought the AWACs airborne radar plane from Boeing in the mid-1980s, these countries valued a commitment by the aircraft manufacturer to purchase certain components for the AWACs in the two countries. This commitment was in addition to prized coproduction agreements calling for Boeing's investment in the French and British manufacturers who supplied components for the plane.

By creating an eventual competitor, U.S. companies try to design an offset that does the least damage to their future sales. This issue is vital for deciding how much technology to transfer.

A U.S. company might bet that technology transferred today will become outmoded in two or three years and, therefore, may not be a threat. The Japanese place great emphasis on technology transfer, stressing it more than any other aspect of the offset concept. In several recent military sales, the Japanese have been aggressive and skillful in extracting a transfer of technology or at least access to it. A succession of military sales to Japan has become increasingly controversial, including Sidewinder missiles from Raytheon, Aegis destroyers from RCA, and FSX planes from General Dynamics (a modified version of the F-16).

The Aegis and FSX were the subject of bitter disputes in Congress during 1988 and 1989 when critics expressed dismay over the large Japanese content in each system and the implications of technology transfer. The companies argued that some sale was better than no sale and that offering a buyer domestic content and access to technology is an accepted marketing technique.

Critics in Congress complained that the United States is simply frittering away its technological advantage and speeding Japan toward its expressed goal of becoming a major exporter of military systems. Japan, they argued, could act more forcefully to reduce the trade deficit by purchasing larger military items "off the shelf" without insisting on the joint venture concept that is so much a part of Japanese business culture and that is central to the notion of offset.

In order to compete, U.S. companies must begin to design offset packages. Japan, South Korea, Australia, Canada (despite the highly touted free-trade agreement), and all European nations have offset policies while the United States does not.

Ideally, no company should negotiate a commitment without a concrete plan for how the commitment will be carried out, even though such precision may not always be possible. Accepting a heavy penalty beyond 3 percent or 4 percent of the unfulfilled offset may be unwise. As with a bank loan, seeking the longest term for carrying out the commitment is often a good idea. Above all, maintaining flexibility for how the offset can be fulfilled is essential. The list of products for export should be as broad as possible, including the right to substitute procurement of components, investment in-country, or the transfer of technology.

General Dynamics has found that investment in-country yields the greatest offset credit for each dollar spent. So far, on a worldwide basis, the company has been able to spend less than $0.04 on average for each $1 of offset credit received.

Coproduction

A key feature of General Dynamics's F-16 sale to Turkey was a coproduction arrangement where the company and its main U.S. subcontractors invested $137 million in an F-16 assembly plant in that country as well as in Turkey's aircraft industry.

Coproduction of this sort, if it can be offered, is becoming a key feature of offsets. For example, in order to sell its twin-jet MD-82 to the Chinese government, McDonnell-Douglas built the first-ever commercial aircraft coproduction factory within the People's Republic. The first airplane in a projected fleet of twenty-five rolled off the assembly line in July 1987.

Compensation

Compensation takes the idea of coproduction one step further. The investing company is repaid with the product of its manufacturing or mining investment while the host government often gives its formal approval and is a partner in the venture.

In the People's Republic of China, where compensation agreements are popular, Occidental Petroleum received a long-term contract to take back ore and refined minerals in return for developing a large mining facility. In Egypt, a major Swiss company, Aluswiss, exports alumina to its newly constructed plant and takes back a portion of the finished aluminum as payment for its investment.

The gradual reduction of trade barriers in the Soviet Union and in the People's Republic of China has spurred countertrade during the past decade. Pepsico has engineered a series of spectacular countertrades with the Soviet Union, trading vodka in the West for soft-drink concentrate over there. More recently, Pepsico agreed to invest in a shipbuilding venture where a portion of the hard currency generated will be used to pay for even more soft-drink sales.

Another factor in the spread of countertrade has been the development of this specialized trade capability within several large U.S. companies in the last ten years, even as Japan and West Germany benefitted more naturally from the prior existence of their large general trading companies. Without a Mitsubishi, a Metallgesellschaft, or a national trading network on which to rely, several U.S. corporations have built successful in-house trading companies. Many additional U.S. companies are being slowly drawn into countertrading through third parties or on their own account. The development of this nascent countertrade structure in the United States suggests at least the perception of countertrade as a longer-term trade strategy.

Countertrade in Corporate Strategy

The role of countertrade as both a financial instrument and a sweetener is illustrated by these three transactions:

Ericsson in Uruguay.   This 1984 sale of a $90 million telephone switching system to Uruguay helps to explain how countertrade can play a critical role in the formulation of an overall strategy to win a large export.

Ericsson, a Swedish telecommunications firm, triumphed mainly for two reasons. First, the company made the best countertrade offer with a coherent plan to implement it. Ericsson asked the British investment banking firm Samuel Montague to offer Uruguay 100 percent offset—in other words, a commitment to export $90 million worth of Uruguayan products, including beef, leather goods, and fish. Samuel Montague traded the products through Surinvest, a joint venture trading and financing house co-owned in Montevideo with Uruguayan partners.

A second reason for Ericsson's success was attractive export credit financing. This financing was offered at a bad time for U.S. companies when potentially comparable financing from the U.S. Export-Import Bank had been sharply cut back.

Both Sweden and Brazil, Ericsson's partners, offered a financing package at subsidized rates. The inclusion of Brazil as a major subcontractor was also a clever political tactic, the next best thing to Uruguayan content in the transaction. Brazil was able to exert more political pressure on neighboring Uruguay than would have been possible from a European country acting on its own.

Westinghouse in Jordan.   Westinghouse devised an equally effective strategy for winning a $100 million air defense radar system. The Pentagon's foreign military sales funds were not available, yet Jordan still wanted to purchase the radar. Commercial bank terms were unacceptable. In the absence of adequate financing, Westinghouse asked Mitsubishi's trading company to sell the phosphate that Jordan was prepared to offer as a form of payment.

The prime contractor was Lor-West of Bermuda, 20 percent owned by Westinghouse and 80 percent owned by Lorad, a subsidiary of Wraxall Group in the United Kingdom. Westinghouse Defense was a subcontractor to Lor-West.

Between June 1985 and December 1987, Mitsubishi was able to sell $70 million in phosphate rock through its worldwide trading network, ahead of the delivery schedule for the radar. The foreign exchange proceeds for the sale were remitted from Mitsubishi back to a special account in the central bank of Jordan.

To establish viable and secure payment procedures, separate contracts were set up between Lor-West and Mitsubishi, Mitsubishi and the central bank, and Lor-West and the central bank. The central bank issued an unconfirmed letter of credit to Lor-West.

As payments for the air defense system were required, they were automatically drawn through the letter of credit out of an escrow account in Chase Manhattan Bank of the United Kingdom's Channel Islands. This offshore payment mechanism, outside either the buying or selling country, provided additional assurance to Lor-West and Westinghouse that funds would be transferred smoothly as the delivery for the radar was met.

N-Ren in Madagascar.   The problems that N-Ren International faced and overcame with countertrade are the stuff of legend.

N-Ren, a small engineering and construction firm based in Brussels, began building a $60 million fertilizer plant in 1979. By 1983, Madagascar ran out of money to pay for the plant, even though the plant was 95 percent complete and 98 percent of the equipment was delivered. The delayed payments created cost overruns and drove up the price of finishing the plant.

Tom Snyder, the U.S. president of N-Ren, personally traveled several times to Tananarive, the capital of Madagascar, trying to resolve the impasse—all to no avail. Finally, when the situation seemed hopeless, a breakthrough occurred. Madagascar proposed to pay for the plant's completion with cloves, a spice for which the country is famous. Snyder obtained approvals from the Ministries of Finance and Agriculture, The Revolutionary Council (or cabinet of ministers), and ultimately President Didier Ransiraka.

Fortunately, the government of Madagascar already had direct and convenient access to the cloves, routinely buying the spice from twelve private sector buyers with local currency (the Malgache franc). Depending on the country, it is not always so easy for the government to buy commodities with local currency. The Malgache franc was also tied to the French franc, giving it a stabler value.

Between 1983 and 1988, four shipments of cloves took place in order to generate hard currency funds for the completion of the factory. The ships docked and took the cloves at Tamatave, the port where the fertilizer factory was also located. The ships then sailed for Rotterdam, the port where Catz International, one of the wold's foremost spice trading companies and N-Ren's partner, was established.

The first two shipments were valued at approximately $10 million each (1,200 tons for the first shipment and 2,000 tons for the next one, as the world's cloves price continued to fall).

For each shipment, numerous technical problems were overcome. N-Ren took out Lloyd's insurance through a Belgian agent. A shipping agent in Hamburg, West Germany, arranged transportation space on a suitable ship. The general manager of the fertilizer plant was at dockside to inspect every 50-kilo bag loaded on board. For each bag, there were about eight to ten documents concerning such issues as weight, origin, quality, and health factors. Nonconforming bags were rejected at dockside. The cloves were sold against documents called bills of lading, whose physical transfer signified the passing of title.

As savvy traders, Catz made N-Ren take title to a portion of the cloves at Tamatave, knowing the price would have fallen further by the time a ship reached port in Rotterdam and offering the prospect of a greater profit on resale. Catz guaranteed payment to N-Ren for the rest of the cloves at a fixed price.

To support this guarantee to N-Ren, Catz opened up a letter of credit with its bank, Credit Anstalt, in London. The letter of credit was confirmed by the American Express bank in Hamburg. Once the ship arrived in Rotterdam, documents were presented to Credit Anstalt; it immediately paid N-Ren under the letter of credit.

In one shipment, the captain persisted in unloading the cloves during violent rainstorms in Rotterdam, despite pleas from N-Ren executives and even though it is well-known that water can damage cloves. He claimed that he was under pressure to meet another contracted shipping schedule and could not wait for a change in the weather.

Catz's bonded warehouse salvaged much of this shipment of cloves by bringing in a specialized kiln company to dry the spice, allowing the bags to be repackaged. A year-long dispute finally resulted in an insurance settlement of several hundred thousand dollars for the damaged portion of the cloves.

In another transfer of the spice, N-Ren's general counsel found that the ship actually vanished for several days. He finally tracked it down in a small port north of Lisbon. Use of the vessel's time had come under legal dispute. N-Ren and French, Swiss, and West German companies with cargo on board all had to make a payment of tribute to the vessel's owner to get the ship's time released. As the fourth and final shipment came to a close, Snyder and the government of Madagascar were hopeful that the proceeds would give the completed plant operating capital during its early years of production.

N-Ren learned many lessons from its experience, aside from the fact that small companies can also do countertrade. The company wisely insisted that local weights govern the transaction since cloves take on weight and water by up to 3 percent in a tropical climate and lose weight in a drier climate. The falling price of cloves over the five-year period created another favorable precondition since, in a strong market, the government would not likely have offered the spice.

Developing a relationship with Catz International was essential, especially for the first two or three shipments because of N-Ren's initial lack of trading experience. Careful attention was paid to all the documentation, which helped during the insurance proceedings related to the one partially damaged shipment. Snyder and his colleagues meticulously monitored the transaction all the way through and resourcefully solved problems each time that they surfaced. Above all, in the crucial early stages, Snyder succeeded in developing a personal relationship with key government officials that helped expedite the transaction.

At this and the previous examples illustrate, countertrade is a way of doing business and thinking about business that raises the almost tribal concept of reciprocity to a new level of importance. The relationship between trading partners is critical, taking on ever greater importance as less cash for products is available and as more barter takes place.

Bloc-Buster Deal

Michael Parks.   *Michael Parks is a* Los Angeles Times *writer.*

The deal was one of the biggest that a U.S. company had ever signed with the Soviet Union, and as far as Pepsico Inc. was concerned probably the best.

Over 10 years, Pepsi-Cola International would double its soft-drink sales here, open two dozen new bottling plants and launch its Pizza Hut restaurants in the country's biggest cities.

To finance the expansion, Pepsico would increase its sales of Russian vodka in the United States and begin a new venture selling and leasing Soviet-built ships abroad.

The retail sales of cola and vodka alone were to total more than $3 billion, according to Pepsico's estimate in 1990, and the ship sales were likely to be worth at least $300 million.

"It was an agreement that people in East–West trade dream about," Karl G. Nigl, a Pepsi-Cola vice president for Russia and Eastern Europe, recounted almost rhapsodically. "Steady growth was locked in over a long term, there was good technology transfer, our partners were able to add value to their exports all along the way, financing was built in. . . .

"It was barter, sure, but there was profit at every step, and structurally it was beautiful, assuring us convertible currency for our profits while financing a massive expansion."

But when the Soviet Union disintegrated late last year, with it went what Pepsico had called its "deal of the century."

The shipyard that was building the double-hulled tankers that Pepsico was selling to finance its Pizza Huts and new bottling plants in Russia was now in a different country, Ukraine, and the new Ukrainian government wanted the revenues from the ship sales.

The chemical plant that was to produce plastic two-liter bottles to expand Pepsi sales was in Belarus, also now independent, but the bottling plants that were to fill them were mostly across the border in Russia.

And the mozzarella cheese needed by the two newly opened Pizza Huts in Moscow had become a very expensive import—it was coming from Lithuania, which wanted to sell the cheese elsewhere or at least to be paid in dollars.

"All of a sudden, the whole thing was in pieces—hundreds of pieces," Donald M. Kendall, Pepsico's retired chairman, who had put the original deal together, said in an

Bartering Billions
Pepsico's complex deal with former Soviet Union includes:

CHEESE FROM RUSSIA—Company obtains mozzarella from southern Russia to supply its Pizza Huts in Moscow.

COTTON FROM UZBEKISTAN—Pepsico buys and then resells farm product to finance sales of cola syrup and equipment. Above, Pepsi stand in Uzbekistan.

SHIPS FROM UKRAINE—Sales of double-hulled tankers helps finance Pizza Huts and bottling plants in Kiev and expansion of Pepsi sales in Ukraine.

Box of vodka rolls off assembly line in Moscow. Pepsi resells the vodka in United States to compensate for supplying cola syrup and bottling equipment to Russians.

Moscow youngster sips soft drink with a straw from Russian-labeled bottle.

interview during a recent visit here. "We had a multibillion-dollar contract with a nonexisting entity—the Soviet Union.

"Put another way, one of our biggest partners, the Soviet Union in this case, had just gone out of business, and that's a major problem for any company."

While Pepsico has been able over the past six months to salvage its deal, Western business people say that scores of others collapsed along with the Soviet state.

And even in success, Pepsico's efforts illustrate the difficulty that American and European companies are having in doing business in Russia and the other former Soviet republics as those independent new states emerge from a single, centrally planned, state-run economy.

Selling to the Soviet Union, as well as other socialist countries, was always difficult because the ruble was not an internationally accepted currency and Moscow's foreign currency holdings were limited. So companies like Pepsico engaged in barter or counter-trade arrangements, taking payments in commodities that it could resell, such as cola syrup for ships.

On top of that longstanding problem, the collapse of the Soviet Union means that old contracts often are simply no longer valid under new regulations. The former Soviet partners may be bankrupt or unable to get raw materials; perhaps they have lost their managers. Suppliers and customers are now frequently in different countries, with tariff barriers going up almost every day. And taxes are imposed at rates that can turn an attractive profit into a serious loss.

Daimler-Benz AG, Germany's largest manufacturing company, for example, signed contracts in late 1990 to produce 2,500 buses a year outside Moscow. With Russia's economy continuing to contract at a rate of more than 15% a year and the country's foreign earnings almost totally consumed by old Soviet debts, Daimler-Benz's partner cannot pay the $132-million fee for the production license and technical assistance, and only limited production is under way.

"We have signed contracts, but they have told us they cannot stand up to the financial commitment," Edzard Reuter, the Daimler-Benz chairman, told a conference on Russian trade this month. Counseling patience, Reuter added, "It is in our interest to do what we can. . . . It's a dramatic transition."

Chevron Corp. had to renegotiate an agreement, it had signed with the former Soviet government to develop the Tengiz oil field in Kazakhstan after the republic became independent—and in the process had to accept a 20% share of after-tax profits compared to the 28% it had originally won. Chevron will now invest about $10.9 billion over 40 years to develop a field likely to produce 700,000 barrels of oil a day and generate $5 billion a year in revenues.

"Chevron will make money in Tengiz, but not nearly as much as it expected," the Moscow representative of another U.S. oil company commented. "What's more, its investment will have to be greater. . . . All in all, it's an OK deal because Tengiz will be another 'Alaska' (as a rich new oil region), but it took a heck of a lot of work to put it back together."

In Pepsi's case, both Nigl and Richard M. Norton, a Vienna-based vice president of Pepsi-Cola International, concluded that the underpinnings of the original counter-trade deal were still sound—that an expansion of company sales here could be underwritten by the increased, profitable export to Western nations of agricultural products and the ships. But the arrangement would have to be divided into separate deals for Russia, Ukraine, Belarus and the other former Soviet republics.

Pepsi negotiated new contracts with a variety of partners—individual bottling plants now owned by their employees, local corporations suddenly freed from Moscow's control, governments of the newly independent republics and a dairy farm in southern Russia that could produce the mozzarella.

It also found its way through a maze of often conflicting laws, regulations and policies adopted by the new governments in Russia, Ukraine and other former republics, each of which has its own program for economic reform.

And it dealt with the broadening collapse of the old Soviet economy, a liquidity crisis that has left customers and suppliers alike unable to pay their bills, and the government's virtual seizure of all foreign currency coming into the country to pay $80 billion in debts.

"We had no option," Norton said, "After two decades of investment and effort to develop business in the Soviet Union, we were not going to walk away. And while we did not have to start from scratch, everything had to be redone in an environment where the only constant was change. . . .

"We had to restructure all the elements of the 1990 contract so that we had the appropriate deal in each republic," Norton said, shaking his head both in disbelief at the speed with which everything fell apart and in amazement at the way it was slowly put back together.

"We were no longer dealing with a highly centralized government in Moscow," Norton continued, "but with new partners in 15 different countries, all independent and sovereign, each with its own policies and approaches to economic reform.

"That has meant, for example, expanding our business much faster in Ukraine—we are bringing in prefabricated Pizza Huts there—in order to use the revenues from the ship construction. But we are really going to have to work to expand our vodka sales in the United States and to buy more apple juice and other products in order [to generate enough cash] to meet the demand for Pizza Huts in Moscow and St. Petersburg.

"And we are looking very hard at what we can buy from Kazakhstan and from other former Soviet republics—timber, tomato paste, fruit juice, industrial waste, cotton, oil maybe—in order to do business in other places. The basic principle is the same, but the partners are different and the business environments are totally different."

There are other problems, according to Norton. "To the major and continuing problem of finding goods we can buy and export to pay for the equipment, services and products we sell, we now must work through dozens of new regulations, tax laws, import and export tariffs and almost daily amendments to them all. With each change, we have to reassess to ensure we are within the law—and still profitable. This is a place you must make sure you don't fall asleep."

Russia, for example, virtually priced its vodka exports out of world markets in January with a new export tax introduced as part of the government's economic reforms. Pepsi warned, as did other Western buyers, that Russian vodka sales would drop to zero unless the tax was cut by three-quarters—and it was.

"The direction in which they are headed is good, and our business will grow as a result," Kendall commented, "but there are many, many missteps along the way."

Lawrence S. Eagleburger, the American deputy secretary of state, warned the Russian government in a recent speech to a business conference here that American businessmen were finding "their ability to contribute as partners to economic recovery is severely, if not fatally, hampered by regulatory and fiscal practices at all levels of government."

A survey of American companies doing business in Russia and the other former Soviet republics by the U.S. Commerce Department last spring concluded: "Firms see high risks and costs . . . but not large profits.

"And they are concerned," the report continued, "that the governments (of the newly independent states) believe the opposite: that (foreign) investors face little risk and can make large profits overnight."

Business executives, economists and government officials attending a top-level meeting here of the World Economic Forum told Russia's new leaders that they had far to go before the country would attract the foreign capital it needs to grow, diversify and compete internationally.

"Russia is a vast potential market, one of the great markets of the future," participants said in a letter sent to the Russian government last week, "but it is not an easy one to penetrate, and it is unlikely that there will be a magic moment when it will suddenly open."

Calling for "a more stable, certain business environment," the group made several recommendations—"a clear indication of who is in charge and who can commit to an agreement," sound commercial laws and courts, a "welcoming" environment for foreign investment through "incentives that justify the risk" and removal of the obstacles to operating a business here.

Reforms must go much faster and deeper if Russia is to develop an economy driven by market forces and entrepreneurship, participants said. They urged the government to abolish the many state controls that remain on the economy, to end the virtual monopolies prevalent in most industries and to accelerate the selloff of state-owned enterprises.

Kendall, a pioneer in Soviet-American trade, agrees on the need for reform. "Clearly, a vibrant, robust, market-oriented economy is the most attractive place to trade in and invest in," he commented. "It will take years, but once we are through this period of upheaval, Russia and the other former Soviet republics are going to look even better to companies like Pepsico than they did before."

He is particularly enthusiastic about opportunities for U.S. companies in agriculture, food processing and distribution. "These are areas where our companies have solved the problems that face Russia," he said, adding the energy sector as another attractive area. "We have solutions we can sell. The trick will be structuring the deals."

Kendall argued, however, that U.S. firms should not wait for everything to be in place, but forge ahead, helping to shape the business environment.

"A lot of people are worried about the political and economic stability here, and they are hesitant to come in," Kendall said. "But if you wait for everything to come right, for a convertible currency, for all the growth curves to head up, then the French, the Japanese and the Germans will be in here so tight Americans won't find a place.

"Truly, the best way we can help Russia is by coming in and doing business. With the trade agreement ratified, small and medium-size companies can get financing from the U.S. Export-Import Bank, guarantees from the Overseas Private Investment Corp.,

---

Diagram of a Deal

Pepsico's operations involve interlocking contracts with nations carved out of the defunct Soviet Union. Some highlights:

What Pepsico Does

1. In Russia

Runs 16 bottling plants for Pepsi, Diet Pepsi, etc. With Moscow city government, operates two Pizza Huts.

With partners, manufacturers Tanez, an orange-flavored soft drink, and Fiesta, a lemon-flavored soft drink, for Soviet market to get ruble income.

Developed bottles, caps, labels used for export production and brought in equipment for the distilleries.

2. In Belarus

Joint venture with Eastman Chemical Co., Chimvolokno and Mposht Textile Mill at Mogilev manufactures polyethylene terephthalate resin, used for new two-liter bottles of Pepsi. Half of production goes to Eastern and Western Europe; the rest to Belarus and Russia, which supplies the raw materials for the Chimvolokno plant.

3. In Ukraine

Runs 7 bottling plants for Pepsi, Diet Pepsi.

What Pepsico Gets

4. From Russia

Stolichnaya, Cristall and Priviet vodka for resale in the United States to compensate for its supply of cola syrup and bottling equipment to Russians.

Miscellaneous oil products in payment for equipment sent to Russia.

Buys tomato paste in southern Russia for use by Pizza Hut and Kentucky Fried Chicken outlets in Western Europe. Also purchases apple juice for use in its products in Western Europe.

5. From Ukraine

Double-hulled tankers, built at Kherson for resale by Pepsi and a Norwegian partner on world market. Proceeds to finance Pizza Huts in Kiev and expansion of Pepsi sales in Ukraine.

6. From Baltics

Buys waste plastic products, which are resold for recycling in Europe, to finance cola and equipment sales.

7. From Uzbekistan

Buys cotton and resells to finance its sales of syrup and equipment.

8. From Kazakhstan

Buys miscellaneous industrial products for resale to finance its cola and equipment sales.

---

and most-favored-nation tariffs. And those small- and medium-size businesses will liven things up and get people the management training a market economy will require."

Kendall recalled how in the early days of Soviet-American trade he would come to Moscow, negotiate with the Soviet minister of foreign trade and be received in the Kremlin by Prime Minister Alexei N. Kosygin. Later, he dealt with Prime Minister Nikolai I. Ryzhkov on reselling Soviet-built ships to pay for increased Pepsi sales.

"Two, three guys made all the decisions at the top, and the deal was sealed in the Kremlin," Kendall said. "Now, the focus will be narrower—'What can we do here, what can we do there?' But this will let smaller companies get into the market, companies that don't have $19 billion in sales a year, but that can make some money for themselves and, in the process, help Russia."

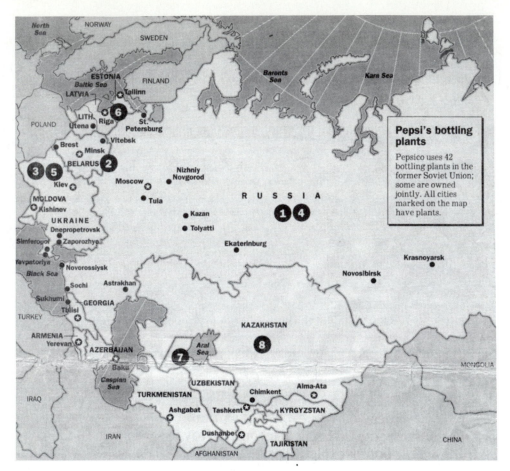

Source: Copyright, 1992, *Los Angeles Times.* Reprinted by permission. Artist: Victor Kotowitz.

Distribution Strategies

The opening paper in this sequence provides a valuable 10-step road map to achieve success in foreign markets. This process begins with an evaluation of a company's readiness to export, combined with an analysis of its strengths and weaknesses, including potential obstacles to exporting. The firm's domestic business plan must be reviewed prior to a global assessment of markets and competition. The next step is the development of a foreign market entry plan, including pricing and budgeting for market entry. Foreign partner selection, compliance with standards and regulations, the development of support services, and market introduction are the remaining steps leading to physical presence in the foreign marketplace.

A related piece is an exporter's guide for the selection of foreign sales agents and distributors. It is important to remember that intermediaries may be difficult and costly to terminate. The author recommends the use of well-drafted agreements with intermediaries and greater attention to their selection.

A paper on export trading companies in world markets reviews the nature and scope of operations of such entities in Japan, Korea, Brazil, and the United States. A model of the external and international factors affecting ETC growth is an important aspect of this contribution.

The International Franchise Association has defined franchising as "a continuing relationship in which the franchisor provides a licensed privilege to do business, plus assistance in organizing, training, merchandising, and management in return for a consideration from the franchise."[1] From a predominately U.S. base, franchising has expanded dramatically during the 1980s. The fourth paper in this section conceptualizes the diffusion of franchise systems using largely Australian cases for illustrative purposes.

The final piece documents the scope of operations and management styles within Korean chaebols. The term *chaebol* refers to a business group of large firms owned and managed by family members or relatives in diversified business areas. Chaebols owe much of their success to government support and their emphasis on increasing sales volume rather than profitability. The authors compare Korean chaebols with Japanese zaibatsu.

---

[1]Andrew Kostecka, *Franchise Opportunities Handbook* (Washington, D.C.: U. Commerce, 1986), p. XXIX.

Executive Insights: The 10-Step Road Map to Success in Foreign Markets

Myron M. Miller.   *Myron M. Miller is director of the International Business Development Center, The Eli Broad Graduate School of Management, at Michigan State University. He was an international business executive with four major multinational corporations for 25 years.*

Even companies that have been quite successful in the U.S. market can find the process of expanding into foreign markets an intimidating prospect. Assuming that a company has been in business long enough to establish a viable presence in the U.S. market, it has learned how to deal with a variety of complexities of business. The company has learned how to develop and market new products and/or services, deal with logistics and customer services, and successfully handle the financial issues involved in developing a growing, successful company.

When the company faces the prospects of going into foreign markets, its experience in dealing with the complexities of U.S. business is helpful, but that experience doesn't ensure success internationally. Looking at a world of dozens and dozens of countries, all with their own unique characteristics, the prospects of choosing markets and investing in the development of those markets can be awesome.

Seminars and workshops designed to help small and medium-sized business get into international markets provide these companies with some understanding of the principal elements of internationalizing a business. Some of these are international finance, marketing, letters of credit and banking, freight forwarding and other aspects of logistics, product planning, and the many complexities of getting into international business. Those programs may also provide insights into the peculiarities of various countries. However, there is something missing when all this information is provided to the prospective exporter (or a company seeking some other type of entry into foreign markets).

Sequence of Steps Required to Get into International Markets

When a company gets information on all the various elements of getting into international business, they have very little idea how to put that into some sequence of action steps.

FIGURE 1   10-Step Road Map to Success in Foreign Markets©

Traditional International Topics		*Traditional International Topics*

	Assessment:	
• International finance *Steps 4, 5, 8, 10*	1. Company readiness to export 2. Company assessment	• Market research *Steps 2, 4, 5, 6, 8*
• Documentation *Steps 5, 8*	**Planning:**	• Pricing *Steps 4, 5, 9*
• Legal *Steps 3, 4, 5, 6, 8, 10*	3. Domestic business plan 4. Global assessment; global strategic design 5. Foreign market entry plan	• Product planning *Steps 3, 4, 5, 7, 9*
• Strategic planning *Steps 1, 3, 4, 5*		• Research and development *Steps 3, 4, 5, 7*
• Accounting and taxes *Steps 5, 8*	**Implementation:**	• Manufacturing *Steps 3, 5, 7, 10*
• Logistics *Steps 4, 5, 8, 9, 10*	6. Foreign partner selection 7. Compliance with standards and regulations 8. Selection of support services 9. Market introduction	• Advertising and promotion *Steps 3, 5, 8*
• Value chain analysis *Steps 2, 4, 5, 8*	10. Physical presence in foreign market	• Channels of distribution *Steps 5, 6, 10*

Michigan International Business Development Center, Michigan State University, March 1993. Copyright 1990 Myron M. Miller. All rights reserved. Permission granted for use by Michigan State University.

Where do I start? In which markets should I begin? What will it cost me to get into international business? How much will it cost to get some help in exporting? A company might get excellent information on all the elements of going international, e.g., marketing, finance, R & D, logistics, etc., yet not be able to see how they are going to put all these elements together into some pathway that will lead them to successful business overseas.

To deal with the lack of sequencing of the steps needed to move into international markets, the **10-Step Road Map to Success in Foreign Markets** was developed.

By putting the activities involved in going international into a sequenced 10-Step Road Map, it becomes much more apparent to a company where it is headed. There is a sense of direction about what it must do to enter foreign markets. No longer is it facing a jumble of activities and functions.

Figure 1 shows on the right and left columns a listing of the traditional topics involved in international business. When managers are taught about these traditional elements of international business, they're not told what they must do next Monday morning, nor the next week nor the next month.

The 10-Step Road Map takes all the content of the traditional elements of international business, and puts those elements in the order that a company must use in developing international business. Figure 1 shows at which steps each of these elements are used. For example, international finance comes into play at steps 4, 5, 8, and 10. Market research is needed at steps 2, 4, 5, 6, and 8. Product planning is involved in the execution of steps 3, 4, 5, 7, and 9.

Overview of the 10-Step Road Map

The following is an overview of the 10-Step Road Map to Success in Foreign Markets, with a brief description of what services are provided at each step. The process is divided into three phases of service:

Assessment Phase

Step #1. Evaluation of a company's readiness to export, or to enter foreign markets by some other method of market entry

Step #2. Company analysis

Planning Phase

Step #3. Reassessment of the domestic business plan

Step #4. Global assessment of markets and competition; global strategic design

Step #5. Development of a foreign market entry plan, including pricing and budgeting for market entry

Implementation Phase

Step #6. Identification and selection of partners in foreign markets

Step #7. Compliance with foreign standards and regulations

Step #8. Selection of service support providers needed in the U.S. and in the foreign market

Step #9. Market introduction of the company's products or services

Step #10. Establish physical presence in foreign market(s)

The Need for a "Coach"—International Business Development Professionals

At each of these ten steps in the road map, management needs to undertake a series of analyses, strategy development, and actions to enable it to continue the process of getting into international business. Without some guidance in this process, it will be very difficult for any company to use this road map successfully. A company will need a "coach" or advisor to help it progress through this analysis, planning and implementation process. It will also need quite a variety of other assistance from international trade experts in such areas as market research, finance, logistics, legal, banking, etc. With the right coach, a company can be directed to the most cost-effective assistance available throughout the process of going international.

Would-be exporters may quickly learn about the availability of expertise in banking, freight forwarders, even international market research firms.[1]

What companies are less likely to find is a "coach" that can help them select the best service providers, distributors, franchisees, and others on whom much depends for success. A new category of international trade and investment intermediary is emerging, the international (or "global") business development concern. It is unlikely that a company can find in any directory a designation for international business development professionals, yet that is what is needed to facilitate a company's internationalization. This new category of service, at its best, is capable of helping a company through the internationalization process. The international group managements of multinationals provide this coaching in-house, though they also must turn to outside services for much of the work in developing new country and product markets.

For small to medium-sized companies, some type of outside international business development assistance is vital to their success in going through the sequence of actions described in the 10-Step Road Map. These new international business development intermediaries can be either private sector or public sector, and the range of capabilities and costs of services varies considerably. The importance of defining the services contained in the 10-Step Road Map is that a company can determine whether a prospective "coach" has the experience and abilities to provide all those services. A company needing assistance in going international should choose the international business development organization most capable and experienced in providing the full range of services, and of directing a company to other capable and economical service providers.

While Traveling through the 10-Step Road Map—Side Trips

Before describing the actions that must be taken throughout the 10-Step Road Map, it is important to recognize that this isn't a road map that one follows wearing blinders. It isn't a systematic process that proceeds down a neat path, step by step. In fact, while a company works its way into international markets, it may jump around from step to step, and take short-term actions that will enable it to take advantage of opportunities to get sales and get market information whenever it can do so.

One of the best ways to learn about market opportunities is to try to secure some export orders. While the 10-Step Road Map doesn't call for selling internationally until the latter part of the process, most companies will want to undertake some international transactions as soon as possible, if only to begin to learn about some of the challenges of selling internationally. If a company attends a trade show and meets someone who wants to place an order, it is well worth the risks involved to obtain that order to get some revenue and go through that learning experience. That experience will help the company do its planning and develop its strategies throughout the 10-Step process.

It is also valuable to do what the fishermen call "chumming," literally placing cut or ground bait on the water to attract fish. In the sphere of international business, this means letting the world know about your business and products so they can locate you. There are various publications in which you can advertise your products—in particular, publications of the U.S. Department of Commerce. A single advertisement in such a publication may reach thousands of prospective buyers. Advertisements in trade journals can also publicize a company's intention to find distributors or agents overseas.

Attendance at trade fairs is part of the "chumming" process, since such fairs provide a great opportunity to meet companies interested in representing a U.S. company. There are offices representing states of the U.S. in various parts of the world, and they often take products from their states on mini-trade missions throughout their part of the world in search of distributors or other partners for the companies in their state. U.S. Department of Commerce Matchmaker programs are a great way to meet potential partners or distributors in foreign countries.

All of these actions can help enhance the systematic process of building international business, as long as these short-term actions do not prevent the company from taking the correct decisions for the long range. For example, in its haste to get overseas business, a company may choose the first distributor it meets in a foreign market, even before the company has assessed the market and looked carefully for the best distributor in that market. A short-term sale might lock the company out of the best long-term relationship and thereby prevent it from getting the maximum benefits from a particular market.

Finally, most enthusiastic would-be exporters are anxious to see some progress in their attempt to go international, and they like to see some results quickly. By integrating these shorter-term chumming efforts into the more systematic 10-Step process, a company can learn some important lessons in exporting and get some profit contribution from sales to help finance the market studies needed, yet ensure that short-term actions do not conflict with longer term strategies.

The following will describe the services required at each step in the 10-Step process. This covers not only what a company will need to go international, but also serves as a guide for a company choosing an international business development "coaching" firm. There are organizations that provide some, but not all, of the range of services. Some economic development firms, for example, may be capable of providing the services described under steps #1 through #3, but may then have to refer their clients to organizations with more experience and capabilities in international management. For companies located far from international business development entities, it may be best to start the process with local intermediaries, then involve the intermediaries with more expertise later.

A Shortcut—Planning, Pricing, and Budgeting for Foreign Market Entry

While we encourage companies to proceed systematically through the 10-Step process, some managers may be anxious to develop a rough plan, to get some idea of the strategies they are likely to pursue, and to get an early idea of the financial implications of their entry into international business. A decision support tool, "Budgeting and Pricing Aids for International Marketers," has been developed at Michigan State University using a computerized spread sheet program, which will be used at Step #5, but can be used earlier if a company wants to develop an earlier vision of the risks and rewards for going international.

This computer-aided program can be used any time after Step # 1, the CORE[2] evaluation, which will be explained later in this chapter. It can then be refined at any time throughout the entire 10-Step process. This tool provides for projecting a company's performance *without* the effects of international operations. It then assists a company to prepare a profit and loss statement for the first three or four years of its international activities, and then shows the impact those international operations will have on total company profitability. For a company's officers and directors, this early view provides information on the financial impact of going international. The earlier a company's officers and board of directors understand the risks and rewards, the more committed the company will be.

Financial Management throughout the Internationalization Process

It is strongly recommended that the company's controller be involved throughout the 10-Step process, to ensure that there is a continual awareness of the financial results of the various plans and actions involved. The company's management and owners will want to know what the internationalization process means to the company. Although financial evaluation is not shown explicitly at each of the 10 steps, it is important that the financial officer be involved and aware of the financial impact of the plans at each step. That person should be involved in key meetings and in the planning sessions throughout this process.

The 10-Step Process

Much of the work during the first five steps can be done in the U.S. Much of the data must still be obtained from foreign markets, but it may not be necessary to go overseas for the information, pay overseas services providers to get the local information, or contact foreign companies and potential customers.

After Step #5, when a Foreign Market Entry Plan has been developed, the other steps require considerable input from foreign markets, involvement with research firms overseas, and personal visits to the market. Steps #6 through #10 require a company to invest more heavily in overseas travel and service costs.

Step #1. Company Readiness to Export (CORE) Evaluation

As any company, regardless of its size and experience, decides to go into international markets, it must determine how ready it is to make that move. Fortunately, a computer-aided decision support tool was developed in 1986 by Dr. S. Tamer Cavusgil, now Executive Director, International Business Centers, Michigan State University. That tool is called CORE, COmpany Readiness to Export. Whether a company is considering exporting, or entering foreign markets by some other method of market entry (e.g., franchising, licensing, retailing, joint venture, etc.), this evaluation is a critical beginning point.

CORE is designed to provide an evaluation of internal company strengths and weaknesses in the context of exporting. It is especially useful for small and medium-sized businesses considering exporting for the first time, but it can also be used by larger firms to reassess their strengths and weaknesses regarding their present performance. CORE provides the user company with a reading on the extent of their readiness to export, as well as specific recommendations relating to export-related tasks. This tool can be used by individual companies for self-assessment, but it can also be used by trainers and consultants.

At the end of this session, the user receives an assessment that includes an indication of what their next steps should be. For some companies, their product and organizational readiness may indicate they are so strong on both attributes that they should proceed into exporting immediately. At the other extreme are the companies that should concentrate on developing their domestic U.S. business and begin the long process of preparing themselves to export some day. In the middle are many companies that are ready to export in some respects, but have some important deficiencies they should correct before proceeding. CORE provides the user with some guidance on what steps they should take before making aggressive commitments.

The end result of the CORE assessment is valuable, but even more valuable is the interaction with a skilled, international business development professional. Possibly 75 percent of the value of the CORE assessment is the definition of issues that arise between the coach and the company.

Step #2. Company Assessment

While the CORE analysis provides a good beginning in assessing a company's readiness to enter foreign markets, the company cannot proceed without making a much more comprehensive analysis of its present strengths and weaknesses, its structure in terms of its value-added activities, and the areas in which it has distinct competitive advantage and a competitive opening.

When a company goes into international markets, it must earn a niche in new markets. It will do that only if it has some competitive advantages in the new markets. Therefore, the company must take the strengths that have made it viable in the U.S. market and transfer those strengths overseas. If it doesn't know why it has been successful in the U.S. market, it won't know how to penetrate foreign markets successfully.

Therefore, a company must analyze its entire spectrum of activities to determine its strengths and weaknesses, and determine where it has unique competitive strengths, sometimes known as its core competencies. The tool for determining this is a variation of the value chain analysis. An analysis of the whole spectrum of company activities, from the sourcing of raw materials and components through R & D, manufacturing, marketing, logistics, and after-sales service, provides the basis for determining which activities should be performed in the U.S. and those which must be done by partners or service organizations overseas. Without a thorough understanding of all company activities in the U.S. market, it is almost impossible to develop a sound strategy for entering foreign markets.

In the process of assessing the company's activities as it begins its planning to go international, it must:

- Evaluate the product
- Evaluate markets and competition
- Evaluate technological and production capabilities
- Assess financial capabilities
- Evaluate the company's position in the home market
- Prepare situation analysis report, with diagnosis of strengths and weaknesses, condensed into a summary of critical issues

The company must evaluate the principal obstacles to the company's entering foreign markets. The following are some of the factors that could immediately prevent a company from starting international activities:

- Legal aspects of representation in a market
- Standards and regulatory issues
- Export controls
- Patent and trademark concerns
- Product adaptations
- Production capacity and equipment restraints
- Financial resources required

Step #3. Reassessment of the Domestic Business Plan

With the assessment completed, the company must reassess its domestic business plan before proceeding to address its first steps in moving into international business.

Some companies attempt to move into international markets with no sound foundation of planning in their domestic business. While there may be some exceptions to the rule, in principle, companies that succeed in foreign markets have established a strong, viable position in the U.S. (or home) market. Companies are often impatient to get into foreign markets and want to get started, without having laid the proper foundation for their business at home.

Using much of the analysis described in Steps #1 and #2 above, the company should ensure that they have a business plan for the next three to four years for domestic operations. That plan should address some of the issues described earlier, and develop the strategies and action programs that will ensure domestic market success. One particular factor often not addressed specifically in the planning in the United States is the issue of foreign competitors there.

While most competitors in the United States previously were domestic manufacturers or service providers, in recent years there has been a significant increase in both the number and the market share of foreign competitors that have established a presence in the United States. Also, foreign companies may have employed a sales agent or distributor in the United States and have indirectly established a significant presence.

Some employees of U.S. manufacturers have left their previous employers and have established distributorships where almost all of their lines are from foreign manufacturers. These foreign companies, whether represented directly or indirectly, must be identified in the domestic business plan and analyzed carefully.

Step #4. Global Assessment of Markets and Competitors and Development of Initial Strategic Plan

This step involves a global assessment of the industry to determine the best country or regional markets for the company's products and the assessment of the best strategies for entering those markets. At the same time, an assessment must be made of the principal competitors throughout the world. In Step #3, information was gathered on those global competitors present in the U.S. market, but it is necessary to look elsewhere in the world to determine who else must be dealt with either "defensively," because of the threat of the new company hurting the business in the U.S. market, or in the "offensive" arena when the company goes into foreign markets.

Based on the assessment of potential opportunities or competitive threats in foreign markets, the company must determine its strategy for entering global markets. It must determine which countries to enter, how many at a time, the proper method for entering those markets, and the financial resources required to execute this plan. It may choose to enter Europe first, and start with one or two countries. Or, it may choose a Pan-American strategy, choosing to start by entering the Canadian and Mexican markets.

In many respects, this is the most difficult and complex part of developing a program to go international. Many companies may be able to start in only one or two markets at a time, because they are limited in financial and human resources. Other companies that have the resources, and where the opportunities are imminent, may want to move on a much broader basis, and faster. Each situation must be evaluated on its own merits.

At this step, it isn't necessary to develop a massive, global strategy. What is required is the development of some guiding strategies regarding the means for beginning the development of an international, or global, presence. Henry Mintzberg (1987) of McGill University refers to this process as "crafting" strategy. Gary Hamel and C. K. Prahalad (1989) have also described a process that is worth reviewing when developing this initial thrust into international markets.

Various models of strategic planning are available to guide a company in the development of its initial global strategic plan. Most would include such elements as:

Mission statement

Statement of objectives and goals

Situation analysis

- Analysis of strengths and weaknesses
- Analysis of threats and opportunities
- Overview of global markets
- Overview of global competition and their market shares
- Environmental issues that affect the industry
- Significant trends in the industry

- Triggers of change in the architecture of the industry
- Benchmark centers of excellence in the industry

Product line and pricing analysis

- Comparison of prices, features and benefits of the company's product lines against its principal competitors in key markets

Characteristics of key functional areas

Assessment of key factors for success in the industry

Critical issues facing the company in its internationalization process

Alternative strategies to deal with the critical issues and take advantage of the opportunities; selection of the most favorable strategies

- Advantages and disadvantages of each alternative
- Financial evaluation of the alternatives
- Reasons for selection of the preferred strategies

Action programs to implement the strategies

- Specific action programs developed related to each strategy, with specific responsibilities assigned for each program and each element of the program, and precise beginning and ending dates for each step in the action program

Projection of human and financial resources required to initiate and implement the plan for the first few years

Because there is so much to learn in developing international markets, this initial strategic plan must be continually modified and updated based on daily experiences.

To assist in this step, the company may be put in contact with various agencies that provide information on key markets throughout the world, such as:

- U.S. Department of Commerce industry sector specialists
- Industry specialists in the U.S. International Trade Commission
- Department of Commerce market research reports on specific industry sectors (particularly information from the NTDB, National Trade Data Bank)
- Data from foreign sources (such as trade associations or industry sector groups) that can provide information on markets within their countries
- Private sector sources, such as Frost and Sullivan, FIND SVP, etc.
- Data on exports to key markets from the U.S. Department of Commerce, United Nations, and the European Community
- JETRO on Japan

The company itself may have contacts in the trade, memberships in associations, information from publications, and visits to industry trade shows or symposia that should be tapped. The company should be encouraged, early in its development, to attend overseas trade shows (many of which may be in Germany) as an effective means of developing a global overview of their business in a short time.

Some of this information can be gathered from secondary sources, but invariably it is necessary for a company to do primary research. Some of the information can be gathered at a very low cost, even free. Eventually, however, it's necessary to pay for important information, and the company must budget for this expense or investment.

When the company has made its global assessment and has chosen its means for entering the global market and has selected its initial target markets, it is ready to move to Step #5, where it will develop specific foreign market entry plans.

Step #5. Foreign Market Entry Planning

Having chosen some initial target markets, the next step is to develop a detailed plan for entering those markets. For each target market, the market entry plan should include such items as:

- The company's objectives for that market, including target market share, sales targets for the first few years, profit objectives, targeted breakeven period, and other quantitative and qualitative objectives.
- Background material on the country relating to the economy, politics, cultural issues, trends in the economy, and other country-related matters that will affect the company's performance in that country. A good starting point for this information is the National Trade Data Bank (NTDB) and a decision support system developed by Michigan State University, *Country Consultant.*
- The opportunities and obstacles in the country for the company in its business sector.
- Strategy for the method of entering the market, whether it be through an agent or distributor relationship, licensing, joint venture, acquisition, or some other method. An important determinant of that strategy will be the company's value adding chain and its selection of the activities it wants to perform in a country and those it wants to retain in the United States.

Having developed an understanding of all the components of a company's value adding chain at Step #2, it is now necessary to configure and coordinate those activities. *Configuring* value chain activities basically involves determining where the various activities should be conducted, whether it be in the U.S. market or in other countries. The determination of the company's core competencies in its value chain will help determine how to configure the various activities. When the various activities have been positioned in the appropriate countries, those activities must be properly *coordinated* between the company's home office and the overseas locations.

- Development of principal strategies for the first three to five years in the country.
- Action plans to implement the strategies.
- Projected financial statements for the company's operations in each country.

Other factors may be included in the preparation of the plan, as determined when a plan is being prepared for a particular country.

In all cases, the U.S. Department of Commerce's capabilities provide the logical starting point, particularly with their country desk officers and the U.S. & Foreign and Commercial Service offices in each country. At a point, it will be necessary to use some private sector consultants in particular countries, and the U.S. & FCS offices in each country can help direct a company to those private sector consultants. Those offices also prepare a Country Marketing Plan that provides excellent material on the country in question. Also, those offices can prepare, for a moderate charge, a Comparison Shopping Survey, which provides very specific information on your market in that country. The latter is a particularly invaluable resource.

Step #6. Identification and Selection of Partners

This step involves the identification, selection, and contracting of the best sales representatives, distributors, licensees, dealers, franchisees, joint venture partners, acquisition candidates, or other types of strategic partners.

To engage in this process, the company must develop a portfolio describing the company, its products, and its services to potential partners in foreign markets and the benefits of association with the U.S. company. Too often a U.S. company just gives its U.S. spec sheets to prospective partners (or to some intermediary to represent the U.S. company), assuming the overseas partner will immediately want to partner with the U.S. company. This is a serious mistake. It is important to prepare first-class material to get a first-class partner, so the U.S. company should assemble first-class visual and printed material to go "courting" for the best possible partners.

From the development of the foreign market entry plan developed at Step #5, information on prospective partners should have been developed. If further analysis is needed to identify the prospects, one way to identify the potential partners is to use the Agent and Distributor Search (ADS) capabilities of the U.S. Department of Commerce (U.S. DOC).

By providing the U.S. DOC with relevant information about the company and its products and services, along with a profile of an ideal partner, the U.S. & FCS can contact prospects in that country to get a reading on their interest in partnering with the U.S. company. When that short list is developed from the feedback, the U.S. company must still visit those companies personally to determine the best partners.

The selection of the best partner should be made using checklists and other methodologies for evaluating all the considerations in this decision. These methodologies have been captured in several computer-aided decision support systems developed at Michigan State University's International Business Centers—one for the selection of distributors in foreign markets, and the other for choosing partners for various types of international collaborative ventures.

Developing a contract with a distributor or strategic alliance partner is critical to the success of the venture, so good legal advice is very important. There are models of good distributor agreements available to guide the company doing this for the first time. It's important, however, to get good legal assistance. In some cases, it is important to use legal assistance in the target market, because they will be aware of what types of agreements are generally acceptable to partners in those markets. They may also be aware of local or regional issues that must be addressed (such as Economic Community matters) in a contract.

At this point in the 10-Step Road Map process, it is important for a small to medium-sized company to be working with competent international business development professionals, located either in the United States or in the foreign market, and/or have good contacts in foreign markets to help in the identification and selection of the best distributors, retailers, franchisees, or other types of alliance partners.

Step #7. Compliance with Standards and Regulations

Often the greatest obstacle to gaining entry into foreign markets is the array of standards and regulations with which it must comply if the company is to market its products or services in that country. One of the first steps in laying the groundwork for doing business in any country is to identify which standards and regulations affect your company, then begin to lay the groundwork for complying with those standards and regulations. These include safety, environment, packaging, labeling, good manufacturing practices, ISO 9000, efficacy (for medical devices, for example), radio frequency interference, electrical standards, patents and trademarks, copyrights, and registrations.

Expert guidance must be selected to help a company identify, then comply with, all the appropriate standards and regulations. There are public sector agencies that can help for moderate fees, and private sector firms that, while more expensive, may have expertise that can ensure a company it will not face legal problems because of failure to comply with some critical regulation.

Step #8. Selection of Service Support Providers

Even if a company chooses to set up an export department, it will need to rely on a group of service support providers both in the United States and overseas. If the company is just exporting, it will still need the help of freight forwarders, to help get the product to the overseas customers; bankers, to help arrange letters of credit and help the company be paid for what it ships; and some legal assistance, to ensure that the company's patents, trademarks, and copyrights will be protected in the target market.

Therefore, as soon as a company faces its first transaction, it will need to choose freight forwarders, bankers, and attorneys to ensure success. Lists of service providers are available from federal and state departments of commerce, as well as from other providers of international business development services. Selecting those firms in the United States is not too difficult, since a company can always meet a number of firms and choose the best one. Michigan State University's International Business Centers has developed a computer-aided decision support system for selecting a freight forwarder, which is a great aid for a company in choosing the best possible freight forwarder.

Selecting service providers is much more difficult in foreign markets. When a company goes beyond exporting, even to the point of choosing an overseas agent or distributor, it is important to use good local services, like attorneys and bankers. Some of the other service providers needed, particularly as a company becomes closer to having a physical presence in a country, include market research firms, tax and accounting firms, advertising and public relations firms, customs brokers, chambers of commerce, and others as appropriate.

Assistance in locating good service suppliers can be obtained from a company's trade association, the American Chamber of Commerce in the particular country, the commercial counselors at the U.S. & FCS offices in the country, and by contacting other non-competing companies operating in the country. These service providers in foreign markets can make or break a company in its foreign markets. Often good services are very expensive for a small to medium-sized company, so the company may not be able to afford the services of the U.S. Big 6 accounting firms, for example. However, some of the local firms don't have the capabilities of the larger firms, so a U.S. company could make a false economy by selecting a small local firm that may not adequately serve the U.S. company.

This is a critical step for small to medium-sized companies expanding into foreign markets, and it should rely on the best advisors in the field of international business development, whether it be the governmental or private sector professionals.

Step #9. Market Introduction of the Company's Products and Services

Many companies choose a distributor in a foreign market, then rely completely on that distributor to do an effective job of introducing that product in the market. That's an unfortunate mistake. The U.S. company should work hand in hand with the distributor to plan and execute the market introduction. The market introduction in the foreign market should be planned with the same care as any market introduction in a new part of the United States.

The U.S. company should work with the foreign distributor to plan every detail of the product launch in that market. A Pert and Gantt chart (or more sophisticated computer-aided planning tool) should be prepared to show every aspect of the market introduction plan, including:

- Preparation and translation of product literature and videos
- Sales training
- Service training
- Advertising and promotion
- Product modification
- Packaging and labeling
- Inventory planning
- Logistics
- Public relations and publicity
- Government relations

One of the great benefits of this mutual planning and execution process is that it brings to light issues that might not have been resolved in the relationship to this point, such as:

- Who will take what responsibility in obtaining approvals for standards and regulations?
- Who will do the translations?
- Who will print the product literature and operating manuals?
- Who will prepare the artwork?

Step #10. Establish a Physical Presence in a Foreign Market

If a company proceeds to the point where it feels confident enough about its progress in getting into foreign markets that it wants a physical presence, it will need to evaluate very carefully the options available. Some presence can be obtained without establishing a legal presence, by using office-sharing facilities available in many countries.

A company can have a telephone answering service, some secretarial support, and part-time office space without having a legal presence. The Office of the U.S. & Foreign Commercial Service can help in locating those services.

When a company wants to establish a legal presence as well as some physical presence, the commitment to that market becomes much greater, with concomitant risks and rewards. When taking this step, it's best to get expert assistance from tax and accounting firms, and legal advisors. These firms, while expensive for the small to medium-sized businesses in the United States, are essential if a company's interests are to be protected properly as they become established in the market. The Big 6 accounting firms have capabilities in providing this assistance and have proven track records.

The U.S. & FCS and the American Chamber of Commerce offices in each country can also provide assistance in this process, as well as the offices of the U.S. states in various regions of the world. Also, professional international business development agencies can provide assistance at this critical point in a firm's internationalization.

The long-term consequences involved in entering, with provision for exiting, a market are very important.

Conclusion

The foregoing 10-Step Road Map to Success in Foreign Markets is like any map between two major points—like Brussels, Belgium, to Milan, Italy, for example. It serves as a guide to getting from one point to another, without saying that there is only one precise way to do it. The 10-Step Road Map doesn't provide a set of rules, rather it consists of some principles that seem to work rather well. A company can undertake some of the steps out of sequence, or do several at a time. It can undertake some export transactions, and it can do some "chumming" to learn where there may be potential customers. All of this can help a company eventually succeed in foreign markets. Properly undertaken, with guidance by international business development professionals, this process can be a great aid to developing a successful exporting or international market presence.

Notes

1. The term "exporter" may be used at times when a company considering going international may decide either to export or to enter foreign markets by one of many other means, such as licensing, R&D partnerships, production-sharing, or establishment of foreign branches or subsidiaries, for example. The issues faced by firms entering foreign markets are similar up to a point, so the term *exporter* can mean any company considering getting into foreign markets.

2. CORE, copyright 1991, S. Tamer Cavusgil. All rights reserved.

3. The U.S. will be referred to as the home market herein, but this process can be used by a company in any country of the world. In the event that a German company is considering expanding into foreign markets, one could substitute Germany for the U.S. throughout this process.

References

Hamel, Gary and C. K. Prahalad. "Strategic Intent." *Harvard Business Review* (May–June 1989): 63–76.

Mintzberg, Henry. "Crafting Strategy." *Harvard Business Review* (July–August 1987): 66–75.

An Exporter's Guide to Selecting Foreign Sales Agents and Distributors

Thomas F. Clasen. *Thomas F. Clasen is a member of the International Business Group of Foley & Lardner, a Milwaukee-based law firm. The author has adapted this article from his new book,* International Agency and Distribution Agreements *(Butterworths, 1991), a multi-volume treatise on the appointment, use, and termination of foreign sales agents and distributors.*

Experts estimate that more than one half of all world trade is handled through agents and distributors. While the use of such sales intermediaries is commonplace, especially for small and medium-sized companies, it is also common for exporters to complain about their foreign agents and distributors. Unsatisfactory sales intermediaries not only cost the exporter sales, but as a result of protective laws in many foreign jurisdictions, they may be difficult and costly to terminate. New Legislation in EC Member States under Directive 86-653, as well as the proposed extension of Article 85 of the Treaty of Rome to "non-integrated" agents, will present additional obstacles to the use of sales intermediaries in Europe.

While exporters can help themselves by using carefully drafted agency and distribution agreements, the best step in minimizing problems is to use more care in selecting the intermediary. It is not uncommon for manufacturing companies to appoint a local agent or distributor without any significant background check at all. This is particularly true where the intermediary appears to be bringing in a significant amount of business or where the market in the country appears marginal. Since costly disputes frequently arise even in these circumstances, however, it is wise to establish a procedure in selecting foreign agents and distributors and stick to that policy in all cases.

An effective agent-distributor selection procedure normally involves a number of steps. While there are variations depending on the industry, the following core elements will generally be present:

1. Examine the legal and business considerations involved in appointing foreign intermediaries, and establish criteria that reflect the particular geographic market;

2. Assemble a list of potential candidates by using the various directories and consulting other sources of information;

3. Qualify such candidates by applying certain criteria and conducting a preliminary interview; and

Reprinted from *The Journal of European Business,* Vol. 3, No. 2, November/December 1991, pp. 28–32. Permission granted by Faulkner & Gray, 11 Penn Plaza, New York, NY 10001.

4. Make a trip to visit the proposed intermediary to obtain additional information about its resources and facilities, to get a proper feel for the intermediary's compatibility with the organization, and to check the assumptions and objectives of the agent or distributor.

Setting the Criteria

Because the qualifications the intermediary should possess differ from country to country, the starting point for the development of criteria may be an analysis of the peculiar characteristics of the market. Is there sufficient demand for the product in the market to justify its own agent or distributor, or could the market be covered well by an intermediary in an adjacent country? Is the market too large to give exclusively to a single agent or distributor? Is it reasonable to expect an agent or distributor not to handle competing goods in the market? To what extent is the market already familiar with and receptive to the product? Will the establishment of a demand require a long-term strategy that can be pursued only by someone with significant financial resources? Is it desirable to go with a well-established intermediary that can immediately provide access to the market even though this may require more sharing of profits?

A related consideration is the nature of the customers. To the extent that the product will be sold exclusively to governmental agencies, it may be critical for the agent or distributor to have access to officials who influence procurement decisions. If the product is sold primarily as part of a larger construction or turnkey project, access to the project coordinators and the ability to work effectively with the project engineers may be key. Each of these would imply a long-term, focused sales effort for which an agent may be better suited than a distributor. In those instances involving sales to a broader base of ordinary consumers, on the other hand, a distributor with an existing network of sales outlets may be more appropriate. For customers that prefer to purchase "local" products, exporters may want to use a distributor that would sell the goods under its own label.

The nature of the product will obviously have a significant effect on the sales approach. For example, is the product of a highly complex, technical nature so that a sales representative will need to employ advanced engineering and technical personnel to sell it effectively? Is the product complementary to another line of products, making it desirable to "piggy back" on distributors of such other products? Is it essential for the intermediary to have sufficient resources to provide service and spare parts or can these be obtained elsewhere? Is the product susceptible to copying so that it is critical to saturate the market completely through a broad distribution network before knockoffs begin to appear?

The special characteristics of the market, the customers, and the product determine many of the criteria the exporter should consider in selecting a foreign intermediary. There are, however, some additional characteristics of the relationship that may influence the choice. Many of these will dictate whether the intermediary will be an agent or a distributor. For example, when it is important to exercise a high level of control over the marketing and sales activities of the representative, an exporter may prefer to use an agent rather than a distributor. An exporter's preference to sell directly to the customer in order to build goodwill in the market may also make an agency arrangement more desirable. On the other hand, if the exporter is unwilling to assume the risk of nonpayment by the customer or is opposed to a commission-based compensation structure, a company may find a distributor to be more consistent with its objectives. As mentioned, distributors are also more likely to inventory product and parts and to provide repair and warranty service.

In addition to the basic criteria, there are a number of characteristics that the exporter should look for in the candidate. For example, what kind of track record has the proposed agent or distributor established in promoting comparable products? Is it clear that it was responsible for its past success? Are there adequate explanations for its past failures? What kind of reputation does the prospective intermediary have within the industry? Do potential customers uniformly regard the agent or distributor as a company with whom they wish to do business?

Another important area of consideration is the prospective candidate's financial condition and resources. Does the intermediary have a sufficient net worth or other sources of income to sustain a long-term promotional effect even if sales are not realized immediately? Has it shown a consistent pattern of paying its creditors and employees? Does the proposed distributor have sufficient credit to justify extending terms? Does it have sufficient funds to stock an inventory or meet its other needs? Does the *del credere* agent (one that guarantees the customers' payment to the exporter) have the financial resources to support its guarantee? Who are the owners and creditors of the prospective agent or distributor, and what is the extent of their commitment to the intermediary? Has the intermediary shown a practice of making necessary commitments of funds for advertising and promotional activities, personnel, and office and shop facilities?

Companies should also consider the level of interest and enthusiasm the candidate demonstrates in representing the product in the market. Did the candidate contact the exporter or vice versa? Has it prepared a business plan or otherwise outlined in detail its proposed strategy for market development? To what extent is it willing to put its own money into advertising and promotion? Is it willing to assume the risks associated with minimum sales or other performance criteria? What would be its expectation for an initial term of the agreement and in what circumstances should it be renewable? Are these consistent with the schedule the exporter believes to be appropriate for establishing a foothold in the market? These and other factors should be examined to confirm the level of the candidate's commitment to the promotion of the product.

While business considerations normally predominate in the choice of a foreign intermediary, legal factors can influence significantly the exporter's costs and risks in using agents and distributors abroad. Many legal considerations can be addressed in the contract regardless of the agent or distributor that is ultimately selected. Others are so fundamental, however, that they should be examined at the outset and included in the exporter's criteria for selecting the intermediary.

Perhaps the most important legal consideration relevant to the exporter's choice of a commercial intermediary is the effect of local law on the use of agents and distributors. Local laws limiting the use of certain types of commercial intermediaries, for example, or requiring the agent or distributor to meet certain conditions for qualification, must obviously be considered in establishing the criteria for selection. In countries where local labor laws extend to protect individual agents, the exporter may require the agent to be a corporate entity. In countries whose protective legislation extends only to distributors, the exporter may decide only to consider agents. On the other hand, if the manner in which local tax law defines taxable "permanent establishments" makes it difficult to use agents without becoming subject to local taxation, the exporter may wish to limit possible candidates to distributors. The risk presented by the implied authority that agents are granted under local law may also favor the use of distributors rather than agents.

Identifying Candidates

Having developed the general criteria that will be used in selecting the foreign agent or distributor, the next step is to assemble a list of prospective candidates that appear to meet the criteria. For many manufacturers new to exporting, this may appear to be a somewhat daunting task. To be sure, the means of developing information on foreign firms that may be able and willing to promote a company's products abroad are not the same as those used to identify domestic representatives. There are, however, a number of specialized sources of information on possible candidates, including a number of directories (such as those identified in *Trade Directories of the World* and other publications of Croner, Dun & Bradstreet, and Thomas), assistance from the U.S. Department of Commerce (particularly under its Agent/Distributor Service and World Traders Data Report Service), and information available from trade associations, the commercial section of foreign embassies and consulates in the United States, commercial banks, international carriers, and other private firms.

Exporters should investigate who their competitors and other firms in related businesses are using abroad. The exporter should also consult with its existing and potential customers in the foreign territory about possible candidates. Customers are perhaps in the best position to provide accurate information about agents and distributors that know the industry and the product, can provide adequate service and support, provide prompt service, and in general enjoy a favorable reputation in the market.

Qualifying Candidates

Once the manufacturer or supplier has located a number of candidates that appear to meet its criteria, the next task is to qualify the prospective candidates. While the qualification process will clearly depend on the industry or product involved and will differ from country to country, it normally will consist of three steps: (1) investigating the background of the candidate based on outside sources, (2) contacting the candidate to determine its interest in serving as an agent or distributor, and (3) reviewing additional background information obtained from the candidate itself. The objective of the qualification process is to narrow the list of potential candidates to a small number of firms that are genuinely interested in the arrangement and that appear to meet the basic criteria the exporter establishes. This will eliminate the need to make a trip to a country to visit firms that are either unqualified for or uninterested in the relationship. It will also allow the exporter to concentrate its time on visiting serious candidates in a market where it identified numerous possible agents or distributors.

Conducting a background investigation on a potential candidate involves looking at many issues. What is the firm's reputation in its industry? How is it regarded by its customers? How extensive are its contacts and market position in the territory? How long has it been in this business? Who are its principals and what are their backgrounds? How strong are its sales and service personnel? Is it qualified to serve the entire market exclusively? Does it have sufficient facilities and personnel? Does it have adequate financial resources? Information on these and similar questions can often be assembled from outside sources. These include trade and other publications, trade associations, foreign and U.S. government agencies and diplomatic posts, banks and consulting firms, and customers in the territory.

The next step is to contact the potential candidates to determine their interest in serving as agents or distributors. For smaller companies with limited resources, this first contact may be made by means of a letter. The letter should describe generally the exporter's plans for appointing an agent or distributor in the territory, provide some background on the exporter, and include complete information on the subject products, including applications and possible sales volume in the territory. The letter may also refer the candidate to existing users of the product in the territory, if any, to give the potential agent or distributor an opportunity to examine the product and discuss it with a customer. The letter should state clearly that it is intended only to determine whether the recipient would have an interest in selling the product, and that the actual appointment of an agent or distributor will be made only following a personal visit and pursuant to a written agreement. It is important to avoid any misunderstanding that the letter itself is an offer to appoint the recipient as the exporter's intermediary.

Before the exporter plans a trip to visit the candidates, it should obtain additional information on any candidates that respond favorably to the initial contact. Like the background investigation, this review is designed to ferret out firms that do not meet the criteria or that are not serious about representing the product line. In this case, the information is secured from the candidate itself. This may include additional information to confirm the accuracy of the information already gleaned from other sources. It should also include more subjective information such as details on how the candidate sees the new product line fitting into its existing business, general information on how the firm would promote the product, and what the firm's requirements might be in terms of compensation. An exporter that has significant bargaining power due to the demand for the product may even require the candidate to prepare a detailed business plan on its proposed marketing and sales strategies.

Meeting with Candidates

Smaller manufacturers and suppliers that have limited financial resources frequently appoint foreign agents and distributors without visiting the intermediary first. They reason that the costs associated with making the trip outweigh the benefit in actually meeting the prospective agent or distributor. They may also feel that they have less to lose than larger companies if the appointment does not work out. In fact, it is probably more important for the exporter with limited resources than for the large multinational to actually meet with the proposed candidates before making a decision—a visit to the candidate's facilities and an opportunity to meet its principals and other personnel is perhaps the best way to confirm that it meets the exporter's criteria. Agents and distributors that meet these criteria are more likely to maximize the exporter's sales in the territory (thus maximizing the exporter's revenue) and less likely to require termination on unfriendly terms (thus minimizing the exporter's costs).

There are at least three separate objectives of meeting with the proposed appointee in person. The first, and most obvious, is to obtain additional information about the candidate's objectives and means of doing business in order to confirm that it is the proper choice. While the exporter should have secured extensive information before the visit, there is normally no substitute for the purely subjective evaluation a supplier can make by actually meeting with the candidate's personnel and spending a reasonable amount of time discussing each other's ideas on how to enter the market and maximize sales. It is not at all unusual for a supplier to conclude after such a meeting that while the candidate looked great on paper, the chemistry just was not right.

If the supplier finds the candidate acceptable, the meeting can help accomplish a second objective of providing the supplier with additional information useful in negotiating the agency or distribution agreement and improving ongoing communication throughout the term of the appointment. Once again, it is clearly possible to negotiate the agreement without actually sitting down together. Experienced negotiators know, however, that it is very difficult to assess the level of the other side's depth of feeling about a particular issue without sitting across the table from him or her. It is obviously possible simply to show the proposed appointee a printed form and tell it to take it or leave it. Even in these cases, however, it is helpful to spend time discussing the issues to determine the likelihood of the candidate's respect for the terms of the agreement after it is executed. An initial meeting also sets an important tone of mutual communication that can last throughout the term of the agreement. An agent or distributor is much more likely to call and discuss problems with an exporter whose salespeople it knows personally.

But if these were the only purposes for the meeting, then it could just as readily take place at the supplier's facilities or at an airport or trade show someplace in between. This is also undesirable. The third and equally important objective of the face-to-face encounter is to give the exporter an opportunity to personally examine the candidate's facilities and to meet more of its personnel to confirm that they are up to the task. The facilities may be more important in the case of a distributor that will be expected to maintain an inventory and provide service for the products. Both agents and distributors should, however, have acceptable means of communicating efficiently with the exporter and its customers (telex, facsimile, cable, etc.) and a sufficient number of trained personnel to handle the responsibilities of the appointment. This will give the exporter first-hand knowledge of the ability of the candidate to provide effective support for the product.

Finally, the visit to the territory should include calling upon potential customers and other sources of information both to develop additional background on the candidate and to obtain additional information on the market.

Maintaining the Relationship

After selecting an agent or distributor, the exporter should take the necessary steps to maintain the intermediary's goodwill. This involves (1) negotiating an agreement that is fair and mutually beneficial, (2) complying in good faith with the terms of the agreement, (3) continuing the communication between the parties, and (4) making occasional adjustments in the relationship in response to changing circumstances.

While there is no sure way to avoid the risks presented by the use of foreign agents and distributors, careful selection of the intermediary by the above steps is the best means of minimizing them.

Export Trading Companies in World Markets: A Conceptual View

Lyn S. Amine.   *Lyn S. Amine is a faculty member in the School of Business Administration, St. Louis University.*

Introduction

The purpose of this article is to examine the numerous types of export trading companies (ETCs) and export groups currently operating in world markets, with a view to defining and modeling the ETC concept. Motivating this attempt is a sense of frustration with published research on ETCs, which is largely descriptive and anecdotal. No attempt has yet been made at categorization or model-building.

The approach adopted here is different. It follows an "evolutionary" line of thought, moving dynamically back and forth between phases of description, comparison, analysis, and conceptualization. This approach has the considerable advantage of anchoring the conceptual inputs onto a firm foundation of empirical evidence.

First, a basic categorization of export trading entities is established. The range of variants is identified, along with critical company variables which may explain some of this variation. Next, some examples of ETCs are presented, classified by country of origin, namely Japan, Korea, Brazil, and the United States. Here, environmental and historical factors are examined which have shaped ETC characteristics and performance. These four nations have been the focus of most of the previous research on ETCs, presumably because companies from these countries are currently the most prominent and active in world markets. In order to structure the comparison of the four nations' ETCs, reference will be made to the critical company variables already identified. This will demonstrate how these variables have combined to create vastly different types of ETCs in each country.

The next step is to move forward from description and comparison to identify modes of competition between these ETCs and the other export trading entities defined at the beginning of the analysis. Here, a model of "competitive clusters" of ETCs will be presented, all positioned relative to the Japanese ETCs which serve as a baseline for the comparison.

Adapted from *Advances in International Marketing,* Vol. 2, pp. 199–238, with permission.

Finally, to complete the analysis, we step back from the definition of current ETC characteristics and activities in order to focus on fundamental aspects of ETC growth and expansion. If a common path for ETC expansion can be identified, similar to the internationalization path assumed to be followed by new exporters (see Cavusgil 1984), this will be a valuable managerial tool for forecasting future ETC growth and performance. It may also indicate which marketing and organizational strategies are appropriate for use by managers during specific phases of ETC development. Thus, this paper offers insights of value to both academics and practitioners.

The analysis and models presented here may have their shortcomings. Nevertheless, the strengths of this research, as well as the weaknesses, should motivate others to continue the challenging task of definition and conceptualization. The analysis is presented in four parts, as follows:

- A typology of ETCs
- Profiles of four nations' ETCs
- A model of competitive clusters of ETCs in world markets
- A generalized model of ETC expansion.

A Typology of ETCs

Attention is drawn to the terms "export trading company" (ETC), "general trading company" (GTC), and "commodity trading company" (CTC). A purist interpretation might state that an ETC is primarily involved in exporting, while a GTC both imports and exports, and a CTC trades in specific commodity markets. However, few companies limit their involvement in world markets simply to one type of activity. As will be shown below in the ETC profiles, exporting may lead to importing, domestic sales, offshore trading, foreign direct investment, or even joint ventures.

Trading companies are not a new concept nor are they limited to any one country. In Japan they date back to the nineteenth century, and in West Europe companies can trace back their origins to colonial times. State-owned and state-managed trading companies have existed for many years in Socialist countries. Even in the less developed countries, general trading companies exist today and demonstrate many of the features of their more established counterparts in developed nations or newly industrializing countries.

These comments highlight a major theoretical problem: how to define an ETC. A loose definition would specify "involvement in export activities" as the principal criterion for classification. A detailed definition might specify official designation or certification as an ETC, conferred on a company by a government agency. Another definition might focus on the type and number of functions performed (such as export financing, assistance in product design, etc.). Yet another approach might focus on the volume of export sales achieved. This approach would eliminate "nominal" or "symbolic" entities involved in only marginal export activities.

Alternatively, attention can be focused on the spread of involvement of the ETC through the distribution function. Involvement may range from that of periodic facilitator of the international flow of goods or services, to a continuing presence in overseas markets as the captain of an international distribution channel. Of course, even these two alternatives are not mutually exclusive.

TABLE 1   Typology of Export Trading Companies

Type	Rationale for Groupings	Some Examples by Country of Origin
I. General trading companies (GTCs)	Historical involvement in generalized import-export activities	Mitsui (Japan), SCOA (France), East Asiatic (Denmark), Jardine Matheson (Hong Kong/Bermuda)
II. Export trading companies (ETCs)	Specific mission to promote growth of exports	Daewoo (S. Korea), Interbras (Brazil), Sears World Trade (U.S.)
III. Federated export marketing groups (FMGs)	Loose collaboration among exporting companies supervised by a third-party and usually market-specific	Fedec (U.K.), SBI Group (Norway), IEB Project Group (Morocco)
IV. Trading arms of multinational corporations (MNC-ETCs)	Import-export and trading activities specific to parent company's operations	General Motors (U.S.), Volvo (Sweden)
V. Bank-based or bank-affiliated trading groups (Bank-ETCs)	Extension of traditional banking activities into commercial fields	Mitsubishi (Japan), Cobec (Brazil), A.W. Galadari Holdings (United Arab Emirates)
VI. Commodity trading companies (CTCs)	Long-standing export trading in a specific market, secretive, fast-paced and high-risk activities	Metallgesellschaft (W. Germany), Louis Dreyfus (France), Amtorg Trading Corp. (U.S.S.R.)

A further complicating factor in the search for a satisfactory definition is the recognition that companies engaged in exporting may also import, diversify into manufacturing abroad, or have originally been involved in domestic manufacturing. Thus, companies from around the world may, on the surface, appear similar, due to their export interests. However, in reality, they may prove to be radically different commercial entities for whom exporting is either a major or a minor priority.

In order to establish baseline definitions for this analysis, a preliminary classification of export trading companies and groups is presented in Table 1. This typology is necessarily very generalized as each type of ETC may appear in more than one country-context. Moreover, one country may be home for several types of trading companies. One type of trading company is, however, specific to certain historical and cultural context, the Sogo Sosha of Japan. Their particular characteristics are detailed in a later section. The other types of trading company defined in Table 1 are discussed briefly below. Short illustrative examples are presented to establish areas of similarity and difference.

GTCs

Among the first group in Table 1 are many long-established, large and diversified general trading companies. Many GTCs remain relatively obscure and unknown to the general public. In some cases, this is due to the nature of their trade, largely among middlemen buyers and sellers. In others, it is due to the dispersion of their activities across scattered market segments, often in developing countries. East Asiatic Company (EAC) of Denmark is diversified, with interests ranging from timber to motor scooter manufacturing. With operations in some 50 countries, EAC is one of the largest and oldest trading houses and traces its origins back to early trade with Thailand in 1884.

ETCs and FMGs

The second group of companies includes ETCs which were either (i) specifically created by their respective governments to stimulate national export growth, or (ii) evolved as a result of enabling legislation by the government. ETCs in South Korea and Brazil illustrate the case of government sponsorship, while ETCs in the U.S. are examples of private, public or quasi-public initiatives. Brief profiles of ETCs from these countries are presented in a later section.

In contrast, the federated marketing groups (FMGs) in group three take part in a loose collaboration supervised by a third-party. This initiative is private, not regulated by legislation, and often lasts only as long as the members' interests are being served—for example, until penetration of a specific geographic market is achieved. Thus, federations are market- rather than product-oriented.

In Morocco, the Irish Export Board (IEB), which is well-known for its assistance to developing countries, identified a group of producers who were both interested in and capable of penetrating the North American market. The Moroccan government established the link between the IEB and individual Moroccan businessmen through the national agency, the Export Promotion Centre based in Casablanca.

MNC-ETCs

The FMGs cited above share common features with the more formalized ETCs and GTCs. In each case, the image of a "mother hen and chicks" emerges, with the "mother hen" being either a commercial company, a consultant, or some other agent. In the case of the MNC-ETCs, the set-up is noticeably different, with the ETC being merely an extension or "trading arm" of the parent company. For example, Motors Trading Corp. is an ETC subsidiary of General Motors. Volvo International Development Corp. is a trading subsidiary set up to promote sales in all geographic areas outside Volvo's major markets, with special emphasis on LDCs.

Bank-ETCs

This group of ETCs differs from MNC-ETCs by being either bank-based or bank-affiliated. Many of these could be alternately classified as GTCs or ETCs, particularly for countries like Japan, Brazil, West Germany, and the United States, where legislation has specifically approved such groupings. Indeed, the Japanese trading companies have derived immense benefits from their historical association with banking institutions, the "zaibatsu." Thus, the Sogo Shosha are able to facilitate trade credit, initiate equity investments, and provide direct loans to their suppliers and customers. Bank-based ETCs are important in Latin American countries where, in many instances, the ETC takes its name from the bank. Also, in the Middle East, banks and trading companies are, in many instances, owned by the same family.

CTCs

The last group from Table 1 includes the commodity trading companies (CTCs). In some respects, these companies are least similar to the preceding groups of ETCs, partly because of their organization and partly because of their business methods. Most CTCs are privately held and are very secretive about their operations due to the highly competitive and fast-paced nature of their business. Like the Japanese Sogo Shosha, these international traders deal in low-margin, high-volume commodities. Their business is characterized by the high levels of risk associated with owning commodities in an era of increased price volatility, floating currencies, and high interest rates. Two Sogo Shosha, Mitsui and Mitsubishi, and two GTCs, Jardine Matheson and East Asiatic Company are often cross-classified as CTCs, on account of their trading in commodities, along with manufactured goods.

Some of the most powerful and secretive CTCs are the state-run trading organizations in the U.S.S.R. Size, secrecy, and the use of bluff are a powerful combination making the dozens of Soviet trading companies both formidable customers and suppliers. Ironically, the very centralization that makes the Soviet economy inefficient at home increases the clout of the trading companies abroad, as a few key decision-makers strive to manipulate world commodity markets.

From the classification in Table 1 and this brief discussion of trading companies and trading groups, it is clear that numerous variants of the ETC format exist. Differences arise with regard to at least fifteen variables. These are listed in Table 2. The listing is not exhaustive, since other descriptive and measurement variables could be included to cover areas such as financial and managerial practices. Moreover, no research has yet been performed to establish the respective weights of these variables in determining ETC performance levels. The following will show how these variables have been combined to create vastly different types of ETCs in four selected nations.

Profiles of Four Nations' Export Trading Companies

In this section, brief profiles of Japanese, Korean, Brazilian, and American ETCs are presented. These were selected because of their prominence in world markets. The

TABLE 2   Variables Determining the Characteristics of Export Trading Companies

Mission	Product type
Planning horizon	Service type
Type of ownership	Market focus
Size	Agent or merchant function
Age	Quality of management
Type of sponsor	Communications capability
Bank involvement	Government regulation and subsidization
	Profitability

purpose here is to present a picture of similarities and differences between these four groups of ETCs. To this end, environmental and historical factors, which have shaped these ETCs' characteristics and performance levels, are considered, and current innovations among these companies are identified. In each case, reference is made to the variables defined in Table 2. Finally, in order to structure this four-way comparison, each profile addresses the following issues:

- origins and missions
- performance levels
- types of diversification (functional, product, area)
- types of competitive advantages, and
- current problems and opportunities.

Japanese General Trading Companies: The Sogo Shosha

The Japanese GTCs have a long history of involvement in the accumulation, transportation, and distribution of goods from a multitude of countries. Cho (1984) has documented the early history of the Japanese GTCs, which were modeled after the European trading houses. Mitsui was set up in 1876, Mitsubishi in 1889, and Nichimen in 1892.

Officially, only nine Japanese GTCs qualify for the impressive name of Sogo Shosha in terms of sales volume and revenues. Table 3 presents a profile of the top nine Sogo Shosha. Another group of seven very large but less well-known GTCs includes: Chori, Itomen, Kawasho, Kinsho-Mataichi, Nozaki, Okura, and Toshoku. Altogether in Japan there are some 8,600 trading companies but most are small, specializing in only a few products and offering only limited services.

From their distant beginnings, the Sogo Shosha have become high-complex international business conglomerates. In addition to importing and exporting, current activities include third-country trade and domestic sales.

The Sogo Shosha also direct turnkey projects, act as financial dealmakers, and serve as investment partners.

TABLE 3 Nine Leading Japanese General Trading Companies (Sogo Shosha) (1988)

Company	Revenue ($ millions)	Net Income ($ millions)	Employees (thousands)
Mitsubishi Corp.	$96,606	$225	13.9
C. Itoh & Co., Ltd.	92,356	126	12.0
Mitsui & Co., Ltd.	88,640	95	11.4
Marubeni Corp.	82,871	54	10.1
Sumitomo Corp.	81,709	184	12.2
Nissho Iwai Corp.	75,441	61	7.3
Toyo Menka Kaisha Ltd.	27,631	19	5.0
Nichimen Corp.	23,240	7	3.0
Kanematsu-Gosho Ltd.	21,160	8	3.5

SOURCE: *Forbes,* "The 500 Largest Foreign Companies," July 25, 1988, p. 228.

The Sogo Shosha are credited with being able to trade in anything "from soup to nuts." Product diversification is only one of their strengths. Area diversification or worldwide coverage is achieved through extensive networks of international offices and sophisticated company telecommunications facilities. For example, Mitsubishi has 140 branches and affiliates in 70 countries, Marubeni has 154 offices in 87 countries, and Mitsui has 5 clearing houses in Tokyo, New York, London, Syndney, and Bahrain. Complementary to these two strengths of product and area diversification is a third key factor, functional diversification.

In recent years, the Sogo Shosha have moved in new directions, from reactive to proactive trading, in response to competitive threats. Each of the principal services traditionally supplied by the top nine Sogo Shosha is now competitively supplied by other Japanese business entities. Moreover, direct exporting by other Japanese manufacturers has reduced the role of the Sogo Shosha as intermediaries. As business opportunities for the Sogo Shosha shrink in the home market, overhead expenses continue to increase, such as the cost of lifetime employment of skilled manpower. Perhaps most critical to the future of the Sogo Shosha is the fact that they have been by-passed in high growth, high-tech industries, since they were fundamentally "general traders" whose principal products came from Japan's low-growth and declining industries.

At least three new types of activity are emerging among the Sogo Shosha: more third-country trade, increased involvement in "mega" projects, and a move into distribution and after-sales service. Third-country trade may take the form of counterpurchase whereby, for example, a foreign government agrees to buy a given volume of product from Japan on condition that Japan buy a specified amount of another product through the Sogo Shosha. In such cases, the product to be purchased by the Sogo Shosha may lack international competitiveness. It may require the special skills of these traders to locate a prospective buyer.

The Sogo Shosha are increasingly serving as organizers, suppliers, and investors, providing "one-stop shopping" for high-risk international "mega" projects. These projects also open the way to subsequent related offshore deals. In entering the realm of high-tech, the Sogo Shosha face the critical problems of developing appropriate sales, engineering, and after-sales capabilities. Sumitomo is gradually moving toward serving the consumer directly. It has been operating a chain of grocery stores for several years in order to gain experience in retailing.

Thus, there are clear indications that the Sogo Shosha are evolving from the traditional import-export houses into global companies which have heavy commitments in overseas manufacturing, resource extraction, high-tech production and innovative business ventures. These new strategies are important because they allow the Sogo Shosha to exert greater control over their product offerings, all the way from manufacturing to retailing, in increasingly protectionist world markets.

Korean Export Trading Companies

The history of Korean ETCs has been documented by Cho (1984), who points to the Japanese GTCs as a model adopted by Korean policy makers. Faced with poor levels of national export performance, the Korean government adopted the ETC concept and in 1975 laid down minimum criteria for the creation of an ETC. These effectively

TABLE 4   Leading Korean Exporters (1988)

Company	Year of Designation as ETC	Revenue ($ millions)	Net Income ($ millions)	Employees (thousands)
Samsung	1975	21,148	250	160.6
Lucky-Gold Star Group	*	14,487	181	88.4
Daewoo Group	1975	13,498	37	94.9
Hyundai Corp.	†	6,387	4	0.9
Hyundai Motor Co.	†	3,972	113	29.8
Sunkyong Group	1976	6,812	91	19.8

*Lucky-Gold Star Group was not officially designated as an ETC.

† Hyundai Group, before its reorganization into two separate entities, was designated as an ETC in 1978.

SOURCE: *Forbes*, ''The 500 Largest Foreign Companies,'' July 25, 1988, p. 222.

positioned the new companies as general export companies, involved in large-scale trading, and diversified with regard to both export products and markets. Functional diversification was not mandated, however.

Subsequently, the minimum criteria were revised six times until 1981, effectively transmuting the original institutionalized ETCs into freewheeling, large trading companies. Wide-ranging subsidies were provided to promote the growth of these fledgling companies. Later, these subsidies were generalized to other large-scale but non-ETC designated exporters.

Table 4 lists selected leading Korean ETCs, their date of designation as an ETC, and performance data for 1988. The minimum requirement for designation is the achievement of 2% of total Korean exports. The ten leading Korean ETCs include Samsumg, Hyundai, Daewoo, Kukje, Hyosung, Ssangyong, Bando, Sunkyong, Kumho, and Koryo. Korean ETCs have achieved a remarkable rate of growth and are now hugh corporations, particularly in terms of number of employees.

Korean ETCs have tended to emphasize heavy industry exports. They have succeeded in diversifying their export markets away from a dependence on developed markets toward the new markets of the Middle East, Latin America, Oceania and Africa. Korean ETCs' involvement in imports is negligible, quite different from the Japanese GTCs, which are responsible for some 55–60% of their country's total imports. New opportunities being pursued by Korean ETCs include joint ventures, vertical integration, and mega projects, as with the Sogo Shosha.

The Lucky-Gold Start Group is family-owned and operated. Its almost $9 billion in annual sales constitute more than 10% of Korea's GNP. Lucy-Gold Star's growth strategy is based on joint ventures, particularly with U.S. firms. Altogether, Lucky has 19 joint ventures and technological cooperation agreements with 50 foreign companies. Advantages of this strategy not only include access to advanced technology and know-how, but also access to U.S. partners' huge world markets.

The Hyundai Group is one of three companies [along with Daewoo Corp. and KIA Industrial Company] which the Korean government approved as automobile manufacturers in 1981. This policy of controlled capacity had its roots in the near-collapse of the car industry in 1980. Hyundai is known as a fiercely independent company, which insists on "going it alone" in exporting and servicing its cars in Canada and Britain. As an automaker from a developing country, Hyundai benefits from duty-free status as an importer into Canada. In return, it procures more locally made automobile parts than all the Japanese importers combined.

In contrast, Daewoo formed a 50–50 joint venture with GM. Daewoo's strategy is less risky than the Hyundai approach, which prefers independence wherever possible. The trade-off affects name recognition abroad. Hyundai cars are already known abroad under the Pony and Stellar names, whereas Daewoo will piggy-back on GM's Pontiac name.

Hyundai is also actively involved in mega projects such as the construction of an Iraqi oil-fired power-station. Korean ETCs are engaged in major projects throughout North Africa and the Middle East and are leading suppliers of manual labor.

These brief examples demonstrate how Korean ETCs are contributing to the growth of their country, as manufacturers of goods which are more sophisticated or have a higher added-value than the steel, ships and textiles which first brought Korea to international prominence. At the core of the nation's export strategy is a concentrated push toward high technology, intensified production, and lower costs.

Korean ETCs have clearly recognized the need to compete effectively in sophisticated markets for high-tech consumer products. Meeting the challenge of worldwide competition is a major preoccupation, as the Koreans struggle to achieve parity in production, marketing, and distribution skills. Korean ETCs have not yet achieved either the area or functional diversification of the Sogo Shosha. If they are to remain competitive in international markets, they must strengthen such functions as information processing, financing (through trade credits, direct loans, and loan guarantees), and risk-reduction procedures.

Brazilian Export Trading Companies

As with Korean ETCs, Brazilian ETCs came into being as a result of specific legislation regulating their format. The concept of ETCs in Brazil was introduced after a visit to Japan by the former Minister of Finance, Antonio Delfim Netto. He believed that it would be possible to transplant the trading company concept to Brazil, and that trading companies would constitute an essential vehicle for promotion of Brazilian exports. Presidential Decree-Law No. 1298 of November 29, 1972, set up conditions for the registration of new enterprises with CACEX (Banco do Brasil's Foreign Trade Department) and allowed local producers to export by selling to an ETC without losing specific export incentives.

Brazilian ETCs account for some 32% of Brazil's world trading operations. Licensed ETCs now number about 180 and have subsidiaries operating in 42 countries. ETCs are making a substantial contribution to the promotion of Brazilian exports through close imitation of Japanese models, and are successfully involving large numbers of smaller Brazilian companies in international trade activities.

Brazilian ETCs are owned either by the government or by private firms. There are two major government-owned groups, Intebras and Cobec. ETCs owned by private firms are of three broad types:

- Leading Brazilian companies combining to promote their own products or services along with those of other suppliers, e.g., Maxitrade, Multitrade, Minal Gerais, Brasil S.A.;
- Export pools formed by producers and even retailers, e.g., Unisider, Madebras, Pao de Acucar Trading; and
- ETCs formed specifically to aid small and medium producers in one industry, e.g., footwear, lace.

The major advantages of joining an ETC for Brazilian companies are the synergistic effects of combined export effort, economies of scale in export financing and documentation, availability of information, easier access to foreign markets, and availability of support services of various kinds. Brazilian ETCs are heavily involved in a large number of industries through a variety of different organizational formats.

Interbras is of particular interest because of (a) its heavy involvement in service exports, (b) its highly diversified activities, and (c) its role in advising suppliers on marketing problems. Interbras serves as a focus for Brazilian architect–engineering (A–E) services by providing information on foreign market opportunities. Interbras also offers assistance in the commercial administration of exporting, financing, payment, and the execution of countertrade. Barter is a frequent requirement when dealing with customers in LDCs, and the exchange of foreign goods for Brazilian services is not unusual. As a subsidiary of Petrobras, the giant government-owned oil-purchasing company, Interbras' trading operations include primary products, manufactured producer goods, and consumer products.

Brazilian A–E firms demonstrate two types of specific competitive advantage. Many are able to draw on the varied political, cultural, and ethnic traits of their employees to overcome barriers of language, climate, and food encountered by traditional Western firms. In addition, Brazilian firms have promoted the concept of "tropicalization," adapting export technology to the tropical conditions prevalent in their LDC markets. These two characteristics are particularly useful in the area of technology transfer to LDCs.

Brazilian ETCs achieve considerable synergy by collaborative action, not just at the level of the individual ETC, but also through the combination of several very large ETCs, ABECE, the Brazilian Association of Commercial Exporting Companies, exports directly or as an agent for third parties. Privately-owned ETCs demonstrate great diversity. For example, Maxitrade and Multitrade include some of the nation's leading industrial goods suppliers and willingly accept to serve competing suppliers. Brasil S.A. is an important ETC which deals mainly with export financing. It is authorized by the Central Bank to give preferential treatment to the ETCs in granting loans. Even states have set up their own ETCs, such as Minas Gerais.

Export pools are formed by producers and even retailers. Each pool specializes in those markets of interest to its members, so greater efficiency and expertise are achieved than would be possible using the general ETCs. Pao de Acucar Supermarkets is the largest retail company in Latin America. Its export subsidiary, Pao de Acucar Trading, handles trade with other Latin American countries as well as Arab and African nations. An important goal of this ETC is to transfer retail technology to rapidly developing markets which do not possess an adequate system of mass distribution.

Two important industries, footwear and handcrafted cotton lace, are also experiencing export growth through the intermediary assistance of ETCs. Brazil is the world's third largest exporter of shoes. ETCs in this industry take several forms, such as consortia of small producers and large private general trading companies. Petrobras even has a special staff for tracking international fashions in the shoe industry. ETCs have been formed in the Recife area to promote lace exports to the United States, Canada, and Europe. Being labor-intensive, lacemaking is a strategic industry and is being extensively supported by ETCs. For example, assistance is given in the area of fashion and design, and added-value items such as hand-embroidered clothing are being developed for export.

ETCs are contributing significantly to Brazilian export growth. There are some 22,000 Brazilian companies doing business abroad, which is comparable to the United States, where about only 10% of the 250,000 manufacturing firms actually engage in any form of international trade. A key organization is responsible for executing Brazil's national trade policy—CACEX (Banco do Brasil's Foreign Trade Department). CACEX controls both import and export activities and operates according to guidelines set by the Finance Ministry and an interministerial National Foreign Trade Council.

U.S. Export Trading Companies

Passage of the Export Trading Company Act in 1982 in the U.S. created considerable excitement among exporters and nonexporters alike. Seminars, conferences and press editorials were numerous and wide-spread during 1982 and 1983. Yet, in 1984, *The Wall Street Journal* featured a front-page article entitled: "Export Trading Firms in the U.S. Are Failing to Fulfill Promise." It seems as though the new ETC concept is not after all the panacea for the national "export problem" that it appeared to be in 1982.

When the ETC Act was passed, optimistic forecasts predicted that U.S. exports would increase by $6–11 billion within five years and that more than 320,000 trade-related jobs would be created by 1985. The Act was expected to help small- and medium-sized firms the most, some 20,000 being considered potential exporters by the Department of Commerce. In reality, major U.S. corporations have demonstrated the strongest response. Ironically, as Czinkota (1984) reports, these MNC-ETC formations would have occurred with or without the ETC legislation. The two major provisions of the 1982 ETC Act (authorization of bank involvement in exporting and prior antitrust protection), apparently have less appeal than expected for current or potential export entities in the U.S.

New ETCs in the U.S.

As a guide for managers interested in forming or joining an ETC, the Department of Commerce developed six hypothetical models which are summarized in Table 5. In reality, new ETCs in the U.S. appear to follow one of four patterns, which are briefly identified as follows. [See Amine *et al.* (1985), and Amine and Cavusgil (1987) for a full discussion.]

TABLE 5 **Summary of Six Hypothetical ETC Models**

Models	Institutional Participants	Products or Services	Domestic Coverage	Foreign Market	Expected Trade Volume by Fourth Year of Operation
Trade stream model	Manufacturer, freight forwarder, bank holding company (BHC)	Narrow product line	Geographic region	Single country	$6.5 million
Single product model	Manufacturers, BHC	Single product line	Nationwide	Worldwide	$10 million
Services model	Architects & engineers	Design & management services	Geographic region	Geographic region	$35 million
Hub model	Port authority, bankers, bank	Multiple product lines	Geographic region	Geographic region	$50 million
Bank holding company	BHC, ocean shipper, insurance company	Multiple product lines	Single state	Worldwide	$65 million
Single product area model	Manufacturers, venture capital institution	Single product area line	Nationwide	Geographic region	$250 million

SOURCE: Adapted from *The Export Trading Company Guidebook,* prepared by Price Waterhouse and The Council for Export Trading Companies for the U.S. Department of Commerce International Trade Administration, Washington, D.C. (February. 1984), p. 42.

1. *ETCs formed by consortia of smaller suppliers*
2. *ETCs formed by service providers* such as banks (bank-ETCs), export management companies (EMC-ETCs), freight forwarders, etc.
3. *ETCs formed by multinational corporations* (MNC-ETCs)
4. *ETCs formed by quasi-public organizations or public entities* such as ports, development councils, state governments, etc.

Groups 3 and 4 above are closest "in spirit" to the Department of Commerce's models ("Single Product" and "Hub"). Most ETC formations have been of the first and third types. Some comments on each type are given below, illustrating the diversity of U.S. ETCs.

1. *Small-Company ETCs.* This type of ETC is likely to remain few in number, whether certified or non-certified, due to the psychological barrier of accepting collaborative action.

2. *EMC-ETCs and Bank-ETCs.* It is ironic to note that the Director of NEXCO (the National Association of Export Management Companies) considers an "ETC" merely a new name for an "EMC," an export management company. This summarizes the attitude of many export service providers who saw in the ETC Act only a source of threat. Some EMC managers feared that new bank-ETCs would lure away their manufacturer-clients. Others feared that banks would use their knowledge of EMCs' financial operations to gain advantage in their own ETC operations. Many EMCs also consider that they are too small to be concerned by or interested in anti-trust protection. Similar mixed or indifferent attitudes toward the ETC Act persist among other export service providers such as ocean carriers, nonvessel operators, and freight forwarders.

Banks' concerns are of a different nature. Czinkota's (1984) research among 37 U.S. bank holding companies or their subsidiaries found that 41% were interested in investing in an ETC, 32% in forming an ETC, and 27% in using an existing ETC. Bankers anticipated two major problems in this field: organizing for countertrade or barter, and finding qualified trading personnel. They were also concerned about maintaining overseas agents, identifying foreign market potential, and supervising trading personnel. Thus, major obstacles for the banks appear to be emotional rather than financial.

More recently, Hu and Maskulka (1985) have identified variations in both knowledge about the ETC Act and attitudes toward the legislation among U.S. banks, depending upon the banks' degree of internationalization. This characteristic was measured in terms of bank size, percentage of international business, and number of offices abroad. Small U.S. banks were found to be mostly unfamiliar with the ETC legislation, whereas large- and medium-sized banks are well-informed and favorable toward the legislation. Differences in attitudes also exist among large banks (money-centers) and medium-sized (regional) banks, concerning future participation in ETCs and the relative importance of ETCs in banks' long-term strategic objectives. Among the larger banks, involvement in ETCs may only be a "matter of time," as they explore the opportunities offered by the legislation.

3. *MNC-ETCs.* The early experiences of MNC-ETCs in the U.S. are proving to be problematic. Virtually none of the U.S. multinational-based ETCs is yet making money. New U.S. MNC-ETCs are finding that it is not enough merely to transfer staff horizontally from domestic units to the trading unit. Genuine trading expertise is a hard-won and expensive skill, as demonstrated by the well-known generous salaries of traders working for commodity firms. Slow growth and perseverance seem to be the keys to success for new MNC-ETCs. Yet, American corporate culture and pressure by shareholders tend to deter managers of MNC-ETCs from taking the long view so typical of the Sogo Shosha.

4. *Public or Quasi-Public ETCs.* As in the case of U.S. banks, port authorities have hesitated to get involved in forming ETCs because of possible conflicts of interest in competition between a port and its customers.

From this brief review of U.S. ETCs, we see that many gray areas remain for clarification. Will ETCs eventually accomplish what the government hoped in 1982? Can a balance be maintained between achieving strong, effective ETCs and checking abuses of the antitrust laws? Can U.S. companies, historically so competitive, learn to work together to the degree that an ETC requires, without a clash of "corporate cultures"? Can U.S managers achieve the skills and mentality of a trader, rather than those of an exporter? Ultimately, it seems that the "people" factor, as opposed to multiple "market" factors, will be critical to the success of U.S. ETCs.

Competitive Clusters of ETCs in World Markets

Presented in Figure 1 are several "competitive clusters" which incorporate the six types of trading companies listed in Table 1. Given that Japanese GTCs span the full range of market involvement activities, other nations' trading companies and groups have been

FIGURE 1

Competitive clusters of ETCs in world markets

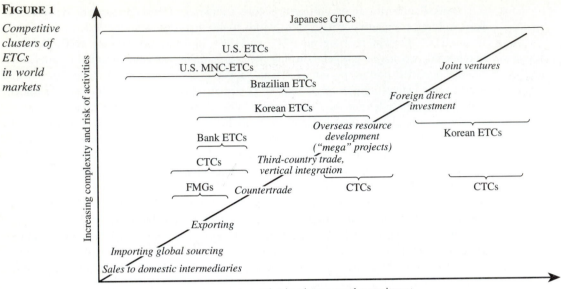

See Table 1 for explanation of acronyms.

positioned relative to them. This approach shows which companies compete directly with one another and which ones are focusing on other areas in order to develop competitive advantages. Again, as in Table 1, we must recognize the broad generalizations and simplification which such an approach entails. Nevertheless, one virtue of this approach is to direct attention to specific aspects of competitive clustering among the world's ETCs.

For example, the Japanese Sogo Shosha's option for proactive trading means that they must now compete across the board with other nations' companies. Faced with such broad-scale and varying types of competition, the Sogo Shosha at least enjoy the advantages of being sufficiently massive and resourceful to be able to choose whether to meet the competition or whether to move into other market segments. The smaller competitors are, in many cases, locked into competition within their segment, with little opportunity to opt out.

This phenomenon of "segment squeeze" can be illustrated by reference to the Korean and Brazilian ETCs. Originally created by their respective governments to promote export growth, both Korean and Brazilian ETCs have recently expanded into resource development in the Middle East. While giants such as Mitsui take on the huge financial burdens and risk of projects such as the Bandar Khomeini petrochemical plant, valued at $3.5 billion, the Koreans and Brazilians serve the specialized niche of supplying construction labor. The Koreans are also beginning to compete directly with Japanese and Western companies to win mega project contracts. Even within this high-risk segment, competition in the Middle East is made more fierce by the appearance of Turkish contracting companies, with their special competitive advantages of geographic proximity to Arab markets and a shared Muslim faith.

In contrast to the Brazilians and Koreans, Japanese GTCs are well established as global competitors. Their major concern is to maintain and even expand their leadership position. At one end of the market spectrum are four low-cost, low-price producers known as the "four tigers," Taiwan, Hong Kong, Singapore, and South Korea. These countries' exports still include such simple consumer items as knit shirts, radios, electric fans, and shoes. But, for all four, the fastest-growing exports have been the more complex electronics products: micro-computer terminals, disk drives, telephone equipment, and semi-conductors. At the other end of the market spectrum, Japanese GTCs are meeting competition head-on from West European and North American multinationals, with their design strengths and technological edge.

One way in which Japanese GTCs have countered the combined threats of globalized competition and market protectionism is through joint ventures with their competitors. It will be noted from Figure 1 that "joint ventures" are positioned at a higher level of increasing involvement, commitment, complexity, and risk than "foreign direct investment." Conventional use of the terms would seem to argue in favor of inverting these positions, but from our point of view, the determining factors are degree of control and duration of the activity. Seen in this light, a 20-year joint-venture agreement, signed between two major ETCs of different nationalities, appears infinitely more fraught with risk than might be the relatively straightforward construction and management of a manufacturing plant overseas. Thus, the risk of losing control of a joint venture, for whatever reason, and the often unpredictable outcomes of a joint venture are the principal arguments which support the positioning of this activity on the continuum in Figure 1.

As we consider the place of U.S. ETCs in this spectrum of competitive clusters, we discover that U.S. corporations appear to be competing both among themselves and against foreign competitors. For example, some of the large joint venture-type ETCs are challenging both the Sogo Shosha, European multinationals, and other large U.S. corporations in the areas of general trading, third-country trade, and vertical integration. Other U.S. companies, which have not formed ETCs, are expanding their international reach through joint ventures, particularly with the Japanese. Thus, it is entirely feasible that, at some time in the future, a Japanese-U.S. JV will compete against a U.S. ETC. This scenario can be developed even further, since Sogo Shosha such as Mitsui have already expressed their willingness to join U.S. ETCs. Such affiliations may be both reasonable and desirable for U.S. companies, particularly as the U.S. Administration appears to be adopting an increasingly "bilateral" approach to international trade. If this trend continues, the main thrust of world competition would be between giant global conglomerates. The small exporter would then either have to become extremely good at nichemanship, identifying small market segments overlooked or discarded by the big companies, or else simply jump on the bandwagon of the ETCs.

This second option, whereby small companies would be constrained to join an ETC in order to get into export markets, is not without its problems. The intricate relationships between manufacturer–suppliers (M–S) and indirect international marketing vehicles such as ETCs are susceptible to instability, either because the ETC serves the M–S too well or not well enough. Thus, if the M–S gets good results from use of an ETC, it may be tempted to "go it alone" and economize on the expense of using the ETC. In the other case, use of the ETC may not produce the results expected by the M–S, if the ETC-parent chooses among its other suppliers for the best deal available.

All the foregoing considerations lead one to question the stability of U.S. ETCs. Will they represent an effective, long term, competitive threat to other nations' ETCs in a particular market or segment? Or will many ETCs be disbanded, because of failure to reach short-term profit objectives? It seems as though the Japanese Sogo Shosha are hedging their bets by offering to join U.S. ETCs and by setting up joint ventures with other U.S. corporations. It will be interesting to see whether U.S. ETCs can survive the initial problems of personnel management, profit planning, and market development, and succeed in building up sufficient critical mass to become successful viable trading entities.

The Brazilians have avoided much international competition and have developed strong competitive advantages by focusing on the supply of basic consumer goods to developing markets. They have also strengthened themselves through collaborative action among their own ETCs, tending to avoid the challenges and risks of international joint ventures. In contrast, the Koreans have chosen the joint venture as a means of rapid expansion into high-tech industries. They have also chosen the strategy of market specialization, based on meeting the needs of sophisticated large-volume Western markets. Similarly, federated marketing groups tend to adopt a single-market geographic focus. In contrast, commodity trading companies have developed specific product or commodity expertise.

U.S. ETCs are remarkable for their wide range of emphases and orientations. Bank-ETCs seem to be opting for functional specialization through the provision of specific export services. The trading arms of some MNCs specialize in a limited range of products, where some manufacturer- or retailer-sponsored ETCs appear to be trying to compete across the board. In so doing, they are of course encountering strong competition from the established and experienced Sogo Shosha, particularly in cases where countertrade is involved.

It will be noted in Figure 1 that "countertrade," "third-country trade," "vertical integration," and "overseas resource development" are positioned adjacent to one another. It could be argued that "countertrade" should serve as a global term for all of these activities, and in the case of the Sogo Shosha, this is probably true. However, as seen in the case of some CTCs, bank-ETCs, U.S., Korean and Brazilian ETCs, there still remains some differentiation, and these variations are reflected in the figure. It will also be noted in Figure 1 that CTCs are shown to be involved in exporting, mega projects, and joint ventures.

In concluding this discussion of competition, one should not forget the vital material and financial support given to Japanese trading companies by MITI (Ministry of International Trade and Industry) to Korean ETCs by their government through MTI (Ministry of Trade and Industry), and to Brazilian ETCs by CACEX (Bank of Brazil's Foreign Trade Department). No such support system has been initiated in the U.S. This probably explains to a large degree why U.S. ETCs experienced such extensive "teething troubles." It is unlikely that compensation for this shortfall will soon occur in the United States, since the concept of a uniform "trade policy" supported by extensive government agencies is still at the discussion stage.

TABLE 6   **External Factors Affecting ETC Growth**

A. Country-Specific Factors

Stage of national economic development
Historical context
Attitudes toward international trade
Status of country's trade balance
Cultural attitudes toward collaborative or group action
Cultural attitudes toward entrepreneurial action
Attitudes toward company organization and operation

B. Market-Specific Factors

Source of initiative for creating ETCs
Constraints imposed on ETC performance
Size of domestic market
Level of domestic competition
Sophistication of domestic companies
Availability and type of marketing support services

A Generalized Model of ETC Expansion

In this final section, information from the foregoing analyses is synthesized. Table 6 presents a listing of external factors likely to affect ETC growth, and Table 7 presents a similar listing of internal company factors. All the factors listed in Tables 6 and 7 are incorporated into the generalized model in Figure 2. It should be noted, as in the case of Table 2, that these listings are not exhaustive. Also, they have not yet been subjected to empirical testing of either their validity or their relative importance in determining the performance of ETCs. These shortcomings are not considered a detriment, but rather a challenge to pursue further research which will validate these conceptualizations.

One of the difficulties in developing the model in Figure 2 is to accommodate the multiple types of activities which an ETC may pursue concurrently. Another difficulty is to allow for flexibility in changing a type of activity, either moving into new areas or returning to previous activities. It will be noticed from Figure 2 that an ETC may conceivably become an importer at home and even get involved in domestic manufacturing—as exemplified by the Sogo Shosha and the Korean ETCs.

Another challenge in modeling ETC expansion is to allow for opposing trends among ETCs. For example, the Sogo Shosha have moved away from general trading toward high-risk investment in overseas resource development. Thus, the traditional import-export houses of Japan have evolved into sophisticated global corporations. U.S. companies which have formed ETCs have followed an inverse pattern of expansion, from specialized manufacturing into general trading of their own and related goods. Korean ETCs, in contrast, are pursuing exporting, along with increased stakes in domestic and overseas production.

As will be seen in Figure 2, all of these variants are accommodated in the model of the ETC expansion path. Attention is drawn to the fact that the model of ETC expansion is not linear, but allows for the possibility of multiple looping, along with movement

TABLE 7   Internal Company Factors Affecting ETC Growth

A. ETC Organization

Type of activity (manufacturing, service provider)
Type of specialization (product, functions, area)
Type of sponsor (private, public, semi-public)
Type of ownership (entrepreneurial, collaborative)
Linkages in domestic market
Linkages in international market
Managerial resources

B. Mission

Prerequisite characteristics for official designation as ETC
Role in national economic development
Sectoral role and importance
Positioning in domestic market regarding suppliers
Positioning in domestic market regarding competitors
Focus (export, import, general trade, countertrade, offshore trade, mega projects, etc.)
Linkages in domestic market (size and anti-trust issues, affiliations with financial institutions and
    government, etc.)

C. Coverage

Number of markets
Location/type of markets
Size of market segments or niches
Overseas channel power
Linkages in overseas markets (cooperation agreements, exclusive contracts, joint ventures, foreign direct
    investments)

---

forward and backward along the path. These characteristics are essential if all the complexities of the ETC concept are to be effectively represented.

As with any conceptualized model, the question of its value arises. The model has at least four major strengths. First, the model aims to be *comprehensive.* Second, the model is *descriptive,* both in its identification of company and market factors affecting ETCs and in the presentation of a range of options for ETC growth and diversification. Third, the model is *dynamic* insofar as it allows for change in the nature of an ETC's activities and even allows for nonlinear ETC development. Fourth, the model aims to serve as both a *diagnostic and planning tool,* providing answers to the questions, "Where are we now?" and "Where do we want to be?"

These four major features of the model offer clear managerial applications. For example, the model identifies a range of diversification and growth options which ETC managers may consider when developing their long-range marketing plan. Moreover, when studied together with the competitive cluster framework, this model will lead ETC managers to reflect upon the implications of selecting specific competitive strategies. For example, managers will be led to consider major strategic issues, such as whether to meet the competition head-on; whether to avoid competition by seeking smaller or more specialized demand segments; or even whether to seek a partner-company in order to develop synergy. Other important decisions identified in the model concern the choice of market position, such as specialization in small market niches or mass marketing

FIGURE 2 *A generalized model of the expansion path for ETCs*

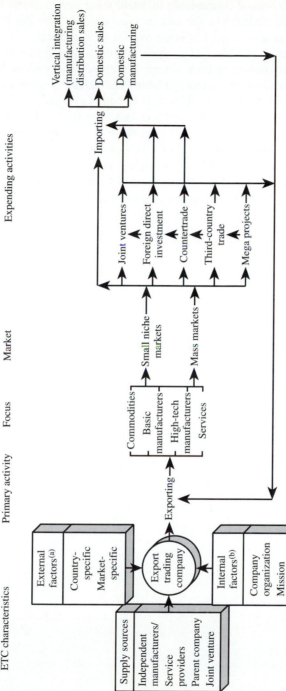

ETC characteristics   Primary activity   Focus   Market   Expending activities

^aSee Table 6; ^bSee Table 7.

503

activities; the role of countertrade in establishing new markets; the mix of products and services to be traded; and the mix of supply sources for the ETC. Clearly, a range of other issues is also implied or made explicit by the model.

In the case of U.S. ETCs, these questions may prove to be critical. U.S. ETCs appear to be competing both among themselves and against foreign competitors. An objective evaluation of current marketing strategies (by reference to the model in Figure 2) would surely help many U.S. ETCs, both large and small, to clarify their market position and to develop a sharper focus than is evident at the present time. The objective of this research was to go beyond mere description of different nations' ETCs in order to identify common characteristics of ETCs and incorporate these into conceptualizations. The generalized model of ETC expansion and the analytical framework of competitive clusters of ETCs together represent valuable aids to both managers and academics in understanding and forecasting future growth patterns for ETCs in world markets.

References

Amine, Lyn S. and S. Tamer Cavusgil, "Issues to Consider When Creating or Joining an Export Trading Company," *Journal of Business and Industrial Marketing* (1987).

Amine, Lyn S., S. Tamer Cavusgil and Robert Weinstein, "Japanese Sogo Shosha and the U.S. Export Trading Companies," *Journal of the Academy of Marketing Science,* Vol. 14, No. 3 (1986), pp. 21–32.

Amine, Lyn S., S. Tamer Cavusgil, A. Coskun Samli, and John R. Nevin, "Toward a New Export Intermediary: Export Trading Companies in the United States," in *Developments in Marketing Science,* VIII, N.K. Malhotra (ed.), (Miami: Academy of Marketing Science, 1985), pp. 85–89.

Cavusgil, S. Tamer, "Differences Among Exporting Firms Based on Their Degree of Internationalization," *Journal of Business Research,* Vol. 12, No. 2 (1984), pp. 195–208.

Cho, Dong Sung, "The Anatomy of the Korean General Trading Company," *Journal of Business Research,* Vol. 12, No. 2 (1984), pp. 241–256.

Czinkota, Michael R., "The Business Response to the Export Trading Company Act of 1982," *Columbia Journal of World Business,* Vol. 19, No. 3 (Fall 1984), pp. 105–111.

Hu, Michael Y. and James M. Maskulka, "U.S. Bankers' Attitudes and Internationalization: The Case of ETCA," *International Journal of Bank Marketing* (Fall 1985), pp. 13–21.

Diffusion of Franchise System Use in International Operations

Lawrence S. Welch.

Although franchising has had a long history, its first significant penetration took place at the end of the nineteenth century in the form of so-called "product and tradename franchising" (U.S. Department of Commerce 1987). This development began in the U.S. and was followed in other Western countries, although concentrated in three main areas: motor vehicle dealerships, service stations and soft drink bottlers—of which Coca Cola is perhaps the best known example.

A new wave of franchising has occurred in the post-World War II period which has been distinguished from the "first generation" by its concern with the transfer of a more complete business system. Often called "business format franchising," it has been defined as being "characterized by an ongoing business relationship between franchisor and franchisee that includes not only the product, service and trademark but the entire business format itself . . . a marketing strategy and plan, operating manuals and standards, quality control and continuing two way communications" (U.S. Department of Commerce 1987, p. 3).

The growth of business format franchising in the post-War period has been particularly rapid, across an ever-broadening front (U.S. Department of Commerce 1987). As a mode of international operations it is being seriously considered by more and more companies in diverse locations as an alternative to the more traditional forms of foreign operations.

In this article the process of global development in franchise system use will be examined, with particular reference to recent Australian experience of companies moving quickly from domestic operations to international franchising.

Development Pattern

The postwar development of franchise system use has tended to follow a path not dissimilar to that argued in the international product life-cycle concept. Initially, the

Reprinted by permission of MCB University Press from *International Marketing Review,* Summer 1989, pp. 7–19, © 1989, MCB University Press.

TABLE 1   **International Franchising by U.S. Companies***

Year	Growth Number of Companies	Total Foreign Outlets
1971	156	3,365
1974	217	9,663
1977	244	14,217
1980	279	20,428
1983	305	25,682
1985	342	30,188

Country or Region	Spread (1985) Number of Franchisors	Number of Outlets
Canada	239	9,054
Japan	66	7,124
Australia	75	2,511
United Kingdom	68	2,291 (69.5%)[†]
Continental Europe	73	4,398
Asia (less Japan and Middle East)	74	1,452
Caribbean	88	803
Mexico	36	542
South America	35	515

*Does not include automobile and truck dealers, gasoline service stations and soft drink bottlers; includes company and franchisee-owned outlets.
[†]Share of total outlets represented by first four countries.

business format franchising system was pre-eminently developed in the U.S. and grew rapidly there in the 1950s and 1960s. Although the focus of growth at the outset was domestic, with successful domestic expansion the attraction of foreign markets became more valid. Research indicates that perceived foreign market potential and foreign franchisee interest were far more important in stimulating the move into foreign markets than any immediate concern about domestic saturation. Nevertheless, the experience, confidence and raised horizons flowing from domestic expansion provided the basic springboard for foreign activity in a manner similar to pre-export patterns.

Thus, in the late 1960s and early 1970s the process of international expansion by U.S. franchisors began in earnest. As Table 1 indicates, there has been a steady growth since 1971. Between 1971 and 1985 the numbers of franchisors operating abroad more than doubled while there was a much larger increase in the number of outlets actually established by these companies in foreign markets. Some of the outlets were set up as company-owned units, but primarily they represented a franchise sale to an individual franchisee or to a master licensee with responsibility for a region or country.

Because of its proximity and low cultural distance, Canada was of course the primary initial target for U.S. franchisors. Although there has been a drop from 1971 when 46% of U.S. franchisors' foreign outlets were located in Canada, in 1985 the corresponding figure was still 30%—making it by far the most important foreign market for U.S. companies (U.S. Department of Commerce 1987). Proximity was stressed in explaining the early move into Canada, but this factor was clearly not of sufficient strength to bring about a similar shift into Mexico. Other important factors undoubtedly come into play. Market potential has already been stressed. There is also the question of how readily an existing franchise format can be applied in a foreign market without major adaptation. Ready transfer is most likely to similarly advanced Western economies with comparable cultural characteristics. The desire to go with an unaltered proven package is strong. In Hackett's survey, 41.2% of companies had reported "no major changes in their franchise marketing package for overseas ventures" (1976, p. 71).

In a similar manner with respect to Canada, the bias towards other culturally similar, advanced countries such as the U.K. and Australia was a natural evolution, despite the proximity factor. The shift into Japan in some strength appears to argue against this trend, although the method of entry was important in supporting this development. The bulk of the penetration in Japan has been through master licenses, minimizing the demands of more direct involvement in developing operations in an alien culture (Grant 1985). As Table 1 indicates, Canada, Japan, Australia and the U.K. accounted for almost 70% of the foreign outlets of franchisors in 1985.

Beyond this core of countries there has been a gradual spread of U.S. franchisors to more and more diverse locations, some to be expected, such as the Scandinavian countries and the newly industrializing countries of Asia, while others have been somewhat surprising. For example, McDonald's is opening restaurants in Yugoslavia and Hungary, and Pizza Hut is negotiating to open 100 outlets in the Soviet Union. The growing importance of global markets to U.S. franchisors is perhaps best illustrated by the experience of McDonald's, where its international segment has become the fastest growing part of the entire organization. Already operating in 44 countries, it has become more dependent on a wide diversity of foreign locations for continued growth.

The Australian Experience

Australia was one of the early favored locations for U.S. franchisors. Despite the adverse distance factor, cultural similarity, a high per capita income, a well developed service sector and a high level of penetration of U.S. firms in general made Australia a strong potential franchising recipient. At the forefront of the Australian invasion were those companies which had been very successful in the U.S., notably the fast food operators. One observer of the Australian franchising scene has commented "that it was the introduction of McDonald's into Australia in the early 1970s and McDonald's entry into franchising in the mid-1970s that gave franchising in Australia its real boost" (Bellin 1984, p. 27). Prior to this stage, as in the U.S., franchising had principally been of the "first generation" variety (product and trade name) in the same areas of motor vehicle dealerships, service stations and soft drink bottlers. Once the "second generation" versions began to spread into the 1970s, franchising's growth was extremely rapid, not only through the entry of foreign (mainly U.S.) franchisors, but also because of the rise of local imitators.

By its very nature franchising is a very open form of operations, offering typically a standardized format, although much of the complexity of the total business system involved remains obscured behind a seemingly simple facade. While a name can be protected, the type of product or service and general style of operation can be readily copied, as the McDonald's imitators in the U.S. and elsewhere have clearly demonstrated, however, not always successfully. In the Australian case the imitators have blossomed, covering a wide spectrum of products and services, including such areas as clothing, chocolates, soaps, tyres, financial services and fitness centers. They have followed very much the format established by the earlier U.S. franchising entrants. Even some well established manufacturing companies with retail outlets have sought to move from a company-owned to a franchised basis as a means of freeing tied up capital and providing a spur to motivation. One Australian bank, the Bank of Queensland, has been setting up new branches of franchised outlets while other banks are examining the possibilities of following suit.

As there are no general statistics maintained on the state of franchising in Australia it is not possible to give any precise figure to the extent of its development. Casual observation at the retail level very quickly indicates that the extent of franchising involvement, both foreign and local, is substantial. Using the broadest definition of franchising (both first and second generation), the Bureau of Industry Economics (1981) found from a survey of small non-manufacturing firms in 1978 that 18.9% were engaged in franchising. More recently, franchising's share of retail sales is estimated to have reached at least 20% and may even be as high as 30%. Despite the limitations of such estimates it is clear that the franchising phenomenon has achieved a deep level of penetration in Australia, particularly in retailing activity, and has grown significantly beyond its U.S. inspired base.

The Outward Move

As a result of early imitation, many Australian companies have been applying the franchising system in a diversity of fields for some time. Inevitably, with their Australian expansion process, similar forces which eventually came into play in the U.S. and led U.S. operators to consider international activity have begun to take effect. The success of domestic expansion likewise pointed to wide possibilities, while these were often exposed by foreign franchisee interest. In Australia's case, the smaller domestic market size quickly exposes the limits of domestic growth. Thus, as shown in Figure 1, we have begun to see a growing outward movement by Australian franchisors.

Included in the target market of interest has been the U.S. Not only is the market potential factor seen as strong but also as the home of franchising it is viewed as having a receptive environment for franchising operations. The Australian pattern is illustrative of a process which is also taking place at different rates in many other countries, so that ultimately the U.S. is likely to become an increasingly important recipient of global franchising activity, in much the same way as it has become the recipient of foreign direct investment operations. A prime example of this pattern is the Italian-based clothing store chain (mainly franchised) Benetton: "With limited room for expansion in Europe, Benetton has launched a major assault on the U.S. market, where it has grown from zero to 650 shops in five years" (Bruce 1987, p. 28).

FIGURE 1

International spread of franchising

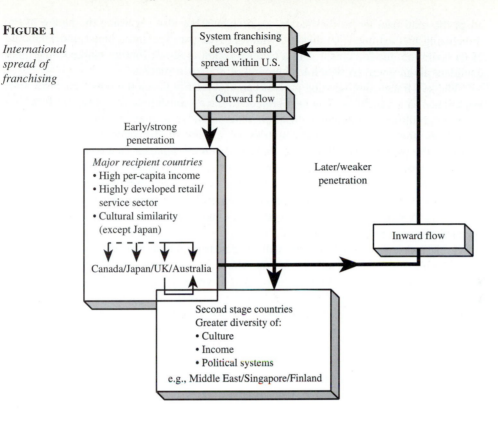

Paths to Foreign Franchising

As Figure 2 indicates, there are a number of feasible paths by which companies might enter foreign franchising operations, with some combination of prior franchising and foreign marketing experience. Although there has been no general empirical research to confirm the pattern, the general impression from reported experience in Australia, and from the particular cases examined in this article, would be that domestic franchising has preceded foreign involvement. This is in line with U.S. experience noted earlier.

There are good reasons for expecting such an approach. The franchising development often begins as a response to a perceived local opportunity, perhaps as an adaptation of a franchising concept already operating in another foreign market. Either way, the market focus is clearly local to begin with. In addition, the local market provides a better environment for testing and developing the franchising format. Feedback from the marketplace and franchises can be more readily obtained because of the ease of communication. Adjustments can be made more quickly because of the close local contact. A whole variety of minor changes in the format may be necessary as a result of early experience in areas such as training, franchisee choice, site selection, organization of suppliers, promotion and outlet decor. The early stages of franchise development represent a critical learning process for the franchisor, not just about how to adapt the total package to the market requirements but also regarding the nature of the franchising method itself. Ultimately, with a proven package and a better understanding of its operation, the franchisor is in a better position to attack foreign markets, and more confident about doing so with a background of domestic success.

The key franchising learning process can also readily develop on the franchisee side. Experience as a franchisee may be a prelude to the establishment of a different franchise chain, and ultimate internationalization. Alternatively, it may be that the company undertakes franchising in other countries on behalf of the international chain. For example, the partners who developed the Wendys Supa Sundaes (ice cream) franchising chain had been franchisees for five years before setting up their own chain; even as the first Wendys outlets were being established they still ran three Wimpy's hamburger restaurants. The transfer of knowledge and experience from franchisee activities parallels the pattern found for a number of Australian companies which switched from international licensee to licensor activities.

It can be expected too that there will be increasing numbers of master licensees for a given country which, having set up the chain locally, seek out the possibilities of expansion for the chain to another country. The master licensee is effectively operating as a franchisor within the country assigned, deriving the benefits of accumulated franchising experience and knowledge in much the same way as a franchisor of domestic origin. The loosely connected Australian end of the worldwide Budget car rental franchising chain moved from its Australian base (mixed company-owned and franchised outlets) to successfully develop South Pacific and then Asian operations, including Japan, under the Budget flag. In these moves the Australian company was the initiator, having obtained rights to these areas from its licensor, Budget America. Originally though, the shift into franchising in domestic operations by Budget Australia, from a system of only company-owned outlets, was heavily based on know-how transferred from the U.S. company: "In large part the experience, assistance and encouragement of Budget U.S. made the franchising experiment work" (Layton 1981, p. 61).

While the most likely path into foreign franchising operations seems to be as an extension of a domestic franchising base, there is every reason to expect some cases whereby the shift is made from other, existing forms of foreign operations. In such cases there is an already established base of foreign experience and knowledge, and perhaps committed facilities, so it is not a blind leap into an unknown foreign environment. The conversion to franchising may be relatively simple, for example, if it is a matter of changing a chain of owned outlets into franchises. As licensing packages broaden and develop a stronger marketing component it can be expected that more will evolve towards a franchising system basis (Welch 1985). The motivation of the franchised owner-operator and the franchisee's capital contribution are strong incentives for the consideration of conversion possibilities. As well, the high international profile of franchising has brought it into stronger focus as a means of foreign operation.

Conversion of foreign operations to franchising in situations where the company also has some domestic franchising experience is a somewhat easier move because of the combination of both franchising and foreign marketing backgrounds. Of course, even for experienced international franchisors like McDonald's, the initial step into a foreign market will often be via a company-owned operation. By such means the company can

FIGURE 2

*Potential paths
to foreign
franchising*

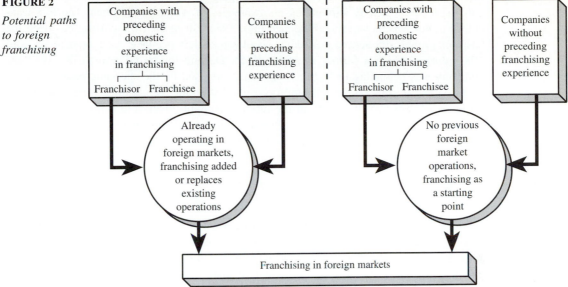

ensure full control and is in a better position to make any required adaptations to portions of the total package, before rolling out on a franchising basis. In this case the alternative method is merely a prelude, or a sounding board, for the ultimate establishment of the franchise system. This process can be seen as part of an overall international franchising strategy.

Amongst the paths to foreign franchising shown in Figure 2, the least likely is that of the inexperienced franchisor starting into franchising first within a foreign market, but without any background of foreign marketing activity. It is possible that, for example, the new franchisor has work experience, lived in the foreign country previously, or is even a migrant from the country. Thus, there is not an unfamiliarity factor to contend with. However, the combination of previously unused techniques in an unfamiliar foreign environment, without previous foreign marketing experience, is a difficult one to contemplate let alone master successfully. The feasibility of such a path probably depends more heavily than in other situations on the ability of the foreign franchisee to develop the system.

Some Australian Cases

As noted already, the assimilation and imitation of franchise system use in Australia has proceeded rapidly since the early 1970s. This process has now led to a growing number of Australian franchisors which have established foreign operations or are seeking to do so. A case in point is the ice-cream franchising chain Wendys Supa Sundaes. It opened its first outlet in 1979 as a company-owned operation. In fact, the initial intention was to establish just four outlets in the one city, Adelaide. At a very early stage though, outside interest in setting up an outlet in a new shopping complex in another city, Melbourne, was expressed—thereby stimulating an awareness of wider possibilities. The first franchised outlet was, however, not opened until 1981. Since then franchising has been the basis of growth throughout Australia: about ten outlets per year were opened up until 1987, during which a further 27 were added. Despite this rapid growth, by 1987 the company was beginning to feel the constraints imposed by the shopping center location of its outlets. Limits on the availability of good shopping center sites were expected to result in a lower rate of growth in the future. Inevitably then, international possibilities presented an alternative source of expansion. The foundation of its initial international interest was, however, laid in its domestic learning curve:

> Things for us on the local front are going extremely well . . . Overseas expansion seems to be the natural progression from here. We have learned a lot during the past eight years and I think we have ironed out most of the bugs in the system. (Burns 1987, p. 50).

The company's initial "pre-export" move was, however, stimulated by an unsolicited inquiry from an Australian with business connections in Hong Kong and South-East Asia. In response, a study tour of the region was undertaken in late 1986, but it was felt that the growth potential was insufficient to justify the set-up expenses. In the background was an interest in U.S. possibilities which had developed through frequent visits and contact with representatives of the U.S. company which supplies its machines—they had stressed the good U.S. market prospects for the concept. After meeting a U.S. franchising consultant at an international franchising conference in 1986, Wendys Supa Sundae has utilized the U.S. franchising consultant to advise on improvements to Australian operations and subsequently to assist in U.S. market entry. The intention has been to establish a joint venture as a basis for U.S. activities, although so far negotiations with potential partners have fallen through.

Dial-a-Dino's, a pizza delivery chain, began in a similar manner to Wendys, at the end of 1984, by establishing company-owned outlets. It was about one year and seven outlets later that the first franchise operation was established. Since then growth has proceeded rapidly throughout Australia via franchising. By late 1987 the company had an Australian chain of 83 outlets.

The founder of Dial-a-Dino's indicates that the intention to set up an international network was present at the outset, and was part of the driving force in the growth of the company. In late 1986 a tour of Asian countries was undertaken because of a perception that it would be easier to develop activities in Japan from an Australian base rather than in Europe or the U.S. As an outcome of the investigations, Japan was seen as a particularly viable market for entry. However, New Zealand was the first foreign market to be penetrated as a result of an unsolicited inquiry. The eventual New Zealand partner was interested in the pizza delivery business and had noticed Dial-a-Dino's operations on a visit to Sydney. The New Zealand entry was relatively straightforward with no capital contribution required: Dial-a-Dino's took a 33% equity in the New Zealand company in exchange for rights to the whole franchise system. From May, 1987, eight outlets had been established by late 1987: five franchised and three company-owned. New Zealand was viewed as an experimental market on which Dial-a-Dino's could cut its teeth before moving to larger and more demanding markets such as Japan.

Japanese market entry was likewise achieved via a joint venture arrangement, with equity exchanged for full access to the franchise system. This involvement was initiated by the Japanese in late 1986 as Dial-a-Dino's was investigating the Japanese market. The President of a Japanese company (Ono Creative) had approached the Australian Trade Commission in Tokyo in search of a potential Australian partner with which to establish a pizza business in Japan, and was put in contact with Dial-a-Dino's. Despite some initial communications difficulties, the joint venture began operations in August, 1987. Some adjustments have been made for the Japanese market—for example, smaller pizzas, lighter dough and smaller delivery vehicles—but in general the franchised package is relatively unchanged.

The move into Japan has been followed quickly by the establishment of a similar joint venture arrangement in the U.K., with the first outlet opened in December, 1987. Such rapid expansion and international penetration are somewhat unusual but can perhaps be explained by a combination of the following factors:

1. Successful franchising of the Australian network and the learning process therefrom;
2. The international outlook of the founder;
3. Fortuitous action by foreign companies interested in the pizza business;
4. The type of entry mode: joint ventures without a capital contribution sharply diminished the financial demands of international expansion.

In another example of rapid expansion, Miniskips, which franchised a waste removal system, considered the possibility of international operations from the outset. Soon after the launch of the company's franchise chain its founders commented they "hope to launch Miniskips in New Zealand and are making inquiries in the U.S. and S.E. Asia, where Singapore and Hong Kong are considered the most likely targets" (Treadgold 1985, p. 113). Such early international interest to some extent runs counter to the earlier stress on expanding domestic operations first. McDonald's took about a decade from its early U.S. spread before initial flirtations with international markets began in the mid-1960s. It was not until the early 1970s that this became a serious international push.

The international interest at the outset by Miniskips can be partly explained by the background of the co-founders. Both were from England, where the system for waste collection and disposal was first seen in operation. They were therefore clearly cognizant of the international possibilities of the business, and of the universality of the need they were serving.

Within 18 months of starting operations in 1985, a national chain of more than 80 franchisees had been established. Such rapid expansion placed a heavy strain on managerial time and resources. This strain was enhanced, since the company's base was in Perth whereas its major markets were on the other (Eastern) side of Australia. Thus, in carrying through its first international move in 1986, it merely sold the rights to the Miniskips package to a New Zealand company for a cash payment and a 14% equity interest, removing the need for direct involvement in establishing a New Zealand network. It had also begun investigations into the U.K. market.

Miniskips was taken over in early 1987 and subsequently went through a period of consolidation. By early 1988 all but 13 franchisees had been bought out. The aim was to establish the business on a sounder basis before resuming any outward push.

Cut-Price Deli is a retail chain of specialty food stores (delicatessens) which is perhaps illustrative of the rapid growth potential of franchising in comparison with company-owned operations. Its first store was acquired in 1974, and by 1982 it had established 16 company-owned stores. However, the company began experiencing significant staff and management problems. In attempting to resolve the situation, the partners who owned and ran the company decided to try franchising, the first franchise being sold in June 1982. Within 12 months, 25 additional franchises had been sold. At the same time the company refined its franchising system by a blending of existing elements (such as an established buying network) with franchising-specific components (for example, a training manual). Since then growth has continued throughout Australia and by early 1987, 110 outlets had been established.

Cut-Price Deli's first international move into New Zealand took place at the beginning of 1987—through a joint venture with a New Zealand investment company (Brierly Investments). A company-owned outlet represented the starting point of operations. The outlet was to function as a pilot store, demonstrating the concept and its viability before rolling out into the full New Zealand market on a franchising basis.

The interest in New Zealand had evolved out of a general recognition of the potential for applying its franchising system in international markets, as well as through direct connections with the New Zealand market via a previous supplier company (Huttons). Cut-Price Deli had used Huttons in Australia for some time until Huttons was taken over by Brierly Investments and withdrew to New Zealand. The move evoked an interest in New Zealand by Cut-Price Deli and eventually contact with Huttons led to the joint venture arrangement with Brierly Investments.

Cut-Price Deli has expressed an intention to ultimately enter the U.S. market although its next move was most likely to be into the U.K. However, the company has found that continuing rapid development in Australia has constrained its ability to take on international markets as rapidly as it would like.

Once again the four Australian franchising cases which have been examined illustrate the way in which the impetus of successful domestic expansion often leads to international interest. While domestic expansion inevitably ties up company commitment for some time, it provides the essential proving ground for the franchising system. The early interest in international possibilities may reflect a more positive environment for such moves in franchising in the 1980s as well as reflecting the nature of the expansion ethos of franchising itself. Success is demonstrated and judged by an ever-widening establishment of franchise outlets, and after initial domestic growth has been proven, the ultimate test is in the international arena.

Franchising from Developing Countries

The main focus of this article has been on the way franchising has spread from the U.S. to other advanced countries, and how these countries have absorbed and applied the technique, as illustrated in the Australian case, and have now begun to franchise internationally themselves. In the same way that the international product life-cycle model predicted the later development of exports of standardized products from the developing countries, it is relevant to ask whether such a pattern could evolve in the use of franchising. Given that the franchising operators have been moving into the developing countries (e.g., McDonald's in the Philippines and Venezuela), the pre-conditions for the type of demonstration effect which operated in the advanced countries are now being established. On that basis we should expect in the future to see the growth of diverse examples of home-grown franchising chains. Already many local versions have emerged in Malaysia (May, 1988). Ultimately, some of these are also likely to move to international operations. The limited scope of the tertiary/retail sector in some developing countries is of course bound to constrain the potential for such a process. Nevertheless franchising is such a well-tried and understood method in the advanced countries, with a developed infrastructure to support its use, that it represents a feasible path for companies from the developing area to consider in penetrating these markets. The ubiquitous franchised clothing chains, for example, in many advanced markets could be emulated, thereby providing a potential for adding value to clothing exports from the developing countries.

Conclusions

From a predominantly U.S. base, business format franchising has moved into global use in the 1980s. Those countries which began as recipients of the system have learned to use it successfully—as illustrated by the Australian experience. The end result of that success, in a growing number of cases, has been to also take its use into international operations, including to the U.S. It is possible to see this process continuing to the point where, like direct foreign investment, there is more balance in the global pattern of franchise system use, and that developing countries will become an identifiable part of this total picture.

Although still in the early stages of outward internationalization, the experience of the Australian franchisors indicates something of the power of franchising and its potential as a driving force in internationalization. The strong expansion ethos which seems to characterize franchising has important implications for the likelihood and speed of internationalization. That a small Australian company could within three years grow from nothing to a chain of 83 domestic outlets and operations in three countries with a "product" as seemingly simple and non-unique as a pizza delivery system is perhaps illustrative of franchising's potential.

However, the expansion ethos can lead to problems, as emerged in the Miniskips case, when companies become over-extended in the domestic expansion process, and then international possibilities emerge as well. There is a clear danger in attempting too much too early: international franchising, even via a master licensing system, is not as understanding as, for example, filling a fortuitous export order. Given the demonstrated importance of the domestic learning curve as a prelude to international operations, it could be argued that franchisor strategy should be to establish a strong domestic base first. However, Australian and U.S. experience has shown just how important foreign franchise interest is in stimulating international involvement. If a franchisor does not respond there is the risk that other operators may be approached and ultimately the market is closed. Would a similar entry opportunity have been available in the New Zealand market to Dial-A-Dino's if it had waited until it was better established in Australia? Thus, the dictum of establishing at home first has to be balanced against the rapid changes in the international environment which are creating new opportunities and pressures for franchising and may require an earlier international responsiveness than was previously considered appropriate.

References

Bellin, H., "Franchising's Promising Future in Australia," *The Chartered Accountant in Australia,* Vol. 54, No. 8, (March 1987), pp. 26–8, 62.

Bruce, L., "The Bright New Worlds of Benetton," *International Management,* No. 42, (November 1987), pp. 24–35.

Burns, W., "Wendys Supa Sundaes Eyes the Big U.S. Market," *Australian Financial Review,* 5 June, 1987, p. 50.

Grant, C., *Business Format Franchising,* (London: Economist Intelligence Unit, 1985).

Hackett, D.W., "The International Expansion of U.S. Franchise Systems," *Journal of International Business Studies,* Vol. 7 (Spring 1976), pp. 65–75.

International Trade Administration, U.S. Dept. of Commerce, *Franchising in the Economy,* 1985–87, (January 1987).

Layton, R.A. (ed.), *Australian Marketing Projects,* (Hoover Awards for Marketing 1980), (Sydney: Macarthur Press, 1981).

Treadgold, T., "Making a Name out of Muck," *Business Review Weekly,* 8 November, 1985, pp. 112–3.

Welch, L.S., "The International Marketing of Technology: An Interaction Perspective," *International Marketing Review,* Vol. 2 (1985), pp. 41–53.

Management Style and Practice of Korean Chaebols

Sangjin Yoo and Sang M. Lee. *Sangjin is a faculty member in Management Science at Bowling Green State University. Sang M. Lee is Regents Distinguished Professor of Management at the University of Nebraska, Lincoln.*

The economic growth of Korea has often been expressed as "The Miracle of the Han River" in comparison to the miracle of the Rhine River (West Germany) and the miracle of the Smida River (Japan).

Over the last two decades, Korea has achieved a truly remarkable economic growth. After World War II, Korea was one of the world's poorest countries, heavily dependent on agriculture and financially dependent upon foreign sources. However, with strong government leadership, sound economic planning, and hard work on the part of her people, Korea has overcome her lack of natural resources and achieved a real annual growth rate of over 9% in GNP. Korea's annual manufacturing output growth rate has been nearly 20% and its export growth rate over 30%. Its per capita income in real terms rose 7.4% annually from only $126 in 1966 to over $2,000 in 1985.[1]

Exports, which reached $100 million for the first time in 1964, amounted to more than $21.6 billion in 1982 and are projected to reach $33 billion in 1986. In 1985, Korean exports ranked 13th in the world and 10 Korean business conglomerates (Chaebols) were ranked in "The Fortune International 500" list. In 1985, Hyundai became the largest exporter of automobiles in Canada in less than 18 months from the introduction of its Ponys.

It is clear that strong leadership and the sound economic planning of the government were important elements of the remarkable economic growth of Korea. However, the efforts of the private business sector, especially those of the Chaebols, have been real catalysts for Korea's economic development.

According to a report by the Korea Federation of Small Business (KFSB), the number of businesses in Korea totalled 917,321 in 1982, compared to 5,510 in 1947.[2] As of 1981, Korea's 30 largest Chaebols held 289 (0.84%) of the total number of mining and manufacturing operations in Korea and produced 38.7% of the nation's total mining and manufacturing output. The same 289 businesses employed 422,000 workers, 19.8%

of the nation's mining and manufacturing employment.[3] Among the 20 largest companies listed in 1983, 15 were owned by the 10 largest Chaebols. In 1984, the five largest Chaebols—Hyundai, Samsung, Lucky-Goldstar, Sunkyung, and Daewoo—had total sales of close to $50 billion, or more than half of the country's GNP. The total exports by eight GTCs (General Trading Companies) owned by the eight largest Chaebols constituted more than 50% of all Korean exports in 1985.[4]

Characteristics of the Korean Chaebols

Evolution of the Korean Chaebols

"Chaebol" stands for a conglomerate or a financial clique in Korea. Korean Chaebols were formed because of the rapid economic growth, although they are different in terms of formation timing and type. Many Chaebols were formed through various support plans initiated by the government. The concept of "Chaebol" originally appeared in Japan. According to Yasuoka, in Japan, the first "Zaibatsu" (Japanese term for Chaebol)—Mitsubishi—was formed in 1893.[5] More Japanese Zaibatsus were established between 1909 and 1920.

Korean Chaebols can be classified in three categories based on the time of their formation: the late 1950s, the 1960s, and the 1970s.[6] Chaebols of the late 1950s—such as Hyundai, Samsung, and Lucky-Goldstar (formerly Lucky)—were established by self-made founders through governmental support such as preferential allotment of grants, disposal of government-vested properties, and preference in taxation and finance. Chaebols of the 1960s—such as Hanjin, Korea Explosive, Hyosung, Sangyong, and Dong-A—came about because of foreign loans induced for a series of five-year plans. Finally, those of the 1970s—such as Daewoo, Sunkyong, Lotte, Kolon, and Doosan—were formed during the economic boom based on a rapid growth of export and domestic demand.

Even though they produce a larger portion of Korean GDP and consist of many related companies like those in Japan, Korean Chaebols are somewhat different from Japanese Zaibatsus in many aspects, especially in terms of ownership and management.

The Korean "Chaebol" vs. the Japanese "Zaibatsu"

In 1984, the fifty largest Chaebols accounted for about 20% of Korean GDP, with the five largest Chaebols representing about 10% of the total.[7] On the other hand, the total sales percentage of the six largest Zaibatsus in Japan—Mitsui, Mitsubishi, Sumitomo, Huyo, Sangwa, and Daiizikangking—was 16.18% of the total of all 1,791 companies whose stocks were listed in 1983. Their gross capital accounted for 15.30% of the total of all 1,791 listed companies.[8] If we consider only these statistics, it appears that the Korean Chaebol and the Japanese Zaibatsu are similar. However, if we take a more analytical look at Chaebols and Zaibatsus, we can find considerable differences between them.

Definition. A Chaebol may be defined as "a business group consisting of large companies which are owned and managed by family members or relatives in many diversified business areas." To be a Chaebol or a Zaibatsu, an organization should satisfy two conditions: it should be owned by family members or relatives; and it should have diversified business operations.[9] Most Korean Chaebols and Japanese Zaibatsus satisfy these two conditions. The owner family of a Chaebol controls 20–40% of a listed company's total shares.[10] The average market share of each Korean Chaebol in manufacturing, banking, insurance, and construction industries is 3–5%.[11] As indicated, this is also true for the Japanese Zaibatsu.

However, there is one basic difference in the concept of "family members or relatives" between Korea and Japan. In Japan, there are two different types of family concepts.[12] One is a "family" which is formed based upon the blood relationship (consanguinity) concept. The other one is "iae" (household, clan), which does not require the blood relationship. In most cases, family and iae represent the same relationship. Nevertheless, in the case of succession, the gap between these two is clear. In Japan, succession of property is often carried out based on the iae concept. Thus, a successor of the property is not necessarily a blood family member. Under this system, there is no change in the value of the iae's property itself. According to Suzuki, the chief of an iae is a successor of the role or status within the iae rather than the blood.[13]

On the other hand, there is only one family concept in Korea, formed strictly on the blood relationship. Under the Korean concept, the blood relationship is the necessary condition of the family. In the case of succession, the eldest son of the family usually becomes the heir of the business. Of course, the other family members would have their own shares. Thus, the property of the family is divided into several portions. Under the Korean system, unlike that of the Japanese, the chief of a family is a successor of the blood.

Ownership.   Japanese Zaibatsus before and after World War II show different characteristics in terms of ownership and management. For comparison purposes, Zaibatsus formed after WW II are probably more suitable than those formed before WW II, since most of these earlier Zaibatsu were broken up and most of the Korean Chaebols were formed after the war.

One of the distinguishing characteristics of Korean management is ownership and management by family. Considering the short history of Korean enterprises, it is understandable that many corporations are still owned by the founder's family members. However, as Table 1 shows, the ratio of family ownership of Chaebols is much higher that those of non-Chaebols. Based on the information provided in Table 1, Chaebols own more than 30% of the listed corporations' stock. Furthermore, larger Chaebols show a relatively higher ratio of family ownership.

Most Korean Chaebols employ one of the following three, somewhat unique structures of ownership:

- sole possession by the owner—the founder of his/her family members and relatives own all affiliated enterprises;
- domination by the core company—the founder or his/her family members or relatives own the core company, which in turn, owns other affiliated enterprises; and
- mutual possession—the founder or his/her family members or relatives own the

TABLE 1   Korean Chaebols: Distribution of Ownership (As of 1982)

	Family & Relatives	Affiliated Enterprises	Total	Level of Power[†]
Chaebol				
Top 10*	13.44%	18.99%	32.43%	20.64
Top 31	19.29%	14.93%	34.22%	29.42
Top 41	18.65%	10.99%	29.64%	39.16
Avg.	17.71%	14.96%	32.67%	29.69
Non-Chaebol	20.96%	2.99%	23.95%	—

*Classified by the amount of paid-in capital, Top 10 means the first 10 Chaebols, Top 31 is the next 21 Chaebols, and Top 41 is the final 10 Chaebols of the study.

[†]The unit for the level of power is points and calculated using the following system; Chairman or President = 10; Vice President = 5; representative director = 4; executive director = 3; and director of the affiliated company = 1.

SOURCE: Edited from Tamio Hattori, "Comparison of Large Corporations in Korea and Japan," in Hakjon Lee and Kuhyun Chung, eds., *The Structure and Strategy of Korean Corporations* (Seoul: Bupmunsa, 1986), p. 182.

TABLE 2   Stock Distribution of Samsung Group (As of 1982, in %)

	Company									
Holder	*A*	*B*	*C*	*D*	*E*	*F*	*G*	*H*	*I*	*J*
Founder	3.40					9.31	2.96		8.17	
2nd Son				2.87				6.20	14.16	
3rd Son	6.02	3.77		5.76			5.30	16.70	1.00	
1st Daughter				2.41		6.99				
2nd Daughter							1.36		0.21	
3rd Daughter		3.46							0.90	
Father-in-law (3rd Son)	0.66	2.18							1.38	
Daughter-in-law										19.28
Company K	1.15			9.47		1.23	9.96	4.60		
Company L	0.50					1.82	2.30			
Company G	3.40		5.75							
Company M	9.66	8.63	9.50	9.47	9.89		8.98	9.60	9.99	
Company J	5.46	4.67		3.86	3.36		1.64			
Company B			22.75	9.54	3.59					
Company H			5.75		9.26		1.00			
Company A					15.24					
Company N							1.39			

Companies A through N represent affiliated enterprises of the Samsung Chaebol.

SOURCE: Edited from Tamio Hattori, "Comparison of Large Corporations in Korea and Japan," in Hakjon Lee and Kuhyxn Chung, eds., *The Structure and Strategy of Korean Corporations* (Seoul: Bupmunsa, 1986), p. 189.

core company and/or some kind of foundation, which in turn owns other affiliated enterprises (affiliated enterprises can possess each other's stocks).

Hattori takes Hanjin, Daewoo, and Samsung as respective examples of these three types.[14] Table 2 shows the distribution of ownership within the Samsung Chaebol.

As of 1982, the Samsung group had 10 listed companies under its control; 12.73% of the total stocks was possessed by family members; and 20.35% by other affiliated companies in the group.[15]

Japanese Zaibatsus, on the other hand, show different aspects of ownership from those of Korean Chaebols. They have enormous influence on the Japanese economy, just as Korean Chaebols do on the Korean economy. In 1981, the six largest Zaibatsus possessed 25.94% of total Japanese corporations' assets and 15.78% of total Japanese corporations' sales, even though they had only 5.11% of the total number of Japanese corporations' employees. However, unlike Korean Chaebols, the average stock-holding ratio of the six largest Zaibatsus was only 1.78% of 1981.[16] In spite of the relatively low stock-holding ratio, a Zaibatsu can maintain 20–30% of the total stock within a group by mutually possessing each other's stock. For example, in 1983, the ratios of mutual possession were 17.67% for Mitsui, 24.39% for Mitsubishi, and 25.06% for Sumitomo.[17]

Management.   To quantify the owners' influence on the Chaebol groups' management, Hattori used a 10-point scale.[18] That is, if the owner or one of the family members is chairman or president that person is given 10 points, the vice president is given 5 points, the representative director 4 points, the executive director 3 points, and the director of the affiliated company 1 point. The far right column of Table 1 shows the point totals.

A study by Lee and Yoo shows that 31% of the executive officers of the top 20 Chaebols in Korea consists of owners' family members.[19] Based upon this information, we may conclude that the owner or his/her family members' influence on management is very strong. However, the power structure of each Chaebol may be different, based upon the number of family members and the owner's management philosophy. While the ratio of family ownership is higher for the larger Chaebols, the owners' influence on management is stronger in the smaller Chaebols (see Table 1). If the structure of ownership is sole possession by the owner, the owner or family members' influence on management is enormous. Even though some non-family members (such as professional managers) may take higher management position in Chaebol groups of the other two ownership types (core company or mutual possession), the most important posts usually belong to the owner's family members.

According to Okumura, six distinctive characteristics have evolved in the Japanese Zaibatsu, especially after World War II.[20] They are:

- stock is owned by affiliated companies (members of the council of presidents) rather than the owner's family;
- presidents of affiliated companies have become members of the council of presidents which makes important decisions in a Zaibatsu;
- an affiliated company owns stock of the other affiliated companies;
- each Zaibatsu owns a bank as its core company to furnish funds;
- each Zaibatsu owns a "Sogoshosha" as its core company (bank and "Sogoshosha" are closely related); and
- each Zaibatsu owns affiliated companies in diversified business areas rather than in one specific area.

Based upon these characteristics, Japanese Zaibatsus show totally different management structure and style from those of Korean Chaebols. Almost no owners' family members are involved in management. Rather, most of the top executives are professional managers who have worked for a specific company for a long time. The ratio of the top executives promoted from within the company is 78.7% for Mitsui, 69.8% for Mitsubishi, and 73.1% for Sumitomo. On the other hand, the ratio of promotion from other affiliated companies is 12.2% for Mitsui, 22.6% for Mitsubishi, and 19.4% for Sumitomo. Outside scouting for the three companies provided 9.1%, 7.6%, and 7.5% of the top executives, respectively.[21]

The Distinctive Management Style of the Korean Chaebol

Founders' Management Philosophy

There are numerous distinctive management characteristics in Korean Chaebols. Among them, self-made founders, management by family, and close government relationships are the most unique features. Before discussing these three in greater detail, an overview of various top management philosophies helps in understanding the Chaebols' management style. Following are five founder-owners' philosophies, drawn from among the top 10 Chaebols:

- Choong-Hoon Cho of the Hanjin Group (Korean Airlines, etc.) has established enterprises through trust and public credibility. He emphasizes management by family rather than professional management. He also attempts to maintain a lifetime employment system because of his concern for the employees' livelihood. His managerial philosophy is: "Business is an art. To make a good work of art, there should be harmony, just as good as an orchestra's."[22]

- Jong-Hyun Choi of Sunkyong Group is a top manager who has used his academic training in chemistry, economics, and management in establishing and managing his company. He rescued Sunkyong Textile Co., Ltd., which was in a precarious situation, through his knowledge of chemistry. He is one of the top managers who tries to avoid management by family, saying: "A firm should exist through all eternity. Thus, management should leave honorably after serving for a firm."[23]

- Ju-Yung Chung of Hyundai Group is a founder-owner who has expanded his business through his deep commitment to the business and through an aggressive management style for which he is called "the entrepreneur." Based on aggressiveness, he established the Hyundai Group, which consists of construction, automobiles, steel, machinery, shipbuilding, and general trading company (GTC) concerns. He tries to maintain an extremely bureaucratic management system combined with management by family, even though professional managers manage some affiliated companies. He is also very proud of the spirit of the Hyundai Group, as expressed by the slogan: "Be very aggressive and become a strong driving force."[24]

- Woo-Choong Kim of the Daewoo Group established his business through hard work and accurate judgment. His acquisition of failing firms and his use of personal connections (based on graduates from the same high school he attended, instead of using family members), have been the main driving forces for the success of the Daewoo group. He is called "the hardest working man in Korea," and "the best salesman in Korea." As his nickname indicates, his managerial philosophy is based on "hard work." Thus, he always requires subordinates to perform an amount of work commensurate with their pay. To accomplish this, he introduced a quite different management philosophy, "requiring hard work through higher compensation."[25] Kim has said, "We work not because of leisure but because of pride."[26]

- Byung-Chull Lee of Samsung Group is one of the senior businessmen in Korea. He tries to keep his authority through various bureaucratic controls. He is the first top manager in Korea to use a competitive recruiting system. He manages personnel based only on performance and ability. As in the case in almost all Korean Chaebols, family members are the mainstream of management, even though Samsung has the highest ratio of non-family member executives. He attempts to develop elites based on two principles: "the right people to the right position," and "incentive compensation." His managerial philosophy is: "Be the number one."[27]

Self-Made Founders

In Korea, the development of enterprises can be classified in terms of historical periods:[28]

- enterprises formed and continued under Japanese colonial rule (1919–1945);
- enterprises established after WW II even though capital was accumulated during the Japanese colonial rule period;
- enterprises established and modernized during the Korean War (1950–1953); and
- enterprises formed based on either foreign aid in the 1950s or loans in the 1960s.

The inauguration mission of Korean enterprises can be classified into five categories, namely:[29]

- the transfer type—modern entrepreneurs succeeded traditional magnates;
- the imitation type—imitation of the American free enterprise system;
- the endemic type—the traditional Korean businesses;
- the managerial type—organizations based on management theory; and
- the welfare type—intended to improve employees' welfare.

Most Korean enterprises have been founded based on one of these inauguration missions. Almost every early Korean company was established by a self-made founder. These self-made founders inaugurated and managed their enterprises under great difficulties, which stemmed from a lack of capital, technology, experience, and education. There were also political problems, especially during the Japanese colonial rule period. Almost every self-founder has devoted his/her entire life to work. These difficulties and the sweatshop work ethic have led to such common Korean entrepreneurial characteristics as: innate diligence and thrift; creativity; strong impellent force; sincerity and creditability; frontier spirit; preference for harmony among family members and employees; preference for stable and bureaucratic organization; top-down decision making; insensitivity to changes in circumstances; non-specific management; preference for management by family; and lack of formal education.[30] These common characteristics still have great impact, both positive and negative, on the management style of Korean Chaebols.

Management by Family

Considering the short history of Korean Chaebols, it is understandable that many companies are still managed by the founder-owner. As companies grow and mature, however, many companies face a shift in generation. The "handing over" of an enterprise is not a simple matter, since it is not simply a transfer of wealth but the inheritance of a living project. Thus, the success or failure of the transfer often determines the future of the company. The success or failure of the transfer is often determined by the method of inheritance. Usually, inheritance in Korea has been based on the Confucian tradition of hierarchical order within the family, the highest priority given to the oldest son in the family. In Korea, according to one study,[31] the ratio of inheritance to the first son is 65.9%, to family members other than the first son is 24.4%, and to non-family members is 9.7%.

In addition to the transfer of control, recruiting becomes an important issue for the growth of a company. During the rapid growth of the economy, the company needs to recruit capable managers. Much of the recruiting has been done, not on the basis of ability but on various connections such as family ties, relatives, common hometown/school, or political ties. One study shows that 31% of the executive officers of the top 20 Chaebols in Korea consisted of family members, 40% of the executive officers are recruited from outside, while 29% are promoted from within.[32] Another study shows that 25.5% of presidents of Korean companies are founders, 18.5% are the second generation of founders, 21.2% are promoted from within, and 35.1% are recruited from outside.[33] Even though more than 50% of CEOs are not family members, the core positions usually belong to the owner's family.

Table 3 presents the structure and number of executive officers and their influence in the Lucky-Goldstar Chaebol. Points for power have again been calculated using Hattori's 10-point scale. As shown in Table 3, the portion of family members is only 10.8% of the total number of executives. However, they exercise 21.6% of the total influence on management. On the other hand, promoted executives' level of influence is only 1.96 times that of family members even though the number of promoted executives is 4.88 times the number of family members. This implies management by family, in which the top-down decision-making style of Korean Chaebols originated.

Close Government Relationship

Undeniably, the incredible growth of Korea was initiated and steered by the government. Since many Korean Chaebols owe their success entirely to government support, a close

TABLE 3   Lucky-Goldstar: Executives and Their Influence (As of 1982)

Company	Number of Executives			Influence (in Points)		
	Family Member	*Promoted Within*	*Outside Scout*	*Family Member*	*Promoted Within*	*Outside Scout*
A	2	15	4	20	29	14
B	4	18	5	26	39	18
C	1	3	4	4	11	17
D	1	6	7	10	13	30
E	2	8	12	5	26	26
F	2	4	4	20	7	13
G		5	1		16	10
H	1	3	2	10	15	4
I	2	13	2	5	41	4
J	1	4	2	10	6	4
K	1	5	4	3	11	13
L	1	3	9	3	12	25
M		1	5		1	16
Total	18	88	61	116	227	194
%	10.8	52.7	36.5	21.6	42.3	36.1

SOURCE: Edited from Tamio Hattori, "Comparison of Large Corporations in Korea and Japan," in Hakjon Lee and Kuhyun Chung, eds., *The Structure and Strategy of Korean Corporations* (Seoul: Bupmunsa, 1986), p. 195.

relationship between government and business has been inevitable. For example, a close relationship with the government has been essential for Chaebols to receive the basic benefits that have been critical to their success, such as: preferential disposal of government-vested properties during the period of confusion (1945–Korean War); preferential allotment of foreign aid and grants during the period of reconstruction (after the Korean War–late 1950s); preference for obtaining loans during the period of development (1960s–early 1970s); designation of GTC and export financing during the take-off period (1970s); preference for taxation and financing; and inclusion in the five-year economic development plans of the government.

In addition, the government's control of the banking system since the early 1960s has made it possible to steer big Chaebols into the industries that the government wanted to develop. Consequently, Chaebols could not help but maintain close relationships with the government if they wanted to be included in the targeted growth areas.

The close government-business relationship in Korea is often referred to as "Korea Inc." However, there are distinct differences between "Korea Inc." and "Japan Inc." For example, "Japan Inc." connotes a government-business partnership in which the policy reflects a consensus between equals. "Korea Inc." means something very different. In Korea, the government sets the policies and businessmen follow, more or less. In this way, Korea is an unusual blend of free enterprise and state direction. The government's strongest weapon is its control of credit. Large Japanese Zaibatsus often have their own banks from which they obtain funds.[34] The Korean government announced banking liberalization plans in 1983, yet the government still does not permit domination of banks by an individual Chaebol.

It is clear that the Korean government's leadership in economic development policy and the close government-business relationship have produced a phenomenal economic growth in Korea. However, government-directed growth policies alone will not achieve *sustained* economic growth, which requires instead a balanced industrial structure, effective competition in the international market, and close cooperation between business and government.

To summarize, the management style of Korean Chaebols consists of:

- clan management
- top-down decision making
- flexible lifetime employment
- a Confucian work ethic
- paternalistic leadership
- loyalty
- compensation based on seniority and merit rating
- bureaucratic conflict resolution
- a very bureaucratic yet low degree of formality and standardized systems
- close government-business relationship
- expansion through conglomeration

Personnel Practice of Korean Chaebols

In general, there are five different concerns in personnel management, which include: security (recruitment), development, compensation, maintenance, and organization. Each area addresses several important issues. For example, recruiting and job assignment are important issues of security, while training, job rotation, performance evaluation, and promotion are important for development policy. Salary, incentives, and welfare are important for compensation, while mobility of workers, retirement policy, and labor relationship are major concerns of maintenance. Finally, task assignment, organization structure, hierarchy, and decision-making style are important issues in the organization area.

According to one study,[35] for security (recruitment), most large Korean corporations classify employees into three categories: core (top management and high-level executives); basic (permanent employees); and temporary. Most Korean companies hire employees through a reference (document) check and a written test for English, knowledge in the major field, and/or common sense. They prefer new college graduates and people with career experience. Once they hire new people, they usually assign the elite group to such core departments as planning, finance, and accounting after a short training period (usually 7–10 days).

For development, Korean corporations adopt uniform training systems for all employees using OJT and experts' lectures. The education and training program is not at all uniform or systematic. It does not closely relate to job assignment, job rotation, and promotion. Thus, employees do not devote themselves to pursuing new knowledge during the education and training period. Naturally, maximum effectiveness of the education and training program is not to be expected. Job rotation in Korean corporations is usually done on an ad hoc basis. Performance evaluation places emphasis on past achievements. Employees in Korean companies are promoted largely based on seniority, dedication, and relationship with top management rather than on contribution and achievement.

Most Korean companies compensate based on seniority. They determine an employee's base salary considering the level of education and seniority, then add some allowances for gross salary. There is a salary difference between college graduates and high school graduates. In addition to a monthly salary, Korean companies pay seasonal bonuses (such as for New Year's, vacations, the Korean Thanksgiving Day, and Christmas). However, most Korean corporations do not yet have complete welfare systems.

In the personnel maintenance area, Korean corporations lay off less important employees (regardless of core, basic, or temporary status) when they face an economic slump. Korean employees retire once they reach a certain age, usually fifty-five. Retiring employees receive a lump sum retirement allowance. They do not usually receive such compensation as a part-time job or consulting position at the company after retirement. In Korea, labor unions have been patterned after the industrial union system. The principles of harmony and paternal authority are emphasized to resolve labor disputes. Labor unions have been kept on a tight leash by law, which forbids outsiders from intervening in a dispute between an employer and his/her workers. These laws make it virtually impossible for a union to help workers bargain with their employers, and regulations on arbitration effectively outlaw strikes.[36]

Finally, in the organization area, most Korean corporations do not have clear job assignment criteria. Usually, middle- or lower-level management do not have much authority to perform their job effectively (more than 80% of the authority resides at the upper management level). Most Korean companies have a people-oriented organization structure. Korean corporations are organized based upon hierarchies with a clear-cut order. Nevertheless, there is no clear description of the relationship between authority and responsibility. Thus, a top-down decision-making style has become typical in Korean corporations. Table 4 shows the distinctive characteristics of the personnel management system in Korea as compared to that of the United States and Japan.

Conclusion

Based on the foregoing discussion, the following conclusions and observations can be made:

- Even though Korean Chaebols are criticized for their "Octopus Arm" style expansion, aggressive infringement in the business areas of small business, lack

TABLE 4 **Comparison of Personnel Management Systems**

Issues	Korea	United States	Japan
Employee Classes	Core, Basic, Temporary	Basic, Temporary	Core, Basic, Some Temporary
Recruitment Criteria	Reference check & written test; prefer both new college	Reference check & interview; prefer experienced	Interview; prefer new college graduates
Job Assignment	Assign elites to important departments	Assign based on the job	Assign field site or floor first
Training & Education	Uniform, OJT, non-systematic	Knowledge & technical OJT, university	OJT, job rotation, informal groups
Job Rotation	Ad hoc basis	Aim at specialists	Regular, periodic; aim at generalists
Evaluation	Non-systematic past-oriented	Systematic, present-oriented	Continuous, future-oriented
Promotion	Seniority	Performance	Combination
Salary Criteria	Education level & seniority	Education level & performance	Education level, age, & performance
Incentive System	Seasonal bonus (uniform)	Performance-based incentive	Performance-based incentive
Welfare	No	Yes	Yes
Employee Lay-Offs	Less important people first	Temporary people & less important departments first	Concentrate on temporary people only
Retirement	Age of 55 (inflexible)	Age of 65 (flexible)	Age of 55–60 (flexible)
Labor Relations	Principles of harmony; no strikes	Contract-oriented; use strikes as a final method	Principles of "wa"; labor disputes start with strike
Job Assignment	No systematic assignment	Individual assignment with detailed job descriptions	Group assignment job descriptions are not detailed
Structure	People-oriented	Work-oriented	Combination
Decision Making	Top-down	Top-down	Bottom-up

SOURCE: Edited from Yookeun Shin, *Structures and Problems of Korean Enterprises* (Seoul: Seoul National University Publishing, 1985), pp. 331–359.

of business ethics, and the concentration of wealth in a small, select group of people, they have been the backbone of Korean economic growth.

· Ownership and management are not separated in most Korean Chaebol groups. This results in management by family even though the proportion of professional managers has increased considerably.

· Many Korean Chaebols adopt certain tactics such as new family ties through marriage to secure their existence and to maintain the family's dominance in management. According to one survey,[37] there are twenty-one marriages between the family members of the top 10 Chaebols.

- Many founders are still in top management position, since Korean Chaebols have had a relatively short history.
- Top-down decision making is common in many Korean Chaebol groups.
- Succession is very important for the success of Korean Chaebols because of their short history and the unique Korean family concept.
- Most Korean Chaebols owe much of their success to government support.
- Most Korean Chaebols' expansion has been largely based upon government policy and with the primary goal of increasing total sales volume rather than profitability.
- Korean Chaebols' management practice reflects many of their unique characteristics.

Korean Chaebols have been able to manage and grow successfully based on their unique characteristics and background. Nevertheless, they may not be able to expect the same favorable situations in the future because: many Korean Chaebols are on the verge of a shift in generation; they are too large to be managed primarily by family members; and the international business environment is becoming increasingly dynamic, with the pressures of protectionism, technological innovation, and stiff international competition.

To manage successfully in this dynamic and difficult environment, Korean Chaebols must devote their efforts to eliminating their weaknesses and making the best use of their strengths. Some of the recommended strategies are:

- continued R&D investment;
- adoption of a continuous training/education concept;
- concentration on high-tech industries;
- improvement of productivity;
- improvement of product quality;
- the fostering of small- and medium-sized firms;
- concentration on technology-intensive industries;
- application of advanced managerial systems;
- positive overseas investment;
- adoption of a permanent employment system;
- the systematization of enterprises;
- positive use of professional management; and
- aggressive international marketing.

References

1. Dennis Holden, "Bank Liberalization in South Korea," *The Oriental Economist,* Vol. 51, No. 872 (June 1983).

2. Daesuk Hwang and Jungyul Yeon, *History of Korean Management* (Seoul, Korea: Sae Yung Publishing Co., 1978).

3. *The Korea Herald,* March 17, 1984.

4. *The Korea Times,* February 18, 1986.

5. Shigeaki Yasouka, *Zaibatsu of Japan* (Tokyo, Japan: Nikkei Shinbunsha (Nihon Keizai Shinbunsha), 1976), p. 33.

6. Myungsu Hwang, "Study about Korean Business Groups and Entrepreneurs," *The Collection of Papers,* Volume 17 (Seoul, Korea: Dankook University, 1973).

7. Tamio Hattori, "Comparison of Large Corporations in Korea and Japan," in Hakjon Lee and Kuhyun Chung, eds., *The Structure and Strategy of Korean Corporations* (Seoul, Korea: Bupmunsa, 1986), p. 149.

8. Ibid.

9. Ibid., p. 151.

10. Tamio Hattori, "Ownership and Management of Modern Korean Corporations," *Azia Keizai (Asian Economy)* (May/June 1984).

11. Il Sakong, "Economic Growth and Chaebol," *Monthly ChoSun* (Seoul, Korea: Chosun Il Bo Sa, September, 1980).

12. Hattori, "Comparison of Large Corporations in Korea and Japan," in Lee and Chung, eds., op. cit., pp. 152–155.

13. Eitaro Suzuki, "Kacho no Iza (Position of the Head of the Family)," *Nihon Noson Shakaigaku Genri (The Principle of Japanese Rural Society)* (Tokyo, Japan: Ji-cho sha, 1940 (Showa15).

14. Hattori, in Lee and Chung, eds., op. cit., p. 183.

15. Ibid., p. 190.

16. Ibid., p. 171.

17. Ibid.

18. Ibid., p. 184.

19. Sang M. Lee and Sangjin Yoo, "The K-type Management: A Driving Force of Korean Prosperity," forthcoming in *International Management Review,* No. 4 (1987).

20. Hiroshi Okumura, *The Largest Six Business Groups in Japan* [Tokyo, Japan: Daiyamondo sha (Diamond Publishing Co.), 1976], pp. 20–25.

21. Hattori, in Lee and Chung, eds., op. cit., p. 171.

22. Chosun Il Bo Sa. *The Twenty-Fifth Hour of Korean Chaebols* (Seoul, Korea: Dongkwang Publishing Co. Ltd., 1984), pp. 151–160.

23. Ibid., pp. 113–128.

24. Ibid., pp. 291–324; and Dongsoon Park, *Inauguration Idea of Korean Chaebols* (Seoul, Korea: Sae Kwang Publishing Co. Ltd., 1983), pp. 160–179.

25. Chosun Il Bo Sa, op. cit., pp. 65–92.

26. *The Korea Times,* Chicago Edition, October 22, 1985.

27. Chosun Il Bo Sa, op. cit., pp. 17–50; and Park, op. cit., pp. 85–102.

28. Park, op. cit., pp. 3–6.

29. Ibid.

30. Lee and Yoo, op. cit.

31. Yookeun Shin, *Structure and Problems in Korean Enterprises* (Seoul, Korea: Seoul National University Publishing, 1985), p. 246.

32. Lee and Yoo, op. cit.

33. Shin, op. cit., p. 245.

34. Norman Pearlstine, "How South Korea Surprised the World," *Forbes,* Vol. 123, No. 9, April 30, 1979.

35. Shin, op. cit., pp. 339–359.

36. Hugh Sandeman, "Asia's Most Ambitious Nation," *The Economist,* Vol. 284, No. 7250, August 14, 1982.

37. Kyunghwan Oh, "Marriage Web of Korean Chaebols I, II," *Jeongkyung Yeon Ku (Research in Politics and Economics)* (Seoul, Korea: Kyunghyang Sin Mun Sa, 1986), Vol. 259 (September): 358–377, and Vol. 260 (October): 154–167.

PART FIVE

ACADEMIC INSIGHTS AND RESEARCH SOURCES

The initial paper in this sequence summarizes the course orientation espoused by the editors. Our research indicates that international and global marketing courses and texts are oriented toward larger multinational firms. But few entry-level international positions are available with multinational firms for individuals holding BS or MBA degrees. Conversely, small and medium-sized firms lack the personnel to plan adequately for export operations. This suggests that greater emphasis should be given in international courses to exporting entrepreneurship. Rather than teaching about marketing on a global scale, we stress export/import opportunities as entrepreneurs, managers, or owners of smaller businesses seeking to possibly expand abroad.

In "Preparing the Exporting Entrepreneur," we cite four barriers that we believe should be included in courses oriented toward smaller firms or entrepreneurs: financial, legal, cultural, and psychological barriers. To reinforce this orientation, we ask our course participants to submit a marketing plan for exporting a product or service from the United States or a plan for importing a product or service from abroad into the United States. It should include all of the elements of a domestic marketing plan—a situation analysis, marketing strategies, action plans, budgets, and a five-year income and expense statement.

An alternative to the import or export term project is an autopsy of an international marketing failure. The failure may range from a fiasco that resulted in a corporate bankruptcy to an international product or service that simply did not achieve forecasted sales and profits. The "failure" may or may not still be on the market. The postmortem should document the initial planning and marketing strategies that resulted in failure and analyze the reasons for failure and what might have been done to avoid or alleviate it. This is a learning project that course participants generally enjoy. We have had considerable success with it.

State trade development services and U.S. Small Business Administration services are summarized in the second paper in this sequence. It includes case histories of entrepreneurs and small businesspeople who have succeeded in international marketing.

Preparing the Exporting Entrepreneur

John L. Graham and Taylor W. Meloan. *John L. Graham is Professor of Marketing, University of California, Irvine, and Taylor W. Meloan is Professor of Marketing, School of Business Administration, University of Southern California, Los Angeles, California.*

According to the United States Department of Commerce, approximately 20,000 U.S. companies could market successfully in foreign markets but currently are not (*Business Week* 1978). Several researchers have investigated the reasons behind this failure to capitalize on target markets abroad. Cavusgil and Nevin (1981) have concluded that "the reluctance of firms to export may largely be attributable to top management's lack of determination to export" (p. 119).

Various marketing researchers and practitioners have suggested key factors and approaches which can facilitate exporting profitably. Reid (1984) reported that executives of firms that export successfully frequently consult informative sources of data on foreign-market entry. Ursic and Czinkota (1984) found that the "younger" firms more often consider exporting as a viable marketing strategy. Reid (1981) summarized revealing studies which suggest a series of managerial characteristics which can contribute to managers' interest in exporting: previous foreign residence, language competence, university education, and youth (i.e., younger managers tend to be more internationally minded). Finally, Suzman and Wortzel (1984) found export-market planning is a crucial factor in successful export ventures.

All of these studies, as well as our own investigations, have suggested that international marketing education should include more emphasis upon exporting for smaller and medium-sized firms. Moreover, a more entrepreneurial focus, in an international context, would be desirable.

In this article we examine these issues in four parts. First, we summarize the findings of a telephone survey undertaken to ascertain the nature and scope of export operations of smaller and medium-sized firms along with their international personnel requirements. Next, we report the findings of a library review of the catalogues of undergraduate and graduate business schools to ascertain the availability and content of international marketing courses. The third aspect is a summary of a telephone survey of selected business school placement officers to ascertain the level of employer interest in internationally educated business students. Finally, we interpret the findings of our

The *Journal of Marketing Education* is published by the Business Research Division of the University of Colorado at Boulder. Reprinted with permission.

research, suggesting recommendations for a career-oriented international marketing curriculum design to prepare exporting entrepreneurs.

Survey of Local Exporting Firms

The telephone survey of selected exporting firms in Southern California had three purposes: (1) to learn how successful exporters began their exporting, (2) to ascertain the scope of their international operations, and (3) to determine the qualifications for employment in their international operations. The interview guide for this telephone survey is found in Appendix A.

Survey Methodology

The universe for this survey consisted of 103 managers of firms listed as "exporters and manufacturers" in the Foreign Trade Association of Southern California Roster and Directory (1984). From the total, 30 large well-known multinationals were eliminated (e.g., Carnation and Bausch and Lomb). This was done to restrict the sample to medium-sized and smaller firms. A recognized marketing research firm was commissioned to telephone a key executive with each of the remaining 73 firms listed in the roster. Subsequently, 24 of the firms were eliminated from the sample because they could not be interviewed: either they refused to respond or were unavailable (i.e., answering machines, disconnected telephones, or frequently out of the office).

The resultant sample consisted of 49 small and medium-sized companies which manufacture for export in Southern California. Their characteristics are listed in Table 1.

Entry Strategies.   Most of the executives indicated that their firms began exporting using a reactive "responder" strategy which Suzman and Wortzel (1984) have defined by noting:

> The responder develops an export business based on unsolicited inquiries and orders, using the market to tell it who is interested in its product. Based on the orders it receives it tries to find out about the customer and simply looks for additional potential customers of similar characteristics. It uses orders and inquiries as a marketing research tool.
>
> The result of this strategy is that the exporting firm may develop an export business that is well diversified geographically, but which is without a particularly strong position in any one market. . . . The responder strategy may be a highly appropriate entry strategy, but it should usually be considered as a first stage leading to a more active stance (pp. 187–188).

TABLE 1   Characteristics of Firms in the Sample

Characteristic	Mean	Range
Years exporting	16.8	3 to 50 years
Export sales	$19.1 million	$5,000 to $40 million
Staff involved in export operations	6.4	1 to 50

TABLE 2   Hiring Qualifications in International Operations

Qualifications	Times Mentioned
Prior experience	28
Language skills	10
International emphasis in school	9
Business school degree	3
M.B.A.	2

Of the executives who replied to the question on entry strategies, 86 percent stated that their firm initiated exporting from inquiries. Only 17 percent indicated that they did any significant research before beginning to export. Few firms employed outside service firms, consultants, or other third parties such as export-management organizations or trading companies. Freight forwarders were the most frequently mentioned outside agency used to facilitate exporting.

Scope of Present Operations.   Suzman and Wortzel (1984) have suggested that an appropriate long-term exporting strategy is to concentrate marketing efforts on a few countries with an entrepreneurial orientation.

> The entrepreneur actively searches for potential markets. It is not concerned with whether particular markets are presently importing significant quantities of similar products from the United States or from anywhere else. It is concerned only about discovering where the large potential markets for its products are and how the potential these markets represent can best be exploited. Successful pursuit of this strategy requires a tenacious, sophisticated firm that is willing to invest considerable time and effort in information collection and analysis (p. 188).

The executives who were interviewed in this survey rarely indicated a progression to "higher" stages of international marketing. In all, 12 stated that their firms had established overseas sales offices and/or retained foreign sales representatives or agents. Most sell in several countries through a variety of dealers and distributors but with no apparent geographical concentration of effort. Further, international operations, when measured by the number of personnel allocated, is a low priority: 23 of the firms employed five or fewer employees in their international operations.

Personnel Qualifications.   Table 2 summarizes the qualifications the executives indicated to be major criteria in appointing personnel in their international operations, listed in decreasing degrees of importance.

Conclusions

The research findings suggest that the small and medium-sized firms in the sample displayed a surprising lack of export planning and commitment. Obviously, they had desirable products for export since their foreign clients continued to order from them. A more entrepreneurial export strategy would probably yield even greater profits for them.

Suzman and Wortzel (1984) have recommended the following planning oriented approach:

> The entrepreneurial firm must perform several tasks in order to make this strategy work. First, it must identify the particular characteristics of markets that indicate probable success, including such factors as size, determinants of buyer behavior, and patterns of competition. Next, the firm must develop marketing plans based upon identified characteristics and on knowledge of the available marketing institutions. The successful pursuit of an entrepreneurial strategy may demand product modification as well as the tailoring of market plans. Often, there is no one to imitate. The firm tries to identify and then satisfy the specific circumstances that lead to the initiation or growth of the market (p. 189).

However, the firms in our sample did not have qualified personnel to implement such aggressive, proactive marketing planning. In addition, it is not clear whether our current international marketing courses are preparing exporting entrepreneurs to be able to implement such plans. To ascertain the focus of courses in this field, and to determine the market for internationally trained graduates, the supplemental work summarized in the next section was undertaken.

Analysis of University International Marketing Programs

International marketing is a popular elective among undergraduate and graduate students for three major reasons: First, it sounds interesting: students want to learn about business policies and systems in other countries. It also seems worthwhile: students recognize the growing importance of exporting and the impact of imported products in the United States. Finally, it appears to offer exciting possibilities: students anticipate traveling and living abroad. But international placement immediately after graduation is rare. Indeed, Cateora (1983) suggests that because of changes in host country laws during recent years, "U.S. companies find they can no longer use foreign assignments for training experience but must send only the more experienced personnel abroad" (p. 503). Most international marketing professors suggest that their students initially seek a domestic position, then request a foreign post after they have learned their jobs and demonstrated their abilities. Indeed, this is the primary career track for international business students within large corporations. But what about students who desire to work for smaller firms? This subject has received scant academic attention.

In this section, we summarize library research and a second telephone survey which we conducted to investigate the focus of current international marketing courses and subsequent international job placement. The findings have led us to propose an alternative orientation for courses in international marketing designed to serve students who desire to join intermediate-sized and smaller firms.

Review of International Marketing Programs in Selected Institutions

Methodology.   The sample consisted of 20 large and/or well-known public and private institutions throughout the United States. We included schools with both undergraduate and graduate programs as well as schools with only graduate programs. To determine the availability of such courses and programs, we studied the catalogues of each institution in our search for international marketing courses and their descriptions.

Findings.   Surprisingly, only 12 of the 20 catalogues listed a course in international marketing, most frequently at the graduate rather than the undergraduate level. The course descriptions seemed to stress a macro orientation with cultural differences as the focus for analyzing the opportunities for large multinational firms. Export and import entrepreneurship was rarely mentioned in the course descriptions.

Although several large, well known business schools did not seem to offer courses in international or multinational marketing, the content may have been covered within other courses in the curricula. Some courses offered under the rubric of "international business" include international marketing content: however, it was difficult to gauge accurately the extent of coverage from the catalogues.

Based on this review, there is no evidence that international marketing is an important focus or area of concentration in major business schools. This situation has not changed in the last 17 years. In a more extensive survey completed in 1968 by Meloan and Taylor with 101 respondents (17 personal interviews and 84 completed mail questionnaires), only two schools offered international marketing as a major or an area of emphasis at that time.

Interviews with Business School Placement Directors

To gain further insight, the placement directors of a dozen of the business schools whose bulletins had been reviewed were telephoned. These were schools with large, well established placement centers. Placement directors were asked to indicate the number of companies during the past three years which have been on campus to interview either American undergraduates or MBAs for initial assignments for international marketing positions in foreign nations. Best estimates were requested rather than precise numbers. In virtually all of the schools, from zero to three firms per year interviewed American students for international foreign assignments.

These firms had typically from one to three positions to fill. Respondents were asked to indicate either the categories or names of firms engaged in such recruiting. Frequently cited replies included large multinational consumer products firms, integrated oil companies, and international banks. Respondents also were asked to say whether the available positions were concentrated in certain countries or regions. The most frequently cited areas were the Pacific rim countries, the Middle East, and Latin American, followed by Europe. In response to a question about desirable applicant characteristics, as one might expect, a specific foreign language competency was highly important. Perceived or proven adaptability and cultural empathy, in conjunction with a strong academic and/or business background, were also mentioned by several of the respondents as very desirable.

The basic conclusion from this telephone survey is that there are very few entering positions in international marketing in foreign nations for new bachelor's degree or MBA graduates. The limited numbers of such positions tends to be filled by MBAs. In spite of the bleak placement picture, graduating seniors and MBAs actively seek such international positions. They consider them to be highly attractive. Their motives are often lifestyle-oriented, and their expectations are too frequently unrealistic. The content of courses in international marketing and business generally tends to mold and reinforce student attitudes and expectations. They learn about large multinational firms which have penetrated foreign markets successfully, and they often want to be a part of this global effort. The placement directors interviewed suggested this to be an important problem resulting in disappointment for many enthusiastic students.

Preparing the Exporting Entrepreneur

Our research indicates that (1) small and medium-sized firms lack the personnel needed to plan adequately export marketing operations, (2) international marketing courses at major business schools are oriented toward larger multinational firms, and (3) few entry level international marketing positions are available with multinational firms for those with new BS or MBA degrees.

The foregoing conclusions suggest that greater emphasis should be given in international marketing courses to exporting entrepreneurship. Rather than teaching about marketing on a "global scale," as one author phrases it, we believe it more appropriate to focus on export and/or import opportunities as entrepreneurs and as managers or owners of smaller businesses desiring to expand abroad. Of primary importance in such a course are the various barriers to international trade and the management options for dealing with them. Such an approach to international marketing also avoids the often-voiced student complaint about the traditional four-Ps approach—"My international marketing course wasn't significantly different from basic marketing, except for the cases and examples used."

The barriers confronting smaller companies and entrepreneurs wishing to export (or import) can be roughly organized into four categories: financial, legal, cultural, and psychological. Financial and legal barriers to trade, although often of critical importance, are perhaps the easiest with which to cope because their effects can be readily identified and measured. That is, tariff schedules and advertising laws are matters of public record. Alternatively, cultural and psychological barriers to trade are much more difficult to manage. Nationalism, differing negotiation styles, prejudice and risk aversion are more subtle barriers to international marketing. Even when clearly identified, the impact of cultural and psychological barriers may be very difficult, if not impossible, to translate into an item on an income statement.

Listed below are the main topics and issues which we feel should be included in an international marketing course oriented toward students planning to work for smaller firms or as entrepreneurs. Each barrier is identified and associated management options are briefly reviewed. Included are the titles of films and videotapes which we have found to be useful teaching aids.

Financial Barriers

Transoceanic shipping costs are perhaps the most obvious barriers to exporting and importing. As industry deregulation and increased efficiency continue, these costs will become less important in the future. Perhaps the best way to inform students about the cost and options is to ask a shipping company representative to speak to the class regarding his or her company's and competitors' services.

Tariffs can have substantial effects on exporters' income statements. Although tariff schedules are complex and ever-changing, tariffs are a matter of public record. Students can be required to ascertain tariffs for particular products and countries as part of a team export market plan project or a shorter assignment. Six management options for dealing with tariff barriers should be reviewed: pay them, protest unfavorable classification and/or valuation decisions, lobby for lowered tariffs through international trade negotiations, use free trade zones, manufacture abroad, and smuggle. We are not suggesting use of the last option. However, international marketers should be aware that competitors may use such tactics and thereby gain an illicit competitive advantage.

The United States has the most cost-effective mass communication system in the world. Consequently, when American products are marketed overseas, managers should anticipate increased promotional expenses as a percentage of sales. Both advertising, on a cost-per-thousand basis, and personal selling will be on a more expensive basis in foreign countries.

Transportation systems in the U.S. are also more efficient than those in most foreign countries. Fuel costs are substantially lower and distribution channels generally more direct. Thus, American firms should plan for increased costs of distribution in foreign markets.

Product homologation costs are perhaps the most important financial barrier facing international marketers. That is, products must be changed to coincide with the tastes and legal requirements of foreign markets. As examples, smaller capacity refrigerators are preferred in many foreign countries, or machine tools may have to be converted to metric specifications.

A financial barrier to exporting (importing) pertains to the various credit and currency risks associated with international transactions. Bankers' fees for letters of credit, foreign credit extension, and currency hedging transaction costs must be considered.

These several financial barriers can consume the profits of international transactions very quickly. The most important management implication stemming from these barriers is that American firms must take a long-term view toward export markets. Hurdling the extra promotional, distribution, and product homologation costs is best accomplished through volume and long production runs and associated economies of scale. American students and managers will, by nature, tend to focus on immediate profits and annual performance criteria.

Legal Barriers

Protectionism tends to vary inversely with national economic performance. Thus, as the world economy recedes, protectionist trade barriers grow. Indeed, during the last few years we have witnessed widespread adoption of quotas, tariffs, boycotts, and subsidies. Moreover, a longer list of more subtle forms of protectionism makes international marketing more difficult—counter-trade requirements; customs and product approval procedures; administrative guidance; and other discriminatory government and company policies. Students of international marketing must be made aware of these protectionist measures, their purposes and implications. Individual firms can influence (and have influenced) the effects of these legal barriers best by voicing complaints through the U.S. trade representative. (Milton Friedman's film. *Tyranny of Control,* provides an excellent discussion of the evils of protectionism and can be obtained from PENN Communications, 8425 Peach Street, Erie, PA 16512.)

In basic marketing courses students are exposed to various laws, federal and state, which constrain marketers' options in the United States. In many cases such laws in the U.S. are more strict than in other countries. For example, tying agreements or price fixing may be permitted in foreign countries. In other cases, however, laws in foreign nations are more stringent. As examples, comparative advertising or puffery may not be permitted. Firms desiring to export must consider the impact of such laws on their marketing operations.

Companies marketing products abroad should anticipate foreign government interference and participation in business transactions. Immigration regulations may preclude substantial American sales representation in a foreign country. In many developing countries and in nations with planned economies, the government may indeed be *the* principal or only buyer.

Home country governments both restrict and promote trade. The U.S. government promotes international trade through five interactive vehicles. The Commerce Department provides an array of marketing services primarily directed toward smaller firms desiring to enter foreign markets. The Department of Agriculture also offers marketing and financing services to encourage exportation of farm products. The U.S. trade representative continuously participates in efforts to reduce foreign protectionism as previously cited. The Export-Import Bank provides a variety of financial services for American firms involved in international trade. Finally, the Federal government gives tax incentives to firms whose revenues are primarily derived from exports. Students of international marketing should be aware of such incentives designed to stimulate international trade. Indeed, local Commerce Department representatives are pleased to have an opportunity to review such services for prospective international markets. However, Reid (1984) suggests that few firms who might, actually do take advantage of such services.

As previously indicated, home country governments also act to restrict trade. U.S. anti-trust laws have been viewed as an obstacle to U.S. firms wishing to export and compete internationally. However, in recent years legislation has been passed to ease restrictions on the formation of trading companies and research and development consortia. U.S. tax laws are considered to be substantial barriers to America's participation in international trade. That is, the United States is one of a small number of countries which tax personal income earned abroad. Such laws make it more economical to hire indigenous nationals to represent American firms in foreign countries. Foreign personnel are less costly in terms of salary, fringe benefits, and supporting services. Because they tend to be less marketing-oriented, they are less likely to report important competitive developments to American headquarters. Although in 1982 the Congress passed legislation to relax such double taxation, recent amendments have slowed the rate of relief.

Many American executives identify the Foreign Corrupt Practices Act as an important disincentive to trade. That is, foreign competitors are said to be "free" to offer "incentives" including bribes to foreign government officials and corporate decision makers, while American firms are less able to do so. But our analysis indicates that the Foreign Corrupt Practices Act has not been a major deterrent to American penetration of international markets (Graham 1983). Finally, the Federal government restricts exporting of several categories of high-tech products for national security purposes and other political reasons. Students of international marketing should be aware of these potential and/or perceived barriers to exporting, and be encouraged to lobby for reforms when their firms are adversely or unfairly affected.

The Japanese government is the only one of which we are aware that *purports* to encourage imports. The Japan External Trade Organization (JETRO), located in Japan Trade Center offices in several large American cities, provides a number of useful audiovisual teaching aids. Particularly appropriate for the discussion of government incentives is their film *The Door Is Open.*

Conflicts are inevitable between international business partners. Because of the expense and complexity of international legal procedures, the importance of arbitration services and clauses should be mentioned. Another management implication associated with conflict resolution is the importance of investing more time in getting to know foreign clients—legal recourse may not be a viable option.

Cultural Barriers

An important but difficult to measure barrier to exporting is foreign country nationalism. "Buy-French" or "Buy Japanese " can be strong influences on industrial and consumer purchases. One needs only to look to Detroit to see how strong. Firms will want to assess the importance of such considerations, and may be required to market abroad under indigenous brand names.

Cultural differences have pervasive implications for marketing research in other countries. Statistical data may not be available (e.g., no adequate census data exists for the Peoples' Republic of China); primary research may not be possible (illiteracy or privacy customs may preclude mail surveys); comparable samples for cross-cultural comparisons may be difficult to implement. *Bottle Babies,* a highly controversial film about marketing baby formula in less developed countries, has proven to be a stimulating teaching aid to illustrate cultural differences and research difficulties. This film can be obtained from the Interfaith Center on Corporate Responsibility, Infant Formula Work Group, Room 566, 475 Riverside Drive, New York, NY 10115, phone (212) 870-2750. "The Corporation Haters," *Fortune,* June 16, 1980, provides an alternative view of the Nestlé's controversy.

Business relationships and practices vary greatly across cultures. Selling processes, negotiation styles, and expectations about agreements are usually quite different from one region or nation to another. The approach or style which works best in the United States may not be appropriate in a given foreign country. Students of international marketing should be sensitized about such differences and taught to be flexible and patient in dealings with foreign clients. JETRO provides an excellent film regarding decision styles in Japanese organizations. This film, *Decision Making in Japan,* clearly summarizes the importance of such cultural differences and communicates their implications for Americans and other foreigners doing business with Japanese clients. *Smart*

Bargaining: Doing Business with the Japanese is an excellent video on negotiations (call 213-740-7140 for information).

Obviously, advertising across cultures is difficult for Americans who are accustomed to a common language, slang, and regulatory norms. Much has been written about the myriad mistakes that multinational companies have made over the years. *The Colonel Goes to Japan,* a movie about the success of Kentucky Fried Chicken in Japan, dramatically demonstrates how advertising (and other marketing strategies) must be adapted to the foreign market and the importance of market research. The film can be obtained from LCA Video Film, 1350 Avenue of the Americas, New York, NY 10019, phone (212) 397-9360.

The structure of distribution systems also varies across cultures. As an example, interorganizational ties in Japanese channels of distribution are stronger and longer-lasting than in the United States. These ties are composed of equity ownership, loans, formal and informal reciprocity agreements, and exchange of personnel. Such strong relationships are largely precluded in the United States by anti-trust laws *and* custom. Such strong interorganizational relationships virtually eliminate opportunities for foreign suppliers (or new Japanese sources) of component parts. But other categories of foreign goods may be marketed more easily in Japan, such as capital equipment, where long-standing commercial relationships are not as pervasive.

A final cultural barrier to international trade pertains to the differing roles of women in society and business. In recent years American women have made real progress toward equality in the workplace. However, this is not the case in most other places in the world. Client relationships with foreign firms are often very difficult for American businesswomen. Over time this should become less of a problem. The first step is awareness of the existence and nature of this issue.

The culture barriers to trade are the most difficult to teach. Little research is available upon which to base prescriptions. Knowledge about a particular culture does not help very much in understanding others. For example, one might expect Japanese bargaining styles and Korean bargaining styles to be very similar. However, having observed both Japanese and Korean businessmen in bargaining situations, we would be hard pressed to find two negotiation styles that are more different! It is dangerous from a marketing standpoint to try to "categorize" cultures. Lastly, it is our feeling that words alone (discussion and text) are an inadequate medium to communicate the richness of cultural diversity. That is why we have included the list of audiovisual aids in our course recommendations.

Psychological Barriers

The last set of barriers to international marketing, the psychological ones, are the least obvious from a manager's point of view. Little has been written about them because they are very difficult to research. We cannot ask executives about decision factors about which they are unaware or loath to reveal. Nonetheless we feel that they deserve mention.

Ethnocentrism might be defined as a belief in the superiority or importance of one's own group. All of us feel this—some more than others. These beliefs find expression in many ways, not the least of which is a Californian's belief that he lives in "God's

Country" or the famous *New Yorker* map of the United States. People all over the world describe their home as the most important place on earth. These ethnocentric feelings can adversely influence sound marketing judgment. They tend to reduce in our minds the importance of learning about and understanding our foreign clients.

Closely related to ethnocentrism are racial and ethnic prejudices. The subject is an uncomfortable one, more so than the sexism cited earlier. Such prejudices do sometimes influence marketing decisions. Particularly troublesome are the vestiges of World War II. We have seen a Dutch sales manager working for an American multinational refuse to hire German sales representatives. We have heard strong misgivings from Philippine businessmen about buying from Japanese suppliers. And in the American press we read about "JapanScam" and so on. Such views hamper sound business judgment.

A third psychological barrier to exporting is risk aversion. Generally, the risks are greater in international trade than in domestic marketing. Certainly actions can be taken to reduce them, including the important initial step of heightened awareness. Other strategies such as gradual stepwise entry to foreign markets or piggy-back distribution also help. But in the final analysis, that first foray into an international market takes courage and commitment. Students should understand that those managers who are risk averse limit their companies' potential.

Focusing on short-term performance criteria also constrains a firm's ability to enter international markets which take time to develop. Profits are generally derived from volume generated over the long run. This requires establishment of long-term business relationships based on mutual trust rather than a tightly written contract. Appropriately designed products, tailored promotional strategies, and efficient distribution systems all take time to ripen in a completely different environment.

Export Marketing Plans

A final and crucial aspect of the curriculum in courses for exporting entrepreneurs is the development of export marketing plans. Ideally, students should be asked to select a product and a country, and complete the required background research to support a well planned entry into a foreign market. The plan should include all the elements of a domestic marketing plan—a situation analysis (including a five-year forecast of sales), marketing strategies, action plans, a budget, and a five-year pro-forma income statement. The local U.S. Commerce Department, U.S. and Foreign Commercial Service can often provide the names of executives and companies who are contemplating exporting and who may be interested in cooperating in student projects.

Conclusions

The four categories of barriers to successful market penetration abroad are especially important to smaller businesses and entrepreneurs. Capital and other resources are often very limited, and "tripping" over any of the financial, legal, cultural, and psychological barriers may prove to be a fatal mistake for them. Yet, the "more global marketplace" of the future holds much promise for knowledgeable marketers of American companies of all sizes and compositions.

In summary, we advance three major reasons for stressing a more entrepreneurial approach to teaching international marketing:

1. Our survey of the practices of local, smaller and medium-sized exporters suggests that most firms tend to "respond" to foreign demand, rather than carefully plan international marketing efforts.

2. Our review of international marketing curricula in several major business schools indicates that business schools offer limited course work to students to prepare them for careers in multinational corporations. Yet, we also discovered that there are few available entry-level positions in the foreign operations of such multinational corporations.

3. Finally, approximately 20,000 American firms are not participating in the international marketplace, primarily because their managers lack the perspective of an exporting entrepreneur.

Thus, international marketing courses designed for fledgling exporting entrepreneurs are needed. We have stressed the critical need for the development of such courses and suggested the content upon which to focus, using recommended audiovisual aids. Such well designed and implemented courses could have a major impact (a) in educating students to become effective exporting entrepreneurs, (b) in enabling them to apply their skills to enhance the profitability of their firms, and, ultimately, (c) in assisting their firms to contribute to a macro increase in export trade and thereby help achieve international business harmony.

Appendix A

Telephone Survey Interview Guide
Exporting Manufacturing Firms

Company _____   Respondent _____

Product Lines _____   Title _____

Hi, I'm _____ from Pendergraft Research. We're doing a study for the School of Business Administration at the University of Southern California, among businesses that manufacture and export products. Are you a manufacturer who exports products to other countries?

　　　　　　YES (PROCEED)　　　　　　　　　　　　　NO (TERMINATE)

1　How many years have you been exporting products? _____ yrs.

2.　When your company first started exporting products, how did you go about deciding to do this? (PROBE: WHO WAS INVOLVED, ONE OR MORE PEOPLE IN THE COMPANY, IN THE DECISION TO EXPORT?)

2a.　Did you originally export products to one country, or more than one? Why is that?

3a. When you first started exporting, how did you get it started? Did you use (READ)?

3b. Do you currently use (READ)?

	3a At Start		3b Currently
Foreign importers	1	....	2
Domestic exporters	1	....	2
Export consultants	1	....	2
Export management companies	1	....	2
Trading companies	1	....	2

Other (specify) _____

_____

4.   How are your export operations organized now?

5.   Do you prefer to hire college graduates to work in your export operations?

YES........ 1   No........ 2

6.   Which of the following are important considerations in hiring such a person?

Business school degree..........................1

MBA 2

International emphasis in school 3

Language skills...............................4

Prior experience 5

Any other? _____

7.   How many people are currently involved in your export operations? _____

8.   How many countries do you export to? _____

9.   Which ones are the most important to your export program? _____

_____

10.   Would you give me an estimate of your sales volume, both in

Domestic $ _____   and International $ _____

Thank you for your help in our research.

Interviewer _____   Date _____

References

Business Week (1978), "The Reluctant Exporter," April 10, 52–54.

Cateora, P. R. (1983), *International Marketing,* Homewood, IL: Richard D. Irwin.

Cavusgil, S. T., and J. R. Nevin (1981), "International Determinants of Export Marketing Behavior, An Empirical Investigation." *Journal of Marketing Research,* 18 (February), 114–119.

Graham, J. L. (1983), "The Foreign Corrupt Practices Act: A Manager's Guide," *Columbia Journal of World Business* (Fall), 89–94.

Meloan, T. W. and D. Taylor (1968), "Internationalizing the Marketing Curricula," in *Internationalizing the Business Curricula,* Bloomington, IN: Bureau of Business Research.

Reid, S. (1984), "Information Acquisition and Export Entry Decisions in Small Firms," *Journal of Business Research,* 12, 141–157.

_____ (1981), "The Decision-Maker and Export Entry and Expansion Decision," *Journal of International Business Studies,* 12 (Winter).

Suzman, C. L. and L. H. Wortzel (1984), "Technology Profiles and Export Marketing Strategies," *Journal of Business Research,* 12, 183–194.

Ursic, M. L. and M. R. Czinkota (1984), "An Experience Curve Explanation of Export Expansion," *Journal of Business Research,* 12, 159–168.

"Who's Who in Foreign Trade," Membership Roster of the Foreign Trade Association of Southern California, Los Angeles, 1983–84.

ARTICLE 47

The Wide World of International Trade

Still bearing scars from the recession, many American small businesses have circled the wagons and limited their focus to this country in an attempt at self-preservation. However, if they are to grow and prosper, just the opposite may be required.

A world of opportunity awaits outside the U.S. borders. Despite calls for protectionism by a number of business and government leaders, trade agreements and the reconfiguration of nations are creating a global marketplace that offers new horizons for companies willing to venture out.

"Small business has to overcome its inward thinking," maintains Tom Gray, formerly with the U.S. Small Business Administration (SBA) and now with the National Federation of Independent Business (NFIB). "Many firms still hold onto the frontier mentality left over from the railroads. But the frontier has moved offshore. Only one-third of U.S. small businesses export and they do it incidentally, not as a purpose. In Europe, every other transaction is a foreign one.

"We have to change our mindset," he stresses. "The World is waiting for us to join, and if we don't someone else will. If your business isn't growing rapidly in your local market, then get thee to a market where it will."

The numbers bear him out. According to NFIB statistics, almost every international market is growing faster than the U.S. For example, Latin America is experiencing annual growth of five percent; the Middle East, nearly that. The Four Tigers—Hong Kong, Singapore, South Korea and Taiwan—and their neighbors Thailand, Malaysia and Indonesia are averaging six percent growth annually—and that's when they're having an unremarkable year. For many of them, the rate is closer to seven or eight percent. And, say many international trade watchers, wait until the Eastern Block countries and the former Soviet Republics begin to fully flex their economic muscles.

U.S. growth rates, on the other hand, have remained comparatively flat. "The average rate for the 90s has been two percent, topping 2.3 percent under the best of circumstances," Gray points out. "These numbers don't mean that the U.S. isn't growing, but rather that other countries are growing so much faster."

Reprinted with permission from *Small Business Success,* Volume VI, produced by Pacific Bell Directory in partnership with the U.S. Small Business Administration, 1993.

A New World Order

Market-driven thinking is sweeping the globe. "People don't talk of countries anymore," notes Dr. N.E. Okeke, former president of the Nigerian Chamber of Commerce and Industry. "They talk of markets." Agrees U.S. Trade Representative Carla Hills, "A new world order of trade is on the horizon."

With this new order some opportunities for small companies that now find their domestic markets have matured or are even shrinking. In fact, firms that market their products and services internationally expect higher growth rates than those which concentrate exclusively on domestic markets, reports financial consulting firm Coopers & Lybrand. In a survey of 328 of the U.S.'s fastest growing companies, globally focused enterprises anticipated 1992 growth rates of 26.4 percent compared to 22.5 percent for firms that aren't involved in selling internationally.

Not only are opportunities more prevalent, but U.S. businesses also have distinct advantages over their foreign competitors. "American companies are more sophisticated and much more capable in many dimensions, including marketing techniques, technology, experience and access to a lot of high quality products," Gray observes. "'Made in America' is still a high-powered statement. And the low value of the U.S. dollar means that our goods are currently so cheap, we have an even greater competitive edge."

Immigrant Entrepreneurs Find Success

Often recent immigrants understand these advantages best. Not only have they had a chance to compare U.S. goods with those of our foreign competitors firsthand, they also maintain ties to their homelands. These ongoing relationships give immigrant entrepreneurs a natural and almost immediate market, and they obviously don't have to worry about learning the nuances of the importing culture.

Michael Gura, a Russian living in Orange County, California, is one such immigrant. The founder of Ortex, an international trading company, Gura exports stereos, personal computers, cars and other Western goods to his native country. His business has become so successful that he now employs 250 people in nine offices around the world. And Gura is not one of a few isolated examples. Stories such as his abound in the Asian, Hispanic and Middle Eastern communities throughout the country as well.

"At first only the big American companies could go abroad and succeed," notes Bill McNutt, owner of International Direct Marketing Consultants in Dallas. "Today, the miracle of the marketplace—fax machines, modems, international 800 telephone numbers and credit cards—has brought a new accessibility. The new technology enables small and medium-size organizations to move to areas where they can prosper as surely as people in the 1800s were able to move to new territories using barbed wire, windmills and other technology of their times."

And don't ignore the human resources factor in the export equation, adds Terence Barber, founder of BHP Associates, a global economic development and management consulting firm in Sacramento, California. "Concentrate on developing a multicultural workforce. Opportunities may arise from informal interpersonal contacts. For example, because of the warming of relations with the West, the Vietnamese market is opening up. Many of the Vietnamese living here have strong links with family and friends still living in their native country. The same is true of the Hispanic population. Owners of small businesses should be looking at an Hispanic workforce as a strategic opportunity."

Beyond your own workforce, other business relationships may prove to be a wellspring for export opportunities. Fred Budetti's United Steel Products of Corona, New York, is now a 50 percent partner in a Russian joint venture thanks to his relationship with a Russian engineer once assigned to his government's New York mission.

The manufacturer of steel security products, such as commercial rolling doors and grills, enjoyed a 15-year relationship with the mission prior to doing business overseas. "We'd provided them with construction services and related security products, including a bullet-proof door for the mission. And when (former Premier Mikhail) Gorbachev came to New York a few years ago, we designed and built security enclosures for wherever he was staying, among them bullet-proof partitions for the windows. It was while working on those projects that I met Vladimir Zinovyev."

Three years ago Zinovyev returned to his country and shortly thereafter invited Budetti to open a similar business there. Together they formed Russato, a multi-division company offering diverse services ranging from architectural and construction services to computer programming and software development for the newly formed Russian stock exchange to installation of high power electrical lines. The company also exports mineral products back to the U.S. from Russia.

Reluctant to put a dollar figure on Russato's profits, Budetti explains you have to think differently when doing business with Russia. "It's difficult to look at exporting to Russia and expect dollars in exchange. It doesn't have the dollar flow other countries have. Instead, you need to find a system that will reap benefits for both sides. In this case, receiving product as payment was the most advantageous arrangement."

He believes the time is opportune to venture into Russia but adds a few words of caution.

"Now is the time to build a foundation there. Russia has the greatest resources in the world. And with global resources getting scarce, it's critical that U.S. manufacturers establish good relations with the state organizations that are now being privatized in the former U.S.S.R.

"But don't go there cold; don't jump on a plane expecting to do business there immediately. Speak first to consultants who can make arrangements as well as to other people already exporting who can help you. If you don't, you'll be spinning your wheels for years."

Where to Begin?

While many companies recognize the potential of the global marketplace, the idea of taking it on can be extremely daunting.

Experts agree that the process starts with a deep commitment. And with that commitment come resources of money, time and effort to research markets, learn about new cultures and create a strategic business plan that specifically addresses the new realities.

"You have to be willing to travel," Gray states emphatically. "You must also be willing to appreciate other people's cultures and learn how to relate to different people and their customs."

Assess Your Export Potential

An important component in making your export commitment is figuring out whether you have anything an international market would want to buy. Perhaps you think you've tapped out your market in the U.S. and believe exporting could breathe some life back into your product. Before you start pouring in time and other resources, step back and candidly assess your potential for success.

This assessment should include a look at industry trends, your firm's domestic position in the industry, the effect exporting will have on your present operations, the status of your resources and the anticipated demand for your commodity. You should also size up your competition and see if there are any market segments these firms have overlooked.

In addition, you may want to test your product's appeal by advertising in the U.S. Department of Commerce's catalog-magazine, *Commercial News USA*. A manufacturer of emergency oxygen packs did just that and received inquiries from every continent. Today, 40 percent of the company's products go to foreign markets.

Identify Your Market

After determining that your product is highly exportable, you need to identify your potential customers. The best way to do this is through market research. To successfully establish your niche, you should target a few selected countries. You will want to investigate national wealth and any cost barriers, such as tariffs and import regulations, as well as taxation laws and restrictions on foreign investments.

Trademark protection and patent law comprise another critical area that requires your attention. A vexing problem for many U.S. companies doing business abroad, especially in developing countries, has been the pirating of intellectual property. The Western idea of "owning" an idea is as foreign to many cultures as the idea of private property.

You should also research existing treaties and any currently under development, such as GATT and the North American Free Trade Agreement (NAFTA). (These trade agreements are still evolving, so be sure to monitor them closely.)

To measure the potential of your target markets, your market study should try to identify:

- Similarities in business culture, practices and the law.
- Language and other possible communication barriers.

- Spending habits.
- National traditions.
- Religious beliefs.
- The stability of the market's economic and political environment.
- Direct and indirect barriers to initial market entry.
- Product standards in the quality, safety and technical areas.
- Current market size and growth potential.
- Existing domestic and foreign competition.

"Moving into foreign markets is not easy," Tom Gray acknowledges. "I liken the process to the type of thinking a small manufacturer engages in when deciding to move a plant or make major renovations to an existing one. The firm that wants to penetrate a foreign market has to consider it an investment project. It will take time to make the critical decision on the country or area it makes sense to enter.

"Penetrate your selected foreign market the way you would a domestic market. Begin in one country, expand to the surrounding region and go on from there. Approach exporting one country at a time.

"For example," Gray adds, "if you do a lot of business with the Latin American market in the U.S., Latin American countries would be a natural for expansion. But don't try to take on Latin America and Europe at the same time."

Your decision to export should also be based on market need. That was the case for H&H Exports in Duluth, Minnesota. The firm's initial decision to venture overseas was triggered by the fact that although American machines are used all over the world and need occasional repairs, it was difficult, if not impossible, to obtain replacement parts. Now, 12 years later, H&H Exports supplies American-made bearings and related power transmission parts to 642 clients around the world.

Get Expert Counseling

Doing business in foreign markets can be very different from doing business here at home, so don't be afraid to ask for help. In fact, most successful exporters say it would have been much more difficult to export if they hadn't done so.

"There's a lot of help out there," Gray encourages. "There are people who can help you from beginning to end." One area in which you should definitely seek assistance is market research. You can get up-to-date information from the U.S. Commerce Department's Trade Information Center and the SBA.

The SBA and its volunteer offshoot, the Service Corps of Retired Executives (SCORE), can also help you with marketing or distributing your commodity.

The Crowning Touch of Medford, Oregon, is now selling its sewing tools in Japan, Australia, the Netherlands, Canada and the United Kingdom thanks to the assistance of four SCORE volunteers. With decades of experience behind them, the retired executives were able to help the five-member firm set up a successful international sales program.

Your bank can also be an excellent resource if you choose one that has an international department and is committed to serving small business. Such an institution can help you with all aspects of an export transaction and introduce you to the federal and state government export financing programs that actively support small firms.

State governments are another prime source of assistance. California has overseas trade offices in five countries and its State Department of Food and Agriculture and California Energy Commission (to name just two agencies) sponsor trade shows and offer financial assistance to prospective exporters.

Industry trade associations are also useful, as are private consulting firms (such as Terence Barber's BHP Associates) and the business departments located within major universities.

Adapt Your Product

What flies off the shelves in Chicago may not necessarily be a big seller in Munich. Cultural differences and varying product standards can present serious barriers if you aren't willing to adapt your commodity to your new target market.

"If you take the attitude that 'We'll sell them what we have,' then it won't work," declares Michael Berman, vice president of sales and marketing at Laser Communications in Lancaster, Pennsylvania. A manufacturer of laser transmission systems, the company has to alter each system it sells to meet the specific product standards of its client countries.

So does Cenogenics Corp., a New Jersey manufacturer of medical diagnostic kits. Not only has the firm become adept at changing its products to suit local needs, but it has also had to change its packaging. "Because their economies can't tolerate our markups, we use less substantial packaging for our markets in West Africa," notes owner Michael Katz.

Ted Teach, president of Spectra-Physics Laserplane of Dayton, Ohio, acknowledges that understanding the requirements and standards of each market is often not easy. "But we must always meet them if we don't want to lose the sale to a local competitor. Throughout our history, whenever we developed a basic product, we quickly worked to adapt it to our target markets overseas."

Select a Selling Technique

The question of how you will sell, deliver and service your product abroad is far more important than you may realize. In answering this question, the first decision you will want to address is method of distribution. You can choose from two basic options: direct and indirect.

The decision to market your product directly or indirectly should be based on several important factors: the size of your firm, the nature of your product, previous export experience, and business conditions in your selected overseas market.

You should also consider after-sales requirements such as service, customary business methods and established distribution channels in the markets you've targeted.

In indirect exporting, rather than dealing with the customer or a foreign importer directly, you may rely on the services of foreign sales representatives or agents (equivalent to a manufacturer's rep), distributors, retailers or government-controlled trading companies.

Foreign distributors and sales representatives generally work on commission, assume no risk or responsibility, and are under contract for a specified period. Distributors purchase goods at a significant discount, acquire title and then market the product. Sales representatives, however, don't purchase goods but instead place orders for them.

Working with distributors or representatives can offer distinct advantages. These individuals can often provide the initial contacts you need in a foreign country. They have already established relationships with buyers of related items and know the local market, which is important in any sales effort.

However, there's another side to the owner-distributor relationship that causes many exporters to urge caution.

"Distributors frequently demand exclusive market rights to your product while reserving the right to service your competitors," warns an article in *World Trade* magazine. "Don't expect commitment. The big complaint of most exporters is distributors who are poised to hop aboard the fastest train and move whatever product is currently hot."

However, the savviest exporters manage to make the relationship work. "The commitment and expertise of the distributor are paramount to use," stresses Cenogenics owner Michael Katz. "Once we've found the right person, the country is no longer difficult. We have a guide through the maze."

Two of the criteria Katz looks for are the distributor's experience selling similar products and a successful track record selling other companies' products. He cautions that the basic business practices of qualifying a dealer remain the same. "We still check references. We have minimized the downside by knowing people for a number of years before committing to partnerships with them."

Going It on Your Own

If you choose to sell your commodity directly, you can market your goods through direct mail, advertising and promotions in magazines with overseas circulation as well as in local publications and other media. The way you market your product in the United States can provide helpful clues for developing methods of selling it internationally.

If you have found that direct mail has paid off for you at home, chances are good that it will also help you reach buyers in foreign markets. Well-drafted cover letters and informative, well-designed product and company brochures can be very effective in getting started in a targeted segment of an overseas market. However, given the cost of foreign mailings, be conscious of the weight of your direct mail package.

Some of the most likely sources of mailing lists are your local Department of Commerce office, foreign trade association membership directories, your state office of international trade, and the U.S. Chamber of Commerce. The World Trade Centers Association computerized NETWORK service can also provide valuable leads.

If you advertise to your U.S. market, you may also want to consider advertising to a new overseas one. However, the decision to include paid-for advertising in your budget depends on the extent you believe advertising influences your end customers. If brand name is relatively unimportant, or if your market is limited and concentrated, then media advertising will probably play a minor role in your overall promotion efforts.

One of the best ways to build overseas sales is by participating in trade shows, both here in the United States and overseas. A considerable amount of business is often written during these shows. But more than this, an attendee can view the offerings of competitors and gain insights into market preferences and trends.

Hundreds of major exhibitions and fairs, both general and specialized, are held each year, and most of them are open to any firm in the particular industry. When participating in these events, you benefit from a full range of promotional and display assistance. In return, you pay a specific sum to offset the cost of the services received. Many of the same organizations that sponsor trade shows and fairs—such as the SBA, industry groups and government agencies—also sponsor trade missions to target countries that enable you to hear from local officials and meet prospective buyers.

Whatever methods you choose to promote your products, you'll find that direct exporting offers distinct advantages: lower inventory, control over your product, potentially higher profits and a closer relationship to foreign buyers and the marketplace. However, these advantages come with a price. If you choose to export directly, you must be willing to devote more time, money, personnel and other company resources.

The Price Is Right

Pricing can be one of your most effective competitive weapons, but it is often the most challenging for new exporters to use effectively.

When establishing your export price, begin by taking into account your customers' perception of value, what differentiates your product from that of your competitors and the role price will play in sales volume and profit.

You also need to weigh many of the same factors you would when pricing for domestic markets, such as the costs of production, packaging, transportation and handling as well as promotion and selling expenses. In addition, you should try and pinpoint the price the market is willing to pay, relative to market demand and the competition. And don't forget the export objectives of your firm.

In defining their price, most exporters choose from three common methods. You can base your overseas price on your domestic one, then add in export costs. You can use incremental cost pricing, determining a basic unit cost that takes into account production and exporting costs plus an additional markup for profit. Or you can reduce the quality of your product, using cheaper materials or simplifying production processes.

Formulate an Export Strategy

Once you have made your export commitment, chosen your market and distribution method and established a price, you need to translate that information into a strategic exporting plan. In doing so, you may want to take a cue from your company's business plan. That is, outline the country or countries in which you plan to do business; identify your export objectives, both immediate and long-term; define the specific tactics you will use to achieve these objectives, such as a marketing and promotional plan and strategies; specify your distribution system and pricing; establish implementation and milestone schedules that reflect your objectives and tactics; and detail your allocation of resources.

Your plan should also include an executive summary, an export policy commitment statement, background analysis market and product selection, personnel and organization, and methods of evaluating the success of your efforts.

Financing Your Overseas Operations

Similar to domestic expansion, moving into international markets requires capital. You need funds for inventory, receivables and promotion activities. In addition, if you intend to open foreign branch offices, you'll need cash for facilities and related operating expenses.

Most owners of small businesses venturing overseas often don't have the extra capital they need and must turn to outside financing sources. In recognition of the importance of exporting building at all governmental levels, new sources of funding are springing up.

"Support for export financing is one of the most aggressive programs state governments have undertaken to enhance export performance by smaller companies," notes Irene Fisher, director of the California State World Trade Commission's Export Finance Office. "Such programs range from counseling, loan packaging and interfacing with the financial community to providing direct loans and loan guarantees. Some programs are tied into state or local economic development funds, while others have special funding sources dedicated to supporting exports. All of the existing programs are designed to streamline access to available funds, to support programs of federal agencies, or both.

"Alaska, California, Oregon, Utah and Washington have been particularly active in export promotion with Arizona, Hawaii, Idaho and Nevada next in also having taken some steps."

Your bank can be an additional good source of financing. For doing business overseas, you will want to choose one that offers short-term and medium-term export financing, foreign credit, commercial letters of credit, collection or discount export drafts, and purchase and sale of foreign exchange. Such services are very valuable and can help you maintain your cash flow.

If you are unable to find a bank that meets your needs, the federal government provides financial assistance through a number of agencies:

- **The Export-Import Bank of the United States,** whose primary purpose is to facilitate the export of American products and services through its various financing programs, including discount and direct loans. Eximbank also arranges financing for the overseas buyer and consequently underwrites the transaction. And to help exporters reduce their risk, Eximbank offers credit insurance through its agent, the Foreign Credit Insurance Program.

STATE TRADE DEVELOPMENT SERVICES

Sources of Assistance by State	Seminars/ Conferences	One-on-One Counseling	Market Studies Prepared	Language Bank	Ref. to Local Export Servcs	Newsletters	How-to Handbook	Sales Leads Disseminated	Trade Shows	Trade Missions	Foreign Office Reps.	Operational Financing Pgm.
Alabama	■	■			■		■	■	■	■	■	
Alaska									■	■	■	
Arizona	■	■	■			■		■	■	■		
Arkansas	■	■	■	■	■	■		■	■	■	■	
California	■	■		■		■(a)	■(b)	■	■	■		■
Colorado	■	■	■		■			■	■	■		
Connecticut	■	■	■		■	■		■	■		■	
Delaware	■				■			■	■			
Florida	■	■	■					■	■	■	■	
Georgia	■	■	■		■			■	■	■	■(c)	
Hawaii	■	■			■			■	■			
Idaho	■							■	■	■		
Illinois	■	■	■		■			■	■	■	■	■
Indiana	■	■		■				■	■	■	■	■
Iowa	■	■	■	■			■	■	■		■	
Kansas	■	■			■	■		■	■	■		
Kentucky	■	■			■		■	■	■	■	■	
Louisiana (d)												
Maine	■							■	■			
Maryland	■	■				■		■	■		■	
Massachusetts	■	■	■		■				■			
Michigan	■	■	■			■	■	■	■		■	
Minnesota	■	■			■	■		■	■	■	■	■
Mississippi	■	■	■			■	■	■	■	■		■
Missouri	■	■	■		■	■		■	■	■	■	
Montana	■	■	■		■		■	■	■	■		
Nebraska	■	■		■	■		■	■	■			
Nevada	■			■		■					■	
New Hampshire	■	■			■			■	■			
New Jersey	■	■			■	■		■	■	■		
New Mexico	■	■			■		■	■			■	
New York	■	■			■	■	■	■	■	■	■	
North Carolina	■	■	■	■	■	■		■	■	■	■	
North Dakota	■	■						■	■			
Ohio	■	■	■	■	■	■		■	■	■	■	■
Oklahoma	■	■	■	■	■	■	■	■	■	■		
Oregon	■	■				■	■	■	■			
Pennsylvania	■	■	■		■	■		■	■		■	
Rhode Island	■	■	■		■	■		■	■	■	■	
South Carolina	■	■	■					■	■	■	■	
South Dakota	■	■	■	■				■				
Tennessee	■				■		■	■	■	■		
Texas	■	■					■	■			■	
Utah	■	■					■	■	■	■	■	
Vermont	■										■	
Virginia	■	■	■				■		■		■	
Washington	■	■	■	■	■	■	■	■	■	■	■	
West Virginia	■										■	
Wisconsin	■	■				■	■	■	■	■	■	
Wyoming										■		

State Trade Development Services Explanations

Seminars/Conferences
State sponsors seminars for exporters, either basic, specific function, or specific market.

One-on-One Counseling
State staff provides actual export counseling to individual businesses in addition to making appropriate referrals.

Market Studies Prepared
State staff prepares specific market studies for individual companies.

Language Bank
State program to match foreign-speaking visitors with bilingual local residents who provide volunteer translation services.

Referrals to Local Export Services
Matching exporters with exporter services, e.g., matchmaker fair, export service directory and individual referrals.

Newsletter
State publishes an international trade newsletter.

How-to Handbook
State publishes a basic how-to-export handbook.

Sales Leads Disseminated
State collects and distributes sales leads to in-state businesses.

Trade Shows
State assists with and accompanies business on trade missions.

Foreign Offices/Representatives
State office or contractual representative located abroad.

Operational Financing Program
State export financing assistance program that is currently operational.

(a) California issues a bimonthly column to local chambers and trade groups for publication in their newsletters.
(b) California produces a "road map" to low cost and free trade services.
(c) Georgia's foreign offices are only active in attracting reverse investment.
(d) Louisiana has recently established a new Office of International Trade, Finance and Development within the Department of Commerce and Industry. The Office is expected to offer a full range of trade promotion services.

U.S. SMALL BUSINESS ADMINISTRATION INTERNATIONAL TRADE INFORMATION MATRIX

A quick reference for matching international trade business needs with the assistance offered by public and private sector organizations.

Use →

If You Want ↓

If You Want	U.S. Department of Commerce	U.S. Small Business Administration	Export-Import Bank of the United States	Overseas Private Investment Corporation	U.S. Department of Agriculture	U.S. Department of State	Department of the Treasury	General Agreement of Tariffs & Trade	United Nations	Embassies and Consulates	World Bank	Inter. American Development Bank	Asian Development Bank	State Departments of Commerce	Chambers of Commerce	Port Authorities	Commercial Banks	Export Management Companies (EMCs)	Trade Associations	Export Packers	Freight Forwarders	Custom House Brokers	Consulting Firms	Transportation Carriers	Credit Reporting Firms	Universities
Export/Import Training Program	■	■	■											■	■											
General Export Information	■	■			■			■	■					■	■	■	■		■		■		■	■	■	■
General Import Information					■				■					■	■	■							■	■		
Potential Foreign Markets	■	■		■	■	■		■	■	■				■	■	■	■	■	■				■			■
Trade Statistics	■						■	■										■	■							
Foreign Buyers and Representatives	■			■										■	■	■	■	■	■					■		
Foreign Sources of Supply	■								■					■	■	■	■		■	■		■				
Overseas Projects	■				■						■	■	■	■			■	■								
Overseas Investment Opportunities	■		■					■						■		■							■	■		
Foreign Firm Credit/Reliability	■	■							■							■									■	
Corresponding Overseas	■													■	■			■	■							
Translation Assistance									■					■	■		■						■			■
Overseas Travel				■																						
Product Sales Promotion	■			■											■			■	■				■			
Export Financing	■	■	■	■	■	■					■	■	■				■	■					■			
Insurance of Overseas Shipments/Investments		■	■															■				■				
Tax Incentives	■				■																					
Foreign Trade Zones	■				■																					
Collection Documents	■													■	■		■	■			■		■			
Shipping Documents	■																	■		■	■	■				
Packaging and Shipping	■													■	■	■	■	■	■	■	■		■			

- **The SBA Export Loan Guarantee Program,** which guarantees up to $500,000 of commercial financing to companies that want to establish or expand their export operations. To qualify, you must meet the SBA criteria for a small business. Qualification requirements vary according to industry, so contact your local SBA office for details. In addition, the program also offers an Export Revolving Line of Credit, which can be used to finance pre-export production; purchase labor, supplies, materials and inventory; and fund marketing development overseas.
- **The Private Export Funding Corporation,** which is a private corporation owned by a group of commercial banks that works with Eximbank in using private capital to finance U.S. exports. Loans are made to foreign borrowers who need medium- to long-term financing to purchase U.S. goods and services.

In for the Long Haul

William J. Dennis, Jr., senior research fellow at The NFIB Foundation (an affiliate of the National Federation of Independent Business), interjects a cautionary note. "I don't agree that exporting is the right idea for many small businesses," he asserts. "First of all, before embarking on an overseas effort, a business must be very, very sure that a demand really exists for its particular product or service. Also, if a company's current markets include St. Louis, Chicago and Houston, for example, wouldn't it make more sense to expand domestically into Los Angeles and New York, rather than into Japan or Europe? The bottom line I'm advocating is careful forethought and prudence. Exporting is not an easy undertaking, nor does it make sense for everyone."

Those who do decide to venture abroad must realize that exporting success is not achieved overnight. The requirements are the same as when you first started your business in this country. That is, you must be willing, even enthusiastic, about making a long-term commitment, agree many experienced exporters.

"You can't expect to succeed in foreign marketing in a short period of time," believes Steve Henn of ITW Lubricating Systems in Kent, Washington. "You have to think long term. It takes awhile to get established in an overseas market because every country is different."

Concurs Susan Oleson of Global Computer Products in Boca Raton, Florida, "International trade is very much a long-term business relationship which takes time to develop."

But there's no question that for many entrepreneurs the time is worth spending. "It's a must to go international," declares Herb Austin of the SBA's New York District Office. "If you don't, you're missing the boat. Limiting yourself to the U.S. market no longer means 'we are here and they are there.' We are quickly becoming a global market and it's a necessity to explore exporting opportunities."

Business Etiquette Abroad: The Hidden Factor in International Export Success

When it comes to marketing abroad, your success may have less to do with your product and more to do with your adaptability to another country's style of doing business.

Although many business people in other countries speak English and are university-trained in U.S. business theories and practices, they—like you and everyone else worldwide—operate from their own distinct set of cultural assumptions.

These include clear notions about how business should be conducted and what behaviors prove you're the sort of person—and from the sort of company—they would feel confident having as a business partner.

These unspoken rules of protocol vary with every region or country. Yet certain fundamental courtesies are applicable everywhere, as summarized in the following five rules:

Rule 1: Do Your Homework. Before going abroad, bone up on a country's political, social and cultural history. Have your business cards printed bilingually, one language per side, and include any appropriate academic titles or credentials. Make sure your visual aids are translated into appropriate languages. Lastly, memorize the names of people you'll be meeting. If you can't ascertain in advance how to address them, ask them ("What would you like me to call you?") upon introduction.

Rule 2: Dress the Part. Wear conservative, inconspicuously correct business clothes. For men, designer suits may be a plus.

Rule 3: Avoid U.S. Jargon and Gestures. Speak so that someone who learned English as a foreign language can easily understand you. Use impeccable textbook grammar. Avoid slang, sports metaphors, buzzwords, techno-speak, folksiness and euphemisms. Standardize your accent as much as possible. Similarly, avoid conversational gestures, such as thumbs up for "okay," which too often can have embarrassingly different local meanings.

Rule 4: Follow Your Host's Lead. Get down to business when your host is ready, and conduct business on your host's timetable. Eat the food your host offers you. Try to follow your host's style of greeting, loudness of voice, extent of eye contact, and physical distance during conversation. Adapt to your host's relaxed or formal style of sitting, standing and walking.

Rule 5: Do Your Part to Stop Misunderstandings. If English isn't your host's own language, speak slowly—but not condescendingly so—and put the onus on yourself for making things clear ("I sometimes talk too quickly. Shall I go over that again?"). Follow up meetings with a conference memo to help ensure you haven't misconstrued the discussion.

These rules, though essential, are only the start. Even if you're conducting business through a local liaison—a choice that experts recommend, particularly in Asia—you still need to know a country's business customs and decorum. Some excellent books, articles and workshops are available. And to start you off, here are overviews for four regions where U.S. companies frequently do business.

Canada

America's largest trading partner, Canada is slightly more formal, reserved and conservative than the U.S. Thus a polite, professional tone is appropriate, with last names used at least initially. Meetings proceed as they do in the U.S., conducted with direct discussion and oriented towards results. Still, decision-making often takes longer in Canada, and the number of players may be smaller than in America because Canada has only one-tenth the total U.S. population.

One advantage of conducting business in Canada is that language differences are minimal, since Canadians pick up. U.S. slang from American television. Note, however, that Canada is officially bilingual, so package copy, for example, must appear in both English and French.

Your business card should also be bilingual if your dealings take you to Quebec.

Western Europe

Europeans are far more reserved, formal and hierarchical than Americans and Canadians. Last names and organizational or academic titles ("Doctor Halbritter") are used, and punctuality is a must, except in Greece and Spain. In addition, there is an insistence on proper decorum; no hands in pockets, no slouching or gum-chewing, no legs on furniture, no casual gossip or personal chitchat. Business cards are unfailingly exchanged. In Germany, another unspoken rule is to walk respectfully to the left of senior officers.

Meetings are for presenting and coordinating information, not for roundtable discussion. Emphasis is placed on exhaustively analytical, number-filled planning documents and reports—involving far more information and intensely detailed discussion than Americans are used to. Business people are sized up by their analytical competence, so participants come to meetings fully prepared and would never present an unsolved problem to colleagues without a tentative solution and plenty of data to support it.

Nevertheless, off-the-record meetings are also important. And business is often accomplished within a hidden hierarchy, which outsiders can identify only by watching and listening for subtle clues as to who is in charge.

There are, of course, exceptions to this business profile. For example, many Italian companies run on a family model with an autocratic, patriarchal leader whose subordinates implement his decisions. Here the real work sessions, and an outsider's best route of approach, are informal meetings with these subordinates, who will pave the way to the company head.

Asia

Politeness and patience are the keys to conducting business in Asia. Punctuality, use of last names (except in Thailand) and titles, respect for age and position, deference to others in the sense of letting them enter a room or sit down first, correct posture and comportment, and exquisite manners are all part of Asian business etiquette.

continued

There is also great concern that nobody "lose face." As a result, negative responses are phrased in roundabout, tactful, face-saving ways and public criticism of anyone—even gentle, joking comments—is strictly avoided.

Business dealings may take months or even years, largely because business commitments are viewed as long-term, if not lifetime, relationships. They are relationships of harmony and mutual trust built gradually through social conversations, numerous social activities, and private exchanges of executive gifts. (Liquor, fine pens, and tasteful logo-imprinted items are good choices.) They are relationships which begin with social talk that may continue over the course of several or more meetings before any business is even broached.

And they are relationships advanced through behaviors that demonstrate trustworthiness: concise and thoughtful speech, reflective silences before speaking, a less logical and more intuitive viewpoint, modesty combined with resolute personal strength and loyalty to one's team above oneself.

Asians are extremely wary of instant and pat overly logical answers. More important, they distrust "I'm my own man" statements and will exploit group disunity, particularly when individuals seem willing to break with their team for personal gain. Asians themselves traditionally work collectively and may discuss a proposal together for more than a year—then give little ground on the elaborately group-refined positions they bring to a meeting

In Asia, a business relationship is far more important than any contact developed within it. To promote this relationship, Asians tend to be flexible about changes requested after a contract is signed. In contrast, Americans, who equate business not with relationships but with contracts, will give little ground at this point.

Likewise, Asians rely less on contracts and more on the painstakingly detailed verbal agreements worked out in meetings. So American companies should keep their paperwork simple and consult their lawyers in private to avoid any semblance of using legalese to circumvent these unbreachable agreements.

Finally, Asians are uncomfortable when age and high rank do not correspond. They them-selves appoint highly placed younger colleagues as "liaisons". or " advisors,". outside the hierarchical line-up, to avoid having young people outrank their elders. Similarly, U.S. companies do well in Asia by giving their young top managers an honorary title and making an older person the apparent officer in charge.

Mexico

Mexican companies, though considerably less formal than Asian ones, maintain conservative business decorum and traditional business values. Last names are used along with professional titles ("Architect Rodrigues"), and respect is paid to the person in charge. Moreover, Mexicans judge others not only on their business qualities, such as reliable follow-through on promises, but also on individual qualities such as personal presence and concern for children, family and education. Punctuality is relaxed in Mexican business etiquette. While people try to be on time, Mexico City's heavy traffic, for example, may delay meetings for an hour or more.

Mexican business relationships include somewhat more socializing than in the U.S. Meetings begin with social conversation and get down to business more slowly than Americans are used to. As the relationship progresses along both social and business lines, Mexican business people look for assuring signs of not only the quality of a product but, more important, the solidity of a company. Fortunately, U.S. companies already have a reputation for efficiency, pragmatism and dependability. This reputation helps to excuse Americans' shortcuts on etiquette, such as their impatience to start talking business, and advances the cause of new U.S. companies entering the Mexican market.

Furthermore, because Mexican firms are familiar with many U.S. companies, able to research new ones easily, and predisposed to work with American enterprises, business can be concluded efficiently and fairly rapidly to the satisfaction of all concerned.

Keep in mind that Mexican business people may sometimes, in the enthusiasm of the occasion, intend more than reality can allow and set delivery dates or numbers that will later have to be modified. Flexibility in this regard is essential.

BIBLIOGRAPHY

The international marketing bibliography is an especially prepared summation of sources—bibliographies, directories, marketing guides, sources of demographic data, and key periodicals. They should be valuable to course participants seeking data for their research projects.

International Marketing Bibliography

Judith A. Truelson.   *Dr. Judith A. Truelson is Director of the Crocker Business and Accounting Libraries, University of Southern California.*

Bibliographies

Ball, Sarah. *The Directory of International Sources of Business Information.* London: Pitman; Philadelphia: Distributed by Trans-Atlantic Publications, 1989.

With an emphasis on organizations and databases, covers business information sources with primary focus on companies, markets, finance, securities and economics; appendices include directories of publishers of market research reports and database hosts and producers.

Multinational Enterprise: An Encyclopedic Dictionary of Concepts and Terms. Compiled by Ankie Hoogvelt with Anthony G. Puxty. New York: Nichols Pub., 1987.

Clearly defines theoretical and technical terms drawn from accounting, management, marketing and related fields; also contains an index of terms grouped under 13 broad categories, including international marketing.

Weekly, James K. *Information for International Marketing: An Annotated Guide to Sources.* (Bibliographies and Indexes in Economics and Economic History, No. 3) New York: Greenwood, 1986.

Lists and briefly annotates more than 190 government publications, databases, periodical and basic reference sources. Appendixes present brief directory listings for publishers, state trade contacts, U.S. foreign service offices in foreign countries, foreign embassies in the U.S., the U.S. International Trade Administration, and international marketing journals.

Directories

American Export Register. New York: Thomas International Publishing Co. Annual.

Includes an alphabetical product list as well as lists of U.S. and foreign embassies and consulates, Chambers of Commerce, world trade center clubs, U.S. and world ports, and banks.

Judith A. Truelson, Director, U.S.C. Crocker Business and Accounting Libraries.

565

Directory of American Firms Operating in Foreign Countries. 12th ed. New York: World Trade Academy Press, 1991.

Alphabetically lists U.S. firms with foreign subsidiaries and affiliates operating in over 125 countries; also lists the foreign operations grouped by countries.

Arpan, Jeffrey S. *Directory of Foreign Manufacturers in the United States.* 4th ed. Atlanta: Publishing Services Division, College of Business Administration, Georgia State University, 1990.

Lists nearly 6,000 foreign-owned manufacturing firms in the U.S.

Directory of United States Exporters. New York: Journal of Commerce. Annual.

Lists U.S. exporters/importers with an alphabetical listing of exported products with their Harmonized Commodity Codes, and information on important customs regulations and procedures.

Directory of World Markets. Waltham, MA: World Economic Development Congress and DRI/McGraw-Hill, Annual.

Contains market analysis and power structure analysis for the largest nations in the world, based on gross product ranking.

Directory of the World's Largest Service Companies. New York: Moody's Investors Service and United Nations Centre on Transnational Corporations. Annual.

Offers a detailed description of more than 200 firms in 14 alphabetically arranged industry categories, including industry rankings and profiles.

Duns Europa. High Wycombe, England: Dun and Bradstreet Europe. Annual.

Lists the largest companies in all 12 European Community countries, Austria, and Switzerland, arranged by country then alphabetically by company name.

European Directory of Trade and Business Journals. London: Euromonitor, 1990.

Lists and describes more than 2,000 major European journals concerned with Western European markets and industries.

Export Yellow Pages. Washington, DC: Delphos International; produced in cooperation with the Office of Export Trading Company Affairs and International Trade Administration; also available through *National Trade Data Bank.* Annual.

Provides detailed information on over 12,000 export service providers and trading companies, agents, distributors and companies outside the U.S.; also includes a product/service index and an alphabetical index.

International Brands and Their Companies. Detroit: Gale, 1990– . Annual.

Lists nearly 65,000 international consumer brand names attributed to 15,000 manufacturers, importers, and distributors, giving for each brand a description of the product, company name, and a code for the source from which the information was taken.

International Companies and Their Brands. Detroit: Gale, 1990– . Annual.

Lists 15,000 manufacturers, importers and distributors and the brand names attributed to them, giving for each company the firm's address and telephone number and an alphabetical listing of its trade names.

International Directory of Corporate Affiliations. Skokie, IL: National Register Publishing Co. Semi-annual.

Contains listings for 5,612 parent companies doing business worldwide; listings are divided into two sections: non-U.S. parent companies and U.S. parent companies.

International Directory of Importers. Healdsburg, CA: Interdata. Annual.

Contains classified listings of worldwide importing firms, as well as special sections containing detailed company information covering geographical regions of the world, including North America, South/Central America and Asia/Pacific.

International Tradeshow. Frankfurt: m+a Publishers for Fairs, Exhibitions and Conventions Ltd. Semi-annual.

Contains detailed information on global trade fairs and exhibitions which are of national and international significance.

Principal International Businesses. Parsippany, NJ: Dun's Marketing Services. Annual.

Covers approximately 55,000 companies in 140 countries, listing businesses by product classification and alphabetically.

Worldwide Franchise Directory. Detroit: Gale. Irregular.

Provides information concerning some 1,574 franchising companies in 16 countries, arranged by type of business in more than 80 categories.

Marketing Guides

Exporters' Encyclopaedia. Parsippany, NJ: Dun and Bradstreet Information Services. Annual.

Comprehensive world marketing guide, in five sections; section two, "Export Markets," gives important market information for specific countries (import and exchange regulations, shipping services, communications data, postal information, currency, banks, and embassies); other sections contain general export information.

International Business Handbook. New York: Haworth Press, 1990.

Includes a global overview as well as separate chapters on 15 countries or regions, covering such topics as consumer cultures, business customs, methods of entry, and global strategies.

Japan Marketing Handbook. London: Euromonitor, 1988.

Analyzes Japan's economy and major industries and the Japanese consumer market and discusses doing business in Japan, with coverage from the mid-1980s through the rest of the 20th century; also contains a directory of government and government-related bodies, importers' associations, market research and consultancy firms, and newspapers.

Overseas Business Reports. Washington, DC: U.S. Department of Commerce, International Trade Administration; distributed by the Superintendent of Documents, U.S. Government Printing Office. Irregular.

Reports on industry trends, foreign trade, banks and credit, trade regulations, and market policies for over 100 countries.

Pacific Rim Almanac. New York: HarperCollins Publishers, 1991.

Includes such topics as marketing, trade, money, ecology and environment and the infrastructure; also lists the PacRim top 500 companies, Pacific Rim trade organizations, world trade centers, embassies in the United States, research organizations and universities, and regional publications.

Van Horn, Mike. *Pacific Rim Trade: The Definitive Guide to Exporting and Investment.* New York: AMACOM, 1988.

Reports on trading opportunities, choosing markets, exporting, trade barriers, and financing; includes profiles of the Pacific Rim countries.

Reference Book for World Traders: A Guide for Exporters and Importers. Jericho, NY: Croner Publications. Looseleaf.

Provides information required for market research and for planning and executing exports and imports to and from all foreign countries; under each country provides listing of services to exporters and importers, including marketing research organizations, marketing publications, and custom brokers.

U.S. Custom House Guide. Philadelphia, PA: North American Pub. Co.. Annual.

Provides a comprehensive guide to importing, including seven main sections: import how-to, ports, directory of services, tariff schedules (Harmonized Tariff Schedules of the U.S.), special and administrative provisions, custom regulations, and samples of import documents.

Demographic Data

Asian Market Atlas. Hong Kong: Business International, 1991.

Contains a wide range of data on macro and micro economies in graphic form.

Canadian Markets. Toronto: Financial Post Information Service, 1926– . Annual.

Contains demographic, economic, and consumer sales data for Canada, its provinces, census metropolitan areas, divisions and subdivisions. Other sections contain rankings, estimates, and projections of population, retail sales, and personal income.

Consumer Europe. London: Euromonitor, 1976– . Irregular.

Provides demographic data on computer products for the major countries of Europe, Eastern Europe, totals for the European Community, and comparison between the European Community, Japan, and the U.S.

National Trade Data Bank [CD-ROM file]. Washington, DC: U.S. Department of Commerce, Economics and Statistics Administration, Office of Business Analysis. Monthly.

Contains information on economic and demographic conditions in over 250 countries, market research reports from the United States and Foreign Commercial Service, plus exports and imports data from the Census Bureau. The *Foreign Traders Index* can be used to identify potential trading partners.

PTS International Forecasts [computer file]. Cleveland, OH: Predicasts, 1972– .

> Machine-readable version of *Worldcasts* which combines the forecasts contained in the product and regional sections of *Worldcasts* with the added advantage of monthly updates. Updated monthly, available online on Data-Star and DIALOG.

Trade Inflo. Rockville, MD: Trade Inflo. Irregular.

> Series of reports which examine state's or industry's activity in the international marketplace; "State Export Report" provides two-digit SIC level data for the agriculture, mining, and manufacturing industries, including state exports by port, country of destination by industry, and value of shipments by state and by industry.

Worldcasts. Cleveland, OH: Predicasts. Quarterly.

> Compiles forecasts on products, markets, industry and economic aggregates as reported by experts in the trade and business press; forecasts are grouped by SIC code; forecasts are arranged by product number and by country; print version of *PTS International Forecasts.*

Periodical Indexes

ABI/Inform [computer file and CD-ROM]. Louisville, KY: UMI/Data Courier. Weekly.

> Indexes and abstracts articles from some 800 business and management periodicals published worldwide. More than half the journals are indexed cover-to-cover, the others selectively. Abstracts are about 200 words long; available online on DIALOG, ORBIT, BRS, VU/TEXT, Data-Star, NEXIS, Dial Com, Human Resource Information Network and in CD-ROM as ABI/INFORM **ondisc.**

Predicasts F & S Europe [print file, computer file and CD-ROM]. Foster City, CA: Predicasts. Monthly.

> Covers company, product, and industry information for the European Community (Common Market), Scandinavia, other regions in Western Europe, the USSR, and East European countries in financial publications, business-oriented newspapers, trade magazines and special reports; available online on DIALOG, ORBIT, BRS, VU/TEXT, Data-Star, NEXIS, Dial Com, Human Resource Information Network and in CD-ROM as *Predicasts F & S International.* Abstracts in the computer file and on CD-ROM vary in length from 400 to 600 words and contain full text for many shorter articles.

Predicasts F & S International [print file, computer file and CD-ROM]. Foster City, CA: Predicasts. Monthly.

> Covers company, product, and industry information for Canada, Latin America, Africa, the Mideast, Asia, and Oceania in financial publications, business-oriented newspapers, trade magazines and special reports; available online on DIALOG, ORBIT, BRS, VU/TEXT, Data-Star, NEXIS, Dial Com, Human Resource Information Network and in CD-ROM as *Predicasts F & S International.* Abstracts in the computer file and on CD-ROM vary in length from 400 to 600 words and contain full text for many shorter articles.

Periodicals

Business International Publications on International Business Trends. *Business Asia, Business China, Business Eastern Europe, Business Europe, Business International, Business Latin America, China Hand,* and *Investing Licensing and Trading Abroad.* New York: Business International. Biweekly or monthly.

Reports issued for each title provide current news about companies, products, markets, and recent developments in laws and practices.

East Asian Business Intelligence. Washington, DC: International Executive Reports. Biweekly.

Provides sales and contracting opportunities for East Asian countries, including a brief description of the business opportunity, the person to contact, address, plus phone and fax numbers.

Marketing in Europe. London: Economist Intelligence Unit. Monthly.

Contains detailed studies of markets for consumer products in France, Germany, Italy, Belgium, and the Netherlands, including food, drink, tobacco, clothing, furniture, leisure goods, chemists' goods, household goods, and domestic appliances.

PART SEVEN

SELECTED CASES

This section includes six in-depth cases about actual firms and products: the SWATCH Watch, the Roots Shoe, Club Med, Cuisinart, Nestlé, and Euro Disney. The firms are all companies that course participants will recognize, and several of them have an entrepreneurial flavor. The final citation is an especially prepared interna-tional simulation, Siberian Petroleum Production Association. It provides the opportunity for interactive negotiations by participant teams. These cases offer the possibility of team or individual analysis of the problems and opportunities the companies faced.

The SWATCH Project

Susan W. Nye and Barbara Priovolos.

"This watch is the product which will reintroduce Switzerland to the low and middle price market. It is the first step of our campaign to regain dominance of the world watch industry," said Dr. Ernst Thomke, President of ETA SA, a subsidiary of Asuag and Switzerland's largest watch company. Ernst Thomke had made this confident declaration about SWATCH to Franz Sprecher, Project Marketing Consultant, in late spring 1981. Sprecher had accepted a consulting assignment to help ETA launch the watch, which was, at that time, still in the handmade prototype phase and as yet unnamed. This new watch would come in a variety of colored plastic cases and bracelets with an analog face. ETA had designed an entire production process exclusively for SWATCH. This new process was completely automated and built the quartz movement directly into the watch case. Sprecher's key concern was how to determine a viable proposal for moving this remarkable new product from the factory in Grenchen, Switzerland into the hands of consumers all over the world.

Company Background: ETA, Ebauches and Asuag

SWATCH was only one brand within a large consortium of holding companies and manufacturing units controlled by Allgemeine Schweizer Uhrenindustrie (Asuag, or General Company of Swiss Watchmaking). SWATCH was to be produced by ETA, a movement manufacturer, which was part of Ebauches SA, the subsidiary company overseeing watch movement production within the Asuag organization (Exhibits 1 and 2).

Asuag was founded in 1931 when the Swiss government orchestrated the consolidation of a wide variety of small watchmakers. The major purpose of this consolidation was to begin rationalization of a highly fragmented, but vital, industry suffering the

This case was prepared by Susan W. Nye and Barbara Priovolos under the direction of Visiting Professor Jean-Pierre Jeannet as a basis for class discussion rather than to illustrate either effective or ineffective handling of an administrative situation. Copyright © 1985 by IMEDE, Lausanne, Switzerland. The International Institute for Management Development (IMD), resulting from the merger between IMEDE, Lausanne, and IMI, Geneva, acquires and retains all rights. Not to be used or reproduced without written permission from IMD, Lausanne, Switzerland.

EXHIBIT 1   Asuag Organization

Subsidiaries	Movements	Components	Industr. Components Equip./Measure Tools/Services
Ebauches SA, Neuchatel (ESA)	x	x	x
ETA, Fabriques d'Ebauches SA, Grenchen	x	x	
Les Fabriques d'Assortiments Reunies SA,			
Le Locle (FAR)		x	x
Nivarox SA, La Chaux-de-Fonds (NIV)		x	x
Pierres Holding SA, Bienne (PH)		x	x
General Watch Co. Ltd., Bienne	x	x	x
Eterna SA, Grenchen			
Eterna	x	x	
Compagnie des Montres Longines,			
Francillon SA, St. Imier			
Longines	x	x	x
Montres Rado SA, Longeau			
Rado	x	x	
Mido, G. Schaeren & Co. SA, Bienne			
Mido	x	x	
Fabrique de Montres Rotary SA,			
La Chaux-de-Fonds			
Rotary		x	
Era Watch Co. Ltd., Bienne			
Edox	x		
Certina, Kurth Frères SA, Grenchen			
Certina	x	x	
Gunzinger SA, Fabrique d'Horlogerie			
Technos, Bienne			
Technos		x	
Endura SA, Bienne			
Microma, Dynasty	x		
Diantus Watch SA, Castel San Pietro			
Dafnis, Diantus	x		
Oris Watch Co. SA, Hölstein			
Oris	x	x	x

Number of employees at the end of December 1980 by subsidiary:

Industries	Switzerland	Abroad	Total
Ebauches SA	6739	719	7458
Fabriques d'Assortiments Reunies SA	1573	39	1612
Nivarox SA	383	—	383
Pierres Holding SA	880	571	1451
Societe du Produit Termine (GWC, ARSA et ATLANTIC)	2733	435	3168
ASU Components SA/Statek Corp.	194	978	1172
DG Asuag, Asam SA, Asulab SA	330	—	330
Total:	12832	2742	15574

EXHIBIT 2   Summary of Financial Activity for Asuag (In Million Swiss Francs)

Asuag Group/31 December	1972	1973	1974	1975	1976	1977	1978	1979	1980
Consolidated sales	1081	1264	1404	1073	1041	1169	1195	1212	1332
Number of employees	19350	19720	20230	17205	15725	16351	16195	15289	15574
Current assets	696	761	878	786	786	813	782	761	788
Long-term assets	263	272	287	309	319	341	338	324	390
Debt	443	479	589	542	418	483	552	580	680
Equity	1352	1384	1436	1372	1364	1352	1063	998	979

	1980/1981 Francs	1979/1980 Francs
Income Statement		
Dividends from subsidiaries	4,507,001.65	4,938,768.43
Remittances from affiliates	14,225,219.10	10,604,457.95
Interest income	9,910,303.23	10,517,844.92
	28,642,523.98	26,061,071.30
Expenses		
General administrative costs	6,296,053.53	5,404,093.33
Research and development	1,809,858.13	2,050,212.05
Information and promotion	3,550,406.81	3,943,119.75
Taxes	692,994.85	698,932.00
Amortization	2,539,096.00	1,622,761.80
Interest paid	8,985,565.05	7,872,187.46
Profit	4,768,549.61	4,469.764.91
	28,642,523.98	26,061,071.30

Companies or Groups of Companies	Sales 1st Half 1981 Francs Millions	Difference 1st Half 1981/1980	Sales 1980 Francs Millions	Difference 1980/1979
Sales Development of Affiliated Companies				
Ebauches SA	389.2	+ 18.7%	670.7	+ 16.2%
Fabriques d'Assortiments Reunies SA	61.0	+ 4.4%	109.8	+ 9.9%
Nivarox SA	13.3	− 2.8%	25.8	+ 4.1%
Pierres Holding SA	38.4	+ 11.1%	66.8	+ 4.1%
Soc. du Produit Termine (GWC, ARSA, Atlantic)	282.1	+ 23.2%	569.9	+ 6.7%
ASU Components SA, Statek Corp.	39.8	+ 31.4%	62.4	+ 44.4%

effects of one world war and a global depression. By 1981 Asuag had become the largest Swiss producer of watches and watch components. Asuag was the third largest watch-maker in the world behind two Japanese firms, Seiko and Citizen. Asuag had a total of 14,499 employees, 83 percent of whom worked within Switzerland. Asuag accounted for about one third of all Swiss watch exports, which were estimated at Sfr. [Swiss francs] 3.1 billion in 1980.[1] Major activities were movement manufacture and watch assembly. Bracelets, cases, dials and crystals were sourced from independent suppliers.

Ebauches SA, a wholly owned subsidiary of Asuag, controlled the various move-ment manufacturers. The Swiss government played an important role in encouraging and

---

[1]US$ = SFR 2.00/1 SFR = US $0.50

funding Ebauches' formation in 1932. An "Ebauche" was the base upon which the movement was built and Ebauches companies produced almost all of the movements used in watches produced by Asuag group companies. Sixty-five percent of Ebauches production was used by Asuag group companies, and the rest was sold to other Swiss watch manufacturers. Ebauches SA recorded sales of Sfr. 675.0 million in 1980, a 3.1 percent increase over the previous year. Ebauches companies employed a total of 6,860 people, 90 percent of them in Switzerland.

ETA SA, the manufacturer of SWATCH, produced a full range of watch movements and was known as the creator of the ultra-thin movements used in expensive watches. The quality of ETA movements was so renowned that some watches were marked with "ETA Swiss Quartz" as well as the name brand. ETA movements were distributed on a virtual quota basis to a select group of watch manufacturers. The demand for its movements had always equalled or exceeded its production capacity. In 1980 ETA employed over 2000 people and produced more than 14 million watch movements for revenues of approximately Sfr. 362 million and profits of about Sfr. 20 million.

Dr. Ernst Thomke had joined ETA as president in 1978. Early in his career, he had worked as an apprentice in production at ETA. He left the watch industry to pursue university degrees in chemistry and cancer research, earning both a Ph.D. and a medical degree. He then moved on to a career in research at British-owned Beecham Pharmaceutical. Thomke did not stay in the lab for long. He moved into the marketing department where he boosted Beecham sales with ski trips and concerts for physicians and their families. His unorthodox selling techniques led to skyrocketing sales. He looked for a new challenge when faced with a transfer to another country. His colleagues at Asuag and throughout the watch industry described Thomke as a tough negotiator and as iron willed. After joining ETA he agreed to provide advertising and support allowances to movement customers. However, these agreements stated that ETA only provided aid if it had a role in product planning and strategy formulation.

The Global Watch Industry

To understand the global watch industry three key variables were considered: watch technology, watch price and the watch's country of origin.

Watch Movement Technology

Watch design underwent a revolutionary change in the early 1970's when traditional mechanical movement technology was replaced with electronics. A mechanical watch's energy source came from a tightened mainspring which was wound by the user. As the spring unwound it drove a series of gears to which the watch hands were attached: the hands moved around the analog (or numerical) face of the watch to indicate the time. Highly skilled workers were required to produce and assemble the movements in accurate mechanical watches and the Swiss were world renowned in this area.

The first electronic watch was built by a Swiss engineer, Max Hetzel, in 1954, but it was U.S. and Japanese companies that first commercialized electronic technology. Bulova, a U.S. company, was the first to bring an electronic watch to market in the early

1960's, based upon tuning-fork technology. A vibrating tuning-fork stimulated the gear movements and moved the hands on a traditional analog face. At the end of the decade, quartz crystal technology began to appear in the market place. An electric current was passed through a quartz crystal to stimulate high frequency vibration. This oscillation could be converted to precise time increments with a step motor. Quartz technology was used to drive the hands on traditional analog watches and led to an innovation: digital displays. Digital watches had no moving parts and the conventional face and hands were replaced with digital readouts. Electronic watches revolutionized the industry because for the first time consumers could purchase an inexpensive watch with accuracy within 1 second per day or less.

Ebauches owned companies had been involved in electronic watch technology since its pioneering stages. In 1962, Ebauches was among a number of Swiss component manufacturers and watch assembly firms which established the "Centre Electronique Horlogère" (CEH). The center's immediate goal had been to develop a movement which could compete with Bulova's tuning-fork movement. CEH was never able to successfully produce a tuning-fork movement which did not violate Bulova's patents. In 1968 Ebauches entered into a licensing agreement with Bulova to manufacture and sell watches using Bulova's tuning-fork technology. In 1969 CEH introduced its first quartz crystal models and Ebauches subsequently took over manufacture and marketing for the new movement, introducing its first quartz line in 1972.

Ebauches also worked with the U.S. electronics firm Texas Instruments and FASEC[2] in the early 1970's to pursue integrated circuit and display technology. By 1973 Ebauches was producing movements or watches for three generations of electronic technology: tuning-fork, quartz analog and digital. Ebauches did not stay in the assembled watch market for long, and returned to its first mission of producing and supplying watch movements to Asuag companies. Between 1974 and 1980 the Swiss watch industry as a whole spent Sfr. 1 billion towards investment in new technology and Asuag accounted for half the expenditure. Ebauches Electronique on Lake Neuchâtel was a major use of investment funds and was created to produce electronic components.

Price

Price was the traditional means of segmenting the watch market into three categories. "AA" and "A" watches were sold at prices above Sfr. 1200 and accounted for 42 percent of the total value of watches sold and 2 percent of total volume. "B" watches priced at Sfr. 120–1200 made up 25 percent of the market in value and 12 percent in units. "C" watches were priced under Sfr. 120 and accounted for 33 percent of the market in value and 86 percent of total units.

Players in the Global Watch Industry

Japan, Hong Kong and Switzerland together accounted for almost 75 percent of total world watch production. In 1980 watch producers worldwide were faced with inventory

---

[2]FASEC was a laboratory for joint research in semiconductors, integrated circuits and lasers. It was formed in 1966 by the Swiss Watch Federation (FHS), Brown Boveri, Landis & Gyr and Philips of the Netherlands.

buildups at factory warehouses and retail stores. A worldwide recession had slowed demand for watches and overproduction compounded the problem. 1980 projections were not being met, and factory-based price cutting, particularly by large producers, was becoming common as a substitute for production cuts.

The Swiss Watch Industry

The Swiss watchmakers' position was viewed by many industry observers as being more precarious than others. Since 1970, when the Swiss accounted for 80 percent, their share of the world watch market in units had declined to 25 percent of the world's watch exports. The Swiss ranked third in unit production but remained first in the value of watches sold. Twenty-five percent of all Swiss watch factories were permanently shut down during the 1970's and 30,000 workers lost their jobs.

Despite extensive factory and company shut-downs within the Swiss industry, in 1981 the Swiss still owned the rights to 10,000 registered brand names, although less than 3,000 were actively marketed. Most Swiss watches were priced in the mid- to expensive price ranges, above Sfr. 100 ex-factory and Sfr. 400 retail. In 1981, industry analysts were congratulating the Swiss for their adherence to the upper price segments, as the low-price segments were beginning to turn weak. Industry observers noted that the Swiss seemed to be emerging from a decade of uncertainty and confusion and were focusing on higher quality segments of the watch market. Swiss component manufacturers had been supplying their inexpensive components to Far East assemblers and it was felt that this practice would continue.

Swiss watch manufacturers generally fell into one of three categories. First, there were the well established, privately owned companies which produced expensive, handmade watches. These firms included Rolex, Patek-Philippe, Vacheron Constantin, Audemars-Piguet and Piaget. For the most part, these firms were in good health financially. Stressing high quality as the key selling point, these manufacturers maintained tight control through vertical integration of the entire production and marketing processes from movement and component production through assembly and out into the market. The recession had cost them some customers, but these had been replaced by new Middle Eastern clients.

Second, there were a number of relatively small privately owned companies that concentrated on watch components—bracelets, crystals, faces, hands or movements. This group included an ETA competitor, Ronda SA. The financial health of these companies was mixed.

The third sector of the industry were the largest participants. Asuag and Société Suisse pour l'Industrie Horlogère (SSIH). SSIH was an organization similar to but smaller than Asuag, producing 10 percent of all Swiss watch and movements output. Its most famous brand, Omega, had for years been synonymous with high quality. Omega had recently run into trouble and had been surpassed by the Asuag brand Rado as Switzerland's best selling watch. In June 1981, SSIH announced a loss of Sfr. 142 million for the fiscal year ending March 31, 1981. This loss gave SSIH a negative net worth of Sfr. 27.4 million. A consortium of Swiss banks and the Zurich trading group Siber Hegner & Co., AG, were brought together to save the company.

In the late 1970's Asuag and SSIH began working in a cooperative effort to cut costs through the use of common components. However, this effort did not affect individual brand identities or brand names. Industry analysts did not rule out the eventual possibility of a full merger. Asuag was noted for its strength in production and quality, but was reported to have a weakness in the marketing function. SSIH was noted for strong marketing skills, but had recently been faced with a slippage in product quality. It was believed that both companies would stand to gain from closer ties in research and production.

The watch industry played a significant role in Switzerland's economy. The banks and the government took a serious interest in its operations and the performance of individual companies. Between 1934 and 1971 the Swiss government made it illegal to open, enlarge, transform or transfer any watch manufacturing plant without government permission. This action was justified as a defensive move to combat potential unemployment due to foreign competition. It was also illegal to export watch components and watch making technology without a government issued permit. The government essentially froze the industry by dictating both prices and the supplier-manufacturer relationship. These constraints were gradually removed, beginning in 1971, and by 1981 were no longer in effect.

The Japanese Watch Industry

Japan was the world's second largest watch producer in 1980 with approximately 67.5 million pieces, up from 12.2 million pieces in 1970. The growth of the watch industry in Japan was attributed to the Japanese watchmakers' ability to commercialize the electronic watch. K. Hattori, which marketed the Seiko, Alba and Pulsar brands, was Japan's largest watchmaker, and responsible for approximately 42 million units. Selling under 3 different brand names allowed Hattori to compete across a broad price range. Seiko watches fell into the "B" category. Alba and Pulsar competed in the "C" range.

Casio entered the watch market in 1975 selling low cost digital watches. Philip Thwaites, the U.K. marketing manager, described Casio as follows: "Casio's strategy is simple, we aim to win market share by cutting prices to the bone." Casio's product line was exclusively digital. The company was noted for adding "gadgetry" to its watches, such as timers, stop watches and calculators. In Casio's view the watch was no longer just a time piece but a "wrist instrument."

In contrast to Switzerland, Japan's "big 3" watch producers: the Hattori group, Casio and Citizen, had a combined product line of fewer than 12 brands. All three firms were fully integrated: producing movements, most components, assembling and distributing worldwide through wholly owned distribution subsidiaries. These watchmakers made extensive use of automated equipment and assembly line production techniques.

The Watch Industry in Hong Kong

Hong Kong manufacturers had only entered the market in 1976 but by 1980 unit output had reached 126 million units. Ten major producers accounted for an estimated 70 percent of total volume. Watch design costs were minimized by copying Swiss and Japanese products. As many as 800 "loft workshops" were in operation in the late

1970's. These facilities could be started at low cost and ran with minimum overheads. The expanded capacity led to the rapid fall of Hong Kong watch prices; prices of simple watches in the Sfr. 15–20 range in 1978 and dropped to Sfr. 10 the next year with margins of less than Sfr. 1. Hong Kong watches were sold under private label in minimum lot sizes of 1000–2000 units with average ex-factory costs of Sfr. 20 for mechanical watches and Sfr. 50 for quartz analog and Sfr. 10 for electronic digitals. Most watchmaking activity in Hong Kong was concentrated on assembly. The colony had become Switzerland's largest client for watch components and movements. Swiss movement exports to Hong Kong had grown from 13.3 million pieces in 1977 to 38.5 million pieces in 1980.

The "Popularius" Project

The SWATCH project began under the code name "Popularius." Thomke's goal had been to discover what the market wanted and then to supply it. He told his engineers that he wanted a plastic, analog watch that could be produced at less than Sfr. 10 and sold ex-factory at Sfr. 15. He also wanted to use the technology which ETA had developed for its high priced, ultra-thin "Delirium" movements to enter the low priced watch segment. Thomke was convinced that ETA's long term viability and profitability depended on increasing the company's volume and integrating downstream into fully assembled watch production and marketing. Thomke had seen the demand for ETA movements dwindle when exports of finished Swiss watches declined from 48 million pieces in 1970 to 28.5 million in 1980. The mass market "C" watch all but disappeared from Swiss production and was replaced by inexpensive Japanese and Hong Kong models. The Swiss manufacturers pushed their products up-market and sales value of exports moved from Sfr. 2,383.7 million in 1970 to Sfr. 3,106.7 million in 1980.

With electronic technology, movements were no longer a major cost factor in the end price of a watch. The average price of an ETA movement was Sfr. 18 and applied whether the watch sold ex-factory at Sfr. 80 or Sfr. 500. Thomke wanted to increase ETA volume output and knew that Asuag transfer pricing policies made this difficult. Asuag was a loose consortium of companies, each operating as an independent profit center. Transfer pricing reflected this fact. At each point of production and sales: movements, components, assembly and through the distribution channels, a profit was taken by the individual unit. Thomke believed that this system weakened the Swiss brands' competitive position for the volume business which his movement business needed to be profitable. Thomke believed that if he wanted to introduce a successful new product, he would need to sell it to 1 percent of the world's population, which amounted to about 10 percent of the "C" market segment. He knew that the Japanese companies were fully integrated and that Hong Kong assemblers, which already operated with low overheads, were moving increasingly towards full integration (Exhibit 3).

Thomke knew he could turn over the "Popularius" project to another Asuag unit, but he did not have a great deal of confidence in the production and marketing capabilities of Asuag branded watch assemblers. ETA was the only company within the Asuag group which had extensive experience in automated manufacturing. If the "Popu-

EXHIBIT 3   Breakdown of Costs and Margins for Traditional "B" Watches (By Country of Origin)

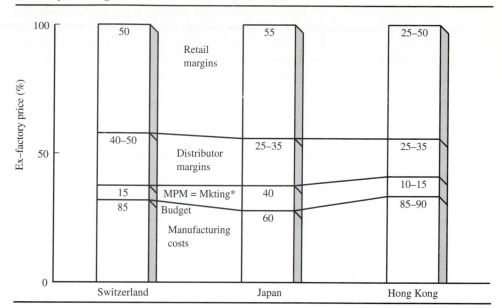

*Manufacturing and profit margins.

EXHIBIT 4   Comparison of Ebauches SA Sales to World Market

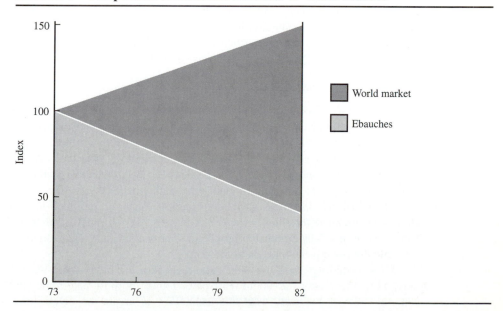

larius" was to succeed as the latest entry in the low price market, it would have to be produced in an automated environment. Furthermore, Thomke had watched many of the finished watch companies steadily lose market share to Japanese and Hong Kong competitors over the last decade and he had little confidence in their marketing capabilities. ETA currently sold 65 percent of its output to Asuag companies and Thomke wanted to reduce this dependence. He planned to use the "Popularius" as ETA's own entry into the finished watch market (Exhibit 4).

ETA engineers and technicians, responding to Thomke's specifications, developed the "Popularius." To meet the low unit ex-factory price was no small accomplishment. A cost analysis at that time showed that the required components without assembly would have cost Sfr. 20. Quartz technology provided accuracy within one second per day, and the watch was waterproof, shock resistant and powered by a readily available and inexpensive 3 year battery. The watch weighed 20 grams and was 8 mm thick with an analog face. The face and strap were made of durable mat finished plastic and the strap was attached with a special hinge that was flush with the face. It was considered stylish and attractive. Further aesthetic enhancements could be made with the careful selection of color and face design. Ultrasonic welding produced a finished product which would not be reopened after it left the assembly line. In the event of failure, designers believed that the watch was essentially unrepairable and would be replaced rather than repaired. Batteries were replaceable by the owner and inserted in the back of the watch.

The product line was, at that time, limited to one size, a large "man's" watch, which could be produced in a number of solid colors with several designs or patterns on the face. Although a 25 percent smaller version for women and children was being considered, no definite introduction plans had as yet been developed. Management believed that the young were a potentially strong secondary market for the new product. A number of ideas were in development for "novelty" watches with special functions, a button watch and special colors and motifs. A day/date calendar with a quick reset feature was available. The production system was designed for strict quality control conditions to produce highly reliable watches. The movement was designed with a theoretical life of 30 years and "Popularius" would be sold with a one year guarantee.

Manufacturing Systems for "Popularius"

The ability to produce and sell a watch with the "Popularius" features, for a low price, was largely dependent upon unique production technology developed at ETA. ETA's product development staff was respected throughout the watch industry for its technical abilities in mass production. Its production technology was considered by industry observers to be equal to that of the best Japanese companies. In the early stages of electronic movement production, even with high priced luxury movements, automated assembly was not only possible but a practical means of production. The production equipment planned for "Popularius" was entirely Swiss made, and would in its final form consist of a fully automated production line that consumed raw materials at one end and delivered complete watches at the other.

ETA technology built the movement right into the base of the watch and required only 51 parts versus the 90 to 150 parts found in most electronic and mechanical watches. ETA had already used this technology to create the "Delirium," the world's thinnest movement measuring .98 mm at its thickest point. These movements were used in high precision, luxury watches measuring 2.4 mm at their thickest point and selling at retail for Sfr. 40,000.

The "Popularius" production process and the equipment that made the technology possible were protected by seven patents. The ETA technical staff felt that it would be impossible for a competitor to duplicate "Popularius," especially at a low ex-factory price, because the watch was closely linked to its unique production process. ETA engineers had already invested nearly two years on this project, including the efforts of 200 employees and more than Sfr. 10 million in research and development funds.

Production was still limited to hand production of prototype watches and watches for test marketing purposes. ETA expected the line to have semi- but not full automation with forecasted production levels of 600,000 men's watches and 150,000 smaller versions for women or children in the first year. Fully automated lines which would produce 2 million units per year were targeted for the second year. Production goals of 3 million units had been set for the third year. Production quotas for later years had not yet been finalized. Management expressed the desire to reach production and sales levels of 5 million units after 3 years.

Initially it was expected that full unit cost could go as high as Sfr. 16. As volume increased, the per unit cost would drop and the full unit cost was expected to be less than Sfr. 10 at production levels of 5 million watches per annum. The project was not considered technically feasible at annual production levels below 5 million, and higher volume was expected to drive the unit price just below Sfr. 7. Asuag pricing and costing policy suggested that individual projects should reach contribution margins of 60 percent for marketing, sales and administrative expenses, fixed costs and profits. Each size model would require a separate production line. Within each line economic order runs were 10,000 units for each color and 2,000 units for each face style. Maximum annual production per line was 2 million units and the initial cost of installing a line was Sfr. 5 million, including engineering costs of Sfr. 2 million. Additional assembly lines could be installed at an estimated cost of Sfr. 3 million. Production costs included depreciation of this equipment over 4 years. The equipment occupied space which was already available and no additional real estate investments were expected.

ETA had applied for special financing packages with local authorities. No response had as yet been received. However, obtaining the necessary financing was not viewed as a problem.

Initial plans suggested a marketing budget of Sfr. 5 per unit. The brand was expected to break even in the third year and begin earning profits for ETA in the fourth year. Per unit marketing costs were expected to decline as volume increased. Decisions as to how the budgeted marketing funds would be distributed had not been finalized. It was expected that they would be divided between ETA and its distributors, but on what basis and how the "campaigns" would be coordinated could not be decided until distribution agreements had been finalized. Thomke was a firm believer in joint ventures and wanted to develop 50/50 relationships with distributors.

Still to be decided were questions of packaging, advertising, production line composition and distribution. Packaging alternatives centered around who should do it. ETA needed to decide if the product would leave the factory prepackaged and ready to hang or display, or shipped in bulk and packaged by the distributor or retailer or even sold "as is." Advertising budgets and campaigns had not been finalized. The size of the budgets and the question of whether or not advertising costs would be shared between ETA and the distributors were still open. The advertising agencies had not yet been chosen and no media decisions had been finalized.

Distributing "Popularius"

Sprecher felt that distribution was the most important and problematic of the issues still outstanding. Discussions at ETA on developing an introduction strategy were confined to five industrial markets. Although it was not as yet definitive, the emerging consensus seemed to be that distribution would begin in Switzerland, the U.S., the U.K., France and West Germany. Distribution in Japan, other industrialized countries and certain developing countries was also being discussed for a later date.

Market and Country Selection

A major motivation in choosing the target entry markets would be the probability of gaining high volume sales and meeting Thomke's goal of selling a watch to 1 percent of the world population. The U.S. would be an important market for "Popularius" success. It was the world's single largest watch market and success with a product in the U.S. often signaled global success. Thomke planned to keep the watch priced below $30 in the U.S. Germany and the U.K. were significantly large in terms of population, but could be difficult markets to enter because they were known to be particularly price sensitive. Germany was also noted as being particularly slow in accepting new innovations in consumer goods. Switzerland was chosen because it was the home market. ETA management assumed that their next move would be into Canada and the rest of Europe. If ETA decided to enter Japan and the LCDs, management would have some special considerations. Japan would be a particularly difficult market to crack because almost all "B" and "C" class watches sold in Japan were produced domestically. Furthermore, Sprecher had heard that Seiko was considering plans for introducing a new quartz analog watch which would be priced under Sfr. 50. The LCDs of Africa and Latin America provided ETA with opportunities for volume sales. Sprecher expected that consumers in these markets would use price as the only criterion for choosing a watch. Selling the "Popularius" to LCDs would put ETA in competition with the Hong Kong producers' inexpensive digital watches.

Selecting Distributing Organizations

Within each market there was a range of distribution alternatives. But a fundamental need was a central marketing, sales and distribution unit within ETA with sole responsibility for "Popularius." However, at that time, there was no marketing or sales department within the ETA organization. ETA's products, watch movements, had always been distributed to a select and consistent group of users. Distribution at ETA had essentially been a question of arranging "best way" shipping, letters of credit and insurance. The

FIGURE 1

Projected marketing costs and profits for SWATCH

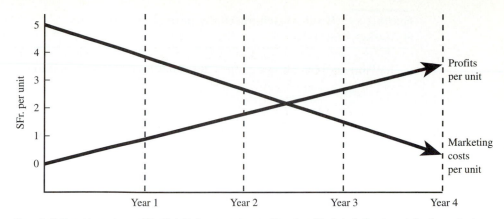

Per unit: Full cost to produce = SFr. 10 (with long range target of less than SFr. 7, including depreciation for production machinery). Ex-factory price = SFr. 15. Contribution margin for marketing costs and profit = SFr. 5.

annual cost of establishing a central marketing division within ETA was estimated at Sfr. 1–1.5 million. This figure would cover management and administrative salaries for a marketing manager, regional managers, product managers, service, sales planning and advertising and promotion planning. Sprecher believed that 8 to 10 people would be required for adequate staffing of the department. Furthermore, he estimated that wholly owned subsidiaries in any of the major target markets could be staffed and run at a similar cost.

Contracting individual, independent marketing organizations in each country and then coordinating the marketing, sales and distribution from the Grenchen office would, Sprecher believed, allow ETA to retain a much greater degree of control over the product. He felt that this type of organization would allow ETA to enter the market slowly and to learn about it gradually without having to relinquish control.

Following Thomke's suggestion, throughout the summer of 1981 Sprecher took a number of trips to the U.S. to determine possible solutions to this and other marketing problems. Sprecher's agenda included visits to a number of distributors, advertising agencies and retail stores. Sprecher completed his investigation with visits to some of the multinational advertising agencies' Zurich offices. Sprecher made his rounds with a maquette which he described as an "ugly, little black strap." The "Popularius" prototype still had a number of bugs to iron out and Sprecher could only make promises of the variety of colors and patterns which were planned.

The U.S. would be essential to "Popularius" success because it was the world's largest watch market. Thomke and Sprecher also believed that the U.S. market would be more open to this new idea and felt they would gain the best advice from U.S. distributors and advertising agencies (Exhibits 5A to 5D).

Retailer and Wholesaler Reactions

Sprecher began his first U.S. trip with a visit to Zales Corporation. The Zales organization included both a large jewelry and watch wholesale business and a chain of jewelry

EXHIBIT 5A   Retail Watch Purchases in the U.S. (Summary of Market Research)

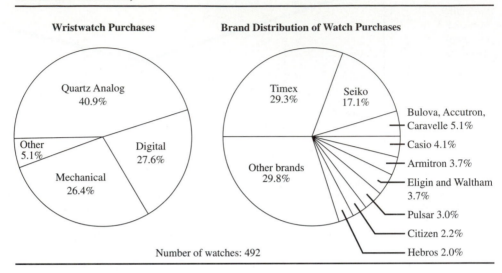

Wristwatch Purchases

- Quartz Analog 40.9%
- Digital 27.6%
- Mechanical 26.4%
- Other 5.1%

Brand Distribution of Watch Purchases

- Timex 29.3%
- Seiko 17.1%
- Other brands 29.8%
- Bulova, Accutron, Caravelle 5.1%
- Casio 4.1%
- Armitron 3.7%
- Eligin and Waltham 3.7%
- Pulsar 3.0%
- Citizen 2.2%
- Hebros 2.0%

Number of watches: 492

stores. Sprecher met with a high level marketing manager who responded positively to the product, but said that Zales could not seriously consider it at this early stage. He invited Sprecher to return when the project was further along. Zales management did advise Sprecher that if ETA decided to go ahead with the project and start production and sales, then "do it right." Doing it "right" meant heavy spending on advertising, point-of-purchase displays, merchandising and aggressive pricing.

Sprecher also paid a visit to Gluck and Company. Gluck was a jewelry, watch and accessory wholesaler operating in the low price end of the market. An aggressive trader, Gluck operated mainly on price and much of its business involved single lots or short term arrangements to catalogue and discount houses. Gluck executives told Sprecher that they did not believe in advertising, but relied on low prices to push goods through the distribution chain and into the hands of the customer. If Gluck agreed to take on "Popularius" it would have to be sold with a retail price of under Sfr. 40. Sprecher attempted to discuss the possibility of a long term relationship between ETA and Gluck, but the wholesaler did not appear particularly interested.

Sprecher's reception at Bulova's New York offices was very different from Gluck. Andrew Tisch's, president of the company, first reaction was that the "Popularius" should be packaged as a fashion watch. Tisch had had substantial experience in consumer goods marketing and believed that "Popularius" should be heavily advertised and promoted, suggesting a budget of Sfr. 20 million. He was sufficiently impressed with the project, and voiced some interest in establishing a separate company with ETA to market the watch.

EXHIBIT 5B   Watch Purchases by Retail Price (Sample Size = 465)

	% Quartz Analog	*% Digital*	*% Mechanical*
(Number of watches)	(200)	(135)	(130)
Price Categories			
$1,000 or more	.5	.7	1.5
$300 to $999	4.0	.7	1.5
$100 to $299	38.0	8.9	14.6
$50 to $99	33.5	31.9	35.4
$30 to $49	24.0	57.8	47.0

46.6 percent of all watches are purchased on sale or discount.

EXHIBIT 5C   Retail Watch Purchases in the U.S.
(Watch Purchases by Outlet Type [Sample Size = 485])

	% Watches (All)	*% Analog Quartz*	*% Digital*
(Number of items)	(485)	(198)	(134)
Jewelry store	27.6	34.3	12.0
Department store	26.2	26.3 ·	27.6
Discount store	16.7	14.7	23.1
Catalog showroom	10.3	14.7	10.4
Mail order	5.4		11.2
Wholesaler	2.1		1.5
Drug store	5.1		6.0
Flea market	0.4		
Other outlets	6.2		7.5

EXHIBIT 5D   Distribution of Watch and Jewelry Purchase Prices by Age of Purchaser

	18–24 Yrs	*25–34 Yrs*	*35–54 Yrs*	*55 and Over*
(Number of customers)	(150)	(419)	(821)	(431)
$25 to $49	39.4%	39.6%	35.7%	32.3%
$50 to $99				
$100 to $299	20.7%	24.8%	25.3%	28.5%
$300 to $999	27.3%	25.3%	26.7%	27.6%
$1,000 or more	11.3%	8.8%	9.0%	10.4%

Considering OEM Arrangements

Sprecher was concerned that he might be taking a "hit-or-miss" approach to his investigation and decided to pay a visit to Arthur Young and Company. Arthur Young was among the largest accounting firms in the world, one of the "Big Eight," and was noted for its industry analysis and consulting. Sprecher visited Arthur Young to see if their consultants might have some suggestions on potential partners for ETA. The accounting firm put together a proposal on how to attack the problem of finding a distribution partner. Sprecher was well aware that his investigation was still incomplete, and he returned to Switzerland with the Arthur Young proposal to work out a new agenda of visits.

Included in the Arthur Young proposal was the possibility of turning all marketing responsibilities of "Popularius" over to an independent company. Sprecher investigated this possibility and entered into negotiations with two well-known multinational consumer good companies: Timex and Duracell. Both of these companies had their own extensive and established distribution channels. ETA executives believed that an agreement with either of these two firms might provide "Popularius" with a virtual guarantee of high volume sales due to the extensive and intensive marketing resources at both.

The Duracell Proposal

Duracell produced and distributed high quality batteries worldwide and was interested in becoming the exclusive distributor of "Popularius." Contact was initiated with the U.S. battery company's general manager in Zurich and followed up with a visit at Duracell's U.S. headquarters. The company had a distribution system in place which covered the entire globe. Duracell batteries were sold through drug stores, supermarkets and hardware stores. Duracell made batteries for watches as well and therefore had some contacts in the retail watch trade. The company employed an experienced and well trained sales force and had a wealth of marketing knowledge. Duracell had unused distribution capacity and its management was looking for extensions to the product line and felt that an electronic watch could be complementary to and a logical extension of Duracell batteries.

Sprecher felt that an agreement with Duracell could be interesting but was concerned that ETA was being relegated to the role of product supplier with little or no impact on marketing decisions. Duracell wanted to establish itself in an original equipment manufacture relationship with ETA. Duracell would buy the watch from ETA and then control the product's marketing strategy. ETA would be supplying the product, the product's name and some marketing funds, but would be left out of most mass marketing decisions. Furthermore, while Duracell continued to express interest, they were proceeding at what ETA executives considered to be a snail's pace. In late summer, Duracell management informed ETA that they were continuing their evaluation of "Popularius" as a product and that their investigation of its potential market was still incomplete.

The Timex Organization

Timex was known for producing durable, inexpensive watches. The U.S.–based company had become famous in the late 1950's and 1960's for circumventing traditional watch outlets, jewelry stores and distributing through mass outlets such as drug, department and hardware stores and even cigar stands. At its peak, Timex had sold watches through an estimated 2.5 million retail outlets. In 1982 Timex had an estimated 100,000 to 150,000 worldwide. Timex and ETA were considering the possibility of ETA production of a limited range of watches under the Timex name. The Timex "Popularius" would be produced in black with a different, but ETA approved, design. The hinge which attached the plastic strap to the watch case would be different and "Swiss Made" would not be stamped on the face. Timex was willing to guarantee a minimum annual order of 600,000 units, at Sfr. 10 ex-factory price.

Sprecher knew that ETA executives considered private label production as a viable option which could be implemented in either the introductory phase of distribution or later when the brand was well established. However, they felt that the Timex arrangement had some drawbacks. First, they perceived the Timex organization as somewhat stodgy and bureaucratic and ETA executives were unsure as to how close a working relationship they could establish with Timex management. Second, Timex seemed to want "Popularius" for "nothing." Sprecher did not think that they could keep "Popularius" to a Sfr. 50 retail price and gain a profit in the Timex agreement. Sprecher considered the Timex distribution system very costly. Sprecher estimated that Timex watches were distributed with a retail price of 4 to 4.5 times the ex-factory watch price. ETA wanted to maintain a 3 to 3.5 ex-factory ratio. Sprecher believed that the Timex system was costly because it used a direct sales force as well as two middlemen (distributor and broker) to get watches into the retail store. Finally, ETA management was also concerned with Timex's most recent performance. The company had been steadily losing market share.

Positioning Options

Towards the end of his second trip to the States, Sprecher hit upon the "perfect" name for the new product—SWATCH. He had arranged to spend two weeks with the advertising agency Lintas SSC&B to work on developing a possible product and advertising strategy. This arrangement initiated a quasi-partnership between the two firms; Lintas invested its time and talent in the "Popularius" project and would receive payment later if they were to get the advertising account.

Lintas had been influenced by their work with another client, Monet, a producer of costume jewelry. Monet supported its products with heavy point of sale promotion activities. Lintas believed that this kind of promotion would be beneficial to "Popularius."

Lintas saw a number of positioning options for the "Popularius," a (new) Swiss watch, a second watch, an activity watch, a fashion watch or a combination of images. The agency had suggested approaching the "Popularius" positioning with a combination of a fashion and sports image while emphasizing the watch's Swiss origin. The copy staff was excited about stressing the Swiss watch concept and the contraction S'watches was repeated throughout their notes. Sprecher looked at the abbreviation and was struck by the idea of taking it one step further to SWATCH and the "Popularius" finally had a name.

Considering Direct Mail

Back in Switzerland, Sprecher continued interviewing advertising agencies. He visited the Zurich office of McCann-Erickson, a large multinational advertising agency, to discuss advertising strategy and to look into the mail order market. McCann-Erickson made an investigation of the mail order market for the SWATCH in West Germany. The purpose of this study was to demonstrate what a mail-order approach might accomplish for SWATCH.

McCann-Erickson's proposal suggested using mail order as an initial entry strategy for SWATCH. This arrangement would later be expanded into a mail-order business through specialized companies with a full range of watches and jewelry. Target group would be young men and women between 20 and 29 years as well as people who "stay young." The target group would be motivated and interested in fashion, pop culture, and modern style.

To achieve sufficient penetration of the target market, which the agency estimated at 12.5 million, advertising support of about Sfr. 1 million would have to be spent. Orders were estimated anywhere from 50,000 units to 190,000. This estimate included volume of 4,500 to 18,000 for a test market, with total advertising costs of about Sfr. 150,000. The effort would be organized in two waves, one in spring and a second in the fall.

Additional costs to be considered were mailing at Sfr. 2.50 per unit sold as well as an unknown amount for coupon handling. Furthermore, experience indicated that about 10 percent of all orders would not be paid.

Considering an Exclusive Distributorship

Zales had suggested that Sprecher contact Ben Hammond, a former Seiko distributor for the southwestern region of the U.S. Sprecher was unable to make this contact, but Thomke followed up on this lead on a separate visit to the U.S. in late summer. Ben Hammond, president of Bhamco, was interested in the exclusive distribution rights for North America for SWATCH and a second Asuag brand, Certina. Bhamco was a gem stone firm and Hammond had been in the jewelry and watch business in the southwest for several years. Up until the recent past he had been the southwest distributor for Seiko. Hammond reported that he and Seiko had had a falling out when the Japanese manufacturer opened a parallel distribution system, selling its watches through new distributors to mass merchandise and discounters in direct competition to its traditional outlets and "exclusive" distributors. He proposed to start a new company, Swiss Watch Distribution Center (SWDC), and wanted an agreement for three years. Hammond was very enthusiastic about the SWATCH and told Thomke that he could "sell it by the ton." Hammond projected first year sales of 500,000 units growing to 1.2 million and 1.8–2 million in years two and three and then leveling off at 2.5 million.

Hammond felt that the watch should be positioned as a fashion item and sold through jewelry and fine department stores. He believed that a heavy advertising and point of sale budget would be important to gaining large volume sales and felt that a Sfr. 5 per watch was a reasonable figure. Furthermore, after his experience at Seiko, he promised a careful monitoring of consumer take-off and a close relationship with retail buyers to avoid discounting and to give service support. Based in Texas, Hammond had substantial financial backing from a group of wealthy investors. He planned to begin initial efforts in the southwest and then promised to spread rapidly to all major U.S. cities and Canada.

Next Week's Meeting

Thomke had just returned from the U.S. and briefed Sprecher on his meeting with Ben Hammond. Thomke was anxious to get moving on the project and planned to make a proposal to Pierre Renggli, the president of Asuag, in mid-September, less than three weeks away. At the end of the briefing they had scheduled a strategy planning session for the next week to evaluate his information and to prepare his proposals for Thomke in preparation for their final presentation to Renggli. Sprecher knew that Thomke expected to receive approval for ETA production and marketing of SWATCH at that presentation. Sprecher knew that his proposals to Thomke needed to be operationally feasible, and with target launch date of 1 January 1982, available implementation time was short. Sprecher knew that they could pursue negotiations with some of the companies which he had visited or "go it alone" with a direct sales force. Sprecher needed to balance the economic restraints which required minimum annual sales volume of 5 million with Thomke's desire to keep strategic control of the product within ETA. Sprecher needed to consider ETA's lack of marketing experience and what that would mean in the international marketplace.

Discussion Issues

1. The case cites a range of possible distributor alternatives. Which should be selected for the SWATCH launch in the United States?
2. Do you prefer another distribution mode in preference to those summarized in the case? If so, explain. If not, why not?

Roots in Europe

Frederick E. Webster, Jr.

On an overcast day in February 1978, Mr. Alan Jackson sat in his office overlooking the Lake of Geneva, in Geneva, Switzerland, and commented to his visitor, "Our business has reached a critical stage but I'll have to take a somewhat roundabout route to bring you to the point where you can understand my problem. Let me tell you the story of the Roots Shoe and how I came to be where I am today." What follows is Jackson's narrative:

Anna Kelso and the Earth Shoe

The 1978 story of Roots really begins almost 20 years ago in Copenhagen, Denmark, with a woman named Anna Kelso. She was a health enthusiast, a yoga practitioner, into health foods, and very much given to developing her body and doing the things which she thought made for a natural type of living. She noticed in her deep breathing exercises that it was important to tilt her pelvis and to hold her body in a certain way in order to get maximum breath. She also noticed that if she stood on the floor and put a book or other item underneath the front of her feet so that the balls of her feet were slightly elevated, it changed her pelvic position and she felt that this improved her deep breathing. Then on long walks in the country on soft ground and particularly on the hard-packed beach, she noticed as she walked along that her heels came down first and took the impact and then she rolled off the side of her feet and across the ball of her foot and off her toes, and she looked back on the imprint and saw that the heel left the deepest impression.

Working these ideas through in her mind, Anna Kelso came up with a wooden sandal in which the foot was placed so that the heel was lower. Now this made it rather awkward to walk since the wooden sandal didn't bend, so she developed a little rocker front end so that the whole wooden sandal could pivot forward. Slowly the concept of a sandal developed into a shoe which she felt allowed the wearer to walk in a natural way. It had a sole with a deeply recessed heel (which she called a "negative" heel) and a high arch support. It also had the rocker front end so that without bending the sole itself you could have a natural swing forward. She went to a few small craftsmen who made shoes in rather primitive ways and had them make up shoes along these designs.

Anna Kelso called her shoe design the Earth Shoe. She began to sell them in a little shop in the central part of Copenhagen. In order to keep the "natural" feeling, she decorated with lots of plants and rather rough-hewn natural wood. She put pebbles and sand in the window to emphasize the naturalness of walking on the beach. She talked about it being the best way to stand and walk and how it changed your stance. And for almost 20 years, nobody ever heard of Anna Kelso and her Earth Shoe except a few fanatics in and around Copenhagen. These were people who were into deep breathing exercises, yoga, meditation, vegetarian eating, health foods, etc. But for the population at large, even in Copenhagen, not very many people had heard of Anna Kelso.

The Earth Shoe Introduced in the United States

Sometime about 1969, an American photographer, Ray Jacobs, and his wife were in Copenhagen and, as the story goes, Mrs. Jacobs suffered from some kind of back ailment and wasn't feeling very well, Apparently, they met in Copenhagen someone who told them about the Anna Kelso Earth Shoe and decided at least to try a pair. After purchasing them, they continued along their way in their trip throughout Europe. Two weeks later, Mrs. Jacobs' backache was gone. They rushed back to Copenhagen, according to the story, and ended up negotiating North American rights to import and distribute the Anna Kelso Earth Shoe. Just like Anna Kelso, Ray Jacobs was not a retail sales oriented person. He simply duplicated in New York City what Anna Kelso had in Copenhagen. He picked a site in a low-rent district, not a very commercial area, and duplicated her kind of store—a store in a location that didn't have a lot of walk-by traffic. He furnished the store with rather rough-hewn furniture and put pebbles and sand in the window. He had these rather crudely made shoes with the negative heel. He had the health charts showing the spine straightening out and gave the Anna Kelso story. He opened that store in 1970. There was no effort to do much advertising; no effort to do much in the way of public or press relations. Nevertheless, in 1970, a few of the North American health fanatics (we might even say "health nuts") slowly began to find their way to his New York store. Three years later, it's our understanding there were three stores then opened by Ray Jacobs: the original one in New York City, another in Cambridge, Massachusetts, and the third in Ann Arbor, Michigan.

Any American who wore a tie in 1972 would most probably not have heard of Anna Kelso and the Earth Shoe. The only people who had by this time become familiar and adopted the shoe were truly the counterculture—those who had turned their backs on the so-called American materialism and had been looking for nature. They found in Anna Kelso and the background of the Earth Shoe a new meaning, a return to nature, the natural way to walk, the simple way to dress. Soon they were standing in line waiting for the next shipment to come in from Copenhagen.

In addition to the real counterculture and nature nuts, there were those university students and faculty that somewhat envied the counterculture but weren't prepared to make the entire change. They became familiar with this Earth Shoe phenomenon though it still had received no notice in the mainstream press. There still was practically no advertising. The Earth Shoe was, after three years in North America, a practically unknown item except for the counterculture group and the university campuses.

Don Green and Michael Budman in Toronto

In Toronto, at that same time, were living two young men from the Detroit area, Don Green and Michael Budman. Don was 23 years old and Michael 27. Michael had graduated from Michigan State University in Lansing and had gone to live in Toronto; Don had attended the university but not graduated. They had lived at the same place in Lansing. The two boys had known each other since childhood, and attended the same camp in Ontario, Canada, had lived in the same area, gone to the same high school, and, despite the four years' difference in age, knew each other well. They had not done anything of a commercial nature and were really just hanging out in Toronto. Michael was working at a few odd jobs to earn some money. They occasionally visited family and friends in Detroit, and on one of those trips back home in 1972, they visited friends in Ann Arbor and were introduced to the Anna Kelso Earth Shoe.

At that time, it took some effort to become accustomed to the shoe. The negative heel was at a very severe angle, the arch support was very high, and for most people accustomed to wearing normal heeled shoes or even flat-soled shoes, there was quite a period of adjustment. The stretching of heel cord tendons and muscles and the adaptation of the arch all required some time, and it was only upon the encouragement of those who had already gone through the process that many people continued to persevere and wear the shoes until their bodies adapted. It took Don and Michael several weeks before they could wear the Earth Shoe for long periods of time, but after that period of adjustment, they really were converts. They felt the shoe was something not commercial; it was something worthwhile, it was back to nature. Since they liked the whole scene, they thought it would be nice if they could have a small store in Toronto similar to the one in Ann Arbor, where they could busy themselves with something meaningful—they could sell the Earth Shoe in Canada.

With this in mind, they contacted Ray Jacobs, and thus began a whole series of "lucky" circumstances that resulted in today's Roots Shoe and the company Natural Footwear Limited. The first result of the contact was Ray Jacobs' refusal to grant them exclusive distribution rights in Canada. It was really rather presumptuous of these two young men to approach Ray Jacobs and ask for the total Canadian rights to the Earth Shoe. Of course he wasn't going to grant that. They then tried to negotiate rights for Toronto with an option on the rest of Canada if this proved successful. Then began a long series of negotiations into which Don's father, a very successful businessman, was called to help. After considerable time, Don and Michael came to the conclusion that it would be impossible to develop a meaningful relationship with Ray Jacobs and his Earth Shoe.

By this time, late 1972, the Earth Shoe had been on the North American market for a full three years. Don and Michael came to the conclusion that they could just as easily have a similar shoe manufactured locally in Toronto and equip the store themselves and sell it under a different name. The rejection by Ray Jacobs was their first bit of luck. The second bit of luck was when they went through the Yellow Pages of the Toronto telephone book looking for someone or some company to manufacture the shoes. Obviously, they could not go to a very large manufacturer because the quantities involved for one little store wouldn't justify it. Looking through the Yellow Pages of the telephone directory, they located the Boa Shoe Company and the Kowalewski family. The Boa Shoe Company consisted of John Kowalewski, a Polish immigrant whose father had made boots for the officers of Czar Nicholas II, and his four sons, who were, essentially, handmaking snakeskin shoes primarily for the Florida tourist trade. When Don and Michael showed John Kowalewski and his sons the recessed heel (or negative heel-type shoe), the first reaction of the Kowalewskis was that it was a very cheaply made, low-quality shoe. Construction details had been ignored, and materials weren't of the best quality. The manufacturing details were primitive; in fact, they were designed to be primitive by Mrs. Kelso and had not been improved over the years that she had been manufacturing.

John Kowalewski indicated that if he was going to be involved, he would want to make a quality shoe. He would like to look for the best quality leathers. He wanted double stitching where it was required. He felt they had to have counters in the heel to support the shoe over a long period of time. When Don and Michael talked with him about the long period of adaptation because of the severe angle, he reached the conclusion that the arch support was too high and was placed too far back. Thus began a period of examining the Anna Kelso Earth Shoe to modify its construction both from a quality standpoint as well as from a functional standpoint in order to make it a more readily usable, more beneficial shoe. (See Exhibit 1.)

The next bit of luck was the discovery of Robert Burns. Robert Burns was an Englishman who had come to Canada and set up his own design and graphics shop. Working with Robert, the group came up with company logos, company brochures, and descriptive material that was definitely of an international standard in quality and design and gave a corporate image considerably more sophisticated than that of the Earth Shoe Company. Looking for a trade name, they wanted something close to nature. Knocking around ideas with friends one evening, a girlfriend came up with the name Roots, meaning roots in the sense of the foundation of life. So with the name Roots and with Robert Burns' graphics, they began to develop a corporate image that could appeal to a wide cross-section of the population.

Graphics and a name, of course, aren't enough, so a fourth piece of luck came along when Robert Burns introduced them to a Welshman who had also immigrated to Canada and had a flair for writing. He was a copywriter and editorialist, and his name was David Perry. David Perry's subtly sophisticated, deceptively simple language fit very nicely with the image that they were trying to create. It blended nicely with the natural feeling of the product and with Robert Burns' graphics.

Their luck in finding people at this critical time continued when they met Fred Kondo, a Japanese Canadian who was a master woodworker. He made fine furniture and agreed to equip the stores with a style of fixtures manufactured out of polished oak and in keeping with the Earth Shoe concept. At the same time, they met Renny Delessing, an

EXHIBIT 1   The Roots Shoe

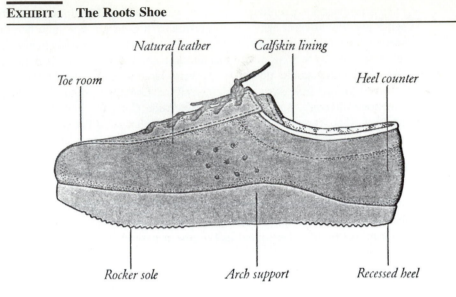

interior architect with a good grasp for space. And so in a very short time in this dynamic city of Toronto, they stumbled across, built up, and put together a creative team. There were Don Green and Michael Budman, who by the refusal of Ray Jacobs were thrown into the necessity of creating their own company. By chance they stumbled across these Polish immigrants John Kowalewski and his four sons, who just happened to be master shoemakers in the Old World tradition and were able to create from the original Earth concept a better quality product.

The first Roots store in North America opened in Toronto on August 15, 1973. It followed the tradition established by Anna Kelso and Ray Jacobs in New York City almost four years earlier, but it was definitely a higher quality presentation because of the contributions of these talented people in the areas of shoemaking, graphic arts, writing, and design.

Growth beyond Toronto

The results were more than anyone expected. A couple of weeks after opening the store, with a little bit of advertising display in the city buses, the blue jean-wearing, semi-counterculture crowd of Toronto went for the Roots recessed heel shoes in a big way. Sales were more than either Don or Michael had ever dreamed of, and of course, this was quickly transmitted to their families. Don's father had a neighbor who was in the shoe business and operated several retail shoe stores in the Detroit area. Upon hearing the boasting of Don's father, the neighbor agreed to visit Toronto and look at the operation. That look was enough to persuade him to open a new Roots store in the Detroit area. Shortly thereafter, in early 1974, a Roots franchise outlet was opened in Birmingham, Michigan, by another neighbor of Green's father. Green also had a brother in San Francisco, who decided that because Don was having so much success, he would also open a store; thus, San Francisco was activated. Michael Budman's brother, who resided in Los Angeles, hopped onto the bandwagon. Therefore, in early 1974, the Roots operations had spread from Toronto to Detroit, San Francisco, and Los Angeles.

Simultaneously, the Earth group began to grant franchises to outsiders. As a result, by the spring of 1974, the countercultural devotees, the nature enthusiasts, the vegetarians, and the yoga people were beginning to hear about the recessed heel, or the negative heel shoe, with the Earth Shoe best known but Roots coming along fast.

Don's father, Irwin Green, had, 10 years earlier, entered a joint venture in Western Europe with another young man from Detroit, Alan Jackson. I had been living in Geneva, Switzerland, since 1957 and had been involved as a consultant primarily in international operations between Europe and the United States, with an emphasis on market development. I had, in fact, developed a European market for the products of a factory owned by Irwin Green, and the developments of that market led to a three-way venture in which those products were manufactured in Italy. The manufacturing facility was owned jointly by Irwin Green, myself, and an Italian businessman. Irwin Green sold out of the venture about 1970 but remained in close contact with me. Thus, I was kept informed of Don's development of the shoe business. In 1973, when production was first started, I was asked to provide some assistance in expediting the delivery from Europe of molds for soles.

The Situation in Europe

In the spring of 1974, Irwin Green suggested that perhaps I might be interested in helping Don actually get established in Western Europe. After studying the possibilities, Don and Michael and I agreed on a joint venture for the development of the European market for Roots. That development was to take the form of setting up test stores in some of the leading European cities—the first in Munich and the second in Amsterdam.

By mid-1974, the Earth Shoe and the Roots shoe were in full international development, and the basic product concept was gaining favor with the public. In the United States, Earth Shoe and Roots franchises increased rapidly. By the spring of 1975, there were experimental Roots stores in Munich and Amsterdam, about 14 Roots stores across Canada and the United States, and roughly 30 to 40 Earth Shoe stores across the United States. And that was just the beginning.

The activity developed differently in North America than in Europe for a number of reasons. The first is that neither Ray Jacobs, for Earth, nor Don Green and Michael Budman, for Roots, had had any previous marketing experience, whereas in Western Europe, we had been consulting for many large international companies in many kinds of business activities. Therefore, I had somewhat more working experience and training in both general business practices and the very special field of new market development.

Another reason for the difference was that Earth became a generic term in North America—it was *the* negative heel shoe, it was *the* recessed heel shoe, it was first in the marketplace, and it expanded most rapidly. Earth was the leader. In this way it was able to sell, at a relatively high price, a product that was not of the highest quality but had the magic of its introductory name. Roots, on the other hand, sold its products at the same price as Earth but had a product that was superior, presented in an atmosphere that was of a higher quality, and with advertising and promotional material that showed outstanding design and creativity. The competitive race was on. The product concept caught on in the United States as a fad, and neither Earth nor Roots could obtain enough shoes to satisfy their market. Earth bought manufacturing facilities in New England and began manufacturing on its own, while Roots bought out the Kowalewskis, took over the Boa Shoe Company, and expanded its manufacturing facilities.

The Growth Stage

It was an exciting time as stores opened and the market seemed endless. Inventory turnovers were exceptionally high, and profits were therefore also high. Drawn into the business as franchisees were people who were university graduates but who had no experience in the retail business; people who were quite intelligent, but who had no business training. Franchises were granted to people who were undercapitalized. They could make money during this period of huge demand, but had yet to face a difficult time.

By 1975, the national press began to take notice of Earth, and major magazines carried editorial comments. Earth began to spend money on national advertising and on public relations. It was an exciting period with booming sales. Looking back, a store located anywhere could sell whatever it could get. By mid-1975, there were about 40 Roots stores in North America and perhaps 60 or 80 Earth stores. Most significantly, middle-class America was taking notice. The negative heel Earth shoe was definitely a roaring success.

At the first meeting of all the Roots franchises and management, the Roots versus Earth situation was discussed. It was June 1975. Roots was not quite two years old in North America and only a few months into Europe.

Although they had virtually no consumer data or market analysis, Roots management believed that there were two different kinds of customers in this rush for the negative heel shoe. First, there were the Earth Shoe customers. These, according to Roots management, were the young blue jean-wearing kids, the real counterculture who were going into these rather seedy looking, rather neglected, rather rough Earth Shoe stores and buying the inflated priced, crudely made Earth Shoes. The second part of the market was the more affluent suburban middle-class consisting of somewhat older people looking for higher quality. This segment was more selective and willing to pay a higher price. They were the Roots customers.

With this in mind, Roots felt that they should direct their marketing approach towards the somewhat more affluent group. They selected a Madison Avenue advertising agency that had good experience in selective, upscale marketing—Lord, Geller, and

Frederico—who had accounts like Tiffany's and the *New Yorker* magazine. At the June 1975 meeting of the franchisees, Lord, Geller, and Frederico were presented as the latest word in promotion for Roots. It was announced that there would be a major fall 1975 advertising program in national media for the brand, including advertisements in major magazines, large newspaper display ads, television, and heavy promotion. And Lord, Geller, and Frederico were going to give Roots the image which Roots felt it had—that of the quality product, the well-designed recessed heel shoe which was head and shoulders above Earth in quality and function.

The program proved to be a fiasco. The ads were not effective, the media were wrong; too much money was spent. It was a failure. Some $250,000 to $300,000 was spent across the United States, but the spending was poorly planned and poorly managed. The expected increase of sales did not result, and the entire effort proved very distasteful to management. From that time on, there was no major national advertising in North America for Roots; there was no consistent program of introducing and maintaining the company's name and product to the public.

The year 1975 did, however, draw the attention of U.S. shoemakers to the roaring success of both Earth and Roots across the country. By the end of 1975, there were 40 or 50 Roots stores across North America and more than double that in Earth Shoes. The U.S. shoemaking industry couldn't ignore this trend, and so 40 to 50 U.S. manufacturers introduced copies. Some of them actually did have recessed or negative heels, while others only looked like they had. Fortunately for both Earth and Roots, these manufacturers felt that the product was overpriced. So all of the copies, whether Florsheim at the higher end of the range or Thom McAn at the lower, entered with shoes (called Terra Firma, Nature Shoe, the Natural Shoe, and so on) priced one third to one half that of the Earth or the Roots shoe. The copies were introduced as fashion items, put into conventional shoe stores, and sold as conventional shoes. They were displayed right along with the other casual and dressy shoes. There was nothing dramatically different about the way they were sold. It was just "this year's shoe." They did, in fact, become "this year's shoe;" there were an estimated 20 million pairs of recessed or negative heel-type shoe sold in North America in 1976. Of that 20 million, probably less than 5 percent (less than 1 million) were sold by Earth and Roots combined. Earth and Roots were the only ones selling the shoes in a distinctive atmosphere. They were the only ones that had specialized shoe stores selling only their products. All of the competing brands were sold as conventional shoes under conventional methods, but they were successful. Mr. and Mrs. Middle-class America and Middle-class America's children swept into the recessed heel shoe. It was in all the fashion magazines; it was in all the newspapers. Promotion was heavy. It was a roaring success.

At the same time, Roots had a very active public and press relations campaign. Unfortunately, practically all of it was devoted to the success story of the company, to the great growth the company was having, to the exciting personalities of Don Green and Michael Budman. Emphasis was not on the product. In 1976, both Earth and Roots began to feel the problems created by not having adequate local management and not being familiar with all of the tiny details necessary to manage retail stores and national distribution. Store site selection was one of the critical details that Roots management lacked familiarity with and which was to become a problem for them. Personnel supervision was another.

The European Situation

At the same time in Europe, things were developing differently. In 1975, three stores had been opened, Amsterdam, Munich, and Paris; early 1976 saw the opening of a second store in Holland in the Hague and a store in London. Sales in each of the five stores reached 80 to 100 pairs per week during the first year. Those stores all began to sell modestly and correctly, following the basic Roots concept. They all had advertising and promotion programs from day one, with heavy emphasis on press and public relations since the single stores couldn't afford much ordinary paid-for advertising. Contacts were made with physiotherapists, orthopedists, and nurses. We contacted people in the health area, who are on their feet during much of the day and who take care of their feet. We also contacted other professionals like models, photographers, and fashion people who also spend long days standing. We wanted to establish Roots as a healthy, fashionable shoe. We called these people on the telephone, wrote letters to them, demonstrated Roots, and let them test the shoe with no obligation. We wanted them talking about us. We also went to the press, especially journalists who write about fashion, sports, business, and outdoor life. We stressed that Roots was an exciting, new, healthy, fashionable concept. We told them about Roots and let them wear them. We didn't have money to spend, but we had the time to spend. There was an organized press relations activity and an organized direct-mail activity. Store site selections had been made with a great deal of care. Standard store operating procedures had been established. It was a relatively well-organized business. Furthermore, Roots was alone in the European marketplace; Earth was not active.

Market Maturity and Management Problems in North America

In North America, by the end of 1976, the craze for the Earth-type shoe was over. Earth and Roots were both in difficulty, and some of the things which they had been ignoring were beginning to show up. In the fall of 1975, there had been no national product advertising emphasizing the functional features of the product by Roots. Promotional material provided to the dealers did not emphasize the product's functions or its characteristics. There had been absolutely no contact by the factory with the field salespeople. There had been only the most minimal contact between the factory and the franchisees and the store managers. Roots owned and operated more than 20 of its own stores in the United States. There was no proper organization for that activity; none of the generally accepted techniques for management, motivation, or control were used. The people at Roots in Toronto were concerned with producing the product but not with contact in the field—not with organizing and managing their own stores or with the kinds of guidance and help that the franchisees required. It was a catastrophic situation producing shoes of better and better quality but not with the necessary marketing follow-through. At the same time they lost control of their accounts receivable, they also lost control of some of their production statistics, and sales began to fall.

Similar problems were developing with Earth. As a matter of fact, the Earth home office in New York was building up very sizable overhead, and by the end of 1976, they had more than 120 people in their central offices. There were about 120 stores, almost all of which were franchise Earth stores that never seemed to have on hand, ready for sale, the product styles that were selling. Back at the factory, however, and in the warehouse, there was a reported 250,000-pair inventory—always in the wrong style, the styles that weren't selling—whereas the stores were screaming for the shoes they could sell. It was a catastrophic situation for Earth.

In Europe, the success of the Roots stores continued; every store was profitable. Expansion was planned. The success was most prevalent in Holland where, at a very early date, the press had shown particular interest in the shoes and the Roots people were able to generate a favorable rapport with the press. Stories about the shoe constantly appeared in the Dutch press. This resulted in some interesting statistics. For example, the Amsterdam store averaged 104 pairs of shoes sold per week in its first year, 1975. It needed only about 60 pairs a week to break even. The 1976 sales were 194 pairs per week, so it was an exceptionally profitable store which encouraged some aggressive developments in Europe in 1977. These positive signs in Europe were to be compared with the devastation coming to North America.

By spring of 1977, both Earth and Roots were in disaster situations in the United States. The total mismanagement of the Earth Shoe Company resulted in the company's forced bankruptcy on March 4, 1977. Roots was somewhat different. The failure to pick proper sites and the failure to perform the functions necessary for the successful marketing of name brand products began to have disastrous results. However, back in the factory in Toronto, although acknowledging some of the management faults as well as the failure to promote and manage, the real reason for the North American failure was said to be the fickle public's attitude. The fad was over, management believed. The recessed heel shoe was dead as a fashion item in management's opinion, and a decision was made to go into other products. In spring of 1977, Toronto made the decision to produce other types of shoes with a normal raised heel and to change its image from that of a manufacturer of the quality recessed heel shoe to one of a manufacturer of quality comfortable casual shoes. A fall 1977 line was designed based on a wedge sole.

Market Growth Continues in Europe

In Western Europe, however, the emphasis was still along the conventional product line, and considerable expansion took place. First of all, the company opened a number of additional stores. Secondly, the company went into leased departments in major department stores, where it recreated within the department store the same kind of selling environment it had in its own stores including natural wood furniture, green plants, and very little product in a small but well-defined physical space. Well, success was immediate. In 1977, previous sales records were exceeded in all of the European stores and particularly in Holland. The Amsterdam sales figures were almost unbelievable. On Thursday nights when the stores were open for late shopping and on Saturdays, they had to close the door and let customers in only when customers came out.

What had happened was that, in 1975 and 1976, the European public was buying Roots primarily for its natural comfort feature. All the promotion emphasized the natural comfort. The company was careful to make no medical claim in its promotion but observed that most normal people seemed to feel less tired after a long day of standing or walking in Roots recessed heel shoes. That message, repeated over and over again, was accompanied by the secondary message of high-quality materials and high-quality Canadian craftsmanship. The European market in 1975 and 1976 was a cross-section of the European public in terms of age and economic status. What they all seemed to have in common was interest in foot comfort. Little old ladies were driven there by their chauffeurs; young athletes came in; fashion models came in—all kinds of people came in. Somewhere in that group of people must have been some young fashion trendsetters, perhaps from the Amsterdam and the Hague high schools, because by the spring of 1977, the Roots shoe became a *must* in the minds of young teenagers in Holland. Sales in the Amsterdam store, for example, that had been 104 pairs per week the first year and 194 the second year, shot up to 400, 500, and 600 pairs a week until they reached 700 pairs Easter week 1977. And they maintained astronomical levels—500 and 600 pairs per week well into the summer. It was at this point that we began opening leased departments in department stores.

By fall 1977, there were 10 outlets in Holland, 5 company stores and 5 leased stores, and sales were booming. During the second year, however, sales in London, Paris, and Munich had remained more or less constant, with problems developing in sales in those stores when inventories were not properly managed and orders were either not placed or not filled properly. This experience in England, France, and Germany emphasized the importance of attention to the details of inventory and store management. These conclusions combined with the tremendous success in the Netherlands convince me that our marketing strategy and the Roots concept were basically sound.

There were also rumors of competition coming as in North America, bringing in some of the cheap shoes that had been sold in the United States. Roots European management came to the decision that it was important to get additional outlets quickly, at least in Holland where the success was phenomenal. A Roots authorized dealer program was created. Rather than just let the product loose, as Florsheim and Thom McAn had done in the United States, the Roots authorized dealer program was established on the basis that there would be one or at least a limited number of authorized dealers in each major city, that the dealer who was selected would be furnished with a lot of marketing and merchandising assistance, and that he would be obligated to use it. For example, the shoes had to be displayed in a Roots corner or a Roots wall area. The basic display fixtures would be furnished at cost to the dealer, and he would be required to use them. The dealer was provided with a detailed program of training and other material. The program was announced to the Dutch retail industry in November 1977. Meetings were held in December to which potential dealers came and heard about the program in detail. In January 1977, 40 Dutch dealers were selected; the program actually opened, with tremendous success, on March 1, 1978.

The Turnaround in North America

In the meantime back in North America, Earth had gone bankrupt, the Roots organization in the United States had had to close about 20 dealers and about 25 of its own retail stores, had to write off as an unrecoupable loss perhaps a half a million dollars in accounts receivable, and had completely changed its marketing goal. In addition to developing its range of wedged shoes, it came out with a line of classic shoes with rubber soles and rubber heels and with styles somewhat reminiscent of the 1950s, along with some very new styles.

In March 1978, Natural Footwear Limited (the manufacturing arm of Roots) was able to offer the remaining Roots Company stores and franchises in Canada and the United States a truly outstanding line of casual footwear of high quality and high price, beginning with the original concept of the Roots recessed heel shoe, going on to a wedge, and continuing to a classic sole. However, the company was not able to offer its retail outlets any of the supporting material and assistance commonly required of successful name brand products. In fact, the owner-management of Natural Footwear had decided that it did not want to be directly involved in retail activities. They had successfully obtained as outlets Saks Fifth Avenue in the United States and the Eaton chain in Canada, and they were negotiating with Bloomingdale's in New York. Each of these retailers was expected to produce a significant portion of Roots' total sales. The feeling of the Toronto management of Natural Footwear was that they would be able to market directly to these major department store chains without the necessity and cost of providing a log of backup material and backup assistance.

In March of 1978, none of the established Roots dealers were obtaining from the factory the full quantity of shoes they were ordering. All of them were enthused about the new styles and were prepared to slowly change the outlook of their retails stores. It's difficult to know exactly what North American sales were, but it seems that about 4,000 pairs a week were being sold in Canada and the United States.

Continued Success in Europe

At the same time, the boom in Europe was continuing. Including the Dutch authorized dealer program, there were now almost 60 retail outlets in Europe. Sales were about 4,500 pairs a week, slightly above the North American rate, and there was a major program to develop franchises and leased departments in France and Germany. Consumer demand for the recessed heel was continuing, and this is the crux of today's problem. The Toronto management is frightened that this so-called fad for the recessed heel will die in Europe as it did in the United States and that the European operation is in for a very difficult time. On the other hand, I feel strongly that when the fad dies, when the teenagers walk away, if the store site locations have been properly selected and if the sales people have been properly dealt with, if the store managers received the same kind of continuing contact and the buildup required, and if the dealers are serviced properly, then the residual market is still a very substantial and successful market and need not die as it did in the United States.

Backing this up is the fact that, despite the introduction of the wedge and the classic heel and despite the fact that the recessed heel had not been promoted since the fall of 1975, the sale of the few remaining recessed heel shoes offered in the franchise stores represented 40 to 60 percent of the volume, it was learned in the March dealer meetings.

I am against the introduction, even on the test basis, of anything that would reduce the impact of the Roots advertising and promotional message in Europe. Our emphasis on the "natural" look and way of walking in Roots shoes, carried over into our store design, is almost anti-fashion, and I don't think we can switch to a fashion orientation. In Europe, I want to stick with the basic Roots concept of a comfortable, high-quality casual shoe whose comfort is based not only on the high quality of its materials and construction, but also on the unique recessed heel design. Whereas my colleagues in Toronto think we should prepare for the end of the recessed heel fad in Europe by the introduction of new products during the height of the fad, I believe that a better approach is to rely upon adequate promotion of the product and strong relationships with all the retail outlets, so that when abnormal fad sales fall off, the remaining sales will still be very, very profitable.

In a typical Roots store in Europe, selling only the recessed heel, some 20 styles are sold, and the average inventory is between 1,000 and 2,000 pairs, with inventory turnover between 7 and 20 times a year. In the Roots stores in North America, where the expanded line includes wedges and classic soles, the number of styles is perhaps 40 to 60, with larger inventories and lower turnovers. As you go into a conventional shoe store, the numbers of models increase dramatically, and inventory turnovers fall equally dramatically. It's a different kind of business. It seems that with the unique recessed heel approach, the business can be managed profitably in much simpler terms and with a more direct method. Anyway, that's the problem today to decide: whether the company can successfully continue in Europe along the lines originally established by the company in Toronto in 1973 and 1974, but abandoned by the company when the sales fell dramatically in North America.

The plan for Holland is to have approximately 50 Roots authorized dealers. So far, the typical outlet is selling about 30 pairs per week from an inventory of 120 to 150 pairs. The normal shoe retailer expects to turn his inventory only three times per year, so this is very good. If there is a fad component in our current sales, there is also a comfort component that should at least guarantee sales of 15 to 20 pairs per week per outlet or continuing sales of 750 to 1,000 pairs per week through the authorized dealers network in Holland alone. Our five company-owned stores can also be expected to generate sales of 500 pairs per store per week when the fad dies and the five leased departments another 375 to 500 each. Furthermore, the situation in the test store in Munich has finally improved in terms of both personnel and inventory management, and sales are now running at more than 150 pairs per week. A new franchise store in Berlin is selling over 200 pairs per week. This positive evidence of the growing German acceptance of the Roots concept opens the way for creating a national distribution pattern in Germany similar to the one so successfully established in the Netherlands. A reasonable objective would be between 10 and 20 German franchise stores selling at 150 to 200 pairs per week, while the fad lasts, and at half that rate thereafter. This could be followed in 1979 by a program to start about 100 leased departments. Similar efforts are also possible in France and England. Then I see a potential for 3,000 pairs per week in Europe *after* the fad has passed.

Discussion Issues

1. If you had been in a decision-making capacity at Roots Shoe, what would you have done differently to enhance domestic and international sales and profits? Explain.

2. If you had been in charge at Earth Shoe, what would you have done to avoid bankruptcy? Explain.

Club Med, Inc.: The Special Challenge of Growth

Warren J. Keegan and Charles Anderer.

Introduction

Gerald Martin, assistant vice president/marketing, and Jean Prevert, vice president/marketing,[1] had what each called a good working relationship as well as an understanding of each other's point of view. Martin, a native of New York City with extensive experience in the American leisure and lodging industry, had been lured to Club Med, Inc.,[2] by Prevert, a Parisian whose 20 year affiliation with Club Med had been mostly spent with the parent firm, Club Mediterranee, S.A.

The two men had been wrestling with the issue of how to broaden Club Med's appeal to capture a bigger piece of the American market. Prevert, who had seen Club Med successfully market a basically standardized product offering on a global scale, felt that success depended on educating American consumers rather than tailoring the product to them. Once Americans understood what made Club Med a different and rewarding experience, he reasoned, they would naturally choose to spend their hard-earned vacation time in one of his company's lovely villages. Martin saw things a little differently. While he agreed that educating the American consumer was important, he felt that certain concessions had to be made to American tastes as well. He believed that the Club Med product concept had global appeal, but he was more inclined to make adjustments to local market conditions than Prevert. Whatever their disagreements on methods, both agreed that the key to long-term success of Club Med, Inc., would lie in its ability to succeed in America.

The Strategic Problem

After three decades of nearly unqualified success, Club Mediterranee, S.A. was at a crossroads. Both outside and internal research reports confirmed that its subsidiary, Club

---

This case was written by Charles Anderer under the supervision of Warren J. Keegan, Professor of International Business and Marketing, Director, Institute of Global Business Strategy, Pace University, New York 10038. Reprinted from Warren J. Keegan, *Global Marketing Management,* fifth edition, Prentice Hall, Inc., 1995.

TABLE 1   **Club Med, Inc.**

Income Data (Million $)

Year Ended Oct. 31	Revs.	Oper. Inc.	% Oper. Inc. of Revs.	Net Bef. Taxes	Net Inc.	% Net Inc. of Revs.
1985	280	23.8	8.5%	16.8	14.2	5.1%
1984	235	21.2	9.0	13.4	12.0	5.1
1983	211	16.6	7.8	10.9	9.7	4.6
1982	207	13.3	6.4	9.0	7.1	3.5

Balance Sheet Data (Million $)

Oct. 31	Cash	Current Assets	Liab.	Ratio	Total Assets	Ret. on Assets	Ret. on Equity
1985	47.5	78.4	46.5	1.7	269	5.9%	10.5%
1984	38.7	75.5	40.9	1.8	212	5.6	11.7
1983	27.3	47.1	40.9	1.2	158	7.1	19.8
1982	20.6	38.3	38.7	1.0	115	NA	NA

Revenues (Million $)

Quarter	1985–6	1984–5	1983–4	1982–3
Jan.	85.4	71.9	62.1	—
Apr.	107.9	87.3	76.0	123.8*
July		62.3	47.6	—
Oct.		58.2	49.6	87.7*

*Six months.

SOURCE: Standard NYSE stock reports.

Med, Inc., had enormous and untapped growth potential. Part of Club Med, Inc.'s, territory included North America, and a considerable effort was being made to expand its share of potential customers. The fundamental issue facing Gerald Martin and Jean Prevert was how to win the maximum share of the American market while at the same time retaining the identity and the formula that had always served Club Med so well.

The Club Med Concept

That Club Med would distinguish itself as a unique company should have been apparent from the start. How many successful companies, after all, are run by former journalists whose political inclinations are decidedly to the left, and the far left at that? Club Med's chairman, Gilbert Trigano, was a member of the French Resistance and, subsequently, a reporter for the Communist paper *L'Humanite*. Trigano joined Club Med as managing director in 1954 and founded the company's first "village" in Greece the following year. Under his leadership, Club Med became a veritable tourism empire composed of 104 villages (and three "auxiliary" ones), located in France and some 30 foreign countries or French overseas territories.

Central to Club Med's success is its concept of what vacationers need in order to truly feel removed from the everyday pressures they seek to escape. Villages are

Table 2   Club Med, Inc.—Operations

Geographic Region	Villages	Number of Beds
North America/Caribbean	Eleuthera-Bahamas	600
	Paradise Island-Bahamas	750
	Punta Cana-Dominican Republic	600
	Caravelle-Guadeloupe	600
	Fort Royal-Guadeloupe	304
	Magic Isle-Haiti	700
	Buccaneer's Creek-Martinique	750
	Cancun-Mexico	750
	Ixtapa-Mexico	750
	Playa Blanca-Mexico	580
	Sonora Bay-Mexico	750
	Copper Mountain-Colorado, USA	470
	Turkoise-Turks and Caicos	490
	St. George's Cove-Bermuda	680
	Five Archeological Inns-Mexico	400
Pacific Basin	Chateau Royal-New Caledonia	550
	Bora Bora-Tahiti	102
	Moorea-Tahiti	700
Indian Ocean	Pointe aux Canonniers-Mauritius	374
	Le Lagon-Reunion	120
Asia	Cherating-Malaysia	600
	Thulagiri-Maldives	60
	Farukolhufushi-Maldives	250
	Phuket-Thailand	600
	Bali-Indonesia	700

Source: Drexel Burnham Lambert.

typically located in beautiful, warm-weather areas (see Table 2). Within each village, Club Med creates an environment that stresses the similarities between people. Its villages are closed societies where beads are used instead of money (everything is prepaid except for side trips and drinks, so the need for money is hardly acute), where there are no locks on doors, where the rooms are identical, where dining is done together at round tables and where the style of dress, excepting the company's ski villages, is minimalist (some might call it skimpy). Simply put, the spirit of competition in the outside world is replaced by a spirit of cooperation that evokes a simpler, less complicated way of life.

Nowhere is the spirit of cooperation more apparent than in the relationship between Club Med guests, who are called GMs (gentils membres—congenial members) and Club Med staff, who are known as GOs (gentils organisateurs—congenial organizers). The GOs are the constant companions of the GMs. They eat with the guests, their rooms are similar as is their style of dress. Each village has around 100 GOs. They work 14-hour days and serve as the guests' teachers, entertainers and friends.

The prepaid package that Club Med offers includes accommodations, all meals, sports and leisure activities, as well as air transportation, and land transfers (see Table 3). Unlike any number of "package deals" that are available to consumers. Club Med's

TABLE 3   The Price of a Club Med Vacation: The Caribbean Example

	One-Week Stays (Not Including Airfare)	
Villages	*Lowest Price (Early Nov.)*	*Highest Price (Early March)*
Caribbean		
Buccaneer's Creek	$470	$ 980
Caravelle	600	980
Magic Isle	525	600
Punta Cana	450	660
St. Lucia	—	700
Turkoise	735	1,070

	One-Week Rates with Air & Transfers	
Villages	*Lowest Price (Early Nov.)*	*Highest Price (Early March)*
Caribbean		
Buccaneer's Creek	$ 879	$1,470
Caravelle	999	1,470
Magic Isle	824	925
Punta Cana	799	1,080
St. Lucia	—	1,090
Turkoise	1,049	1,425

Rates are for the winter/spring 1986–87 season. All rates are per person, double occupancy, and subject to Club Med's terms and conditions.
SOURCE: Company brochure.

offerings are decidedly upscale. The company only builds villages in exclusive coastal or mountainside locations. The villages themselves are normally equipped with everything from tennis courts to discotheques and the food is reputed to be excellent.

1985—A Warning against Complacency

Club Mediterranee, S.A., received a warning of sorts when its financial results for the year ended October 31, 1985, were reported. In a marked contrast to previous years, the company experienced a modest rise in net profit of 8.3 percent to FFr [Franch francs] 266.6 million ($28.5 million) on revenues that increased by 17.3 percent to FFr 6 billion. This represented an increase in earnings per share of only 0.8 percent in a year when consumer prices in France rose by 5 percent. This per share decline in real terms was all the more surprising in that the Paris stock market experienced a boom year in 1985. As a result of its lackluster performance, Club Med fell from its position of the 16th largest firm on the Paris exchange in terms of stock market capitalization to the 28th largest.

The parent company bounced back in the first six months of 1986 and realized a 22 percent increase in net profits. In fact, this figure would have been even greater had the dollar not weakened. This impressive first-half reinforced Club Med's overall image as a highly profitable, well-run company. Those who ran the company had been at it for over three decades and had developed some foolproof ways to generate revenues and cut costs.

Firstly, since all of its vacations are paid anywhere from three to eight weeks in advance, Club Med makes upwards of $3 million a year in annual interest income from this source alone. Furthermore, since it transports most of its guests in groups, Club Med can strike a hard bargain with airlines for bulk rates. The company makes a substantial amount of money (17 1/2 percent of gross operating profits in 1983) buying air transport at wholesale prices and selling it to its vacationers at the going retail rate. While this policy often resulted in taxing the patience of its clientele (flights were often with "second-tier" airlines at odd hours of the day and rarely non-stop), the profits realized were too good to pass up. As for its villages, Club Med often builds at the request of host country governments in remote areas that would not otherwise be developed. The company can afford to do this because the success of its concept does not hinge on a specific locale or destination. By bringing business to distant areas, Club Med often gets the host country to put up much of the necessary capital (more than one-third of its $240 million North American/Asian expansion plan was being financed this way), while it takes a less than 10 percent ownership position in order to minimize tax liabilities (*The Economist,* 7/12/86).

In spite of its strong financial condition, however, Club Med was not about to be lulled into a false sense of security. The company's product was at different levels of life cycle in each of its major markets. In France, for example, the product was fast reaching saturation. The United States and West Germany were still in the growth stage, and the product was still in the introductory phase in markets such as Japan and Brazil. Of all these markets, none carried the importance that the American market held. It was becoming more and more obvious that, in order for Club Med to realize its true growth potential, its American customer base had to be expanded.

Selling Club Med to America

Gerald Martin just knew he had the answers. When Jean Prevert asked him what he thought Club Med, Inc., needed to do in order to expand in America, he submitted the following:

1. The villages had to be internationalized. That is, English-speaking villages where the number of French GMs was necessarily limited needed to be created. Even more importantly, the number of American GO's needed to be substantially increased.

2. The popular perception of Club Med as a haven for young and virile singles had to be altered somewhat. The demographics of the travel industry and Club Med's clientele had changed. More mature customers, many of whom were married and had children, needed to feel that a Club Med village was an appropriate place for them to spend a vacation. American consumers, in short, needed to be better informed on the advantages that Club Med offered them.

3. Americans took less vacation time than almost any other country in the developed world. They were far more likely to take a long weekend than a week or two in the sunshine. It was therefore a considerable challenge for Club Med to persuade them that it was beneficial for them to spend an important portion of the time they had away from their jobs in one of its villages.

4. Americans are very attached to convenience. While Club Med finds it lucrative to place many of its customers on flights that are marked by poor service and erratic scheduling. Martin felt that Club Med, Inc.'s, long-term interests would be better served by a more flexible approach to air travel. Martin also pushed for added amenities in the villages, such as telephones in the rooms.

The Need for More American GOs

Martin considered GOs to be the key to the success of any American expansion. He felt that the same personnel policies used with French GOs could not work with American GOs because their expectations are different. French GOs had a significantly lower turnover rate than American GOs and it appeared that the major problem was money. Martin felt that it would be beneficial to the company to reward those American GOs who show promise or who are already good at what they do with good salaries. American GOs needed to feel that they were not making an unnecessary financial sacrifice by staying with Club Med (see Appendix). Presently, they had that feeling (they are paid $100 per week including room and board) and it showed in their turnover rate.

Prevert thought it would be destabilizing to pay American GOs more than the French GOs who worked alongside them. Of course, they could raise everybody's salary, but that would be too costly. Prevert also thought Martin was overestimating the importance of American GOs to begin with. Club Med, Inc.'s, French GOs were required to speak fluent English, so what was the big deal?

American GOs were important, Martin thought, because American GMs feel so much more comfortable around them than is the case with French GOs. Martin knew that the French GOs, whether deservedly or not, sometimes had a reputation among American GMs as being arrogant toward them. This could simply be a result of the misunderstanding that takes place between members of different cultures or the result of a popularly held perception amongst Americans who travel that the French are simply an arrogant group of people. Martin believed that many French were guilty until proven innocent when it came to the question of arrogance. However unfair this might be, it remained absolutely necessary, in Martin's view, that Club Med cultivate a solid group of American GOs.

The French Accent: Asset or Liability?

Even though the Club Med concept stresses the similarities between people, the villages themselves inevitably have a strong French feeling to them. The dominant language in the large majority of Club Med's enclosed villages is, quite naturally, French. While the French accent does lure Americans to underdeveloped countries that they would be otherwise hesitant to visit, it can be intimidating to non-French speakers. Many Americans have no doubt either heard the usual horror stories from friends about those legendary, ill-mannered Parisians or have themselves had humbling experiences during the course of their visit(s) to France. Some industry observers surmise that the company's strong French accent serves as a barrier to growth. For example, France's sometimes playfully antagonistic neighbor from across the Channel, the United Kingdom, accounted for only 10,800 GMs in 1985 (a 48 percent increase from the previous year) compared to the French total of 365,200. The British, it might be added, can also vacation at the villages of Club Mark Warner, an anglicized version of the Club Med concept.

Being French, Prevert was naturally sensitive about the charge of arrogance. Although he thought Americans such as Martin exaggerated the problem, he favored the development "international villages." At these villages, English is the dominant language spoken and the proportion of French GMs is limited to 25 percent. In Europe, 18 such villages were established in 1986 whereas another 14 were planned for the rest of the world. It remained to be seen, according to Martin, if "internationalizing" a mere one-third of its villages would be enough to enable Club Med to substantially increase the number of American GMs.

Juggling the Image to Satisfy the Market

For years, the mere mention of the name "Club Med" evoked an alluring imagery of hedonism that only single people could enjoy in good conscience. In fairness to the company, Club Med had only passively cultivated this sort of image. Of course, the gates to its villages were not graced with signs reading "For Singles Only." On the other hand, once inside a Club Med village, one was far more likely to encounter single people than married couples. An example of how firmly entrenched this image was (and still is) in the minds of some was provided by members of Bermuda's political opposition in March of 1986, who called Club Med and its villages in the harbors of Castle and St. George immoral.

By 1984, Club Med would state in its annual report that significant changes in the makeup of its guest population had taken place. Nowhere was this change more apparent than among the American GMs. About half of them were married, the median age was said to be 37 years old, and more than half of them reported an annual income of at least $50,000. Club Med has catered to this demanding group of affluent baby boomers by offering more luxury, more options, special clubs for parents with children and a wider range of villages within reasonable travel time from the northeastern United States. American GMs are therefore steered to the village that best fits their personal tastes.

Even though Club Med's unstated goal was to portray itself as a provider of vacations for a maturing group of people, it initially found it difficult to resist the lure of selling the simple concept of sun and fun with beautiful people. A 1986 advertising campaign which revolved around the theme, "The perfect climate for body and soul," illustrates this point. Although the ads promoted such ideas as self-discovery, friendship, and improved communications between married couples, these messages were clearly marked by visuals of young, beautiful people flaunting toned-up physiques.

TABLE 4   Club Mediterannee, SA, and Club Med, Inc., Membership by Nationality (Percent of Total)

	1981	*1982*	*1983*	*1984*	*1985E*	*1986E*
Europe and Africa						
France	49.0	46.6	44.6	43.4	42.0	40.0
Italy	5.9	5.6	5.3	5.1	4.8	4.6
Belgium	5.2	5.1	4.8	4.7	4.5	4.4
W. Germany	4.5	4.4	3.8	4.5	4.4	4.4
Switzerland	2.9	2.7	2.6	2.5	2.3	2.2
Other	7.1	7.6	8.1	7.2	6.5	6.4
	74.6	72.0	69.2	67.4	64.5	62.0
North and Central America						
U.S./Canada	16.2	17.5	19.5	21.9	24.0	26.0
Other	1.5	2.1	2.3	1.7	2.0	2.0
	17.7	19.6	21.8	23.6	26.0	28.0
Asia, Indian Ocean and South Pacific						
Australia	2.7	2.6	2.2	1.7	1.8	2.0
Japan	0.9	1.2	1.5	1.5	1.5	1.7
Other	2.1	2.4	2.8	2.7	2.7	2.8
	5.7	6.2	6.5	5.9	6.0	6.5
South America	2.0	2.2	2.5	3.1	3.5	3.5
Total	100.0	100.0	100.0	100.0	100.0	100.0

SOURCE: Drexel Burnham Lambert.

Americans: Anything but Vacation

As of 1986, in spite of some undeniable gains Club Med, Inc., still saw itself as underperforming with respect to the number of American guests it attracted per year. This view was no doubt reinforced by a 1985 study done by the investment bank Drexel Burnham Lambert (see Tables 4–7.) Drexel calculated that the French were over nine times more likely to be a Club Med GM than Americans. If the concept could only become half as popular in the United States as it is in France (meaning an increase in GM's per 1,000 people from 0.7 to 3.0), then North America alone could support 90 villages, or six times the number of villages it had in 1985.

Drexel's optimistic numbers notwithstanding, Martin still saw a large problem. The group that was to fuel Club Med's ambitious growth plans, the Americans, took less vacation time than the French, the British or the Germans (see Table 8.) Europeans, who were responsible for Club Med's initial success, enjoy a decidedly more relaxed lifestyle than Americans. Vacations in Europe are traditionally taken in four to six week blocks in July or August.

Why is there such a big difference in vacation time between America and other developed countries? The reasons are mainly cultural in nature. American society is outwardly more competitive than those in Western Europe. The difference might be summed up by a commonly held notion among Europeans who have either worked in America or for American companies in Europe: Americans live to work and Europeans work to live. In any event, a typical American manager would be downright afraid to

TABLE 5   Selected Propensities to Visit Club Med

Country	Approx. No. of Native GM's per Year	% of Total GM's	Pop. (1980)	GM's per Thousand Inhabit.
Europe				
France	356,000	39.6%	53,580,000	6.6
Italy	106,000	11.8	57,080,000	1.9
Belgium	38,800	4.3	9,890,000	3.9
W. Germany	35,000	3.9	61,480,000	0.6
Switzerland	20,800	2.3	6,250,000	3.3
North America				
USA/Canada	179,800	20.0%	258,302,604	0.7
Asia, Indian Ocean and South Pacific				
Japan	12,000	1.3%	119,680,000	0.1
Australia	18,000	2.0	15,535,000	1.2

SOURCE: Drexel Burnham Lambert.

TABLE 6   Estimated Potential Club Med Market

	Current Propensity to Visit Club Med (GM's per 1,000 Pop.)	Estimated Potential Propensity (GM's per 1,000 Pop.)	Extrapolated Potential Number of GM's
Europe			
France	6.6	6.6	356,000
Italy	1.9	2.0	114,200
Belgium	3.9	4.0	39,600
W. Germany	0.6	3.5	215,250
Switzerland	3.3	4.0	25,200
North America			
Canada	0.7	2.5	62,750
U.S.A.	0.7	3.0	717,300
Asia, Indian Ocean and South Pacific			
Japan	0.1	2.5	299,250
Australia	1.2	2.5	38,750

SOURCE: Drexel Burnham Lambert.

take that much time off in one stretch and most wouldn't even begin to contemplate the notion. In order to ease the guilt, Martin was able to convince Prevert, after some arm-twisting, to equip 7 villages with computer workshops.

Toying with the Concept

Martin's controversial approach to the Club Med concept was largely based on his interpretation of Club Med's initial success with the French. At the heart of his success,

TABLE 7   **Current vs. Estimated Potential**

	Approx. Current No. of GM's	Estimated Potential	Estimated % Growth Potential	Approx. Growth Potential as a % of Total Growth Potential
Europe				
France	356,000	356,000	0%	0.0%
Italy	106,000	114,000	8	0.6
Belgium	38,000	39,600	2	0.1
W. Germany	35,000	215,250	515	12.6
Switzerland	20,800	25,200	21	0.3
North America				
USA/Canada	179,800	780,050	334%	42.1%
Asia, Indian Ocean and South Pacific				
Japan	12,000	299,250	2.934%	20.1%
Australia	18,000	38,750	115	1.5

SOURCE: Drexel Burnham Lambert.

TABLE 8   **Holidays with Pay (Annual Averages)**

	Statutory	Collective Agreements and Practice	Paid Public Holidays
Belgium	4 weeks	4 weeks	10 days
Canada	2 weeks	3 weeks	6–9 days
France	5 weeks	5 weeks	*
W. Germany	3 weeks	5–6 weeks	11–13 days
Italy	10days	4 weeks	10 days
Japan	6 days	—	12 days
The Netherlands	3 weeks	4–4.5 weeks	8 days
Sweden	5 weeks	5 weeks	11 days
Switzerland	2–3 weeks	3–4 weeks	4–5 days
England	*	4 weeks	8 days
USA	*	1–2 weeks	*

*No generally applicable statutory provisions.
SOURCE: International Labor Office.

he believed, was Club Med's ability to give people a home away from home. Martin believed very little in the notion of global Club Med villages where the people of the world comfortably coexist. He saw room for a little international flair, but he felt that Americans, in particular, did not want to spend their vacations in an environment basically alien to them and surrounded by GOs who do not speak their language.

On the other hand, Martin saw the Club Med concept as a natural for Americans because of their basic social instincts. There was no reason why the concept could not be successful here. The main problem, as Martin saw it, was management's ability to properly implement its growth strategy. One area where Martin was successful was in air travel. As stated above, the company buys air travel wholesale and sells it retail. Martin fought hard to ensure that the company would not risk losing customers for the sake of avoiding a decrease in interest income from the sale of airfare. As a result of his efforts, air travel for the American market was upgraded.

Martin was still worried by Prevert's reluctance to change the company's winning ways. An example was the horror with which Prevert greeted Martin's proposal to put telephones in guests' rooms. "A telephone is a direct link with the outside world and all of its miseries," sniffed Prevert, fully aware of the fact that his company had somehow managed to survive before Gerald Martin was hired. "Cut off the outside world, and you cut off the very anxieties that the guests are trying to escape. Computer workshops and better travel arrangements, yes. Telephones in the rooms, never."

Discussion Issues:

1. Gerald Martin felt that Club Med had to make concessions to American tastes. Do you agree or disagree?
2. How can Club Med broaden its appeal to Americans? Explain.

Endnotes

[1]These characters, as well as their discussions, are fictitious. Their purpose is to highlight some of the issues facing the company described herein.

[2]Club Med, Inc., is a Grand Cayman Island company, traded on the New York Stock Exchange; 73 percent of its shares outstanding are owned by its French parent, Club Mediterranee, S.A. It has exclusive rights to the sale of Club Med packages and the operations of Club Med resorts in North and Central America and the Caribbean, the Pacific Basin, Oceania, Asia and the Indian Ocean (see Table 1).

APPENDIX

A Day in the Life of a Club Med GO

What are the difficulties that Club Med faces in cultivating a solid group of American GOs? One problem is that, by American standards, the GOs actually are underpaid for the amount of work they do. One former American GO who lasted six months as a dance instructor at the Punta Cana resort in the Dominican Republic said that a major factor in her decision to leave was the rigorous schedule that she faced every day of the week:

7:30–10 a.m.	Breakfast duty. Greet and seat guests.
11–12	Teach dance class in the theater.
12–1:30 p.m.	Host luncheon buffet or perform mime skit with the animateur (club jester) in the dining room as guests eat lunch.
1:30–3 p.m.	Rehearsals in the theater.
3–6 p.m.	FREE! If I didn't have Arrivals and Departures, a GO meeting or a team meeting, or have to help prepare the set or costumes for the evening performance.
6–7 p.m.	Teach another dance class in the theater.
7–8 p.m.	Cocktail hour. Model a dress from the boutique and flirt with guests at the bar.
8–9:30 p.m.	SMILE! Host dinner or perform a mime skit.
9:30–10 p.m.	Change out of boutique dress or mime costume and gulp down dinner.
10–11 p.m.	Change into another costume and perform in show.
11–12 p.m.	Clean up backstage and mingle with guests at the bar.
12–1 a.m.	Midnight rehearsal if scheduled.
1–?	Disco. Lure shy guests onto the dance floor.

How Cuisinart Lost Its Edge

N. R. Kleinfield.

It is the sort of fabled brand name that marketers usually only dream about. If you were in the copier business, you would wish your name were Xerox. If tissues were your product, it would be nice to be named Kleenex. But if you were going to make your fortune in food processors, you couldn't do better than to possess the name Cuisinart.

That, at least, was what a group of investors thought when they took on a mountainous debt and bought Cuisinarts Inc. early in 1988 from Carl Sontheimer, the inspired founder of the company and an almost deific figure in the kitchenware industry. They acquired not only the Rolls-Royce of food processors, but also a venerated name with such cachet that it could probably be stamped on alarm clocks or cat beds and produce a bonanza.

Two years later, the bonanza has proved elusive and Cuisinarts lies enfeebled. The group of investors who bought it, led by Robert Fomon, the controversial former head of E. F. Hutton, and George Barnes, a housewares veteran with a checkered history, are gone. Meanwhile, Cuisinarts collapsed into bankruptcy and it was auctioned off at the end of December at a significantly marked-down price to the Conair Corporation, the hair-dryer people. Resurrecting Cuisinarts, though, may be a perilous mission.

How could such a conspicuous name become crippled so quickly? Like so many other fast-dollar artists of the 1980s, Fomon and Barnes rooted their dreams in borrowed money. Despite the wonder of the name, Cuisinarts was the wrong prospect at the wrong time to pile borrowings on. Starting with a poor hand, the owners seemed to make matters worse through a procession of bad gambles.

Carl Sontheimer, a portly, rumpled, retired physicist, grew up in France, where his father labored in the export division of an American company. A graduate of the Massachusetts Institute of Technology, he holds 40-odd patents, mostly for various electronic components. Ever since he was a child, however, cooking has been his private obsession. He would grow excited over a new goulash recipe the way that other youngsters would thrill over the latest muscle car. Those who know him describe Sontheimer, who declined to be interviewed for this article, as stunningly intelligent, a perfectionist and stubborn to a fault.

Before Cuisinarts, Sontheimer formed an electronics business called CGS Laboratories. However, he got into a quarrel with a partner and unloaded his stake. In 1960, he established Anzac Electronics, which invented several electronic devices that found their way to the moon. But Sontheimer was frustrated being a minuscule player in the high-technology world and so, in 1967, he sold Anzac to another electronics company.

Sontheimer was 53 and well enough fixed that he could have retired to limitless shuffleboard. But he couldn't imagine simply taking an early slide. Mulling over new roads to follow—maybe burglar alarms, he thought—he pondered his longstanding lust for cooking. He and his wife, Shirley, were visiting a French cookery show in 1971 in the hope of finding products fit for a franchise operation in the United States, when a bulbous, clumsy-looking device caught Sontheimer's eye: it was a food processor for restaurant chefs. Invented by Pierre Verdun in 1963, it was being manufactured by Verdun's company, Robot-Coupe, France's biggest maker of restaurant equipment. The machine didn't mop up or defrost the refrigerator, but it did just about anything—cut, slice, knead, chop, dice, grate, grind—to whatever food was shoved into it. It made redundant many of the numerous gadgets crowding the counter top. As he studied the device, Sontheimer sensed that the mechanical marvel, if adapted for home use, could become an important product in the United States. In short order, he signed a distribution agreement to sell a modified version of the machine in America under the trade name Cuisinart. "For Carl," an associate remembered, "finding that machine was like finding the Holy Grail."

Returning to his home in Greenwich, Conn., Sontheimer set up offices and began selling cookware. Meanwhile, for more than 18 months, with an absorption approaching obsession, he modified the blades and slicing and shredding disks and improved the safety of the processor. In January 1973, he unveiled it at the National Housewares Show in Chicago.

Shortly thereafter, a small band of salesmen began calling on upscale department and specialty stores to pitch the quirky-looking product. At first sight, it seemed too astonishing to believe. When the salesmen mentioned that the suggested retail price was $175, buyers would often flash "Oh, brother!" looks and laugh until their eyes welled with tears.

No matter the blandishments of the salesmen, sales amounted to only a few hundred thousand dollars until a glowing article appeared in 1975 in *Gourmet* magazine entitled "The Phenomenal Food Processor."

"When that article hit," recalled a former executive, "mass hysteria struck." A host of other notable culinary experts—James Beard, Julia Child—raved about the device. Craig Claiborne wrote that it was perhaps the greatest food invention since toothpicks.

Suddenly Cuisinarts Inc. found itself with more business than it could handle. It paved the way for an entirely new kitchen appliance category, and before long people began offering classes teaching how to cook meals with the new gadget.

Within a few years, food processors arrived from Farberware, Waring, General Electric, Hamilton Beach and the French company Moulinex. Some sold for half the price of a Cuisinart, but none matched its performance. For one thing, Sontheimer was fastidious about quality. In 1977, all the makers sold an estimated 500,000 units, with half of them believed to be Cuisinarts. Contradicting the normal rule of American enterprise, the most expensive product was the biggest seller.

Heady with success, Cuisinarts brought out more deluxe models. In 1979, when competing machines were selling for around $70, the company introduced a more powerful processor priced at $275. It was a time when fancy home cooking had become the rage, and the device sold briskly.

Sontheimer, however, became increasingly dismayed over quality control at Robot-Coupe, and so, like many leaders of American companies, he struck a deal with a Japanese maker. Before long, he was selling more Japanese than French models. Miffed executives at Robot-Coupe grumbled that he wasn't adequately promoting their machines and severed ties with him.

By 1981, Robot-Coupe was on the offensive. It hired Alvin Finesman, who had been Cuisinarts' marketing head, to direct an American incursion of a machine carrying the Robot-Coupe name. Finesman, a spunky man with an Ichabod Crane body, was born to slap backs. His family owned a cigar and tobacco business, and when he was 15, Finesman himself was hawking cigars to pharmacists in Ohio. He had grown disgruntled with his treatment at Cuisinarts. He maintains that Sontheimer promised him an equity stake in the company, but according to Finesman, when he approached Sontheimer and asked about the promise, Sontheimer's reply was, "My wife won't let me."

Finesman said, "After 30 seconds, I quit."

To get things rolling in his new job, Finesman developed an advertising campaign in which the copy read, "Robot-Coupe. It's pronounced Robo-Coop. (It used to be pronounced Cuisinart.)"

Sontheimer didn't find the campaign amusing and filed a lawsuit charging deceptive advertising. Though Robot-Coupe was compelled to alter its slogan, the publicity engulfing the case was a stupendous boost to Robot-Coupe. But the battle of the cutters proved to be a dud. Robot-Coupe, Finesman allows, failed to deliver any more than a me-too product. Sales evaporated, Finesman left and the device today clings to a tiny share of the American market. It remains, however, France's leading food processor.

Cuisinarts itself received a black eye in the early 1980s, when a Connecticut grand jury and the Justice Department charged it with conspiring to fix prices by refusing to supply machines to stores that sold it below the suggested price. Sontheimer pleaded no contest and paid a fine of $250,000. Consumers, however, attacked with class-action suits. Sontheimer finally agreed to allow anyone who bought a Cuisinart between 1973 and 1981 to buy up to $200 worth of Cuisinart kitchenware at half price.

The next important moment in the history of the processor occurred in 1985, in the form of a tiny device that was initially scorned as a "gum-ball machine."

The Sunbeam Company had undertaken a study of the market the previous year and was stunned to discover that half of all food processors were collecting dust in closets because their owners felt they were either too big, too complicated or too hard to clean—or all of those. Taking its cue from the study, Sunbeam built a little machine that it dubbed Oskar (an acronym standing for Outstanding Superior Kitchen All-Rounder, an "all-rounder" being a person who plays all positions on a rugby team). It was half the size of the standard Cuisinart and sold for as little as $60. When he got a look at it, Sontheimer sneered and decided it was just a gimmick.

The first year, Oskar sold 750,000 units, as many as Sunbeam could manufacture. The next year, sales soared to 1.4 million.

It would have been sensible for Cuisinart to develop its own small machine, but Sontheimer chose not to. "When someone spits in your face, you don't say it's raining outside," Finesman says. Not until several years later was a compact Cuisinart introduced, too late to blossom into a big success.

By the middle 1980s, the days of breakneck growth for the food-processor market had ceased and it began to shrink. Many people who wanted the devices had them; fancy cooking was less voguish. Cuisinart's sales began to erode, and its profit margins were further compressed by the fact that the company's chief sources of supply were Japan and Hong Kong and the dollar had sunk in relation to the yen. What's more, a protracted problem began to catch up to the company: the failure to mine the prestigious Cuisinart name.

Perhaps the best thing about a potent brand name is you can plaster it on all manner of supplemental products and then count the money. Cuisinart did introduce a bread pan, a meat-yeast thermometer, and a rolling pin, but little else. From early on, the company had examined hordes of products, but had never gotten them out the door. Former executives blame Sontheimer's fussiness. he didn't want to bring out just a good toaster. It had to practically fly.

Several years ago, Sontheimer was quoted by a *Forbes* magazine reporter as saying: "We could put pebbles in a can, and if we put the Cuisinart name on it, it would sell. But after that, the name would be absolutely worthless. If we don't feel we can make a better product, we don't enter the market."

Besides Sontheimer's perfectionism, he also had a decided lack of capitalistic vision. Cooking was his obsession. In the words of one associate: "Carl could be in a meeting where one person was going to jump out the window because of something going sour in his life, the Premier of Russia and the President were waiting to see him and someone else had arrived to show him a new recipe. The guy with the recipe is the person he would talk to."

In the early part of 1987, getting up in years and strained by the decline of his company, Sontheimer agreed to sell Cuisinart. The buyer—for $45 million—was to be a group headed by Dick Tarlow, a friend who ran Tarlow Advertising and handled Cuisinarts' advertising. Tarlow landed the account by a quirk. Sixty-two agencies competed for it, and when it was Tarlow's turn to perform, Sontheimer asked him one question, "Dick Tarlow, if you could do anything with your life, what would it be." Years before, Tarlow had been a baseball pitcher, with enough talent that a dozen professional teams dangled contracts. He turned them all down because he found watching baseball boring and didn't want to have to sit on the bench during days he wasn't on the mound. He glanced at Sontheimer and said, "I wish I were in baseball." Sontheimer gave him the account because he said that was the only interesting response he had heard.

The night before Tarlow was to close on the deal, he got cold feet and told Sontheimer he was backing out. As he explained his change of heart recently: "What scared me was we were paying a lot of money and we wouldn't have enough capital in the company to expand it."

Others bidders, however, stepped forth, and Sontheimer sold Cuisinart for $42 million, the bulk of it borrowed from the Bank of Boston, to a group of investors led by George Barnes, Robert Fomon and the Washington National Investment Corporation. People in the industry felt the price was far too steep. Also, the deal was a leveraged buyout, the prevalent financial phenomenon of the 1980s, in which much of the purchase price is borrowed and secured by assets of the company. By conventional wisdom, Cuisinart was hardly an apt candidate for a leveraged buyout. Usually, such deals are done with growing companies with marketable assets that can be sold to pay down some of the awesome debt. Cuisinarts' sales had fallen for five consecutive years and it didn't have assets to sell. It needed an infusion of money to steer the company into new products. Several well-informed people proclaimed the deal to be ridiculously ill conceived.

The acquisition was completed in January 1988. George Barnes arrived at the Stamford, Conn., headquarters and was installed as Cuisinarts' new chief executive.

At this point the company had been losing money for several years. Matters, however, became considerably more precarious under the new regime. They did not enter the picture with the best of reputations. Bob Fomon, an intense, imperious man, presided over E. F. Hutton for 16 years, during which time the company slipped badly and, in 1985, was engulfed by scandal when it pleaded guilty to 2,000 felony counts for illegal bank overdrafting. Fomon steadfastly refused to relinquish power at the company until at the end of 1986 the board forced him out as chief executive. George Barnes is a stocky man with thinning gray hair, with a knack for promoting himself and a peripatetic past. After stints at Waring Products, Westbend, Gillette and Schick, he founded the National Appliance Company in 1979. It went into liquidation in 1982.

Because of its heavy debt, Cuisinarts sorely needed higher sales. To accomplish that, Barnes embarked on what one observer termed "panic salesmanship." Ignoring the fact that the Cuisinart was an upscale product whose customers shopped in higher-priced department and specialty stores, the places where the device had primarily been sold, Barnes approached major deep discounters such as Caldor, Target Stores and Price Club and sold them big orders. He put them in different boxes and made other small cosmetic changes to make it seem that the discount stores were getting a different model from the department stores.

The tack quickly foundered. Fewer Caldor shoppers than had been anticipated bought Cuisinarts. Compounding matters, many of the stores that had been loyal Cuisinart customers were enraged by the move. Dick Silk, a Cuisinart representative who sells the machine in the Southwest, says the new strategy "killed us."

"Our orders dropped substantially," he says. "There was a loss of credibility. The Cuisinart name meant quality and all of a sudden that changed overnight. And that had a very adverse effect on the specialty stores and department stores that had built the business. And so the Cuisinart went from the front aisle to the back aisle."

Meanwhile, management failed to deal with the fact that its machines were coming over from Japan and Hong Kong, and its cookware from France, at a cost significantly higher than could be gotten in places like Taiwan or Korea. Yet no new supplier arrangements were struck.

Strapped for money, the owners were also unable to take the most important step: exploiting the Cuisinart name. Though Barnes planned to bring out can openers and slow cookers, the funds weren't there to market them. Undoubtedly, the owners didn't sense how much the market for processors had contracted. Nineteen eighty-six proved to be the peak year, when sales hit six million units. Last year, they sagged to half that and makers anticipate a similar performance this year. Cuisinarts Inc., which had peak sales of some $70 million a year in the early 1980s, watched its revenues slump to around $56 million in 1988. Now that an estimated 43 percent of homes have a food processor, the product has become mature, and the arrival in 1987 of a tiny new device—the chopper/grater—has also pinched sales.

As is so often characteristic in takeovers, personal pride began to play a part in the unraveling of Cuisinarts. More money was necessary, and increasingly it seemed clear that the only way to get it was to sell some equity in the company. But the owners clung to their dreams. "People in these deals usually can't handle the reality when things go sour," noted a businessman familiar with mergers and acquisitions. "They want to hold on to it and thrash it while there's still life left in it."

George Barnes's stay at Cuisinarts was stormy and brief. As the company failed to achieve the monthly sales targets set by the principal investors, the board began to lose faith in Barnes. Last April, he was dismissed. Replacing him was Donald Luke, a docile, well-groomed man who had been president of Actmedia, a marketing and advertising company. Barnes is quick to exempt himself from any blame. He maintains that his strategy was clicking but that too much had been paid for the company. He says that he exhorted the board to recapitalize the company but that it refused. When Barnes is pointing fingers, he likes to aim at Luke. "Luke probably set a North American record for running a company into bankruptcy," he says. "He didn't know what the hell he was doing." Luke refused to comment on Barnes's remarks.

Once he settled in, Luke de-emphasized the policy of selling to mass discounters. He trimmed the work force to 100 people from 150, and readied two new housewares products for introduction. Few forward steps could be taken, because there was just too much bleeding. It became clear that the company's only hope was to find a new partner who could provide the money necessary to expand. Consequently, Cuisinarts filed for bankruptcy, listing the assets of $34.5 million and liabilities of $43.2 million, and was put on the auction block. "We're trying to save every buck that we can," Luke said near the end of last year. Soon afterward, Luke left Cuisinarts to become chief executive of the Senior Service Corporation, which supplies services to people over 50.

At first, more than 60 potential buyers expressed interest in Cuisinarts, but within weeks, the list shrank to about two dozen. Among those said to be in the hunt were Farberware, Proctor-Silex, Dansk International, Conair, Hamilton Beach and Toastmaster. Dansk, as it happens, recently bought an electrical products concern run by Al Finesman. If Dansk bought Cuisinarts, Finesman expected to take command.

Oddly enough, George Barnes even tried to put together investors to mount a bid to once again buy the company. He isn't ruffled much by the fact that he is often portrayed as the heavy.

"Yeah, I understand that," he said. "They've got to put the blame somewhere. Like every industry, this one is full of gossip and innuendo."

At the end of December, Conair came out on top when it agreed to acquire most of Cuisinarts' assets for $17.1 million, less than half of what the Barnes group had paid. Lee Rizzuto, Conair's chairman, who founded the company in 1959 with his parents with a paltry $100, vows to exploit the Cuisinart name with a blizzard of products, including a coffee maker, a juicer and Cuisinart coffee beans. He hopes to pump up interest by winning endorsements from celebrated chefs. He says he thinks he can boost the company's sales, which dwindled to some $40 million last year, to $100 million within two years.

Carl Sontheimer, now in his mid-70s, and his wife continue to live in Greenwich and no doubt are eagerly watching as the next act of the Cuisinarts saga unfolds. Those who know him say he is bitterly disappointed over what has become of his company.

Clearly Conair faces a problematic task. As Dick Silk says, "You need to pull a rabbit out of a hat."

Discussion Issues

1. What steps should have been taken to avoid the fate that overtook Cuisinart? Be specific.
2. What has happened to Cuisinart since 1990? Has the company regained its pre-eminence? Explain.

Nestlé—The Infant Formula Incident

J. Alex Murray, Gregory M. Gazda, and Mary J. Molenaar.

Nestlé Alimentana of Vevey, Switzerland, one of the world's largest food-processing companies with worldwide sales of over $8 billion, has been the subject of an international boycott. For over 10 years, beginning with a Pan American Health Organization allegation, Nestlé has been directly or indirectly charged with involvement in the death of Third World infants. The charges revolve around the sale of infant feeding formula which allegedly is the cause of mass deaths of babies in the Third World.

In 1974 a British journalist published a report that suggested that powdered-formula manufacturers contributed to the death of Third World infants by hard-selling their products to people incapable of using them properly. The 28-page report accused the industry of encouraging mothers to give up breast feeding and use powdered milk formulas. The report was later published by the Third World Working Group, a lobby in support of less-developed countries. The pamphlet was entitled, "Nestlé Kills Babies," and accused Nestlé of unethical and immoral behavior.

Although there are several companies who market infant baby formula internationally, Nestlé received most of the attention. This incident raises several issues important to all multinational companies. Before addressing these issues, let's look more closely at the charges by the Infant Formula Action Coalition (INFACT) and others and the defense by Nestlé.

The Charges

Most of the charges against infant formulas focus on the issue of whether advertising and marketing of such products have discouraged breast feeding among Third World mothers and have led to misuse of the products, thus contributing to infant malnutrition and death. Following are some of the charges made:

- A Peruvian nurse reported that formula had found its way to Amazon tribes deep in the jungles of northern Peru. There, where the only water comes from a highly contaminated river—that also serves as the local laundry and toilet—formula-fed babies came down with recurring attacks of diarrhea and vomiting.

An update of "Nestlé in LDCs," case written by J. Alex Murray, University of Windsor, Ontario, Canada, and Gregory M. Gazda and Mary J. Molenaar, University of San Diego. Originally appeared in P. R. Cateora, *International Marketing,* 8th ed., Richard D. Irwin, © 1993.

- Throughout the Third World, many parents dilute the formula to stretch their supply. Some even believe the bottle itself has nutrient qualities and merely fill it with water. The result is extreme malnutrition.

- One doctor reported that in a rural area, one newborn male weighed 7 pounds. At four months of age, he weighed 5 pounds. His sister, aged 18 months, weighed 12 pounds, the weight one would expect a 4-month-old baby to weigh. The children had never been breast-fed, and since birth, their diets were basically bottle feeding. For a four-month baby, one tin of formula should have lasted just under 3 days. The mother said that one tin lasted two weeks to feed both children.

- In rural Mexico, the Philippines, Central America, and the whole of Africa, there has been a dramatic decrease in the incidence of breast feeding. Critics blame the decline largely on the intensive advertising and promotion of infant formula. Clever radio jingles extoll the wonders of the "white man's powder that will make baby grow and glow." "Milk nurses" visit nursing mothers in hospitals and their homes and provide samples of formula. These activities encourage mothers to give up breast feeding and resort to bottle feeding because it is "the fashionable thing to do or because people are putting it to them that this is the thing to do."

The Defense

The following points are made in defense of the marketing of baby formula in Third World countries:

- First, Nestlé argues that the company has never advocated bottle feeding instead of breast feeding. All its products carry a statement that breast feeding is best. The company states that it "believes that breast milk is the best food for infants and encourages breast feeding around the world as it has done for decades." The company offers as support of this statement one of Nestlé's oldest educational booklets on "Infant Feeding and Hygiene," which dates from 1913 and encourages breast feeding.

- However, the company does believe that infant formula has a vital role in proper infant nutrition as (1) a supplement, when the infant needs nutritionally adequate and appropriate foods in addition to breast milk and (2) a substitute for breast milk when a mother cannot or chooses not to breast feed.

- One doctor reports, "Economically deprived and thus dietarily deprived mothers who give their children only breast milk are raising infants whose growth rates begin to slow noticeably at about the age of three months. These mothers then turn to supplemental feedings that are often harmful to children. These include herbal teas, and concoctions of rice water or corn water and sweetened, condensed milk. These feedings can also be prepared with contaminated water and are served in unsanitary conditions."

- Mothers in developing nations often have dietary deficiencies. In the Philippines, a mother in a poor family who is nursing a child produces about a pint of milk daily. Mothers in the United States usually produce about a quart of milk each day.

For both the Philippine and U.S. mothers, the milk produced is equally nutritious. The problem is that there is less of it for the Philippine baby. If the Philippine mother doesn't augment the child's diet, malnutrition develops.

- Many poor women in the Third World bottle feed because their work schedules in fields or factories will not permit breast feeding.

- The infant feeding controversy has largely to do with the gradual introduction of weaning foods during the period between three months and two years. The average well-nourished Western woman, weighing 20 to 30 pounds more than most women in less-developed countries, cannot feed only breast milk beyond five or six months. The claim that Third World women can breast feed exclusively for one or two years and have healthy, well-developed children is outrageous. Thus, all children beyond the ages of five to six months require supplemental feeding.

- Weaning foods can be classified as either native cereal gruels of millet or rice, or commercial manufactured milk formula. Traditional native weaning foods are usually made by mixing maize, rice, or millet flours with water and then cooking the mixture. Other weaning foods found in use are crushed crackers, sugar and water, and mashed bananas.

   There are two basic dangers to the use of native weaning foods. First, the nutritional quality of the native gruels is low. Second, microbiological contamination of the traditional weaning foods is a certainty in many Third World settings. The millet or the flour is likely to be contaminated, the water used in cooking will most certainly be contaminated, the cooking containers will be contaminated, and therefore, the native gruel, even after it is cooked, is frequently contaminated with colon bacilli, staph, and other dangerous bacteria. Moreover, large batches of gruel are often made and allowed to sit, inviting further contamination.

- Scientists recently compared the microbiological contamination of a local native gruel with ordinary reconstituted milk formula prepared under primitive conditions. They found both were contaminated to similar dangerous levels.

- The real nutritional problem in the Third World is not whether to give infants breast milk or formula; it is how to supplement mothers' milk with nutritionally adequate foods when they are needed. Finding adequate locally produced, nutritionally sound supplements to mothers' milk and teaching people how to prepare and use them safely is the issue. Only effective nutrition education along with improved sanitation and good food that people can afford will win the fight against dietary deficiencies in the Third World.

The Resolution

In 1974, Nestlé, aware of changing social patterns in the developing world and the increased access to radio and television there, reviewed its marketing practices on a region-by-region basis. As a result, mass media advertising of infant formula began to be phased out immediately in certain markets and, by 1978, was banned worldwide by the company. Nestlé then undertook to carry out more comprehensive health education programs to ensure an understanding of the proper use of their products reached mothers, particularly in rural areas.

"Nestlé fully supports the WHO (World Health Organization) Code. Nestlé will continue to promote breast feeding and ensure that its marketing practices do not discourage breast feeding anywhere. Our company intends to maintain a constructive dialogue with governments and health professionals in all the countries it serves with the sole purpose of servicing mothers and the health of babies." This quote is from *Nestlé Discusses the Recommended WHO Infant Formula Code.*

In 1977 the Interfaith Center on Corporate Responsibility in New York compiled a case against formula-feeding in developing nations and the Third World Institute launched a boycott against many Nestlé products. Its aim was to halt promotion of infant formulas in the Third World. The Infant Formula Action Coalition (INFACT, successor to the Third World Institute) along with several other world organizations successfully lobbied the World Health Organization (WHO) to draft a code to regulate the advertising and marketing of infant formula in the Third World. In 1981 by a vote of 114–1 (three countries abstained and the United States was the only dissenting vote), 118 member nations of WHO endorsed a voluntary code. The eight-page code urged a worldwide ban on promotion and advertising of baby formula and called for a halt to distribution of free product samples and/or gifts to physicians who promoted the use of the formula as a substitute for breast milk.

In May 1981 Nestlé announced it would support the code and waited for individual countries to pass national codes that would then be put into effect. Unfortunately, very few such codes were forthcoming. By the end of 1983, only 25 of the 157 member nations of the WHO had established national codes.

Accordingly, Nestlé management determined it would have to apply the code in the absence of national legislation and in February 1982 issued instructions to marketing personnel, delineating the company's best understanding of the code and what would have to be done to follow it.

In addition, in May 1982, Nestlé formed the Nestlé Infant Formula Audit Commission (NIFAC) chaired by former Senator Edmund J. Muskie, and asked the commission to review the company's instructions to field personnel to determine if they could be improved to better implement the code. At the same time, Nestlé continued its meetings with WHO and UNICEF to try to obtain the most accurate interpretation of the code.

NIFAC recommended several clarifications for the instructions that it believed would better interpret ambiguous areas of the code; in October 1982, Nestlé accepted those recommendations and issued revised instructions to field personnel.

Other issues within the code, such as the question of a warning statement, were still open to debate. Nestlé consulted extensively with WHO before issuing its label warning statement in October 1983, but there was still not universal agreement with it. Acting on WHO recommendations, Nestlé consulted with firms experienced and expert in developing and field-testing educational materials, so that it could ensure that those materials met the code.

When the International Nestlé Boycott Committee (INBC) listed its four points of difference with Nestlé, it again became a matter of interpretation of the requirements of the code. Here, meetings held by UNICEF proved invaluable, in that UNICEF agreed to define areas of differing interpretation—in some cases providing definitions contrary to both Nestlé's and INBC's interpretations.

It was the meetings with UNICEF in early 1984 that finally led to a joint statement by Nestlé and INBC on January 25. At that time, INBC announced its suspension of boycott activities, and Nestlé pledged its continued support of the WHO code.

Nestlé Supports WHO Code

The company has a strong record of progress and support in implementing the WHO Code, including:

- Immediate support for the WHO Code, May 1981; and testimony to this effect before the U.S. Congress, June 1981.
- Issuance of instructions to all employees, agents, and distributors in February 1982 to implement the code in all Third World countries where Nestlé markets infant formula.
- Establishment of an audit commission, in accordance with Article 11.3 of the WHO Code to ensure the company's compliance with the code. The commission, headed by Edmund S. Muskie, was composed of eminent clergy and scientists.
- Willingness to meet with concerned church leaders, international bodies, and organization leaders seriously concerned with Nestlé's application of the code.
- Issuance of revised instructions to Nestlé personnel, October 1982, as recommended by the Muskie committee to clarify and give further effect to the code.
- Consultation with WHO, UNICEF, and NIFAC on how to interpret the code and how best to implement specific provisions, including clarification by WHO/UNICEF of the definition of children who need to be fed breast milk substitutes, to aid in determining the need for supplies in hospitals.

Nestlé Policies

In the early 1970s Nestlé began to review its infant formula marketing practices on a region-by-region basis. By 1978 the company had stopped all consumer advertising and direct sampling to mothers. Instructions to the field issued in February 1982 and clarified in the revised instructions of October 1982 adopt articles of the WHO Code as Nestlé policy and include:

- No advertising to the general public.
- No sampling to mothers.
- No mothercraft workers.
- No use of commission/bonus for sales.
- No use of infant pictures on labels.
- No point-of-sale advertising.
- No financial or material inducements to promote products.

- No samples to physicians except in three specific situations: a new product, a new product formulation, or a new graduate physician; limited to one or two cans of product.
- Limitation of supplies to those requested in writing and fulfilling genuine needs for breast milk substitutes.
- A statement of the superiority of breast feeding on all labels/materials.
- Labels and educational materials clearly stating the hazards involved in incorrect usage of infant formula, developed in consultation with WHO/UNICEF.

Even though Nestlé stopped consumer advertising, they were able to maintain their share of the Third World infant formula market. By 1988 a call to resume the seven-year boycott was called for by a group of consumer activist members of the Action for Corporate Accountability. The group claimed that Nestlé was distributing free formula through maternity wards as a promotional tactic that undermines the practice of breast feeding. The group claims that Nestlé and others have continued to dump formula in hospitals and maternity wards and that as a result "babies are dying as the companies are violating the WHO resolution."[1]

The boycott focus is Taster's Choice Instant Coffee, Coffeemate Nondairy Coffee Creamer, Anacin aspirin, and Advil.

Representatives of Nestlé and American Home Products rejected the accusations and said they were complying with World Health Organization and individual national codes on the subject.

The Issues

Many issues are raised by this incident. Such questions as: How can a company deal with a worldwide boycott of its products? Why did the United States decide not to support the WHO Code? Who is correct, WHO or Nestlé? But a more important issue concerns the responsibility of an MNC marketing in developing nations. Setting aside the issues for a moment, consider the notion that, whether intentional or not, Nestlé's marketing activities have had an impact on the behavior of many people, that is, Nestlé is a cultural change agent. And, when it or any other company successfully introduces new ideas into a culture, the culture changes and those changes can be functional or dysfunctional to established patterns of behavior. The key issue is—what responsibility does the MNC have to the culture when, as a result of its marketing activities, it causes change in that culture?[2]

Discussion Issues

1. What could Nestlé have done to avoid the accusations of "killing Third World babies" and still market its products?
2. After Nestlé's experience, how do you suggest it or any other company protect itself in the future?

Endnotes

[1] "Boycotts: Activists' Group Resumes Fight against Nestlé, Adds American Home Products," Associated Press, October 5, 1988.

[2] This case draws from the following: "International Code of Marketing of Breastmilk Substitutes," World Health Organization, Geneva, 1981; INFACT Newsletter, Minneapolis, Minn., February 1979; John A. Sparks, "The Nestlé Controversy—Anatomy of a Boycott," Grove City, Pa., Public Policy Education Fund, Inc.; "Who Drafts a Marketing Code," *World Business Weekly,* January 19, 1981, p. 8; "A Boycott over Infant Formula," *Business Week,* April 23, 1979, p. 137; "The Battle over Bottlefeeding," *World Press Review,* January 1980, p. 54; "Nestlé and the Role of Infant Formula in Developing Countries: The Resolution of a Conflict," (Nestlé Company, 1985); "The Dilemma of Third World Nutrition," (Nestlé S.A., 1985), 20 pp.; Thomas V. Greer, "The Future of the International Code of Marketing of Breastmilk Substitutes: The Socio-Legal Context," *International Marketing Review,* Spring 1984, pp. 33–41; James C. Baker, "The International Infant Formula Controversy: A Dilemma in Corporate Social Responsibility," *Journal of Business Ethics,* no. 4, 1985, pp. 181–90; Shawn Tully, "Nestlé Shows How to Gobble Markets," *Fortune,* January 16, 1989, p. 75.

Mickey's Trip to Trouble: Euro Disney

Jolie Solomon.

The spires of Sleeping Beauty's castle are glistening, there's no line for Aladdin's cave and a yellow Mickey Mouse slicker costs only $5. It's late January, and the cold rain in France's Marne-la-Vallee is soft but relentless. In the Disneyland Hotel's luxurious lobby, a fire is burning in the grate, but there aren't many guests to enjoy it. Of 500 rooms only 35 are occupied. A supervisor tries a little humor to cheer up his bored and lonely desk clerks: "Welcome to the Phantom Disneyland Hotel," he tells them. "I'm sure you've counted the crystals in the chandelier 100 times. . . ." This is Euro Disneyland in the "low season."

The low season has lasted longer than the folks at Disney ever imagined when they opened the park near Paris in April 1992. Despite howls from the intelligentsia about Disney's threat to French culture, France had laid out the red carpet. French children have always loved Mickey, and in 1985 when Disney announced its plans the grown-ups were newly enamored of the kind of American capitalism Disney does so well. Sixty international banks plunked down billions of francs, the government flooded Disney with incentives, and workers from all over Europe lined up for piece of the American dream. Even the Roman Catholic Church saw an angle; for the first time in decades, it assigned a priest to the fallow farm area east of Paris.

But Euro Disney has fallen short of the dream. A stunning 19 million people have visited the park since it opened, a fact the company trumpets with devotion. But it isn't enough. The guests don't spend enough time or money at the park, and no one will buy the hotels Euro Disney had built and planned to sell. Euro Disney is drowning in debt, and its stock has plunged.

Last week Euro Disney announced a first-quarter loss 30 percent bigger than last year's. Least happy to get this bulletin were Disney's bankers. They met for hours to debate Disney's proposal that half of the $3.5 billion in debt be restructured, with the loss split 50–50 between the banks and Disney. Bondholders, shut out of the negotiations, threatened to sue. The bad news has been flowing since the fall, when the park said it would cut 950 jobs. But time is running out: Walt Disney Co., which owns 49 percent of Euro Disney, has injected $175 million to keep the park running through March. The parent company took a $514.7 million charge last year for its share of losses, but it is making plenty elsewhere. Still, in December, chairman Michael Eisner said the magic words: Euro Disney might shut down. Eisner was simply rattling sabers, say the bankers, though the warning had one happy consequence. Brussels travel agent Ajnes Van De Velde finally saw a surge in bookings: "People want to go before it closes."

Don't rush to your booking office. Euro Disney will probably remain open and even prosper. Disney's other parks struggled at first, and too many people have too much riding on this one. Eisner has approved a new business plan that slashes prices on everything from admission to hamburgers. The park itself is a fantasia, richly detailed inside and out, from the wainscoting in Walt's restaurant to the handmade Aubusson tapestries in Sleeping Beauty's castle. The inventive rides are expertly engineered: "Brilliant," says Bob Hoffman of Dublin as he flies over London with Peter Pan.

But that's only part of the picture. Far from showing Europe the fairest face of American capitalism, Disney has for many become the corporate embodiment of the ugly American. A Spanish newspaper runs a cartoon of Mickey panhandling near the Eiffel Tower. A Swiss satire portrays Euro Disney in 2001 as a camp for Paris's homeless. And a French taxi driver laughs when he hears the name. France, he says, has become Disney's "Berezina," the icy Russian river where Napoleon lost 10,000 men in his retreat from Moscow.

Disney executives refused to be interviewed for this story. A spokesman disputes some figures (but won't provide his own) and delivers the company line: the problem is the economy. Europe's recession *has* been fierce. But critics see Euro Disney as something akin to Coke's 1985 decision to change its formula—a remarkable stumble by a master marketer. *Newsweek* interviewed dozens of former and current employees, as well as bankers, government officials, marketing and financial experts. They draw a picture of blinding arrogance—and two foolish assumptions: Disney always triumphs and economies don't slow down. Disney is putting the lesson to work as it plans a new park in northern Virginia. But for any business looking abroad, it's a powerful cautionary tale.

Eisner and his team came by their hubris in the usual way: a long run of success. It was Walt Disney himself, of course, who built the first park; he'd found inspiration in Copenhagen's Tivoli Gardens. In 1955 he opened his own version in Anaheim, Calif., and declared it "The Happiest Place on Earth." When Eisner took over the company almost 80 years later, one of his top priorities was to expand Disney's presence abroad.

Disney in 1984 was a hugely powerful brand name, but it had stalled financially. While Disney people combed Europe for the best site, Eisner's team was remaking the company. It built 100 retail stores in four years, pushed the movie studio to number three from number 12 and rejuvenated animation art by creating new hits such as *The Little Mermaid.* They jacked up prices in the parks but crowds poured in, thanks largely to all the baby boomers who were now having babies of their own.

To top it all off, there was Disney's newest park, in Tokyo. Nervous about their first foreign and cold-climate park, Eisner's predecessors had let the Japanese build it; they just took royalties. But by the late 1980s Tokyo was booming, a rare trophy for an American company in the decade of Japan Inc. Disney profits and stock kept climbing. But it wasn't enough. "They always need to top themselves," says a former executive. "It's like, 'We're a shark. If we're not moving forward, we're dead.'"

In Europe, Eisner was determined to exploit the market more than his predecessors had done in Tokyo—by taking only royalties—or in Orlando, where they'd failed to control hotel development and now own only 14 percent. So Disney thought big. It would build the park complex, 5,200 hotel rooms, thousands more square feet of offices, a golf course and 570 homes. That was just phase one.

The huge development plan only boosted competition for the park in Europe, giving Disney the perfect climate to drive one of its famously hard bargains. By late 1985 the finalists were sites near Paris and Barcelona, Spain had a lot going for it, most of all sunshine. (Mild Spanish winters make it one of Britain's top vacation destinations.) But there were downsides, particularly Spain's location farther from Europe's heart, its older trains and smaller airports.

France, meanwhile, was turning cartwheels. The Socialist government, facing tough elections, was determined to bag the Disney prize and prove, says the then culture minister, Jack Lang, that it was a "modern" party, receptive to private enterprise. Many Europeans were euphoric over plans to unite all of Europe in 1992. Europe would be one big happy family, the perfect Disney market. In 1987 France agreed to cut taxes, build rail lines and provide low-interest loans. Banks and investors would put up about $3.6 billion; Disney would cough up only $200 million, most of it for a 49 percent share of the new company. The stock was later offered at about $11.50, but Disney paid about $1.50 a share. A complex financial web largely insulated Disney from risk, and it was guaranteed royalty and management fees. "Everyone in the U.S. knew [the projections] were hyped," says one analyst. Asked why he barely looked at Disney's numbers, one banker just shrugs: "Disney was a magic name."

Eisner's team told itself—and the public—that it was headed for glory. As construction began, one executive called the venture "something immortal, [like] the Pyramids." But back at headquarters, some lower-level executives were nervous. Sure, Disney characters were popular in Europe. Millions of children had read *Le Journal de Mickey* since 1934, and *Jungle Book* has the world's record for home-video sales. But did that mean people would spend days at Disney hotels, with Paris just 20 miles away? And wasn't sunshine part of the Disney experience? "I'm not sure the Europeans will stand in line in winter," ventured one executive in a strategy meeting. "The answer" from Eisner's guys, recounts a former Disney executive, was: "'The Japanese do.' No one said, 'The Japanese are different.'"

Disney insiders these days can catalog those differences: Europeans' per-capita income is lower than the Japanese, and they like to spread it out over long vacations, not four-day spending sprees. Japanese employees eagerly conformed to Disney's famous mandate: smile at all times. The French were hardly specialists in service. But, says the executive, "The people in that room" didn't want to hear it.

At Marne-la-Vallee, the budget kept growing. One winter day Eisner warmed himself by a fire in a Paris hotel lobby and ordered more than a dozen wood-burning fireplaces for Euro Disney, despite the added cost of chimneys and upkeep. The roller coaster on Big Thunder Mountain was redesigned to splash down into water, making it necessary to dig tunnels. Just months before opening Disney realized it had to borrow another $6.6 million to build 3,500 dorm rooms for employees.

Bankers raised questions, especially as the economy weakened, but Disney brushed aside all concerns. Chairman Robert Fitzpatrick told *Business Week* in 1990: "We're seeing Cartesian skepticism meeting American can-do-ism."

On opening day, April 12, 1992, traffic was hurt by a rail workers' strike. But the sparkling new park was a hit. By October, 6.8 million visitors had streamed in. The spirits of "cast members," as Disney calls employees, were high. Some were annoyed to find rules forbidding facial hair, makeup and nails longer than 0.2 inches. But they were delighted that managers wanted to be addressed by their first names and to be told that these weren't just jobs, but careers. While it's often hard to move up in European companies, this promise was "pure American," says Roger Dupont, a union official: "Everyone would climb the corporate ladder according to his abilities."

But the tremors of culture shock had just begun. When customers ordered lunch or dinner, they were stunned to discover that there was no beer or wine. Especially when they'd been standing in line so long. Unlike Americans, who will wander around, hot dog in hand, Europeans seemed determined to eat at a set time. Everyone would converge on the restaurants at 12:30.

Food wasn't the only problem. Some customers seemed taken aback to find as many shops in the park as attractions—and by the prices. A tiny figurine of Prince Charming for $14? But worst of all was the European's short attention span. Disney was used to Orlando, where families may stay a week, filling hotels. Many visitors to Euro Disney were day-trippers. And if they stayed longer, they didn't always stay in Disney's six carefully "themed" hotels. Paris had more variety, cheaper options and it was, well, Paris. Approaching Orlando's 94 percent occupancy rate was only a dream.

Disney managers in Marne-la-Vallee could have used some sympathy from top brass. But the learning curve seemed steep. One executive, fresh from Burbank, was furious to see a guest's Mercedes standing outside the Cheyenne, an "economy" hotel, remembers one visitor. He raged at a marketing manager: Mercedes drivers should be staying at the luxury Disneyland Hotel! Someone took him aside to explain: not every Mercedes driver in Europe was wealthy. This was a Mercedes 190, roughly equivalent to a Buick. It wasn't until last summer, when business plummeted, that the message came home. Beer and wine appeared on the menu. It was a start.

In the Walt Disney annual report issued late last year, Eisner gave Euro Disney a "D"—and blamed the recession. He hasn't said much to the press lately. That tough job has fallen to Jacques-Henri Eyraud, who did press duty for the French military during the gulf war. In flawless English, he declares: "There is no cultural resistance to the product." But then he goes on to catalog the changes: A "softer" ad campaign has begun, targeting only Disney-friendly territory. New attractions will open, with a stronger emphasis on European figures such as Jules Verne.

But what Euro Disney really needs is a second park. Construction should have started by now on MGM Studio, the second "gate" critical to draw and keep customers. But those plans are on the shelf for now. England's *Independent* called Euro Disney a "cultural Vietnam." The military metaphor is apt; Disney can't afford to commit more, and it can't afford to pull out. For the moment, hopes are pinned on the English Channel tunnel, opening this spring, and a new high-speed rail line. Bankers have called another big meeting for later this month; they'll hear from auditors who are checking Disney's math. If everyone can agree on how much medicine to swallow, there may yet be a happy ending.

Euro Disney's Rough Start

December 1985
France triumphs over Spain as the site for Disney's new park. Says the left-leaning daily *Liberation*: "The little Hollywood mouse prefers Brie cheese to Spanish paella."

March 1987
French Prime Minister Jacques Chirac and Disney CEO Michael Eisner sign the final contract for the $2 billion park. A clause requires the new park to respect French culture.

October 1989
Euro Disney's stock offering (at $11.30 a share) announced with hoopla in Paris. Eisner and Mickey are pelted with ketchup and eggs; protestors shout, "Mickey go home."

April 1992
Opening-day ceremonies broadcast to 30 countries. Stock price: $28.18 a share. But that fall, Banque Paribas issues a "sell" recommendation on the stock, which then nosedives.

January 1993
Euro Disney slashes its entrance prices; the 1,098-room Newport Bay Club Hotel closes for the winter. Dismal first-quarter results reported: $92.4 million loss.

June 1993
Euro Disney drops its ban on beer and wine in the park. But, despite the summer weather, there are fewer visitors from outside France, and spending is down too.

November 1993
Euro Disney says it lost more than $900 million for the fiscal year; its stock drops to $7. Walt Disney Co. calls on banks to restructure debt; it will supply cash through March.

January 1994
A month after Eisner says that the park could shut down, Euro Disney announces a first-quarter loss worse than last year's. Negotiations with the banks continue.

But others are busy crunching the numbers, too. Last month Euro Disney's bankers were invited to an ornate hall at the Georges V Hotel. While a harpist played softly, the sixtysomething financiers were treated to champagne by some new American capitalists. This time they were thirtysomething Wall Streeters who've mastered the art—new to France—of buying and repackaging bad debt. The message: hey, we'll give you 50 cents on the dollar. Really, it's a great deal.

Discussion Issues

1. In your view, what should be done to revitalize Euro Disney?
2. What is your prognosis for the future of Euro Disney? Explain.

Siberian Petroleum Production Association: A Negotiation Simulation

John L. Graham. *University of California, Irvine.*

Recently Harland Smith, vice president of marketing for Bolter Turbines International (BTI), attended a two-day conference in Houston sponsored by the U.S. Commerce Department. The purpose of the conference was to stimulate trade between American companies in the oil and gas industry and potential Russian customers. Details regarding the conference and associated programs were reported in a recent article in *Business America.*[1]

A 40-member Russian delegation of oil and gas government officials and industry experts, led by Deputy Minister of Fuel and Energy Audrey Konoplyanik, visited Houston, Texas, April 28–May 7. The mission, hosted by the U.S. government and organized by the Department of Commerce, was sponsored by the U.S. Agency for International Development through the U.S. Energy Association.

The trip was the result of an agreement by both the U.S. and Russian governments during the first meeting of the U.S.–Russia Oil and Gas working group, which decided to hold a conference and meeting in conjunction with the Houston Offshore Technology Conference, the largest annual trade show covering oil and gas equipment. (The oil and gas working group is one of seven industrial sector working groups established under the auspices of the Business Development Committee, an organization co-chaired by Commerce Secretary Ronald H. Brown and Russian Deputy Prime Minister Alexander Shokhin.)

The delegation's program was organized by the Commerce Department's Basic Industries division, which was assisted by the Greater Houston Partnership and other federal agencies. The agenda consisted of a conference on "Opportunities in Russia for U.S. Oil and Gas Firms," attended by more than 200 U.S. oil and gas industry representatives (April 29–30); the second U.S.–Russia Oil and Gas working group meeting, May 1–2; and visits to the Offshore Technology Conference, May 3–6. In addition, the delegation participated in private meetings with American firms, special briefings, and social events hosted by U.S. companies. The conference on opportunities in Russia for U.S. oil and gas firms was presented by Russian officials representing Russian federation ministries, regional administrations, and state/commercial enterprises. It was structured to provide a variety of settings within which American companies could interact with the entire Russian delegation. The conference consisted of a general session in the morning, followed by concurrent roundtable discussions and private meetings in the afternoon. Presentations at the general sessions covered the main direction of Russian energy policy, particularly concepts for attracting foreign investors, access to resources and licensing, state enterprise transformation to stock holding companies, and privatization. Methods of cooperation in the main business activities of the oil and gas subsectors, specifically exploration, production, refining, supply of oil products, and gas services, were also addressed.

The roundtable discussions elaborated on the subjects presented in the plenary sessions. During the private meetings conducted concurrently with the roundtables in the afternoon, a number of U.S. companies were able to discuss specific projects with members of the Russian delegation and establish contacts for future contracts or business collaboration.

American businesses participating in the conference and those involved in hosting the delegation appeared to have benefited from the interchange. "The great value of this conference," said Richard Hildahl of Ernst & Young, "was that key Russian government and industry representatives met with their counterparts in the United State to discuss the challenges and possible solutions to the complexity of doing business in Russia."

William Gottfried, an American petroleum consultant, said, "The conference format allowed the American participants to work directly with the key decision makers from the Russian oil and gas industry. This conference served as a real catalyst for American investment and cooperation in the Russian oil and gas sector."

Rod A. Johnson, president of OptiMarket, a U.S. firm promoting investment projects in the Russian Federation's Krasnoyarsk region, offered this view, saying, "The Department of Commerce has created a milestone in world energy affairs. Every major issue of cooperation between the United States and Russia has been identified and addressed by the countries' governments and industry representatives at one forum in two days. A generation of errors and mistakes will be avoided. In an international energy market marked by embargoes and energy cartels and energy price escalations, we are seeing two great world energy powers bring their industry leaders together to maximize and facilitate their countries' energy resources and energy technologies. We are seeking not just solutions, but the format for future solutions. This conference sets the precedence, procedure, and pace for future Russian/American business and government cooperation, which will stimulate the economies and futures of the United States and Russia."

The Russian delegation appeared to be equally satisfied with the results of the conference. The leader of the Russian delegation, Audrey Konoplyanik, commented, "The value of the conference was in the discussion of key issues characterizing the situation in the oil and gas sector of Russia. This allowed the American participants to understand better possible ways of interacting with Russian federal and regional bodies, as well as with commercial entities."

Aladimir Filanovsky, president of the Kamneft Joint Venture, who moderated the round-table on priorities of the subsectors, expressed his views on the conference: "The discussions showed the necessity for the development of an effective mechanism for the financing of joint ventures with American companies for the manufacturing of oil extraction equipment based on conversion of Russian defense enterprises. These discussions also showed the need for providing U.S. companies with detailed information clarifying the procedures for involvement in the Russian oil market."

At the second U.S.–Russia Oil and Gas working group meeting, the results of the conference were discussed in detail. Both the U.S. and Russian sides agreed that important joint government actions needed to be taken to realize the full potential of U.S. commercial capabilities in assisting Russia to modernize its oil and gas sector. It became clear to the group that financing of trade and investment is clearly one of the major constraints for U.S. firms seeking to do commercial business in Russia in the oil and gas sector.

The Working Group also discussed its work plan for the next 12 months, tentatively agreeing to four priority projects to be completed over the next six months, including:

- preparing and publishing proceedings for the "Opportunities in Russia for U.S. Oil and Gas Firms" conference,
- assisting Russian officials in preparing an information directory on the Russian oil and gas sector,
- jointly organizing a series of expert workshops on western approaches to financing, accounting, taxes, and selected legal issues, and
- distributing to the American business community the 19 defense conversion projects selected by the Russians as priority projects and assisting U.S. firms in structuring business ventures.

During the last four days of their visit to Houston, the Russian delegation attended the Offshore Technology Conference. The Russian delegation members were able to view in person and discuss advanced oil and gas field products, services, and systems with more than 1,200 petroleum equipment exhibitors.

In addition to organized briefings given by major U.S. equipment manufacturers, there were a number of one-on-one meetings that enabled smaller U.S. firms to gauge the potential interest for their products in Russia.

The Russian delegation attended a number of social events hosted by U.S. companies. Among the firms involved were McDermott Marketing Services, Dresser Industries, Butler Taper Joint, Inc., CIS American Chamber of Commerce, Enron Corporation, Gulf Publishing Company, Petroleum Advisory Forum, Smith Meter Inc., Wheatley TXT Corporation, and Bolter Turbines International.

At the conference Harland Smith met Leonid Vihansky, the director of the newly formed Siberian Petroleum Production Association (SPPA). SPPA is a quasigovernment-owned oil and gas production company with operations in northwestern Siberia and offices in Moscow. SPPA, like many other former Soviet industrial concerns, is now being privatized as part of the most recent economic reforms in Russia.

Vihansky's job is to increase the production of oil and gas of his production unit *at a profit*. The last stipulation, at a profit, is a new one to Vihansky, and he and his associates are still learning the ropes of western-style free enterprise. But they are learning quite fast.

Vihansky is interested in buying equipment from BTI. In the months following the conference in Houston, SPPA and BTI representatives met several times in both Moscow and Los Angeles to discuss equipment needs of SPPA. These meetings resulted in an initial price quotation for the first of what SPPA describes as a series of orders to revitalize the production capacity of its Siberian fields.

You have been assigned by Smith to participate in the final negotiations for this initial order from SPPA. Your team consists of three people, your Europe regional sales manager, a sales representative, and an applications engineer. You are to meet with three representatives of SPPA: Vihansky, his chief production engineer, and a trade representative. The last, Oleg Evenko, is very experienced in dealings with Western companies. He formerly worked for the Soviet Foreign Trade Organization involved in purchasing oil field equipment. Your team will be meeting with the SPPA people in Nice, France, to close the deal.

Your marketing research unit has provided you with a briefing regarding the cultural nuances of the Russian negotiation style. Included in that briefing are excerpts from a recent article in the *California Management Review*.[2] (See Article 22 page 252.)

A price quotation and a schematic of the JR2000 are attached. More details about your assignment will soon be provided by Smith. Good Luck!

Bolter Turbines, Inc.

Price Quotation

For Siberian Petroleum Product Association	Installation: Timon
Arbotov 687	Perchora Field,
Moscow, Russia	Northwest Siberia

Model JR2000 Natural Gas Compressor Set	$2,500,000
(the standard package includes an XJ1 compressor)	
Product options	
Custom-built Cold Weather Shelter	400,000
XJ3 Compressor (replacement for XJ1)	500,000
Service contract (2 years normal maintenance, parts, and labor)	150,000
Total Price	$3,550,000

Standard Terms and Conditions

Delivery	6 months
Penalty for late delivery	$10,000/month
Cancellation charges (if client cancels order)	10% of contract price
Warranty (for defective machinery)	Parts, one year
Terms of payment	COD
Inflation escalator	10% per year

Model JR2000 Natural Gas Compressor Set

Endnotes

[1]Joseph Yanick (Office of Energy) and Marianne Vanatta (Basic Industries, U.S. Department of Commerce), "U.S.–Russian Oil and Gas Officials Establish Close Links for Future," *Business America,* May 31, 1993.

[2]Mahesh N. Rajan and John L. Graham, "Nobody's Grandfather Was a Merchant: Understanding the Soviet Commercial Negotiation Process and Style," *California Management Review,* Spring 1991.

DATE DUE

8/18/97			
NOV 2 2 2004			
MAY 0 1 2005			
12/4			